Italian Texts and Studies on Religion and Society

Edmondo Lupieri, *General Editor*

Italian religious history has been pivotal to the formation and growth of European and Western civilization and cultures. Unfortunately, many texts that are fundamental for the understanding of its importance have long remained inaccessible to non-Italian readers. Similarly, the exciting developments of Italian scholarship in the field of the studies of religion have not always come into the public eye outside of Italy. Particularly since the end of World War II there has been continuous expansion in the field, and at the moment Italian scholars, combining the old and solid Italian tradition of philological and historical studies with new and innovative ideas and methodologies, are emerging as a new force.

Italian Texts and Studies on Religion and Society (ITSORS) is a new series. Its publications are all English translations of works originally published in Italian. The main aim of ITSORS is to have readers in the English-speaking world become acquainted with Italian socioreligious history and with the best of Italian scholarly research on religion. For this reason ITSORS will include *Texts*, *Historical and Philological Studies*, and *Theological Essays*.

Texts consist of classical works and are intended to be useful as sources for a better comprehension of important events in religious history. Many are texts that have never been translated into English or are not readily available. *Historical and Philological Studies* comprise original works of contemporary Italian scholarship that offer a methodological contribution to research and/or make inroads into seldom-studied areas. *Theological Essays* are books written by Italian theologians who construct a new dialogue between religious tradition and our modern or postmodern contemporary cultural world.

ITALIAN TEXTS
& STUDIES
ON RELIGION
& SOCIETY

BOOKS PUBLISHED

Bruno Forte
The Essence of Christianity

Bruno Forte
To Follow You, Light of Life

Edmondo F. Lupieri
A Commentary on the Apocalypse of John
(Sponsored by Segretariato Europeo per le Pubblicazioni Scientifiche)

Edmondo Lupieri
The Mandaeans: The Last Gnostics
(Sponsored by the Italian Ministry of Foreign Affairs)

Odoric of Pordenone
The Travels of Friar Odoric
(Sponsored by the Chamber of Commerce of Pordenone, Italy)

A COMMENTARY ON THE

APOCALYPSE OF JOHN

Edmondo F. Lupieri

Translated by

Maria Poggi Johnson and Adam Kamesar

WILLIAM B. EERDMANS PUBLISHING COMPANY
GRAND RAPIDS, MICHIGAN / CAMBRIDGE, U.K.

Originally published in Italian under the title *L'Apocalisse di Giovanni*
© 1999 Fondazione Lovenzo Valla

English translation © 2006 Edmondo F. Lupieri

Wm. B. Eerdmans Publishing Co.
2140 Oak Industrial Drive N.E., Grand Rapids, Michigan 49505 /
P.O. Box 163, Cambridge CB3 9PU U.K.
www.eerdmans.com

Printed in the United States of America

11 10 09 08 07 06   7 6 5 4 3 2 1

ISBN-10: 0-8028-6073-7 / ISBN-13: 978-0-8028-6073-6

The translation of this work has been funded by SEPS
Segretariato Europeo per le Pubblicazioni Scientifiche

Via Val d'Aposa 7
40123 Bologna
Italy

seps@alma.unibo.it / www.seps.it

Contents

Preface

1. Can a place be found in our culture for the Apocalypse? If ever there were a book brimming with angels and devils, with monsters and catastrophes, with heavenly and supernatural visions, with spiritual journeys through a geocentric and pre-Galileo cosmos, surely it is that of the visionary of Patmos. The book is deeply anchored in an ancient worldview. Moreover, there is no part of the NT so full of threats and scenes of warfare: the blood of the slain reaches the horses' nostrils, and mercy seems to have given way before the sword. Even the rewards given to the chosen ones, in particular Christ's famous millennial reign with the resurrected on earth, are problematic for churches rooted in and ordered around the realities of this world. There are indeed many and various reasons why the Christian churches have felt ill at ease with John's book of prophecy. Throughout the history of the book and of its interpretation, many ecclesiastical authorities have sensed the need to neutralize it before allowing it to be read or heard by people whom they deemed improperly qualified. Conversely, the unrestrained use of the Apocalypse has always accompanied surges of religious enthusiasm that often expressed itself in radical political or social action and sometimes truly did end in blood or fire. There may be few for whom the daily reading of the Bible remains a habit, yet the mystery of the Apocalypse, at the conclusion of the book, still stands and, at the dawn of the third Christian millennium, continues to fascinate the readers. The strange and archaic cadences of its language, the swell of its images, like the waves of a sea moved by distant winds, even the obscurity of its meaning are attractive in themselves.

The Apocalypse is a controversial text that needs to be approached cautiously. Even modern criticism, which rose out of the struggles of the Enlightenment, produced a host of contradictory and irreconcilable interpretative theories and in doing so echoed the earlier conflicts among ecclesiastical interpretations. This has become so clear in the world of contemporary biblical scholarship that the exegesis of the Apocalypse has become a prime target for the assaults of postmodern criticism. Postmodern criticism was born *from/of* the conviction that positivistic science had failed to attain its goals in all areas of human knowledge because any investigation styling itself "scientific" inevitably produces nothing but a projection of the researcher's subjectivity. Postmodernism is difficult to summarize, but it has pushed to the limit the process of relativizing every other form of research and in doing so has created a new kind of cultural apocalypse. It has been compared to a monster that swallows every earlier expression of cultural patrimony, thumbing its nose at reason and readying itself for the final sublime ecstasy of devouring itself. Consistency demands that the tools used to demolish modern science also be used on postmodern methods, which are every bit as subjective and relative as those that present themselves as rational and scientific; the end result should be silence.

2. In such a cultural climate as this, what goals should a commentary on the Apocalypse set for itself? We must from the beginning abandon any hope of an interpretation that explains absolutely everything. Readings of the Apocalypse that pretend to make everything fit together in fact do nothing of the sort. They usually derive from the commentator's preconceived ideas: from theological agendas or personal convictions that are often little short of monomaniacal.

This commentary aims to be open, to suggest new and hopefully convincing interpretations, to take due note of knotty interpretive problems. The work's primary goal is to bring the reader as close as possible to our reconstruction of the thinking of a 1st-century Jewish follower of Jesus. The introduction is dedicated to the task of illuminating this world. It is the world of Jesus of Nazareth, John the Baptist, Paul of Tarsus, and many others, from the ultra-observant Essenes at Qumran to the fully Hellenized Jewish leaders. It is not a monolithic, self-contained world, but one able to blend in various and at times disconcerting cultural currents. We can see this in the fortunes of Josephus, who became the official historian of the Flavii, those very generals who initiated the destruction of that world. And Berenice is also emblematic of this moment. She was a Hebrew and the "queen" of the Jews, she was the sister and lover of Agrippa II (the last of the little Jewish kings to be recognized by Rome), and she became the lover of Titus as well, whom she followed to the Palatine in Rome, where she almost became the empress.

3. This book was published in Italy in 1999 in a series dedicated to Greek and Latin Writers ("Scrittori Greci e Latini" of the Lorenzo Valla Foundation), and it follows the general rules of that series. Every volume has an introduction, the text in the original language accompanied by a new translation with the apparatuses, and a line-by-line commentary. The Apocalypse of John was the first NT book to appear in the series, and the result has been very encouraging (11,000 copies and four reprints).

As Joseph Sievers stresses (Sievers 2000), the Italian edition of the book aims mostly at readers used to the classics but not so much at ease with the Bible, people who still know their Greek but do not have the Nestle-Aland at hand. Therefore, it also offers readers the Greek text, which reproduces, with a few variants, the most recent critical edition of the Apocalypse available, and that most used in scholarly circles.[1] Honesty should force us to admit that there is no such thing as a real critical edition of any book in the NT. Instead we have a recently constructed harmonization of the texts of various ancient editions, the story of which we can hypothetically trace to the period between the 2nd and 4th centuries CE. It is a theoretical text, a text that never actually existed in antiquity, but that corresponds to what, on the basis of the manuscripts that have survived to our day, we think the author might have written. That we have the texts we do rather than others is mere accident, the result of external circumstances such as the fact that they escaped destruction by fire, or that they survived in a dry location. Nonetheless, they provide us with as good a starting point as we have for most other ancient texts, most of which have also been pieced together in the modern or contemporary period. If there are any more remarkable discoveries of texts, as there have been at Qumran and Nag Hammadi, they will probably present us with new variants, the validity of which will be open to debate; such variants will doubtless differ in many external points from the ones we now possess. Also, in the first centuries CE pronunciation was in the process of changing, and words were often

---

1. The Greek text I reproduce here is that of Nestle-Aland 26th, which remained unchanged in Nestle-Aland 27th, with the following six variants (mostly privileging the text of the Codex Vaticanus A, concerning which see Hoskier 1929): 2:22 μετανοήσουσιν ℵ A Nestle-Aland 25th/ -σωσιν C 𝔐 Nestle-Aland 26th; 6:17 ὀργῆς αὐτοῦ A 𝔐/ὀργῆς αὐτῶν ℵ C Nestle-Aland 26th; 7:2 ἀνατολῶν A/ἀνατολῆς 𝔐 Nestle-Aland 26th; 13:15 προσκυνήσουσιν ℵ/-σωσιν 𝔐 Nestle-Aland 26th; 16:12 ἀνατολῶν A 𝔐ᴬ/ἀνατολῆς ℵ C Nestle-Aland 26th; 19:7 δώσομεν ℵ² A Nestle-Aland 25th/-σωμεν 𝔐ᴬ Nestle-Aland 26th. The Italian edition also contained a simplified and positive critical apparatus, which we decided not to reproduce, as the interested American reader may easily find it in her or his own critical edition. Similarly, we decided not to reproduce the apparatus containing sources and parallels, as the biblical ones can be found in the critical editions, while the many nonbiblical ones (mostly Qumran, Apocrypha, and Rabbinica) are discussed at length in the line-by-line commentary.

written as they were pronounced. The text we are using has in fact been adapted to bring it into line with classical Greek orthography, and does not actually reflect the way the language was written, especially not the way it was written by those who had not undertaken serious study.

4. The translation was no small task, and I am very grateful to Adam Kamesar, who translated into English my Italian translation of the Apocalypse and reread the final version of the whole book, and to Maria Poggi Johnson, who assumed the task of translating the introduction and the line-by-line commentary.

John's Greek is harsh and often difficult. It is certainly impossible to render in another language the same linguistic flavor of any original work, particularly of an ancient one, and even more of a text like the Apocalypse. Nevertheless, we must ask ourselves *how* the Greek text of the Apocalypse would have sounded to the ears of an educated Greek person at the end of the first century CE. Therefore my Italian translation is very literal and attempts to reproduce some of the linguistic harshness and syntactical difficulties of the original. This made it impossible to simply translate into English my Italian translation of the Greek. Adam Kamesar carefully checked my translation against John's Greek and rendered my interpretation in a new English version that is faithful to both the Greek and the Italian, and hopefully acceptable to the English reader.

No lesser problems emerged from the translation of the rest of the book. Not only did an often stylistically Baroque Italian text have to be transposed into a more pragmatic English, but there was again the problem of translating the translations. I had translated directly from the Greek all passages from the NT and the LXX, and checked against the Hebrew the OT passages of the MT, offering a new translation, usually more literal than the most common Italian translations of the Bible. Here, too, we had to choose a solution that would not sound too odd to the English reader but that at the same time would be such as not to betray the literal faithfulness to the original texts. Maria Poggi Johnson checked every biblical passage against the NRSV and, when possible, reproduced its wording. The result is that almost every biblical quotation in this book is "NRSV altered."

A similar case is that of the Apocrypha and Pseudepigrapha of the OT. Besides translating all Latin and Greek texts and checking, wherever possible, the other texts against their originals, for the Italian edition I had already used Charlesworth I 1983 and II 1985, and also the collection of Italian translations edited in Sacchi I 1981 and II 1989. Here, too, Poggi Johnson checked every passage against Charlesworth I and II. The result is, then, a new "Charlesworth altered" translation.

The matter was more complex for the Qumran texts. During the prepara-
tory work for this commentary, I had access to the then published volumes of
the DJD (former DJDJ) series, to other editions, like Newsom 1985, and to
García Martínez 1994. But I could also make good use of the Italian edition of
this last work, by C. Martone, who corrects many mistakes of the English edition and, in general, offers a more literal Italian translation (see now Martone
2003). In the meantime, though, García Martínez–Tigchelaar I 1997 and II
1998 (working edition) appeared; therefore Poggi Johnson had to check each
quotation against the new and more accurate English translation. So, again,
the Qumranic texts that can be found in this book are usually a "García
Martínez–Tigchelaar altered" translation.

For the sake of brevity and readability, however, I have decided to avoid
inserting on each occasion in the commentary "author's translation," or
"NRSV/NRSV altered," or "Charlesworth/Charlesworth altered," or "García
Martínez–Tigchelaar/García Martínez–Tigchelaar altered," or any other indication of this type.

5. The general editor of the Italian series and I had decided that the main goal
of this commentary was to be the understanding of the Apocalypse of John in
light of its historical and cultural background, with as little as possible in the
way of linguistic or philological commentary, analysis of manuscript variants,
and discussion of the subsequent history of images or ideas from the Apocalypse. Again for the sake of readability and brevity (we had to produce no
more than one volume, with fewer than 400 pages), comparisons with or between the various critical positions have been reduced to discussions of general ideas, and the commentary proceeds with as few bibliographical references as possible. In this way we were able to contain the dimension of the
bibliography (actually a "list of shortened titles of the quoted works") within
reasonable limits (for bibliographical discussions, see Aune 1997-98). More
demanding readers, however, will find references to works that develop at
greater length subjects that I only touch on here, and more specialized readers
will be able to spot my indebtedness to major works of many scholars whose
names do not appear in the above-mentioned list.

Furthermore, in the years that have elapsed between the first Italian edition and today, many new works have been published, and a number of them
are rich in suggestions and corrections (esp. the Italian works by Corsini 2002
and Biguzzi 2001[1] and 2001[2]), some of which I was able to take into consideration for the present English edition. Also, I was able to take full advantage of
other works, such as an excellent Italian edition of the *Book of Similitudes*
(Chialà 1997), and of new ideas. In this way I could expand on or deepen my

discussion of many passages of my commentary, which may now be regarded as a new, enlarged, and corrected edition.

Finally, the American reader will also notice that, from a strictly formal perspective, there is little gender correctness in this book. The world of John is androcentric, and the predominance of the male emerges from his patriarchal worldview so as to permeate his language and imagery. I do not think that we should take the liberty, at least in a scholarly work, of modernizing an old text so that it conforms better to our ideas and feelings. It also seemed somehow unnatural to transform my original conceptually neutral but linguistically male-oriented sentences by adding, for instance, "he or she" where it would have been deemed suitable by some. Nevertheless, I hope that the American reader (she and he) will be able to enjoy reading this book.

EDMONDO F. LUPIERI

Bibliography

Acerbi 1989.

A. Acerbi, *L'Ascensione di Isaia: Cristologia e profetismo in Siria nei primi decenni del II secolo.* Milan, 1989.

Adam 1995.

A. K. Adam, *What Is Postmodern Biblical Criticism?* Minneapolis, 1995.

Allegro 1968.

J. M. Allegro, *Qumran Cave 4, I, 4Q158-4Q186.* Discoveries in the Judaean Desert of Jordan V. Oxford, 1968.

Arnold 1994.

J. P. Arnold, "The Davidian Dilemma — To Obey God or Man?" In J. R. Lewis (ed.), *From the Ashes: Making Sense of Waco.* Lanham, Md. and London, 1994, pp. 23-31.

Aune 1997-98.

D. E. Aune, *Revelation.* 3 vols. Word Biblical Commentary 52 A-C. Dallas, 1997-98.

Avigad 1990.

N. Avigad, "Jerusalem Flourishing: A Craft Center for Stone, Pottery, and Glass." In H. Shanks and D. P. Cole (eds.), *Archaeology and the Bible: The Best of BAR II: Archaeology in the World of Herod, Jesus, and Paul.* Washington, 1990 (orig. 1983).

Baillet 1982.

M. Baillet, *Qumran Grotte 4, III, 4Q482-4Q520.* Discoveries in the Judaean Desert VII. Oxford, 1982.

Barclay 1958-59.

W. Barclay, "Great Themes of the New Testament, 5: Revelation xiii." *The Expository Times* 70 (1958-59) 297.

Bauckham 1993.

R. Bauckham, *The Climax of Prophecy: Studies on the Book of Revelation.* Edinburgh, 1993.

Baumgarten 1996.
A. I. Baumgarten, "The Temple Scroll, Toilet Practices, and the Essenes." *Jewish History* 10 (1996) 9-20.

Beagley 1987.
A. J. Beagley, *The 'Sitz im Leben' of the Apocalypse: With Particular Reference to the Role of the Church's Enemies*. BZNW 50. Berlin and New York, 1987.

Beale 1996.
G. K. Beale, "The Old Testament Background of Revelation 3:14." *New Testament Studies* 42 (1996) 133-52.

Betz 1966.
H. D. Betz, "Zum Problem des religionsgeschichtlichen Verständnisses der Apokalyptik." *Zeitschrift für Theologie und Kirche* 63/4 (1966) 391-409.

Biguzzi 1996.
G. Biguzzi, *I settenari nella struttura dell'Apocalisse: Analisi, storia della ricerca, interpretazione*. RivistBSup 31. Bologna, 1996.

Biguzzi 2001[1].
G. Biguzzi, "Gli enigmi di Ap 17 e le sue allusioni alla storia contemporanea." *RivistB* 49 (2001) 173-201.

Biguzzi 2001[2].
G. Biguzzi, "Interpretazione antiromana e antigerosolimitana di Babilonia in Ap." *RivistB* 49 (2001) 439-71.

Boccaccini 1987.
G. Boccaccini, "È Daniele un testo apocalittico?" *Henoch* 9 (1987) 267-99.

Boccaccini 1998.
G. Boccaccini, *Beyond the Essene Hypothesis: The Parting of the Ways between Qumran and Enochic Judaism*. Grand Rapids, 1998.

Boccaccini 2005.
G. Boccaccini (ed.), *Enoch and Qumran Origins: New Light on a Forgotten Connection*. Grand Rapids, 2005.

Bogaert 1969.
P. Bogaert (ed.), *Apocalypse de Baruch*. Vol 1. Sources chrétiennes 144. Paris, 1969.

Boismard 1949.
M.-É. Boismard, "'L'Apocalypse' ou 'les Apocalypses' de S. Jean." *Revue biblique* 66 (1949) 507-54.

Bousset 1896.
W. Bousset, *The Antichrist Legend: With a Prolog on the Babylonian Dragon Myth*. London, 1896.

Bousset 1906.
W. Bousset, *Die Offenbarung Iohannis*. Göttingen, 1906.

Bowman 1968.
J. W. Bowman, *The First Christian Drama: The Book of Revelation.* Philadelphia, 1968.

Brox 1991.
N. Brox, *Der Hirt des Hermas.* Kommentar zu den Apostolischen Vätern 7. Göttingen, 1991.

Caquot–Geoltrain 1963.
A. Caquot and P. Geoltrain, "Notes sur le texte éthiopien des Paraboles d'Hénoch." *Semitica* 13 (1963) 51-54.

Charles I-II 1920.
R. H. Charles, *A Critical and Exegetical Commentary on the Revelation of St. John.* 2 vols. Edinburgh, 1920.

Charlesworth I 1983; II 1985.
J. H. Charlesworth (ed.), *The Old Testament Pseudepigrapha.* 2 vols. New York, 1983, 1985.

Charlesworth 1985.
J. H. Charlesworth, "The Jewish Roots of Christology: The Discovery of the Hypostatic Voice." *Scottish Journal of Theology* 39 (1985), 19-41.

Charlesworth 1987.
J. H. Charlesworth, *The New Testament Apocrypha and Pseudepigrapha: A Guide to Publications, with Excursuses on Apocalypses.* ATLA Biblical Series 17. Metuchen, N.J., and London, 1987.

Chialà 1997.
S. Chialà, *Libro delle Parabole di Enoc.* Brescia, 1997.

***Computer Concordance* 1985.**
Computer Concordance to the Novum Testamentum Graece of Nestle-Aland, 26th Edition, and to the Greek New Testament, 3rd Edition. Berlin and New York, 1985.

Corsini 1980.
E. Corsini, *Apocalisse prima e dopo.* Torino, 1980.

Corsini 1983.
E. Corsini, *The Apocalypse: The Perennial Revelation of Jesus Christ.* Wilmington, Del., 1983.

Corsini 2002.
E. Corsini, *Apocalisse di Gesù Cristo secondo Giovanni.* Torino, 2002.

Delcor 1957.
M. Delcor, "Un Psaume messianique de Qumran: Traduction et commentaire." In *Mélanges Bibliques André Robert.* Travaux de l'Institut Catholique de Paris 4. Paris, 1957, pp. 334-40.

Destro–Pesce 1992.
A. Destro and M. Pesce, "Il rito ebraico di Kippur: Il sangue nel tempio, il peccato nel deserto." In G. Galli (ed.), *Interpretazione e perdono*. Genoa, 1992, pp. 47-73.

Destro–Pesce 1995.
A. Destro and M. Pesce, "Conflits et rites dans le Temple de Jérusalem d'après la Mishna: Le rite de Yom Kippur (Traité Yoma) et l'ordalie des eaux amères (Traité Sota)." In *Le Temple lieu de conflit*. Les Cahiers du Centre d'Étude du Proche-Orient Ancien 7. Leuven, 1995, pp. 127-37.

Diels 1901.
H. Diels, *Poetarum Philosophorum Fragmenta*. Berlin, 1901.

Dupont-Sommer 1955.
A. Dupont-Sommer, "La mère du Messie e la mère de l'Aspic dans un hymne de Qumran." *Revue de l'Histoire des Religions* 147 (1955) 174-88.

Endleman 1993.
R. Endleman, *Jonestown and the Manson Family: Race, Sexuality, and Collective Madness*. New York, 1993.

Fabbro 1995.
F. Fabbro, *Destra e sinistra nella Bibbia: Uno studio neuropsicologico*. Rimini, 1995.

García Martínez 1992.
F. García Martínez, "The Last Surviving Columns of 11QNJ." In F. García Martínez and C. J. Labuschagne (eds.), *The Scriptures and the Scrolls, in Honour of A. S. Van der Woude*. Leiden, 1992.

García Martínez 1994.
F. García Martínez, *The Dead Sea Scrolls Translated: The Qumran Texts in English*. Translated by W. G. E. Watson. Leiden, 1994.

García Martínez–Tigchelaar 1997.
F. García Martínez and E. J. C. Tigchelaar (eds.), *The Dead Sea Scrolls*. 2 vols. Grand Rapids, 1997, 1998.

Gieschen 1994.
C. A. Gieschen, "The Angel of the Prophetic Spirit: Interpreting the Revelatory Experiences of the *Shepherd of Hermas* in Light of *Mandate* XI." *SBL 1994 Seminar Papers*. Atlanta, 1994, pp. 790-803.

Gieschen 1995.
C. A. Gieschen, "Angelomorphic Christology." Diss., University of Michigan, Ann Arbor, 1995.

Goodenough 1964.
E. R. Goodenough, *Jewish Symbols in the Graeco-Roman Period: Symbolism in the Dura Synagogue*. Vol. 10: *Text* and vol. 11: *Illustrations*. New York, 1964.

Grabbe 1987.
L. L. Grabbe, "The End of the Desolation of Jerusalem: From Jeremiah's 70 Years to Daniel's 70 Weeks of Years." In *Early Jewish and Christian Exegesis.* Atlanta, 1987, pp. 67-72.

Gruenwald 1980.
I. Gruenwald, *Apocalyptic and Merkavah Mysticism.* Leiden, 1980.

Gundry 1994.
R. H. Gundry, "Angelomorphic Christology in the Book of Revelation." *SBL 1994 Seminar Papers.* Atlanta, 1994, pp. 662-78.

Haak 1992.
R. D. Haak, *Habakkuk.* VTSup 44. Leiden, 1992.

Hall 1995.
R. G. Hall, "The Angelic Spirit and the Ascension of Isaiah." Paper presented at the SBL Annual Meeting, Philadelphia, 1995.

Halperin 1988.
D. J. Halperin, *The Faces of the Chariot: Early Jewish Responses to Ezekiel's Vision.* Tübingen, 1988.

Halperin 1993.
D. J. Halperin, *Seeking Ezekiel: Text and Psychology.* University Park, Penn., 1993.

Hoskier 1929.
H. C. Hoskier, *Concerning the Text of the Apocalypse: Collations of All Existing Available Greek Documents, with the Standard Text of Stephen's Third Edition, Together with the Testimony of Versions, Commentaries, and Fathers.* 2 vols. London, 1929.

Humphrey 1995.
E. McE. Humphrey, *The Ladies and the Cities: Transformation and Apocalyptic Identity in Joseph and Aseneth, 4 Ezra, the Apocalypse, and the Shepherd of Hermas.* Sheffield, 1995.

Jenks 1991.
G. C. Jenks, *The Origins and Early Development of the Antichrist Myth.* BZNW 59. Berlin, 1991.

Karrer 1986.
M. Karrer, *Die Johannesoffenbarung als Brief. Studien zu ihrem literarischen, historischen, und theologischen Ort.* Göttingen, 1986.

Klijn–Reinink 1973.
A. F. J. Klijn and G. J. Reinink, *Patristic Evidence for Jewish-Christian Sects.* NTSup 36. Leiden, 1973.

Körtner 1983.
U. H. J. Körtner, *Papias von Hierapolis: Ein Beitrag zur Geschichte des frühen Christentums.* FRLANT 133. Göttingen, 1983.

Kraft 1974.
H. Kraft, "Die Offenbarung des Johannes." In *Handbuch zum Neuen Testament*. Vol. 16a. Tübingen, 1974.

Lang 1881.
C. Lang, *L. Annaei Cornuti Theologiae Graecae Compendium*. Leipzig, 1881.

Lemaire 1976.
D. and G. Lemaire, *Les OVNI de l'Apocalypse*. 2 vols. Bruxelles, 1976.

Levison 1995.
J. R. Levison, "The Angelic Spirit in Early Judaism." *SBL 1995 Seminar Papers*. Atlanta, 1995, pp. 464-93.

Loader 1990.
J. A. Loader, *A Tale of Two Cities: Sodom and Gomorrah in the Old Testament, Early Jewish and Early Christian Traditions*. Kampen, 1990.

Lupieri 1985.
E. Lupieri, "La purità impura: Giuseppe Flavio e le purificazioni degli esseni." *Henoch* 7 (1985) 15-42.

Lupieri 1990.
E. Lupieri, "Esegesi e simbologie apocalittiche." *Annali di Storia dell'Esegesi* 7/2 (1990) 379-96.

Lupieri 1992.
E. Lupieri, "The Seventh Night: Visions of History in the Revelation of John and the Contemporary Apocalyptic." *Henoch* 14 (1992) 113-32.

Lupieri 1997.
E. Lupieri, "Halakhah qumranica e halakhah battistica: Due mondi a confronto." In R. Penna (ed.), *Qumran e le origini cristiane*. Ricerche Storico-Bibliche 11/2. Bologna, 1997, pp. 69-98.

Lupieri 1997².
E. Lupieri, "Fra Gerusalemme e Roma." In G. Filoramo and D. Menozzi (eds.), *Storia del Cristianesimo*. Vol. 1. Bari and Roma, 1997, pp. 5-137.

Lupieri 1999.
E. Lupieri, "Sex and Blood: Some New Approaches to the *Apocalypse of John*." *Folia Orientalia* 35 (1999) 85-92.

Lupieri 2002.
E. Lupieri, *The Mandaeans: The Last Gnostics*. Grand Rapids, 2002.

Lupieri 2005.
E. Lupieri, "Dodici, sette, undici, ventiquattro: Numeri, chiese e fine del mondo." *Annali di Storia dell'Esegesi* 22/2 (2005) 357-71.

Maier 1989.
J. Maier, "The Architectural History of the Temple in Jerusalem in the Light of the

Temple Scroll." In G. J. Brook (ed.), *Temple Scroll Studies.* Journal for the Study of the Pseudepigrapha, Suppl. Ser. 7. Sheffield, 1989.

Massyngberde Ford 1975.
J. Massyngberde Ford, *Revelation.* Anchor Bible 38. Garden City, N.Y., 1975.

Mealy 1992.
J. W. Mealy, *After Thousand Years: Resurrection and Judgment in Revelation 20.* JSNTSup 70. Sheffield, 1992.

Mengozzi 1997.
A. Mengozzi (ed.), *Trattato di Sem e altri testi astrologici.* Testi del Vicino Oriente Antico 7/1. Brescia, 1997.

Meyers 1993.
C. M. and E. M. Meyers, *Zechariah 9–14: A New Translation with Commentary.* Anchor Bible 25. New York, 1993.

Milgrom 1978.
J. Milgrom, "Studies in the Temple Scroll." *Journal of Biblical Literature* 97 (1978) 501-23.

Moraldi 1986.
L. Moraldi, *I manoscritti di Qumran.* Torino, 1986².

Morgenthaler 1958.
R. Morgenthaler, *Statistik des neutestamentlichen Wortschatzes.* Zürich, 1958.

Mussies 1971.
G. Mussies, *The Morphology of Koine Greek, As Used in the Apocalypse of St. John: A Study in Bilingualism.* Suppl. NT 27. Leiden, 1971.

Nestle-Aland 26th.
E. Nestle et al., *Novum Testamentum Graece.* Stuttgart, 1983⁷.

Nestle-Aland 27th.
E. Nestle et al., *Novum Testamentum Graece.* Stuttgart, 1993.

Newsom 1985.
C. Newsom, *Songs of the Sabbath Sacrifice: A Critical Edition.* Harvard Semitic Studies 27. Atlanta, 1985.

Newsom 1988.
C. Newsom, "The 'Psalm of Joshua' from Cave 4," *Journal of Jewish Studies* 39 (1988) 56-73.

Norelli 1983.
E. Norelli, "Sulla pneumatologia dell'Ascensione di Isaia." In M. Pesce (ed.), *Isaia, il Diletto e la Chiesa: Visione ed esegesi profetica cristiano-primitiva nell' "Ascensione di Isaia."* Brescia, 1983, pp. 211-76.

Norelli I-II 1995.
E. Norelli (ed.), *Ascensio Isaiae: Textus and Commentarius.* Corpus Christianorum, Ser. Apocr. 7-8. Turnhout, 1995.

Olck 1899.
F. Olck, "Citrus." In *RE* 3/2 (1899): cols. 2621-24.

Pesce 1990.
M. Pesce, "Mangiare e bere il proprio giudizio. Una concezione culturale comune a 1 Cor. e Sotah?" *RivistB* 38 (1990) 495-513.

Philonenko 1997.
M. Philonenko, "Dehors les chiens (Apocalypse 22.6 et 4QMMT B 58-62)." *New Testament Studies* 43 (1997) 445-50.

Pincherle 1925.
A. Pincherle, "Da Ticonio a Sant'Agostino." *Ricerche Religiose* 1 (1925) 443-66.

Pippin 1992.
T. Pippin, *Death and Desire: The Rhetoric of Gender in the Apocalypse of John.* Literary Currents in Biblical Interpretation. Louisville, 1992.

Pippin 1994.
T. Pippin, "Peering into the Abyss: A Postmodern Reading of the Biblical Bottomless Pit." In E. S. Malbon and E. V. McKnight (eds.), *The New Literary Criticism and the New Testament.* JSNTSup 109. Sheffield, 1994, pp. 251-67.

Puech 1987.
É. Puech, "Notes sur le manuscrit de XIQMelchîsédeq," *Revue de Qumran* 12/48 (1987) 483-513.

Qimron-Strugnell 1994.
E. Qimron and J. Strugnell, *Qumran Cave 4, V, Miqsat Ma'as'e ha-Torah.* Discoveries in the Judaean Desert X. Oxford, 1994.

Raguse 1993.
H. Raguse, *Psychoanalyse und biblische Interpretation: Eine Auseinandersetzung mit Eugen Drewermanns Auslegung der Johannes-Apokalypse.* Stuttgart, 1993.

Ramsay 1909.
W. M. Ramsay, *The Letters to the Seven Churches of Asia and Their Place in the Plan of the Apocalypse.* London, 1909.

Routh 1974.
M. J. Routh, *Reliquiae Sacrae.* Vol. 2. Oxford, 1846 (repr. Hildesheim, 1974), pp. 238-308.

Sacchi 1976.
P. Sacchi, "L'esilio e la fine della monarchia davidica." *Henoch* 11 (1976) 131-48.

Sacchi I 1981; II 1989.
P. Sacchi (ed.), *Apocrifi dell'Antico Testamento.* Vols. 1 and 2. Torino, 1981 and 1989.

Sacchi 1990.

P. Sacchi, *L'apocalittica giudaica e la sua storia*. Brescia, 1990.

Sacchi 1994.

P. Sacchi, *Storia del Secondo Tempio: Israele tra VI secolo a.C. e I secolo d.C.* Torino, 1994.

Scholem 1960.

G. Scholem, *Jewish Gnosticism, Merkabah Mysticism, and Talmudic Tradition*. New York, 1960.

Sievers 2000.

J. Sievers, "A Unique Commented Edition of the Book of Revelation." *Rivista di Storia e Letteratura Religiosa* 36 (2000) 487-89.

Simonetti 1983.

M. Simonetti, "Note sulla cristologia dell'*Ascensione di Isaia*." In M. Pesce (ed.), *Isaia, il Diletto e la Chiesa: Visione ed esegesi profetica cristiano-primitiva nell' 'Ascensione di Isaia'*. Brescia, 1983.

Simonetti 1986.

M. Simonetti, "Il problema dell'unità di Dio a Roma da Clemente a Dionigi." *Rivista di Storia e Letteratura Religiosa* 22 (1986).

Strack I-VI.

L. Strack and P. Billerbeck, *Kommentar zum Neuen Testament aus Talmud und Midrasch*. 6 vols. München, 1922-61.

Strozier 1994.

C. B. Strozier, *Apocalypse: On the Psychology of Fundamentalism in America*. Boston, 1994.

Stuckenbruck 1995.

L. T. Stuckenbruck, *Angel Veneration and Christology: A Study in Early Judaism and in the Christology of the Apocalypse of John*. WUNT 77. Tübingen, 1995.

Sussmann 1994.

Y. Sussmann, "Appendix 1: The History of the Halakha and the Dead Sea Scrolls: Preliminary Talmudic Observations on Miqsat Maʿasʾe ha-Tora (4QMMT)." In Qimron–Strugnell 1994.

Thomas 1935.

J. Thomas, *Le mouvement baptiste en Palestine et Syrie (150 av. J.-C.–300 ap. J.-C.)*. Gembloux, 1935.

Tigchelaar 2004.

E. Tigchelaar, "Sodom and Gomorrah in the Dead Sea Scrolls." In E. Noort and E. Tigchelaar, *Sodom's Sin: Genesis 18–19 and Its Interpretations*. Themes in Biblical Narratives 7. Leiden, 2004, pp. 47-62.

Vanni 1980.
U. Vanni, "Il simbolismo nell'Apocalisse." *Gregorianum* 71/3 (1980) 461-506.

Vanni 1980².
U. Vanni, *La struttura letteraria dell'Apocalisse*. Brescia, 1980².

Walch 1987.
J. G. Walch (ed.), *Dr. Martin Luthers sämtliche Schriften etc.* Vol. 14. Gross Oesingen, 1987 (repr. of St. Louis, Mo., 1880-1910²).

Yarbro Collins 1976.
A. Yarbro Collins, *The Combat Myth in the Book of Revelation*. Missoula, 1976.

Yarbro Collins 1984.
A. Yarbro Collins, "Numerical Symbolism in Jewish and Early Christian Apocalyptical Literature." In W. Haase (ed.), *Aufstieg und Niedergang der römischen Welt*. Vol. 21/2. Berlin and New York, 1984, pp. 1221-87.

Yarbro Collins 1987.
A. Yarbro Collins, "Women's History and the Book of Revelation." In *SBL 1987 Seminar Papers*. Atlanta, 1987.

Abbreviations

I. Biblical Books

Gen	Genesis	Mic	Micah
Exod	Exodus	Nah	Nahum
Lev	Leviticus	Hab	Habakkuk
Num	Numbers	Zeph	Zephaniah
Deut	Deuteronomy	Hag	Haggai
Josh	Joshua	Zech	Zechariah
Judg	Judges	Matt	Matthew
1, 2 Sam	1, 2 Samuel	Mark	Mark
1, 2 Kings	1, 2 Kings	Luke	Luke
1, 2 Chr	1, 2 Chronicles	John	John
Ezra	Ezra	Acts	Acts
Neh	Nehemiah	Rom	Romans
Esth	Esther	1, 2 Cor	1, 2 Corinthians
Ps(s)	Psalms	Gal	Galatians
Prov	Proverbs	Eph	Ephesians
Eccl	Ecclesiastes	Phil	Philippians
Song	Song of Solomon	Col	Colossians
Isa	Isaiah	1, 2 Thess	1, 2 Thessalonians
Jer	Jeremiah	1, 2 Tim	1, 2 Timothy
Lam	Lamentations	Tit	Titus
Ezek	Ezekiel	Heb	Hebrews
Dan	Daniel	James	James
Hos	Hosea	1, 2 Pet	1, 2 Peter
Joel	Joel	1, 2, 3 John	1, 2, 3 John
Amos	Amos	Jude	Jude
Jonah	Jonah	Apoc	Apocalypse of John

II. Apocrypha

Bar	Baruch
Jdt	Judith
1, 2 Macc	1, 2 Maccabees
Sir	Sirach
Tob	Tobit

III. Old Testament Pseudepigrapha

Ahikar	*Ahikar*
Apoc. Abr.	*Apocalypse of Abraham*
Apoc. El.	*Apocalypse of Elijah*
Apoc. Isa.	*Apocalypse of Isaiah*
Apoc. Mos.	*Apocalypse of Moses*
Apoc. Zeph.	*Apocalypse of Zephaniah*
Asc. Isa.	*Ascension of Isaiah*
2, 3 Bar.	*2, 3 Baruch*
1 Enoch	*1 Enoch*
BA	*Book of Astronomical Writings*
BD	*Book of Dreams*
BS	*Book of Similitudes*
BW	*Book of the Watchers*
EE	*Epistle of Enoch*
2, 3 Enoch	*2, 3 Enoch*
4 Esdr.	*4 Esdras (Ezra)*
Jub.	*Jubilees*
Par. Jer.	*Paraleipomena of Jeremiah*
Ps. Sol.	*Psalms of Solomon*
Sib. Or.	*Sibylline Oracles*
T. Abr.	*Testament of Abraham*
T. Adam	*Testament of Adam*
T. Levi	*Testament of Levi*
T. Mos.	*Testament of Moses*

IV. Dead Sea Scrolls

CD	*Damascus Document*
1QapGen	*Genesis Apocryphon*
1QH	*Thanksgiving Hymns*
1QM (WS)	*War Scroll*
1QpHab	*Pesher (Commentary) on Habakkuk*
1QpPs[a]	*Pesher on Psalms*

1QS	*Manual of Discipline*
1QSa	*Rule of the Congregation*
1QSb	*Rule of the Blessings*
4QapLamA	*Lamentations Apocryphon*
4QBéat	*Beatitudes*
4QBer[a, b]	*Berakot[a, b]*
4QDibHam[a]	*Words of the Luminaries*
4QEn[c] ar	*Book of the Watchers*
4QEnastr[b-c]	*Book of the Astronomical Writings*
4QH	*Hodayot (Hymns)*
4QMMT *(HL)*	*Halakhic Letter*
4QMyst[b]	*Mysteries*
4QpGen[a]	*Pesher on Genesis*
4QpIsa	*Pesher on Isaiah*
4QpsMos[c, e]	*Pseudo-Moses*
4QpNah	*Pesher on Nahum*
4QpPs[a]	*Pesher on Psalms*
4QShir[b]	*Shirot, Songs of the Sages*
4QShirShabb	*Song of the Sabbath Sacrifice*
4QTanh	*Tanhumim*
4QTest	*Testimonies*
4QTLevi ar[b, d]	*Testament of Levi*
4QTNaph	*Testament of Naphtali*
11QBer	*Berakot*
11QMelch	*Melchizedek*
11QNJ *(NJ)*	*New Jerusalem*
11QPs[a]	*Psalms Scroll*
11QT[a] (TS)	*Temple Scroll*

V. Rabbinic Works

Ber.	*Berakot*
'Eduy.	*'Eduyyot*
Gen. Rab.	*Genesis Rabbah*
Hal.	*Hallah*
Hul.	*Hullin*
Kel.	*Kelim*
Mid.	*Middot*
Miqw.	*Miqwa'ot*
Ned.	*Nedarim*
Pes.	*Pesahim*
Pirqe R. El.	*Pirqe Rabbi Eliezer*
Sheq.	*Sheqalim*

Sot.	*Sotah*
Yoma	*Yoma*

VI. Apostolic Fathers

Barn.	*Barnabas*
Did.	*Didache*
Herm. *Sim.*	Hermas, *Similitudes*
Herm. *Vis.*	Hermas, *Visions*
Ign. *Eph.*	Ignatius, *Ephesians*
Ign. *Epist.*	Ignatius, *Epistles*

VII. New Testament Pseudepigrapha

Apoc. Pet.	*Apocalypse of Peter*
Gos. Pet.	*Gospel of Peter*

VIII. Greek and Latin Works

Augustine, *Civ. Dei*	Augustine, *Civitas Dei*
Clement, *Protr.*	Clement, *Protrepticus*
Epiphanius, *Pan.*	Epiphanius, *Panarion*
Eusebius, *Hist. eccl.*	Eusebius, *Historia ecclesiastica*
Ezekiel Trag., *Exag.*	Ezekiel the Tragedian *Exagoge*
Hesiod, *Theog.*	Hesiod, *Theogonia*
Hippolytus, *Adv. haer.*	Hippolytus, *Adversus haereses*
Antichr.	*De Antichristo*
In Dan.	*In Danielem*
Homer, *Il.*	Homer, *Iliad*
Od.	*Odyssey*
Irenaeus, *Adv. haer.*	Irenaeus, *Adversus haereses*
Josephus, *A.J.*	Josephus, *Antiquities of the Jews*
J.W.	*Jewish War*

Justin,	Justin,
Dial.	*Dialogus cum Tryphone Iudaeo*
Philo,	Philo,
De conf. ling.	*De confusione linguarum*
Pliny,	Pliny,
Nat. hist.	*Naturalis historia*
Plutarch,	Plutarch,
Mor.	*Moralia*
Pseudo-Philo,	Pseudo-Philo,
Lib. Ant. Bib.	*Liber antiquitatum biblicarum*
Suetonius,	Suetonius,
Nero	*Nero*
Theophilus,	Theophilus,
Ad Autol.	*Ad Autolycus*

XI. Secondary Sources

ATLA	American Theological Library Association
BA	*Biblical Archaeologist*
BAR	*Biblical Archaeology Review*
BG	Berlin Gnostic Codex
BZNW	Beihefte zur Zeitschrift für die altesttamentliche Wissenschaft
DJD	Discoveries in the Judean Desert
DJDJ	Discoveries in the Judean Desert of Jordan
FRLANT	Forschungen zur Religion und Literatur des Alten und Neuen Testaments
GCS	De griechischen Schriftsteller der ersten drei Jahrhunderte
JSNTSup	Supplement to *Journal for the Study of the New Testament*
NHC	Nag Hammadi Codices
NHL	J. A. Robinson, ed., *The Nag Hammadi Library in English* (New York, 1977)
NTS	*New Testament Studies*
PG	Patrologia Graeca
RE	*Paulys Real-Enzyklopädie der klassischen Altertumswissenschaft*
RivistB	*Rivista biblica*
SBL	Society of Biblical Literature
TU	*Texte und Untersuchungen*
VTSup	Supplements to *Vetus Testamentum*
WUNT	Wissenschaftliche Untersuchungen zum Neuen Testament
ZTK	*Zeitschrift für Theologie und Kirche*

X. General

ad loc.	at the place
BCE	before the Common Era
CE	the Common Era
chs.	chapters
cod.	codex
col.	column
diss.	dissertation
ed.	edition, edited by
e.g.	*exempli gratia,* for example
ET	English translation
et al.	*et alia,* and the others
etc.	*et cetera,* and the rest
ff.	following
frr.	fragments
ibid.	*ibidem,* in the same place
i.e.	*id est,* that is
IT	Italian translation
lit.	literally
LXX	the Septuagint
mss.	manuscripts
MT	Masoretic Text
n.	note
nos.	numbers
NRSV	New Revised Standard Version
NT	New Testament
OT	Old Testament
repr.	reprinted
ser.	series
suppl.	supplement
s.v.	*sub vide,* see under
Theod.	Theodotion
trans.	translated by
Vg.	Vulgate
vol.	volume
vv.	verses

A Note on the Translation of the Greek Text

It has been a pleasure and an honor to work with Professor Lupieri on the preparation of this American edition of his *Apocalisse di Giovanni*. The making of an English version of his Italian translation of the Greek has been an engaging task. Of particular importance in carrying it out was a daylong face-to-face session I had with Lupieri in Toronto in November of 2002, when we were able to go over a very large portion of the text together. I thank him for his patience on that occasion and in subsequent detailed correspondence. At this juncture, it may be helpful to point out a couple of features of the translation.

As Lupieri explains in his preface (p. x), his intention has been to produce a version that is highly literal, so that the modern reader might get a sense of the strangeness that a cultured Greek person would have felt when reading/hearing the Apocalypse. For the Apocalypse falls well short of the literary standards that were in vogue at the time. The language of the text is often ungrammatical and anacoluthic, and reflects a lack of Hellenic education. It is also permeated with Semitisms, derived both from a living Semitizing Greek and from a written biblical Greek (see pp. 40-42 below). Many of these have been retained in the present translation: the superfluous repetition of a personal pronoun in a relative clause, noun clauses without the verb "to be," the use of the third person plural in an indefinite construction ("they" for "one"). The attempt to re-create the stylistic impression the book may have made in educated Greek circles around A.D. 100 is tentative. This is chiefly because biblical style in general, even in translated form, became "naturalized" in a Western cultural setting in the course of the Latin Middle Ages. This appreciation of the literary quality of the Scriptures, acquired over centuries, was retained in the course of the transition to the use of vernacular translations. Accordingly, it is very difficult to return to pre-medieval literary sensibilities, and the perspective of a Cleomedes (*Caelestia* 2.1, p. 61 [Todd]; cf. Arnobius, *Adversus nationes* 1.58-59 and H. Lewy, in *Sefer Dinaburg* [1949], pp. 104-6) may be lost forever. In any case, the effort has been made to maintain a version that is as literal as possible. This may lead to a certain degree of obscurity in some cases.

In general, I have used the Italian as the model, but the translation is in essence from both the Italian and the Greek. In many instances it has been a matter of transferring Lupieri's system of translation to an English setting. This does not mean, however, that the English version is without any Italian flavor. The text has been "poured into the third jar," as Jerome would have put it (*Praefatio in libros Salomonis*), and thus retains some of the taste of the second. I hope that a positive result will follow, namely, that the reader may move closer to Lupieri's understanding of the Greek.

ADAM KAMESAR
Cincinnati, March 2006

Introduction

I. The Meanings of a Text

1. By the latter half of the second century the various strands of Christianity had produced works of literature bearing witness to a wide spectrum of opinions on the Apocalypse. Many Christians acknowledged it as an inspired book, written by the apostle John, the disciple of the Lord and the author of the Fourth Gospel and of some epistles. This approach is well attested within the mainstream church, where Justin, Irenaeus, and then Hippolytus formed a moderate interpretive tradition[1] that held that after a period of great tribulation Christ would return in glory and then, with the resurrected saints, begin a thousand-year reign on the earth, based in Jerusalem. It is possible that this "millenarian" interpretation is based on ancient oral traditions stretching back to the "elders," the disciples of the Lord's disciples. Papias of Hierapolis, a city in Asia Minor not far from Laodicea, bears witness to words of these elders, who themselves recall the instruction of John.[2] In the millennial reign every vine would have ten thousand branches, and every branch ten thousand shoots, and every shoot ten thousand buds, and every bud ten thousand bunches, and every bunch ten thousand grapes, and every grape would yield twenty-five measures of wine.[3] John supposedly had similar things to say about grain and fruits: the millennium rejoiced in this fertility, and in the universal docility of animals.

Ideas such as these, which would later appear naive to different audiences,

---

1. Justin, *Dial.* 81.14; Irenaeus, *Adv. haer.* 5, particularly 5.26-33; Hippolytus, *De Antichristo* and *Commentarium in Danielem,* particularly 5.

2. Eusebius, *Hist. eccl.* 3.39, particularly in 11ff.

3. Irenaeus, *Adv. haer.* 5.33.3ff. A "measure" is 39.4 liters. For this image in a non-Christian Jewish apocalyptic context, which is probably familiar with Christian traditions, see *2 Bar.* 29:5.

were held in varying ways and to various degrees in a number of ecclesiastical environments. The more radical groups, who were also inspired by the preaching of new prophets, anticipated an imminent return of Christ and interpreted contemporary crises as apocalyptic tribulations. The most famous of these prophets was Montanus from Asia Minor, who initially founded a Christian movement and eventually a separate church. The Montanists believed, among other things, that the New Jerusalem of Apoc 21:2 would physically descend from heaven to a place in Phrygia known as Pepuza. Interpretations of this sort, which attempt to relate the Apocalypse to contemporary history, tend to find there the first signs of the fulfillment of the prophecies. Hippolytus claimed that the seven heads of the beast were the seven millennia of history. According to a chronology quite well known at the time,[4] Jesus was born 5500 years after creation, and thus the end of the sixth millennium and the beginning of Christ's reign will be 500 years after his coming in the flesh: fairly soon, but not as soon as the heretics claimed. Well into the fourth century the Donatist Tyconius[5] explained the three and a half days of Apoc 11:9 as referring to 350 years of the witness of the church, from Jesus' death to his return. Tyconius was a committed allegorist who did not understand the millennium in a strictly literal sense: Christ's final triumph and the end of the world were so imminent (380 CE by his prediction) that there was no time for a thousand-year reign. For Tyconius, whose Donatist church was persecuted by ecclesiastical authorities aligned with the Roman Empire, the text of the Apocalypse offered an explanation for the suffering of a Christian minority under the persecution of other Christians.

Also outside the mainstream church in the second century, but in the other direction, we find the first critics of the Apocalypse. Tertullian tells us that Marcion,[6] who accepted only a few letters of Paul and a revised version of Luke's Gospel, rejected the Apocalypse wholesale, considering it a Judaizing work that Jesus' Jewish disciples used to hide his real message. Other, equally radical criticisms came from the "Alogi,"[7] so called because of their denial of

---

4. It is defended in the *Chronographia* of Julius Africanus, from shortly after 220; fragments in PG 10, coll. 63-94; critical edition in Routh 1974, 2:238-308. Hippolytus's text is *In Dan.* 4.23.

5. The Donatists were a rigorist schismatic group: they did not recognize the authority of any member of the Christian clergy who had turned over sacred books during the Diocletian persecution in 304-5, and who were therefore called *traditores*. Donatism was born in Africa, and spread throughout the Christian empire in the fourth and fifth centuries, giving birth to an alternative church with different clergy and places of worship from the official church.

6. Marcion came from Sinope, on the northern coast of Asia Minor, and was active in Rome around the middle of the second century.

7. The name was invented by Epiphanius (*Pan.* 51.1-35).

Johannine Logos theology, and thus, by a pun, also called "irrational." Little is known about the movement beyond that it was active in Asia Minor and was strongly opposed to that of the Montanists. The conviction developed among them that the Apocalypse and the Fourth Gospel were not the work of the apostle John, but of his bitter foe, the gnostic Cerinthus. This would have been a matter of small importance had not a presbyter named Caius,[8] in the course of an anti-Montanist polemic, advanced the very same ideas from an orthodox pulpit in Rome itself. Caius was forcibly criticized, and his ideas did not win a following within the mainstream church, but their very existence shows how genuine difficulties could arise in the handling of a text like the Apocalypse.

The principal interpretive tradition of orthodox Christianity took shape with the explosion of Christian exegesis in third-century Alexandria. These circumstances held that the Apocalypse, like the OT, could be understood only by means of allegorical interpretation. Moreover, in a polemic with a millennialist bishop, one of Origen's disciples, Dionysius of Alexandria, argued on strictly literary grounds that the apostle John, the author of the Gospel and of the letters, could not have written a text with such bad Greek as that found in the Apocalypse and that the author must have been the other John of the two recorded as having tombs in Ephesus.[9] Most orthodox authors, however, did not really doubt that the Apocalypse was written by the John who wrote the Gospel; they used the tools of allegory to shore up the entire text. Even Methodius,[10] an opponent of Origen, could calmly assert that the seven heads of the dragon, who is the devil, are the seven principal sins. This made it possible to dehistoricize the Apocalypse when the Christianization of the empire in the fourth century left little room for a political and anti-Roman reading of John's visions. Eusebius, writing in the wake of Constantine's victory, returned to the Dionysian theory of the "second John" and crushed Papias with a harsh judgment that would carry weight for centuries against this disciple of the elders.[11] What is more, since the height of the persecutions before the Christian victory, Eusebius had drawn up a new universal chronology in which (in an obvious, if never explicit, polemic against Julius Africanus) he proved on philological grounds that the biblical chronologies for the period before Abraham were not reliable; we do not even know

8. Or Gaius, in the time of the bishop Zephyrinus (199-217).

9. In Eusebius, *Hist. eccl.* 7.24ff. Dionysius does not dispute the canonicity of the Apocalypse: he explicitly rejects attempts to attribute it to Cerinthus; but by ascribing it to another John, a figure of lesser importance from the apostolic period, he diminishes the text's weight.

10. Possibly the bishop of Olympus in Lycia, he was martyred in 311.

11. *Hist. eccl.* 3.39, particularly 11ff.; see Körtner 1983.

how long Adam spent in paradise, it is impossible to date the birth of Christ in relation to the creation of the world,[12] and thus it is also impossible to sustain any kind of millennial interpretation of the Apocalypse. When Augustine took up Tyconius's idea and stated authoritatively that the millennium of Apoc 20 is to be understood symbolically as referring to the age of the church on earth, the first phase of the interpretation of the Apocalypse came to an end.[13]

There were still some problems in the East: the Apocalypse was not included in the Greek liturgy and thus did not appear in lectionaries. Some Greek ecclesiastical writers from the Syro-Palestinian region still felt the same hesitation as had Eusebius: they do not appear to make use of the Christian apocalypse, and some, like Cyril of Jerusalem, did not consider it canonical. The first Syriac translation appeared rather late, and the text does not appear in the scriptural corpus of the Syrian church. The Western church, however, did not question the text's apostolicity or inspiration, although it was convinced that it demanded an allegorical interpretation. The literal interpretation of the Apocalypse became synonymous with an ignorant, millennialist, sectarian, Judaizing, and indeed heretical reading.

Ancient and medieval Christian exegetes initiated discussions that continue to this day. They identified the presence in the text of groups of seven entities ordered in sequence (letters, seals, bowls . . .) called "septets," claimed that these were symbolic descriptions of human history, and debated whether they represented different and successive periods or whether all the sequences referred to the same events, with each list "recapitulating" what had been said in the previous one.[14] They tried to understand the overall structure of the book, which seemed to be made up of seven sections, and they attributed a deliberate symbolic value to this fact.

The passionate and powerful interpretation of Joachim of Fiore blew like a whirlwind into this painstaking process. The Calabrian peasant who had joined the Cistercians, the most learned of the monastic orders, took the Apocalypse and the rest of Scripture as the basis for his own view of reality; the originality and autonomy of his thought can be accounted for only on the basis of the fact that he saw himself as a prophet. The whole of human history is divided into three ages, each of forty-two generations or 1260 years.[15] The

12. He counted the years from the birth of Abraham in 2016-2015 BCE. What is left of his text is in the version prepared and updated by Jerome, edited by R. Helm in GCS 47 (1956).

13. *Civ. Dei* 20.7-17. See Pincherle 1925, pp. 443-66.

14. See Biguzzi 1996.

15. A month is thirty days, and a generation is thirty years; by this means Joachim could give a new explanation to the numbers in Dan 7:25 and Apoc 11:2 and 12:6.

first, the Age of the Father, ended with the end of the OT; the second, the Age of the Son, was drawing to a close as Joachim wrote; and the third, the Age of the Spirit, would begin in 1261. In this last age — and this is where millennialism comes into play[16] — Christ would reign personally on the earth, and happiness, peace, and prosperity would be guaranteed by a new monastic order of celibates who would be his collaborators and soldiers; the "virgins" of Apoc 7 and 14 are a prophecy of the order founded by Joachim himself at the monastery of St. John in Fiore.[17] The beast that comes up from the sea (Apoc 13) is Islam, and its seemingly mortal wound is that inflicted by the Crusades, but now Saladin has reconquered Jerusalem, to the astonishment of the whole world, and may be destined to fulfill the prophecy about the little horn in Dan 7:8, 11.

Today we tend to consider Francis and his movement (or rather the swarm of movements that drew their inspiration from him) to be the true heirs of Joachim and his ideas. These movements held Joachim's exegetical and prophetic works (a trilogy whose central part was a commentary on the Apocalypse) to be the *evangelium aeternum* that the abbot of Fiore had predicted would appear to announce and sustain the Age of the Spirit. Even Dante, who was born after the fateful year, placed Joachim in paradise among the holy prophets, and the *Divine Comedy,* the last great apocalypse of medieval Europe, is imbued, from the vision on the greyhound onward, with themes and tones reminiscent of Joachim. From our point of view the importance of Joachim and his followers lies in the way in which they fully reintegrated John's text into the history of their own times and interpreted it in a political as well as a simply historical sense. From the end of the twelfth century (Joachim's commentary dates from 1195) countless groups and movements derive the pattern for their own religious and political activities from the pages of the Apocalypse that describe the millennium and the heavenly Jerusalem.[18] Antiecclesiastical and antipapal themes resonated clearly, especially during the Avignon papacy, which included, with the "Great Schism," the entire 14th and the beginning of the 15th centuries: a spiritual order of vir-

---

16. We now define as millennialist any movement that expects Christ to reign on the earth, regardless of whether or not this reign lasts exactly a thousand years. Joachim believed it would last 1260 years. He saw the Apocalypse as being divided into eight parts; the first six (each of which was in its turn subdivided into seven elements) describe the first six periods of the church's trials in the Age of the Son, the seventh (20:1-11) is the millennium, the Age of the Spirit, and the eighth is the final and eternal blessedness of the New Jerusalem.

17. The name is mysterious and possibly has a symbolic significance that escapes us.

18. These pages are often read in tandem with Luke's description in Acts of the primitive Christian community in Jerusalem.

gins (usually the Franciscans) would save the true church, while the official ecclesiastical hierarchy was compromised and corrupted by this world (see Apoc 14:4). Petrus Joannis Olivi held that the papacy itself was the Antichrist, Ubertino da Casale that Boniface VIII was the beast that rose from the sea.

The next phase was the Reformation. In his hasty *Introduction* of 1522 Luther claimed that he did not think the Apocalypse was either apostolic or inspired but rather was similar to *4 Ezra*. He said that while he did not want to force anyone to share his views, he preferred those biblical books that presented Christ in a "clear and pure" way.[19] However, in 1534 he decided to write a brief *Commentary* that was firmly political and anti-Roman in tone. Here the two beasts of Apoc 13 are the empire (then led by Charles V) and the papacy. This latter is the beast with two horns because, Luther says, the papacy is also an earthly kingdom.[20] By and large, although with some notable exceptions,[21] Protestant exegesis after Luther takes up this anti-Roman interpretation of the text. Catholics for their part, particularly Spanish Jesuit exegetes, produced ever-longer commentaries on the Apocalypse, in which we see a historicization of many parts of the text that makes the debates of the 17th and 18th centuries very similar to our contemporary discussions. There is full and open debate about the identity of the seven emperors, and a clear awareness of the issue of the text's date, which was given as coming between the reign of Nero and that of Domitian. In his 1619 *Commentary* the Jesuit Juan de Mariana revived the legend of Nero returned to life as a plausible way of making sense of Apoc 13:3. In this type of exegesis, which is close to meeting our definition of scientific, we see the beginnings of those internal issues that will characterize later exegesis when it is the work of churchmen; if John really believed in Nero restored to life — a diabolical imitation of Christ's resurrection — is a modern-day believer obliged to believe in it too? Catholics and Protestants from the major groups were united, however, in their rejection of the millennium: this was usually interpreted allegorically as the spiritual reign of Christ through the church. A chiliastic interpretation reappears in the pietistic movement in German Protestantism at the dawn of the 18th century; there is a 1693 work to this effect by Spener.

The exegetical transformation that began with the Enlightenment and continues today was the accompaniment and result of a genuine theological

19. Walch 1987, pp. 140-41.
20. Walch 1987, pp. 130-39.
21. In the middle of the 16th century the learned Bibliander put the Apocalypse back into its historical context, identifying the various "kings" with the succession of Roman emperors. The beast is the Roman Empire, its "mortal" wound the death of Nero, and its recovery the restoration of Vespasian.

revolution, the work primarily of British and French thinkers. In the arena of Christology, a conceptual distinction was made between the human Jesus and Christ. The figure who emerges from the NT is the man Jesus, the preacher from Nazareth, who is studied primarily or exclusively with respect to his humanity. This study is the province of reason, and reason uses its own tools and does not concern itself with speculations about the divinity of Christ, which come to be considered "the Christian myth." Secular and historicist investigations of this sort come to be defined as "exegesis" to distinguish them from "hermeneutics," meaning study with an ecclesiastical orientation that attempts to comprehend the religious dimension of a text which it considers sacred.

It is within the area of exegesis that we find the first attempts to understand the Apocalypse in relation to the Judaism or Jewish Christianity of its time. The learned French Jesuit Jean Hardouin, who was famous for his eccentric views and died after subscribing the condemnation of his works, was convinced that the Apocalypse must be situated in the Palestinian context: the seven letters were addressed to the Jewish Christians of Jerusalem, and even if the beast's seven heads were the Roman emperors up to Nero, Babylon was Jerusalem. Hardouin's commentary on the NT, which came out in a posthumous pirated edition in Le Havre in 1741, was already on the Index by 1742. The Protestant rationalist Firmin Abauzit also held that John's prophecy was about the end of Jerusalem in 70 CE: Babylon is Jerusalem, the seven mountains are the seven hills on which it is built, and the seven heads are the city's last seven high priests. His commentary, published in 1770, is dedicated to demonstrating that Christianity is the only "rational religion"; it was put on the Index in 1774. The completely or primarily anti-Jewish interpretation of the Apocalypse, however, continued to be the opinion of a minority, despite the appearance of works of considerable erudition, full of parallels from rabbinic literature,[22] and notwithstanding the wholehearted agreement of a Romantic and, at least in part, anti-Enlightenment figure such as Johann Gottlieb Herder.[23]

Major German exegesis never questioned the Jewish roots of the Apocalypse, but continued to hold that the text is imbued with a spirit of fierce anti-Romanism. Luther's judgment (or prejudice) is ever present: Babylon can only be imperial Rome, a prophecy of papal Rome. As long as it is properly historicized, this interpretation is acceptable both to traditional Catholics, for

22. A work along these lines, by the Protestant theologian and orientalist Johann Cristoph Harenberg, appeared in 1759.
23. His book on the Apocalypse appeared in 1779.

whom the reference is exclusively to pagan Rome, and to more progressive Catholics, who have no great quarrel with the institution of the papacy in itself but who regard the apocalyptic Babylon as a prefiguration of the church's embroilment in worldly affairs and its need for purification. In the course of the 19th century a sort of consensus took shape under the influence of German-speaking Protestant exegetes. The author of the Apocalypse[24] is a Judaizing Christian who expects the imminent collapse of Rome and the end of the world. This position brings with it a significant hermeneutical problem in that the prophecies were not realized; Rome did not fall when he expected it, nor did the world end. This is not a problem for those exegetes without ecclesiastical commitments, who refer rather to the principle that a prophecy corresponding with historical events must have been written after those events and therefore attempt to assign a precise date to the Apocalypse, as was done in the case of Daniel. The evidence does not always line up in the Apocalypse, however, because everything in the text is open to debate and some elements seem to contradict others. This led to the supposition that the text was rewritten by the same prophet, who adapted his account of his visions to new circumstances and possibly to new visions.

In the second half of the 19th century, and particulary in its last two decades, a flood of new hypotheses destroyed the literary unity of the work. Scholars began to posit that the existing text was a collage of apocalypses by different authors (Cerinthus, John Mark, the elder, or unknown others) from different periods, which had been put together by a redactor. The oldest texts were held to hail from the era of Claudius or Caligula or Nero, while the redactor — or even a series of different redactors — was said to have been active as late as the era of Trajan or even of Hadrian. In the same period E. Vischer, a disciple of Harnack, made what seemed to be an indisputable observation: certain parts of the text could not have been written by a Christian. What faithful Christian could have prophesied the birth of a Messiah like the one described in ch. 12, where the child is caught up into heaven the moment he is born and kept isolated there until his triumphant return at the end? Within the existing text, then, at least one and possibly two Jewish apocalypses were reworked by a Christian redactor who is responsible for the final changes to the book. Scholarship in the history of religions joined with literary criticism in bringing to light the different cultural backgrounds of various parts of the Apocalypse. From this was born a kind of "theory of fragments,"

---

24. Only Catholics still believe that John was the apostle; Protestant exegesis usually attributes the book to John the elder, the author of 2 John and 3 John, to John Mark from Acts 12:12, or to another John not otherwise known.

according to which a Christian redactor reworked fragments from very old traditions, whose origins can be traced back for centuries or even millennia, rooted as they were in ancient myths of Babylonian or Persian or even Egyptian origin, all of which had been more or less filtered through Judaism. Each fragment has its own history, different from that of the other fragments. This method was notably espoused by Wilhelm Bousset, who produced an epoch-making study of the myth of the Antichrist, which was supposed to have existed first in pre-Christian and then in Christian form.

There were still scholars who, while making use of the tools of historical and literary criticism and the history of religions, tried to preserve the book's profound unity. The work of Robert Henry Charles was notable for the way in which it set the Apocalypse within the context of the Jewish apocalyptic tradition. He reinstated the figure of the author, a Christian prophet called John who was different from the author of the Gospel, but he was compelled to admit the involvement of an editor, whom he called "fanatical and celibate," "stupid" and "ignorant," and who mangled the text, especially the final part, cutting, moving passages, and inserting phrases of his own that were inconsistent with John's real message.[25] The work of the contemporary exegete lies essentially in the reconstruction of the original text and the identification of every single interpolation.

More recent work emphasizes the importance of the book's redaction, and defends more firmly the unity of the text, sometimes on the basis of modern theories of literary[26] or even of dramatic structure: the Apocalypse should be seen as a drama in seven acts with seven scenes each.[27] Catholic circles, on the other hand, have seen the birth of the "Johannine school." On the basis of Papias's testimony about the presbyters of Asia Minor, they hold John to have had a group of disciples who listened to his preaching and then produced at various times the various works attributed to their master. This solution protects the basic unity of the Johannine corpus of the NT,[28] preserves its inspiration and apostolicity, and even explains the dual ending of the Fourth Gospel, the variety of language among the vari-

---

25. His rants against the phantom reviser can be attributed to the exegete's frustration at the difficulty of the text, while his dislike for celibacy and "obscurantism" are to be expected from an author who at the time was the archdeacon of Westminster (see in particular Charles I 1920, pp. 50-55); for Bousset see the English edition: Bousset 1896 and Jenks, 1991.

26. These theories study the work as an epistle (Karrer 1986) or as a text designed for liturgical use (Vanni 1980[2]).

27. Bowman 1968.

28. The concept of a "school" is applied to other teachers (Paul, Peter, Matthew) and is used to explain the existing condition of almost all of the NT.

ous writings attributed to John, and the theological shifts or developments within the corpus.[29]

The various forms of historical-critical research are united in the conviction — born of the Enlightenment and filtered through the experience of positivism — that an inherently secular approach is the only guarantee of scientific objectivity. Beginning with this assumption, scholars incessantly point out each other's "theological" presuppositions. Exegetes and theologians both religious and secular, however, are in agreement on the dangers of a hermeneutic not founded on scientific exegesis. There are many dissenters from this new orthodoxy. Some, like those who see the angels and devils of the Apocalypse as the manifestation of life-forms from other planets, do not really seem very dangerous.[30] What is more worrisome is the rich religious and cultural world that feeds on irrationalism and apocalyptic themes. This is a complex phenomenon. Recent studies claim that at least a quarter of the population of the United States belong to Christian groups or movements of a kind that are usually called fundamentalist, and that are distinguished by their belief that after a cosmic crisis Christ will return to reign on earth; scholars use the presence of this belief to distinguish fundamentalist from other groups.[31] Beyond or within the broader world of fundamentalist churches there are radical subgroups whose obsession with the Apocalypse can lead to mass suicide or to armed resistance to the state, which they see as the manifestation of Satanic power. In contemporary literature the tragedy of Jonestown has recently been superseded by the massacre of the preacher and apocalyptic prophet David Koresh, together with his followers, the Branch Davidians, in Waco, Texas.[32]

29. This allows some Catholic scholars to break up the text as their Protestant or secular colleagues do, while still maintaining an orthodox position (e.g., Boismard 1949). In any case, the various redactors operating after John all belong to the same school, the presence of John in which guarantees its authority.

30. In the work of Dalila and Gérard Lemaire the curious reader can find everything from flying saucers to prophecies of the pyramid of Cheops, Padre Pio, and Sun Myung Moon (Lemaire 1976).

31. In past years the crisis was usually identified with nuclear war, but now after the "red dragon" (Apoc 12:3) of Soviet communism has collapsed without precipitating a world war, the expected crisis is more often the slower but not less inevitable collapse of the ecosystem (Strozier 1994).

32. The "white night" that saw the suicide of more than 900 followers of Jim Jones took place on November 18, 1978; see Endleman 1993. David Koresh (Vernon Wayne Howell) believed that he was the Lamb who would offer himself up, while his followers probably thought that they were witnessing the opening of the fifth seal of the Apocalypse on April 19, 1993 (see Arnold 1994, pp. 23-31). The massacre in Oklahoma City seems to have been conceived as an act of revenge for the events at Waco.

Historical-critical exegesis — the necessary prelude to a "scientifically correct" hermeneutic — seemed to have the power to secure rational Christianity against the excesses of the sects. Conservative theologians could deploy historical readings against all those interpretations that they considered to be "wild" and that would relate the book directly to the contemporary world, including those interpretations associated with liberation theology, according to which John's anti-Romanism and antiimperialism are merely prophetic symbols of the modern antiimperialism that should be proper to the church. In any case, historical criticism provided a logical defense against what it saw as the fantastical, deviant, and unfounded claims of the new apocalypticism. In the last decades, however, after a critical ferment that began between the wars, "postmodern" positions have mounted a frontal attack on earlier certainties.[33] This is less an organized movement than a form of thought that seems to have roots in both literary and psychological reflection. Its first step is the awareness that when historical-critical inquiry claims to reconstruct the historical context of a text and to situate it, its author, and the first readers or hearers therein, it is in fact making an illegitimate claim. In reality when we read a text (the Apocalypse) we cannot reach the historical figure of its author (John), but only the image of himself that he wants to give us in that particular text. The real author is lost to us, and all that remains for us to work with is a virtual image.

The same is true of the readers. We learn nothing from the text about the historical situation of the audience of the seven letters; we see only the image of them created by John. The first readers or hearers of the Apocalypse are ideal Christians imagined by John, and if we rely exclusively on the text we cannot construct a realistic history or sociology. This leaves the exegete in a Pirandellian limbo of virtual characters with even more virtual authors. It is only with the next step, however, that the final blow falls. Every text is stillborn in the moment of its writing, when it becomes precisely a text, and it is we who bring it (back) to life by reading or listening to it. All we can actually reach is our own mental reconstruction of a text. Thus any historical research, however decked with the trappings of scientific objectivity, can generate only subjective theories. More important than the text itself are the contexts and the pretexts — all the cultural baggage that we bring to the text and that we rediscover in the results of our research. "Postmodernism" is characterized by the awareness that communication is impossible. The first disturbing result of this is that all interpretations, all methodological approaches, are equally legitimate, or illegitimate. The Jesus of Bultmann or of the most secular of

33. Adam 1995.

secular exegetes is no more nor less valuable than the Christ of David Koresh or the most bigoted of contemporary apocalyptic sects. This relativism has two consequences that lead in opposite directions. At the conservative pole all those biblical interpretations, even the most irrational or traditionalist, that had been sidelined by historical-critical research are reappearing and trying to stake out a holding within scientific territory. At the progressive pole new exegetical methods are taking heart and finding their feet, so much so that it is no longer possible to ignore psychoanalytical[34] or feminist[35] readings of the Apocalypse.

2. In this volume I offer an analysis of the Apocalypse that aims to reconnect with the traditions of historical-critical research. "Postmodernism" has brought a breath of fresh air to what was becoming a stale atmosphere, but its tendency to relativize absolutely everything seems to me to be counterproductive, and not merely for pragmatic reasons. From a strictly methodological point of view an important distinction must be maintained. While it is true that in and of itself the object of scientific research is inaccessible to us, it is equally true that there is an area of human reality to which we do have access. Beyond its borders, the absolute truth is not within our grasp — a fact that I believe was acknowledged by Western philosophy and theology even before the advent of "postmodern" criticism. In absolute terms the 1st century is beyond our reach, and even if we could reach it, we could not fully describe it. The man John, in his individuality, is indeed lost to us forever. Despite this, however, if we accept the imprecision that characterizes the human sciences, we can indeed make an approach to the 1st century, to John, and to the Apocalypse.

I see the Apocalypse as a unified text, the work of a historical figure by the name of John. I agree with the recent critical tendency that claims that John wrote his text in the expectation that it would be read at several levels.[36] This emerges from the fact that the text has a deep coherence that is evident only

---

34. E.g., Raguse 1993. The author is a German psychologist and theologian of the Freudian school who is in polemic with Jungian interpretations of the text. One of the limitations of this or similar works lies in its connection with traditional historical-critical exegesis: if the historical interpretation changes, so do the functions of the figures in the story, as does their relation with the author, thus threatening the collapse of the psychoanalytic interpretation (see Lupieri 1999).

35. E.g., Pippin 1992 and 1994. Her work is an enlightening attempt to explain to male exegetes and ecclesiastics what a woman of the 20th century experiences when she reads a text like the Apocalypse, whose author seems to be deeply androcentric and antifeminist. The Apocalypse can be salvaged only for its antiimperial (and thus antiimperialist) sentiments, which can serve a "liberationist" function (see Lupieri 1999).

36. Bauckham 1993.

on serious study. A superficial reader or hearer, for instance, who did not reflect on the text at length, would not notice that it contains seven blessings, but since this very probably has symbolic value, it must be the case that the text requires in-depth study as well as superficial reading. At the deeper level in particular the text requires allegorical interpretation, and in this case such interpretation is not an escape hatch for an exegete who finds himself forced to deal with a text that has, with the passage of time, come to seem improbable and whose relevance he somehow needs to restore. When handling the Apocalypse, it is both legitimate and necessary to proceed allegorically, in a way which I will clarify later.

What we must ask, then, is whether it is historically possible for a 1st-century author to expect his work to be read at several levels, and to demand from his reader allegorical reading and reflection. I will argue that it is indeed possible, inasmuch as John places himself conceptually and literarily within the tradition of Jewish thought that we call apocalyptic.

II. Apocalypse and Apocalyptic

What we call the *Jewish apocalyptic tradition*[37] was formed in the period after the exile, in reaction to the exaltation of the Law and of the rules of observance. This sometimes extreme exaltation of the Law had been introduced as part of the reform attributed to Ezra, the goal of which was the ethnic and ritual purity of the people. The earliest form of Jewish apocalyptic literature of which we know appears in the *Book of the Watchers* (*BW;* 4th-3rd century

37. The terms *apocalyptic* and *apocalypticism* are generally used in reference to three different phenomena. In their broadest sense they designate an extremely long-lived literary phenomenon that is not exclusively Jewish and that still exists in the religious cultures that derive from Jewish/Christian/Islamic roots. In recent years *apocalypticism* has been defined as a literary genre that includes all the texts that resemble the Apocalypse in some way or other. The first element that distinguishes an apocalypse from other texts is that it is the account of a "revelation" that in Greek is precisely ἀποκάλυψις, "apocalypse." As is the case with all literary genres, the formal resemblances between apocalyptic texts do not imply that they all share a point of view: two apocalypses that may have been written centuries apart will not express the same ideology. In its second sense *apocalyptic* can refer to a vision of the world that is apocalyptic in nature. Not only can this be shared by members of different faiths, but it can also appear in texts that are not apocalypses in the literary sense; it is possible, for instance, to speak of an "apocalyptic discourse" in a Gospel. In its third sense *apocalyptic* refers to a particular Jewish tradition that has produced a series of texts (almost all of them apocalypses) and behind which we can imagine an originally distinct conceptual school within Judaism. See Sacchi 1990; for a further historical contextualization see Sacchi 1994; Lupieri 1997², 1:5-137.

BCE), which was inspired by the lost *Book of Noah*. In this book the existence of evil is attributed not to the sin of Adam or Eve but rather to the sin of the Watchers.[38] In the age of Jared, the father of Enoch, some angels became infatuated with women because of "their beauty." Their sexual union violated a distinction imposed by God, who had made reproduction permissible to humans because their nature is mortal, but not to immortal angels.[39] The commixture of the two natures, angelic and human, resulted in the contamination of the whole created world.[40] The giants who were born from the coupling of angels and women (see Gen 6:1-4) committed unspeakable abominations: they tormented men to the point of eating their flesh and drinking their blood, thus bringing the world's defilement to an unbearable level. At this point God intervened, and by the mediation of the holy angels had the rebels imprisoned and all the giants killed. Their immortal souls, though, continued to torment men in the form of evil spirits; this concept marks the birth of the devils. *BW* is part of the *First Book of Enoch (1 Enoch)*, so called for the name of the seer.[41] He acquires all knowledge, to the point of becoming God's scribe and acting as God's intermediary both to humans and to the sinful angels. The account, which is hostile to Ezra's reform, has two implications. First of all, it is not pure-blooded Jews who contaminate themselves with foreign women, but rather it was the angels who contaminated all of hu-

38. "Watchers" were a particular category of angels charged with overseeing the created world and men; the rebellion occurred among their number.

39. One level of the redaction of *BW* specifies that the sin of the angels consists in having divulged to their human wives the secrets of heaven (astronomy) and earth (medicine): sinful knowledge moves from the sexual to the intellectual arena. We can detect here the presupposition behind the demonic interpretation of Eve's sin: the serpent was not an animal but an evil angel (i.e., to use more modern terminology, a devil) who had shared forbidden knowledge with the woman. It is possible that the Enochic tradition was influenced in this detail by the tradition of Genesis, which was originally more interested in gnosiological problems than in sexual sins.

40. This resolves a problem within the Genesis account: if only man sinned, why do the animals suffer too? Moreover, and also unlike the Genesis account, death is not a punishment but a mere fact of nature, which had been established by God before sin.

41. *1 Enoch* is made up of five Jewish apocalyptic texts, of which *BW* is the first and the most ancient. Together they are attributed to Enoch, the antediluvian patriarch, and the seventh man after Adam. The Bible does not say that he died but rather that, after 365 years (a year of years), he "walked with God" (Gen 5:24). Inasmuch as he is not dead but still alive with God (see comments on 11:3), Enoch becomes a central figure in apocalyptic texts. *1 Enoch* survives in its entirety in Ethiopic; there is a summary and fragments in Greek, as well as fragments of the Aramaic original discovered at Qumran. For the translations from Ethiopic I rely on the English text of Isaac (Charlesworth I 1983), which I compared with the Italian text of Fusella (Sacchi I 1981).

manity by their union with women; nobody, not even Ezra and the Jews who returned from exile, can claim to be pure.⁴² Secondly, it is impossible for man to purify himself, since evil originates in a higher realm against which he is powerless. Observance is thus impossible. On the other hand, if man cannot by his own powers free himself from an evil that dominates him in his very nature, then salvation must come from a power that is also greater than man.

The first apocalyptic works introduced several new ideological themes into Judaism, such as individual survival after death, whether in the form of an eternal soul in an otherworld of reward and punishment, or in the form of a resurrection of the dead, in which holy humans receive in a new life what they did not receive in their first. The apocalyptic insistence that sin is inevitable for men means that this life after death will take the form of eternal condemnation for most of the human race; the saved are a small minority. The more recent strata of *BW* do not think that the sin of the angels in the time of Jared adequately accounts for all of the evil on the earth; the sin of Cain came first.⁴³ Consequently, the book posits the existence of a sin that preceded mankind; on the fourth day of creation seven "luminary" angels, that is, seven stars, refused to accept the cosmic order willed by God. These are seven errant heavenly bodies, the planets,⁴⁴ whose rebellious orbits show how the whole of creation was disfigured from its very beginning. The *Book of Astronomical Writings (BA)*,⁴⁵ which appeared at the end of the 3rd century BCE, saw astronomy as the supreme knowledge that God granted to Enoch, and thus suggested a new approach to the problem whereby everything is predetermined and there is no such thing as angelic sin nor personal responsibility. Heavenly tablets, kept in God's court, bear written record from all eternity of the destiny of all. Man is sinful because he was created as such, and there would be no salvation for him had not God decided to save a few. The text is probably woven into *1 Enoch* because of its determinism, which denies the possibility of a covenant with God and renders any observance useless.⁴⁶

42. This is still an androcentric mode of thought. Contamination arises from sexual relations between a superior male being (angels; pure-blooded Jews) and an inferior feminine being (women in general; non-Jewish women). Whatever the responsibility of the male, the motive for the sin lies in the very nature of the feminine.

43. According to this tradition, Adam did not sin.

44. The Greek πλάνητες means precisely "wanderers" (see n. 76) and is used to indicate the Sun and Moon and the five planets known to the ancients (Mercury, Venus, Mars, Jupiter, and Saturn).

45. This apocalypse is another part of *1 Enoch*: fragments of it were discovered at Qumran. The Aramaic text is rather fuller than the Ethiopic version known to us.

46. This book is probably contemporary with the *Book of the Giants*, about which we knew almost nothing before its discovery at Qumran. As far as we can tell, in this book the demons re-

Judaism in the 2nd century BCE was characterized by the armed struggle against the forced imposition of Hellenism and the Hasmonean rise to power. Various positions arose that gave rise to the "schools" (as Josephus calls them): to the political, cultural, and religious parties familiar to modern scholars. Various groups of observant Jews decided to separate themselves from the rest of the people and to observe the Law in such a way as to guarantee their salvation within a corrupt world. The largest group was that of the Pharisees (the term itself means "separated"), while the most famous today are the Essenes, who at the time were second to the Pharisees in number. The period of the uprising produced two texts, the *Book of Dreams* (*BD*, from 163 BCE)[47] and Daniel. According to *BD*, Enoch dreamed the whole of human history from his own time up to the war, which is possible because all of future history is already contained in the divine present. The sin of the angels reappears in this text, in which the rebel angels have a leader who leads angels and men astray; we saw the birth of the devils in *BW* and now see the birth of the devil. Evil is so rooted in the world that neither the angels who remained faithful to God nor the flood was able to uproot it. The period after the exile is a bad one as well: God sends seventy angel-shepherds to lead the flock of Israel, but they go astray and thus are to be imprisoned and punished. The text's judgment on the priestly world of Jerusalem, spiritually represented by these sinful angels, is thus as pointed as is its ideological departure from that world: there is no such thing as a covenant between God and man. Although Enoch dreams all of history, his dream does not include Sinai.[48] Daniel, on the other hand, reaffirms the validity of the covenant with God and the ideological pillars of the tradition of Ezra thanks to its notion of resurrection, which makes possible personal retribution in a future world. For Daniel, as for the apocalypses of the Enochic tradition, this world is under condemnation: God's will can be realized only in a future world but, thanks again to the

---

pent and receive God's forgiveness and salvation. This eschatology may have been judged deviant since the book is not included in *1 Enoch*, although it is attributed to Enoch. It seems to have been used by the Manicheans.

47. We can be precise in dating these texts because they are linked to certain political and religious elements of the Maccabean war: events whose dates we know and that the text describes as still to happen. After the last event that the authors were familiar with, the prophecy becomes more vague and imprecise, or else the end of the world comes and with it the triumph of the righteous.

48. There is not even such a thing as free will and thus, as there is no personal responsibility, there is no room for observance or for retribution: the "just" are the elect, chosen by God. Unlike other Enochic texts, this one does not include immortality or personal survival; after the judgment and the purification of this world there will be a future world, governed by the eschatological Messiah, in which everyone will be just.

resurrection, the just, meaning the observant, will be saved in that world. Daniel thus uses both typically Enochic ideas and the literary form of apocalyptic to defend the spirituality of the tradition of Ezra. It is for this reason that, after some hesitation, Daniel entered into the Jewish and Christian canons, while *BD* became part of the *First Book of Enoch*.

In the political arena the Hasmonean period saw profound changes throughout the Middle East, as two new powers emerged — Rome and the Parthians. Torn apart by bitter dynastic struggles, the royal family finally ceded power to the Idumean Herod, called the Great. His unscrupulous political conduct kept him on the throne for an unusually long period of time (37-4 BCE), and he even died in his bed. As a subject-king of Rome, he succeeded in maintaining a position of stability and relative independence through difficult times. During times of peace he dedicated himself to an intense program of building: his contemporaries could view him as a benefactor. In the religious arena he had a policy of being "all things to all men": he was a pagan among pagans and among Jews he observed the Law. The greatest symbol of his political and religious conscientiousness was his rebuilding of the temple in Jerusalem. An extremely important pilgrimage site, and the focus of enormous religious and economic interests,[49] the temple and its cult became more than ever the center of Jewish religious life. After Herod Roman control over the region grew until they took over the administration of Judea where, according to Josephus's account, the Roman administrators' greed, arrogance, and ignorance of Judaism were possibly the main factors in the progressive deterioration of the social and political situation. Armed rebellion broke out in 66 CE.

In this period the final parts were added to the *Book of Enoch* — the *Book of the Similitudes (BS)* and the *Epistle of Enoch (EE)*. In the *BS* individuals seem to be predetermined. The sin of the angels also appears in this text, as does the leader of sinners, the devil, who is distinct from his followers. The angels' sin lies in their having revealed science, the arts, and above all the construction of weapons of war to their human wives. All knowledge is thus sin,[50] and all power the fruit of a diabolic education. The "just" — always in the sense of the elect rather than the observant — are the "poor," the little ones whom God chooses (the readers and hearers of the text did not reap any benefits from the power of the Hasmoneans, Herod, or the Romans). Salva-

49. The Jerusalem temple, like pagan temples, functioned as a bank for the sovereign, for individuals, and even for foreigners.

50. Knowledge as sin — or sin as knowledge — echoes the Genesis account (see n. 39). *BS* contains an attempt to reconcile the Enochic myth with that of Genesis: one of the leaders of the rebel angels is said to be the seducer of Eve.

tion, like sin, will be a cognitive revelation from the heavenly realm. The Son of Man,[51] a being created before the stars (and thus destined for the salvation of men even before the sin of the angels), reveals to men where the righteousness of God really lies: God's righteousness is his mercy. The Son of Man, identified at the end of the book with Enoch himself, will execute justice, and will then live among men. As we can see, this book has many similarities to what is found in primitive Christianity. *EE* stands out from the other texts of the Enochic tradition, although its author wants to be considered one of them.[52] According to this book, there was no angelic sin, and the Watchers, who have always remained faithful to God, will execute God's judgment on the human world. There is a verse that states that the mountains cannot be slaves of woman, by which is intended that the heavenly angels (the mountains) cannot become infatuated with women, or allow themselves to be seduced by them.[53] Although the stages of history are predetermined, human sin and personal responsibility do exist.

The period from the rise of the Maccabeans to the war with Rome saw the flowering of the Essene movement and literary production at Qumran, where texts from the Enochic tradition were read, if not composed.[54] It is likely that not all of the texts found at Qumran originated with the Essenes or expressed the ideas of the sectarians who lived there; it is certain, however, that apocalyptic ideas (sometimes linked to the figure of Enoch) were current at Qumran, and possibly a topic of discussion. The phenomenon of Qumran and the Essenes was neither particularly short-lived nor especially enduring within Jewish history; we can trace a development lasting about two hundred years, during which time there were changes in their theology and view of the world. Certain ideas, such as angelology and its implications, seem to have been firmly established, at least among a majority of the Essenes, at the beginning of the Christian era. According to the Essene view, God created two angelic princes at the very beginning: the prince of light, that God might love

51. The term comes from Daniel, but it seems to be used here to represent an exalted, even a "superangelic," spiritual being. The fact that it appears in non-Christian Judaism at the time of the birth of Christianity helps us to understand what people in Palestine might have thought when the phrase was applied to Jesus and became a title.

52. This text utilized the so-called *Apocalypse of the (Ten) Weeks*, an otherwise lost Enochic text that perhaps dates from the 2nd century BCE, in which the seer contemplates the whole of human history, from creation to judgment, divided into ten weeks of times.

53. *1 Enoch* 98:4. This passage is probably a criticism of *1 Enoch* 18:13–19:1 *(BW)*. For the identity of angels, mountains, and stars, see part 3 below.

54. It seems quite clear now that the Enochic texts reached Qumran only during the early stage of the settlement. The scrolls of *1 Enoch* are among the oldest, and do not seem to have been copied later (on this matter see Boccaccini 1998 and 2005).

him, and the prince of darkness, that he might hate him. The spiritual world is divided in two, and the numberless ranks of the angels of light and the angels of darkness confront each other, just as the human world is divided into good and evil. The "sons of light" are the holy minority of men (holy because they are chosen by God), who are surrounded by the multitude of the "sons of darkness," the corrupt and impure remainder of humanity that includes first of all non-Essene Jews with their rulers and priests. Worship in Jerusalem has been corrupted by the impurity of wicked priests who do not follow the precepts of the Teacher of Righteousness, the founder of the sect and himself a priest. Jerusalem is still holy despite this: the *Temple Scroll (TS)* and the text entitled *New Jerusalem (NJ)* contain detailed descriptions of features and dimensions of the eschatological temple and the city. By the inscrutable decree of God the entire human world is following the forces of darkness and is headed toward the final conflict, after which the elect will share in the eschatological victory of the forces of light. The *War Scroll (WS)* contains minute instructions about the human part in this cosmic struggle. The ages and numbers of the true Jews — the members of the sect — are given: they will be exhorted by seven priests, who will sound their trumpets at various moments in the battle, and they will fight for a jubilee of years ($7 \times 7 = 49$ years), resting one year in every seven, until they have conquered the entire world. Two Anointed Ones will appear, one from David's line and one from Aaron's. According to a characteristically priestly concept, the Davidic Anointed will be merely a military commander, and will be subject to the Aaronic. When war really did break out against the Romans, the Essenes joined in the armed resistance, and one of them, named John, was one of the first leaders of the insurrection.

66 CE was the beginning of a terrible period for the Jews. Within seventy years Judaism had largely vanished from Judea, and the Romans had even changed the region's name (to *Syria Palestina*) to blot out any trace of its Jewish past. We have an exceptional and passionate account of the first war (which culminated in the taking of Jerusalem in 70 CE but did not end until the fall of Masada in 74) from Josephus, a participant and eyewitness. His work describes the horrors of war, which in ancient times was often aimed at the extermination of the enemy population, in a tone that can readily be described as apocalyptic. The second Jewish insurrection, from 115 to 117 CE, does not seem to have involved Judea, but instead devastated Egypt, much of Roman North Africa, Crete, Cyprus, and possibly part of Mesopotamia. This rebellion probably broke out in the expectation that the Romans would be defeated by the Parthians (Trajan was still advancing toward the Persian Gulf); Jews rose up in various places, slaughtered hundreds of thousands of

their pagan neighbors, and were in their turn massacred in the Roman repression. A semblance of order was reestablished that lasted until 132. When Hadrian, having banned circumcision throughout the empire, decided to construct a pagan city on the ruins of Jerusalem and a temple to Jupiter on the site of the Jewish temple,[55] the Jews rose up again and named as their leader Bar Kosiba, known to his followers as Bar Kochba, "Son of the Star." His messianic nature was acknowledged by many, including the famous Rabbi Aqibah, who was later executed by the Romans. The war (132-35 CE) was merciless and bitter; the Roman's policy of destruction is described in rabbinic sources that tell us that the Romans "ploughed" Jerusalem before building Aelia Capitolina, which nobody circumcised was permitted to enter.

Some Jews attempted to explain to themselves and to other Jews how it could be that God had decided to abandon Jerusalem and the temple although he was no less faithful to his promises or to his love for his people, and a considerable number of apocalyptic texts appeared between 70 and 135. Several contain speculations about the cosmic week: just as the world was created in one week, so has God determined that it will continue through seven periods of varying length. There is a widespread sense of living in the end times, although some texts refuse to predict a precise date and envisage a longer period before the end. There is an expectation that God will intervene in history through the appearance of a messianic figure and the overturning of the present painful state of affairs. The destruction of Jerusalem is explained as God's punishment for the sins of Israel, in keeping with the interpretation of history in 1 and 2 Chronicles. The nature of the sins varies, although it usually has to do with inadequate observance of the Law and with idolatry, whereas in Christian texts the decisive guilt lies in the rejection and killing of Jesus. There is a corresponding variety in the conclusions of the apocalypses and of human history. In non-Christian Jewish texts the punishment of Jerusalem is temporary; the people will be pardoned and the city and temple rebuilt as already happened in the time of Nebuchadnezzar. In Christian texts, on the

---

55. There is a contemporary debate on the extent of the destruction of Jerusalem in 70 CE. Some buildings, including synagogues, remained standing; the temple itself was burned, but it was not razed to the ground by the Romans. The site was regarded as somehow sacred even by pagans: Josephus recounts that the Romans offered sacrifices to the imperial eagle within the sacred enclosure of the temple itself, and that he himself went "to the temple" where the Romans had gathered captured women and children. Titus and his immediate successors did not prevent the Jews from returning to Jerusalem, nor did they forbid the practice of the Jewish religion. It is thus possible that some form of worship, albeit in a very reduced form, was again practiced after 70 in the sacred site of the temple, the ruins of which must therefore still have stood.

other hand, the guilt cannot be expiated and no stone of the temple will remain on another (Mark 13:2).

The *Fourth Book of Ezra (4 Ezra)* must have appeared before 100 CE because it predicts that the messianic kingdom will come and Israel's enemies be defeated exactly thirty years after the destruction of Jerusalem (70 + 30 = 100). The kingdom will last for 400 years and will end with the death of the Messiah. As human history seems to be subdivided into six periods of twenty jubilees each (20 × 49 = 980 years), this kingdom will occupy the last part of the sixth and final period.[56] After the messianic kingdom will come the final kingdom of God, like a cosmic Sabbath. One of the book's visions involves an old woman mourning for her only son, who died just before his marriage; she is Jerusalem/Israel, who at the end will be transfigured into a glorious city, the eschatological Jerusalem.[57] The book, which is set in Babylon during the exile, is troubled throughout by the question of why God would allow the destruction of his own people and the triumph of the wicked. It arrives at an unsatisfactory theodicy by concluding that God's plans are inscrutable. The visionary is not allowed to reflect on the fact that "many were created but few will be saved," but must simply abandon himself to God's will, which permitted Adam and his descendants to have a "wicked heart."

The *Second Book of Baruch (2 Bar.),* which is also set during the Babylonian destruction of Jerusalem, seems to have a later date. The most famous vision in this work is that of a great cloud that pours onto the earth alternate torrents of water of darkness and water of light. This is a summary of all of human history, which is defined as dark or as light according to Israel's obedience to the will of God. Past history consists of six nights followed by six days, for a total of six cosmic days, according to the Jewish way of measuring time, which puts night before day. The first night is the sin of Adam; an alternating series of nights and days lead to the sixth night, which is the destruction of Jerusalem by the hand of Nebuchadnezzar, and to the sixth day, which is the luminous period of the Second Temple. The present is the seventh night, the darkest moment in all of history, when Jerusalem lies wasted by the hands of Rome. As deep as is this darkness, the final moment of light, when the Messiah will illuminate the world like lightning and will destroy the power of the pagans, will be correspondingly bright. In this book, which is certainly Jewish, the Messiah will rule over the seventh period and God over the eighth,

---

56. Thus the world is destined to end in the 500th year after the birth of Jesus Christ. As we saw above, this idea was also shared by some Christians. For the relevant calculations see Lupieri 1992, pp. 117-24.

57. For the transfiguration of female figures in apocalyptic texts, see Humphrey 1995.

which will never end; the author was probably familiar with Christian ideas and was engaged in polemic against them. Jerusalem's destruction represents the focal point of all of human history — a painful but necessary preface to the coming of the Messiah.[58] *2 Baruch* also makes clear that Israel will never lack for trustworthy guidance while she is being punished: the Messiah will indeed come some day, but prophecy of his coming refers to a point in the future that is not specified and cannot be calculated. For this reason the apocalypse is often linked with rabbinic spirituality and dated to the first decades of the 2nd century.

The *Fourth Book of Baruch,* or the *Paraleipomena of Jeremiah (Par. Jer.)* was definitely produced before the Bar Kochba revolt. This book also is set during Nebuchadnezzar's destruction of Jerusalem, and contains a prophecy that the messianic reign and the liberation of Israel will come sixty-six years after the destruction, which means that the text was written before 136 CE (70 + 66), at which point the rebellion had already drowned in blood.[59]

The *Coptic Apocalypse of Elijah (Apoc. El.),* a strange text of Egyptian Judaism, probably dates from before 115-17 CE. The existing text has been Christianized, but gives evidence of a Jewish author who knew Christian traditions and was deliberately entering into competition with them.[60] Several scenes present a series of struggles against the Antichrist on the part of the "virgin Tabitha" (see Acts 9:36-41?), sixty martyrs, and Elijah and Enoch, who return to earth to be killed by the Antichrist (the Bible reports that neither of them died) and who come back to life after three and a half days. The parallel with the two unnamed "witnesses" of Apoc 11 is clear and, I believe, deliberate.

Some of the characteristic elements of Enochic texts also appear in apocalypses that do not feature Enoch, while on the other hand the figure of Enoch appears to have been an annoyance to some groups who nevertheless expressed their thought in the form of apocalypses. The *Apocalypse of Abraham*

---

58. In *4 Ezra* the destruction of Jerusalem — a terrible punishment that cannot be explained in human terms — does not in itself constitute a particular epoch in history, but occurs within one of the periods of history.

59. It is extremely difficult to date the *Third Letter of Baruch (3 Bar.),* which survives in Paleoslavic and Greek (this latter is more recent and is Christianized: it certainly dates from later than *Par. Jer.*). It is yet another lament over the fall of Jerusalem, but here Baruch is consoled by the contemplation of the heavens, of which he sees five, by acquiring the knowledge of the mysteries of the cosmos and by seeing the punishment of God's enemies (human beings appear in the form of composite animals). Because the coming redemption of Israel is not given a specific date, it is very difficult to tie the account to any precise historical moment besides the destruction of Jerusalem, which has already occurred.

60. The text's dependence on the NT is so great that some scholars consider it to be entirely Christian: Charlesworth 1987.

(Apoc. Abr.), which has also been dated between 70 and 135, includes at least four significant features found in Enochic texts, although Enoch does not appear in it. First of all, the seer contemplates past, present, and future in a "likeness of heaven"[61] that appears under his feet. The original Greek may have used ὁμοίωμα οὐρανοῦ to imply a belief in the existence of an intermediate dimension between human and divine where visions occur, and which is a "likeness of heaven": a reflection below of the spiritual sky above such as can be contemplated by mortal man.[62] Secondly, the *Apocalypse of Abraham* accepts the angelology and demonology of *BW*, at least to the extent that Azazel is the head of the fallen angels. Thirdly, it takes on the idea that the human visionary can act as an intermediary between a higher being and the fallen angels, as did Enoch in *BW*: here Abraham reproaches Azazel on obedience to the command of Iaoel.[63] Fourthly, it blends the myth of the angelic sin with that of Adam's sin, such that Azazel himself is the seducer of Adam and Eve, according to the system that we also find in *BD, BS* (where the seducer is Gader'el, an angelic leader),[64] and the Apocalypse (where the "ancient serpent" is also the chief of "his angels").[65] Within the Enochic tradition in the narrow sense — meaning that Enoch himself is the seer — is the *Second Book of Enoch (2 Enoch)*, which probably dates from the same years, and whose finale is almost a text in its own right. In this last section, the main figure is no longer Enoch, who is denied a role as an intercessor before God, but Melchizedek. He has both priestly and messianic attributes: he is born, weaned, and wearing priestly garments, from the corpse of his aged mother who became pregnant without having sexual relations. He is spared from the flood, caught up into heaven, and destined to serve as an intermediary before God. The extraordinary glorification of Melchizedek appears earlier in 11QMelchizedek, which can be dated to the second half of the 1st century BCE and which offers clues as to the meaning of some phrases in Hebrews.[66] The exaltation of a priestly messianic figure suggests that a spirituality connected to the priesthood persisted among non-Christian Jewish groups after 70 and possibly after 135. On the other hand, the transferal to Melchizedek of Enochic functions suggests that the figure of Enoch, possibly in the wake of *BS*, was still exalted in quite unique ways.

---

61. *Apoc. Abr.* 21:2.

62. For the rather complex organization of the heavens see Excursus VI in Norelli II 1995, pp. 375-80.

63. Iao-el contains, and sometimes is, the mystical name of Yahweh; see *Apoc. Abr.* 17:13.

64. *1 Enoch* 69:6.

65. Apoc 12:9.

66. Heb 7:1-17.

2 Enoch 64:5 (in the long version, which is the latest one) demonstrates that there were people who believed in Enoch's ability to "carry away" the sins of humanity. This must have given rise to some degree of hostility, at least in some rabbinic circles, as is confirmed by the so-called *Third Book of Enoch (3 Enoch)*. This text, which survives in Hebrew and is extremely difficult to date,[67] is a *sefer Hekalot*.[68] In it Enoch is identified with Metatron,[69] although his name does not appear in the traditional title, and not he but Rabbi Ishmael is the visionary. Enoch is certainly exalted by being identified with Metatron, but at the same time this identification rules out the possibility that Enoch is a messianic figure, as there is no chance that Metatron might "return." Enoch is also humbled in *3 Enoch* 16, which asserts that he cannot be the second power in heaven.[70] If we consider *3 Enoch* together with *2 Enoch* 65, where Enoch appears to deny his own salvific function, and especially with the Melchizedekian ending of *2 Enoch,* we must conclude that the ancient patriarch had become too burdensome, or too closely involved with some cultural reality (religious or sociopolitical) that had come to be seen as undesirable.

---

67. The final redaction may have been completed in the 6th century CE, but it definitely contains material from ancient traditions.

68. Or *Book of the Palaces:* the traditional title of accounts in which the visionary (usually a teacher following rabbinic tradition) undertakes a celestial journey that leads him to contemplate the "Palaces" — the heavenly temple in all its manifestations. As in *1 Enoch* 14, the divine heavenly temple is constructed like a Chinese box, into which the visionary enters, going deeper into himself at the same time as he rises through the heavens. It is difficult to assign a date to the origins of Jewish mysticism, but a text of which several copies were found at Qumran and Masada (called *Song of the Sabbath Sacrifice* or *ShirShabb;* the mss. are identified as 4Q ShirShabb/Masada ShirShabb) is full of speculations about multiple "dwellings" and of "carriage *(merkabot)* — thrones" of God and the angels in various heavens. These speculations tell us that the roots of medieval Jewish mysticism are in the Hellenistic-Roman era.

69. In much Jewish mystical speculation Metatron is the great angel, the prince of the heavenly host, who sits beside God's throne (the name seems to derive from μετά + θρόνος). He is identified with the OT angel who speaks in the name of God (e.g., Gen 16:7-13) and becomes the manifestation of God himself among men; there is a clear analogy between this figure and the Son of Philonian and Christian speculations.

70. This idea might also be directed against Christians, who are guilty precisely of introducing a "second power" into heaven, besides God. The scene in which Enoch/Metatron is humiliated describes him as "seated" next to the throne, in such a way that the visionary is led to believe that there must be another divine power in heaven, a "second principle" who can remain seated in the presence of God. Rabbi Ishmael is astonished, and God intervenes by having Metatron lashed with a whip of flame, so that there can be no doubt as to his own supreme authority. At the time of the text's redaction the rabbis may already have decided that the angels had no joints in their legs, so that they could not sit in God's court. That Enoch could sit probably reflects the role of heavenly scribe that is traditionally attributed to him; he was also of human origin and thus able to bend his knees (see the comments on 4:9-10).

If we bear in mind that other Jewish apocalyptic texts were produced (before they were censored by the rabbis, who were careful not to permit the circulation of books that might annoy the Romans), and that there were oracular texts produced in Egypt by Jews and attributed to the Sibyl,[71] it becomes apparent that much of the Jewish world was concerned with apocalyptic tremors. The final destruction of Judea in 135 seemed to put an end to Jewish hopes for revenge against the empire, and the cultural inheritance of Second Temple Judaism began to pass into the hands of rabbinic Judaism and a Christianity that was no longer Jewish.

III. Visions and Reality

The God of the prophets had accustomed Israel to receive symbolic messages in the form of visions of objects that indicated other realities. Jeremiah, for instance, sees two baskets, one of good and one of bad figs, which represent the destinies awaiting the two kingdoms into which Israel had been divided (24:1-10). The visions of other prophets became more complex and dynamic; Ezek 17, for example, involves two eagles, a cedar, and a vine. In Ezek 1:5-12 composite animals, some of them with human parts, appear and are interpreted as angelic figures. In *BD* animals of various types and colors represent humanity. Their coupling with the sinful angels is represented as stars falling from the sky among bovids (the first human generation): "I saw all of them (the fallen stars) extending their sexual organs like horses and commencing to mount the heifers [bovids]; and they all became pregnant and bore elephants, camels, and donkeys."[72] The angels who did not fall, on the other hand, are represented by human figures, and in particular by those "shepherds" to whom is given the task of governing Israel.[73] Daniel uses monsters composed of parts of different

71. In one of these the eruption of Vesuvius (79 CE) is treated as the beginning of the divine punishment of Rome, which is guilty of the destruction of Jerusalem. The idea must have been reasonably widespread since there is even a wall in Pompeii bearing the graffito SODOM AND GOMORRAH, as much as if to say that Pompeii was receiving the punishment of Sodom and Gomorrah. It is unlikely that a pagan would have thought of the Bible under such circumstances.

72. *1 Enoch* 86:4. Camels and donkeys are impure according to the Law (Lev 11:4ff.; Deut 14:7 — the impurity of the donkey can be deduced from the context), and elephants were making their appearance in Judea in those days as terrible weapons of war in the ranks of the Syrian army (1 Macc 6:30-46; 2 Macc 13:15).

73. See especially *1 Enoch* 89:59-71 and 90:20-25. Animal symbolism in visions about different peoples or categories of people were also probably developed under the influence of the parabolic language of wisdom literature; see, e.g., several cases in the *Book of Ahikar* (nos. 11, 12, 15-20, 25-29, etc.).

animals to show the diabolical and bestial aggression of the kingdoms of this world, the enemies of God and of his people.[74]

In some cases the prophet found himself impelled to perform symbolic gestures, which could be extremely demanding. Ezekiel was not only compelled to lie in chains first on one side and then the other for days on end, eating only small rations of impure food (Ezek 4:4-17), but also had to watch his wife, "the delight of his eyes," die, without shedding a tear (Ezek 24:15-27). Hosea's story was less tragic; he was obliged by God to marry a prostitute, to have three children with her, and finally to buy himself an adulteress, to show how God was going to behave in regard to Israel (Hos 1 and 3). In her relationship with a patriarchal God Israel could only play the part of a woman whose "unfaithfulness" takes the form of adultery and prostitution.[75] From the earliest accounts of prophetic and apocalyptic visions the visionary is called to enter into the vision and take part in what he sees. In Isa 6:5-7 the prophet sees one of the seraphs taking up "with tongs" a live coal from the altar before the Glory of God and touching his lips with it. Ezekiel receives and obeys an order to eat a scroll containing a written text (Ezek 2:9–3:3). It makes sense that the prophets' mouths should be involved, as their task is to speak.

Just as Jesus' "parable" about the fig tree in spring (Mark 13:28ff. and parallels) was immediately comprehensible to anyone living in the Mediterranean region, so too was Jeremiah's vision of the almond branch that refers allegorically to the watchfulness of God who will soon bring to pass what he has promised and threatened. It is just as comprehensible to us today. Conversely, when we read in Enoch about a star that falls from heaven (1 Enoch 86:1) we do not naturally think about the sin and fall of an angel. In antiquity, indeed, it was not a form of allegory to say that a star is an angel or vice versa; rather, it was both the statement of a religious truth and a widely accepted scientific hypothesis. All stars, whether fixed or moving, were spiritual beings.[76] Nobody in

74. Daniel 7. In Daniel and *BD* the visions treat of large sections of human history. There are considerable similarities in symbolic language, for example, the growth of a horn on a special animal: *1 Enoch* 90:9 (Judas Maccabeus), Dan 7:8 (Antiochus IV), and Dan 8:5 (Alexander the Great).

75. E.g., Hosea 2. The symbolism is helped by the fact that "Israel" is a feminine name. The prophets often describe Israel and her cities as one or more prostitutes; the most elaborate example is that of Ezekiel, who describes Samaria and Jerusalem, the capitals of the two kingdoms, as two young girls who threw away their virginity as whores in Egypt and continue in their prostitution until they are slaughtered, mutilated, burned, and destroyed by their own lovers (Ezek 23).

76. The fixed stars were attached to the vault of heaven, which circled the earth; those that moved either moved along it on their own orbits or were attached to vaults of their own contained within the vault of heaven. These hemispheric vaults had to be both strong enough to

the ancient world, whether pagan, Jewish, or Christian, doubted for a moment that the stars influenced the sublunar world, although different groups had different understandings of the nature of that influence. The pagans saw the stars as gods who, like all gods, could act both for good and for evil. Many Jews and Christians saw the star-gods as fallen angels who had rebelled against God — devils with power much greater than that of humans. The entire world from the heavenly vault downward was under their influence, and they had created paganism to procure for themselves the worship and offerings of men and, at the same time, eternal damnation for their followers. Devils know that they are damned and are moved by jealousy to seek the ruin of men as well; they trick them with more or less illusory miracles, and they steer them toward the sin of idolatry to ensure that they will not be saved either. The devils' power is limited by God, but it will last to the end of the world. Indeed, they have control over chronological time, since the sun and the moon determine the length of days and nights, of months and years. All the irregularities of the calendar, and the fact that the solar and lunar calendars do not coincide,[77] are a result of their willful rebellion. Disorder is a characteristic of demonic power and is evident not only in calendrical irregularity but also in the unpredictable dangers of atmosphere and weather. In a pre-scientific and flat cosmos there is no significant distance between the clouds and the moon or between "the sun and the other stars" (Dante, *Paradiso* 33.145), and thus atmospheric and astronomical phenomena are closely linked. Enoch is shown the storehouses of the rain, hail, and snow, which angels are instructed to throw onto the earth. Thunder and lightning are also angels, and even the pagans recognize their voice as prophetic or divine.[78]

---

prevent the star from falling and transparent, and must therefore probably be made of crystal or of some material that God had "solidified"; see Isa 42:5, taken up in Herm. *Vis.* 1.3.4. The intermediate heavens within the Jewish and Christian traditions do not always contain the planets, however; a varying number of them (usually between 3 and 7) are the seats of nonplanetary angels and form the steps of a cosmic ladder that brings the visionary (or the souls of the dead) to the heaven where God dwells.

77. God had designed a year of 364 days, which is exactly 52 weeks, or 13 lunar months of 28 days (4 weeks) each. What we have instead is a year with 365¼ days, and lunar months that vary in length, and that the ancients rounded up to 29½ days each. Other groups had different ideas: *1 Enoch (BS)* 41:5-9 depicts the sun and moon as angels faithful to the pact who "neither increase nor decrease (their orbits)." In other texts, stars are angels (or vice versa) (e.g., *1 Enoch [BW]* 21:3-6, *1 Enoch [BD]* 86:1-3; and 1QH 9:9-13). See also Jude 12-13.

78. See the comments on 4:5. The "mystery" of thunder and lightning is among many that occupied ancient scientific and religious speculation (see *1 Enoch* 17:3; 59:1-3; 60:13-15; 69:23; *2 Enoch* 40:9; *3 Enoch* 42:1, 4-5). 4Q318 fr. 2, 2, shows that even observant Jews practiced "brontology," a method of divination that attempted to predict the future by interpreting thun-

BA sees the universe as being closely controlled by God by means of his angels, and shows that not all Jews were in agreement on the topic, but it is nonetheless safe to say that the majority of 1st-century Jews thought the universe was in the hands of Satan. God's territory lies beyond the starry vault that, like the intermediate heavenly vaults, had doors through which good angels traveled in both directions, maintaining the relationship between God and his faithful. Daniel shows that there could even be angelic wars, as God had assigned an angel to each nation to be its "prince":[79] earthly battles are merely the reflection of angelic battles. Michael becomes the prince-protector of Israel.

The universe is inhabited by innumerable spiritual beings, which pagans saw as gods and Jews and Christians as demons. Winds, rivers, springs, trees, and mountains all were, or had, a divinity or a fallen angel. There is a close correspondence between stars in heaven and mountains on earth. The seven planetary stars — rebel angels — are the same as the seven enormous mountains whose punishment Enoch sees in his vision of flaming mountains (*1 Enoch* 18:13-16; 21:3 [*BW*]); their final punishment, still to come, is awaited in hope and fear. If the entire universe is comprised of or held up by devils, then liberation from them will come when the structures of this world collapse and the world itself is destroyed. "I saw in a vision the sky being hurled down and snatched and falling upon the earth. And when it fell upon the earth I saw the earth being swallowed up into the great abyss, and the mountains being suspended upon mountains, and the hills sinking down upon the hills, and tall trees being cut from their stumps, and thrown and sinking into the deep abyss. . . . And I said, 'The earth is being destroyed!'" (*1 Enoch* 83:3-5 [*BS*]).[80]

The ancient Greek notion of a "cosmos" — of a good, harmonious and probably eternal world under God's providential guidance — had ceased to hold together in the centuries before the Christian era, and it is apocalyptic notions of Jewish origin that survive the crises of late antiquity.[81] Their demonization of the universe was so complete that they situated hell within

---

der, which was a particularly important divine messenger. For divination and meteorological practices in ancient Judaism see Mengozzi 1997.

79. Dan 10:12-14, 20-21; see *Asc. Isa.* 7:9. There were traditionally 70 or 72 nations and a corresponding number of angels.

80. Unless otherwise stated, quotations from the OT Pseudepigrapha are taken or adapted from Charlesworth 1985.

81. An anonymous pagan during the restoration of Julian (in Macarius of Magnesia, *Apocriticon* 4.7, TU 37 [Lipsiae, 1991], pp. 78-79) condemned as impious the quotation of Isa 34:4 that he could still read in a no longer existing redaction of *Apocalypse of Peter:* "And every power of the sky itself will dissolve, and the heaven will roll itself up like a scroll, and all the stars will fall like leaves from a vine and like leaves from a fig tree." But he was fighting a losing battle — so much so that his words reach us only in the form of a Christian refutation.

various heavens, the seats of the rebel angels,[82] but in the long run it was the more popular ideas, shared by many, including Christians and Jews, that hell lay under the earth that prevailed. The realm under the earth was the seat of the dead, who were there separated into different caves for the good and the evil;[83] the existence of volcanoes and of springs showed that it also contained fire and water, and at least the columns that must have been somewhere holding up the earth from beneath. The need to explain the sea gave rise to the idea that dry land was a sort of platform on piles and that the sea led into a space under the earth, probably with gates between the subterranean and submarine realms.[84]

To a Middle-Eastern Jew the Great Sea was the Mediterranean. In its western parts lie "the islands": all the lands to the west, beginning with Crete and Cyprus, which we would call islands, from the small marine rocks of the Aegean to Sicily, and to the lands over the sea to the west — Greece, Italy, and Spain.[85] Beyond these lands, as pagans in particular believed, there was a great sea or river, the Ocean, that surrounded all the land. Finally, under everything there must be another, solid layer, a sort of pavement of the lower regions, that held up the pillars or foundations of the land and the islands, and that contained the seas from below. Many others believed that below this, further down still, was the Abyss.

For a believer in antiquity none of this was to be understood as allegory, any more than was his expectation that God would destroy this world and then create another one. Some held that God had created this future world from all eternity and was keeping it above the physical sky until it should be revealed to men as new. Enoch saw God's seven holy mountains — his faithful angels — perpetually at the ready in his service.[86] There was also a special mountain, God's holy mountain, which is the base of God's throne, or God's

82. This theme appears in Christian and Jewish apocalypses from the Christian era (*2 Enoch, 3 Baruch, Apocalypse of Zephaniah, Apocalypse of Peter*) as well as in Gnosticism and Mandaeanism.

83. From *1 Enoch* 22:9ff. on there is no such thing as a "beyond" without such a distinction (Sheol) — at least for many Jews. Various ideas about the condition of the dead persisted since the idea of a beyond divided into areas of reward and of punishment — an idea whose roots are outside of Judaism — is different from the traditional idea of a "life" for the dead that is not really a life, but just a shadowy condition.

84. Thus Herm. 1.3 (*Vis.* 1.3).4 paraphrases Ps 136:6 (135:6, LXX) and says that God "laid the foundations of the earth upon the waters."

85. Sometimes defined as "tongues (of land)," meaning peninsulas.

86. *1 Enoch* 24:1ff. *(BW)*. "And in those days the mountains will leap like he-goats, and the hills will rejoice like lambs full of milk, and they will all be angels in the sky"; phrases of this sort make little sense unless we acknowledge that even here, in a text that comes perhaps from the 1st century CE, the mountains are angels (*1 Enoch* 51:4 [*BS*]).

throne itself (*1 Enoch* 25:3 [*BW*]), or, better yet, the throne of his Glory. The throne, like the many heavenly thrones that serve as seats of powers, dominions, and principalities, is itself an angelic being, like all the other angelic categories. These were common ideas in Judaism, as we can see from the way that Paul refers to them (Rom 8:38), and the discoveries at Qumran have shown that among some groups at least they were fully developed.[87]

The mountain-throne that concerns us has a terrestrial counterpart in this transitory world: Zion, the seat of the temple and of Jerusalem, the city by antonomasia. Zion is the subject of Ps 48,[88] whose opening in Hebrew says, by and large, "Great is the LORD and to be abundantly praised in the city of our Lord, which is the mount of his Glory. . . . Mount Zion, bowels of the north, is the city of the great king."[89] The holy mountain is identified with the holy city that is built on it.[90] Since Zion is "the center of the navel of the earth,"[91] Jerusalem becomes the center and the pinnacle of the world, the mountain to which God descends to meet the man who ascends it.[92] Thus the analogy is a very close one; the mountain-angel of God is the throne where his Glory, his manifestation,

87. It used to be believed that speculations on the throne-chariot of Ezek 1 were later material, possibly even linked to medieval Kabbalism, until the Sabbath liturgies found at Qumran with their descriptions of infinite praying throne-chariots, hard though they are to interpret, showed that such ideas had existed from a much earlier date (see n. 68).

88. Cited in Matt 5:35.

89. Ps 48:2-3. Unless otherwise stated, quotations from the Bible (other than those from the Apocalypse) are taken or adapted from the New Revised Standard Version. The expression "bowels of the north" refers to the sacred mountain situated to the north and regarded throughout the Middle East, even in non-Jewish traditions, to be the seat of God (the Mandaeans, e.g., still regard it as such today). The psalmist identifies this mountain with Zion.

90. This privileged relationship makes sense in the context of the usual practice throughout the ancient world of building cities on high places; see Cornutus, *Theologiae Graecae compendium*, 6 (Lang 1881, p. 6) and Matt 5:14b.

91. *Jub.* 8:19 (many people in antiquity believed that the body begins, develops, and grows from the navel). *Jubilees,* like *Enoch,* is an alternative account of the events narrated in Genesis and Exodus, from the creation to the giving of the Law on Sinai. It was very well known in antiquity, and there were several copies at Qumran, but it did not make its way into the canon. The only complete version that survives is the Ethiopic translation.

92. This aspect of Jerusalem was emphasized not only by geography but also by literary usage: humans "go up" to Jerusalem and "go down" from it, not vice versa. Mount Zion has been the center of the universe from eternity, and in fact the temple contains "the rock" by antonomasia, the rock of foundation that God took from his own throne to begin the creation of the world. The ark rested on it, and it indicated the exact spot of the threshing floor of Araunah the Jebusite where David saw the angel of God and made a burnt offering (2 Sam 24:16-25; 1 Chr 21:15-30); it is the spot on Mount Moriah where Abraham prepared to sacrifice Isaac (see already 2 Chr 3:1); it is Adam's tomb. In the Muslim era, under the Omayyad dynasty, it became the place from which Mohammed began his journey into heaven.

dwells, and the earthly Zion is the seat of Jerusalem, the city of the temple that is the earthly Dwelling of the Glory of God, as Ezek 11:23 and 43:1-4 show.

Philo, the Alexandrian Jewish philosopher, became intensely involved in speculations within which the temple and even its component parts correspond to the universe, which he saw as reflecting the creative project of God. Philo operated more in a Platonic than in an apocalyptic framework, but there are also apocalyptic works in which a heavenly temple is the model of the earthly one[93] and may be destined to replace it at the end of time in the new creation that must include a new Jerusalem, built on eschatological Zion.[94] In whatever manner the heavenly and the earthly temples were understood to reflect each other, the importance of the latter was evident. During the Herodian reconstruction a thousand young men from priestly families were instructed in the crafts of architecture and masonry, and thus the absolute sacredness of the new building was assured by the fact that only priests who conformed to strict laws of purity had been in contact with the building materials and tools. Herod's architects leveled hills and filled a valley[95] to enlarge the plain from which the sanctuary arose, making it into an enormous four-sided plateau whose sides were "almost" parallel.[96] The foundations, which held together the material used to fill up the valley and raise the ground to a single level, were made of several layers of enormous rectangular parallelepiped stone blocks.[97] The sanctuary building was as white as snow on the outside; it had a square façade (as broad as it was tall) with a portico; its height and breadth were greater than those of the body of the building, and were in fact identical not only to each other but also to the length of the temple.[98] Solomon's temple had been

93. The existence of a heavenly temple was clear since *1 Enoch* 9:1 (the Greek text, confirmed by the Aramaic), that is, since *BW*.

94. The prophecy, which is repeated in Isa 2:2 and in Mic 4:1, reads, "it will happen at the end of days: the mountain of the house of the Lord will be set above [lit., on the head] of the mountains." "At the end of days" merely means "in the future," but LXX renders it: "The mount of the Lord will be very visible *in the last days*, and the house of God on the peak of the mountains."

95. Josephus, *J.W.* 5(5.1).188; note the apocalyptic value of such an undertaking (see, e.g., Hab 3:6; *1 Enoch* [*BS*] 52:6).

96. The excavations of 1988 revealed the measurements to be 1590 × 1035 × 1536 × 912 feet; this is almost a rectangle, but the sides are all of different lengths and not all the corners can be exactly right angles (see the comments on 21:16).

97. It has been calculated that the largest of these blocks to be identified at this point and still in place weighs more than 400 tons.

98. The floor plan was in the shape of a T, whose cross stroke — the façade — was the same length as the down stroke — the length of the temple. The entrance was in the middle of the façade.

richly decorated with painted images,[99] and Herod's must have been also. On the portico at the entrance there was a golden vine on whose branches pilgrims could hang as offerings vine leaves and bunches of grapes, also of gold, which were made for the purpose and later collected by the priests. The inside of the building had walls set with richly decorated golden tiles that were periodically removed and exhibited outside for pilgrims to admire. Two enormous curtains, woven and embroidered by pre-pubescent girls from priestly families, to avoid contamination, set off the most sacred part. They were hung parallel to each other, with each one a slight distance from one of the side walls, one to the right and the other to the left. The priest would come in from one side, proceed along the corridor between the curtains, and come into the Holy of Holies at the other side. These two curtains were embroidered with stars and eagles, and represented the vault of heaven; priests passed through its openings to reach God.[100]

During major festivals the temple square could hold hundreds of thousands of pilgrims. Hundreds of barefoot priests,[101] accompanied by singing and by the music of the Levites, performed thousands of sacrifices or made sure that they were done correctly. John Hyrcanus had constructed a slaughterhouse within the temple precincts: a canopy with many columns and rings to which animals could be tied by the head so that their throats could be cut in the proper manner.[102] The blood that gushed from the animals' throats was collected in golden basins and poured on the walls of the altar, which was then washed. A channel ran around the altar and carried the blood beneath it and thence into a system of channels that brought the liquids from the temple into the valley of Kedron.[103] Not only was the temple the earthly image of God's heavenly dwelling, but the worship there represented spiritually the angelic liturgies and a prophetic anticipation of the worship that men and angels together would raise to God at the end of time. The temple spirituality,

---

99. See Ezek 41:17-20 and 1 Kings 6:29.

100. These precious curtains, like the golden tiles, were periodically exhibited to the faithful, and thus everybody knew about the stars and eagles embroidered on the "veil of the temple."

101. They were obliged to purify their hands and feet constantly. Moreover, *m. Ber.* 9:5 seems to assume that all the pilgrims climbed the Temple Mount with bare feet as a sign of respect (see Exod 3:5).

102. Before the cultural reforms of John Hyrcanus (135-105 BCE) cattle and sheep had their skulls shattered with a special sacred axe, as in pagan sacrifices. The high priest John, as he is called in rabbinic sources, thought that no bone of a sacrificial animal, not even the skull, could be broken.

103. This river of blood and water was used as fertilizer. The owners of the gardens paid a tax to the temple, since nothing sacred could be used for a mundane purpose unless it had been "redeemed" or bought.

which was probably linked to the priestly classes, must have included eschato-logical expectations.

Apocalypticists followed a different path. A man,[104] not necessarily from a priestly family, was chosen by God to "see" spiritual reality directly. The visions occurred in different places and forms; in some an angel comes down through the heavens to reveal himself or a message to the visionary; in some the heavens open and allow the visionary to see what lies beyond the vault of heaven; in others the visionary is himself transported through the heavens until he reaches the realities beyond them. By whatever means, the visionary is transported into another dimension, which is, however, not the dimension of God. Nobody can see God, and it would be heretical for a visionary to say that he had.[105] He sees God's Throne, Robe, Glory, Face, or Hand: expressions that denote a visible image of God, God made manifest to man, a divine reality that some Jewish and Christian groups interpreted as an angelic being, Metatron, the Prince of princes, the Word, the Son, the second Person of the Trinity.[106] In this intermediate dimension between human and divine, the visionary not only contemplates the visible aspect of God but also grasps the whole history of the universe. In the eternity of God all spatial and temporal reality is present at once, and can be seen all together by the human visionary.

To us the content of these visions and auditions looks like a mass of symbols, but to a believer of the 1st century the issue was more complicated. There are beings that are spiritual in nature but are absolutely real: the angels, the heavens and their doors, the stars, the heavenly temple and its furnishings, the throne of God. These and other real angelic beings participate in "performances" in which they carry out actions, handle objects, wear garments, and make utterances all of which must be explained to the visionary (usually by another angel called an "interpreter") because in themselves they are not comprehensible to humans. Thus there is a need for a first level of allegory, in which objects or actions are explained by analogy and take on different meanings, which meanings constitute the content of the message revealed to the visionary. There can be several levels of allegorization and even extremely

104. We have no ancient apocalypses attributed to female figures. Probably for most Jewish and Jewish-Christian groups the ritual impurity involved in being a woman would have made it impossible for a woman to approach God spiritually. This trend changes in later Christianity with the apocalyptic exaltation of Mary, who is, however, a figure of exceptional purity. There were prophetesses among the first generations of Christians, but their words or possible writings have not survived.

105. See n. 148.

106. See John 1:18 ("God, no one has ever seen him; God the firstborn [Son], who is in the breast of the Father, has revealed him"); 14:9 ("Who sees me sees the Father"); etc.

complex visions in which almost everything has a symbolic value. The composite beasts in Daniel, for instance, can also be seen as the visible manifestations of the angelic (meaning demonic) principles of various kingdoms and kings, but the visionary's interest is in their composition and behavior. Nevertheless, if it were possible for us to question a visionary, he would most likely tell us that what he had seen was not allegorical at all, but rather the true reality of the spirit. In the eternal present of God, all events are realized, and human history is merely the representation of those events in fleshly form. Corrupt angelic beings who display their corruption to the visionary by appearing as composite wild beasts devour each other in the spiritual dimension, and the earthly kingdoms that are their counterparts down below destroy and supersede each other throughout human history. Human kings are no more than puppets who contain all the power of the kingdoms on top of which they sit in their illusory thrones; the reality behind them is the beasts, goats and horns that Daniel sees, or the "crushing mountain" that appears to Jeremiah (51:25).

Most believers do not ordinarily have visionary experiences of their own. They have access to the spiritual realm only through the words and writings of prophets and visionaries, and their role is to scrutinize the historical realities around them for signs that the true prophecies are being fulfilled.[107] Thus there is a process of rereading, interpretation, and adjustment of earlier prophecies. It emerges from some Qumranic texts that the divine inspiration granted to the Teacher of Righteousness had convinced him and his followers that they were able to understand the true meaning of Scripture and to apply it to their own world. This application, often an allegorical process that "updates" old prophecies by referring words from the past to things in the present, takes place in commentaries, or *pesharim,* on the prophets.[108] In a *Commentary on Nahum* (4QpNah) all of the prophecy's geographical elements (seas, rivers, mountains) are interpreted as representing the fate of the commentator's enemies, while the oracle on Nah 3, originally directed against Nineveh ("Woe to the city of bloodshed, utterly deceitful, full of booty . . . prostitute"[109]), is referred as a whole to Jerusalem.[110] The schism within Judaism, and one group's sense of itself as being unjustly persecuted, make them

107. The distinction between true and false prophecies is always made after the fact: true prophets are those whose words are fulfilled. See, e.g., Jer 26; 28:9; 29:23.

108. The term *pesher,* which is translated as "commentary" or "interpretation," is used to denote texts that comment on the Bible pericope by pericope.

109. Unless otherwise stated, quotations from the Dead Sea Scrolls are taken or adapted from García Martínez–Tigchelaar 1997.

110. For 4QpNah and the analogous 1QpHab see comments on 17:5, 6, 9 and 18:6.

feel justified in turning on contemporary Jerusalem the insults and threats that the ancient prophets had used against foreign enemies.[111]

The first Christians also undertook this kind of contemporary application of prophecies, and interpreted the events of Jesus and the early church as the realization or "fulfillment" of the Scriptures. According to the Christian tradition, Jesus himself did and said things that could be understood in this sense.[112] After his death, Jesus' followers were firmly convinced that the Spirit who had been promised and given to them would help them understand the sacred text correctly, and undertook a hermeneutical project that led to a complete reinterpretation of the Jewish scriptures, which they had come to see as Christian. Groups of men and women of the first Christian generations had a palpable experience of the presence of the Spirit and went beyond the rereading of the sacred text in the light of Jesus to create new texts. New prophecies, in the literary form that today we call apocalyptic, circulated among the churches. We have seen that this literary activity was particularly rich and intense within Judaism, especially in some periods such as that between 70 and 135 CE. John, the visionary of Patmos, a Jewish follower of Jesus, left what is probably for us the oldest Christian prophetic writing; it became the apocalyptic pattern for the Christian churches.[113]

IV. A Prophet Called John

1. The author of the Apocalypse presents himself to us as a Jew, indeed as a true Jew,[114] by the name of John, a follower of Jesus Christ. He presents his book as containing a prophecy:[115] in its finale the angelic figure who "showed" him the things that he had seen declares himself to be "fellow servant" of John and his "brothers, the prophets" (22:8-9). John sees himself as a prophet within a group of Jews who believe in Jesus Christ. There is some de-

---

111. The commentator probably thinks that Jerusalem will meet the same fate as Nineveh if it does not become an Essene city. Commenting on Nah 2:12 (about lions not being disturbed by enemies), he says that Jerusalem will remain under God's protection despite the perversions of her kings "from Antiochus until the appearance of the commanders of the Kittim [who must be the Romans], but then she will be trampled" (an echo of Daniel and an allusion to Pompey or to the future). The immediate context in Nahum does not call for this echo of Daniel, which must therefore have been added by the author of the *pesher*.

112. See especially Luke 4:21.

113. But not for apocryphal apocalypses: Charlesworth 1987.

114. As opposed to those who falsely call themselves Jews: 2:9 and 3:9.

115. See 1:3; 22:7, 10, 18-19.

bate about the extent of prophetic phenomena within primitive Christianity and even about the nature of primitive Christian prophecy. 1 Cor 12–14 shows, on the one hand, that there must have been a definite category of prophets within the community; Paul gives them second place, after "apostles"[116] and before "teachers."[117] On the other hand, however, Paul seems to oppose the community's tendency to allow different groups to focus exclusively on particular spiritual gifts: "you can all prophesy," albeit "one by one."[118] The gift of prophecy consists in the ability to speak comprehensibly to other people for "their building up and encouragement and consolation."[119] Paul does not specify the exact content of prophecy, but explains that the prophet reads the hearts of others (1 Cor 14:24-25 and see Apoc 2:23). The Samaritan woman (John 4:19, 39) also recognizes Jesus as a prophet when he tells her "everything [I have] ever done."

Paul nowhere says that it is a particular or primary task of the prophet to foresee the future, but we can infer that edification, consolation, and encouragement might be based on such foresight. In fact, it is clear from the whole NT that although it may not be their principal function, prophets do foresee future events. The ancient prophets were such because their words were fulfilled in Jesus;[120] for Christians John the Baptist was a prophet in that he foresaw the coming of the one "greater than [himself]," who was Jesus. In Luke 1:67 Zechariah speaks a "prophecy" about the son of David and his own son. Furthermore, Anna is described as a "prophetess"[121] but then "gives thanks to

116. Not, obviously, the Twelve, but a group of believers who were held in great esteem.

117. 1 Cor 12:28-29. There are other lists in Eph 3:5; 4:11. See Acts 13:1-3.

118. 1 Cor 14:31. Paul treats it as a matter of course that women do prophesy, but recommends (or insists) that they cover their heads (1 Cor 11:5-15); shortly afterward, however, he recommends (or orders) that women in general "should be silent in the meetings. For they are not permitted to speak" (1 Cor 14:34).

119. 1 Cor 14:3 (Paul says that prophets "speak to men," but, as is often the case in Greek, the term does not exclude women). In Eph 2:20 the "building up" is on the foundation of the apostles and prophets; in Acts 15:32 Judas and Silas speak as prophets for the encouragement of the believers. In Rom 12:6-8, however, Paul makes a distinction between prophecy and exhortation, as if they were different spiritual gifts.

120. See Peter's speech in Acts 2:30-31 about David the prophet, who foresaw the resurrection of Christ.

121. Luke appears at first glance to have no problems with the idea that women can prophesy, since besides Anna he records the daughters of Philip as being prophetesses (Acts 21:9) and in Peter's speech in Jerusalem he cites the text of Joel 2:28 according to which both sons and daughters prophesy. However, in both contexts that he mentions flesh-and-blood prophetesses the predictions about the future are made by men (Simeon and Agabus). Moreover, Anna's words are not recorded in direct speech, and he says nothing about Philip's daughters. Luke apparently thought that celibacy was a requirement for prophecy, at least for women; the four

God" and begins to "speak about him [whether about the child or about God is left unclear] to all who were looking for the redemption of Jerusalem," while Simeon, who is not said to be a prophet, makes an explicit prediction about the future, including that of Mary.[122] The Christian prophet Agabus is introduced once in Antioch, where he foresees a famine, and once in Caesarea, where he foresees Paul's imprisonment.[123] Even Caiaphas is said to "prophesy" when he predicts the future, not on his own account but because he is "the high priest" (John 11:51), and in Tit 1:12 Epimenides is called a prophet because he described the future behavior of the Cretans during the time of the apostles. Jesus foresees the destruction of the temple and of Jerusalem, and possibly the end of the world, in connection with the end of Jerusalem (Mark 13 and parallels); he uses both his own words and those of the prophets, especially of Daniel. Matt 24:15 even has Jesus mention Daniel by name as he quotes him. According to Josephus, a Jesus son of Ananias ("an ignorant peasant") for "seven years and five months" predicted the fall of Jerusalem as well as his own eventual death. His prophecy, which mentions cosmic and angelic "voices" against Jerusalem and the temple, reworks Jeremiah (7:34; 16:9; 25:10) in its threats against "bridegrooms and brides."[124] Thus in the cultural world of 1st-century Judaism and Christianity it makes sense for a prophet to be primarily, although not exclusively, one who foresees the future. There is no historical or literary reason not to read the Apocalypse literally when it speaks of "things that are to come" or that "will come soon" or that have "not yet" come, nor to resist the book's orientation toward the future, which is precisely what one would expect from a book of prophecy by a Jewish-Christian prophet of the 1st century.

---

daughters of Philip are all virgins, and Anna first "lived with her husband for seven years after her virginity," then as a widow to the age of eighty-four, and thus has been living celibately for around 77 years (Luke 2:36-37); Mary is a virgin too (1:46-55), and Elizabeth is an exceptional case (1:41-45; see 1:7).

122. Luke 2:25-38. In any case, the expectation of Jerusalem's redemption looks to the future.

123. Acts 11:28 and 21:10. At Agabus's last appearance his prediction is accompanied by a symbolic gesture (he binds his hands and feet with Paul's belt), which puts him firmly in the tradition of the biblical prophets.

124. *J.W.* 6(5.3).300-309. Prophets were certainly expected to produce signs and miracles as well as oracles; Luke says that Jesus is called a "great prophet" after the resurrection of the widow's son (Luke 7:16) because he has reproduced Elijah's miracle (1 Kings 17:17-24 and Luke 4:25-26), while according to John the blind man explains his cure by calling Jesus a prophet (John 9:17). See also John 6:14, where the crowd proclaims Jesus a prophet after the miracle of the multiplication. The "false prophets" and "false messiahs" of the last times will also perform amazing feats (Mark 13:22 and parallel).

2. How much can we know about the life of an early Jewish-Christian prophet? The Gospel of Matthew, which is the Gospel most interested in the spread of Christianity through the region that he calls "Syria" and that today we could call the Middle East,[125] makes allusion to the existence of prophets who had to be welcomed because they were sent by Jesus.[126] The few prophetesses we know about seem to live in one place (Philip's four daughters in Caesarea [Acts 21:9]; Jezebel in Thyatira [Apoc 2:20-23]) while the prophets are itinerant. When Agabus appears, he is said to be traveling (from Judea). There is an important confirmation of this in the *Didache (Did.)* or *The Teaching of the Apostles,* a Christian text of great antiquity that seems to be composed of material that reflects the situation from the early 2nd or even the late 1st centuries. Several passages in this text concern apostles, prophets, and teachers, and give the impression that there were prophets who were only prophets (*Did.* 11), apostles who were also prophets (11), and bishops and deacons (presbyters are not mentioned) who "fulfill the duty of prophets and teachers" (15). There is a long paragraph about the proper way to receive apostles and prophets, who cannot stay more than a day or two: "if he stays three days, he is a false prophet."[127] Clearly one can explain the itinerant behavior of the early apostles and prophets in terms of the structure and sociology of primitive Christianity, which was composed of groups of Jews from different "schools" who were united by an intense commitment to proselytism that took some of them outside the world of Jews and their sympathizers. Jesus' own itinerant activity must also have served as a model.[128]

125. See Matt 4:24; the passage has no synoptic parallels.
126. See Matt 10:41 for the reward of those who receive "prophets" and the "righteous" (the passage appears only in Matthew, and the terminology is his own, as we can see from Matt 13:17, which changes the "prophets" and "kings" of Luke 10:24 into "prophets" and "righteous"). See also Matt 7:22 (those who prophesy in the "Name," another passage found only in Matthew) and in particular 23:34, where Jesus himself says that he sends prophets, wise men, and scribes in the present, while Luke 11:49 still casts the sentence as a prophecy in which the Wisdom of God proclaims that it will send prophets and apostles in the future.
127. *Did.* 11:5. The purpose of the passage is to protect the community against abuses and impostors: "if he asks for money he is a false prophet" (11.6); "From their ways (of living) you will know if they are false prophets or prophets" (11.8); "Every prophet who orders a table (to eat) in spirit will not eat from it; otherwise he is a false prophet" (11.9); "If he says in the spirit: give me money or anything else, do not listen to him" (11.12). True prophets may have been itinerants, but they were not parasites.
128. John the Baptist is portrayed as an itinerant prophet in the Fourth Gospel and in Luke 3:3, but not necessarily in Mark, nor in Matthew, which follows Mark, nor in Josephus. In the Apocalypse the one "similar to a son of man" promises or threatens to come to the churches to the angels of which he orders John to write, but it is possible that John, as an instrument of his will, might have seen himself as the one to undertake the task (see also 2 John 12 and 3 John 9-10 and 14).

It is more difficult to determine whether the early Jewish-Christian prophets always acted and prophesied alone, as often appears to have been the case, or whether there were also groups, schools, or real confraternities, with greater or lesser degrees of organization. The *Ascension of Isaiah* (*Asc. Isa.,* a Christian apocalypse that contains sections that may originate from the late 1st and from the early 2nd centuries)[129] recounts Isaiah's martyrdom and an evidently apocryphal prophecy about the future coming of the Beloved (meaning Christ) to this world; it presents Isaiah as being at the head of a group of prophets. The text adds a number of details to its basis in the biblical stories of Elijah and of several groups of prophets, either persecuted or sponsored by the court. The wicked Manasseh is now king, and the corruption of Jerusalem has led Isaiah to abandon both her and Bethlehem to seek refuge in a mountain in the desert (*Asc. Isa.* 2:7). A group of men forms around him; they dress "in sackcloth" and are "all prophets," who are defined as "naked." They lament Israel's (future) destruction and live only on "bitter herbs" (2:9-10). The text seems to bear witness to the existence of organized groups of prophets, which suggests that the term "brothers" in Apoc 22:9 might not be generic, but might refer to actual groups of that sort. However, no other text so explicitly suggests such a level of organization within primitive Christian prophecy. It is likely that Christians who had the gift of prophecy gathered together for prayer, as happens at Antioch in Acts 13:1-3, where some of them come from Jerusalem.[130]

The gift of prophecy, like that of tongues, appears not to be constant. Paul has already had to combat those who opposed it (1 Thess 5:20), and when ecclesiastical structures were established in the 2nd century deacons, presbyters, bishops, teachers, and even exorcists seem to have been organized, while prophets were not. Hermas, who was probably active in Rome around 140 CE, seems to have been a solitary figure, with no affiliation to a school or circle.[131] The Apocalypse presents itself as a letter directed to "all" (22:21) or to the "seven churches" (1:4).[132] Certainly the letter was not addressed exclusively to

---

129. See Norelli I-II 1995.

130. Acts 11:27-28. In Acts 21:8-11, Agabus goes alone to Caesarea, to the house of Philip, whose four daughters are virgin prophetesses, but does not appear to concern himself with them.

131. Contemporary Jewish apocalyptic texts that are attributed to a famous figure from the past also picture this figure as solitary; he may have secretaries who transcribe from dictation the text of his vision (like Ezra in *4 Ezra*), but the prophet himself is usually alone.

132. It is not surprising that the book takes the form of a letter, a form that is characteristic of most of the NT, since 22 of the 27 books are letters (Acts records the content of two other letters); the popularity of the epistolary form is a consequence of the dynamism with which the

prophets (John distinguishes between the one who reads and the many who listen),[133] although he defines himself as their "brother" and "partner" (1:9). The "two witnesses . . . wrapped in sackcloth" (11:3), who are said to be "prophets" (11:10), act alone,[134] and the so-called prophetess Jezebel has followers ("children") rather than colleagues in her teaching (2:20-23). It does not appear from the benedictions and the opening and closing greetings that there are other senders than John himself.[135] The hypothesis that there was a school or circle of prophets around John must remain precisely a hypothesis.

The epistolary form, with an address at the beginning and greetings at the end, provides the literary framework of the Apocalypse. In the face of innumerable attempts to dissect it, the book retains the appearance of a coherent and unified work, despite its many borrowings from earlier works and from traditions with which the author was familiar. After an introductory section there is the account of the first vision and audition, which provokes the writing of seven messages to seven angels charged with the guidance and care of seven Christian churches (1:9–3:22). "After these things" the visionary moves through "a door that was open in heaven" (4:1) and embarks on a long series of visions and auditions that are connected in various interlocking ways;[136] this series ends with the last chapter.

The style is very idiosyncratic. John must have been trilingual: he could compose (whether by writing or by dictating) in Greek, he knew biblical Hebrew, and he probably spoke Aramaic as well.[137] It is also clear that, whether or not he did so in his daily life, when he wrote the text of the Apocalypse he made use of expressive forms typical of Jewish religious language as he knew it from texts that, whether or not they are part of today's canon, he held to be

---

proselytizing movement was rapidly spreading over great distances. Texts from the *Baruch* cycle in particular show how a prophetic work can take the form of an epistle: *2 Baruch* closes with a letter that Baruch sends to the tribes of the diaspora and mentions a second letter to the Jews of Babylon (see the *Letter of Jeremiah* [LXX = *Bar.* 6, Vg.]); *1 Bar.* [=*Baruch*, LXX] takes the form of a letter sent from Babylon to Jerusalem, and a letter from Baruch to Jeremiah appears in *Paraleipomena of Jeremiah* (Karrer 1986, pp. 48-83, deals with an ample range of similar material, but stresses the way in which the Apocalypse differs from other works).

133. Apoc 1:3. For a similar "liturgical" dimension in a letter see Col 4:16; 1 Thess 5:27; *2 Bar.* 86:1.

134. In *Apoc. El.* 4:7-33 Elijah and Enoch fight alone against the Antichrist, while the "righteous," as distinct from "prophets," perish in a group of sixty.

135. Pauline, Petrine, and even Johannine epistles contain multiple greetings.

136. For the use of "interlocking" see Yarbro Collins 1976, pp. 15-16.

137. Evidence that these three languages coexisted in the Jewish world is provided by a group of fifteen letters from the time of the Bar Kochba revolt, which were found in a cave near Nahal Hever; eight of them are in Aramaic, five are in Hebrew, and two in Greek.

sacred. His Greek is not just an example of the so-called "Semitic Greek" spoken by Jews and eastern merchants throughout the Mediterranean basin and in the region of Syria, nor is it merely "biblical Greek" such as appears, for instance, in Greek translations of the Bible or in some parts of Luke. It is rather a combination of these, in a person who does not seem to have undergone a regular curriculum of study according to the norms of Greek *paideia*. The resulting Greek sometimes has parallels in papyrus documents, sometimes in Greek biblical translations, from the LXX to the translations by Aquila and Theodotion (Theod.) that are more faithful to the Hebrew,[138] and sometimes in other primitive Christian texts, such as the *Epistle* attributed to Barnabas or the *Letters* of Ignatius, whose authors have a Jewish cultural background but apparently limited grounding in Greek culture. John does not always pay close attention to the grammatical and syntactical correctness of his Greek.[139] He seems to have used some prepositions and some cases with a freedom that must have driven copyists to exasperation, as we can see from the traditional variants in certain passages, with regard both to prepositions (especially ἐκ, ἐπί, ἀπό)[140] and cases (gen./dat./acc.). There are a number of occasions where infinitive forms and participles are used in contexts where Greek demands the use of the finite forms[141] — a phenomenon that is certainly due to the influence of Semitic linguistic structures. As regards the agreements between nouns and adjectives, John's practice is so irregular as to suggest that he is utterly indifferent to the formal rules of correct Greek,[142] an indifference that

138. I do not know whether John knew the Septuagint, wholly or in part; he probably did, but he did not necessarily use it in composing the Apocalypse. His reworking of biblical and prophetic texts is a mental rather than a literary undertaking; he quite possibly knew the texts from memory and did not need to consult them, least of all in Greek. Thus he sometimes translates and adapts biblical phrases in terms that may recall the LXX or some other translation, or that may be quite new.

139. If we had access to the autograph, we would most likely find that the spelling is careless there as well; there are traces of this in the mss.

140. The preposition ὑπό appears only twice in the text of the critical edition (Apoc 6:8 and 13); in like manner it appears only once in John (in 14:21).

141. For instance, I translate 1:16 as "and from his mouth there extended a . . . sword." The Greek says literally, "and from his mouth a sword . . . coming forth."

142. When using terms with the same root he is fond of creating assonances within the text, sometimes to make a point but often simply for the purpose of personal style. Take, for instance, the play on words in his description of the figure who appears in the opening passage of the book, which translates as "from his mouth there extended a two-edged sword" (1:16). The expression "two-edged" is my rendering of a Greek adjective that translates as "of two mouths," which recalls the mouth from which the sword extends (just as, a few lines earlier, the figure is said to be "girded . . . with a *girdle*" [*sash* in the ET], 1:13). It is normal both in Greek and in Hebrew to say that a sword has one or two "mouths."

might well stem from a multilingual person whose attention was engaged with other problems.

The primary problem engaging John's attention was his sense that the churches in Asia Minor were facing serious and imminent danger. They seem to be on the brink of losing their faith, and thus John, like Enoch, acts as an intermediary between the sphere of God and that of the angels: in John's case the angels of the churches.[143] The divinity appears to him first as "one similar to a son of man," the risen Jesus Christ, and then with the mediation of numerous angels. It is also to angels that the written messages in the first part of the book are directed. There are seven of these, but this is not because there are seven churches in Asia Minor; rather, there must be seven churches in Asia Minor because the angels have to be seven in number. Like the seven churches whom they guide and direct, these angels are in a dangerous and unstable position, halfway between the seven angels who are faithful to God and the seven planetary angels who fell. The example of the seven stars shows the real and present danger of another fall (see in particular 2:5). Some of the communities seem to be faithful but to be in conflict with (other) Jews and with internal minorities (Smyrna); some seem to be seriously divided (Thyatira); in some it appears that John is in contact with only a minority (Sardis); while some others, it appears, will be lost unless they are converted (Laodicea).

The threats come from two fronts that at first glance seem to be opposed. On the one hand there is the threat of religious and social compromise with the Greek world that surrounds the community, possibly as a consequence of preaching an extreme form of Pauline Christianity, while on the other there is the threat from the world of non-Christian Jews. These threats come together in the areas of religious life, since neither Greeks nor Jews acknowledge the divinity of Jesus Christ, and of practical life, since John sees Jews as adapting themselves to and accepting the cultural and economic values of the Greek world. At Sardis itself the Jewish community will buy a pagan basilica and transform it into one of the largest synagogues of the age, indeed the largest of which we know. There is a pattern for this kind of behavior in historical Israel and in Jerusalem, who, according to the prophets, continually fornicated with pagans. Thus the churches are surrounded and threatened by Judaism and paganism. In apocalyptic terms the message of exhortation and encour-

143. In Acts Luke stresses that prophets act as intermediaries between God and men, communicating the Spirit's words and will. See, for instance, Acts 13:1-3, where the community at Antioch appears to be guided by five "prophets and teachers" whom the Spirit directs to "set apart" Barnabas and Saul for the mission to which he "calls" them. This is further confirmed by 1 Tim 1:18 and 4:14, which refer to prophecies about Timothy himself.

agement that forms the matter of John's prophecy is a vision of the universe and above all of history. The beasts of paganism, and Satan who animates them, have already destroyed (or are about to destroy) Jerusalem, who fornicated with them and killed Christ. There has to be a period of tribulation now, but at the end of everything a New Jerusalem, the community of the faithful, will come from heaven. The example of the seven ancient angels and of the history of Jerusalem point out to the faithful the right path: a path that they will pursue by witness and, if necessary, through blood.

3. The Apocalypse is at the same time a Judaizing and an anti-Jewish text. Like Matthew it represents a westward movement on the part of an eastern Christianity. It is both an alternative to non-Christian Judaism and hostile to the "concessions" to the pagan Greek world made by the tradition derived from Paul. Luke represents an attempt at conciliation, but Matthew and the Apocalypse hold to the anti-Greek approach that gained the upper hand in Asia Minor rather than the ideas of Pauline lineage that were nevertheless destined to determine the direction of future Christianity. We are all heirs of Paul's Christianity and of the accommodation with paganism (1 Cor 8–10) rather than of a Christianity that flees from contact with that which defiles (Apoc 2:14, 20). This situation can help to clarify some of the reasons behind the contrast between the Apocalypse on the one hand and the Christian teachers of Alexandria and figures such as Eusebius, who found it difficult to accept the book's attitudes toward Jewish heredity, on the other.

It is no simple matter to determine who was the Jewish Christian called John who wrote the Apocalypse, even if one is not motivated primarily by an ecclesiastical or antiecclesiastical desire to prove that he was or was not John the disciple of the Lord and the son of Zebedee. From a purely stylistic and linguistic perspective it is not possible that the person who wrote the Apocalypse could be the same as the one who wrote the Fourth Gospel. It is not, of course, impossible that he might have been the apostle, but this hypothesis is difficult to prove for other reasons: what author, however apocalyptic, would have designated himself as one of the twelve foundations of the eschatological Jerusalem?[144] In its use of theologically or ecclesiologically meaningful terms the Apocalypse is often aligned with the Gospel of John and thus highlights a conceptual affinity between the two books that critics have often stressed, al-

---

144. Apoc 21:14. It is possible that the author considers himself to be an "apostle," as distinct from the self-styled and false apostles of Apoc 2:2. As in other early Christian texts, the term "apostle" is used to indicate people holding authority within the community, who are not among the Twelve.

though there are passages in which it is more closely aligned with Pauline ter-minology.[145] Thus the author of the Apocalypse was familiar with both Johannine and the Pauline traditions.

There are few reference points that we can use to obtain a precise date for the work.[146] It seems that the fall of Jerusalem in 70 CE has already taken place and that the author is explaining it to his readers just as did all Jewish apoca-lypses of the era, in their various ways.[147] Certainly the fall of Jerusalem was, and would remain, significant to the Christian as well as to the Jewish imagi-nation: in the *Ascension of Isaiah* the prophet is accused precisely of prophe-sying "against Jerusalem and against the cities of Judah, [saying] that they will be laid waste" (3:6) and of "calling Jerusalem [by the name of] Sodom."[148]

The tragic immediacy and violence of the images suggest to me that the Apocalypse was written relatively close to the event, when the author was close, at least mentally, to the experience of war; external factors also support this theory. I believe that both *2 Baruch,* which dates from before 132, and the *Coptic Apocalypse of Elijah,* which is usually assigned a date before 115, are po-lemical responses to the Apocalypse. The Apocalypse, on the other hand, en-gages polemically with the ideas defended in *4 Ezra,* which must date from before 100 and after 70. We thus arrive, by different paths, and without relying on the question of Johannine authorship, at a date very close to the tradi-tional one, namely, between 70 and 100 CE.

---

145. For example, the term ὑπομονή, "constancy, endurance," appears often in the Pauline corpus (18 times in all, as well as twice in Luke, out of a total of 32 occurrences); it does not ap-pear in John but is used all of seven times in the Apocalypse (the five remaining occurrences be-ing three in James and two in 2 Peter).

146. The commentary will show that the seven heads of the beast do not point to seven Ro-man emperors with the precision of a Roman annalist, and in any case critical disagreement in identifying the emperors shows how imprecise and hypothetical this enterprise is.

147. It is also possible that the Apocalypse was written when the tragedy was imminent and the text's readers and hearers saw it as inevitable. If this is the case, then the work was redacted at a time when it was already clear that there would be military action on the part of the Romans. Since we do not have an apologetic agenda, it makes little difference if we move the limit *post quem* from 70 to 67.

148. *Asc. Isa.* 3:10; see Isa 1:10. In the Greek legend Isaiah, as he is dying by being sawed in half with a wooden saw, prophesies the utter destruction of Jerusalem; (*Asc. Isa.* 3:18; Norelli I 1995, pp. 56-59, 448-49). He is also accused of having claimed to have seen God and thus of plac-ing himself above Moses (see Isa 6:5).

TEXT AND COMMENTARY

The Apocalypse of John

1 Ἀποκάλυψις Ἰησοῦ Χριστοῦ ἣν ἔδωκεν αὐτῷ ὁ θεὸς δεῖξαι τοῖς δούλοις αὐτοῦ ἃ δεῖ γενέσθαι ἐν τάχει, καὶ ἐσήμανεν ἀποστείλας διὰ τοῦ ἀγγέλου αὐτοῦ τῷ δούλῳ αὐτοῦ Ἰωάννῃ, 2 ὃς ἐμαρτύρησεν τὸν λόγον τοῦ θεοῦ καὶ τὴν μαρτυρίαν Ἰησοῦ Χριστοῦ ὅσα εἶδεν.

3 Μακάριος ὁ ἀναγινώσκων καὶ οἱ ἀκούοντες τοὺς λόγους τῆς προφητείας καὶ τηροῦντες τὰ ἐν αὐτῇ γεγραμμένα, ὁ γὰρ καιρὸς ἐγγύς.

4 Ἰωάννης ταῖς ἑπτὰ ἐκκλησίαις ταῖς ἐν τῇ Ἀσίᾳ· χάρις ὑμῖν καὶ εἰρήνη ἀπὸ ὁ ὢν καὶ ὁ ἦν καὶ ὁ ἐρχόμενος καὶ ἀπὸ τῶν ἑπτὰ πνευμάτων ἃ ἐνώπιον τοῦ θρόνου αὐτοῦ 5 καὶ ἀπὸ Ἰησοῦ Χριστοῦ, ὁ μάρτυς, ὁ πιστός, ὁ πρωτότοκος τῶν νεκρῶν καὶ ὁ ἄρχων τῶν βασιλέων τῆς γῆς.

Τῷ ἀγαπῶντι ἡμᾶς καὶ λύσαντι ἡμᾶς ἐκ τῶν ἁμαρτιῶν ἡμῶν ἐν τῷ αἵματι αὐτοῦ, 6 καὶ ἐποίησεν ἡμᾶς βασιλείαν, ἱερεῖς τῷ θεῷ καὶ πατρὶ αὐτοῦ, αὐτῷ ἡ δόξα καὶ τὸ κράτος εἰς τοὺς αἰῶνας [τῶν αἰώνων]· ἀμήν.

7 Ἰδοὺ ἔρχεται μετὰ τῶν νεφελῶν, καὶ ὄψεται αὐτὸν πᾶς ὀφθαλμὸς καὶ οἵτινες αὐτὸν ἐξεκέντησαν, καὶ κόψονται ἐπ᾽ αὐτὸν πᾶσαι αἱ φυλαὶ τῆς γῆς. ναί, ἀμήν.

8 Ἐγώ εἰμι τὸ ἄλφα καὶ τὸ ὦ, λέγει κύριος ὁ θεός, ὁ ὢν καὶ ὁ ἦν καὶ ὁ ἐρχόμενος, ὁ παντοκράτωρ.

9 Ἐγὼ Ἰωάννης, ὁ ἀδελφὸς ὑμῶν καὶ συγκοινωνὸς ἐν τῇ θλίψει καὶ βασιλείᾳ καὶ ὑπομονῇ ἐν Ἰησοῦ, ἐγενόμην ἐν τῇ νήσῳ τῇ καλουμένῃ Πάτμῳ διὰ τὸν λόγον τοῦ θεοῦ καὶ τὴν μαρτυρίαν Ἰησοῦ. 10 ἐγενόμην ἐν πνεύματι ἐν τῇ κυριακῇ ἡμέρᾳ καὶ ἤκουσα ὀπίσω μου φωνὴν μεγάλην ὡς σάλπιγγος 11 λεγούσης· ὃ βλέπεις γράψον εἰς βιβλίον καὶ πέμψον ταῖς ἑπτὰ ἐκκλησίαις, εἰς Ἔφεσον καὶ εἰς Σμύρναν καὶ εἰς Πέργαμον καὶ εἰς Θυάτειρα καὶ εἰς Σάρδεις καὶ εἰς Φιλαδέλφειαν καὶ εἰς Λαοδίκειαν.

The Apocalypse of John

See the Note on the Translation of the Greek Text on page xxix.

1 The revelation of Jesus Christ, which God gave to him, in order to show to his servants the things that must take place soon, and which he made manifest by dispatch, through the medium of his angel, to his servant John, 2 who testified to the word of God and to the testimony of Jesus Christ, that is, to all the things that he saw.

3 Blessed is he who reads and those who hear the words of the prophecy and keep the things that are written in it, for the moment is near.

4 John to the seven churches, those in Asia: Grace to you and peace from him who is and who was and who is coming, and from the seven spirits that are in front of his throne, 5 and from Jesus Christ, the faithful witness, the firstborn of the dead, and the ruler of the kings of the earth.

To him who loves us and has freed us from our sins by means of his blood, 6 and has made us a kingdom, priests for his God and Father, to him the glory and the power forever [and ever], amen.

7 Lo, he is coming with the clouds, and every eye will see him, and all those who pierced him through; and all the tribes of the earth will strike themselves in mourning for him. Yes indeed, amen.

8 "I am the Alpha and the Omega," says the Lord God, he who is and who was and who is coming, the Almighty.

9 I, John, your brother and partner in the tribulation and kingdom and endurance in Jesus, was on the island called Patmos because of the word of God and the testimony of Jesus. 10 I was in spirit on the day of the Lord, and I heard behind me a great voice like that of a trumpet 11 which was saying: "That which you see write in a scroll and send it to the seven churches, to Ephesus and to Smyrna and to Pergamum and to Thyatira and to Sardis and to Philadelphia and to Laodicea."

12 Καὶ ἐπέστρεψα βλέπειν τὴν φωνὴν ἥτις ἐλάλει μετ' ἐμοῦ, καὶ ἐπιστρέψας εἶδον ἑπτὰ λυχνίας χρυσᾶς 13 καὶ ἐν μέσῳ τῶν λυχνιῶν ὅμοιον υἱὸν ἀνθρώπου ἐνδεδυμένον ποδήρη καὶ περιεζωσμένον πρὸς τοῖς μαστοῖς ζώνην χρυσᾶν. 14 ἡ δὲ κεφαλὴ αὐτοῦ καὶ αἱ τρίχες λευκαὶ ὡς ἔριον λευκόν ὡς χιὼν καὶ οἱ ὀφθαλμοὶ αὐτοῦ ὡς φλὸξ πυρὸς 15 καὶ οἱ πόδες αὐτοῦ ὅμοιοι χαλκολιβάνῳ ὡς ἐν καμίνῳ πεπυρωμένης καὶ ἡ φωνὴ αὐτοῦ ὡς φωνὴ ὑδάτων πολλῶν, 16 καὶ ἔχων ἐν τῇ δεξιᾷ χειρὶ αὐτοῦ ἀστέρας ἑπτὰ καὶ ἐκ τοῦ στόματος αὐτοῦ ῥομφαία δίστομος ὀξεῖα ἐκπορευομένη καὶ ἡ ὄψις αὐτοῦ ὡς ὁ ἥλιος φαίνει ἐν τῇ δυνάμει αὐτοῦ.

17 Καὶ ὅτε εἶδον αὐτόν, ἔπεσα πρὸς τοὺς πόδας αὐτοῦ ὡς νεκρός, καὶ ἔθηκεν τὴν δεξιὰν αὐτοῦ ἐπ' ἐμὲ λέγων· μὴ φοβοῦ· ἐγώ εἰμι ὁ πρῶτος καὶ ὁ ἔσχατος 18 καὶ ὁ ζῶν, καὶ ἐγενόμην νεκρὸς καὶ ἰδοὺ ζῶν εἰμι εἰς τοὺς αἰῶνας τῶν αἰώνων καὶ ἔχω τὰς κλεῖς τοῦ θανάτου καὶ τοῦ ᾅδου. 19 γράψον οὖν ἃ εἶδες καὶ ἃ εἰσὶν καὶ ἃ μέλλει γενέσθαι μετὰ ταῦτα. 20 τὸ μυστήριον τῶν ἑπτὰ ἀστέρων οὓς εἶδες ἐπὶ τῆς δεξιᾶς μου καὶ τὰς ἑπτὰ λυχνίας τὰς χρυσᾶς· οἱ ἑπτὰ ἀστέρες ἄγγελοι τῶν ἑπτὰ ἐκκλησιῶν εἰσιν καὶ αἱ λυχνίαι αἱ ἑπτὰ ἑπτὰ ἐκκλησίαι εἰσίν.

2 Τῷ ἀγγέλῳ τῆς ἐν Ἐφέσῳ ἐκκλησίας γράψον·
Τάδε λέγει ὁ κρατῶν τοὺς ἑπτὰ ἀστέρας ἐν τῇ δεξιᾷ αὐτοῦ, ὁ περιπατῶν ἐν μέσῳ τῶν ἑπτὰ λυχνιῶν τῶν χρυσῶν· 2 οἶδα τὰ ἔργα σου καὶ τὸν κόπον καὶ τὴν ὑπομονήν σου καὶ ὅτι οὐ δύνῃ βαστάσαι κακούς, καὶ ἐπείρασας τοὺς λέγοντας ἑαυτοὺς ἀποστόλους καὶ οὐκ εἰσὶν καὶ εὗρες αὐτοὺς ψευδεῖς, 3 καὶ ὑπομονὴν ἔχεις καὶ ἐβάστασας διὰ τὸ ὄνομά μου καὶ οὐ κεκοπίακες. 4 ἀλλὰ ἔχω κατὰ σοῦ ὅτι τὴν ἀγάπην σου τὴν πρώτην ἀφῆκες. 5 μνημόνευε οὖν πόθεν πέπτωκας καὶ μετανόησον καὶ τὰ πρῶτα ἔργα ποίησον· εἰ δὲ μή, ἔρχομαί σοι καὶ κινήσω τὴν λυχνίαν σου ἐκ τοῦ τόπου αὐτῆς, ἐὰν μὴ μετανοήσῃς. 6 ἀλλὰ τοῦτο ἔχεις, ὅτι μισεῖς τὰ ἔργα τῶν Νικολαϊτῶν ἃ κἀγὼ μισῶ.

7 Ὁ ἔχων οὖς ἀκουσάτω τί τὸ πνεῦμα λέγει ταῖς ἐκκλησίαις. Τῷ νικῶντι δώσω αὐτῷ φαγεῖν ἐκ τοῦ ξύλου τῆς ζωῆς, ὅ ἐστιν ἐν τῷ παραδείσῳ τοῦ θεοῦ.

8 Καὶ τῷ ἀγγέλῳ τῆς ἐν Σμύρνῃ ἐκκλησίας γράψον·
Τάδε λέγει ὁ πρῶτος καὶ ὁ ἔσχατος, ὃς ἐγένετο νεκρὸς καὶ ἔζησεν· 9 οἶδά σου τὴν θλῖψιν καὶ τὴν πτωχείαν, ἀλλὰ πλούσιος εἶ, καὶ τὴν βλασφημίαν ἐκ τῶν λεγόντων Ἰουδαίους εἶναι ἑαυτοὺς καὶ οὐκ εἰσὶν ἀλλὰ συναγωγὴ τοῦ σατανᾶ. 10 μηδὲν φοβοῦ ἃ μέλλεις πάσχειν. ἰδοὺ μέλλει βάλλειν ὁ διάβολος ἐξ ὑμῶν εἰς φυλακὴν ἵνα πειρασθῆτε καὶ ἕξετε θλῖψιν ἡμερῶν δέκα. γίνου πιστὸς ἄχρι θανάτου, καὶ δώσω σοι τὸν στέφανον τῆς ζωῆς.

12 And I turned to see the voice that was speaking to me, and, having turned, I saw seven golden lampstands, 13 and in the midst of the lampstands one similar to a son of man, who was wearing a long garment and who was girded at the breasts with a golden sash. 14 And his head and his hair were white, like white wool, like snow, and his eyes were like a flame of fire, 15 and his feet similar to orichalcum, as in a furnace with fired orichalcum, and his voice like the voice of many waters, 16 and he had in his right hand seven stars, and from his mouth there extended a two-edged sword, sharp, and his face was like the sun shining with its might.

17 And when I saw him, I fell before his feet as dead, and he placed his right hand upon me, saying: "Do not fear; I am the first and the last, 18 and the living one; and I was dead, and lo I am alive forever and ever, and I have the keys of Death and of Hades. 19 Write therefore the things that you saw, and the things that are, and the things that are to take place after these. 20 This is the mystery of the seven stars that you saw in my right hand and the seven golden lampstands: the seven stars are angels of the seven churches, and the lampstands, seven in number, are seven churches.

2 "To the angel of the church in Ephesus write:
"These are the words of him who holds firmly the seven stars in his right hand, who walks in the midst of the seven golden lampstands: 2 I know your works, and your toil and endurance, and that you are not able to bear evil men; and you have put to the test those who call themselves apostles and are not, and you have found them to be false. 3 And you have endurance, and you have borne up for the sake of my name, and you have not become weary. 4 But I have against you that you have abandoned your love, the first one. 5 Remember therefore from where you have fallen, and repent and do the deeds of before; otherwise I am coming to you, and I will remove your lampstand from its place, if you do not repent. 6 But this you have in your favor, that you abhor the works of the Nicolaitans, which I also abhor. 7 He who has an ear, let him hear what the Spirit says to the churches. To the victor I will give to eat of the wood/tree of life that is in the paradise of God.

8 "And to the angel of the church in Smyrna write:
"These are the words of the first and the last, who was dead and lived [again]: 9 I know your tribulation and your poverty — but you are rich — and the blasphemy coming from those who say they are Jews and are not, but are a synagogue of Satan. 10 Do not fear at all the things that you are to suffer. Lo, the devil is about to throw some of you into prison, in order that you may be tested and endure a tribulation of ten days. Be faithful until death, and I will give you the crown of life.

11 Ὁ ἔχων οὖς ἀκουσάτω τί τὸ πνεῦμα λέγει ταῖς ἐκκλησίαις. Ὁ νικῶν οὐ μὴ ἀδικηθῇ ἐκ τοῦ θανάτου τοῦ δευτέρου.

12 Καὶ τῷ ἀγγέλῳ τῆς ἐν Περγάμῳ ἐκκλησίας γράψον·

Τάδε λέγει ὁ ἔχων τὴν ῥομφαίαν τὴν δίστομον τὴν ὀξεῖαν· 13 οἶδα ποῦ κατοικεῖς, ὅπου ὁ θρόνος τοῦ σατανᾶ, καὶ κρατεῖς τὸ ὄνομά μου καὶ οὐκ ἠρνήσω τὴν πίστιν μου καὶ ἐν ταῖς ἡμέραις Ἀντιπᾶς ὁ μάρτυς μου ὁ πιστός μου, ὃς ἀπεκτάνθη παρ' ὑμῖν, ὅπου ὁ σατανᾶς κατοικεῖ. 14 ἀλλ' ἔχω κατὰ σοῦ ὀλίγα ὅτι ἔχεις ἐκεῖ κρατοῦντας τὴν διδαχὴν Βαλαάμ, ὃς ἐδίδασκεν τῷ Βαλὰκ βαλεῖν σκάνδαλον ἐνώπιον τῶν υἱῶν Ἰσραὴλ φαγεῖν εἰδωλόθυτα καὶ πορνεῦσαι. 15 οὕτως ἔχεις καὶ σὺ κρατοῦντας τὴν διδαχὴν [τῶν] Νικολαϊτῶν ὁμοίως. 16 μετανόησον οὖν· εἰ δὲ μή, ἔρχομαί σοι ταχὺ καὶ πολεμήσω μετ' αὐτῶν ἐν τῇ ῥομφαίᾳ τοῦ στόματός μου.

17 Ὁ ἔχων οὖς ἀκουσάτω τί τὸ πνεῦμα λέγει ταῖς ἐκκλησίαις. Τῷ νικῶντι δώσω αὐτῷ τοῦ μάννα τοῦ κεκρυμμένου καὶ δώσω αὐτῷ ψῆφον λευκήν, καὶ ἐπὶ τὴν ψῆφον ὄνομα καινὸν γεγραμμένον ὃ οὐδεὶς οἶδεν εἰ μὴ ὁ λαμβάνων.

18 Καὶ τῷ ἀγγέλῳ τῆς ἐν Θυατείροις ἐκκλησίας γράψον·

Τάδε λέγει ὁ υἱὸς τοῦ θεοῦ, ὁ ἔχων τοὺς ὀφθαλμοὺς αὐτοῦ ὡς φλόγα πυρὸς καὶ οἱ πόδες αὐτοῦ ὅμοιοι χαλκολιβάνῳ· 19 οἶδά σου τὰ ἔργα καὶ τὴν ἀγάπην καὶ τὴν πίστιν καὶ τὴν διακονίαν καὶ τὴν ὑπομονήν σου, καὶ τὰ ἔργα σου τὰ ἔσχατα πλείονα τῶν πρώτων. 20 ἀλλὰ ἔχω κατὰ σοῦ ὅτι ἀφεῖς τὴν γυναῖκα Ἰεζάβελ, ἡ λέγουσα ἑαυτὴν προφῆτιν καὶ διδάσκει καὶ πλανᾷ τοὺς ἐμοὺς δούλους πορνεῦσαι καὶ φαγεῖν εἰδωλόθυτα. 21 καὶ ἔδωκα αὐτῇ χρόνον ἵνα μετανοήσῃ, καὶ οὐ θέλει μετανοῆσαι ἐκ τῆς πορνείας αὐτῆς. 22 ἰδοὺ βάλλω αὐτὴν εἰς κλίνην καὶ τοὺς μοιχεύοντας μετ' αὐτῆς εἰς θλῖψιν μεγάλην, ἐὰν μὴ μετανοήσουσιν ἐκ τῶν ἔργων αὐτῆς, 23 καὶ τὰ τέκνα αὐτῆς ἀποκτενῶ ἐν θανάτῳ. καὶ γνώσονται πᾶσαι αἱ ἐκκλησίαι ὅτι ἐγώ εἰμι ὁ ἐραυνῶν νεφροὺς καὶ καρδίας, καὶ δώσω ὑμῖν ἑκάστῳ κατὰ τὰ ἔργα ὑμῶν. 24 ὑμῖν δὲ λέγω τοῖς λοιποῖς τοῖς ἐν Θυατείροις, ὅσοι οὐκ ἔχουσιν τὴν διδαχὴν ταύτην, οἵτινες οὐκ ἔγνωσαν τὰ βαθέα τοῦ σατανᾶ ὡς λέγουσιν· οὐ βάλλω ἐφ' ὑμᾶς ἄλλο βάρος, 25 πλὴν ὃ ἔχετε κρατήσατε ἄχρι[ς] οὗ ἂν ἥξω.

26 Καὶ ὁ νικῶν καὶ ὁ τηρῶν ἄχρι τέλους τὰ ἔργα μου, δώσω αὐτῷ ἐξουσίαν ἐπὶ τῶν ἐθνῶν 27 καὶ ποιμανεῖ αὐτοὺς ἐν ῥάβδῳ σιδηρᾷ ὡς τὰ σκεύη τὰ κεραμικὰ συντρίβεται, 28 ὡς κἀγὼ εἴληφα παρὰ τοῦ πατρός μου, καὶ δώσω αὐτῷ τὸν ἀστέρα τὸν πρωϊνόν. 29 Ὁ ἔχων οὖς ἀκουσάτω τί τὸ πνεῦμα λέγει ταῖς ἐκκλησίαις.

11 "He who has an ear, let him hear what the Spirit says to the churches. The victor will not suffer harm from the second death.

12 "And to the angel of the church in Pergamum write:

"These are the words of him who has the two-edged sword, the sharp one: 13 I know where you dwell, where the throne of Satan is; and you hold fast to my name, and you did not deny my faith even in the days of Antipas, my witness, my faithful one, who was killed among you, where Satan dwells. 14 But I have a few things against you, namely, that you have there some who hold fast to the teaching of Balaam, who taught Balak to throw a stumbling block before the children of Israel, that is, to eat food sacrificed to idols and to engage in fornication. 15 So you as well have some who hold fast to the teaching of [the] Nicolaitans, in the same manner. 16 Repent therefore; otherwise I am coming to you soon, and I will fight against them with the sword of my mouth.

17 "He who has an ear, let him hear what the Spirit says to the churches. To the victor I will give some manna, of the hidden kind, and I will give him a white pebble, and on the pebble a new name will be written, which no one knows save the one who receives it.

18 "And to the angel of the church in Thyatira write:

"These are the words of the Son of God, the one who has his eyes like a flame of fire, and his feet are similar to orichalcum: 19 I know your works and love and faith and service, and your endurance and your works, the latter ones of which are better than the first ones. 20 But I have against you that you allow Jezebel to act (freely), she who calls herself a prophet, and she teaches and leads astray my servants, to engage in fornication and eat food sacrificed to idols. 21 And I have given her time that she might repent, but she is not willing to repent and depart from her prostitution. 22 Lo, I am throwing her on a bed, and those who commit adultery with her into great tribulation, if they do not repent and depart from her works; 23 and her children I will kill with death. And all the churches will know that I am he who searches inner feelings and hearts, and I will give to each one of you according to your works. 24 But to you, to the rest of you, who are in Thyatira, all those who do not have this teaching, who have not come to know the depths of Satan, as they say, to you I say, I am casting on you no other burden, 25 except that you hold fast to what you have until I arrive.

26 "And the victor, and he who keeps my works until the end, I will give to him authority over the nations 27 — and he will shepherd them with an iron staff, as he shatters the vessels of clay — 28 just as I have received it from my Father, and I will give him the morning star. 29 He who has an ear, let him hear what the Spirit says to the churches.

3 Καὶ τῷ ἀγγέλῳ τῆς ἐν Σάρδεσιν ἐκκλησίας γράψον·
Τάδε λέγει ὁ ἔχων τὰ ἑπτὰ πνεύματα τοῦ θεοῦ καὶ τοὺς ἑπτὰ ἀστέρας·
οἶδά σου τὰ ἔργα ὅτι ὄνομα ἔχεις ὅτι ζῇς, καὶ νεκρὸς εἶ. 2 γίνου γρηγορῶν καὶ
στήρισον τὰ λοιπὰ ἃ ἔμελλον ἀποθανεῖν, οὐ γὰρ εὕρηκά σου τὰ ἔργα
πεπληρωμένα ἐνώπιον τοῦ θεοῦ μου. 3 μνημόνευε οὖν πῶς εἴληφας καὶ
ἤκουσας καὶ τήρει καὶ μετανόησον. ἐὰν οὖν μὴ γρηγορήσῃς, ἥξω ὡς κλέπτης,
καὶ οὐ μὴ γνῷς ποίαν ὥραν ἥξω ἐπὶ σέ. 4 ἀλλὰ ἔχεις ὀλίγα ὀνόματα ἐν
Σάρδεσιν ἃ οὐκ ἐμόλυναν τὰ ἱμάτια αὐτῶν, καὶ περιπατήσουσιν μετ' ἐμοῦ ἐν
λευκοῖς, ὅτι ἄξιοί εἰσιν.

5 Ὁ νικῶν οὕτως περιβαλεῖται ἐν ἱματίοις λευκοῖς καὶ οὐ μὴ ἐξαλείψω τὸ
ὄνομα αὐτοῦ ἐκ τῆς βίβλου τῆς ζωῆς καὶ ὁμολογήσω τὸ ὄνομα αὐτοῦ ἐνώπιον
τοῦ πατρός μου καὶ ἐνώπιον τῶν ἀγγέλων αὐτοῦ. 6 Ὁ ἔχων οὖς ἀκουσάτω τί
τὸ πνεῦμα λέγει ταῖς ἐκκλησίαις.

7 Καὶ τῷ ἀγγέλῳ τῆς ἐν Φιλαδελφείᾳ ἐκκλησίας γράψον·

Τάδε λέγει ὁ ἅγιος, ὁ ἀληθινός, ὁ ἔχων τὴν κλεῖν Δαυίδ, ὁ ἀνοίγων καὶ
οὐδεὶς κλείσει καὶ κλείων καὶ οὐδεὶς ἀνοίγει· 8 οἶδά σου τὰ ἔργα, ἰδοὺ δέδωκα
ἐνώπιόν σου θύραν ἠνεῳγμένην, ἣν οὐδεὶς δύναται κλεῖσαι αὐτήν, ὅτι μικρὰν
ἔχεις δύναμιν καὶ ἐτήρησάς μου τὸν λόγον καὶ οὐκ ἠρνήσω τὸ ὄνομά μου.
9 ἰδοὺ διδῶ ἐκ τῆς συναγωγῆς τοῦ σατανᾶ τῶν λεγόντων ἑαυτοὺς Ἰουδαίους
εἶναι, καὶ οὐκ εἰσὶν ἀλλὰ ψεύδονται. ἰδοὺ ποιήσω αὐτοὺς ἵνα ἥξουσιν καὶ
προσκυνήσουσιν ἐνώπιον τῶν ποδῶν σου καὶ γνῶσιν ὅτι ἐγὼ ἠγάπησά σε.
10 ὅτι ἐτήρησας τὸν λόγον τῆς ὑπομονῆς μου, κἀγώ σε τηρήσω ἐκ τῆς ὥρας τοῦ
πειρασμοῦ τῆς μελλούσης ἔρχεσθαι ἐπὶ τῆς οἰκουμένης ὅλης πειράσαι τοὺς
κατοικοῦντας ἐπὶ τῆς γῆς. 11 ἔρχομαι ταχύ· κράτει ὃ ἔχεις, ἵνα μηδεὶς λάβῃ τὸν
στέφανόν σου.

12 Ὁ νικῶν ποιήσω αὐτὸν στῦλον ἐν τῷ ναῷ τοῦ θεοῦ μου καὶ ἔξω οὐ μὴ
ἐξέλθῃ ἔτι καὶ γράψω ἐπ' αὐτὸν τὸ ὄνομα τοῦ θεοῦ μου καὶ τὸ ὄνομα τῆς
πόλεως τοῦ θεοῦ μου, τῆς καινῆς Ἰερουσαλὴμ ἡ καταβαίνουσα ἐκ τοῦ
οὐρανοῦ ἀπὸ τοῦ θεοῦ μου, καὶ τὸ ὄνομά μου τὸ καινόν. 13 Ὁ ἔχων οὖς
ἀκουσάτω τί τὸ πνεῦμα λέγει ταῖς ἐκκλησίαις.

14 Καὶ τῷ ἀγγέλῳ τῆς ἐν Λαοδικείᾳ ἐκκλησίας γράψον·

3 "And to the angel of the church in Sardis write:

"These are the words of him who has the seven spirits of God and the seven stars: I know your works, that you have a name that you are alive, and you are dead. 2 Get yourself awake and make firm the things that remain, which were about to die; for I have not found your works fulfilled before my God. 3 Keep in mind therefore how you have received and have heard, and keep it and repent. If therefore you do not awaken, I will come like a thief, and you truly will not know at what hour I will come upon you. 4 But you have a few names in Sardis who did not defile their garments, and they will walk with me in white garments, since they are worthy.

5 "The victor will be wrapped thus in white garments, and I shall not erase his name from the scroll of life, and I will profess his name before my Father and before his angels. 6 He who has an ear, let him hear what the Spirit says to the churches.

7 "And to the angel of the church in Philadelphia write:

"These are the words of the holy one, the true one, who has the key of David, who opens and no one will close, and who closes and no one can open: 8 I know your works; lo, I have set before you an open door, which no one can close, since you have a little power and yet you have kept my word and you have not denied my name. 9 Lo, I will offer some of the synagogue of Satan, of those who say that they are Jews and are not, but lie. Lo, I will make them come and bow down before your feet and know that I have loved you. 10 Since you have kept the word of my endurance, I also will keep you from the hour of trial, the one that is to come upon the entire inhabited world, to put to the test those who dwell on the earth. 11 I am coming soon; hold fast to what you have, so that no one may take your crown.

12 "The victor I will make a pillar in the temple of my God, and he will not venture out any more, and I will write upon him the name of my God and the name of the city of my God, the new Jerusalem that comes down out of heaven from my God, and my name, the new one. 13 He who has an ear, let him hear what the Spirit says to the churches.

14 "And to the angel of the church in Laodicea write:

Τάδε λέγει ὁ ἀμήν, ὁ μάρτυς ὁ πιστὸς καὶ ἀληθινός, ἡ ἀρχὴ τῆς κτίσεως τοῦ θεοῦ· 15 οἶδά σου τὰ ἔργα ὅτι οὔτε ψυχρὸς εἶ οὔτε ζεστός. ὄφελον ψυχρὸς ἦς ἢ ζεστός. 16 οὕτως ὅτι χλιαρὸς εἶ καὶ οὔτε ζεστὸς οὔτε ψυχρός, μέλλω σε ἐμέσαι ἐκ τοῦ στόματός μου. 17 ὅτι λέγεις ὅτι πλούσιός εἰμι καὶ πεπλούτηκα καὶ οὐδὲν χρείαν ἔχω, καὶ οὐκ οἶδας ὅτι σὺ εἶ ὁ ταλαίπωρος καὶ ἐλεεινὸς καὶ πτωχὸς καὶ τυφλὸς καὶ γυμνός, 18 συμβουλεύω σοι ἀγοράσαι παρ' ἐμοῦ χρυσίον πεπυρωμένον ἐκ πυρὸς ἵνα πλουτήσῃς, καὶ ἱμάτια λευκὰ ἵνα περιβάλῃ καὶ μὴ φανερωθῇ ἡ αἰσχύνη τῆς γυμνότητός σου, καὶ κολλ[ο]ύριον ἐγχρῖσαι τοὺς ὀφθαλμούς σου ἵνα βλέπῃς. 19 ἐγὼ ὅσους ἐὰν φιλῶ ἐλέγχω καὶ παιδεύω· ζήλευε οὖν καὶ μετανόησον. 20 Ἰδοὺ ἕστηκα ἐπὶ τὴν θύραν καὶ κρούω· ἐάν τις ἀκούσῃ τῆς φωνῆς μου καὶ ἀνοίξῃ τὴν θύραν, [καὶ] εἰσελεύσομαι πρὸς αὐτὸν καὶ δειπνήσω μετ' αὐτοῦ καὶ αὐτὸς μετ' ἐμοῦ.

21 Ὁ νικῶν δώσω αὐτῷ καθίσαι μετ' ἐμοῦ ἐν τῷ θρόνῳ μου, ὡς κἀγὼ ἐνίκησα καὶ ἐκάθισα μετὰ τοῦ πατρός μου ἐν τῷ θρόνῳ αὐτοῦ. 22 Ὁ ἔχων οὖς ἀκουσάτω τί τὸ πνεῦμα λέγει ταῖς ἐκκλησίαις.

4Μετὰ ταῦτα εἶδον, καὶ ἰδοὺ θύρα ἠνεῳγμένη ἐν τῷ οὐρανῷ, καὶ ἡ φωνὴ ἡ πρώτη ἣν ἤκουσα ὡς σάλπιγγος λαλούσης μετ' ἐμοῦ λέγων· ἀνάβα ὧδε, καὶ δείξω σοι ἃ δεῖ γενέσθαι μετὰ ταῦτα.

2 Εὐθέως ἐγενόμην ἐν πνεύματι, καὶ ἰδοὺ θρόνος ἔκειτο ἐν τῷ οὐρανῷ, καὶ ἐπὶ τὸν θρόνον καθήμενος, 3 καὶ ὁ καθήμενος ὅμοιος ὁράσει λίθῳ ἰάσπιδι καὶ σαρδίῳ, καὶ ἶρις κυκλόθεν τοῦ θρόνου ὅμοιος ὁράσει σμαραγδίνῳ. 4 Καὶ κυκλόθεν τοῦ θρόνου θρόνους εἴκοσι τέσσαρες, καὶ ἐπὶ τοὺς θρόνους εἴκοσι τέσσαρας πρεσβυτέρους καθημένους περιβεβλημένους ἐν ἱματίοις λευκοῖς καὶ ἐπὶ τὰς κεφαλὰς αὐτῶν στεφάνους χρυσοῦς. 5 Καὶ ἐκ τοῦ θρόνου ἐκπορεύονται ἀστραπαὶ καὶ φωναὶ καὶ βρονταί, καὶ ἑπτὰ λαμπάδες πυρὸς καιόμεναι ἐνώπιον τοῦ θρόνου, ἅ εἰσιν τὰ ἑπτὰ πνεύματα τοῦ θεοῦ, 6 καὶ ἐνώπιον τοῦ θρόνου ὡς θάλασσα ὑαλίνη ὁμοία κρυστάλλῳ. Καὶ ἐν μέσῳ τοῦ θρόνου καὶ κύκλῳ τοῦ θρόνου τέσσαρα ζῷα γέμοντα ὀφθαλμῶν ἔμπροσθεν καὶ ὄπισθεν. 7 καὶ τὸ ζῷον τὸ πρῶτον ὅμοιον λέοντι καὶ τὸ δεύτερον ζῷον ὅμοιον μόσχῳ καὶ τὸ τρίτον ζῷον ἔχων τὸ πρόσωπον ὡς ἀνθρώπου καὶ τὸ τέταρτον ζῷον ὅμοιον ἀετῷ πετομένῳ. 8 καὶ τὰ τέσσαρα ζῷα, ἓν καχ' ἓν αὐτῶν ἔχων ἀνὰ πτέρυγας ἕξ, κυκλόθεν καὶ ἔσωθεν γέμουσιν ὀφθαλμῶν, καὶ ἀνάπαυσιν οὐκ ἔχουσιν ἡμέρας καὶ νυκτὸς λέγοντες· ἅγιος ἅγιος ἅγιος κύριος ὁ θεὸς ὁ παντοκράτωρ, ὁ ἦν καὶ ὁ ὢν καὶ ὁ ἐρχόμενος.

"These are the words of the Amen, the faithful and true witness, the beginning of the creation of God: 15 I know your works, that you are neither frigid nor fervent. Would that you were frigid or fervent! 16 So, since you are lukewarm, and neither fervent nor frigid, I am going to spew you out of my mouth. 17 Because you say: I am rich, and I have become rich, and I have need of nothing. And you do not know that you are the wretched one and pitiable and beggarly and blind and naked; 18 I advise you to buy from me gold fired by fire, so that you may become rich, and white garments, so that you may wrap yourself up and the shame of your nakedness will not be visible, and eyesalve to anoint your eyes, so that you may see. 19 All those whom I love, I reprove and discipline. Be zealous, therefore, and repent. 20 Lo, I am standing in front of the door and knocking; if someone hears my voice and opens the door, I [also] will come in to him and I will dine with him, and he with me.

21 "The victor I will grant to sit with me on my throne, as I also was victorious and sat down with my Father on his throne. 22 He who has an ear, let him hear what the Spirit says to the churches."

4 After these things I saw, and, lo, a door that was open in heaven; and the voice, the one from before, which I had heard like that of a trumpet speaking with me, was saying: "Come up here, and I will show you the things that must take place after these."

2 Straightaway I was in spirit, and lo a throne was set in heaven, and on the throne was one seated, 3 and the one seated was, to the sight, similar to a jasper stone and a carnelian, and there was a rainbow around the throne, to the sight, similar to an emerald. 4 And around the throne I saw twenty-four thrones, and seated on the thrones twenty-four elders, wrapped in white garments, and on their heads golden crowns. 5 And from the throne come forth lightnings, voices, and thunders, and seven torches of fire burning before the throne, which are the seven spirits of God, 6 and before the throne there is something like a sea of glass, similar to crystal. And in the middle of the throne and around the throne are four living creatures, full of eyes, in front and in back: 7 the first living creature similar to a lion, and the second living creature similar to a calf, and the third living creature with its face like that of a man, and the fourth living creature similar to a flying eagle. 8 And the four living creatures, each one of them with six wings apiece, are full of eyes all around and inside, and have no rest day or night, saying, "Holy, holy, holy, is the Lord God, the Almighty, he who was and who is and who is coming."

9 Καὶ ὅταν δώσουσιν τὰ ζῷα δόξαν καὶ τιμὴν καὶ εὐχαριστίαν τῷ καθημένῳ ἐπὶ τῷ θρόνῳ τῷ ζῶντι εἰς τοὺς αἰῶνας τῶν αἰώνων, 10 πεσοῦνται οἱ εἴκοσι τέσσαρες πρεσβύτεροι ἐνώπιον τοῦ καθημένου ἐπὶ τοῦ θρόνου καὶ προσκυνήσουσιν τῷ ζῶντι εἰς τοὺς αἰῶνας τῶν αἰώνων καὶ βαλοῦσιν τοὺς στεφάνους αὐτῶν ἐνώπιον τοῦ θρόνου λέγοντες· 11 ἄξιος εἶ, ὁ κύριος καὶ ὁ θεὸς ἡμῶν, λαβεῖν τὴν δόξαν καὶ τὴν τιμὴν καὶ τὴν δύναμιν, ὅτι σὺ ἔκτισας τὰ πάντα καὶ διὰ τὸ θέλημά σου ἦσαν καὶ ἐκτίσθησαν.

5 Καὶ εἶδον ἐπὶ τὴν δεξιὰν τοῦ καθημένου ἐπὶ τοῦ θρόνου βιβλίον γεγραμμένον ἔσωθεν καὶ ὄπισθεν κατεσφραγισμένον σφραγῖσιν ἑπτά. 2 καὶ εἶδον ἄγγελον ἰσχυρὸν κηρύσσοντα ἐν φωνῇ μεγάλῃ· τίς ἄξιος ἀνοῖξαι τὸ βιβλίον καὶ λῦσαι τὰς σφραγῖδας αὐτοῦ; 3 καὶ οὐδεὶς ἐδύνατο ἐν τῷ οὐρανῷ οὐδὲ ἐπὶ τῆς γῆς οὐδὲ ὑποκάτω τῆς γῆς ἀνοῖξαι τὸ βιβλίον οὔτε βλέπειν αὐτό. 4 καὶ ἔκλαιον πολύ, ὅτι οὐδεὶς ἄξιος εὑρέθη ἀνοῖξαι τὸ βιβλίον οὔτε βλέπειν αὐτό. 5 καὶ εἷς ἐκ τῶν πρεσβυτέρων λέγει μοι· μὴ κλαῖε, ἰδοὺ ἐνίκησεν ὁ λέων ὁ ἐκ τῆς φυλῆς Ἰούδα, ἡ ῥίζα Δαυίδ, ἀνοῖξαι τὸ βιβλίον καὶ τὰς ἑπτὰ σφραγῖδας αὐτοῦ.

6 Καὶ εἶδον ἐν μέσῳ τοῦ θρόνου καὶ τῶν τεσσάρων ζῴων καὶ ἐν μέσῳ τῶν πρεσβυτέρων ἀρνίον ἑστηκὸς ὡς ἐσφαγμένον ἔχων κέρατα ἑπτὰ καὶ ὀφθαλμοὺς ἑπτὰ οἵ εἰσιν τὰ [ἑπτὰ] πνεύματα τοῦ θεοῦ ἀπεσταλμένοι εἰς πᾶσαν τὴν γῆν. 7 καὶ ἦλθεν καὶ εἴληφεν ἐκ τῆς δεξιᾶς τοῦ καθημένου ἐπὶ τοῦ θρόνου.

8 Καὶ ὅτε ἔλαβεν τὸ βιβλίον, τὰ τέσσαρα ζῷα καὶ οἱ εἴκοσι τέσσαρες πρεσβύτεροι ἔπεσαν ἐνώπιον τοῦ ἀρνίου ἔχοντες ἕκαστος κιθάραν καὶ φιάλας χρυσᾶς γεμούσας θυμιαμάτων, αἵ εἰσιν αἱ προσευχαὶ τῶν ἁγίων, 9 καὶ ᾄδουσιν ᾠδὴν καινὴν λέγοντες· ἄξιος εἶ λαβεῖν τὸ βιβλίον καὶ ἀνοῖξαι τὰς σφραγῖδας αὐτοῦ, ὅτι ἐσφάγης καὶ ἠγόρασας τῷ θεῷ ἐν τῷ αἵματί σου ἐκ πάσης φυλῆς καὶ γλώσσης καὶ λαοῦ καὶ ἔθνους 10 καὶ ἐποίησας αὐτοὺς τῷ θεῷ ἡμῶν βασιλείαν καὶ ἱερεῖς, καὶ βασιλεύσουσιν ἐπὶ τῆς γῆς.

11 Καὶ εἶδον, καὶ ἤκουσα φωνὴν ἀγγέλων πολλῶν κύκλῳ τοῦ θρόνου καὶ τῶν ζῴων καὶ τῶν πρεσβυτέρων, καὶ ἦν ὁ ἀριθμὸς αὐτῶν μυριάδες μυριάδων καὶ χιλιάδες χιλιάδων 12 λέγοντες φωνῇ μεγάλῃ· ἄξιόν ἐστιν τὸ ἀρνίον τὸ ἐσφαγμένον λαβεῖν τὴν δύναμιν καὶ πλοῦτον καὶ σοφίαν καὶ ἰσχὺν καὶ τιμὴν καὶ δόξαν καὶ εὐλογίαν. 13 καὶ πᾶν κτίσμα ὃ ἐν τῷ οὐρανῷ καὶ ἐπὶ τῆς γῆς καὶ ὑποκάτω τῆς γῆς καὶ ἐπὶ τῆς θαλάσσης καὶ τὰ ἐν αὐτοῖς πάντα ἤκουσα λέγοντας· τῷ καθημένῳ ἐπὶ τῷ θρόνῳ καὶ τῷ ἀρνίῳ ἡ εὐλογία καὶ ἡ τιμὴ καὶ ἡ δόξα καὶ τὸ κράτος εἰς τοὺς αἰῶνας τῶν αἰώνων. 14 καὶ τὰ τέσσαρα ζῷα ἔλεγον· ἀμήν. καὶ οἱ πρεσβύτεροι ἔπεσαν καὶ προσεκύνησαν.

9 And when the living creatures grant glory and honor and thanks to the one sitting on the throne, to the one who lives forever and ever, 10 the twenty-four elders will fall down before the one sitting on the throne, and will bow down to the one who lives forever and ever, and will throw their crowns before the throne, saying: 11 "You are worthy, Lord and our God, to receive the glory and the honor and the power, because you created all things, and by your will they were and were created."

5 And I saw in the right hand of the one seated on the throne a scroll, written on the inside and on the back, sealed with seven seals. 2 And I saw a strong angel proclaiming with a great voice: "Who is worthy to open the scroll and to loose its seals?" 3 And no one in heaven or on earth or below the earth was able to open the scroll or even look at it. 4 And I wept much, because no one was found worthy to open the scroll or even look at it. 5 And one of the elders says to me: "Do not weep; lo, the Lion has prevailed, the one from the tribe of Judah, the root of David, to open the scroll and its seven seals."

6 And I saw, in the midst of the throne and the four living creatures and in the midst of the elders, a Lamb standing, as if slaughtered, with seven horns and seven eyes, which are the [seven] spirits of God sent out to all the earth. 7 And he came and took it from the right hand of the one seated on the throne.

8 And when he had taken the scroll, the four living creatures and the twenty-four elders fell down before the lamb, each of them having a lyre and golden bowls full of fragrances — these are the prayers of the holy ones — 9 and they sing a new song, saying: "You are worthy to take the scroll and open its seals, because you were slaughtered and you purchased for God, by your blood, men of every tribe and language and people and nation, 10 and you made them a kingdom and priests for our God, and they will reign upon the earth."

11 And I saw, and I heard a voice of many angels around the throne and the living creatures and the elders, and their number was myriads of myriads and thousands of thousands, 12 and they were saying with a great voice: "Worthy is the Lamb, the one slaughtered, to receive the power and riches and wisdom and strength and honor and glory and blessing!" 13 And every creature in heaven and on earth and under the earth and on the sea, and everything in them, I heard saying: "To the one sitting on the throne and to the Lamb be the blessing and the honor and the glory and the power forever and ever!" 14 And the four living creatures said: "Amen." And the elders fell and bowed down.

6Καὶ εἶδον ὅτε ἤνοιξεν τὸ ἀρνίον μίαν ἐκ τῶν ἑπτὰ σφραγίδων, καὶ ἤκουσα ἑνὸς ἐκ τῶν τεσσάρων ζῴων λέγοντος ὡς φωνὴ βροντῆς· ἔρχου. 2 καὶ εἶδον, καὶ ἰδοὺ ἵππος λευκός, καὶ ὁ καθήμενος ἐπ' αὐτὸν ἔχων τόξον καὶ ἐδόθη αὐτῷ στέφανος καὶ ἐξῆλθεν νικῶν καὶ ἵνα νικήσῃ.

3 Καὶ ὅτε ἤνοιξεν τὴν σφραγῖδα τὴν δευτέραν, ἤκουσα τοῦ δευτέρου ζῴου λέγοντος· ἔρχου. 4 καὶ ἐξῆλθεν ἄλλος ἵππος πυρρός, καὶ τῷ καθημένῳ ἐπ' αὐτὸν ἐδόθη αὐτῷ λαβεῖν τὴν εἰρήνην ἐκ τῆς γῆς καὶ ἵνα ἀλλήλους σφάξουσιν καὶ ἐδόθη αὐτῷ μάχαιρα μεγάλη.

5 Καὶ ὅτε ἤνοιξεν τὴν σφραγῖδα τὴν τρίτην, ἤκουσα τοῦ τρίτου ζῴου λέγοντος· ἔρχου. καὶ εἶδον, καὶ ἰδοὺ ἵππος μέλας, καὶ ὁ καθήμενος ἐπ' αὐτὸν ἔχων ζυγὸν ἐν τῇ χειρὶ αὐτοῦ. 6 καὶ ἤκουσα ὡς φωνὴν ἐν μέσῳ τῶν τεσσάρων ζῴων λέγουσαν· χοῖνιξ σίτου δηναρίου καὶ τρεῖς χοίνικες κριθῶν δηναρίου, καὶ τὸ ἔλαιον καὶ τὸν οἶνον μὴ ἀδικήσῃς.

7 Καὶ ὅτε ἤνοιξεν τὴν σφραγῖδα τὴν τετάρτην, ἤκουσα φωνὴν τοῦ τετάρτου ζῴου λέγοντος· ἔρχου. 8 καὶ εἶδον, καὶ ἰδοὺ ἵππος χλωρός, καὶ ὁ καθήμενος ἐπάνω αὐτοῦ ὄνομα αὐτῷ [ὁ] θάνατος, καὶ ὁ ᾅδης ἠκολούθει μετ' αὐτοῦ καὶ ἐδόθη αὐτοῖς ἐξουσία ἐπὶ τὸ τέταρτον τῆς γῆς ἀποκτεῖναι ἐν ῥομφαίᾳ καὶ ἐν λιμῷ καὶ ἐν θανάτῳ καὶ ὑπὸ τῶν θηρίων τῆς γῆς.

9 Καὶ ὅτε ἤνοιξεν τὴν πέμπτην σφραγῖδα, εἶδον ὑποκάτω τοῦ θυσιαστηρίου τὰς ψυχὰς τῶν ἐσφαγμένων διὰ τὸν λόγον τοῦ θεοῦ καὶ διὰ τὴν μαρτυρίαν ἣν εἶχον. 10 καὶ ἔκραξαν φωνῇ μεγάλῃ λέγοντες· ἕως πότε, ὁ δεσπότης ὁ ἅγιος καὶ ἀληθινός, οὐ κρίνεις καὶ ἐκδικεῖς τὸ αἷμα ἡμῶν ἐκ τῶν κατοικούντων ἐπὶ τῆς γῆς; 11 καὶ ἐδόθη αὐτοῖς ἑκάστῳ στολὴ λευκὴ καὶ ἐρρέθη αὐτοῖς ἵνα ἀναπαύσονται ἔτι χρόνον μικρόν, ἕως πληρωθῶσιν καὶ οἱ σύνδουλοι αὐτῶν καὶ οἱ ἀδελφοὶ αὐτῶν οἱ μέλλοντες ἀποκτέννεσθαι ὡς καὶ αὐτοί.

12 Καὶ εἶδον ὅτε ἤνοιξεν τὴν σφραγῖδα τὴν ἕκτην, καὶ σεισμὸς μέγας ἐγένετο καὶ ὁ ἥλιος ἐγένετο μέλας ὡς σάκκος τρίχινος, καὶ ἡ σελήνη ὅλη ἐγένετο ὡς αἷμα 13 καὶ οἱ ἀστέρες τοῦ οὐρανοῦ ἔπεσαν εἰς τὴν γῆν, ὡς συκῆ βάλλει τοὺς ὀλύνθους αὐτῆς ὑπὸ ἀνέμου μεγάλου σειομένη, 14 καὶ ὁ οὐρανὸς ἀπεχωρίσθη ὡς βιβλίον ἑλισσόμενον καὶ πᾶν ὄρος καὶ νῆσος ἐκ τῶν τόπων αὐτῶν ἐκινήθησαν. 15 καὶ οἱ βασιλεῖς τῆς γῆς καὶ οἱ μεγιστᾶνες καὶ οἱ χιλίαρχοι καὶ οἱ πλούσιοι καὶ οἱ ἰσχυροὶ καὶ πᾶς δοῦλος καὶ ἐλεύθερος ἔκρυψαν ἑαυτοὺς εἰς τὰ σπήλαια καὶ εἰς τὰς πέτρας τῶν ὀρέων 16 καὶ λέγουσιν τοῖς ὄρεσιν καὶ ταῖς πέτραις· πέσετε ἐφ' ἡμᾶς καὶ κρύψατε ἡμᾶς ἀπὸ προσώπου τοῦ καθημένου ἐπὶ τοῦ θρόνου καὶ ἀπὸ τῆς ὀργῆς τοῦ ἀρνίου, 17 ὅτι ἦλθεν ἡ ἡμέρα ἡ μεγάλη τῆς ὀργῆς αὐτοῦν, καὶ τίς δύναται σταθῆναι;

6 And I saw when the Lamb opened one of the seven seals, and I heard one of the four living creatures saying, like a voice of thunder: "Come!" 2 And I saw, and, lo, a white horse, and he who was sitting upon it was holding a bow, and a crown was given to him, and he went out as a victor and in order that he might be victorious again.

3 And when he opened the second seal, I heard the second living creature saying: "Come!" 4 And another horse, fiery red, came out, and to him who was sitting upon it, to him it was granted to remove peace from the earth — and that they might slaughter one another — and a large dagger was given to him.

5 And when he opened the third seal, I heard the third living creature saying: "Come!" And I saw, and, lo, a black horse, and he who was sitting upon it had a scale in his hand. 6 And I heard something like a voice in the midst of the four living creatures, saying: "A choenix of wheat for a denarius, and three choenices of barley for a denarius, and do not ruin the oil and the wine!"

7 And when he opened the fourth seal, I heard a voice of the fourth living creature saying: "Come!" 8 And I saw, and, lo, a green horse, and he who was sitting upon it, his name was Death, and Hades was following him, and to them was given authority over the fourth part of the earth, to kill with sword and with famine and with death and by the agency of the wild beasts of the earth.

9 And when he opened the fifth seal, I saw underneath the sacrificial altar the souls of those slaughtered for the word of God and for the testimony that they held. 10 And they shouted with a great voice, saying: "Until when, you who are the Master, the holy and true, will you not judge and avenge our blood on them who dwell upon the earth?" 11 And to them, to each one, was given a white robe, and it was said to them that they will rest for a short time more, until their fellow servants and their brothers should also be fulfilled, the ones who are to be killed as they.

12 And I saw when he opened the sixth seal, and there was a great quake, and the sun became black, like sackcloth of hair, and the entire moon became like blood, 13 and the stars of the sky fell to the earth, as a fig tree throws down its unripe fruits, shaken by a great wind, 14 and the heaven drew back like a scroll that is rolled up, and every mountain and island was moved from its place. 15 And the kings of the earth and the chief men and the commanders and the rich and the strong and every slave and freeman hid themselves in the caves and among the rocks of the mountains, 16 and they say to the mountains and to the rocks: "Fall upon us and hide us from the countenance of him who is sitting on the throne and from the rage of the Lamb, 17 because the day has arrived, the great day of his rage, and who will be able to stand?"

7Μετὰ τοῦτο εἶδον τέσσαρας ἀγγέλους ἑστῶτας ἐπὶ τὰς τέσσαρας γωνίας τῆς γῆς, κρατοῦντας τοὺς τέσσαρας ἀνέμους τῆς γῆς ἵνα μὴ πνέῃ ἄνεμος ἐπὶ τῆς γῆς μήτε ἐπὶ τῆς θαλάσσης μήτε ἐπὶ πᾶν δένδρον. 2 Καὶ εἶδον ἄλλον ἄγγελον ἀναβαίνοντα ἀπὸ ἀνατολῶν ἡλίου ἔχοντα σφραγῖδα θεοῦ ζῶντος, καὶ ἔκραξεν φωνῇ μεγάλῃ τοῖς τέσσαρσιν ἀγγέλοις οἷς ἐδόθη αὐτοῖς ἀδικῆσαι τὴν γῆν καὶ τὴν θάλασσαν 3 λέγων· μὴ ἀδικήσητε τὴν γῆν μήτε τὴν θάλασσαν μήτε τὰ δένδρα, ἄχρι σφραγίσωμεν τοὺς δούλους τοῦ θεοῦ ἡμῶν ἐπὶ τῶν μετώπων αὐτῶν.

4 Καὶ ἤκουσα τὸν ἀριθμὸν τῶν ἐσφραγισμένων, ἑκατὸν τεσσεράκοντα τέσσαρες χιλιάδες, ἐσφραγισμένοι ἐκ πάσης φυλῆς υἱῶν Ἰσραήλ· 5 ἐκ φυλῆς Ἰούδα δώδεκα χιλιάδες ἐσφραγισμένοι, ἐκ φυλῆς Ῥουβὴν δώδεκα χιλιάδες, ἐκ φυλῆς Γὰδ δώδεκα χιλιάδες, 6 ἐκ φυλῆς Ἀσὴρ δώδεκα χιλιάδες, ἐκ φυλῆς Νεφθαλὶμ δώδεκα χιλιάδες, ἐκ φυλῆς Μανασσῆ δώδεκα χιλιάδες, 7 ἐκ φυλῆς Συμεὼν δώδεκα χιλιάδες, ἐκ φυλῆς Λευὶ δώδεκα χιλιάδες, ἐκ φυλῆς Ἰσσαχὰρ δώδεκα χιλιάδες, 8 ἐκ φυλῆς Ζαβουλὼν δώδεκα χιλιάδες, ἐκ φυλῆς Ἰωσὴφ δώδεκα χιλιάδες, ἐκ φυλῆς Βενιαμὶν δώδεκα χιλιάδες ἐσφραγισμένοι.

9 Μετὰ ταῦτα εἶδον, καὶ ἰδοὺ ὄχλος πολύς, ὃν ἀριθμῆσαι αὐτὸν οὐδεὶς ἐδύνατο, ἐκ παντὸς ἔθνους καὶ φυλῶν καὶ λαῶν καὶ γλωσσῶν ἑστῶτες ἐνώπιον τοῦ θρόνου καὶ ἐνώπιον τοῦ ἀρνίου περιβεβλημένους στολὰς λευκὰς καὶ φοίνικες ἐν ταῖς χερσὶν αὐτῶν, 10 καὶ κράζουσιν φωνῇ μεγάλῃ λέγοντες· ἡ σωτηρία τῷ θεῷ ἡμῶν τῷ καθημένῳ ἐπὶ τῷ θρόνῳ καὶ τῷ ἀρνίῳ.

11 Καὶ πάντες οἱ ἄγγελοι εἱστήκεισαν κύκλῳ τοῦ θρόνου καὶ τῶν πρεσβυτέρων καὶ τῶν τεσσάρων ζῴων καὶ ἔπεσαν ἐνώπιον τοῦ θρόνου ἐπὶ τὰ πρόσωπα αὐτῶν καὶ προσεκύνησαν τῷ θεῷ 12 λέγοντες· ἀμήν, ἡ εὐλογία καὶ ἡ δόξα καὶ ἡ σοφία καὶ ἡ εὐχαριστία καὶ ἡ τιμὴ καὶ ἡ δύναμις καὶ ἡ ἰσχὺς τῷ θεῷ ἡμῶν εἰς τοὺς αἰῶνας τῶν αἰώνων· ἀμήν.

13 Καὶ ἀπεκρίθη εἷς ἐκ τῶν πρεσβυτέρων λέγων μοι· οὗτοι οἱ περιβεβλημένοι τὰς στολὰς τὰς λευκὰς τίνες εἰσὶν καὶ πόθεν ἦλθον; 14 καὶ εἴρηκα αὐτῷ· κύριέ μου, σὺ οἶδας. καὶ εἶπέν μοι· οὗτοί εἰσιν οἱ ἐρχόμενοι ἐκ τῆς θλίψεως τῆς μεγάλης καὶ ἔπλυναν τὰς στολὰς αὐτῶν καὶ ἐλεύκαναν αὐτὰς ἐν τῷ αἵματι τοῦ ἀρνίου. 15 διὰ τοῦτό εἰσιν ἐνώπιον τοῦ θρόνου τοῦ θεοῦ καὶ λατρεύουσιν αὐτῷ ἡμέρας καὶ νυκτὸς ἐν τῷ ναῷ αὐτοῦ, καὶ ὁ καθήμενος ἐπὶ τοῦ θρόνου σκηνώσει ἐπ᾽ αὐτούς. 16 οὐ πεινάσουσιν ἔτι οὐδὲ διψήσουσιν ἔτι οὐδὲ μὴ πέσῃ ἐπ᾽ αὐτοὺς ὁ ἥλιος οὐδὲ πᾶν καῦμα, 17 ὅτι τὸ ἀρνίον τὸ ἀνὰ μέσον τοῦ θρόνου ποιμανεῖ αὐτοὺς καὶ ὁδηγήσει αὐτοὺς ἐπὶ ζωῆς πηγὰς ὑδάτων, καὶ ἐξαλείψει ὁ θεὸς πᾶν δάκρυον ἐκ τῶν ὀφθαλμῶν αὐτῶν.

7 After this I saw four angels standing upon the four corners of the earth, holding firmly the four winds of the earth, so that no wind might blow on the earth nor on the sea nor upon any tree. 2 And I saw another angel coming up from where the sun rises, with the seal of the living God, and he shouted with a great voice to the four angels to whom it was granted to harm the earth and the sea, 3 saying: "Do not harm the earth nor the sea nor the trees until we mark with a seal the servants of our God on their foreheads."

4 And I heard the number of those marked with the seal, one hundred forty-four thousands: men marked with the seal from every tribe of the children of Israel. 5 Of the tribe of Judah twelve thousands: men marked with the seal; of the tribe of Reuben twelve thousands; of the tribe of Gad twelve thousands; 6 of the tribe of Asher twelve thousands; of the tribe of Naphtali twelve thousands; of the tribe of Manasseh twelve thousands; 7 of the tribe of Simeon twelve thousands; of the tribe of Levi twelve thousands; of the tribe of Issachar twelve thousands; 8 of the tribe of Zebulun twelve thousands; of the tribe of Joseph twelve thousands; of the tribe of Benjamin twelve thousands: men marked with the seal.

9 After these things I saw, and, lo, a great throng, which no one could count it, from all nations and tribes and peoples and languages, standing before the throne and before the Lamb, wrapped in white robes and with palm branches in their hands. 10 And they shout with a great voice, saying: "Salvation to our God, to him who sits on the throne, and to the Lamb."

11 And all the angels were standing around the throne and the elders and the four living creatures, and they fell on their faces before the throne and bowed down to God, 12 saying: "Amen; the blessing and the glory and the wisdom and the giving of thanks and the honor and the power and the strength to our God forever and ever! Amen."

13 And one of the elders answered, saying to me: "These who are wrapped in the white robes, who are they and from where did they come?" 14 And I said to him: "My lord, you know!" And he said to me: "These are the ones who come from the tribulation, the great one, and they washed their robes and bleached them in the blood of the Lamb. 15 For this reason they are before the throne of God, and they render service to him day and night in his temple, and he who sits on the throne will abide upon them. 16 They will not feel hunger any more, nor feel thirst any more, nor shall the sun fall upon them, nor any burning, 17 because the Lamb, the one in the middle of the throne, will shepherd them and lead them to the springs of the water of life, and God will wipe away every tear from their eyes."

8 Καὶ ὅταν ἤνοιξεν τὴν σφραγῖδα τὴν ἑβδόμην, ἐγένετο σιγὴ ἐν τῷ οὐρανῷ ὡς ἡμιώριον.

2 Καὶ εἶδον τοὺς ἑπτὰ ἀγγέλους οἳ ἐνώπιον τοῦ θεοῦ ἑστήκασιν, καὶ ἐδόθησαν αὐτοῖς ἑπτὰ σάλπιγγες.

3 Καὶ ἄλλος ἄγγελος ἦλθεν καὶ ἐστάθη ἐπὶ τοῦ θυσιαστηρίου ἔχων λιβανωτὸν χρυσοῦν, καὶ ἐδόθη αὐτῷ θυμιάματα πολλά, ἵνα δώσει ταῖς προσευχαῖς τῶν ἁγίων πάντων ἐπὶ τὸ θυσιαστήριον τὸ χρυσοῦν τὸ ἐνώπιον τοῦ θρόνου. 4 καὶ ἀνέβη ὁ καπνὸς τῶν θυμιαμάτων ταῖς προσευχαῖς τῶν ἁγίων ἐκ χειρὸς τοῦ ἀγγέλου ἐνώπιον τοῦ θεοῦ. 5 καὶ εἴληφεν ὁ ἄγγελος τὸν λιβανωτὸν καὶ ἐγέμισεν αὐτὸν ἐκ τοῦ πυρὸς τοῦ θυσιαστηρίου καὶ ἔβαλεν εἰς τὴν γῆν, καὶ ἐγένοντο βρονταὶ καὶ φωναὶ καὶ ἀστραπαὶ καὶ σεισμός.

6 Καὶ οἱ ἑπτὰ ἄγγελοι οἱ ἔχοντες τὰς ἑπτὰ σάλπιγγας ἡτοίμασαν αὐτοὺς ἵνα σαλπίσωσιν.

7 Καὶ ὁ πρῶτος ἐσάλπισεν· καὶ ἐγένετο χάλαζα καὶ πῦρ μεμιγμένα ἐν αἵματι καὶ ἐβλήθη εἰς τὴν γῆν, καὶ τὸ τρίτον τῆς γῆς κατεκάη καὶ τὸ τρίτον τῶν δένδρων κατεκάη καὶ πᾶς χόρτος χλωρὸς κατεκάη.

8 Καὶ ὁ δεύτερος ἄγγελος ἐσάλπισεν· καὶ ὡς ὄρος μέγα πυρὶ καιόμενον ἐβλήθη εἰς τὴν θάλασσαν, καὶ ἐγένετο τὸ τρίτον τῆς θαλάσσης αἷμα 9 καὶ ἀπέθανεν τὸ τρίτον τῶν κτισμάτων τῶν ἐν τῇ θαλάσσῃ τὰ ἔχοντα ψυχὰς καὶ τὸ τρίτον τῶν πλοίων διεφθάρησαν.

10 Καὶ ὁ τρίτος ἄγγελος ἐσάλπισεν· καὶ ἔπεσεν ἐκ τοῦ οὐρανοῦ ἀστὴρ μέγας καιόμενος ὡς λαμπὰς καὶ ἔπεσεν ἐπὶ τὸ τρίτον τῶν ποταμῶν καὶ ἐπὶ τὰς πηγὰς τῶν ὑδάτων, 11 καὶ τὸ ὄνομα τοῦ ἀστέρος λέγεται ὁ Ἄψινθος, καὶ ἐγένετο τὸ τρίτον τῶν ὑδάτων εἰς ἄψινθον καὶ πολλοὶ τῶν ἀνθρώπων ἀπέθανον ἐκ τῶν ὑδάτων ὅτι ἐπικράνθησαν.

12 Καὶ ὁ τέταρτος ἄγγελος ἐσάλπισεν· καὶ ἐπλήγη τὸ τρίτον τοῦ ἡλίου καὶ τὸ τρίτον τῆς σελήνης καὶ τὸ τρίτον τῶν ἀστέρων, ἵνα σκοτισθῇ τὸ τρίτον αὐτῶν καὶ ἡ ἡμέρα μὴ φάνῃ τὸ τρίτον αὐτῆς καὶ ἡ νὺξ ὁμοίως.

13 Καὶ εἶδον, καὶ ἤκουσα ἑνὸς ἀετοῦ πετομένου ἐν μεσουρανήματι λέγοντος φωνῇ μεγάλῃ· οὐαὶ οὐαὶ οὐαὶ τοὺς κατοικοῦντας ἐπὶ τῆς γῆς ἐκ τῶν λοιπῶν φωνῶν τῆς σάλπιγγος τῶν τριῶν ἀγγέλων τῶν μελλόντων σαλπίζειν.

8 And when he opened the seventh seal, there was silence in heaven for something like a half an hour.

2 And I saw the seven angels, those who stand before God, and seven trumpets were given to them.

3 And another angel came and stood on the sacrificial altar with a golden censer, and much incense was given to him, so that he might impart it to the prayers of all the holy ones upon the sacrificial altar, the golden one, the one before the throne. 4 And the smoke of the incense rose to the prayers of the holy ones from the hand of the angel before God. 5 And the angel took the censer and filled it with the fire of the sacrificial altar and threw it to the earth, and there were thunders and voices and lightnings and a quake.

6 And the seven angels, those with the seven trumpets, prepared themselves to sound them.

7 And the first sounded: and there was hail and fire mixed with blood, and they were thrown to the earth, and the third part of the earth burned up, and the third part of the trees burned up, and all green grass burned up.

8 And the second angel sounded, and something like a great mountain, burning with fire, was thrown into the sea, and the third part of the sea became blood, 9 and the third part of the creatures in the sea, those having souls, died, and the third part of the ships were destroyed.

10 And the third angel sounded: and there fell from heaven a large star, burning like a torch, and it fell upon the third part of the rivers and upon the springs of water. 11 And the name of the star is called Wormwood, and the third part of the waters became wormwood, and many among men died from the waters, because they became bitter.

12 And the fourth angel sounded: and the third part of the sun was hit, and the third part of the moon, and the third part of the stars, in order that the third part of them would be darkened, and the day would not shine with the third part of its light, and likewise the night.

13 And I saw, and I heard a solitary eagle flying in high heaven, saying with a great voice: "Woe, woe, woe to those who dwell on the earth, from the remaining voices of the trumpet of the three angels who are about to sound!"

9 Καὶ ὁ πέμπτος ἄγγελος ἐσάλπισεν· καὶ εἶδον ἀστέρα ἐκ τοῦ οὐρανοῦ πεπτωκότα εἰς τὴν γῆν, καὶ ἐδόθη αὐτῷ ἡ κλεὶς τοῦ φρέατος τῆς ἀβύσσου 2 καὶ ἤνοιξεν τὸ φρέαρ τῆς ἀβύσσου, καὶ ἀνέβη καπνὸς ἐκ τοῦ φρέατος ὡς καπνὸς καμίνου μεγάλης, καὶ ἐσκοτώθη ὁ ἥλιος καὶ ὁ ἀὴρ ἐκ τοῦ καπνοῦ τοῦ φρέατος. 3 καὶ ἐκ τοῦ καπνοῦ ἐξῆλθον ἀκρίδες εἰς τὴν γῆν, καὶ ἐδόθη αὐταῖς ἐξουσία ὡς ἔχουσιν ἐξουσίαν οἱ σκορπίοι τῆς γῆς. 4 καὶ ἐρρέθη αὐταῖς ἵνα μὴ ἀδικήσουσιν τὸν χόρτον τῆς γῆς οὐδὲ πᾶν χλωρὸν οὐδὲ πᾶν δένδρον, εἰ μὴ τοὺς ἀνθρώπους οἵτινες οὐκ ἔχουσι τὴν σφραγῖδα τοῦ θεοῦ ἐπὶ τῶν μετώπων. 5 καὶ ἐδόθη αὐτοῖς ἵνα μὴ ἀποκτείνωσιν αὐτούς, ἀλλ' ἵνα βασανισθήσονται μῆνας πέντε, καὶ ὁ βασανισμὸς αὐτῶν ὡς βασανισμὸς σκορπίου ὅταν παίσῃ ἄνθρωπον. 6 καὶ ἐν ταῖς ἡμέραις ἐκείναις ζητήσουσιν οἱ ἄνθρωποι τὸν θάνατον καὶ οὐ μὴ εὑρήσουσιν αὐτόν, καὶ ἐπιθυμήσουσιν ἀποθανεῖν καὶ φεύγει ὁ θάνατος ἀπ' αὐτῶν.

7 Καὶ τὰ ὁμοιώματα τῶν ἀκρίδων ὅμοια ἵπποις ἡτοιμασμένοις εἰς πόλεμον, καὶ ἐπὶ τὰς κεφαλὰς αὐτῶν ὡς στέφανοι ὅμοιοι χρυσῷ, καὶ τὰ πρόσωπα αὐτῶν ὡς πρόσωπα ἀνθρώπων, 8 καὶ εἶχον τρίχας ὡς τρίχας γυναικῶν, καὶ οἱ ὀδόντες αὐτῶν ὡς λεόντων ἦσαν, 9 καὶ εἶχον θώρακας ὡς θώρακας σιδηροῦς, καὶ ἡ φωνὴ τῶν πτερύγων αὐτῶν ὡς φωνὴ ἁρμάτων ἵππων πολλῶν τρεχόντων εἰς πόλεμον, 10 καὶ ἔχουσιν οὐρὰς ὁμοίας σκορπίοις καὶ κέντρα, καὶ ἐν ταῖς οὐραῖς αὐτῶν ἡ ἐξουσία αὐτῶν ἀδικῆσαι τοὺς ἀνθρώπους μῆνας πέντε, 11 ἔχουσιν ἐπ' αὐτῶν βασιλέα τὸν ἄγγελον τῆς ἀβύσσου, ὄνομα αὐτῷ Ἑβραϊστὶ Ἀβαδδών, καὶ ἐν τῇ Ἑλληνικῇ ὄνομα ἔχει Ἀπολλύων.

12 Ἡ οὐαὶ ἡ μία ἀπῆλθεν· ἰδοὺ ἔρχεται ἔτι δύο οὐαὶ μετὰ ταῦτα.

13 Καὶ ὁ ἕκτος ἄγγελος ἐσάλπισεν· καὶ ἤκουσα φωνὴν μίαν ἐκ τῶν [τεσσάρων] κεράτων τοῦ θυσιαστηρίου τοῦ χρυσοῦ τοῦ ἐνώπιον τοῦ θεοῦ, 14 λέγοντα τῷ ἕκτῳ ἀγγέλῳ, ὁ ἔχων τὴν σάλπιγγα· λῦσον τοὺς τέσσαρας ἀγγέλους τοὺς δεδεμένους ἐπὶ τῷ ποταμῷ τῷ μεγάλῳ Εὐφράτῃ. 15 καὶ ἐλύθησαν οἱ τέσσαρες ἄγγελοι οἱ ἡτοιμασμένοι εἰς τὴν ὥραν καὶ ἡμέραν καὶ μῆνα καὶ ἐνιαυτόν, ἵνα ἀποκτείνωσιν τὸ τρίτον τῶν ἀνθρώπων. 16 καὶ ὁ ἀριθμὸς τῶν στρατευμάτων τοῦ ἱππικοῦ δισμυριάδες μυριάδων, ἤκουσα τὸν ἀριθμὸν αὐτῶν.

17 Καὶ οὕτως εἶδον τοὺς ἵππους ἐν τῇ ὁράσει καὶ τοὺς καθημένους ἐπ' αὐτῶν, ἔχοντας θώρακας πυρίνους καὶ ὑακινθίνους καὶ θειώδεις, καὶ αἱ κεφαλαὶ τῶν ἵππων ὡς κεφαλαὶ λεόντων, καὶ ἐκ τῶν στομάτων αὐτῶν ἐκπορεύεται πῦρ καὶ καπνὸς καὶ θεῖον. 18 ἀπὸ τῶν τριῶν πληγῶν τούτων ἀπεκτάνθησαν τὸ τρίτον τῶν ἀνθρώπων, ἐκ τοῦ πυρὸς καὶ τοῦ καπνοῦ καὶ τοῦ θείου τοῦ ἐκπορευομένου ἐκ τῶν στομάτων αὐτῶν. 19 ἡ γὰρ ἐξουσία τῶν ἵππων ἐν τῷ στόματι αὐτῶν ἐστιν καὶ ἐν ταῖς οὐραῖς αὐτῶν, αἱ γὰρ οὐραὶ αὐτῶν ὅμοιαι ὄφεσιν, ἔχουσαι κεφαλὰς καὶ ἐν αὐταῖς ἀδικοῦσιν.

9 And the fifth angel sounded: and I saw a star fallen from heaven to the earth, and the key of the pit of the abyss was given to it. 2 And it opened the pit of the abyss, and smoke rose from the pit like the smoke of a large furnace, and the sun became dark, and so did the air, from the smoke of the pit. 3 And from the smoke locusts came out toward the earth, and to them was given power, as the scorpions of the earth have power. 4 And it was said to them that they should not harm the grass of the earth nor any green thing nor any tree, but only men, namely, those who do not have the seal of God on their foreheads. 5 And it was granted them that they not kill them but that they be tormented for five months, and their torment was like the torment of a scorpion when it stings a man. 6 And in those days men will seek death and will not find it, and they will desire to die, and death flees from them.

7 And the likenesses of the locusts were similar to horses prepared for war, and on their heads was something like crowns, similar to gold, and their faces were like faces of men, 8 and they had hair like the hair of women, and their teeth were like those of lions, 9 and they had breastplates like iron breastplates, and the voice of their wings was like the voice of many chariots with horses, rushing to war. 10 And they have tails similar to scorpions, and stings, and in their tails is their power to harm men for five months. 11 They have over them as king the angel of the abyss; his name in Hebrew is Abaddon, and in Greek he has the name Apollyon.

12 The first woe has gone; lo, a woe is coming twice more after these things.

13 And the sixth angel sounded: and I heard a voice from the [four] corners of the sacrificial altar, the golden one, the one before God, 14 and the altar said to the sixth angel, the one with the trumpet: "Untie the four angels, the ones bound at the great river, the Euphrates." 15 And the four angels were untied, those who were prepared for the hour and day and month and year, to kill the third part of mankind. 16 And the number of the troops of cavalry was two myriads of myriads; I heard their number.

17 And thus I saw the horses in the vision and those who were sitting upon them, with breastplates of fire and of hyacinth and of sulfur, and the heads of the horses were like the heads of lions, and from their mouths comes forth fire and smoke and sulfur. 18 By these three plagues the third part of mankind was killed, by the fire and by the smoke and by the sulfur, which came forth from their mouths. 19 For the power of the horses is in their mouth and in their tails; for their tails are similar to snakes since they have heads, and with them they cause harm.

20 Καὶ οἱ λοιποὶ τῶν ἀνθρώπων, οἳ οὐκ ἀπεκτάνθησαν ἐν ταῖς πληγαῖς ταύταις, οὐδὲ μετενόησαν ἐκ τῶν ἔργων τῶν χειρῶν αὐτῶν, ἵνα μὴ προσκυνήσουσιν τὰ δαιμόνια καὶ τὰ εἴδωλα τὰ χρυσᾶ καὶ τὰ ἀργυρᾶ καὶ τὰ χαλκᾶ καὶ τὰ λίθινα καὶ τὰ ξύλινα, ἃ οὔτε βλέπειν δύνανται οὔτε ἀκούειν οὔτε περιπατεῖν, 21 καὶ οὐ μετενόησαν ἐκ τῶν φόνων αὐτῶν οὔτε ἐκ τῶν φαρμάκων αὐτῶν οὔτε ἐκ τῆς πορνείας αὐτῶν οὔτε ἐκ τῶν κλεμμάτων αὐτῶν.

10 Καὶ εἶδον ἄλλον ἄγγελον ἰσχυρὸν καταβαίνοντα ἐκ τοῦ οὐρανοῦ περιβεβλημένον νεφέλην, καὶ ἡ Ἶρις ἐπὶ τῆς κεφαλῆς αὐτοῦ καὶ τὸ πρόσωπον αὐτοῦ ὡς ὁ ἥλιος καὶ οἱ πόδες αὐτοῦ ὡς στῦλοι πυρός, 2 καὶ ἔχων ἐν τῇ χειρὶ αὐτοῦ βιβλαρίδιον ἠνεῳγμένον. καὶ ἔθηκεν τὸν πόδα αὐτοῦ τὸν δεξιὸν ἐπὶ τῆς θαλάσσης, τὸν δὲ εὐώνυμον ἐπὶ τῆς γῆς, 3 καὶ ἔκραξεν φωνῇ μεγάλῃ ὥσπερ λέων μυκᾶται. καὶ ὅτε ἔκραξεν, ἐλάλησαν αἱ ἑπτὰ βρονταὶ τὰς ἑαυτῶν φωνάς. 4 καὶ ὅτε ἐλάλησαν αἱ ἑπτὰ βρονταί, ἤμελλον γράφειν, καὶ ἤκουσα φωνὴν ἐκ τοῦ οὐρανοῦ λέγουσαν· σφράγισον ἃ ἐλάλησαν αἱ ἑπτὰ βρονταί, καὶ μὴ αὐτὰ γράψῃς.

5 Καὶ ὁ ἄγγελος, ὃν εἶδον ἑστῶτα ἐπὶ τῆς θαλάσσης καὶ ἐπὶ τῆς γῆς, ἦρεν τὴν χεῖρα αὐτοῦ τὴν δεξιὰν εἰς τὸν οὐρανὸν 6 καὶ ὤμοσεν ἐν τῷ ζῶντι εἰς τοὺς αἰῶνας τῶν αἰώνων, ὃς ἔκτισεν τὸν οὐρανὸν καὶ τὰ ἐν αὐτῷ καὶ τὴν γῆν καὶ τὰ ἐν αὐτῇ καὶ τὴν θάλασσαν καὶ τὰ ἐν αὐτῇ, ὅτι χρόνος οὐκέτι ἔσται, 7 ἀλλ᾽ ἐν ταῖς ἡμέραις τῆς φωνῆς τοῦ ἑβδόμου ἀγγέλου, ὅταν μέλλῃ σαλπίζειν, καὶ ἐτελέσθη τὸ μυστήριον τοῦ θεοῦ, ὡς εὐηγγέλισεν τοὺς ἑαυτοῦ δούλους τοὺς προφήτας.

8 Καὶ ἡ φωνὴ ἣν ἤκουσα ἐκ τοῦ οὐρανοῦ πάλιν λαλοῦσαν μετ᾽ ἐμοῦ καὶ λέγουσαν· ὕπαγε λάβε τὸ βιβλίον τὸ ἠνεῳγμένον ἐν τῇ χειρὶ τοῦ ἀγγέλου τοῦ ἑστῶτος ἐπὶ τῆς θαλάσσης καὶ ἐπὶ τῆς γῆς. 9 καὶ ἀπῆλθα πρὸς τὸν ἄγγελον λέγων αὐτῷ δοῦναί μοι τὸ βιβλαρίδιον. καὶ λέγει μοι· λάβε καὶ κατάφαγε αὐτό, καὶ πικρανεῖ σου τὴν κοιλίαν, ἀλλ᾽ ἐν τῷ στόματί σου ἔσται γλυκὺ ὡς μέλι.

10 Καὶ ἔλαβον τὸ βιβλαρίδιον ἐκ τῆς χειρὸς τοῦ ἀγγέλου καὶ κατέφαγον αὐτό, καὶ ἦν ἐν τῷ στόματί μου ὡς μέλι γλυκὺ καὶ ὅτε ἔφαγον αὐτό, ἐπικράνθη ἡ κοιλία μου. 11 καὶ λέγουσίν μοι· δεῖ σε πάλιν προφητεῦσαι ἐπὶ λαοῖς καὶ ἔθνεσιν καὶ γλώσσαις καὶ βασιλεῦσιν πολλοῖς.

11 Καὶ ἐδόθη μοι κάλαμος ὅμοιος ῥάβδῳ, λέγων· ἔγειρε καὶ μέτρησον τὸν ναὸν τοῦ θεοῦ καὶ τὸ θυσιαστήριον καὶ τοὺς προσκυνοῦντας ἐν αὐτῷ. 2 καὶ τὴν αὐλὴν τὴν ἔξωθεν τοῦ ναοῦ ἔκβαλε ἔξωθεν καὶ μὴ αὐτὴν μετρήσῃς, ὅτι ἐδόθη τοῖς ἔθνεσιν, καὶ τὴν πόλιν τὴν ἁγίαν πατήσουσιν μῆνας τεσσεράκοντα [καὶ] δύο.

20 And the remainder of mankind, those who were not killed by these plagues, did not even repent of the works of their hands, so as not to bow down to the demons and the idols, those of gold and those of silver and those of bronze and those of stone and those of wood, which can neither see nor hear nor walk, 21 and they did not repent of their murders nor of their poisons nor of their prostitution nor of their thefts.

10 And I saw another strong angel descending from heaven, wrapped in a cloud, and the rainbow was over his head, and his face was like the sun, and his feet like pillars of fire, 2 and he was holding in his hand a small scroll, opened. And he placed his right foot on the sea and his left on the land, 3 and he shouted with a great voice, as a lion roars. And when he shouted, the seven thunders spoke their voices. 4 And when the seven thunders spoke, I was about to write, and I heard a voice from heaven saying: "Seal closed the things that the seven thunders said, and do not write them."

5 And the angel, whom I saw standing on the sea and on the land, raised his hand, the right one, toward heaven 6 and swore by the one who lives forever and ever, who created heaven and the things in it, and the earth and the things in it, and the sea and the things in it, that time will be no more, 7 but that in the days of the voice of the seventh angel, when he is about to sound, the mystery of God was also completed, as he proclaimed with good report to his servants, the prophets.

8 And the voice that I heard from heaven, when again talking to me, was saying: "Go on, take the open scroll in the hand of the angel standing on the sea and on the land." 9 And I went toward the angel, saying to him: "Give me the scroll." And he says to me: "Take and swallow it, and it will make your stomach bitter, but in your mouth it will be sweet as honey."

10 And I took the scroll from the hand of the angel, and I swallowed it, and in my mouth it was sweet as honey, and when I ate it, my stomach was made bitter. 11 And they say to me: "It is necessary for you to again prophesy about numerous peoples and nations and languages and kings."

11 And a reed similar to a staff was given to me, saying: "Arise and measure the temple of God and the sacrificial altar and those who bow down in it. 2 And the court, the one outside the temple, throw outside and do not measure it, because it was given to the nations, and they will trample on the holy city for forty-two months.

3 Καὶ δώσω τοῖς δυσὶν μάρτυσίν μου καὶ προφητεύσουσιν ἡμέρας χιλίας διακοσίας ἑξήκοντα περιβεβλημένοι σάκκους. 4 οὗτοί εἰσιν αἱ δύο ἐλαῖαι καὶ αἱ δύο λυχνίαι αἱ ἐνώπιον τοῦ κυρίου τῆς γῆς ἑστῶτες. 5 καὶ εἴ τις αὐτοὺς θέλει ἀδικῆσαι πῦρ ἐκπορεύεται ἐκ τοῦ στόματος αὐτῶν καὶ κατεσθίει τοὺς ἐχθροὺς αὐτῶν· καὶ εἴ τις θελήσῃ αὐτοὺς ἀδικῆσαι, οὕτως δεῖ αὐτὸν ἀποκτανθῆναι. 6 οὗτοι ἔχουσιν τὴν ἐξουσίαν κλεῖσαι τὸν οὐρανόν, ἵνα μὴ ὑετὸς βρέχῃ τὰς ἡμέρας τῆς προφητείας αὐτῶν, καὶ ἐξουσίαν ἔχουσιν ἐπὶ τῶν ὑδάτων στρέφειν αὐτὰ εἰς αἷμα καὶ πατάξαι τὴν γῆν ἐν πάσῃ πληγῇ ὁσάκις ἐὰν θελήσωσιν.

7 Καὶ ὅταν τελέσωσιν τὴν μαρτυρίαν αὐτῶν, τὸ θηρίον τὸ ἀναβαῖνον ἐκ τῆς ἀβύσσου ποιήσει μετ᾽ αὐτῶν πόλεμον καὶ νικήσει αὐτοὺς καὶ ἀποκτενεῖ αὐτούς. 8 καὶ τὸ πτῶμα αὐτῶν ἐπὶ τῆς πλατείας τῆς πόλεως τῆς μεγάλης, ἥτις καλεῖται πνευματικῶς Σόδομα καὶ Αἴγυπτος, ὅπου καὶ ὁ κύριος αὐτῶν ἐσταυρώθη. 9 καὶ βλέπουσιν ἐκ τῶν λαῶν καὶ φυλῶν καὶ γλωσσῶν καὶ ἐθνῶν τὸ πτῶμα αὐτῶν ἡμέρας τρεῖς καὶ ἥμισυ καὶ τὰ πτώματα αὐτῶν οὐκ ἀφίουσιν τεθῆναι εἰς μνῆμα. 10 καὶ οἱ κατοικοῦντες ἐπὶ τῆς γῆς χαίρουσιν ἐπ᾽ αὐτοῖς καὶ εὐφραίνονται καὶ δῶρα πέμψουσιν ἀλλήλοις, ὅτι οὗτοι οἱ δύο προφῆται ἐβασάνισαν τοὺς κατοικοῦντας ἐπὶ τῆς γῆς.

11 Καὶ μετὰ τὰς τρεῖς ἡμέρας καὶ ἥμισυ πνεῦμα ζωῆς ἐκ τοῦ θεοῦ εἰσῆλθεν ἐν αὐτοῖς, καὶ ἔστησαν ἐπὶ τοὺς πόδας αὐτῶν, καὶ φόβος μέγας ἐπέπεσεν ἐπὶ τοὺς θεωροῦντας αὐτούς. 12 καὶ ἤκουσαν φωνῆς μεγάλης ἐκ τοῦ οὐρανοῦ λεγούσης αὐτοῖς· ἀνάβατε ὧδε. καὶ ἀνέβησαν εἰς τὸν οὐρανὸν ἐν τῇ νεφέλῃ, καὶ ἐθεώρησαν αὐτοὺς οἱ ἐχθροὶ αὐτῶν. 13 καὶ ἐν ἐκείνῃ τῇ ὥρᾳ ἐγένετο σεισμὸς μέγας καὶ τὸ δέκατον τῆς πόλεως ἔπεσεν καὶ ἀπεκτάνθησαν ἐν τῷ σεισμῷ ὀνόματα ἀνθρώπων χιλιάδες ἑπτὰ καὶ οἱ λοιποὶ ἔμφοβοι ἐγένοντο καὶ ἔδωκαν δόξαν τῷ θεῷ τοῦ οὐρανοῦ.

14 Ἡ οὐαὶ ἡ δευτέρα ἀπῆλθεν· ἰδοὺ ἡ οὐαὶ ἡ τρίτη ἔρχεται ταχύ.

15 Καὶ ὁ ἕβδομος ἄγγελος ἐσάλπισεν· καὶ ἐγένοντο φωναὶ μεγάλαι ἐν τῷ οὐρανῷ λέγοντες· ἐγένετο ἡ βασιλεία τοῦ κόσμου τοῦ κυρίου ἡμῶν καὶ τοῦ χριστοῦ αὐτοῦ, καὶ βασιλεύσει εἰς τοὺς αἰῶνας τῶν αἰώνων. 16 καὶ οἱ εἴκοσι τέσσαρες πρεσβύτεροι [οἱ] ἐνώπιον τοῦ θεοῦ καθήμενοι ἐπὶ τοὺς θρόνους αὐτῶν ἔπεσαν ἐπὶ τὰ πρόσωπα αὐτῶν καὶ προσεκύνησαν τῷ θεῷ 17 λέγοντες· εὐχαριστοῦμέν σοι, κύριε ὁ θεὸς ὁ παντοκράτωρ, ὁ ὢν καὶ ὁ ἦν, ὅτι εἴληφας τὴν δύναμίν σου τὴν μεγάλην καὶ ἐβασίλευσας. 18 καὶ τὰ ἔθνη ὠργίσθησαν, καὶ ἦλθεν ἡ ὀργή σου καὶ ὁ καιρὸς τῶν νεκρῶν κριθῆναι καὶ δοῦναι τὸν μισθὸν τοῖς δούλοις σου τοῖς προφήταις καὶ τοῖς ἁγίοις καὶ τοῖς φοβουμένοις τὸ ὄνομά σου, τοὺς μικροὺς καὶ τοὺς μεγάλους, καὶ διαφθεῖραι τοὺς διαφθείροντας τὴν γῆν.

19 Καὶ ἠνοίγη ὁ ναὸς τοῦ θεοῦ ὁ ἐν τῷ οὐρανῷ καὶ ὤφθη ἡ κιβωτὸς τῆς διαθήκης αὐτοῦ ἐν τῷ ναῷ αὐτοῦ, καὶ ἐγένοντο ἀστραπαὶ καὶ φωναὶ καὶ βρονταὶ καὶ σεισμὸς καὶ χάλαζα μεγάλη.

3 "And I will grant to my two witnesses, and they will prophesy for one thousand two hundred and sixty days, wrapped in sackcloth." 4 These are the two olive trees and the two lampstands, which stand before the Lord of the earth. 5 And if someone wants to harm them, fire comes forth from their mouth and devours their enemies; and truly, if someone should wish to harm them, in this manner he must be killed. 6 These men have the power to close heaven, so that rain does not fall during the days of their prophesying, and they have power over the waters, to turn them into blood, and to smite the land with every plague, as many times as they desire.

7 And when they have completed their testimony, the beast that comes up out of the abyss will make war with them and will defeat them and will kill them. 8 And their corpse will lie on the square of the city, the great one, which spiritually is called Sodom and Egypt, where also their Lord was crucified. 9 And some of the peoples and tribes and languages and nations watch their corpse for three days and a half and do not allow their corpses to be placed in a tomb. 10 And those who dwell on the land rejoice over them and jubilate, and will bring gifts to one another, because these two prophets tormented those who dwell on the land.

11 And after the three days and a half a spirit of life from God entered into them, and they stood on their feet, and great fear fell on those watching them. 12 And they heard a great voice from heaven saying to them: "Come up here!" And they went up to heaven in the cloud, and their enemies looked at them. 13 And in that hour there was a great quake, and the tenth part of the city fell, and in the quake names of men, seven thousand, were killed, and the rest were frightened and rendered glory to the God of heaven.

14 The second woe has gone; lo, the third woe is coming soon.

15 And the seventh angel sounded; and there were great voices in heaven, saying: "The kingdom of the world of our Lord and of his Anointed has been realized, and he will reign forever and ever." 16 And the twenty-four elders, [those] before God, seated on their thrones, fell on their faces and bowed down to God, 17 saying: "We render thanks to you, Lord God almighty, who is and who was, for you have taken your power, which is great, and you realized your kingdom. 18 And the nations became angry, and your anger came, and the moment for the dead to be judged and to give payment to your servants the prophets, and to the holy ones, and to those who fear your name, the small and the great, and to destroy those who destroy the land."

19 And the temple of God, the one in heaven, was opened, and the ark of his covenant was seen in his temple, and there were lightnings and voices and thunders and a quake and great hail.

12 Καὶ σημεῖον μέγα ὤφθη ἐν τῷ οὐρανῷ, γυνὴ περιβεβλημένη τὸν ἥλιον, καὶ ἡ σελήνη ὑποκάτω τῶν ποδῶν αὐτῆς καὶ ἐπὶ τῆς κεφαλῆς αὐτῆς στέφανος ἀστέρων δώδεκα, 2 καὶ ἐν γαστρὶ ἔχουσα, καὶ κράζει ὠδίνουσα καὶ βασανιζομένη τεκεῖν. 3 καὶ ὤφθη ἄλλο σημεῖον ἐν τῷ οὐρανῷ, καὶ ἰδοὺ δράκων μέγας πυρρὸς ἔχων κεφαλὰς ἑπτὰ καὶ κέρατα δέκα καὶ ἐπὶ τὰς κεφαλὰς αὐτοῦ ἑπτὰ διαδήματα, 4 καὶ ἡ οὐρὰ αὐτοῦ σύρει τὸ τρίτον τῶν ἀστέρων τοῦ οὐρανοῦ καὶ ἔβαλεν αὐτοὺς εἰς τὴν γῆν. καὶ ὁ δράκων ἔστηκεν ἐνώπιον τῆς γυναικὸς τῆς μελλούσης τεκεῖν, ἵνα ὅταν τέκῃ τὸ τέκνον αὐτῆς καταφάγῃ. 5 καὶ ἔτεκεν υἱὸν ἄρσεν, ὃς μέλλει ποιμαίνειν πάντα τὰ ἔθνη ἐν ῥάβδῳ σιδηρᾷ. καὶ ἡρπάσθη τὸ τέκνον αὐτῆς πρὸς τὸν θεὸν καὶ πρὸς τὸν θρόνον αὐτοῦ. 6 καὶ ἡ γυνὴ ἔφυγεν εἰς τὴν ἔρημον, ὅπου ἔχει ἐκεῖ τόπον ἡτοιμασμένον ἀπὸ τοῦ θεοῦ, ἵνα ἐκεῖ τρέφωσιν αὐτὴν ἡμέρας χιλίας διακοσίας ἑξήκοντα.

7 Καὶ ἐγένετο πόλεμος ἐν τῷ οὐρανῷ, ὁ Μιχαὴλ καὶ οἱ ἄγγελοι αὐτοῦ τοῦ πολεμῆσαι μετὰ τοῦ δράκοντος. καὶ ὁ δράκων ἐπολέμησεν καὶ οἱ ἄγγελοι αὐτοῦ, 8 καὶ οὐκ ἴσχυσεν οὐδὲ τόπος εὑρέθη αὐτῶν ἔτι ἐν τῷ οὐρανῷ. 9 καὶ ἐβλήθη ὁ δράκων ὁ μέγας, ὁ ὄφις ὁ ἀρχαῖος, ὁ καλούμενος Διάβολος καὶ ὁ Σατανᾶς, ὁ πλανῶν τὴν οἰκουμένην ὅλην, ἐβλήθη εἰς τὴν γῆν, καὶ οἱ ἄγγελοι αὐτοῦ μετ' αὐτοῦ ἐβλήθησαν. 10 καὶ ἤκουσα φωνὴν μεγάλην ἐν τῷ οὐρανῷ λέγουσαν· ἄρτι ἐγένετο ἡ σωτηρία καὶ ἡ δύναμις καὶ ἡ βασιλεία τοῦ θεοῦ ἡμῶν καὶ ἡ ἐξουσία τοῦ χριστοῦ αὐτοῦ, ὅτι ἐβλήθη ὁ κατήγωρ τῶν ἀδελφῶν ἡμῶν, ὁ κατηγορῶν αὐτοὺς ἐνώπιον τοῦ θεοῦ ἡμῶν ἡμέρας καὶ νυκτός. 11 καὶ αὐτοὶ ἐνίκησαν αὐτὸν διὰ τὸ αἷμα τοῦ ἀρνίου καὶ διὰ τὸν λόγον τῆς μαρτυρίας αὐτῶν καὶ οὐκ ἠγάπησαν τὴν ψυχὴν αὐτῶν ἄχρι θανάτου. 12 διὰ τοῦτο εὐφραίνεσθε, [οἱ] οὐρανοὶ καὶ οἱ ἐν αὐτοῖς σκηνοῦντες. οὐαὶ τὴν γῆν καὶ τὴν θάλασσαν, ὅτι κατέβη ὁ διάβολος πρὸς ὑμᾶς ἔχων θυμὸν μέγαν, εἰδὼς ὅτι ὀλίγον καιρὸν ἔχει.

13 Καὶ ὅτε εἶδεν ὁ δράκων ὅτι ἐβλήθη εἰς τὴν γῆν, ἐδίωξεν τὴν γυναῖκα ἥτις ἔτεκεν τὸν ἄρσενα. 14 καὶ ἐδόθησαν τῇ γυναικὶ αἱ δύο πτέρυγες τοῦ ἀετοῦ τοῦ μεγάλου, ἵνα πέτηται εἰς τὴν ἔρημον εἰς τὸν τόπον αὐτῆς, ὅπου τρέφεται ἐκεῖ καιρὸν καὶ καιροὺς καὶ ἥμισυ καιροῦ ἀπὸ προσώπου τοῦ ὄφεως. 15 καὶ ἔβαλεν ὁ ὄφις ἐκ τοῦ στόματος αὐτοῦ ὀπίσω τῆς γυναικὸς ὕδωρ ὡς ποταμόν, ἵνα αὐτὴν ποταμοφόρητον ποιήσῃ. 16 καὶ ἐβοήθησεν ἡ γῆ τῇ γυναικὶ καὶ ἤνοιξεν ἡ γῆ τὸ στόμα αὐτῆς καὶ κατέπιεν τὸν ποταμὸν ὃν ἔβαλεν ὁ δράκων ἐκ τοῦ στόματος αὐτοῦ. 17 καὶ ὠργίσθη ὁ δράκων ἐπὶ τῇ γυναικὶ καὶ ἀπῆλθεν ποιῆσαι πόλεμον μετὰ τῶν λοιπῶν τοῦ σπέρματος αὐτῆς τῶν τηρούντων τὰς ἐντολὰς τοῦ θεοῦ καὶ ἐχόντων τὴν μαρτυρίαν Ἰησοῦ. 18 καὶ ἐστάθη ἐπὶ τὴν ἄμμον τῆς θαλάσσης.

12 And a great sign was seen in heaven, a woman wrapped in the sun, and the moon was under her feet, and a crown of twelve stars on her head, 2 and she is pregnant and cries out, feeling the pangs and suffering travail to deliver. 3 And another sign was seen in heaven, and lo a great dragon, fiery red, with seven heads and ten horns and seven diadems on its heads, 4 and his tail drags the third part of the stars of heaven and threw them to the earth. And the dragon stands before the woman about to give birth, so as to swallow her child when she gives birth. 5 And she gave birth to a son, a male, who is to shepherd all the nations with an iron staff. And her child was snatched up toward God and toward his throne. 6 And the woman fled into the desert, where she has there a place prepared by God, so that there they would nourish her for one thousand two hundred and sixty days.

7 And there was war in heaven, Michael and his angels fighting with the dragon. And the dragon fought and his angels, 8 and he was not strong, nor was their place found anymore in heaven. 9 And the great dragon was thrown down, the ancient serpent, called Devil and Satan, the one who leads the entire inhabited world astray; he was thrown down to earth, and his angels were thrown down with him. 10 And I heard a great voice in heaven, saying: "Now the salvation has come, and the power and the kingdom of our God, and the power of his Anointed, because the accuser of our brothers was thrown down, he who accuses them before our God day and night. 11 And they defeated him with the blood of the Lamb and with the word of their testimony, and they did not love their soul, up until death. 12 Rejoice, therefore, O heavens, and you that abide in them! Woe to the land and to the sea, because the devil has come down toward you with great wrath, knowing that he has little time!"

13 And when the dragon saw that he was thrown to the earth, he pursued the woman who had given birth to the male child. 14 And the two wings of the eagle, the great one, were given to the woman, in order that she might fly to the desert, to her place, where she is nourished for a time and times and half a time, far from the countenance of the serpent. 15 And the serpent cast from his mouth water, like a river, after the woman, to cause her to be drowned. 16 And the earth came to the aid of the woman, and the earth opened its mouth and swallowed the river that the dragon had cast out of his mouth. 17 And the dragon became angry with the woman, and went to make war against the remnant of her seed, those who keep the commandments of God and have the testimony of Jesus. 18 And he stood on the sand of the sea.

13 Καὶ εἶδον ἐκ τῆς θαλάσσης θηρίον ἀναβαῖνον, ἔχον κέρατα δέκα καὶ κεφαλὰς ἑπτὰ καὶ ἐπὶ τῶν κεράτων αὐτοῦ δέκα διαδήματα καὶ ἐπὶ τὰς κεφαλὰς αὐτοῦ ὀνόμα[τα] βλασφημίας. 2 καὶ τὸ θηρίον ὃ εἶδον ἦν ὅμοιον παρδάλει καὶ οἱ πόδες αὐτοῦ ὡς ἄρκου καὶ τὸ στόμα αὐτοῦ ὡς στόμα λέοντος. καὶ ἔδωκεν αὐτῷ ὁ δράκων τὴν δύναμιν αὐτοῦ καὶ τὸν θρόνον αὐτοῦ καὶ ἐξουσίαν μεγάλην. 3 καὶ μίαν ἐκ τῶν κεφαλῶν αὐτοῦ ὡς ἐσφαγμένην εἰς θάνατον, καὶ ἡ πληγὴ τοῦ θανάτου αὐτοῦ ἐθεραπεύθη.

Καὶ ἐθαυμάσθη ὅλη ἡ γῆ ὀπίσω τοῦ θηρίου 4 καὶ προσεκύνησαν τῷ δράκοντι, ὅτι ἔδωκεν τὴν ἐξουσίαν τῷ θηρίῳ, καὶ προσεκύνησαν τῷ θηρίῳ λέγοντες· τίς ὅμοιος τῷ θηρίῳ καὶ τίς δύναται πολεμῆσαι μετ᾿ αὐτοῦ;

5 Καὶ ἐδόθη αὐτῷ στόμα λαλοῦν μεγάλα καὶ βλασφημίας καὶ ἐδόθη αὐτῷ ἐξουσία ποιῆσαι μῆνας τεσσεράκοντα [καὶ] δύο. 6 καὶ ἤνοιξεν τὸ στόμα αὐτοῦ εἰς βλασφημίας πρὸς τὸν θεὸν βλασφημῆσαι τὸ ὄνομα αὐτοῦ καὶ τὴν σκηνὴν αὐτοῦ, τοὺς ἐν τῷ οὐρανῷ σκηνοῦντας. 7 καὶ ἐδόθη αὐτῷ ποιῆσαι πόλεμον μετὰ τῶν ἁγίων καὶ νικῆσαι αὐτούς, καὶ ἐδόθη αὐτῷ ἐξουσία ἐπὶ πᾶσαν φυλὴν καὶ λαὸν καὶ γλῶσσαν καὶ ἔθνος. 8 καὶ προσκυνήσουσιν αὐτὸν πάντες οἱ κατοικοῦντες ἐπὶ τῆς γῆς, οὗ οὐ γέγραπται τὸ ὄνομα αὐτοῦ ἐν τῷ βιβλίῳ τῆς ζωῆς τοῦ ἀρνίου τοῦ ἐσφαγμένου ἀπὸ καταβολῆς κόσμου.

9 Εἴ τις ἔχει οὖς ἀκουσάτω. 10 εἴ τις εἰς αἰχμαλωσίαν, εἰς αἰχμαλωσίαν ὑπάγει· εἴ τις ἐν μαχαίρῃ ἀποκτανθῆναι αὐτὸν ἐν μαχαίρῃ ἀποκτανθῆναι. Ὧδέ ἐστιν ἡ ὑπομονὴ καὶ ἡ πίστις τῶν ἁγίων.

11 Καὶ εἶδον ἄλλο θηρίον ἀναβαῖνον ἐκ τῆς γῆς, καὶ εἶχεν κέρατα δύο ὅμοια ἀρνίῳ καὶ ἐλάλει ὡς δράκων. 12 καὶ τὴν ἐξουσίαν τοῦ πρώτου θηρίου πᾶσαν ποιεῖ ἐνώπιον αὐτοῦ, καὶ ποιεῖ τὴν γῆν καὶ τοὺς ἐν αὐτῇ κατοικοῦντας ἵνα προσκυνήσουσιν τὸ θηρίον τὸ πρῶτον, οὗ ἐθεραπεύθη ἡ πληγὴ τοῦ θανάτου αὐτοῦ. 13 καὶ ποιεῖ σημεῖα μεγάλα, ἵνα καὶ πῦρ ποιῇ ἐκ τοῦ οὐρανοῦ καταβαίνειν εἰς τὴν γῆν ἐνώπιον τῶν ἀνθρώπων, 14 καὶ πλανᾷ τοὺς κατοικοῦντας ἐπὶ τῆς γῆς διὰ τὰ σημεῖα ἃ ἐδόθη αὐτῷ ποιῆσαι ἐνώπιον τοῦ θηρίου, λέγων τοῖς κατοικοῦσιν ἐπὶ τῆς γῆς ποιῆσαι εἰκόνα τῷ θηρίῳ, ὃς ἔχει τὴν πληγὴν τῆς μαχαίρης καὶ ἔζησεν.

15 Καὶ ἐδόθη αὐτῷ δοῦναι πνεῦμα τῇ εἰκόνι τοῦ θηρίου, ἵνα καὶ λαλήσῃ ἡ εἰκὼν τοῦ θηρίου καὶ ποιήσῃ [ἵνα] ὅσοι ἐὰν μὴ προσκυνήσουσιν τῇ εἰκόνι τοῦ θηρίου ἀποκτανθῶσιν. 16 καὶ ποιεῖ πάντας, τοὺς μικροὺς καὶ τοὺς μεγάλους, καὶ τοὺς πλουσίους καὶ τοὺς πτωχούς, καὶ τοὺς ἐλευθέρους καὶ τοὺς δούλους, ἵνα δῶσιν αὐτοῖς χάραγμα ἐπὶ τῆς χειρὸς αὐτῶν τῆς δεξιᾶς ἢ ἐπὶ τὸ μέτωπον αὐτῶν 17 καὶ ἵνα μή τις δύνηται ἀγοράσαι ἢ πωλῆσαι εἰ μὴ ὁ ἔχων τὸ χάραγμα τὸ ὄνομα τοῦ θηρίου ἢ τὸν ἀριθμὸν τοῦ ὀνόματος αὐτοῦ.

18 Ὧδε ἡ σοφία ἐστίν. ὁ ἔχων νοῦν ψηφισάτω τὸν ἀριθμὸν τοῦ θηρίου, ἀριθμὸς γὰρ ἀνθρώπου ἐστίν, καὶ ὁ ἀριθμὸς αὐτοῦ ἑξακόσιοι ἑξήκοντα ἕξ.

13 And I saw a beast coming up from the sea, with ten horns and seven heads, and on his horns ten diadems and on his heads a name of blasphemy. 2 And the beast that I saw was similar to a leopard, and its feet were like those of a bear, and its mouth was like the mouth of a lion, and the dragon gave it his power and his throne and great authority. 3 And I saw one of its heads, as though slaughtered to death, and its death-wound was healed.

And the entire earth marveled after the beast 4 And they bowed down to the dragon because he gave the authority to the beast, and they bowed down to the beast, saying: "Who is similar to the beast, and who is able to fight against it?"

5 And a mouth was given to it to utter great things and blasphemies, and authority was given to it to act for forty-two months. 6 And it opened its mouth in blasphemies toward God, to blaspheme his name and his abode, that is, those who abide in heaven. 7 And to it was granted to make war on the holy ones and to defeat them, and authority over every tribe and people and language and nation was given to it. 8 And all those who dwell upon the earth will bow down to it, everyone whose name is not written in the scroll of life of the Lamb, the one slaughtered from the establishment of the world.

9 If anyone has an ear, let him hear. 10 If anyone must go into captivity, into captivity he goes; if anyone must be killed by the sword, he must be killed by the sword. Here is the endurance and faith of the holy ones.

11 And I saw another beast coming up out of the earth, and it had two horns similar to a lamb and spoke like a dragon. 12 And it accomplishes all of the authority of the first beast in the latter's presence, and it makes the earth and those that dwell in it bow down to the first beast, whose death-wound was healed. 13 And it accomplishes great signs, so as to make even fire come down from heaven to earth before men. 14 And it leads astray those who dwell on the earth on account of the signs that were given to it, to accomplish before the (first) beast, saying to those who dwell on the earth to make an image to the beast, the one who has the wound of the sword and lived.

15 And to it was granted to provide spirit to the image of the beast, so that the image of the beast might also speak and cause all those who would not bow down to the image of the beast to be killed. 16 And it causes all, the small and the great, the rich and the poor, the free and the slave, it causes that they should give them a brand on their right hand or on their forehead, 17 and that no one can buy or sell except he who has the brand, the name of the beast or the number of its name.

18 Here is wisdom. Let him who has intellect calculate the number of the beast, because it is the number of a man; and its number is six hundred sixty-six.

14 Καὶ εἶδον, καὶ ἰδοὺ τὸ ἀρνίον ἑστὸς ἐπὶ τὸ ὄρος Σιὼν καὶ μετ' αὐτοῦ ἑκατὸν τεσσεράκοντα τέσσαρες χιλιάδες ἔχουσαι τὸ ὄνομα αὐτοῦ καὶ τὸ ὄνομα τοῦ πατρὸς αὐτοῦ γεγραμμένον ἐπὶ τῶν μετώπων αὐτῶν. 2 καὶ ἤκουσα φωνὴν ἐκ τοῦ οὐρανοῦ ὡς φωνὴν ὑδάτων πολλῶν καὶ ὡς φωνὴν βροντῆς μεγάλης, καὶ ἡ φωνὴ ἣν ἤκουσα ὡς κιθαρῳδῶν κιθαριζόντων ἐν ταῖς κιθάραις αὐτῶν. 3 καὶ ᾄδουσιν [ὡς] ᾠδὴν καινὴν ἐνώπιον τοῦ θρόνου καὶ ἐνώπιον τῶν τεσσάρων ζῴων καὶ τῶν πρεσβυτέρων, καὶ οὐδεὶς ἐδύνατο μαθεῖν τὴν ᾠδὴν εἰ μὴ αἱ ἑκατὸν τεσσεράκοντα τέσσαρες χιλιάδες, οἱ ἠγορασμένοι ἀπὸ τῆς γῆς.

4 Οὗτοί εἰσιν οἳ μετὰ γυναικῶν οὐκ ἐμολύνθησαν, παρθένοι γάρ εἰσιν, οὗτοι οἱ ἀκολουθοῦντες τῷ ἀρνίῳ ὅπου ἂν ὑπάγῃ. οὗτοι ἠγοράσθησαν ἀπὸ τῶν ἀνθρώπων ἀπαρχὴ τῷ θεῷ καὶ τῷ ἀρνίῳ, 5 καὶ ἐν τῷ στόματι αὐτῶν οὐχ εὑρέθη ψεῦδος, ἄμωμοί εἰσιν.

6 Καὶ εἶδον ἄλλον ἄγγελον πετόμενον ἐν μεσουρανήματι, ἔχοντα εὐαγγέλιον αἰώνιον εὐαγγελίσαι ἐπὶ τοὺς καθημένους ἐπὶ τῆς γῆς καὶ ἐπὶ πᾶν ἔθνος καὶ φυλὴν καὶ γλῶσσαν καὶ λαόν, 7 λέγων ἐν φωνῇ μεγάλῃ· φοβήθητε τὸν θεὸν καὶ δότε αὐτῷ δόξαν, ὅτι ἦλθεν ἡ ὥρα τῆς κρίσεως αὐτοῦ, καὶ προσκυνήσατε τῷ ποιήσαντι τὸν οὐρανὸν καὶ τὴν γῆν καὶ θάλασσαν καὶ πηγὰς ὑδάτων.

8 Καὶ ἄλλος ἄγγελος δεύτερος ἠκολούθησεν λέγων· ἔπεσεν ἔπεσεν Βαβυλὼν ἡ μεγάλη ἣ ἐκ τοῦ οἴνου τοῦ θυμοῦ τῆς πορνείας αὐτῆς πεπότικεν πάντα τὰ ἔθνη.

9 Καὶ ἄλλος ἄγγελος τρίτος ἠκολούθησεν αὐτοῖς λέγων ἐν φωνῇ μεγάλῃ· εἴ τις προσκυνεῖ τὸ θηρίον καὶ τὴν εἰκόνα αὐτοῦ καὶ λαμβάνει χάραγμα ἐπὶ τοῦ μετώπου αὐτοῦ ἢ ἐπὶ τὴν χεῖρα αὐτοῦ, 10 καὶ αὐτὸς πίεται ἐκ τοῦ οἴνου τοῦ θυμοῦ τοῦ θεοῦ τοῦ κεκερασμένου ἀκράτου ἐν τῷ ποτηρίῳ τῆς ὀργῆς αὐτοῦ καὶ βασανισθήσεται ἐν πυρὶ καὶ θείῳ ἐνώπιον ἀγγέλων ἁγίων καὶ ἐνώπιον τοῦ ἀρνίου. 11 καὶ ὁ καπνὸς τοῦ βασανισμοῦ αὐτῶν εἰς αἰῶνας αἰώνων ἀναβαίνει, καὶ οὐκ ἔχουσιν ἀνάπαυσιν ἡμέρας καὶ νυκτὸς οἱ προσκυνοῦντες τὸ θηρίον καὶ τὴν εἰκόνα αὐτοῦ καὶ εἴ τις λαμβάνει τὸ χάραγμα τοῦ ὀνόματος αὐτοῦ. 12 ὧδε ἡ ὑπομονὴ τῶν ἁγίων ἐστίν, οἱ τηροῦντες τὰς ἐντολὰς τοῦ θεοῦ καὶ τὴν πίστιν Ἰησοῦ.

13 Καὶ ἤκουσα φωνῆς ἐκ τοῦ οὐρανοῦ λεγούσης· γράφον· μακάριοι οἱ νεκροὶ οἱ ἐν κυρίῳ ἀποθνήσκοντες ἀπ' ἄρτι. ναί, λέγει τὸ πνεῦμα, ἵνα ἀναπαήσονται ἐκ τῶν κόπων αὐτῶν, τὰ γὰρ ἔργα αὐτῶν ἀκολουθεῖ μετ' αὐτῶν.

14 And I saw, and, lo, the Lamb standing on Mount Zion, and with him one hundred forty-four thousands who had his name and the name of his Father written on their foreheads. 2 And I heard a voice from heaven, like a voice of many waters and like a voice of great thunder, and the voice that I heard was like that of lyrists playing on their lyres. 3 And they sing [something like] a new song before the throne and before the four living creatures and the elders, and no one was able to learn the song save those one hundred forty-four thousands, those who were purchased and taken away from the earth.

4 These are the ones who have not defiled themselves with women, for they are virgins; these are the ones who follow the Lamb wherever he goes. These were purchased and taken away from among men, a first offering for God and for the Lamb. 5 And in their mouth no lie was found; they are blameless.

6 And I saw another angel flying in high heaven with an eternal gospel to proclaim with good report to those who reside on the earth and to every nation and tribe and language and people, 7 saying with a great voice: "Fear God and give him glory, for the hour of his judgment has come, and bow down to him who made the heaven and the earth and the sea and the springs of water."

8 And another angel, a second, followed, saying: "Fallen, fallen, is Babylon the great, she who has given all the nations to drink of the wine of the wrath of her prostitution."

9 And another angel, a third, followed them, saying with a great voice: "If anyone bows down to the beast and to its image and receives the brand on his forehead or on his hand, 10 he also will drink of the wine of the wrath of God, the one poured unmixed into the cup of his rage, and he will be tormented with fire and sulfur before the holy angels and before the Lamb. 11 And the smoke of their torment rises forever and ever, and they have no rest, day or night, those who bow down to the beast and to its image and if anyone receives the brand of its name." 12 Here is the endurance of the holy ones, those who keep the commandments of God and the faith of Jesus.

13 And I heard a voice from heaven saying: "Write: Blessed are the dead, those who die in the Lord from this time onward." "Yes — says the Spirit — "so that they will rest from their toils; for their works follow them."

14 Καὶ εἶδον, καὶ ἰδοὺ νεφέλη λευκή, καὶ ἐπὶ τὴν νεφέλην καθήμενον ὅμοιον υἱὸν ἀνθρώπου, ἔχων ἐπὶ τῆς κεφαλῆς αὐτοῦ στέφανον χρυσοῦν καὶ ἐν τῇ χειρὶ αὐτοῦ δρέπανον ὀξύ. 15 καὶ ἄλλος ἄγγελος ἐξῆλθεν ἐκ τοῦ ναοῦ κράζων ἐν φωνῇ μεγάλῃ τῷ καθημένῳ ἐπὶ τῆς νεφέλης· πέμψον τὸ δρέπανόν σου καὶ θέρισον, ὅτι ἦλθεν ἡ ὥρα θερίσαι, ὅτι ἐξηράνθη ὁ θερισμὸς τῆς γῆς. 16 καὶ ἔβαλεν ὁ καθήμενος ἐπὶ τῆς νεφέλης τὸ δρέπανον αὐτοῦ ἐπὶ τὴν γῆν καὶ ἐθερίσθη ἡ γῆ.

17 Καὶ ἄλλος ἄγγελος ἐξῆλθεν ἐκ τοῦ ναοῦ τοῦ ἐν τῷ οὐρανῷ ἔχων καὶ αὐτὸς δρέπανον ὀξύ. 18 καὶ ἄλλος ἄγγελος [ἐξῆλθεν] ἐκ τοῦ θυσιαστηρίου [ὁ] ἔχων ἐξουσίαν ἐπὶ τοῦ πυρός, καὶ ἐφώνησεν φωνῇ μεγάλῃ τῷ ἔχοντι τὸ δρέπανον τὸ ὀξὺ λέγων· πέμψον σου τὸ δρέπανον τὸ ὀξὺ καὶ τρύγησον τοὺς βότρυας τῆς ἀμπέλου τῆς γῆς, ὅτι ἤκμασαν αἱ σταφυλαὶ αὐτῆς. 19 καὶ ἔβαλεν ὁ ἄγγελος τὸ δρέπανον αὐτοῦ εἰς τὴν γῆν καὶ ἐτρύγησεν τὴν ἄμπελον τῆς γῆς καὶ ἔβαλεν εἰς τὴν ληνὸν τοῦ θυμοῦ τοῦ θεοῦ τὸν μέγαν. 20 καὶ ἐπατήθη ἡ ληνὸς ἔξωθεν τῆς πόλεως καὶ ἐξῆλθεν αἷμα ἐκ τῆς ληνοῦ ἄχρι τῶν χαλινῶν τῶν ἵππων ἀπὸ σταδίων χιλίων ἑξακοσίων.

15 Καὶ εἶδον ἄλλο σημεῖον ἐν τῷ οὐρανῷ μέγα καὶ θαυμαστόν, ἀγγέλους ἑπτὰ ἔχοντας πληγὰς ἑπτὰ τὰς ἐσχάτας, ὅτι ἐν αὐταῖς ἐτελέσθη ὁ θυμὸς τοῦ θεοῦ.

2 Καὶ εἶδον ὡς θάλασσαν ὑαλίνην μεμιγμένην πυρὶ καὶ τοὺς νικῶντας ἐκ τοῦ θηρίου καὶ ἐκ τῆς εἰκόνος αὐτοῦ καὶ ἐκ τοῦ ἀριθμοῦ τοῦ ὀνόματος αὐτοῦ ἑστῶτας ἐπὶ τὴν θάλασσαν τὴν ὑαλίνην ἔχοντας κιθάρας τοῦ θεοῦ. 3 καὶ ᾄδουσιν τὴν ᾠδὴν Μωϋσέως τοῦ δούλου τοῦ θεοῦ καὶ τὴν ᾠδὴν τοῦ ἀρνίου λέγοντες· μεγάλα καὶ θαυμαστὰ τὰ ἔργα σου, κύριε ὁ θεὸς ὁ παντοκράτωρ· δίκαιαι καὶ ἀληθιναὶ αἱ ὁδοί σου, ὁ βασιλεὺς τῶν ἐθνῶν· 4 τίς οὐ μὴ φοβηθῇ, κύριε, καὶ δοξάσει τὸ ὄνομά σου; ὅτι μόνος ὅσιος, ὅτι πάντα τὰ ἔθνη ἥξουσιν καὶ προσκυνήσουσιν ἐνώπιόν σου, ὅτι τὰ δικαιώματά σου ἐφανερώθησαν.

5 Καὶ μετὰ ταῦτα εἶδον, καὶ ἠνοίγη ὁ ναὸς τῆς σκηνῆς τοῦ μαρτυρίου ἐν τῷ οὐρανῷ, 6 καὶ ἐξῆλθον οἱ ἑπτὰ ἄγγελοι [οἱ] ἔχοντες τὰς ἑπτὰ πληγὰς ἐκ τοῦ ναοῦ ἐνδεδυμένοι λίνον καθαρὸν λαμπρὸν καὶ περιεζωσμένοι περὶ τὰ στήθη ζώνας χρυσᾶς. 7 καὶ ἓν ἐκ τῶν τεσσάρων ζῴων ἔδωκεν τοῖς ἑπτὰ ἀγγέλοις ἑπτὰ φιάλας χρυσᾶς γεμούσας τοῦ θυμοῦ τοῦ θεοῦ τοῦ ζῶντος εἰς τοὺς αἰῶνας τῶν αἰώνων. 8 καὶ ἐγεμίσθη ὁ ναὸς καπνοῦ ἐκ τῆς δόξης τοῦ θεοῦ καὶ ἐκ τῆς δυνάμεως αὐτοῦ, καὶ οὐδεὶς ἐδύνατο εἰσελθεῖν εἰς τὸν ναὸν ἄχρι τελεσθῶσιν αἱ ἑπτὰ πληγαὶ τῶν ἑπτὰ ἀγγέλων.

16 Καὶ ἤκουσα μεγάλης φωνῆς ἐκ τοῦ ναοῦ λεγούσης τοῖς ἑπτὰ ἀγγέλοις· ὑπάγετε καὶ ἐκχέετε τὰς ἑπτὰ φιάλας τοῦ θυμοῦ τοῦ θεοῦ εἰς τὴν γῆν.

14 And I saw, and, lo, a white cloud, and on the cloud I saw one seated, similar to a son of man, who had a crown of gold on his head and a sharp sickle in his hand. 15 And another angel came out from the temple shouting with a great voice to him who was sitting on the cloud: "Dispatch your sickle and reap, for the hour to reap has come, for the harvest of the earth has dried." 16 And he who was sitting on the cloud threw his sickle upon the earth, and the earth was reaped.

17 And another angel came out of the temple, the one in heaven, he also having a sharp sickle. 18 And another angel [came out] from the sacrificial altar, [the one] who has power over fire, and he shouted with a great voice to him who had the sharp sickle, saying: "Dispatch your sharp sickle, and gather the clusters of the vine of the earth, because its grapes have ripened." 19 And the angel threw his sickle to the earth and gathered the vine of the earth and threw the grapes into the winepress of the wrath of God, which is great. 20 And the winepress was trodden, outside the city, and blood came out of the winepress as high as the bridles of horses, for one thousand six hundred stades.

15 And I saw another sign in the sky, great and wondrous, seven angels with seven plagues, the last ones, because in them the wrath of God has been completed.

2 And I saw something like a transparent sea, mixed with fire, and the conquerors of the beast and of its image and of the number of its name, standing on the transparent sea with lyres of God. 3 And they sing the song of Moses, the servant of God, and the song of the Lamb, saying: "Great and wondrous are your works, Lord God almighty! Just and true are your ways, you who are the king of the nations! 4 Who does not fear, O Lord, and will not glorify your name? Because you alone are holy, because all the nations will come and bow down before you, because your judgments of justification have been made manifest."

5 And after these things I saw, and the temple of the tent of the testimony was opened in heaven, 6 and the seven angels came out, [those] with the seven plagues, from the temple, dressed in pure bright linen and girded at the breast with golden sashes. 7 And one of the four living creatures gave to the seven angels seven golden bowls, full of the wrath of God, the one who lives forever and ever. 8 And the temple was filled with smoke from the Glory of God and from his power, and no one was able to enter the temple until the seven plagues of the seven angels were completed.

16 And I heard a great voice from the temple, saying to the seven angels: "Go and pour the seven bowls of the wrath of God on the earth."

2 Καὶ ἀπῆλθεν ὁ πρῶτος καὶ ἐξέχεεν τὴν φιάλην αὐτοῦ εἰς τὴν γῆν, καὶ ἐγένετο ἕλκος κακὸν καὶ πονηρὸν ἐπὶ τοὺς ἀνθρώπους τοὺς ἔχοντας τὸ χάραγμα τοῦ θηρίου καὶ τοὺς προσκυνοῦντας τῇ εἰκόνι αὐτοῦ.

3 Καὶ ὁ δεύτερος ἐξέχεεν τὴν φιάλην αὐτοῦ εἰς τὴν θάλασσαν, καὶ ἐγένετο αἷμα ὡς νεκροῦ, καὶ πᾶσα ψυχὴ ζωῆς ἀπέθανεν τὰ ἐν τῇ θαλάσσῃ.

4 Καὶ ὁ τρίτος ἐξέχεεν τὴν φιάλην αὐτοῦ εἰς τοὺς ποταμοὺς καὶ τὰς πηγὰς τῶν ὑδάτων, καὶ ἐγένετο αἷμα. 5 καὶ ἤκουσα τοῦ ἀγγέλου τῶν ὑδάτων λέγοντος· δίκαιος εἶ, ὁ ὢν καὶ ὁ ἦν, ὁ ὅσιος, ὅτι ταῦτα ἔκρινας, 6 ὅτι αἷμα ἁγίων καὶ προφητῶν ἐξέχεαν καὶ αἷμα αὐτοῖς [δ]έδωκας πιεῖν, ἄξιοί εἰσιν. 7 Καὶ ἤκουσα τοῦ θυσιαστηρίου λέγοντος· ναὶ κύριε ὁ θεὸς ὁ παντοκράτωρ, ἀληθιναὶ καὶ δίκαιαι αἱ κρίσεις σου.

8 Καὶ ὁ τέταρτος ἐξέχεεν τὴν φιάλην αὐτοῦ ἐπὶ τὸν ἥλιον, καὶ ἐδόθη αὐτῷ καυματίσαι τοὺς ἀνθρώπους ἐν πυρί. 9 καὶ ἐκαυματίσθησαν οἱ ἄνθρωποι καῦμα μέγα καὶ ἐβλασφήμησαν τὸ ὄνομα τοῦ θεοῦ τοῦ ἔχοντος τὴν ἐξουσίαν ἐπὶ τὰς πληγὰς ταύτας καὶ οὐ μετενόησαν δοῦναι αὐτῷ δόξαν.

10 Καὶ ὁ πέμπτος ἐξέχεεν τὴν φιάλην αὐτοῦ ἐπὶ τὸν θρόνον τοῦ θηρίου, καὶ ἐγένετο ἡ βασιλεία αὐτοῦ ἐσκοτωμένη, καὶ ἐμασῶντο τὰς γλώσσας αὐτῶν ἐκ τοῦ πόνου, 11 καὶ ἐβλασφήμησαν τὸν θεὸν τοῦ οὐρανοῦ ἐκ τῶν πόνων αὐτῶν καὶ ἐκ τῶν ἑλκῶν αὐτῶν καὶ οὐ μετενόησαν ἐκ τῶν ἔργων αὐτῶν.

12 Καὶ ὁ ἕκτος ἐξέχεεν τὴν φιάλην αὐτοῦ ἐπὶ τὸν ποταμὸν τὸν μέγαν τὸν Εὐφράτην, καὶ ἐξηράνθη τὸ ὕδωρ αὐτοῦ, ἵνα ἑτοιμασθῇ ἡ ὁδὸς τῶν βασιλέων τῶν ἀπὸ ἀνατολῶν ἡλίου. 13 καὶ εἶδον ἐκ τοῦ στόματος τοῦ δράκοντος καὶ ἐκ τοῦ στόματος τοῦ θηρίου καὶ ἐκ τοῦ στόματος τοῦ ψευδοπροφήτου πνεύματα τρία ἀκάθαρτα ὡς βάτραχοι· 14 εἰσὶν γὰρ πνεύματα δαιμονίων ποιοῦντα σημεῖα, ἃ ἐκπορεύεται ἐπὶ τοὺς βασιλεῖς τῆς οἰκουμένης ὅλης συναγαγεῖν αὐτοὺς εἰς τὸν πόλεμον τῆς ἡμέρας τῆς μεγάλης τοῦ θεοῦ τοῦ παντοκράτορος. 15 ἰδοὺ ἔρχομαι ὡς κλέπτης. μακάριος ὁ γρηγορῶν καὶ τηρῶν τὰ ἱμάτια αὐτοῦ, ἵνα μὴ γυμνὸς περιπατῇ καὶ βλέπωσιν τὴν ἀσχημοσύνην αὐτοῦ. 16 καὶ συνήγαγεν αὐτοὺς εἰς τὸν τόπον τὸν καλούμενον Ἑβραϊστὶ Ἁρμαγεδών.

17 Καὶ ὁ ἕβδομος ἐξέχεεν τὴν φιάλην αὐτοῦ ἐπὶ τὸν ἀέρα, καὶ ἐξῆλθεν φωνὴ μεγάλη ἐκ τοῦ ναοῦ ἀπὸ τοῦ θρόνου λέγουσα· γέγονεν. 18 καὶ ἐγένοντο ἀστραπαὶ καὶ φωναὶ καὶ βρονταὶ καὶ σεισμὸς ἐγένετο μέγας, οἷος οὐκ ἐγένετο ἀφ' οὗ ἄνθρωπος ἐγένετο ἐπὶ τῆς γῆς τηλικοῦτος σεισμὸς οὕτω μέγας. 19 καὶ ἐγένετο ἡ πόλις ἡ μεγάλη εἰς τρία μέρη καὶ αἱ πόλεις τῶν ἐθνῶν ἔπεσαν. καὶ Βαβυλὼν ἡ μεγάλη ἐμνήσθη ἐνώπιον τοῦ θεοῦ δοῦναι αὐτῇ τὸ ποτήριον τοῦ οἴνου τοῦ θυμοῦ τῆς ὀργῆς αὐτοῦ. 20 καὶ πᾶσα νῆσος ἔφυγεν καὶ ὄρη οὐχ εὑρέθησαν. 21 καὶ χάλαζα μεγάλη ὡς ταλαντιαία καταβαίνει ἐκ τοῦ οὐρανοῦ ἐπὶ τοὺς ἀνθρώπους, καὶ ἐβλασφήμησαν οἱ ἄνθρωποι τὸν θεὸν ἐκ τῆς πληγῆς τῆς χαλάζης, ὅτι μεγάλη ἐστὶν ἡ πληγὴ αὐτῆς σφόδρα.

2 And the first one went and poured his bowl on the earth, and there was a sore, wicked and evil, upon men, those who had the brand of the beast and those who bowed down to its image.

3 And the second one poured his bowl on the sea, and it became blood like that of a dead man, and every living soul died, those in the sea.

4 And the third one poured his bowl on the rivers and the springs of water, and there was blood. 5 And I heard the angel of the waters saying: "You are just, the One who is and who was, the Holy One, because you have decreed these things, 6 because they poured out blood of holy ones and prophets, and you gave them blood to drink; they are worthy of it." 7 And I heard the sacrificial altar saying: "Yes, Lord, God almighty, true and just are your judgments!"

8 And the fourth one poured his bowl on the sun, and to it was granted to scorch men with fire. 9 And men were scorched with a great heat, and they blasphemed the name of God, the one who has the power over these plagues, and they did not repent so as to render him glory.

10 And the fifth one poured his bowl on the throne of the beast, and its kingdom was darkened, and they gnawed their tongues because of the pain. 11 And they blasphemed the God of heaven for their pains and for their sores, and they did not repent of their works.

12 And the sixth one poured his bowl on the great river, the Euphrates, and its water was dried up, so that the way of the kings might be prepared, those who come from where the sun rises. 13 And I saw emerging from the mouth of the dragon and from the mouth of the beast and from the mouth of the false prophet three impure spirits, like frogs. 14 For they are spirits of demons, accomplishing signs, that go forth to the kings of the entire inhabited world, to gather them for the war of the great day of God almighty. 15 "Lo, I am coming like a thief. Blessed is he who is awake and keeps his garments so that he may not walk naked, and they may not see his indecency." 16 And he assembled them in the place called in Hebrew Harmagedon.

17 And the seventh one poured his bowl on the air, and a great voice came out of the temple, from the throne, saying: "It has happened." 18 And there were lightnings and voices and thunders, and there was a great quake, such as has not occurred since man has been on the earth, so large a quake, so great. 19 And the city, the great one, came to be in three parts, and the cities of the nations fell. And Babylon the great was remembered before God, so as to give to her the cup of the wine of the wrath of his rage. 20 And every island fled, and no mountains were found. 21 And great hailstones, of something like the weight of a talent, come down from heaven on men, and men blasphemed God for the plague of the hail, because the plague of it is great, very much so.

17 Καὶ ἦλθεν εἷς ἐκ τῶν ἑπτὰ ἀγγέλων τῶν ἐχόντων τὰς ἑπτὰ φιάλας καὶ ἐλάλησεν μετ' ἐμοῦ λέγων· δεῦρο, δείξω σοι τὸ κρίμα τῆς πόρνης τῆς μεγάλης τῆς καθημένης ἐπὶ ὑδάτων πολλῶν, 2 μεθ' ἧς ἐπόρνευσαν οἱ βασιλεῖς τῆς γῆς καὶ ἐμεθύσθησαν οἱ κατοικοῦντες τὴν γῆν ἐκ τοῦ οἴνου τῆς πορνείας αὐτῆς. 3 Καὶ ἀπήνεγκέν με εἰς ἔρημον ἐν πνεύματι. καὶ εἶδον γυναῖκα καθημένην ἐπὶ θηρίον κόκκινον, γέμον[τα] ὀνόματα βλασφημίας, ἔχων κεφαλὰς ἑπτὰ καὶ κέρατα δέκα. 4 καὶ ἡ γυνὴ ἦν περιβεβλημένη πορφυροῦν καὶ κόκκινον καὶ κεχρυσωμένη χρυσίῳ καὶ λίθῳ τιμίῳ καὶ μαργαρίταις, ἔχουσα ποτήριον χρυσοῦν ἐν τῇ χειρὶ αὐτῆς γέμον βδελυγμάτων καὶ τὰ ἀκάθαρτα τῆς πορνείας αὐτῆς 5 καὶ ἐπὶ τὸ μέτωπον αὐτῆς ὄνομα γεγραμμένον, μυστήριον, Βαβυλὼν ἡ μεγάλη, ἡ μήτηρ τῶν πορνῶν καὶ τῶν βδελυγμάτων τῆς γῆς. 6 καὶ εἶδον τὴν γυναῖκα μεθύουσαν ἐκ τοῦ αἵματος τῶν ἁγίων καὶ ἐκ τοῦ αἵματος τῶν μαρτύρων Ἰησοῦ. καὶ ἐθαύμασα ἰδὼν αὐτὴν θαῦμα μέγα.

7 Καὶ εἶπέν μοι ὁ ἄγγελος· διὰ τί ἐθαύμασας; ἐγὼ ἐρῶ σοι τὸ μυστήριον τῆς γυναικὸς καὶ τοῦ θηρίου τοῦ βαστάζοντος αὐτὴν τοῦ ἔχοντος τὰς ἑπτὰ κεφαλὰς καὶ τὰ δέκα κέρατα. 8 τὸ θηρίον ὃ εἶδες ἦν καὶ οὐκ ἔστιν καὶ μέλλει ἀναβαίνειν ἐκ τῆς ἀβύσσου καὶ εἰς ἀπώλειαν ὑπάγει, καὶ θαυμασθήσονται οἱ κατοικοῦντες ἐπὶ τῆς γῆς, ὧν οὐ γέγραπται τὸ ὄνομα ἐπὶ τὸ βιβλίον τῆς ζωῆς ἀπὸ καταβολῆς κόσμου, βλεπόντων τὸ θηρίον ὅτι ἦν καὶ οὐκ ἔστιν καὶ παρέσται.

9 ὧδε ὁ νοῦς ὁ ἔχων σοφίαν. αἱ ἑπτὰ κεφαλαὶ ἑπτὰ ὄρη εἰσίν, ὅπου ἡ γυνὴ κάθηται ἐπ' αὐτῶν. καὶ βασιλεῖς ἑπτὰ εἰσιν· 10 οἱ πέντε ἔπεσαν, ὁ εἷς ἔστιν, ὁ ἄλλος οὔπω ἦλθεν, καὶ ὅταν ἔλθῃ ὀλίγον αὐτὸν δεῖ μεῖναι.

11 Καὶ τὸ θηρίον ὃ ἦν καὶ οὐκ ἔστιν καὶ αὐτὸς ὄγδοός ἐστιν καὶ ἐκ τῶν ἑπτά ἐστιν, καὶ εἰς ἀπώλειαν ὑπάγει.

12 Καὶ τὰ δέκα κέρατα ἃ εἶδες δέκα βασιλεῖς εἰσιν, οἵτινες βασιλείαν οὔπω ἔλαβον, ἀλλὰ ἐξουσίαν ὡς βασιλεῖς μίαν ὥραν λαμβάνουσιν μετὰ τοῦ θηρίου. 13 οὗτοι μίαν γνώμην ἔχουσιν καὶ τὴν δύναμιν καὶ ἐξουσίαν αὐτῶν τῷ θηρίῳ διδόασιν. 14 οὗτοι μετὰ τοῦ ἀρνίου πολεμήσουσιν καὶ τὸ ἀρνίον νικήσει αὐτούς, ὅτι κύριος κυρίων ἐστὶν καὶ βασιλεὺς βασιλέων καὶ οἱ μετ' αὐτοῦ κλητοὶ καὶ ἐκλεκτοὶ καὶ πιστοί.

15 Καὶ λέγει μοι· τὰ ὕδατα ἃ εἶδες οὗ ἡ πόρνη κάθηται, λαοὶ καὶ ὄχλοι εἰσὶν καὶ ἔθνη καὶ γλῶσσαι. 16 καὶ τὰ δέκα κέρατα ἃ εἶδες καὶ τὸ θηρίον οὗτοι μισήσουσιν τὴν πόρνην καὶ ἠρημωμένην ποιήσουσιν αὐτὴν καὶ γυμνὴν καὶ τὰς σάρκας αὐτῆς φάγονται καὶ αὐτὴν κατακαύσουσιν ἐν πυρί. 17 ὁ γὰρ θεὸς ἔδωκεν εἰς τὰς καρδίας αὐτῶν ποιῆσαι τὴν γνώμην αὐτοῦ καὶ ποιῆσαι μίαν γνώμην καὶ δοῦναι τὴν βασιλείαν αὐτῶν τῷ θηρίῳ ἄχρι τελεσθήσονται οἱ λόγοι τοῦ θεοῦ.

17

And one of the seven angels came, of those who have the seven bowls, and spoke with me, saying: "Come here, I will show you the condemnation of the prostitute, the great one, the one who is seated on many waters, 2 with whom the kings of the earth fornicated and those who inhabit the earth became drunk with the wine of her prostitution."

3 And he carried me in spirit into a desert. And I saw a woman sitting on a scarlet beast, full of names of blasphemy, with seven heads and ten horns. 4 And the woman was wrapped in purple and scarlet, and adorned with gold and precious stone and pearls, with a golden cup in her hand, full of abominations — the impurities of her prostitution — 5 and on her forehead a name was written — a mystery — "Babylon the great, the mother of the prostitutes and of the abominations of the earth." 6 And I saw the woman drunk with the blood of the holy ones and with the blood of the witnesses of Jesus. And seeing her, I marveled, with great wonder.

7 And the angel said to me: Why did you marvel? I will tell you the mystery of the woman and of the beast who bears her, the one that has the seven heads and the ten horns. 8 The beast that you saw was, and is not, and is about to come up from the abyss, and goes to perdition. And those who dwell upon the earth will marvel, those whose names are not written in the scroll of life from the establishment of the world, seeing the beast, because it was, and is not, and will be present.

9 "Here is the intellect that has wisdom. The seven heads are seven mountains, where the woman sits upon them. And they are seven kings. 10 Five have fallen, one is, the other has not yet come, and when he comes, he must remain for a short while.

11 "And the beast that was, and is not, and he himself is eighth, and consists of the seven, and goes to perdition.

12 "And the ten horns that you saw are ten kings, who have not yet received the kingdom, but they receive authority as kings for one hour only with the beast. 13 These have only one purpose, and they give over to the beast their own power and authority. 14 They will do battle with the Lamb, and the Lamb will defeat them because he is Lord of lords and King of kings, and those with him are called and chosen and faithful."

15 And he says to me: The waters that you saw, where the prostitute is seated, are peoples and throngs and nations and tongues. 16 And the ten horns that you saw and the beast, these will hate the prostitute, and will make her desolate and naked, and will eat her flesh and will burn her with fire. 17 For God has put into their hearts to do his purpose, a single purpose, and to give their kingdom to the beast, until the words of God should be fulfilled.

18 Καὶ ἡ γυνὴ ἣν εἶδες ἔστιν ἡ πόλις ἡ μεγάλη ἡ ἔχουσα βασιλείαν ἐπὶ τῶν βασιλέων τῆς γῆς.

18 Μετὰ ταῦτα εἶδον ἄλλον ἄγγελον καταβαίνοντα ἐκ τοῦ οὐρανοῦ ἔχοντα ἐξουσίαν μεγάλην, καὶ ἡ γῆ ἐφωτίσθη ἐκ τῆς δόξης αὐτοῦ. 2 καὶ ἔκραξεν ἐν ἰσχυρᾷ φωνῇ λέγων· ἔπεσεν ἔπεσεν Βαβυλὼν ἡ μεγάλη, καὶ ἐγένετο κατοικητήριον δαιμονίων καὶ φυλακὴ παντὸς πνεύματος ἀκαθάρτου καὶ φυλακὴ παντὸς ὀρνέου ἀκαθάρτου [καὶ φυλακὴ παντὸς θηρίου ἀκαθάρτου] καὶ μεμισημένου, 3 ὅτι ἐκ τοῦ οἴνου τοῦ θυμοῦ τῆς πορνείας αὐτῆς πέπωκαν πάντα τὰ ἔθνη καὶ οἱ βασιλεῖς τῆς γῆς μετ᾽ αὐτῆς ἐπόρνευσαν καὶ οἱ ἔμποροι τῆς γῆς ἐκ τῆς δυνάμεως τοῦ στρήνους αὐτῆς ἐπλούτησαν.

4 Καὶ ἤκουσα ἄλλην φωνὴν ἐκ τοῦ οὐρανοῦ λέγουσαν· ἐξέλθατε ὁ λαός μου ἐξ αὐτῆς ἵνα μὴ συγκοινωνήσητε ταῖς ἁμαρτίαις αὐτῆς, καὶ ἐκ τῶν πληγῶν αὐτῆς ἵνα μὴ λάβητε, 5 ὅτι ἐκολλήθησαν αὐτῆς αἱ ἁμαρτίαι ἄχρι τοῦ οὐρανοῦ καὶ ἐμνημόνευσεν ὁ θεὸς τὰ ἀδικήματα αὐτῆς. 6 ἀπόδοτε αὐτῇ ὡς καὶ αὐτὴ ἀπέδωκεν καὶ διπλώσατε τὰ διπλᾶ κατὰ τὰ ἔργα αὐτῆς, ἐν τῷ ποτηρίῳ ᾧ ἐκέρασεν κεράσατε αὐτῇ διπλοῦν, 7 ὅσα ἐδόξασεν αὐτὴν καὶ ἐστρηνίασεν, τοσοῦτον δότε αὐτῇ βασανισμὸν καὶ πένθος. ὅτι ἐν τῇ καρδίᾳ αὐτῆς λέγει ὅτι κάθημαι βασίλισσα καὶ χήρα οὐκ εἰμὶ καὶ πένθος οὐ μὴ ἴδω. 8 διὰ τοῦτο ἐν μιᾷ ἡμέρᾳ ἥξουσιν αἱ πληγαὶ αὐτῆς, θάνατος καὶ πένθος καὶ λιμός, καὶ ἐν πυρὶ κατακαυθήσεται, ὅτι ἰσχυρὸς κύριος ὁ θεὸς ὁ κρίνας αὐτήν.

9 Καὶ κλαύσουσιν καὶ κόψονται ἐπ᾽ αὐτὴν οἱ βασιλεῖς τῆς γῆς οἱ μετ᾽ αὐτῆς πορνεύσαντες καὶ στρηνιάσαντες, ὅταν βλέπωσιν τὸν καπνὸν τῆς πυρώσεως αὐτῆς, 10 ἀπὸ μακρόθεν ἑστηκότες διὰ τὸν φόβον τοῦ βασανισμοῦ αὐτῆς λέγοντες· οὐαὶ οὐαί, ἡ πόλις ἡ μεγάλη, Βαβυλὼν ἡ πόλις ἡ ἰσχυρά, ὅτι μιᾷ ὥρᾳ ἦλθεν ἡ κρίσις σου.

11 Καὶ οἱ ἔμποροι τῆς γῆς κλαίουσιν καὶ πενθοῦσιν ἐπ᾽ αὐτήν, ὅτι τὸν γόμον αὐτῶν οὐδεὶς ἀγοράζει οὐκέτι 12 γόμον χρυσοῦ καὶ ἀργύρου καὶ λίθου τιμίου καὶ μαργαριτῶν καὶ βυσσίνου καὶ πορφύρας καὶ σιρικοῦ καὶ κοκκίνου, καὶ πᾶν ξύλον θύϊνον καὶ πᾶν σκεῦος ἐλεφάντινον καὶ πᾶν σκεῦος ἐκ ξύλου τιμιωτάτου καὶ χαλκοῦ καὶ σιδήρου καὶ μαρμάρου, 13 καὶ κιννάμωμον καὶ ἄμωμον καὶ θυμιάματα καὶ μύρον καὶ λίβανον καὶ οἶνον καὶ ἔλαιον καὶ σεμίδαλιν καὶ σῖτον καὶ κτήνη καὶ πρόβατα, καὶ ἵππων καὶ ῥεδῶν καὶ σωμάτων, καὶ ψυχὰς ἀνθρώπων.

14 Καὶ ἡ ὀπώρα σου τῆς ἐπιθυμίας τῆς ψυχῆς ἀπῆλθεν ἀπὸ σοῦ, καὶ πάντα τὰ λιπαρὰ καὶ τὰ λαμπρὰ ἀπώλετο ἀπὸ σοῦ καὶ οὐκέτι οὐ μὴ αὐτὰ εὑρήσουσιν.

18 "And the woman that you saw is the city, the great one, the one that has rule over the kings of the earth."

18

After these things I saw another angel coming down from heaven with great authority, and the earth was illuminated by his glory. 2 And he shouted with a strong voice, saying: "Fallen, fallen is Babylon the great, and has become an abode of demons and a haunt of every impure spirit and a haunt of every impure and hateful bird [and a haunt of every impure beast], 3 because all the nations have drunk of the wine of the wrath of her prostitution, and the kings of the earth fornicated with her, and the merchants of the earth became rich through the power of her unrestrained pride."

4 And I heard another voice from heaven, saying: "Go out, O my people, from her, so as not to have a share in her sins, and not receive of her plagues, 5 because her sins have been piled up to heaven, and God has remembered her iniquities. 6 Render to her as even she has rendered, and double it in double fashion according to her works: into the cup with which she has poured, pour for her a double amount. 7 To the degree that she has glorified herself and has become proud without restraint, to the same degree give her torment and mourning. Because in her heart she says: 'I sit as a queen, and I am not a widow, and I shall not see mourning.' 8 On account of this, in a single day her plagues will come, death and mourning and famine, and she will be burned with fire, because a strong Lord is God, the one that has judged her."

9 And the kings of the earth will weep and strike themselves in mourning for her, those who fornicated with her and became proud without restraint, when they see the smoke of her burning, 10 as they stand from afar, for fear of her torment, saying: "Woe, woe, O great city, Babylon, O strong city, because in a single hour your judgment has come!"

11 And the merchants of the earth weep and mourn over her, since no one buys their cargo any more, 12 a cargo of gold and of silver and of precious stone and of pearls and of fine linen and of purple and of silk and of scarlet, and every sort of thyine wood, and every article of ivory, and every article of very precious wood and of bronze and of iron and of marble, 13 and cinnamon and amomum and incense and myrrh and frankincense and wine and oil and fine flour and wheat and herds and flocks, and of horses and of carriages and of bodies, and souls of men.

14 "And your seasonal fruit, the object of the soul's desire, has departed from you, and all the sumptuous things and the splendid things are lost for you and they will never find them again."

15 Οἱ ἔμποροι τούτων οἱ πλουτήσαντες ἀπ᾽ αὐτῆς ἀπὸ μακρόθεν στήσονται διὰ τὸν φόβον τοῦ βασανισμοῦ αὐτῆς κλαίοντες καὶ πενθοῦντες 16 λέγοντες· οὐαὶ οὐαί, ἡ πόλις ἡ μεγάλη, ἡ περιβεβλημένη βύσσινον καὶ πορφυροῦν καὶ κόκκινον καὶ κεχρυσωμένη [ἐν] χρυσίῳ καὶ λίθῳ τιμίῳ καὶ μαργαρίτῃ, 17 ὅτι μιᾷ ὥρᾳ ἠρημώθη ὁ τοσοῦτος πλοῦτος.

Καὶ πᾶς κυβερνήτης καὶ πᾶς ὁ ἐπὶ τόπον πλέων καὶ ναῦται καὶ ὅσοι τὴν θάλασσαν ἐργάζονται, ἀπὸ μακρόθεν ἔστησαν 18 καὶ ἔκραζον βλέποντες τὸν καπνὸν τῆς πυρώσεως αὐτῆς λέγοντες· τίς ὁμοία τῇ πόλει τῇ μεγάλῃ; 19 καὶ ἔβαλον χοῦν ἐπὶ τὰς κεφαλὰς αὐτῶν καὶ ἔκραζον κλαίοντες καὶ πενθοῦντες λέγοντες· οὐαὶ οὐαί, ἡ πόλις ἡ μεγάλη, ἐν ᾗ ἐπλούτησαν πάντες οἱ ἔχοντες τὰ πλοῖα ἐν τῇ θαλάσσῃ ἐκ τῆς τιμιότητος αὐτῆς, ὅτι μιᾷ ὥρᾳ ἠρημώθη.

20 Εὐφραίνου ἐπ᾽ αὐτῇ, οὐρανὲ καὶ οἱ ἅγιοι καὶ οἱ ἀπόστολοι καὶ οἱ προφῆται, ὅτι ἔκρινεν ὁ θεὸς τὸ κρίμα ὑμῶν ἐξ αὐτῆς.

21 Καὶ ἦρεν εἷς ἄγγελος ἰσχυρὸς λίθον ὡς μύλινον μέγαν καὶ ἔβαλεν εἰς τὴν θάλασσαν λέγων· οὕτως ὁρμήματι βληθήσεται Βαβυλὼν ἡ μεγάλη πόλις καὶ οὐ μὴ εὑρεθῇ ἔτι. 22 καὶ φωνὴ κιθαρῳδῶν καὶ μουσικῶν καὶ αὐλητῶν καὶ σαλπιστῶν οὐ μὴ ἀκουσθῇ ἐν σοὶ ἔτι, καὶ πᾶς τεχνίτης πάσης τέχνης οὐ μὴ εὑρεθῇ ἐν σοὶ ἔτι, καὶ φωνὴ μύλου οὐ μὴ ἀκουσθῇ ἐν σοὶ ἔτι, 23 καὶ φῶς λύχνου οὐ μὴ φάνῃ ἐν σοὶ ἔτι, καὶ φωνὴ νυμφίου καὶ νύμφης οὐ μὴ ἀκουσθῇ ἐν σοὶ ἔτι· ὅτι οἱ ἔμποροί σου ἦσαν οἱ μεγιστᾶνες τῆς γῆς, ὅτι ἐν τῇ φαρμακείᾳ σου ἐπλανήθησαν πάντα τὰ ἔθνη, 24 καὶ ἐν αὐτῇ αἷμα προφητῶν καὶ ἁγίων εὑρέθη καὶ πάντων τῶν ἐσφαγμένων ἐπὶ τῆς γῆς.

19 Μετὰ ταῦτα ἤκουσα ὡς φωνὴν μεγάλην ὄχλου πολλοῦ ἐν τῷ οὐρανῷ λεγόντων· ἀλληλουϊά· ἡ σωτηρία καὶ ἡ δόξα καὶ ἡ δύναμις τοῦ θεοῦ ἡμῶν, 2 ὅτι ἀληθιναὶ καὶ δίκαιαι αἱ κρίσεις αὐτοῦ· ὅτι ἔκρινεν τὴν πόρνην τὴν μεγάλην ἥτις ἔφθειρεν τὴν γῆν ἐν τῇ πορνείᾳ αὐτῆς, καὶ ἐξεδίκησεν τὸ αἷμα τῶν δούλων αὐτοῦ ἐκ χειρὸς αὐτῆς.

3 Καὶ δεύτερον εἴρηκαν· ἀλληλουϊά· καὶ ὁ καπνὸς αὐτῆς ἀναβαίνει εἰς τοὺς αἰῶνας τῶν αἰώνων.

4 Καὶ ἔπεσαν οἱ πρεσβύτεροι οἱ εἴκοσι τέσσαρες καὶ τὰ τέσσαρα ζῷα καὶ προσεκύνησαν τῷ θεῷ τῷ καθημένῳ ἐπὶ τῷ θρόνῳ λέγοντες· ἀμὴν ἀλληλουϊά.

5 Καὶ φωνὴ ἀπὸ τοῦ θρόνου ἐξῆλθεν λέγουσα· αἰνεῖτε τῷ θεῷ ἡμῶν πάντες οἱ δοῦλοι αὐτοῦ [καὶ] οἱ φοβούμενοι αὐτόν, οἱ μικροὶ καὶ οἱ μεγάλοι.

15 The merchants of these things, those who became rich owing to her, will stand from afar, for the fear of her torment, weeping and mourning, 16 saying: "Woe, woe, to the great city, wrapped in fine linen and purple and scarlet, and adorned with gold and precious stones and pearls, 17 because in a single hour such wealth was laid waste."

And every helmsman and everyone who sails locally and seamen and all those who practice trade by sea stood from afar, 18 and shouted, seeing the smoke of her burning, saying: "What city was similar to the great city?" 19 And they threw ashes on their heads and shouted, weeping and mourning, saying: "Woe, woe, to the great city, in which all those who have ships in the sea became rich owing to her wealth, because in a single hour she was laid waste.

20 "Rejoice over her, O heaven, with the holy ones and the apostles and the prophets, because God has judged your judgment against her."

21 And a strong angel lifted by himself a stone, like a great millstone, and threw it into the sea, saying: "In this manner, with violence, Babylon, the great city, will be thrown down, and shall never again be found. 22 And the voice of lyrists and of minstrels and of flute players and of trumpeters shall never again be heard in you; and no craftsman of any craft shall ever again be found in you; and the voice of a millstone shall never again be heard in you; 23 and the light of a lamp shall never again shine in you; and the voice of groom and bride shall never again be heard in you; because your merchants were the chief men of the earth, because by your poisoning all the nations were led astray. 24 And in you was found the blood of prophets and of holy ones and of all those slaughtered upon the earth."

19 After these things I heard something like a great voice of a large throng in heaven, and they said: "Hallelujah. The salvation and the glory and the power belong to our God, 2 because true and just are his judgments; because he judged the prostitute, the great one, who destroyed the earth by her prostitution, and he avenged on her hand the blood of his own servants."

3 And for the second time they said: "Hallelujah! And her smoke rises up forever and ever."

4 And the elders fell, the twenty-four, and the four living creatures, and bowed down to God, to him who sits on the throne saying: "Amen. Hallelujah!"

5 And a voice came out from the throne, saying: "Praise our God, all of you, his servants, [and] those who fear him, the small and the great."

6 Καὶ ἤκουσα ὡς φωνὴν ὄχλου πολλοῦ καὶ ὡς φωνὴν ὑδάτων πολλῶν καὶ ὡς φωνὴν βροντῶν ἰσχυρῶν λεγόντων· ἀλληλουϊά, ὅτι ἐβασίλευσεν κύριος ὁ θεὸς [ἡμῶν] ὁ παντοκράτωρ. 7 χαίρωμεν καὶ ἀγαλλιῶμεν καὶ δώσομεν τὴν δόξαν αὐτῷ, ὅτι ἦλθεν ὁ γάμος τοῦ ἀρνίου καὶ ἡ γυνὴ αὐτοῦ ἡτοίμασεν ἑαυτὴν 8 καὶ ἐδόθη αὐτῇ ἵνα περιβάληται βύσσινον λαμπρὸν καθαρόν· τὸ γὰρ βύσσινον τὰ δικαιώματα τῶν ἁγίων ἐστίν.

9 Καὶ λέγει μοι· γράψον· μακάριοι οἱ εἰς τὸ δεῖπνον τοῦ γάμου τοῦ ἀρνίου κεκλημένοι. καὶ λέγει μοι· οὗτοι οἱ λόγοι ἀληθινοὶ τοῦ θεοῦ εἰσιν. 10 καὶ ἔπεσα ἔμπροσθεν τῶν ποδῶν αὐτοῦ προσκυνῆσαι αὐτῷ. καὶ λέγει μοι· ὅρα μή· σύνδουλός σού εἰμι καὶ τῶν ἀδελφῶν σου τῶν ἐχόντων τὴν μαρτυρίαν Ἰησοῦ· τῷ θεῷ προσκύνησον. ἡ γὰρ μαρτυρία Ἰησοῦ ἐστιν τὸ πνεῦμα τῆς προφητείας.

11 Καὶ εἶδον τὸν οὐρανὸν ἠνεῳγμένον, καὶ ἰδοὺ ἵππος λευκός καὶ ὁ καθήμενος ἐπ' αὐτὸν [καλούμενος] πιστὸς καὶ ἀληθινός, καὶ ἐν δικαιοσύνῃ κρίνει καὶ πολεμεῖ. 12 οἱ δὲ ὀφθαλμοὶ αὐτοῦ [ὡς] φλὸξ πυρός, καὶ ἐπὶ τὴν κεφαλὴν αὐτοῦ διαδήματα πολλά, ἔχων ὄνομα γεγραμμένον ὃ οὐδεὶς οἶδεν εἰ μὴ αὐτός, 13 καὶ περιβεβλημένος ἱμάτιον βεβαμμένον αἵματι, καὶ κέκληται τὸ ὄνομα αὐτοῦ ὁ λόγος τοῦ θεοῦ.

14 Καὶ τὰ στρατεύματα [τὰ] ἐν τῷ οὐρανῷ ἠκολούθει αὐτῷ ἐφ' ἵπποις λευκοῖς, ἐνδεδυμένοι βύσσινον λευκὸν καθαρόν. 15 καὶ ἐκ τοῦ στόματος αὐτοῦ ἐκπορεύεται ρομφαία ὀξεῖα, ἵνα ἐν αὐτῇ πατάξῃ τὰ ἔθνη, καὶ αὐτὸς ποιμανεῖ αὐτοὺς ἐν ράβδῳ σιδηρᾷ, καὶ αὐτὸς πατεῖ τὴν ληνὸν τοῦ οἴνου τοῦ θυμοῦ τῆς ὀργῆς τοῦ θεοῦ τοῦ παντοκράτορος, 16 καὶ ἔχει ἐπὶ τὸ ἱμάτιον καὶ ἐπὶ τὸν μηρὸν αὐτοῦ ὄνομα γεγραμμένον· Βασιλεὺς βασιλέων καὶ κύριος κυρίων.

17 Καὶ εἶδον ἕνα ἄγγελον ἑστῶτα ἐν τῷ ἡλίῳ καὶ ἔκραξεν [ἐν] φωνῇ μεγάλῃ λέγων πᾶσιν τοῖς ὀρνέοις τοῖς πετομένοις ἐν μεσουρανήματι· Δεῦτε συνάχθητε εἰς τὸ δεῖπνον τὸ μέγα τοῦ θεοῦ 18 ἵνα φάγητε σάρκας βασιλέων καὶ σάρκας χιλιάρχων καὶ σάρκας ἰσχυρῶν καὶ σάρκας ἵππων καὶ τῶν καθημένων ἐπ' αὐτῶν καὶ σάρκας πάντων ἐλευθέρων τε καὶ δούλων καὶ μικρῶν καὶ μεγάλων.

19 Καὶ εἶδον τὸ θηρίον καὶ τοὺς βασιλεῖς τῆς γῆς καὶ τὰ στρατεύματα αὐτῶν συνηγμένα ποιῆσαι τὸν πόλεμον μετὰ τοῦ καθημένου ἐπὶ τοῦ ἵππου καὶ μετὰ τοῦ στρατεύματος αὐτοῦ. 20 καὶ ἐπιάσθη τὸ θηρίον καὶ μετ' αὐτοῦ ὁ ψευδοπροφήτης ὁ ποιήσας τὰ σημεῖα ἐνώπιον αὐτοῦ, ἐν οἷς ἐπλάνησεν τοὺς λαβόντας τὸ χάραγμα τοῦ θηρίου καὶ τοὺς προσκυνοῦντας τῇ εἰκόνι αὐτοῦ· ζῶντες ἐβλήθησαν οἱ δύο εἰς τὴν λίμνην τοῦ πυρὸς τῆς καιομένης ἐν θείῳ. 21 καὶ οἱ λοιποὶ ἀπεκτάνθησαν ἐν τῇ ρομφαίᾳ τοῦ καθημένου ἐπὶ τοῦ ἵππου τῇ ἐξελθούσῃ ἐκ τοῦ στόματος αὐτοῦ, καὶ πάντα τὰ ὄρνεα ἐχορτάσθησαν ἐκ τῶν σαρκῶν αὐτῶν.

6 And I heard something like a voice of a large throng, and like a voice of many waters, and like a voice of strong thunders, saying: "Hallelujah, because [our] God, the almighty, has reigned as Lord. 7 Let us rejoice and exult, and we will give the glory to him, because the marriage of the Lamb has come, and his woman has prepared herself, 8 and fine linen, bright, pure, was given to her so that she could wrap herself with it. For the fine linen is the justifications of the holy ones.

9 And he says to me: "Write: Blessed are they who are called to the marriage supper of the Lamb." And he says to me: "These are the true words of God." 10 And I fell before his feet to bow down to him. And he says to me: "Take care not to do that. I am a fellow servant of yours and of your brothers, those who have the testimony of Jesus; bow down to God. For the testimony of Jesus is the spirit of prophecy."

11 And I saw the heaven opened, and, lo, a white horse, and he who was sitting upon it, [called] faithful and true, and by means of righteousness he judges and makes war. 12 And his eyes are [something like] a flame of fire, and on his head are many diadems, with a name written that no one knows save he himself, 13 and wrapped in a garment dipped in blood, and his name is: the Word of God.

14 And the troops, [those] in heaven, follow him on white horses, dressed in fine linen, white, pure. 15 And from his mouth extends a sharp sword, to smite the nations with it, and he will shepherd them with an iron staff, and he will tread the winepress of the wine of the wrath of the rage of God, the almighty. 16 And he has a name written on his garment and on his thigh: "King of kings and Lord of lords."

17 And I saw an angel by himself, standing in the sun; and he shouted with a great voice saying to all the birds, those flying in high heaven: "Come, gather yourselves for the supper, the great supper of God, 18 to eat flesh of kings and flesh of commanders and flesh of strong men and flesh of horses and of those that sit upon them and flesh of all, of freemen and of slaves, and of small and of great."

19 And I saw the beast and the kings of the earth and their troops gathered to make war on him who sits on the horse and on his army. 20 And the beast was seized, and with it the false prophet, he who accomplished the signs before it, with which he led astray those who received the brand of the beast and those who were bowing down to its image. The two were thrown alive into the marsh of fire, fire of a marsh burning with sulfur. 21 And the rest were killed by the sword of him who sits on the horse, the one extending from his mouth, and all the birds ate of their flesh to repletion.

20 Καὶ εἶδον ἄγγελον καταβαίνοντα ἐκ τοῦ οὐρανοῦ ἔχοντα τὴν κλεῖν τῆς ἀβύσσου καὶ ἄλυσιν μεγάλην ἐπὶ τὴν χεῖρα αὐτοῦ. 2 καὶ ἐκράτησεν τὸν δράκοντα, ὁ ὄφις ὁ ἀρχαῖος, ὅς ἐστιν Διάβολος καὶ ὁ Σατανᾶς, καὶ ἔδησεν αὐτὸν χίλια ἔτη 3 καὶ ἔβαλεν αὐτὸν εἰς τὴν ἄβυσσον καὶ ἔκλεισεν καὶ ἐσφράγισεν ἐπάνω αὐτοῦ, ἵνα μὴ πλανήσῃ ἔτι τὰ ἔθνη ἄχρι τελεσθῇ τὰ χίλια ἔτη. μετὰ ταῦτα δεῖ λυθῆναι αὐτὸν μικρὸν χρόνον.

4 Καὶ εἶδον θρόνους καὶ ἐκάθισαν ἐπ᾽ αὐτοὺς καὶ κρίμα ἐδόθη αὐτοῖς, καὶ τὰς ψυχὰς τῶν πεπελεκισμένων διὰ τὴν μαρτυρίαν Ἰησοῦ καὶ διὰ τὸν λόγον τοῦ θεοῦ καὶ οἵτινες οὐ προσεκύνησαν τὸ θηρίον οὐδὲ τὴν εἰκόνα αὐτοῦ καὶ οὐκ ἔλαβον τὸ χάραγμα ἐπὶ τὸ μέτωπον καὶ ἐπὶ τὴν χεῖρα αὐτῶν. καὶ ἔζησαν καὶ ἐβασίλευσαν μετὰ τοῦ Χριστοῦ χίλια ἔτη. 5 οἱ λοιποὶ τῶν νεκρῶν οὐκ ἔζησαν ἄχρι τελεσθῇ τὰ χίλια ἔτη. αὕτη ἡ ἀνάστασις ἡ πρώτη. 6 μακάριος καὶ ἅγιος ὁ ἔχων μέρος ἐν τῇ ἀναστάσει τῇ πρώτῃ· ἐπὶ τούτων ὁ δεύτερος θάνατος οὐκ ἔχει ἐξουσίαν, ἀλλ᾽ ἔσονται ἱερεῖς τοῦ θεοῦ καὶ τοῦ Χριστοῦ καὶ βασιλεύσουσιν μετ᾽ αὐτοῦ [τὰ] χίλια ἔτη.

7 Καὶ ὅταν τελεσθῇ τὰ χίλια ἔτη, λυθήσεται ὁ Σατανᾶς ἐκ τῆς φυλακῆς αὐτοῦ 8 καὶ ἐξελεύσεται πλανῆσαι τὰ ἔθνη τὰ ἐν ταῖς τέσσαρσιν γωνίαις τῆς γῆς, τὸν Γὼγ καὶ Μαγώγ, συναγαγεῖν αὐτοὺς εἰς τὸν πόλεμον, ὧν ὁ ἀριθμὸς αὐτῶν ὡς ἡ ἄμμος τῆς θαλάσσης. 9 καὶ ἀνέβησαν ἐπὶ τὸ πλάτος τῆς γῆς καὶ ἐκύκλευσαν τὴν παρεμβολὴν τῶν ἁγίων καὶ τὴν πόλιν τὴν ἠγαπημένην, καὶ κατέβη πῦρ ἐκ τοῦ οὐρανοῦ καὶ κατέφαγεν αὐτούς. 10 καὶ ὁ διάβολος ὁ πλανῶν αὐτοὺς ἐβλήθη εἰς τὴν λίμνην τοῦ πυρὸς καὶ θείου ὅπου καὶ τὸ θηρίον καὶ ὁ ψευδοπροφήτης, καὶ βασανισθήσονται ἡμέρας καὶ νυκτὸς εἰς τοὺς αἰῶνας τῶν αἰώνων.

11 Καὶ εἶδον θρόνον μέγαν λευκὸν καὶ τὸν καθήμενον ἐπ᾽ αὐτόν, οὗ ἀπὸ τοῦ προσώπου ἔφυγεν ἡ γῆ καὶ ὁ οὐρανὸς καὶ τόπος οὐχ εὑρέθη αὐτοῖς. 12 καὶ εἶδον τοὺς νεκρούς, τοὺς μεγάλους καὶ τοὺς μικρούς, ἑστῶτας ἐνώπιον τοῦ θρόνου. καὶ βιβλία ἠνοίχθησαν, καὶ ἄλλο βιβλίον ἠνοίχθη, ὅ ἐστιν τῆς ζωῆς, καὶ ἐκρίθησαν οἱ νεκροὶ ἐκ τῶν γεγραμμένων ἐν τοῖς βιβλίοις κατὰ τὰ ἔργα αὐτῶν. 13 καὶ ἔδωκεν ἡ θάλασσα τοὺς νεκροὺς τοὺς ἐν αὐτῇ καὶ ὁ θάνατος καὶ ὁ ᾅδης ἔδωκαν τοὺς νεκροὺς τοὺς ἐν αὐτοῖς, καὶ ἐκρίθησαν ἕκαστος κατὰ τὰ ἔργα αὐτῶν. 14 καὶ ὁ θάνατος καὶ ὁ ᾅδης ἐβλήθησαν εἰς τὴν λίμνην τοῦ πυρός. οὗτος ὁ θάνατος ὁ δεύτερός ἐστιν, ἡ λίμνη τοῦ πυρός. 15 καὶ εἴ τις οὐχ εὑρέθη ἐν τῇ βίβλῳ τῆς ζωῆς γεγραμμένος, ἐβλήθη εἰς τὴν λίμνην τοῦ πυρός.

20

And I saw an angel coming down from heaven with the key of the abyss and a great chain in his hand. 2 And he took firm hold of the dragon, the ancient serpent, who is the Devil and Satan, and bound him for a thousand years, 3 and he threw him into the abyss, and closed it, and put a seal upon it, in order that he would no longer lead astray the nations until the thousand years would be completed. After these years he must be loosed for a short time.

4 And I saw thrones, and they sat upon them, and judgment was given to them, and I saw the souls of those decapitated on account of the testimony of Jesus and on account of the word of God, and all those who did not bow down to the beast nor to its image and did not receive the brand on their forehead and on their hand. And they lived and reigned with Christ for a thousand years. 5 The rest of the dead did not live until the thousand years were completed. This is the resurrection, the first one. 6 Blessed and holy is he who has a share in the first resurrection. Over these the second death has no power, but they will be priests of God and of Christ, and will reign with him for [the] thousand years.

7 And when the thousand years are completed, Satan will be loosed from his prison, 8 and he will come forth to lead astray the nations that are at the four corners of the earth, Gog and Magog, to gather them for war, whose number is like the sand of the sea. 9 And they came up upon the plain of the earth and encircled in siege the camp of the holy ones and the city, the beloved one. And fire came down from heaven and devoured them. 10 And the devil, he who leads them astray, was thrown into the marsh of fire and sulfur, where also the beast and the false prophet are, and they will be tormented day and night forever and ever.

11 And I saw a great white throne and him who was sitting upon it, from whose face the earth fled and the heaven, and no place was found for them. 12 And I saw the dead, the great and the small, standing before the throne. And scrolls were opened, and another scroll was opened, which is the one of life, and the dead were judged on the basis of the things written in the scrolls, according to their works. 13 And the sea gave up the dead that were in it, and Death and Hades gave up the dead that were in them, and they were judged, each according to their works. 14 And Death and Hades were thrown into the marsh of fire. This is the second death, the marsh of fire. 15 And whoever was not found written in the scroll of life was thrown into the marsh of fire.

21 Καὶ εἶδον οὐρανὸν καινὸν καὶ γῆν καινήν. ὁ γὰρ πρῶτος οὐρανὸς καὶ ἡ πρώτη γῆ ἀπῆλθαν καὶ ἡ θάλασσα οὐκ ἔστιν ἔτι. 2 καὶ τὴν πόλιν τὴν ἁγίαν Ἰερουσαλὴμ καινὴν εἶδον καταβαίνουσαν ἐκ τοῦ οὐρανοῦ ἀπὸ τοῦ θεοῦ ἡτοιμασμένην ὡς νύμφην κεκοσμημένην τῷ ἀνδρὶ αὐτῆς. 3 καὶ ἤκουσα φωνῆς μεγάλης ἐκ τοῦ θρόνου λεγούσης· ἰδοὺ ἡ σκηνὴ τοῦ θεοῦ μετὰ τῶν ἀνθρώπων, καὶ σκηνώσει μετ᾽ αὐτῶν, καὶ αὐτοὶ λαοὶ αὐτοῦ ἔσονται, καὶ αὐτὸς ὁ θεὸς μετ᾽ αὐτῶν ἔσται [αὐτῶν θεός], 4 καὶ ἐξαλείψει πᾶν δάκρυον ἐκ τῶν ὀφθαλμῶν αὐτῶν, καὶ ὁ θάνατος οὐκ ἔσται ἔτι οὔτε πένθος οὔτε κραυγὴ οὔτε πόνος οὐκ ἔσται ἔτι, [ὅτι] τὰ πρῶτα ἀπῆλθαν.

5 Καὶ εἶπεν ὁ καθήμενος ἐπὶ τῷ θρόνῳ· ἰδοὺ καινὰ ποιῶ πάντα καὶ λέγει· γράφον, ὅτι οὗτοι οἱ λόγοι πιστοὶ καὶ ἀληθινοί εἰσιν. 6 καὶ εἶπέν μοι· γέγοναν. ἐγώ [εἰμι] τὸ ἄλφα καὶ τὸ ὦ, ἡ ἀρχὴ καὶ τὸ τέλος. ἐγὼ τῷ διψῶντι δώσω ἐκ τῆς πηγῆς τοῦ ὕδατος τῆς ζωῆς δωρεάν. 7 ὁ νικῶν κληρονομήσει ταῦτα καὶ ἔσομαι αὐτῷ θεὸς καὶ αὐτὸς ἔσται μοι υἱός. 8 τοῖς δὲ δειλοῖς καὶ ἀπίστοις καὶ ἐβδελυγμένοις καὶ φονεῦσιν καὶ πόρνοις καὶ φαρμάκοις καὶ εἰδωλολάτραις καὶ πᾶσιν τοῖς ψευδέσιν τὸ μέρος αὐτῶν ἐν τῇ λίμνῃ τῇ καιομένῃ πυρὶ καὶ θείῳ, ὅ ἐστιν ὁ θάνατος ὁ δεύτερος.

9 Καὶ ἦλθεν εἷς ἐκ τῶν ἑπτὰ ἀγγέλων τῶν ἐχόντων τὰς ἑπτὰ φιάλας τῶν γεμόντων τῶν ἑπτὰ πληγῶν τῶν ἐσχάτων καὶ ἐλάλησεν μετ᾽ ἐμοῦ λέγων· δεῦρο, δείξω σοι τὴν νύμφην τὴν γυναῖκα τοῦ ἀρνίου. 10 καὶ ἀπήνεγκέν με ἐν πνεύματι ἐπὶ ὄρος μέγα καὶ ὑψηλόν, καὶ ἔδειξέν μοι τὴν πόλιν τὴν ἁγίαν Ἰερουσαλὴμ καταβαίνουσαν ἐκ τοῦ οὐρανοῦ ἀπὸ τοῦ θεοῦ 11 ἔχουσαν τὴν δόξαν τοῦ θεοῦ, ὁ φωστὴρ αὐτῆς ὅμοιος λίθῳ τιμιωτάτῳ ὡς λίθῳ ἰάσπιδι κρυσταλλίζοντι. 12 ἔχουσα τεῖχος μέγα καὶ ὑψηλόν, ἔχουσα πυλῶνας δώδεκα καὶ ἐπὶ τοῖς πυλῶσιν ἀγγέλους δώδεκα καὶ ὀνόματα ἐπιγεγραμμένα, ἅ ἐστιν [τὰ ὀνόματα] τῶν δώδεκα φυλῶν υἱῶν Ἰσραήλ· 13 ἀπὸ ἀνατολῆς πυλῶνες τρεῖς καὶ ἀπὸ βορρᾶ πυλῶνες τρεῖς καὶ ἀπὸ νότου πυλῶνες τρεῖς καὶ ἀπὸ δυσμῶν πυλῶνες τρεῖς. 14 καὶ τὸ τεῖχος τῆς πόλεως ἔχων θεμελίους δώδεκα καὶ ἐπ᾽ αὐτῶν δώδεκα ὀνόματα τῶν δώδεκα ἀποστόλων τοῦ ἀρνίου.

21

And I saw a new heaven and a new earth. For the first heaven and the first earth passed away, and the sea is no more. 2 And the holy city, a new Jerusalem, I saw coming down out of heaven from God, prepared like a bride adorned for her husband. 3 And I heard a great voice from the throne, saying: "Lo, the abode of God among men, and he will abide with them, and they will be his peoples, and God himself will be with them, [their God], 4 and he will wipe away every tear from their eyes, and death will be no more, neither will there be mourning nor crying nor pain any more; [because] the first things have passed away."

5 And he who sits on the throne said: "Lo, I make all things new." And he says: "Write: These are the faithful and true words." 6 And he said to me: "They have happened! I [am] the Alpha and the Omega, the beginning and the end. To the one who is thirsty I will give of the spring of the water of life, free of charge. 7 The victor will inherit these things, and I will be his God, and he will be my son. 8 But as for the cowardly and unfaithful and abominable and murderers and prostitutes and poisoners and idolaters and all the liars, their share is in the marsh, the one burning with fire and sulfur, which is the second death."

9 And one of the seven angels came, of those who have the seven bowls and who are full of the seven plagues, the last ones, and he spoke to me, saying: "Come here; I will show you the bride — the woman — of the Lamb." 10 And he carried me in spirit upon a mountain, great and high, and he showed me the city, the holy Jerusalem, coming down out of heaven from God, 11 with the Glory of God, her splendor similar to a very precious stone, like a stone of crystalline jasper. 12 She had a wall, great and high, with twelve gates, and on the gates twelve angels and names written, which are [the names] of the twelve tribes of the children of Israel: 13 on the east three gates, and on the north three gates, and on the south three gates, and on the west three gates. 14 And the wall of the city had twelve foundations, and on them twelve names of the twelve apostles of the Lamb.

15 Καὶ ὁ λαλῶν μετ' ἐμοῦ εἶχεν μέτρον κάλαμον χρυσοῦν, ἵνα μετρήσῃ τὴν πόλιν καὶ τοὺς πυλῶνας αὐτῆς καὶ τὸ τεῖχος αὐτῆς. 16 καὶ ἡ πόλις τετράγωνος κεῖται καὶ τὸ μῆκος αὐτῆς ὅσον [καὶ] τὸ πλάτος. καὶ ἐμέτρησεν τὴν πόλιν τῷ καλάμῳ ἐπὶ σταδίων δώδεκα χιλιάδων, τὸ μῆκος καὶ τὸ πλάτος καὶ τὸ ὕψος αὐτῆς ἴσα ἐστίν. 17 καὶ ἐμέτρησεν τὸ τεῖχος αὐτῆς ἑκατὸν τεσσεράκοντα τεσσάρων πηχῶν μέτρον ἀνθρώπου, ὅ ἐστιν ἀγγέλου. 18 καὶ ἡ ἐνδώμησις τοῦ τείχους αὐτῆς ἴασπις καὶ ἡ πόλις χρυσίον καθαρὸν ὅμοιον ὑάλῳ καθαρῷ. 19 οἱ θεμέλιοι τοῦ τείχους τῆς πόλεως παντὶ λίθῳ τιμίῳ κεκοσμημένοι· ὁ θεμέλιος ὁ πρῶτος ἴασπις, ὁ δεύτερος σάπφιρος, ὁ τρίτος χαλκηδών, ὁ τέταρτος σμά-ραγδος, 20 ὁ πέμπτος σαρδόνυξ, ὁ ἕκτος σάρδιον, ὁ ἕβδομος χρυσόλιθος, ὁ ὄγδοος βήρυλλος, ὁ ἔνατος τοπάζιον, ὁ δέκατος χρυσόπρασος, ὁ ἑνδέκατος ὑάκινθος, ὁ δωδέκατος ἀμέθυστος, 21 καὶ οἱ δώδεκα πυλῶνες δώδεκα μαργαρῖται, ἀνὰ εἷς ἕκαστος τῶν πυλώνων ἦν ἐξ ἑνὸς μαργαρίτου. καὶ ἡ πλατεῖα τῆς πόλεως χρυσίον καθαρὸν ὡς ὕαλος διαυγής.

22 Καὶ ναὸν οὐκ εἶδον ἐν αὐτῇ, ὁ γὰρ κύριος ὁ θεὸς ὁ παντοκράτωρ ναός αὐτῆς ἐστιν καὶ τὸ ἀρνίον. 23 καὶ ἡ πόλις οὐ χρείαν ἔχει τοῦ ἡλίου οὐδὲ τῆς σελήνης ἵνα φαίνωσιν αὐτῇ, ἡ γὰρ δόξα τοῦ θεοῦ ἐφώτισεν αὐτήν, καὶ ὁ λύχνος αὐτῆς τὸ ἀρνίον. 24 καὶ περιπατήσουσιν τὰ ἔθνη διὰ τοῦ φωτὸς αὐτῆς, καὶ οἱ βασιλεῖς τῆς γῆς φέρουσιν τὴν δόξαν αὐτῶν εἰς αὐτήν, 25 καὶ οἱ πυλῶνες αὐτῆς οὐ μὴ κλεισθῶσιν ἡμέρας, νὺξ γὰρ οὐκ ἔσται ἐκεῖ, 26 καὶ οἴσουσιν τὴν δόξαν καὶ τὴν τιμὴν τῶν ἐθνῶν εἰς αὐτήν. 27 καὶ οὐ μὴ εἰσέλθῃ εἰς αὐτὴν πᾶν κοινὸν καὶ [ὁ] ποιῶν βδέλυγμα καὶ ψεῦδος εἰ μὴ οἱ γεγραμμένοι ἐν τῷ βιβλίῳ τῆς ζωῆς τοῦ ἀρνίου.

22 Καὶ ἔδειξέν μοι ποταμὸν ὕδατος ζωῆς λαμπρὸν ὡς κρύσταλλον, ἐκπορευόμενον ἐκ τοῦ θρόνου τοῦ θεοῦ καὶ τοῦ ἀρνίου. 2 ἐν μέσῳ τῆς πλατείας αὐτῆς καὶ τοῦ ποταμοῦ ἐντεῦθεν καὶ ἐκεῖθεν ξύλον ζωῆς ποιοῦν καρποὺς δώδεκα, κατὰ μῆνα ἕκαστον ἀποδιδοῦν τὸν καρπὸν αὐτοῦ, καὶ τὰ φύλλα τοῦ ξύλου εἰς θεραπείαν τῶν ἐθνῶν. 3 καὶ πᾶν κατάθεμα οὐκ ἔσται ἔτι. καὶ ὁ θρόνος τοῦ θεοῦ καὶ τοῦ ἀρνίου ἐν αὐτῇ ἔσται, καὶ οἱ δοῦλοι αὐτοῦ λατρεύσουσιν αὐτῷ 4 καὶ ὄψονται τὸ πρόσωπον αὐτοῦ, καὶ τὸ ὄνομα αὐτοῦ ἐπὶ τῶν μετώπων αὐτῶν. 5 καὶ νὺξ οὐκ ἔσται ἔτι καὶ οὐκ ἔχουσιν χρείαν φωτὸς λύχνου καὶ φωτὸς ἡλίου, ὅτι κύριος ὁ θεὸς φωτίσει ἐπ' αὐτούς, καὶ βασιλεύ-σουσιν εἰς τοὺς αἰῶνας τῶν αἰώνων.

6 Καὶ εἶπέν μοι· οὗτοι οἱ λόγοι πιστοὶ καὶ ἀληθινοί, καὶ ὁ κύριος ὁ θεὸς τῶν πνευμάτων τῶν προφητῶν ἀπέστειλεν τὸν ἄγγελον αὐτοῦ δεῖξαι τοῖς δούλοις αὐτοῦ ἃ δεῖ γενέσθαι ἐν τάχει. 7 καὶ ἰδοὺ ἔρχομαι ταχύ. μακάριος ὁ τηρῶν τοὺς λόγους τῆς προφητείας τοῦ βιβλίου τούτου.

15 And he who was speaking with me had a measure, a golden reed, to measure the city and her gates and her wall. 16 And the city is laid out foursquare, and her length is as large as her width. And he measured the city with the reed, at twelve thousand stades; the length and the width and height of her are equal. 17 And he measured her wall: a hundred forty-four cubits, by measure of a man, that is, of an angel. 18 And the construction of her wall was of jasper, and the city was pure gold, similar to pure glass. 19 The foundations of the wall of the city were adorned with every precious stone: The first foundation was jasper; the second, sapphire; the third, chalcedony; the fourth, emerald; 20 the fifth, sardonyx; the sixth, carnelian; the seventh, chrysolite; the eighth, beryl; the ninth, topaz; the tenth, chrysoprase; the eleventh, hyacinth; the twelfth, amethyst. 21 And the twelve gates were twelve pearls; each of the gates, one after the other, was made of a single pearl. And the square of the city was pure gold, like transparent glass.

22 And I saw no temple in her; for the Lord, God Almighty, is her temple, and the Lamb. 23 And the city has no need of the sun, nor of the moon, to give her light; for the Glory of God gave her light, and the lamb is her lamp. 24 And the nations will walk by the help of her light, and the kings of the earth bring their glory into her. 25 And her gates will surely not be closed by day — for there will be no night there — 26 and they will bring the glory and the honor of the nations to her. 27 And surely no profane thing will enter her, nor anyone practicing abomination and lies, but only those who are written in the Lamb's scroll of life.

22 And he showed me a river of water of life, bright like crystal, coming forth from the throne of God and of the Lamb. 2 In the middle of her square, and on one side of the river and on the other, there is a tree of life producing twelve fruits, yielding its fruit each month, and the leaves of the wood/tree for the healing of the nations. 3 And there will no longer be any curse. And the throne of God and of the Lamb will be in her, and his servants will render worship to him, 4 and they will see his face, and his name will be on their foreheads. 5 And there will be no night any more, and they do not have need of light of lamp or light of sun, because the Lord God will shine light upon them, and they will reign forever and ever.

6 And he said to me: "These are the faithful and true words, and the Lord, the God of the spirits of the prophets, sent his angel to show to his servants the things that must take place soon. 7 And lo, I am coming soon! Blessed is he who keeps the words of the prophecy of this scroll."

8 Κἀγὼ Ἰωάννης ὁ ἀκούων καὶ βλέπων ταῦτα. καὶ ὅτε ἤκουσα καὶ ἔβλεψα, ἔπεσα προσκυνῆσαι ἔμπροσθεν τῶν ποδῶν τοῦ ἀγγέλου τοῦ δεικνύοντός μοι ταῦτα. 9 καὶ λέγει μοι· ὅρα μή· σύνδουλός σού εἰμι καὶ τῶν ἀδελφῶν σου τῶν προφητῶν καὶ τῶν τηρούντων τοὺς λόγους τοῦ βιβλίου τούτου· τῷ θεῷ προσκύνησον.

10 Καὶ λέγει μοι· μὴ σφραγίσῃς τοὺς λόγους τῆς προφητείας τοῦ βιβλίου τούτου, ὁ καιρὸς γὰρ ἐγγύς ἐστιν. 11 ὁ ἀδικῶν ἀδικησάτω ἔτι καὶ ὁ ῥυπαρὸς ῥυπανθήτω ἔτι, καὶ ὁ δίκαιος δικαιοσύνην ποιησάτω ἔτι καὶ ὁ ἅγιος ἁγιασθήτω ἔτι.

12 Ἰδοὺ ἔρχομαι ταχύ, καὶ ὁ μισθός μου μετ᾽ ἐμοῦ ἀποδοῦναι ἑκάστῳ ὡς τὸ ἔργον ἐστὶν αὐτοῦ. 13 ἐγὼ τὸ ἄλφα καὶ τὸ ὦ, ὁ πρῶτος καὶ ὁ ἔσχατος, ἡ ἀρχὴ καὶ τὸ τέλος.

14 Μακάριοι οἱ πλύνοντες τὰς στολὰς αὐτῶν, ἵνα ἔσται ἡ ἐξουσία αὐτῶν ἐπὶ τὸ ξύλον τῆς ζωῆς καὶ τοῖς πυλῶσιν εἰσέλθωσιν εἰς τὴν πόλιν. 15 ἔξω οἱ κύνες καὶ οἱ φάρμακοι καὶ οἱ πόρνοι καὶ οἱ φονεῖς καὶ οἱ εἰδωλολάτραι καὶ πᾶς φιλῶν καὶ ποιῶν ψεῦδος.

16 Ἐγὼ Ἰησοῦς ἔπεμψα τὸν ἄγγελόν μου μαρτυρῆσαι ὑμῖν ταῦτα ἐπὶ ταῖς ἐκκλησίαις. ἐγώ εἰμι ἡ ῥίζα καὶ τὸ γένος Δαυίδ, ὁ ἀστὴρ ὁ λαμπρὸς ὁ πρωϊνός.

17 Καὶ τὸ πνεῦμα καὶ ἡ νύμφη λέγουσιν· ἔρχου. καὶ ὁ ἀκούων εἰπάτω· ἔρχου. καὶ ὁ διψῶν ἐρχέσθω, ὁ θέλων λαβέτω ὕδωρ ζωῆς δωρεάν.

18 Μαρτυρῶ ἐγὼ παντὶ τῷ ἀκούοντι τοὺς λόγους τῆς προφητείας τοῦ βιβλίου τούτου· ἐάν τις ἐπιθῇ ἐπ᾽ αὐτά, ἐπιθήσει ὁ θεὸς ἐπ᾽ αὐτὸν τὰς πληγὰς τὰς γεγραμμένας ἐν τῷ βιβλίῳ τούτῳ, 19 καὶ ἐάν τις ἀφέλῃ ἀπὸ τῶν λόγων τοῦ βιβλίου τῆς προφητείας ταύτης, ἀφελεῖ ὁ θεὸς τὸ μέρος αὐτοῦ ἀπὸ τοῦ ξύλου τῆς ζωῆς καὶ ἐκ τῆς πόλεως τῆς ἁγίας τῶν γεγραμμένων ἐν τῷ βιβλίῳ τούτῳ.

20 Λέγει ὁ μαρτυρῶν ταῦτα· ναί, ἔρχομαι ταχύ. Ἀμήν, ἔρχου κύριε Ἰησοῦ.

21 Ἡ χάρις τοῦ κυρίου Ἰησοῦ μετὰ πάντων.

8 And I, John, am he who hears and sees these things. And when I heard and saw, I fell to bow down before the feet of the angel who was showing me these things. 9 And he says to me: "Take care not to do that! I am a fellow servant of yours and of your brothers the prophets, and of those who keep the words of this scroll. Bow down to God!"

10 And he says to me: "Do not seal closed the words of the prophecy of this scroll, for the moment is near. 11 Let him who is unjust still commit injustice, and him who is defiled still defile himself, and let the just man still do justice, and the holy man still make himself holy.

12 "Lo, I am coming soon, and my payment with me, to give to each one accordingly, as is his work. 13 I am the Alpha and the Omega, the first and the last, the beginning and the end."

14 Blessed are those who wash their robes, so that their authority will be over the wood/tree of life and that they may enter into the city by the gates. 15 Out with the dogs and the poisoners and the prostitutes and the murderers and the idolaters and anyone who loves and practices lies.

16 "I, Jesus, sent my angel to testify to these things to you concerning the churches. I am the root and the offspring of David, the bright star of the early morning."

17 And the Spirit and the bride say: "Come!" And let him who hears say: "Come!" And let him who is thirsty come; let him who desires take water of life free of charge.

18 I testify to everyone who listens to the words of the prophecy of this scroll: if someone adds to these things, God will add to him the plagues, those written in this scroll.

19 And if someone takes away from the words of the scroll of this prophecy, God will take away his share from the wood/tree of life and from the holy city, that is, the things written in this scroll.

20 He who testifies to these things says: "Yes, I am coming soon." Amen, come, Lord Jesus!

21 The grace of Lord Jesus be with all.

Commentary

1 :1 Ἀποκάλυψις Ἰωάννου. Ἀποκάλυψις Ἰησοῦ Χριστοῦ. The Greek term must be translated in two different ways ("Apocalypse of John," "Revelation of Jesus Christ"), even in two occurrences so close to each other in the text. The book's title almost certainly does not originate with John, but dates from a period at which this text was already considered an "apocalypse" (as far as we know, the earliest to be referred to by its author as an "apocalypse" might be 2 *Baruch;* cf. Bogaert 1969, 1:96; ET by A. F. J. Klijn, in Charlesworth I 1983; IT by P. Bettiolo in Sacchi II 1989). For John, the term means "revelation" and describes the content of the book, which is disclosed by Jesus Christ. Jesus is both the subject and the object of the revelation; he manifests himself in this book, whose form indeed is that of a manual of Christology cast in the form of images. I believe, however, that in this passage John means to emphasize the role of Jesus Christ as the *subject* of the revelation. There is a kind of hierarchy of authority at work: the revelation originates first with God, who "gives" it to Jesus Christ. He in turn "makes it known by sending his angel" to John, who, finally, "testifies."

The content of John's testimony is expressed in v. 2 in an ostensibly simple sentence. The main verb, "testified," has two objects joined by "and" ("the word — λόγος — of God" and "the testimony of Jesus Christ") followed by a relative clause "to all the things that he saw," which seems to be an explanation of what precedes it. The element of repetition, "testified, testimony" (ἐμαρτύρησεν–μαρτυρίαν), sets up a parallel between the two parts of the sentence, for the purpose of showing that Jesus Christ is the Word-Logos of God. The καί thus acquires the epexegetic sense of "that is." The meaning of the sentence, therefore, is "John testified to the word of God, that is to say, he gave testimony about Jesus Christ. This testimony consists of all the things that he saw and wrote down" (for ὅσα with and without the preceding πάντα see Matt 13:44 and 46). ὅσα εἶδεν is probably deliberately ambiguous and refers both to what precedes it (the things that John saw are the "word" and "Jesus Christ," or rather his "testimony") and to what follows it, namely, all the visions that the book recounts. By using this phrase as a "hinge" John wants to indicate that the visions recorded in the book are his testimony about Jesus Christ. John, as we shall see, considers his own work to be a "prophecy," which makes sense of 19:10, "For the testimony of Jesus is the spirit of prophecy" (see 19:10 and 1:3).

τοῖς δούλοις αὐτοῦ. In the Apocalypse the genitive follows the noun in 321 cases as opposed to only eleven cases where it precedes the noun; this reflects Semitic linguistic usage. The Greek term δοῦλος, conventionally translated "servant," in fact implies a relationship of slavery toward the person or body to whom the servant belongs.

διὰ τοῦ ἀγγέλου αὐτοῦ. It is not immediately clear what John means when he speaks of the angel of Jesus Christ. "Angel" can be used to refer to any manifestation of divinity or to any spiritual reality between God and humanity (see Levison 1995). To put it differently, in the first century every reality that we would term "spiritual" could be interpreted as angelic. This is the only way to explain why, in Acts 12:15, the Jerusalem believers thought that it was Peter's "angel" and not Peter himself who was knocking at the gate.

That the first manifestation of God toward humanity is of an angelic nature superior to all others makes plain that there is a pyramidal angelic hierarchy. There are texts in which the first manifestation or image of God is a being very close to God himself ("Iaoel [Yahweh-God] of the same name" in *Apoc. Abr.* 10:3 and 17:13). At this point in time it is not yet a heresy to say that Jesus Christ, insofar as he is the visible image or the audible word of God, is an angel of God, or rather *the* angel of God; there are actually traces of angelic Christology in the Apocalypse (Karrer 1986, pp. 141-49; the current term is "angelomorphic christology"; Gundry 1994, Stuckenbruck 1995, Gieschen 1995). However, inasmuch as Jesus Christ is close to, or taken up into, God, he reveals himself in his turn by means of an angel. It is common for a superior angelic nature to use other angels as means of communicating with humans or of acting in the world. In the *Shepherd of Hermas,* the Shepherd himself is an angelic being sent to Hermas by another, higher, angelic being, who is defined variously as Glorious Man, Glorious Angel, Angel of the Lord, or Michael, and who, in the last analysis, appears to be either the heavenly Christ or the Holy Spirit (Gieschen 1994). In *1 Enoch* 60:4 (*BS; 1 Enoch* 60 contains an ancient fragment of a lost "history" of Noah), Michael sends "another angel from among the holy ones" to communicate with the visionary, but the dialogue between Michael and the visionary goes on as if there were no such intermediary (1 *Enoch* 60:5). Thus there are "angels of angels" who, like the biblical angels of God, tend to become confused with their sender, at least in the eyes of the human beings with whom they communicate. In the case of the Apocalypse the angel of Christ could be the Voice, the medium whereby the Word renders itself perceptible to the human ear (see 1:12). It could also be the interpreting angel who explains the visions to John, and who seems to be identified with the first of the seven angels who stand near God (in 1 *Enoch* 60 also the angel sent by Michael appears to take on the role of interpreting angel). Even as Jesus Christ is the Angel of God because he is his image, so this "angel" is the image of Jesus Christ (see the comments on 10:1 and 22:16). In Mark 13:27, too, the Son of Man, at the parousia, sends some angels; in Matt 16:27 and 24:31, on the other hand, these become "his angels," thus establishing a contrast with Satan and "his angels" in 25:41.

1:3   Μακάριος. This is the first of the seven blessings in the book, the others being in 14:13, 16:15, 19:9, 20:6, and 22:7, 14. In four cases the blessing is in the singular, "blessed is he," and in three cases in the plural, "blessed are they." In some cases the blessing is dictated to John by a Voice, in others it is probably pronounced by Jesus Christ. It is not clear here whether the blessing forms part of a message John receives or whether it is an exclamation by him. It is not structurally important that there are seven blessings in the text, as the blessings do not represent a self-contained segment, nor do they signal the beginning or end of distinct sections of the work. Thus that there are seven of them is most likely part of a deliberate numerical strategy that shows that the author expected his work to receive close and careful analysis, since nobody reading or hearing the text for the first time would be aware that there were seven blessings. This notion is further supported by the fact that John uses the same terms in similar sentences in various parts of the book. Here, for instance, we find for the first time the word "keep," which will reappear another ten times and will often have as its grammatical or logical object terms like "word/words" or "laws" — of God, of Christ, or of prophecy. By this method John creates a series of internal correspondences within the text; a web of references and echoes that lends the book a striking compactness and consistency.

This construction of a web of parallels is not purely a literary technique. Both Jewish and early Christian students of Scripture were acutely aware of the principle that Scripture itself is the primary key for the interpretation of Scripture. Ancient biblical exegesis operated by gathering passages that contained the same words and that were thus understood to cast light on each other, with the more transparent passages illuminating the more obscure ones. The deliberate method of the Apocalypse's composition suggests that the author, who considers himself to be inspired, expects that his book will be subjected to the kinds of investigation typically reserved for the other inspired texts. There are two implications. In the first place the book is designed to receive both superficial readings or hearings, and profound study. In the second place, the author's strategy of constructing a web of parallels within the text leads him to repeat the same terms many times, which in its turn can help to explain the "poverty" of the Apocalypse's vocabulary. The Apocalypse contains somewhat fewer than 900 different terms, which recur about 9800 times altogether. Hebrews, which is approximately half as long as the Apocalypse, has over 1000 terms, which are repeated almost 4950 times. There are other indicators of the "poverty" of John's Greek, for instance, his frequent use of καί, which occurs on average twelve times every hundred words. Hebrews, by way of comparison, uses it about five times every hundred words, and in Acts, which contains almost twice as many words as the Apocalypse (about 18,400), καί appears almost the same number of times. δέ appears correspondingly infrequently: at most seven times, or approximately every 1400 words, as opposed to, for instance, Luke, where δέ occurs roughly every thirty-five words.

John's strategy of repeating similar expressions many times in different contexts for the purpose of creating internal consistency within the text probably induced him also to expand the range of meaning of each word, or rather to give to each word a variety of nuances. When taken together with the "poverty" of John's Greek, this expansion leads to an abundance of, for instance, the verbs "to give" and "to do," and to a scarcity of compound verbs composed of prepositions that serve precisely to emphasize nuances of meaning. In the Apocalypse only 4.6 percent of the verbs are combined with prepositions, as opposed to, for instance, 20.5 percent in Luke and 21.1 percent in Acts. Luke uses the highest percentage of these verbs in the NT, and John the lowest (see Bauckham 1993, pp. 22-30; the numerical data here and elsewhere is derived from Morgenthaler 1958 and checked on *Computer Concordance* 1985).

ὁ ἀναγινώσκων . . . γεγραμμένα. The author anticipates that the text will be read publicly in a gathering of the faithful. He appears to imagine this event as being relatively structured, involving at least a "lector" distinct from the other participants. Although it is impossible today to reconstruct fully and credibly the Christian liturgy at the time of the Apocalypse's composition, it does seem clear that John expects the text to be put to some liturgical use.

I have used the first blessing to argue that the author expected his text to receive detailed and profound study; it is also, curiously enough, the verse that most clearly suggests that the book was intended for public reading. Moreover, in view of the exhortation to "keep," which is most appropriately addressed to a normal community of the faithful, it seems that the meeting of such a community is precisely what John had in mind, much more than the meeting of a school or of a confraternity of prophets (see Introduction, pp. 39-40; see also 22:9).

ὁ γὰρ καιρὸς ἐγγύς. The Apocalypse uses two terms for "time": χρόνος, which refers to time as linear and without precise limits inherent to it, as in 2:21, 6:11, 10:6, and 20:3, and καιρός, which implies a limited "period" (12:12 and 14 [three times]) or a "moment" (1:3, 11:18, and 22:10). By qualifying with adjectives the terms for "time" John reveals all his propensity for an eschatology close to its realization: the "moment" is said to be "near" in two out of three cases, in 1:3 and 22:10, at the beginning and end of the book, "a short time more" in 6:11, and "a short time" in 20:3. In 10:6 John affirms that "time will be no more." It is hard to deny the presence of this strong propensity in the Apocalypse, in particular because it is also present in works both already traditional and contemporary with John (see, e.g., Isa 26:20 [LXX]; *2 Bar.* 20:1; *1 Enoch* 51:2; *4 Ezra* 8:18, 61; 14:18; Mark 13:20; Luke 22:28; Heb 10:37).

1:4 ἑπτά. It is no longer tenable to argue that in the first century the number "seven" indicates perfection (see Yarbro Collins 1984). The power of the number "seven" to indicate the completeness of that to which it refers is often linked to chronological phenomena because of its obvious connection to the number of days in a week. In the Apocalypse it is probable that some groups of seven serve symbolically to represent the division of human history in its entirety into seven stages, or at least to the occurrence of seven successive events or periods. Some scholars hold that the "seven churches" themselves represent seven stages of salvation history, while others firmly reject this interpretation and maintain instead that the seven messages to the seven churches do not even represent a real "septet" (see the comments on 5:1).

There have been innumerable attempts to explain why the churches are seven in number, and why these particular churches and not others are mentioned. Some of these explanations rest on reasonable and restrained hypotheses about seven Christian communities actually known to John, situated in a confined area and connected by a good system of Roman roads that made it possible to send the letter to multiple destinations (this is the thesis defended by Ramsay 1909). There are also a number of rather farfetched explanations. An examination of the contemporary map of Turkey has led some to conclude that John uses the seven cities to construct a kind of "geographical menorah" — that the cities correspond to the seven lamps of a huge, imaginary, seven-branched lampstand. It is not plausible that John, in the 1st century, had access to a map, or that he could conceivably have come up with such a concept as he moved, most likely on foot, from place to place across Asia. In any case, it seems to me that John took little interest in the geographical aspect of this transitory earth. I would suggest instead that John mentions seven churches precisely for the purpose of having seven angels to whom he can write, in keeping with the model of prophetic behavior found in the Enochic tradition (see the comments on 1:20 and 2:1). We have no way of knowing whether John chose only seven churches from among many possibilities for symbolic purposes, or whether he was personally familiar with these particular churches, and judged them to be the only ones in need of messages from Christ. If the latter possibility is correct, then the fact that there were seven of them — as many as there are fallen angels — must have struck him as significant, and have increased the urgency with which he felt he must intervene.

ἀπὸ ὁ ὤν. It seems that what we have here is an instance of ἀπό with the nominative. We can also suppose that since he is dealing with a divine attribute John uses the expression as a formula, as seems to be the case with "one similar to a son of man" in 1:13. The divine attribute "who is and who was and who is coming" appears three times in the Apocalypse, in 1:4 and 8, and in 4:8, with the order of the terms changed. A similar formula, but with two terms, appears in 11:17 (see commentary ad loc.) and 16:5. Most English translations soften the syntactical harshness of the Greek, which puts the three grammatically different terms in syntactical parallel: literally, "the Being and the He Was and the Coming." In the Hebrew Bible there are several occurrences of finite verbal forms preceded by the article. It seems reasonably clear that John's intended meaning is expressed exactly by the standard English translation; nonetheless, the Johannine phrase must have looked rather ponderous to a cultivated Greek.

τῶν ἑπτὰ πνευμάτων. The presence of the definite article might be taken to suggest that John was counting on his readers and hearers already knowing what he was talking about. Alternatively perhaps he meant to say by antonomasia that these are "the seven spirits." The context suggests that John is developing some kind of (pre-)Trinitarian thinking, as he refers to God, in the formula discussed above, to a spiritual reality, and to Jesus Christ. It is typically maintained that the seven here is indicative of the totality, perfection, and fullness of the Spirit. Seven, however, is not the only number used to indicate the totality of something (Yarbro Collins 1984; see above). As angels appear in groups of seven, or of four, or alone, or in myriads, it would seem that when John speaks of "seven angels" he is referring not to the totality of them but to one of their functions (see Lupieri 1990, n. 48; see 4:5 for an attempt to explain the number). Many of the beings who appear in groups of seven are angelic beings, either faithful or rebellious; perhaps the fact that there are seven spirits is the result of John's reflection on the angelic nature of the Spirit. It would not be surprising to find an angelic or angelomorphic pneumatology in a text of this date (Gieschen 1994 and 1995). The spirits are, however, carefully distinguished from Jesus Christ; see 5:6 for their relationship with him. There appears to be a deliberate contrast between these seven spirits and the three spirits sent forth by the Satanic triad in 16:13. Finally, there is a list of seven spirits in *1 Enoch (BS)* 61:11; here the seven spirits appear to describe the "spiritual qualities" of angels and saints.

ἃ ἐνώπιον . . . αὐτοῦ. The connection between the seven spirits, or the Spirit, and the throne, is emphasized throughout the book (see, e.g., 4:5), and indeed, if I am correct in my interpretation, this connection, which reappears at the close of the book, with the "river of the water of life . . . coming forth from the throne," constitutes a motif of the entire book. The throne thus makes its first appearance here in the context of a theological reflection within which the divinity seems to be understood in Trinitarian terms. We have, in fact, he who sits on the throne, the seven spirits, and Jesus Christ. What does John's decision to introduce the throne in this context tell us about his understanding of its nature? What is its function, and why are the spirits in front of it? We can find valuable clues in the bewildering landscape of Jewish mystical traditions, whose existence in the first century can by now be regarded as an established fact (Scholem 1960; Gruenwald 1980; Halperin 1988). The throne, which is also the chariot in Ezekiel and later Jewish mysticism, is not merely a divine seat that the visionaries perceive on the model of earthly kings' thrones. It is, rather, an extremely powerful angelic being, of manifold and at times monstrous attributes, at once dazzling and terrifying. It is the first perceptible manifestation of the God who cannot be described by humans (he who "sits on the throne"). Inasmuch as the throne represents the transcendent God's self-projection into immanence, it can be seen as equivalent to the *shekinah,* God's presence or indwelling in the created world. Even the creation could, indeed, be said to proceed from it more or less directly because what comes from it really comes from God (see the commentary on 4:6 and 22:3).

1:5 τῆς γῆς. The term γῆ appears over eighty times, making it one of the most common words in the *Apocalypse.* There is a rather difficult ambiguity to the term: it is not always clear what γῆ refers to. At times — almost certainly in this passage, for instance — John is thinking of the entire inhabited earth, or rather of the earth as part of creation, along with the sea and the sky. In other cases he appears to be referring to the land of Israel, the Holy Land that God promised to his people (for such an antonomastic use of the term "land" at Qumran, see 1QM 12:5). The interpretation of entire sections of the book rests on the question of whether John is referring to the whole human world, or to Israel; however, it is often impossible to settle with complete certainty on one or the other possibility (see the comments on 1:7).

1:5-6 Τῷ ἀγαπῶντι . . . ἀμήν. See Gal 1:3-5 for a doxology immediately after the greeting.

1:6 καὶ ἐποίησεν . . . ἱερεῖς. The phrase, and its echo in 5:10, presented a serious syntactical problem even in the ancient world; taken at face value "priests" can be seen as an apposition, probably in the nominative, to "kingdom." It is possible, on the other hand, that John is adhering closely to the Hebrew structure of Exod 19:6, to which this phrase refers, and which signifies "a priestly kingdom." "Kingdom-priests" is how Symmachus and Theodotion also translate into Greek the expression in Exod 19:6. The priesthood of the angels and holy men is emphasized in mystic texts discovered at Qumran: "and they shall be priests, the people of his justice, his army and servants, the angels of his glory" (4QShir^b = 4Q511 fr. 35, 3-4; Baillet 1982, pp. 237-38). "[Because he has established] the most holy ones among the eternal holy ones, and they became priests for him" (4QShirShabb^a = 4Q400 fr. 1, 3; for the connection between angelhood and the priestly and military dimensions of "holy ones," see Newsom 1985, pp. 30-33).

ἀμήν. This term, which has both declarative and exclamatory senses, occurs seven times, in direct discourse, at the beginning or end of a sentence (1:6, 7; 5:14; 19:4, 22:20). On one occasion, in 7:12, it even appears at the beginning and end of the same doxology. In many manuscripts it also appears at the end, as the book's final word in 22:21, although this might be an addition. An eighth occurrence in 3:14, where the word is used as an epithet of Christ — "the Amen" — is certainly original. The number of repetitions — seven and one — does not seem to me to suggest anything: the fact that an isolated term appears seven times, or another number that often carries symbolic significance, does not in itself indicate that the author attaches particular importance or sacredness to that term (e.g., ἄβυσσος, as even Bauckham observes; cf. Bauckham 1993, p. 35). The relative pronoun ὅδε — ἥδε — τόδε also appears seven times, but this indicates only that it is used as a deliberate archaism in the seven opening messages (the formula τάδε λέγει occurs approximately 250 times in LXX; see Acts 21:11).

1:7 Ἰδού. The deictic particle "lo" appears twenty-six times in the Apocalypse. By the time John wrote it had long since lost its ancient sense of the imperative of the verb "to see" or "to look." The use of such expressions as ἰδοὺ ἐγώ, meaning "Here I am!" rather than "Look at me!" (Gen 22:1; Acts

9:10, etc.), clearly tells against the argument that John wants to involve the hearer or reader in the vision by inviting him to "look" or to "see" what is happening. The particle serves simply to indicate the urgency and inevitability of the decision or prophecy. Thus there is no foundation to the commonly heard argument that falsely attributes to ἰδού a heightened degree of significance and thus infers the presence of indemonstrable ecclesiological or psychological implications (see, e.g., Raguse 1993, p. 149 and cross references).

ἔρχεται μετὰ τῶν νεφελῶν. The "clouds" are a very common mode of transportation in apocalyptic texts, including Christian ones (see, e.g., Acts 1:9; *4 Ezra* 13:3; Apoc 11:12). Nonetheless, when a first-century follower of Jesus says that Jesus Christ will come "with" the clouds, we must ask ourselves what he understands the nature of the clouds to be (we should also note that John does not say "on the clouds," as in Matt 24:30 and 26:64, and Dan 7:13 in the LXX, but "with the clouds," as in Mark 14:62 and Dan 7:13 in Theod.). The antecedent of the clouds that accompany a revelation of the divine is the pillar of cloud in Exod 13:21-22 that accompanies the Hebrews in their exodus and that indicates the presence of Yahweh; the pillar is, in fact, Yahweh's angel. In the period and cultural climate in which John wrote, all clouds were probably thought to be in some degree angelic or demonic, and their shape could therefore contain a sign or a message from God or from demons. This becomes relatively apparent in Bar (Ep. Jer.) 6:61 (LXX). The clearest text, however, is perhaps that of *Apoc. Abr.* 14:5, where the heredity of Azazel is said to be "with the stars and with the men born by the clouds." "Stars" and "clouds" are here the fallen angels who united themselves to women according to the myth of the books of *Enoch;* the "men" are the giants whose spirits are actually the devils (see *1 Enoch* 15:8-9). The "clouds," on the other hand, not only "rush" the visionary into heaven but also "call" him (*1 Enoch* 14:8-9). In this context the "clouds" are placed on the same level as "fog," "stars," "lightning," and "winds" (see Bar 6:61 and Introduction, pp. 27-28). In the Christian traditions as well (see Mark 9:7 and parallels), a voice comes from the cloud that represents the presence of God. Thus to say that the Risen One or another superhuman figure "comes with the clouds" is quite similar to saying that he will "come with (his holy) angels" (see Mark 8:38 and Matt 16:27; for the connection between an angelic figure and the cloud see the comments on 10:1).

καὶ οἵτινες. "And all those who"; it is the second part of the subject of "will see."

κόψονται . . . αἱ φυλαὶ τῆς γῆς. This is another ambiguous use of the term γῆ (see the comments on 1:5). John is paraphrasing Zech 12:10, which, in the version known by ancient writers, including John 19:37, reads, "they will look on [me, who am] the one whom they have pierced." MT has, "they will look on me because of him whom they have pierced." Zech 12:12 reads "the land shall mourn, tribe by tribe." This is also the rendering of LXX, although the term translated as "tribe," φυλή, really indicates a clan, midway between a tribe and a family (see Meyers 1993, p. 345). We may note in passing that the land is hypostatized to such a degree that it is capable of mourning by "beating" its breast. The context of Zechariah refers entirely to Jerusalem: the book records both the suffering of the besieged city and the promise of God that his anger will fall on the heads of their enemies when the penitent Jews turn back to him. The person whom they "pierced" is perhaps Gedaliah, assassinated by rebels against the government imposed by Babylon at about 586 BCE (2 Kings 25:22-26), or possibly, as others claim, Zerubbabel. Christian readings, of course, interpret "he whom they [the Jews!] have pierced" as Jesus Christ; the beating of the breast as a sign of mourning in fact occurs in Luke 23:48, immediately after the death of Jesus. Matt 24:30, on the other hand ("and then the sign of the Son of Man will appear in heaven, and then all the tribes of the earth will beat their breasts and will see the Son of Man coming on the clouds of heaven"), transfers this vision to the parousia, and removes any reference to the piercing and death of Jesus — the tribes mourn because of the cosmic disruption of Matt 24:29, not because they witness the passion. The effect is to broaden the significance of γῆ to its universal meaning. The context of the phrase in this verse of the Apocalypse is unique, uniting the suffering of the passion with the triumph of the parousia. It is not fully clear whether "those who pierced him" are the Jews, as distinct from the rest of humanity who are represented by "every eye," or whether the whole of humanity shares responsibility. Likewise it is not fully clear whether the land with its tribes is the Jewish world, as in Zechariah and perhaps Luke, or the whole world. I would prefer a universalistic reading, which renders the text less available to be used in an anti-Jewish way, but I must admit that a reading that makes the distinction between "every eye" and "those who pierced him" does seem to be more consistent with the context and with the biblical tradition from which the passage derives.

1:8 Ἐγώ . . . ὦ. This sentence, with minimal variations, occurs three times: here at the beginning, and twice at the end of the book. It is the self-definition of a divine person who, here and in 21:6-7, seems to be God the Father, and in 22:12-13 seems instead to be the glorified Jesus Christ. The first and last letters of the alphabet (in John's time the last letter was called not *omega* but simply *o*) together indicate that the figure is a spatio-temporal totality and may correspond to "Aeon," αἰών. That this expression appears to designate both the Father and Christ can be accounted for in two ways. In the first place, the phrase is so broad and generic as to be able to indicate two different levels within a unified whole, in such a way as not to exclude the idea of generation being applied to the Son. In the second place, the Risen One could be so fully assumed into the Father that the epithets applied to the one can be smoothly transferred to the other (see comments on 1:17).

1:9 Ἐγὼ Ἰωάννης. This first person interjection by the author marks the end of the preamble and the beginning of the narrative proper, with its account of the beginning of the visions. Scholars who maintain that the Apocalypse is addressed exclusively or primarily to a group of prophets stress the fact that on two other occasions, in 19:10 and 22:9, the term "brother," which appears a total of five times, is used to indicate the brotherhood of prophets. In 12:10, on the other hand, there is nothing to suggest that the brothers accused by the devil are prophets. In view of the reference to John's own share in the "tribulation . . . in Jesus," I would suggest rather that the closest parallel is perhaps in 6:11, where "brothers" and "fellow servants" are the martyrs.

1:10 φωνὴν μεγάλην. The adjective "great" is used more frequently in the Apocalypse than in any other NT book (it is repeated 80 times out of 194 occurrences in the whole NT; in the Gospel of John it appears only five times, in contrast to the frequent use of the comparative adjective μείζων, which does not appear in the Apocalypse). Not only is it John's favorite adjective, but, after articles and prepositions and such verbs as "to be," "to have," or "to say," it is one of the most frequently used words, slightly behind "God" with 95 repetitions, and γῆ with 82 but ahead of "angel" with 67. This cannot be accidental, nor can it be a result only of the poverty of the author's vocabulary (see comments on 1:3). Rather, it is evidence that the word, like the root *rb* in some Semitic mystical literature, is used to indicate a superhuman or spiritual quality in the noun it qualifies. The presence of the adjective indicates that the noun stands apart from the physical sphere of human life. It is not always easy to decide when the adjective does and does not carry this implication, or whether it always does so, but by and large I would say that the Apocalypse is brimming not so much with gigantic beings and deafening shouts as with beings who are superhuman, angelic, spiritual, and thus "great" in comparison to humans (see Acts 8:10). When the adjective qualifies the noun "voice," as it does twenty times in the Apocalypse, it can indicate that the voice comes from heaven, from the throne, or from the temple, or that it is the voice of Christ, or of one or more angels, or of an eagle who might be an angelic creature. It can also be the voice of a crowd: always a heavenly multitude of angels and/or of the saved (7:10; 19:1).

It might be coincidence that the word "voice" is never associated with an act of the forces of evil, although the forces of evil are capable of speech, and even of making the statue of the beast speak in 13:15. I do not think that it is co-incidence, however, that the expression "a great voice" is associated exclusively with the forces of good. What is more, its usage in other books of the NT suggests that the expression must have had a particular significance, at least in certain Christian circles. In Mark it is used to describe the two cries of the dying Jesus, and on two other occasions, the cry of exorcised devils (Mark 1:26; 5:7; 15:34, 37). In Matthew, on the other hand, it is reserved exclusively for the cries of the dying Jesus (Matt 27:46, 50), and it may appear in an apocalyptic context, in variants on 24:31 in which the Son of Man sends "his angels with a trumpet [with a] great [voice]." In John it appears only once, to describe how Jesus calls Lazarus back to life (11:43). Except in Luke and Acts (Paul does not use the expression) it is never used of an ordinary human being.

1:10-11 ὡς σάλπιγγος λεγούσης. Strictly speaking, the participle should refer to the voice and not to the trumpet. However, the parallel with 4:1 suggests that John really intends to say that the voice was like a trumpet speaking to him. In texts with apocalyptic content the trumpet is an important instrument, used to announce the coming of the ἔσχατα (see 1 Thess 4:16 [parousia and resurrection]; 1 Cor 15:52 [resurrection]; Matt 24:31 [probably resurrection in the context of the parousia]; for contemporary Jewish apocalypses see *4 Ezra* 6:23 and *Apoc. Abr.* 31:1). The original of this trumpet must be in the Sinai theophany in Exod 19:16, 19 (see also Heb 12:19) filtered through texts such as Zech 9:14. In the Matthew passage, the trumpet of God seems to be coextensive or merged with the voice of the archangel. The expression usually translated "the sound of a trumpet" in Exod 19, MT is "the voice of a trumpet" *(shofar)*, which is rendered in LXX as φωνὴ/αἱ τῆς σάλπιγγος. It was easy, therefore, to make the shift from a tool of God's manifestation or revelation to his hypostasis or personification. Here and in 4:1 the "trumpet" indicates the way in which the "voice" has chosen to manifest itself, which is why the trumpet can talk.

1:12 βλέπειν τὴν φωνήν . . . μετ᾽ ἐμοῦ. The term "voice" appears over 50 times in the Apocalypse, and numerous parallels to contemporary Jewish apocalypticism suggest that in many cases the term probably refers to a distinct angelic reality, the Voice (Charlesworth 1985). This would explain why John writes of "seeing" a voice, and at times uses masculine forms when referring to the feminine term φωνή: he thinks of the Voice as an angel (see 4:1). The Hebrew Bible contains a similar phenomenon whereby verbs in masculine form are used of angelic beings that are described in nonmasculine terms (Levison 1995, p. 467). Other voices appear to be other angelic beings: individual ones as in 9:13, or ones belonging to specific categories such as thunder and lightning that are also to be considered as angelic beings (see 4:5 and comments, 8:5, 11:19, and 16:18). As for the possible relationship between the Voice and Christ, in *Asc. Isa.* 9:2 and 5 one of the Voices appears to be identified with "your Lord" (for the text see Norelli II 1995, pp. 452-53).

εἶδον ἑπτὰ λυχνίας. I have chosen the literal translation "lampstands" over "candlesticks" or "candelabras" because they (as well as candles) had probably not yet appeared in the Middle East in NT times (candles and candelabras seemingly originated with the Etruscans, and spread through the empire only in the 2nd century). In its simplest form the lampstand is a base with a post to which is attached an oil lamp (see 18:23). This lamp is a terra-cotta or metal pot (with at least one opening), which is filled with oil: the fuel burns, with or without a wick, and sheds light. Lamps and lampstands were generally used indoors (see 4:5). The menorah of Jewish tradition is an elaborate lampstand with seven branches, on which are placed seven lamps: a menorah without branches appears in the vision of Zech 4:2; here John recovers and alters it for the first time. This technique of modifying and adapting earlier prophecies to new realities is characteristic of Jewish apocalypticism: the clearest example may be *4 Ezra* 12:11-12, where the angel explicitly modifies the prophecy by "your brother Daniel" (see also Apoc 19:10 and 22:9). It is no longer possible to determine whether these adaptations are primarily literary or whether they are founded in an ecstatic experience in which the old vision is seen again and modified by the visionary, but the possibilities are not mutually exclusive.

1:13-14 ὅμοιον υἱὸν ἀνθρώπου . . . χιών. John uses the adjective ὅμοιον 21 times, usually following it with a dative. Whenever he uses the expression "similar to a Son of Man," however, "Son" is in the accusative, being attracted into it by "similar." The probable direct source of the scene is Dan 7:13, which reads ὡς υἱὸς ἀνθρώπου (LXX and Theod.). John appears to see the whole phrase as a sort of title that cannot be declined. The description of the figure that John sees is a conflation of elements from various famous visions. The immediate antecedents are Isa 49:2, "[my] mouth like a sharp sword"; Ezek 1:24, "the sound [of their wings] like the sound of mighty [= many] waters" (ὡς φωνὴν ὕδατος πολλοῦ = LXX); cf. 43:2, MT (this is a frequently referenced text; see, e.g., *4 Ezra* 6:17); Ezek 1:26-27, "a likeness as of the image of a" (ὁμοίωμα ὡς εἶδος ἀνθρώπου = LXX), "fire"; Ezek 9:2 and 11 (LXX), "long robe [to his feet]," "[sapphire] belt at his waist"; Dan 7:9, "the hair of his head like pure/white wool," "clothing . . . as white as snow" (= Theod.), "[throne] as a flame of fire"; Dan 7:13, "like a Son of Man"; Dan 10:5-6, "a man . . . belted [around the waist with linen]," "his waist belted with gold of Uphaz" (Theod.), "his eyes like flaming torches," "his feet like blazing bronze" (ἐξαστράπτων = LXX), "his legs like a vision of burnished bronze" (στίλβοντος = Theod.), "his voice . . . like the voice of a roar" (Theod., "multitude"); *1 Enoch* 14:20-22, "[his cloak] . . .

brighter than the sun . . . whiter than snow," "flame of fire"; *1 Enoch* 46:1 *(BS),* "his head was white like wool," "[his] face was like the appearance of a man"; Judg 5:31, "may those who love him be like the sun as it rises in its powers" (see Matt 17:2, "and his face shone like the sun," said of Jesus at the transfiguration; cf. also *2 Enoch* 1:5 and *4 Ezra* 7:97 on angelic entities).

1:14 οἱ ὀφθαλμοί . . . πυρός. In both apocalyptic and Jewish mystical traditions the visionary often meets a person or persons whose eyes are terrifying to behold. We will return repeatedly to the role of fire in theophany; for the present we need only remark that in a world far removed from modern scientific knowledge, fire was difficult to explain. It can appear to be divine, spiritual or angelic, depending on the context and the religious environment. Bar (LXX) (Ep Jer) 6:59-61 records the fire as an angelic being like the sun, moon, stars, lightning, wind, and clouds, which, like them, is obedient to God.

1:15 οἱ πόδες . . . πεπυρωμένης. Here the "orichalcum" should be an alloy of gold and copper. The idea of precious metal being purified in a fire comes from Ps 12:7 and is well supported (Hodayot [1QH–4QH] 13:16). John does not appear to be quoting directly from any known source (Dan 10:6, which itself is a literal reprise of Ezek 1:7, has "like a vision [lit. an eye] of burnished bronze"). Having just spoken of a flame of fire in reference to the eyes of the figure in the vision, he wants to reaffirm the presence of fire even down to his feet and therefore uses the participle of the verb πυρόω, "to burn," a derivative of πῦρ, "fire," an image that is absent in the immediate source (see also 14:19). The translation "as in a furnace with fired orichalcum" is an attempt to translate ὡς ἐν καμίνῳ πεπυρωμένης. I suppose that the verbal participle, which is a feminine genitive, cannot refer to "furnace," which is feminine dative in Greek. The nearest feminine noun in the text is "orichalcum," and I think it may be implied here. Therefore, I have translated the sentence as if it were ὡς ἐν καμίνῳ χαλκολιβάνου πεπυρωμένης.

1:16 ῥομφαία δίστομος (see Introduction, p. 41, n. 142). Two cutting weapons are mentioned in the Apocalypse: the ῥομφαία, a long sword that usually issues from the mouth of a superhuman personage, and the μάχαιρα, a short saber or dagger (see 6:4 and comments on 6:8); they are different weapons used in different types of combat.

ἡ ὄψις . . . φαίνει. The sentence is grammatically ambiguous, as the subject of the verb could be either "face" or "sun." The comparison of the face of the Risen One with the sun implies that while God's brightness is greater and different than the sun's, John can find no better analogy. The phrase is probably a deliberate prefiguration of the affirmation that Christ will be the only "sun" or "bright star" in the New Jerusalem (see comments on 21:11, 23; 22:16).

1:17 ἔπεσα. It is common in visionary literature for the seer to fall or throw himself to the ground, overwhelmed by the vision of divine reality (Ezek 1:28; Dan 8:17 and 18; 10:9; *1 Enoch* 14:14 and 24-25). The exhortation "Do not be afraid" is also normal (it is repeated many times in Isa 41–44, and often reused as in *1 Enoch* 15:1). Falling "at his feet" is a sign of veneration, which in this case is not rejected (see Matt 28:9-10). The closest parallel in a non-Christian source is perhaps in *T. Abr.* 9:1-3 (rec. A), which includes the details "fell at [his] feet" and "as one dead"; here also the archangel Michael, the object of the visionary's veneration, does not reject the gesture. It is almost impossible to assign a date to the redaction of *Testament of Abraham,* which can be seen as a polemical response to the Christian claims to adore Christ; it is unlikely that a Christian author would propose the worship of Michael except inasmuch as he was identified with Christ by virtue of being an archangel and commander of the heavenly army. The same could be said of *2 Enoch* 1:7-8, in which Enoch adores two angelic beings who accept his worship and exhort him not to fear. The atmosphere, however, is that of *Ascension of Isaiah,* in which the two highest angelic princes, the Beloved, that is, Christ, and the angel of the Spirit, accept the adoration of all inferior angels and of Isaiah, who is set on a level with the angels of the seventh heaven (see 9:27-36). *Ascension of Isaiah* has a rigid angelic hierarchy, ordered in accordance with the spheres of the heavens, within which the lower angels are permitted to adore their superiors; only the Beloved and the angel of the Spirit who is his subordinate receive universal adoration, inasmuch as they are the only ones to adore God directly, and are, in fact, able to sit on the left and right of "the Great Glory" (see 9:40 and 11:32-33; R. G. Hall addressed this topic in Hall 1995; for the superangelic nature of the Beloved, who only at times assumes the "form of an angel," see Simonetti 1983, pp. 185-209, especially p. 192, and Acerbi 1989, pp. 195-209; for the Spirit/Angel of the Spirit see Norelli 1983). Similar themes occur in a slightly different context in *4 Ezra* 10:30. On seeing the vision of the heavenly Jerusalem Ezra falls down "like a corpse"; the angel Uriel responds to his call, takes his right hand, and sets him on his feet.

ὁ πρῶτος καὶ ὁ ἔσχατος (see 2:8). As 22:13 shows, this corresponds to "Alpha and Omega" in 1:8 and 21:6. Inasmuch as he is the beginning and the end (21:6 and 22:13), Christ presents himself not only as the origin of creation (see 3:14) but also as its goal or *telos.* His absolute priority over all creation is probably demonstrated by his resurrection and enthronement (for the resurrection see 1:5 and the variants in ms. A in 1:17 and 2:8; for the enthronement see the many parallels in the Pauline corpus: Eph 1:20-23; Phil 2:6-11; Col 1:15-20). These words open the discourse of Christ that continues until 3:22.

1:18 τὰς κλεῖς . . . τοῦ ᾅδου. The presence of keys in Christ's hand establishes his power over the entities he names, as will become evident in 20:1.

The theme of God's dominion over the forces of evil pervades the entire text, offering to believers a sense of security to balance the distressing visions of blood that also permeate the Apocalypse (see comments on 2:1 and 9:1 for the binding of angelic figures more or less closely identified with the forces of evil). It is certain that Death and Hades are personified, or rather hypostatized as superhuman and therefore angelic figures; only thus can Death be given the authority, as he is in 6:8, to "kill . . . with death." That Hades is hypostatized in *Apoc. Abr.* 10:11 and addressed in both OT prophetic and Pauline texts is testimony to the continuity of the phenomenon in the Jewish world (Hos 13:14; 1 Cor 15:55). It is worth noting in passing that Hosea addresses both Death *(mwt)* and Hades *(š'wl)* while Paul speaks only of Death, and attributes to it the "sting" (thus possibly implying that he envisages it as a scorpion similar to the monsters of Apoc 9:10) that Hosea attributes to Sheol (see comments on 12:2).

1:19 γράψον οὖν . . . μετὰ ταῦτα. The relationship between the three things John is told to write is far from simple. The most common, and probably the best, interpretation is that "the things that you saw" refers to the entirety of the visions and auditions contained in the book (or, perhaps better, to the seven stars and the seven lampstands that already spiritually contain within themselves the content of the whole book), whereas "the things that are" and "the things that are to take place" refer to the apocalyptic meaning of the things he saw. It follows that John conceived of the book as being subdivided into two parts: a vision of what is, that is to say, the historical situation of the seven churches he addresses in the initial chapters, and a vision of what is to take place, from 4:1 to the end. While this is likely the most correct interpretation, we must note that even the letters to the churches foresee future events such as the promises to the victor, and that the second and longer part of the book contains references to events that occurred before John's time; see, for instance, 11:8: "where also their Lord was crucified." The compactness of the text, which the author planned deliberately and emphasizes by his continual use of internal references, mediates against tidy divisions.

1:20 μυστήριον. The term "mystery," here and in 17:7, indicates that the reality perceived by John has a profound meaning of a sort that we would term "allegorical" and that John himself probably would have referred to as "spiritual" (see 11:8). A revelation from a superhuman source is needed to enable the visionary to understand what he is seeing. On this occasion the explanation comes from a person with divine characteristics, while in 17:7 it clearly comes from an angel, specifically one of the seven angels who bear the seven bowls in 17:1. For an apocalyptic writer of the first century what we call allegory is not a method of interpretation that goes beyond the letter of the text but is rather the very heart of a religious revelation — so much so that the Vg. translates the Greek μυστήριον in both passages as *sacramentum*. An allegorical interpretation is not a meaning added by the exegete, but is rather implicit in the vision itself: it is, in fact the true meaning of the vision, which the visionary himself did not know, and for which an "apocalypse" is therefore necessary. Thus what John says here must be of particular significance for him and for the structure of the entire book (see comments on 17:1, 5, 7).

ἐπὶ τῆς δεξιᾶς μου. The expression must be a calque from the Hebrew and mean "in my right hand," and therefore "in my power." The heavenly being who is speaking here has the seven angels in his power and thus may not himself be an angel like them, not even the first among them, as all seven appear to be inferior to him and under his dominion. Behind the scene are traces of the Enochic model of seven sinful angels in chains and at the mercy of God or of his archangel (see *1 Enoch* 10:4, 13; 21:3).

οἱ ἑπτὰ ἀστέρες . . . ἑπτὰ ἐκκλησίαι εἰσίν. This is the first time in the book that the contents of a revelation are explained. "The things that you saw" are stars and lampstands; the reality of what they "are" is angels and churches — the true meaning of John's vision. Angels are not a symbol of the stars (see Introduction, pp. 26-27), but the stars, rather, are both the manifest form of angels in the visible world and their symbol within the vision. The stars stand in the same relation to the angels as the lampstands stand to the churches. That a lampstand, possibly a golden one, could serve as the symbolic representation of a human being before God, possibly in prayer, can be deduced by comparing this passage to the two lampstands of 11:4; they represent the Johannine gloss on the "lampstand all of gold" in Zech 4:2, which in its turn is probably a prophetic gloss on Exod 25:31-40 (see also 37:21-24 and Lev 24:2-4). The Exodus text contains the commands that God gives to Moses about the preparation of the golden menorah for the temple, and underlines the fact that this was made in accordance with the model shown to Moses on the mountain (Exod 25:40). There is thus a heavenly menorah by the side of God that is a central object of Jewish mystical meditation and speculation and that becomes the heavenly symbol of Israel. Lev 24:2-4 emphasizes not only the purity of the cultic object but also the fact that the flames of the seven lamps must always be lit "before the Lord." The lighted menorah is, in fact, Israel at prayer. The unity of the menorah appears to John to be divided into the seven churches, which in their turn represent a unity, whether spatial, temporal, or mystical. Whatever the case, we learn from *ShirShabb* that all the elements of the heavenly temple are living, praying, spiritual beings. In light of this the Johannine connection between the lampstands and the churches appears less farfetched (see comments on 3:12).

The text also suggests, if somewhat less explicitly, yet another parallel: the stars stand in the same relationship to the lampstands as the angels to the churches. Stars and lampstands are intrinsically similar inasmuch as both are associated with light. The stars are sources of spiritual light in the heavens, and these lampstands, although the text does not tell us that they hold lighted lamps, should be the golden and spiritual support of lamps that burn perpetually before God. We can go so far as to say that the seven stars correspond in some way to the seven lamps that we must imagine on the seven lampstands. Maybe the lamps are not explicitly mentioned because they are spiritually represented by the stars. If the seven angels are the angels of the churches, then the seven stars would represent the spiritual light that flows from the seven celestial lampstands (in Josephus [*J.W.* 5(5.5).217] the seven lamps on the menorah in the temple represent the planets). According to this interpretation the angels/stars would represent the spiritual light of the churches/lampstands. If this is the case, then the angels/stars are on the one hand the luminous product of the lampstands and on the other the lampstands' true spiritual nature. In a spiritually stratified world to which an angelomorphic interpretation is applied, and in which every figure represents a level, a reflection of another reality, every earthly church has a lampstand that stands as its own celestial counterpart, and has, or is, also an angel, who, in its turn, appears as a star. The presence, therefore, of angels of the churches derives from apocalyptic patterns of thought (see, e.g., the church as an angelomorphic figure in *Vis.* 2-4 of the *Shepherd of Hermas* with the "explanation" offered in 3.78[*Sim.* 9.1].1-3; Gieschen 1994 and 1995, pp. 238-54). It does not by itself imply the existence of an established hierarchical episcopacy such that the angel is the heavenly counterpart of an earthly pastor, although the existence of the angel could support such an interpretation (see comments on 17:9). The "sevenness" of the angels is a common concept, not only in the Enochic traditions (*1 Enoch* 20; 81:5; 87:2; 90:21; *3 Enoch* 17–18) but also elsewhere, as in *T. Levi* 8:2 and at Qumran, where all of *ShirShabb* describes multiple angelic hierarchies based on the number "seven" (see Newsom 1985, pp. 34-35).

2:1 Τῷ ἀγγέλῳ . . . γράψον. John, a human being, acts as an intermediary between the divine sphere, represented by the Risen One, and a group of angels, to whom he sends messages dictated by Christ. At this point in time it would not seem absurd that a human being might receive a charge from God to address angels, especially fallen angels (see *Apoc. Abr.* 14:5-8 and Introduction, p. 23). This message is *written*, however, which makes the visionary a "divine scribe," and thus the closest antecedent is the episode recounted in *1 Enoch* 12:3–14:7 and 15:1–16:3, where the angels who have remained faithful, acting under orders from God, call Enoch and send him to announce to the sinful and fallen Watchers their condemnation and punishment. The Watchers charge Enoch to write a prayer of supplication and to present it to God; Enoch, through dreams and visions, makes contact with God, who replies in the negative and leaves no hope for the fallen angels. The text even remarks that it should be they who intercede for humans, and not vice versa (15:2; see *2 Enoch* 7:4-5). The divine reproach, called "words of justice," that Enoch is commanded to pass on to "the Watchers of heaven" forms the content of Enoch's book. The analogy with imperial bureaucratic practices might make the idea that God would avail himself of the services of a scribe by ordering him to write seem normal (see Ezra 1:1 and Dan 12:4). On the other hand, it would also have been conceivable that prophetic oracles be directed to the angels. This is the case in Ezek 28:1-19, in which the archon-prince of Tyre could be considered a fallen angel, a cherub, one of the "Elohim" who were cast down to earth (see comments on 2:13). The detail of a written message destined for an angelic rather than a human audience comes from the Enochic tradition. John seems to be presenting himself as the Christian heir of Enoch, the "scribe of righteousness" (see *1 Enoch* 12:4; 15:1, etc.; for the difference from the Enochic tradition, see comments on 2:5).

ὁ κρατῶν . . . ἀστέρας. The verb κρατέω can be used to indicate placing in chains (7:1; 20:1-2), a characteristic punishment for angels, who can, however, be released (see 9:14). In Jewish apocalyptic traditions it is usually another angelic being, a prince or archangel, acting under orders from God, who imprisons or binds or releases the angels (in *1 Enoch* 10:4 it is Raphael; in *1 Enoch* 10:12, Michael; in *Apoc. Abr.* 10:10-11 it is Iaoel, etc.; see also variants in the manuscripts of Jude 5). In *3 Enoch* we see Metatron, like a master of ceremonies in the celestial court, clapping his hands to direct all the angels-stars to leave the firmament and ascend like flames "to the four sides of the throne of the chariot." The reference is presumably to the moment in the morning when the stars disappear from the sky — to return to prayer before God (see Introduction, p. 24, and *3 Enoch* 46:1-4). This dominion over the stars strengthens the implication that the risen Christ is identified with the Prince of angels (see 1:18). At least once, however (*1 Enoch* 18:16), this power is attributed directly to God, although the expressions used in the text do not exclude the possibility that God could have acted by means of angels.

2:5 πόθεν πέπτωκας. John uses the word "fall" over 20 times, 9 times to indicate a gesture of adoration (see comments on 1:17) and the rest with reference to the fall of cities, of stars, or of angelic beings (see comments on 17:10).

Here he describes as fallen the first of the seven angels to whom the Risen One sends his written messages by means of John. The text deliberately refers to the model of the epistolary exchange between God and the fallen angels that appears in *1 Enoch*. In the Apocalypse, however, the messages contain not only reproaches and threats but also invitations to conversion. The possibility of fallen angels repenting and thus being forgiven and attaining salvation must have been thoroughly discussed in Jewish apocalyptic circles, where it was linked to the intercessory activity of Enoch. That the idea is rejected repeatedly within the Enochic texts (see *1 Enoch* 12:4–14:7 and *2 Enoch* 7:4-5) only serves to demonstrate that there were groups with varying ideas on the subject, as we now know from the rediscovered fragments of the *Book of Giants* (see Introduction, p. 15, n. 46).

2:6 τὰ ἔργα τῶν Νικολαϊτῶν. See 2:15: τὴν διδαχὴν [τῶν] Νικολαϊτῶν (maybe "of some Nicolaitans"). We do not know who these Nicolaitans were, nor what their teaching was, let alone what their works were. They were almost certainly followers of a Nicholas, but the identification of this Nicholas with the Hellenist deacon, a proselyte of Antioch mentioned in Acts 6:5, is completely hypothetical. The enemies of the visionary of Patmos, who can be glimpsed in the seven opening letters, appear to belong to different categories. There are those who follow "the teachings of Balaam," and those who accept those of Jezebel: both groups have in common that they eat animals sacrificed to idols and engage in fornication (see 2:14, 20-24). This suggests that they are probably Jewish Christians who have ceased to observe Jewish practices, probably on principles similar to those of Paul, and who seem to John to have compromised too much with paganism (see comments on 2:14). Then there are those who "say they are Jews" but in reality are "a synagogue of Satan" (see 2:9; 3:9); these must be observant Jews, possibly not even followers of Jesus (see comments on 2:9). It might well be simply coincidence that the Nicolaitans are mentioned next to the followers of Balaam, and it is not necessary to insist that the Nicolaitans were Hellenizers. Nonetheless, it is intriguing that they are mentioned twice by name in a text that makes so few references to names and to human individuals. The name could be a cover for groups of Hellenizing Jewish Christians who had "fallen" into positions that John found unacceptable. Certainly John was writing to combat both those who were too Jewish and those who were too Hellenistic, but it might be significant that there are both seven churches and angels whom he addresses and seven so-called "deacons" among whose number was Nicholas; in this case the deacons would have been seen as the human representatives of the churches of Hellenizing Jewish Christians (see comments on 17:9). John would have been familiar with the same traditions as those underlying Acts, or possibly even with the text itself, and would have seen a correspondence between the seven heads of the Hellenistic churches and the seven fallen angels.

2:7 Ὁ ἔχων οὖς ... ταῖς ἐκκλησίαις. This sentence is repeated in exactly this form seven times, contributing to the strong parallel between the letters that is immediately evident on a first encounter with the text. In the first three letters this sentence is followed by a promise to the victor, while in the last four letters the promise immediately precedes the exhortation to listen. The connection between the two thus appears to be deliberate, although it is not clear whether what the Spirit says is actually the promise to the victor. In the last four letters, in fact, references to the Father and to the name of the speaker (2:28; 3:5, 12, 21) make it plain that the promise comes from Jesus Christ. The distinction between the Son and the Spirit is quite plain here after having been stated explicitly in 1:4-5, where we first encountered the seven spirits that we have interpreted as being the fullness of the Spirit revealing himself to man: the different ordering of the seven promises could be an indication of this distinction. In the first three letters the promises do not contain explicit references to the Son as the subject, and thus they appear to be pronounced by the Spirit, whereas in the last four the text of the promises is itself like a continuation of the message dictated in the first person by the Risen One. Nonetheless, in these latter cases in particular the entire letter appears to be pronounced by the Spirit. The mediation of the Spirit thus seems to be an integral part of the act of communication that is the book's *raison d'etre*. The relationship between the action of the Spirit in this regard and that of the angel of Jesus Christ, who first appears in 1:1, still needs to be discussed and clarified. If Jesus Christ is at this stage already enthroned, and if the Spirit proceeds from the throne (see comments on 4:5), then it follows that the Spirit also proceeds from Jesus Christ, at least as regards his mission among men (see comments on 5:6); this is consistent with the teaching on the Paraclete in John (see in particular John 14:26).

φαγεῖν ... τῷ παραδείσῳ. The Greek term ξύλον, like the corresponding Hebrew term, can mean both "wood" and "tree." The phrase is a reference to Gen 3:22, where God forbids the fallen Adam to eat from the tree of life to prevent him from living forever. What was forbidden to Adam is here promised to the victor; this reversal of human destiny is the result of the salvific death of Jesus Christ on the wood of the cross (I have chosen always to translate ξύλον as "wood" to emphasize the connection between the ideas: the tree of life, for Christians, is the wood of the cross; see comments on 22:2, 14). There must have been a centuries-old tradition of Jewish speculation on that mysterious "tree of life" which remained within paradise and which receives no further mention in the Pentateuch after its sudden and unexpected appearance in Gen 3:22. Besides a possible reference to it in Ezek 47:12 (see comments on 22:2), the tree of life is certainly exalted in the apocalyptic literature of the Enochic tradition (*1 Enoch* 24:4; *2 Enoch* 8:3) and in the wisdom tradition. Prov 3:16ff. actually identify the tree of life with Wisdom, in line with the Christian reflection that connects the tree of life to the tree of the cross, to Wisdom, and thus to Christ.

As regards the texts closest to John, in *4 Ezra* 7:53 (123) the prophet laments the destiny of sinful humanity, and the health-giving fruit that is shut in paradise, which is unattainable; he then learns that the tree of life was planted precisely for him and for those like him. Here also, then, the tree of life appears as one of the eschatological gifts for the righteous elect of God (*4 Ezra* 8:52). In *The Life of Adam and Eve* 28:4 the resurrected Adam eats from the tree of life to attain immortality. While speculations about the tree of knowledge are preserved in the legends about Adam and Eve, and emerge into literature from time to time (see, e.g., *La Queste del Saint Graal* 211-19), such speculation tends to fade into the background in the great Jewish and Christian mystical traditions (it does not even appear in the Apocalypse) as the tree of knowledge has already completed its function in the history of mankind, and even made men, to some degree, "like God" (Gen 3:22). These traditions focus instead on the tree of life, whose power to give eternal life was fruitful ground for speculation.

2:8 ἐγένετο . . . ἔζησεν. The expression parallels that in 1:18 and must have been common in primitive Christianity; there is also a close echo in Rom 14:9. The contrast between death and life, which provides a particularly effective summary of the story of Jesus, can easily be extended to apply to the life of the faithful, for whom it has a spiritual meaning (see Luke 15:32 and, with a characteristically Pauline edge, 2 Cor 4:11; 6:9; Gal 2:19; see also 3:1 and comments on 13:3). John hints at this application nearby in v. 10, where he says that believers' fidelity unto death will win them the crown of life.

2:9 συναγωγὴ τοῦ σατανᾶ. This is one of the expressions that has contributed most to discussions of anti-Judaism or anti-Semitism in the Apocalypse (see 3:9). However, I am inclined to see this verse as evidence that John considers himself to be a true Jew, and thus thinks that his followers should consider themselves to be true Jews (see the Introduction, p. 35, n. 114). If this is the case, then we are dealing not with anti-Judaism nor still less with anti-Semitism: the issue is rather the bitter confrontation between contemporary Jewish groups. The sectarian self-identification of a particular group — those followers of Jesus who are in sympathy with John — leads its members to contrast themselves radically to the rest of the religion of which they still consider themselves to be a part. The Dead Sea Scrolls contain numerous, similarly harsh expressions — "son of deceit," "wicked priest," "maggots' assembly," "spat saliva," "molded clay," "sons of Belial," "sons of darkness," etc. (see especially 1QS 9:20-22) — which are directed against priests, Pharisees, and other Jews in general, and show that religious disputes within the Judaism of the period could provoke considerable *animus*. If all the Jews outside of a particular group are regarded by the members of that group as "sons of Belial" — that is, of Satan (see John 8:44; 1 John 3:10) — it stands to reason that their synagogue would also be perceived as an assembly of Satan. In the *Hymns (Hodayot)* there is the similar expression "assembly of Belial" (1QH–4QH 10:22); here the term for assembly is the one normally used by the Essenes to indicate the gatherings of their own community (while John introduces a distinction between the church and the synagogue). The other Jews, whom the sectarians regard as apostate, meet in assembly like the "holy ones," but their assembly is now Satanic. Thus anti-Semitism is not an issue; the reader or hearer of the text is himself a Jew and is by no means encouraged to entertain anti-Jewish sentiments; rather, he must accept this radical phraseology as expressing the sense of being the only one in possession of the truth as well as by the frustration of not being listened to by those he considers his own.

"Satan" is named eight times in the Apocalypse, always preceded by the article — "the Satan" — even where the term appears to be used as a proper name and in parallel to devil, which has no article (12:9; 20:2).

2:10 ἡμερῶν δέκα. This reference to a period of time — the first in the book — is mysterious. The phrase is usually understood to indicate a brief period, in order to encourage the reader or hearer. But while the text undeniably has a hortatory dimension, the presence of the term "days" does not necessarily point either to brevity or to extension — after all, for God a thousand years are like a day (Ps 90:4). More important is the significance of the number "ten." John uses the number only in chs. 12, 13 and 17, and always to refer to the number of "horns" (and in one case of "diadems") of a Satanic beast; in the last of these cases the ten horns are interpreted as being ten kings. The number thus appears to be connected with negative and persecuting forces, while the references to kings and diadems recall the political dimension and manifestation of evil. Thus there appears to be an internal pattern behind John's choice of the number, since the agents in question also have the power to imprison and thus seem to possess some form of political authority. Inasmuch as the number "ten" is also used to designate a totality, it follows that the period in question, regardless of whether it is short or long, represents the whole of the persecution.

τὸν στέφανον τῆς ζωῆς. It is common in apocalyptic literature to represent eternal rewards in terms of clothes, crowns, and thrones, which are connected with light, life, and glory (see, e.g., *Asc. Isa.* 8:26; 9:11-13, etc.). The Qumran community envisaged this kind of reward for the just (i.e., for the Essenes) arriving at the moment of the "visitation" of God, when the reign of injustice was ended (1QS 4:6-8 and 18-19; see comments on 3:11).

2:11 ἐκ τοῦ θανάτου τοῦ δευτέρου. John, as he frequently does, introduces a new concept — in this case the second death — without explaining its significance. The reader or hearer understands from the immediate context that this is not physical death — for this see 12:11 — because it is precisely thanks to physical death that he can expect to receive the crown of life. The life in question, therefore, must be a spiritual life. To it is contrasted the second death, which, in its turn, is distinguished both temporally and conceptually from physical death. The explanation is given only at the close of the book (20:6, 14; and see 21:8). On the "second death" see also *Pirqe R. El.* 34 (18a.4; IV:830-31 and Strack III/2:1177).

2:13 ὁ θρόνος τοῦ σατανᾶ. This is one of only three points in the whole text at which a throne does not constitute a mark of a positive being (see also 13:2; 16:10). Most likely John intends to emphasize the royalty, albeit terrestrial and transitory, of the spiritual force that opposes God. This particular throne of Satan established at Pergamum, the center of the Roman province of Asia, is generally believed to indicate the seat of Roman political power, or, more likely, a particular center of the imperial pagan cult that flourished in Pergamum (see Ramsay 1909, pp. 281-315). In any case, the connection to pagan idolatry is clear (see Ezek 28:2; for medieval legends of the king of Tyre transformed into a Satanic figure and seated on his throne, see Halperin 1988, pp. 241-47), as is demonstrated also by a Qumranic fragment that reads, "upon the throne of evil and upon the heights" (4QBeat [4Q525] fr. 4, 2:2).

2:14 τὴν διδαχὴν Βαλαάμ ... Ἰσραήλ. The long account in Num 22–24 of Balaam, who is sent by the Moabite king Balak to curse the Israelites but ends up blessing them instead, had been retold many times in such a way as to underline Balaam's evil (see Num 31:8, 16; Deut 23:5-6; Josh 13:22; 24:9; Judg 11:25; Neh 13:2, and, finally, Pseudo-Philo, *Lib. Ant. Bib.* 18:13-14). Apart from this passage the "road of Balaam" (2 Pet 2:15), or his "error," by which is intended his going on the wrong way, is explicitly connected to the "road of Cain" (Jude 11). In the NT such errors are meant to denote the doctrines and practices of Christians who belong to groups that differ from the writer's. The sin of these adversaries is always connected also with the sin of Sodom and Gomorrah (see comments on 11:8) and with some unspecified hostility toward the angels, whose authority they despise or reject and whose glory they slander (2 Pet 2:10; Jude 8). The contexts of both 2 Peter and Jude are deeply informed by an Enochic spirituality that accords considerable importance to the myth of the fallen angels (2 Pet 2:4; Jude 6): Jude 14 refers explicitly to Enoch as a prophet and cites 1 *Enoch* 1:9 as Scripture. In the Apocalypse the sin of the followers of Balaam is linked to the consumption of meat that has been offered to idols; the ancient name has apparently come to be associated with Pauline practices (1 Cor 8–10). The consumption of this meat is then linked to fornication. From the perspective of Jewish observance this connection is obvious: it is conventional in prophetic language for any form of Jewish participation in pagan idolatrous practices to be equated with fornication. To eat meat offered to idols puts the individual in spiritual communion with the pagans who carried out the sacrifice and above all with the devil, the fallen angel behind the pagan deity to whom the animal was offered. Thus to "eat food sacrificed to idols" and to "engage in fornication" can be used almost as synonyms. The rather peculiar notion that Balaam suggested that Balak put scandal before the eyes of the children of Israel finds its explanation in the above-mentioned passage in Pseudo-Philo (*Lib. Ant. Bib.* 18), in which Balaam tells Balak to arrange a line of naked girls along the road that the soldiers of Israel would follow to go into battle, so that they would defile themselves with the women, thus becoming impure and unfit for battle (as explained in Deut 23:11).

2:17 δώσω . . . τοῦ μάννα. While the followers of Balaam prostitute themselves by eating meat sacrificed to idols, those who conquer are promised the hidden manna. While the allusion to the exodus is plain (see Exod 16), nonetheless the precise reference to the *hidden* manna indicates a spiritual reality that remained hidden from fleshly Israel (but see comments on 3:21). The text seems quite close to that of John 6:31-58, where the Johannine Jesus describes himself as the true bread from heaven, thus contrasting himself to the manna and opposing the spiritual interpretation given to it in the exodus. In Jewish tradition manna is considered to be the bread of heaven and the food of angels (Ps 78:24-25; 105:40; Wis 16:20), and in Paul it is a "spiritual food" — πνευματικὸν βρῶμα — probably because it is a prefiguration of Christ. Here, as in John, we glimpse a further depreciation of the biblical manna: the Christian manna, which in the past was hidden, must be Jesus Christ himself, who promises to give himself as food (presumably in the Eucharist) to all who conquer (see comments on 2:28). If, on the other hand, the hidden manna is that which according to Exod 16:33-34 Aaron and his descendants preserved in the ark and which in the legends that grew up around the figure of Jeremiah the prophet hid together with the temple vessels (2 Macc 2:5ff.), then the promise would clearly have an eschatological significance. The Apocalypse, however, makes no reference to the rediscovery of the temple vessels, which, like the temple itself, would probably be useless in the New Jerusalem.

ψῆφον λευκήν. The significance of the "white pebble" is not immediately apparent. The term probably refers to the pebbles used for calculation (the Latin is *calculus;* see comments on 12:6; 13:18), while the stone's whiteness probably indicates that it belongs among the things of God (see comments on 3:4). In this case the pebble would correspond to a number and thus to a letter or to a name, in this case the "new name"; this must be the name of Christ, which is new with respect to the old economy (see Ezek 48:35, where the eschatological city takes the name of Yahweh into its own). This name is written on the white pebble. The practice of names being written or inscribed on stones appears in the description of the ephod, an embroidered apron tied in front and held up by two straps, and of the priestly breastplate (see Exod 28 and 39). The ephod had only two precious stones of onyx on which were written, six to each stone, the names of the twelve patriarchs and tribes (see Exod 28:9-10, 39:8). The breastplate, on the other hand, had twelve stones, set in gold, with the name of a patriarch written on each (see Exod 28:21; 39:14). John apparently means that in the new economy of salvation there is no longer a need for twelve precious stones, but that a simple pebble, albeit white, is all that is necessary for the salvation of the faithful (see comments on 17:4; 18:16; 21:19-20). Thus the manna and the pebble would refer to the same christological reality. The use of the term ψῆφος anticipates the correspondence between names and numbers (see 13:28).

2:20 τὴν γυναῖκα Ἰεζάβελ. It is very difficult to be certain whether this is the actual name of a Christian prophetess (who is either of a radical Pauline school or who in any case disregards the laws of purity and of proper Jewish practice), whether the name is symbolic, or indeed whether the entire presentation of the issue is a sort of parable. I am in agreement with the majority of interpreters, who hold that this verse refers to an actual situation possibly involving a woman who believed herself to have been invested with prophetic powers, and certainly involving a fracture within the community, with the formations of groups and factions as in 2-3 John and Jude. The name could be symbolic since the biblical Jezebel was the pagan wife of the Israelite king Ahab and the enemy of Elijah (see 1 Kings 16–22). As the biblical Jezebel was an idolatrous queen of Israel, she could certainly be called a prostitute in the idiom of prophetic language (see comments on 2:14 for the connection between idolatry and fornication). The only female character in the first three chapters is certainly not presented in a positive light. John emphasizes the point further by referring specifically to Jezebel as a woman, as if to say that the femininity is in itself a negative. The language is particularly hard: she leads astray; her followers are adulterers; her business is prostitution. The speaker, finally, threatens to throw her on a bed and to kill her children with death; that is, perhaps, with the help of Death, already mentioned in 1:18. The violence of the language — rare in the NT — is striking, especially if the speaker is the risen Christ, as is implied by the facts that he has dominion over death and that it is his servants whom Jezebel seduces (see comments on 12:1). John's choice of language and imagery reveals an attitude that today we call sexist and misogynist: Jezebel is the only woman who speaks in the Apocalypse and it is necessary that she be silenced (Pippin 1992, p. 77; but see comments on 22:17). The variant τῆς γυναῖκά σου, "your woman," is very ancient, and is widely diffused within the mss. As the message is addressed to the angel of the church, it might mean that the mainstream community and its leaders are of a party hostile to John, as in the case of 3 John. The translation "you allow . . . to act (freely)" is an explanation of the probably meaning of ἀφεῖς.

2:22   εἰς κλίνην. "in a bed." Some scholars (see Corsini 1983) suggest that the Greek term κλίνη does not mean "bed" but rather "coffin" (or possibly the funerary litter on which the bodies of the deceased were brought to be buried). If this is the case, then there are two kinds of punishments for two kinds of "Christians" in Thyatira: the woman and her children are threatened with death, and those who commit adultery with her, with the "great tribulation" if they do not convert. The first category would probably represent the majority, or at least those with power in the community (especially if we accept the variant "your woman"), and the second, those followers of John who are inclining toward the position of the adversaries, but for whom there is still hope of repentance.

2:24   οὐκ ἔγνωσαν . . . τοῦ σατανᾶ. The presence of ὡς λέγουσιν suggests that this phrase reflects an expression typically used in the teaching that is being condemned. It is probable that the group in question claimed to "know the depths" of the Christian message, and that John added the τοῦ σατανᾶ to show his own understanding of the situation. There has been much discussion as to whether this knowledge in depth (τὰ βαθέα) refers to some esoteric teaching, or whether the phrase is a deliberately critical echo of Pauline language (1 Cor 2:10; cf. Rom 11:33) or of gnostic teaching (see, e.g., Hippolytus, *Adv. haer.* 5.6, ed. Wendland, GCS 3 [1916], p. 78, 3). It seems to be a fairly common expression also in the apocalyptic literature of the period (e.g., 2 *Bar.* 14:8), and its presence at Qumran demonstrates the extent and duration of its usage (1QM 10:17). In any case, given the above-mentioned reference to the teaching of Jezebel, we cannot eliminate the possibility that it is an allusion to Paul.

2:28   δώσω . . . τὸν πρωϊνόν. At first glance it is not evident in what the gift of the morning star consists. The star itself might be Venus, and thus be one of the seven angel-planets. But why is it given to the victor? It is not surprising that the glory of beatitude should put a human being in a position of superiority to the angels (see 1 Cor 6:3). However, a "Luciferian" interpretation of this passage — whereby the Risen One promises victory and dominion over the power of Satan/Lucifer (see Isa 14:12, where the reference is to the "king of Babylon") — would seem to contradict 22:16, where Jesus presents himself as "the bright star of the early morning." This confirms our claims that, on the one hand, when John was writing the initial messages he had in mind not only the general plan but the details of the entire work, and that, on the other hand, he sometimes waits until the very last lines of the book to explain a mysterious phrase that appeared earlier. Once we have ascertained that the morning star is Jesus, we still have to determine what the phrase means. The Risen One promises to give the star-Jesus to the victor; does this mean that the star is a being distinct from the Risen One himself? If it is, then what is the relationship between the two figures? Could there have been, as early as the Apocalypse, an understanding of Christology that clearly divides the two? And, in any case, what does it mean to give Jesus as a prize to the victor? A eucharistic interpretation does not seem appropriate, because in an eschatological context such as we are dealing with here the sacramental dimension is rendered obsolete by the presence of God himself. Perhaps we are dealing with a gradually revealed teaching of John, whereby he proclaims at the beginning of the book that the Risen One promises dominion and victory over Satan/Lucifer, and at the end reveals that this victory consists in being identified with Christ in his obedient death on the cross. Thus the gift from Christ turns out to be the gift of himself (see comments on 22:16).

3:4 ὀνόματα. Here and in 11:13 ("names of men . . . were killed") the term indicates persons (also in Acts 1:15: ὄχλος ὀνομάτων); John is probably thinking of men, as he applies to them the masculine adjective ἄξιοι (see 7:4). This is reinforced by the contrast with 14:4, the only other place where the verb μολύνειν occurs and where it is recorded that the men have not defiled themselves with women, whereas in this passage it is their garments that they have not defiled. If this parallel has any significance, it must be that the clothes are the bodies of the faithful. Throughout the book "clothes" are to be "kept" (16:5) from being "defiled" (3:4), and if they are not yet white or are no longer white they must be "washed" (7:14; 22:14 with the verb πλύνω; 19:13 with βάπτω) or "purified" (variant to 1913); the symbolism is clearly baptismal. This is the first appearance of the expression "white garments." The term ἱμάτια, used in the plural, probably has a generic meaning corresponding to the modern "clothes" and referring to the external, visible garments. The expression "white garment" occurs a total of seven times in the Apocalypse, on six of which occasions it is in the plural. On four occasions the noun is ἱμάτια (3:4, 5, 18; 4:4), and on three it is στολή (6:11; 7:9, 13); there is probably no important difference between the meaning of the two terms, especially not when the plural is used. The adjective "white" occurs fifteen times; besides clothing it qualifies, on three occasions, a horse (6:2; 19:11, 14), as well as wool (1:14), the pebble with the number (2:17), a cloud (14:14), fine linen (19:14), and a throne (20:11). Thus the adjective qualifies a total of seven nouns. When we consider all these occurrences together, and bear in mind in particular that horses, clouds, and thrones are all entities on which heavenly beings are borne, it seems plain that the adjective "white" indicates a positive quality in the object that it describes; a quality that is linked to the divine realm. In 6:11 the "white garment" appears to be a gift from God (the verb is a *passivum divinum*). It is not, however, clear, whether this gift is generic — one of the heavenly rewards of the apocalyptic tradition — or whether it refers rather to a particular entity such as a spiritual body, which serves as a vehicle for the soul after death — an idea with a distant Aristotelian pedigree, which will be taken up and discussed by the Church Fathers. In this passage the expression refers to gifts that are destined by God for human beings. While humans can, obviously, have "garments" while they are alive (3:4), it seems that the "white garments" belong exclusively to the otherworldly dimension, and thus refer to an eschatological event.

3:5 ἐκ τῆς βίβλου τῆς ζωῆς. After the "wood of life" (2:7) and the "crown of life" (2:10) we now encounter the "scroll of life." Only at the end of the book (see in particular 20:12, 15) does it become clear what this is. While the wood is the means by which the faithful are or will be saved, and the crown represents the reward they will receive, the scroll, on which are listed the names of the saved, represents the certainty of salvation for those whose names are recorded and of damnation for all others.

ὁμολογήσω . . . τῶν ἀγγέλων αὐτοῦ. The mutual acknowledgment of God and man occurs in various places in the OT (see, e.g., 1 Sam 2:30). In several places in the NT the phenomenon takes a negative form, such that those who do not acknowledge Christ will not be acknowledged by him (Mark 8:38; Luke 9:26; 2 Tim 2:12) while in other passages both positive and negative aspects are present (Matt 10:32-33; Luke 12:8-9; see *4 Ezra* 13:23). This passage suggests a tripartite celestial structure, consisting of the Son, who is speaking, the Father, and his angels. This motif is present as early as Mark 8:38, which speaks of when "the Son of Man . . . comes in the glory of his Father with the holy angels." Luke repeats this, while Matthew eliminates the angels (Matt 10:32-33; Luke 9:26; 12:8-9). The triad of Son–Father–angels is well established in primitive Christianity (see also Mark 13:32). Insofar as the angels represent the whole of the spiritual dimension as distinct from the Father and the Son, this passage constitutes a pre-Trinitarian speculation.

3:7 ὁ ἔχων . . . Δαυίδ. Here supposedly John revives an ancient prophecy about a steward of King Hezekiah of whom God says that he will place on his shoulder "the key of the house of David: he shall open, and no one shall shut; he shall shut, and no one shall open" (Isa 22:22; there is probably an echo of this also in Matt 16:19 in the promise to Peter). It seems strange that a prophecy about the steward of a king rather than about a king himself should be applied to the Risen One, whose lordship is constantly emphasized. I wonder, therefore, whether this "key of David" might not refer to the legend whereby the biblical king, despite having the keys of the ark in which the Law was kept, did not open it, and thus remained in ignorance (for Qumranic developments see the *Damascus Document* [CD] 5:2 ff.). In this case the implication is that Christ, insofar as he is the Davidic king, has the power to offer definitive revelation. The expression must also have seemed strange to the ancient world, leading some mss. to eliminate "key of David" in favor of the more conventional "key of Hades" (see 1:18).

3:9 διδῶ. "I will offer." The word is a by-form of δίδωμι, which here means: "I am ready/determined to give." The Greek object is a double partitive: "[some] of the synagogue . . . of those who say. . . ." "Those who say" are members of the synagogue. Those who receive the present are the faithful, the "you" in the text. The sentence seems to envision a certain number of conversions from the "synagogue" to the "church."

3:11 ἔρχομαι ταχύ. "I am coming soon." Greek ταχύ may refer to the aspect ("quickly") as well as to the time ("soon") of the action. I think "soon" is the correct translation (see 22:7, 12 and comments to 1:3).

τὸν στέφανόν σου. This is probably a reference to the reward promised in 2:10. As it has been promised to the faithful believer, there is a sense in which it already belongs to him, and may be taken from him. The term στέφανος indicates a crown, which always appears on the heads of positive characters, whether human, angelic, or possibly divine: the faithful (2:10), the twenty-four elders (4:4, 10), the one sitting on the white horse (6:2), the heavenly woman (12:1), the one seated on the white cloud (14:14). The demonic monsters who come out of the abyss have false crowns ("And on their heads were something like crowns, similar to gold": 9:7). It would be consistent with the normal usage of the Greek term for these to be symbols of victory rather than of royalty, for which John uses the term "diadems" (12:3; 13:1; 19:12). When these diadems appear in definite numbers, seven or ten, they are on the heads of Satanic beasts; when, on the other hand, they appear in large but indefinite numbers, they adorn the victorious and regal head of the Logos (19:12).

3:12 στῦλον ἐν τῷ ναῷ. This appears to be a reference to the "spiritual temple" that Christians are called to build and thus to the church, as the reference to the New Jerusalem makes plain. The notion of spiritual pillars refers back to the account in Exod 13:21 of the famous column, cloud by day and fire by night, which is the hypostasis of God's presence (see comments on 1:7). All the components of any spiritual temple are themselves living and spiritual; there must have been many and varied speculations on the topic, as *ShirShabb* demonstrates (see Newsom 1985, pp. 5-13). There the components of the heavenly and sevenfold temple participate in the angelic liturgies (see in particular 4Q403 1:41-44 — "foundations," "supporting columns," "corners" ["beams"], "walls"; 2:13 — "decorations of the inner shrine"; 4Q405 frr. 15-16, 4-5 — the veil of the temple and the painted images. See also Newsom 1985, pp. 9-10, 15-16, 53-54). Spiritual columns also appear in other, probably mystical, Qumranic texts ("all the spirits who support the temple" in 4Q286 (= 4QBer^a) fr. 2, 1. The concept appears in Christian apocalypticism in the *Vision of Paul* 44. *2 Bar.* 2:1-2 includes a different understanding of spiritual architecture, according to which "the columns" are good works and "the wall" is prayer.

This passage is an important key to John's view of the spiritual Jerusalem that the church will become. He imagines that a spiritual temple, bearing the name of the New Jerusalem, will exist in the future as a reward for the victor. The New Jerusalem is introduced in 21:2 and is described only in the two closing chapters of the book. As John will stress precisely the temple's absence (21:22), the temple mentioned in this verse cannot be part of the New Jerusalem. But how can the temple that, among the other eschatological entities seen in chs. 2 and 3 (see comments on 3:21), is promised to the victor not be part of the New Jerusalem whose name it bears? I believe that this is the temple that I presume to exist in the "beloved city" where the holy ones will dwell during the millennium (see comments on 20:9). Insofar as this city is an anticipation of the New Jerusalem, it is legitimate for the temple in which the resurrected faithful will offer their spiritual worship to bear its name. Thus we are witnessing a logical and chronological development from the earthly Jewish Jerusalem, which is destined for destruction, to the Christian church. And the church too is something that develops over time. It begins with a reality that, while it is spiritual, is also persecuted and in peril, as is apparent from the seven messages to the angels of the seven churches (see also 11:1-2); it then becomes the spiritual reality of the beloved city during the millennium, and it will finally become the definitive New Jerusalem. While the earlier realities are already spiritual, perhaps to different degrees, they are still transitory, and only the final one will be eternal (see comments on 21:2).

It is normal in primitive Christian literature to refer to humans as pillars of the church (Gal 2:9 and 1 Tim 3:15, where the "household of God," or the temple, is the church. See the symbolic language of 1QS 8:7-9, "tested rampart," "precious cornerstone," "foundation," "most holy dwelling," or 1QSb [1Q28b] 5:23, "tower" or "rampart"). The idea that the pillars of the temple have names is derived from the two enormously tall bronze pillars built by Solomon (18 cubits, according to 1 Kings 7:15; 35 cubits, according to 2 Chr 3:15) called Jachin and Boaz, which might be names or parts of the names of people (1 Kings 7:21 = 2 Chr 3:17; LXX translates the two terms in 2 Chronicles as κατόρθωσις ["uprightness, righteousness"] and ἰσχύς ["strength"]). That the temple had columns was widely known and must have given rise to esoteric speculations that are difficult to identify today, but of which there is evidence (see, e.g., the beginning of the *Apoc. Pet.* [NHC] 7.70.17; see also Mandaean texts in Lupieri 2002, pp. 219-20). The notion that the name of God was written on the temple (see comments on 2:17) appears also in the *Temple Scroll (TS),* where God himself speaks of "a hou]se to set my name upon it" (11QTᵃ [11Q19] 3:4).

3:14 Τάδε λέγει ὁ Ἀμήν. It is not immediately obvious why the Risen One would define himself as "the Amen." The term is an adverbial particle, of Hebrew origin, with an affirmative meaning — the classic example is 1 Chr 16:36 — which is frequently used in liturgical formulae. It could function as a noun in sentences such as "to say the 'Amen,'" and in these cases it was treated as neuter in gender in Greek (see 1 Cor 14:16; 2 Cor 1:20). As early as Isa 65:16 "Amen" appears as an attribute of God — "the God Amen," or "the God of Amen" — and is used to indicate the faithfulness or truth of God (Beale 1996, pp. 133-52). John apparently wants to say that the Risen One himself is the authoritative guarantee of the promise of God, and therefore he is faithful and true — because, that is, he keeps faith with what he or the Father has promised. Finally, just as "Amen" can stand at the beginning or end of a phrase to assert its importance, "the Amen" appears to function here as the first and last seal, the Alpha and Omega, the beginning and the end (see 1:8; 22:13).

ἡ ἀρχή . . . τοῦ θεοῦ. The beginning of creation seems to be a deliberate reference to Gen 1:1, and also calls to mind John 1:1. The identification with the Risen One is clear here, and the effect is to reaffirm his preexistence and to deepen and clarify its significance (see 1:8, 17). This passage connects this preexistence very closely with the "creation of God." John is not aware of any theological difficulty about the createdness of the Son, and thus the text is ambiguous on this point: is the Son, inasmuch as he is the beginning of creation part of creation itself, of which he constitutes the first work, or is he external to it, the creative instrument or intermediary between God the Father and the creation?

3:15-16   ψυχρός . . . ζεστός . . . χλιαρός. John's choice of adjectives is particularly effective in a sentence that presents the reader with a radical choice and that may echo proverbial expressions. It is difficult, however, to be certain exactly what John is referring to. He is undoubtedly exhorting his readers, through the mouth of the Risen One, to be "fervent" in their attitude, probably an allusion to the gold that is "fired by fire" in v. 18. Thus to be fervent means to embrace the new faith wholeheartedly, with a determination that will not recoil from the fires of martyrdom. If this is the case, then frigidity must be a reference to the opposite position, perhaps that of the unconverted Jews of the "synagogue of Satan" or that of the pagans. John, in any case, appears to prefer frigidity to the hypocrisy of false Christians, which is particularly dangerous because it has the power to undermine from within the strength of a community that is still young and small in numbers. The lukewarmness of the Laodiceans, which goes hand in hand with their presumed wealth, is unacceptable to John, who rejects a Christianity of compromises and half-measures. The passage as a whole has been given ethical and social interpretations, and while these are not without validity, the main compromise that the Christian prophet attacks must be that of Christians who submit to the civil and religious values of the world around them, and choose a quiet life over martyrdom.

3:17   Πλούσιός εἰμι . . . πεπλούτηκα. This seems to be a reference to Hos 12:9 (it is closer to LXX than to MT), where Ephraim boasts of his own wealth and impunity. The context, on the other hand, echoes Zech 11:4ff., where God orders the prophet to be the new shepherd and to care for the sheep who have been abandoned by their old shepherds and sold for slaughter. The seller exclaims, "Blessed be the LORD, for I have become rich." As well as their similarity to Enochic traditions, where angelic figures appear with the names and characteristics of shepherds (see Introduction, p. 16) both Zechariah and the Apocalypse contain threats against unworthy leaders: Zechariah, like the new shepherd, disposes of three shepherds in a single month (Zech 11:18).

3:18   χρυσίον πεπυρωμένον. The fire that fires this gold that is so precious might be persecution (see comments on 15:2).

ἡ αἰσχύνη . . . σου. Phrases such as this and 16:15 recall a cultural context in which nudity and the consequent exposure of the genitals were forbidden for reasons of purity. The prohibition appears as early as Exod 28:42-43, in reference to officiating priests, and it is present in Second Temple Judaism. Many Qumranic texts forbid nudity and prescribe punishments for anyone who, unless by necessity, appears naked or uncovered in the assembly (1QS 7:14-15

[= 12-13]; 4Q267 fr. 18, 4; 4Q270 fr. 11; 1QM 7:7 and 10:1). The Pharisees also would have agreed that the very sight of the genitals was inherently contaminating, at least in certain circumstances (e.g., *m. Hal.* 2.3, where the prohibition is applied to anyone kneading bread for the offering). For the Essenes, the condemnation of nudity probably resulted from their conviction of the presence of God or his angelic emissaries; the purity of the angels could not tolerate human nakedness. (For the possible presence of God, see the last verse of the passage of 1QM cited above. On angelic presence and its consequences in Qumran see CD 15:16-17: "None of these should one allow to enter the congregation since the holy angels are in its midst," and cf. 1QSa [1Q28a] 2:3-9; 4Q285 and 11Q14 = 11QBer [the last words of the fragment]; 1QH-4QH 11:21-22; 14:13, "to all the men of your counsel and in the lot, together with the angels of the face, without there being a mediator between . . ."; 19:3-24; and, perhaps, 1QM 12:1 and 4Q400 fr. 2, 2.) The presence of the angels might explain some Essene practices, such as wearing some items of clothing for the baptism of purification, and certain practices connected with defecation (see Lupieri 1985 and Baumgarten 1996). For an analogous Christian conviction, see the strange Pauline passage in 1 Cor 11:10.

3:21 Ὁ νικῶν . . . αὐτῷ. At the end of a series of definitions and promises the victor appears as a faithful follower of Jesus whom John holds up as a model (for the use of "victor/conqueror" as an epithet for the saved, see *4 Ezra* 7:45). Seven promises are made to this exemplary Christian, all of which appear to be oriented toward the future reality to be described further on in the book. The first promise of the Risen One is permission to eat of the tree of life, which is in the paradise of God (see comments on 2:7). Its meaning will become clear only in 22:2, where the tree of life will reappear in the New Jerusalem as a reward for all believers. The second promise, of protection from the second death (see comments on 2:11), makes sense only in the light of chs. 20 and 21. Those who escape the second death enter into the millennial reign and the New Jerusalem (20:6, 14, 21:8). The third promise, of the hidden manna and the white pebble with a new name that no one knows except he who takes it, is the most mysterious (see comments on 2:17, 28). The white pebble itself refers to the number/name of Christ, while the expression "a new name . . . that nobody knows" anticipates both 3:12 and 19:12, with its description of the Word, himself a victor on a white horse (see also 6:2).

The fourth promise strongly suggests that the faithful victor will be identified with the Risen One himself. Its first part, the promise of authority over the nations to rule them with an iron staff (2:26-27), suggests a link to the messianic destiny of the son of the woman in ch. 12 with whom the Risen One seems to identify himself (esp. 2:26, 28). Then, in light of the reference to

130

22:16, the gift of the morning star appears to indicate that the Risen One promises the gift of himself. The fifth promise consists in the white garment (see comments on 3:4), in the victor's name not being blotted out of the Book of Life but rather being proclaimed before the Father and his angels (see comments on 3:5). The mention of the scroll of life, which occurs twice in the book with a negative sense (13:8; 17:8), is a reference to the scene of judgment, as well as to the essential qualification for entrance into the New Jerusalem (20:12, 15; 21:27). Thus the acknowledgment of the conqueror by God is also a reference to the Final Judgment. The sixth promise, that the conqueror will become "a pillar in the temple of my God, and he will not venture out any more, and I will write upon him the name of my God and the name of the city of my God, the New Jerusalem," explicitly refers to the New Jerusalem and to its descent "out of heaven from my God" (3:12; see 21:2, 10). However, the New Jerusalem is explicitly said to have no temple since it has no need for one. So I have interpreted this promise as referring to the millennium, and in particular to the status of Christians during this period of salvation history as the spiritual temple (see comments on 3:12).

The seventh and last promise consists in the conqueror being assimilated with Christ and thus enthroned with God. "I will grant him to sit with me on my throne, as I also was victorious and sat down with my Father on his throne" (3:21). Just as the victorious Christ is σύνθρονος with the Father, so the faithful is σύνθρονος with the Son, and thus with the Father himself. There are many references to the throne in the Apocalypse (the term occurs 47 times, as opposed to only 15 in the rest of the NT, and never at all in John), but the allusion here is probably to the last occurrence of the term, namely, the mention of the "throne of God and of the Lamb" in the New Jerusalem (22:3). In a Qumranic text considered by the editors to be a "messianic apocalypse" enthronement is promised to the believer: "For he [the Lord] will honor the pious upon the throne of an eternal kingdom" (4Q521 fr. 2, 2:7). There is an even closer parallel in the so-called *Song of Michael*, which reads, "He prepared for Israel a throne of strength in the assembly of the Gods, on which none of the Kings of the East will sit, and their nobles will not . . ." (4Q491c fr. 1, 3-5). There seems to be an expectation of superhuman enthronement for the faithful.

On encountering each of the promises the reader or hearer who does not know the final chapters and can form only an imperfect understanding of their meaning, which suggests that the author is following a deliberate plan of gradual revelation (see comments on 2:28). It is reasonable to suppose that the seven opening letters were edited after the completion of the work, or at least at a point when John already had clearly in mind what he was going to say. The complex web of internal references suggests a carefully constructed composition rather than a first draft.

4:1 θύρα ... ἐν τῷ οὐρανῷ. Unlike many of his contemporaries, John does not seem to envisage multiple heavens or celestial vaults. (The plural in 12:12 can be understood as poetic; see comments.) He uses the term "heaven" to mean a transitory reality that can be replaced by the will of God who created it in the beginning (10:6; 14:7; 21:1-5). It is manifest as a physical reality that can be split, or opened, or closed (6:14; 11:6; 19:11) and that, like the earth, is sometimes spiritual, personalized, or at any rate liable to be hypostatized (20:11). From the first to the last occurrences of the term (3:12 and 21:10), heaven is shown in a close relationship with God, who is himself called "God of heaven" (11:13; 16:11). It is the seat not only of the heavenly temple, the angels, the throne, the voices, and all the spiritual forces of good (4:2; 11:19; 15:5) but also, in the past, of Satan and his angels, the stars that are later thrown down to earth (6:13; 8:10; 9:1; 12:4). Both fire and hail can come from it (8:7; 13:13; 16:21; 20:9) since it possesses the "storerooms of hail," according to some popular cosmogonies (1 Enoch 41:3-4; cf. Introduction, p. 27). The ambiguous nature of heaven arises from its intermediary position between the human and divine worlds. For John, it is the "in-between world" where God shows his signs to the visionary and therefore also the screen on which God manifests himself, and at the same time the veil by which divinity is concealed (see comments on 4:2; and cf. 12:1, 3, 15:1 and Sacchi 1990, pp. 55-61). Insofar as it is a place, it has certain architectonic characteristics, first among which are one or more entry doors through which stars and winds pass (these were common in astronomical texts; cf. 1 Enoch 72–76 [BA]; see comments on 21:12).

ἃ δεῖ ... ταῦτα. The change in the visionary's position coincides with a change in the content of the visions. Whatever the structural divisions of the text, this is a transitional moment, and John probably uses the motif of movement to indicate that from now on he will begin to recount events or realities that follow on from the literary chronological setting of the preceding scenes (see comments on 1:19).

4:2 καὶ ἰδοὺ θρόνος. The book's second theophany is a vision of the throne and of the one seated on the throne, a figure usually understood to be God the Father. As in the first vision, John emphasizes the fact that he is "in spirit" (cf. 1:10). He does this at only two other crucial moments: before the vision of the prostitute and before the vision of the New Jerusalem (17:3; 21:10), which suggests that he considers this to be a scene of particular importance. The passage contains traditional elements, of which many, including the rainbow, appear in the initial vision of Ezekiel (1:28). John's general dependence on Ezekiel goes beyond the details of derivation, and makes sense if we consider the context in which the prophet of the exile composed his book. Ezekiel wrote in a period of terrible crisis for Israel, when Jerusalem was conquered and destroyed by Nebuchadnezzar. Ezekiel regarded as the true Israel those Israelites who found themselves in exile in the pagan land of Babylon, and took upon himself the spiritual and physical reconstruction of the Jewish world. He explained to the exiles that the Almighty had abandoned the old Jerusalem to follow them eastward, and that God had planned a new Jerusalem, of which Ezekiel is able to give the plans, complete with dimensions. John's situation is similar; Jerusalem has been destroyed because of her own sins, and God will replace her with a heavenly Jerusalem, the New Jerusalem. In like manner Judaism must be re-founded, this time centered on the Christian figure of the sacrificed Lamb who replaces the old, discarded, sacrificial cult. While John's Christianity distinguishes him from the ancient prophet in certain fundamental aspects such as the reconstruction of Jerusalem and the temple, nonetheless the similarities between their situations and their intentions lead him to reflect carefully on Ezekiel's text.

ἔκειτο ἐν τῷ οὐρανῷ. The verb κεῖμαι occurs only twice in the Apocalypse: here, where it refers to the throne, and in 21:16, where it is used to indicate the position of the New Jerusalem. The eschatological Jerusalem is a sort of throne for God and for the Lamb, which may explain why John uses the same verb for the throne in this passage (see comments on 21:16). In any case, I have translated the verb in the original sense of "to be set" (the passive of τίθημι), which leaves open the possibility that John meant to say that he has seen the throne being put into place before his eyes, in which case ἰδού indicates the immediacy of the action. This would emphasize further that for John heaven is an intermediary place in which God prepares visions so that he may see them. The content of the visions, in fact, exists so that John can contemplate it, and is distinct both from its own existence in God, which is not accessible to human contemplation, and from its existence in human history, which is usually in the future.

4:3 ὅμοιος ὁράσει. John might mean "like the vision of a stone/an emerald" (see the meaning of ὅρασις in 9:17). His carelessness with the Greek use of cases is particularly evident in this chapter. (In v. 4 ἐπὶ τοὺς θρόνους . . . καθημένους; in v. 9 τῷ καθημένῳ ἐπὶ τῷ θρόνῳ; and in v. 10 τοῦ καθημένου ἐπὶ τοῦ θρόνου. Apparently John is inclined to put words governed by ἐπί in the same case as that of the nouns that govern them.) Moreover, the noun "rainbow" (ἶρις) is feminine, whereas the adjective "similar to" (ὅμοιος), which should agree with it, is masculine. Maybe John shifts to the masculine because he is aware that he is in fact describing an angelic nature (see comments on 1:12). The rainbow, like the thunder and lightning, is difficult to explain in the ancient world. No one had any idea of the phenomenon of refracted light, and therefore the pagans saw the rainbow as the minor deity Iris, who, as she was a spiritual being, was from a Jewish perspective an angel. (For the pagans also Iris's job was that of carrying messages, and thus she does function as an "angel" between the gods; see Hesiod, *Theog.* 780-86. For the presence of the rainbow in visions of God and for its spiritual essence, see Halperin 1988, pp. 250-61.)

4:4 εἴκοσι τέσσαρας πρεσβυτέρους καθημένους. The identity of these twenty-four elders is mysterious, and there are several persuasive explanations. As early as Isa 24:23 we encounter a theophany in Jerusalem, in which God "before his elders manifests his glory"; the number of the elders is not mentioned. The more famous theophany of Exod 24 is also useful: here a group of "seventy elders of Israel" appears repeatedly (see Num 11:16). These seventy, because they are "elect" or "privileged," are admitted to the presence of God without being harmed. Their number is increased by the presence of Nadab and Abihu (Exod 24:1, 9), who bring the total to seventy-two: twenty-four elders would be a third of this number (see comments on 8:7). In any case, there are biblical texts that stress the presence of "elders" in the context of a theophany, once at Sinai and once in Jerusalem. It is uncertain whether John sees these figures as angelic or as glorified human beings. That they are seated might count against their being angels (see comments on 5:6), although in an early Christian text such as the *Martyrdom of Perpetua* 12 the "four elders to the left and right" of the throne and the "many others" who appear in the course of the theophany constitute the celestial, and almost certainly the angelic, court of God. The same is probably true also of the *Vision of Paul* 44, which is influenced by the Apocalypse. "Elders" also appear as angelic figures in *2 Enoch* 4:1 (see also F. I. Andersen's comment, in Charlesworth I 1983, pp. 110-11). In any case, the elders in John's text behave in a ritually significant way, which seems to suggest a link with the twenty-four categories of Jewish priests (Halperin 1998, pp. 88-89). They appear also to be the holy counterparts of the "seventy . . . elders" and the "about twenty-five men" of the vision in Ezek 8:9-16, who commit base and abominable acts of idolatry in the Jerusalem temple itself (it is possible that "about twenty-five" might be for Ezekiel a veiled way of saying twenty-four, or, at any rate, that John might have interpreted it as such. On this extremely mysterious chapter of Ezekiel see Halperin 1993). If they are glorified humans with priestly roles, perhaps they represent the praying church under its celestial aspect, which is the fullness of Judaism. In this case they might represent the twelve patriarchs and the twelve apostles who appear together in Apoc 21:12 and 14, where they constitute essential structural elements of the New Jerusalem. In the same way they might represent here the unity of the two historical components of the church. The distinction between glorified humans and angels is more significant in terms of our categories than of those of the first century; there is no reason why we cannot see the twenty-four elders as being the celestial dimension of the church that is always with God, and thus as the "angels" of the patriarchs and apostles. If past, present, and future coexist in the present of God, and if the Lamb is "slaughtered, from the establishment of the world" (see comments on 13:8), it is not unreasonable to imagine that an angelic dimension of an earthly reality might be present with God (for the elders' crowns, see comments on 3:11).

4:5 ἀστραπαί . . . καὶ βρονταί. These must be angels. *1 Enoch* 59:1-3 *(BS)* appears to support this in spite of the poor condition of the text, but the Amaric translation of *1 Enoch* 59:2 is more explicit: it mentions "the voice of the lightning and thunder," and if the lightning has a voice, it is probably an angel (see 10:4). In *1 Enoch* 44:1 (also *BS*), the lightning is a kind of star that "cannot dwell with the rest," and in *1 Enoch* 43:2 lightning is generated by "revolutions" of the stars; this confirms their spiritual nature. Finally, in Greek, there is a possible etymological connection between "star" (ἀστήρ) and "lightning" (ἀστραπή < ἀστ(ε)ροπή). There are, at all events, angels associated with thunder and lightning (see *Jub.* 2:2; *T. Adam* 4:3). *3 Enoch* 14:4 gives their names: Baraqi'el for the lightning and Ra'ami'el for the thunder. The contemporary understanding, different from ours, was that thunder was more dangerous because thunderbolts fall from heaven and strike, while lightning is a good omen (according to *1 Enoch* 59:2-3; 60:13-15 there are "winds" who hold back the thunder by its "bridle" so that it arrives after the lightning to which it is originally joined).

λαμπάδες. The term means "torch," a short stick of wood, with one end covered in pitch or some other flammable material. It could be carried around or attached to a wall by a fixture, and it was used to give light outdoors, especially when on the move. John may have seen the seven torches coming forth from the throne together with the lightning, thunder, and voices, as there are moving torches inside or under the throne in Ezek 1:13, although the participle καιόμεναι ("burning"), which refers to "torches," most probably corresponds to a finite form; therefore, the sentence means: "And seven torches . . . *are* burning" (for the movement and the fiery nature of the seven spirits, and for Qumranic parallels, see Halperin 1988, p. 54). In any case, John uses the verb "come forth" (ἐκπορεύομαι) to indicate that spiritual, probably angelic, beings issue from the throne of God (22:1), from the mouth of Jesus Christ, from those of the punishing angels (the horselike locusts with lions' heads of ch. 9), the components of the Satanic triad (16:14), or the two witnesses (11:5). The entity that issues "from the mouth" is usually defined as fire or a sword, with the exception of the "three impure spirits" that are emitted from the mouths of the dragon, the beast, and the false prophet in diabolic imitation of divine action (16:13 and see 12:15). As regards the emission of spiritual or angelic beings from the mouth (see Ps 33:6) or from the face (of God), see Levison 1995, pp. 478-79; the cases discussed there reveal a connection between the "spirit" and the creating "word": there the Logos is the Spirit, or a spiritual being. The fact that the torches, which are the "seven spirits of God," issue from the throne emphasizes the contrast with the "three impure spirits" that issue from the mouth of the three components of the Satanic trinity. After the conclusion of human history the spiritual river of 22:1 will flow from the throne, reflecting the limitlessness of the divine gift of life, which by this stage has moved beyond human chronological time into the eternity of God. We are to understand that whenever the Spirit comes forth in human history, and indeed whenever there is any angelic intervention, it must be sevenfold, in contrast to the Satanic dominion. That this dominion is in fact sevenfold is shown by the fact that the various demonic beasts always have seven heads, which in its turn probably reflects Satan's dominion over the seven periods into which the duration of this world seems to be divided (see comments on 5:6; 17:10 and 11). The sevenfold pattern of the Spirit's interventions thus probably indicates the constant presence of the Spirit throughout the duration of human history.

4:6 ὡς θάλασσα . . . κρυστάλλῳ. This is probably the vault of heaven, which reappears in 15:2, and which derives from Ezek 1:22-23, where it is also portrayed as glassy or crystalline. Here it is compared to a sea, an image that does not appear in Ezekiel but that is present in *1 Enoch* 14:11. The presence of water in the sky is connected with the belief in the waters above the earth, which served to explain the phenomenon of rain (e.g., in Gen 8:2). In mystical texts, on the other hand, these celestial seas take on an arcane significance that can be grasped only by those mystics who not only make the journey but really understand the nature of heavenly reality (cf. Scholem 1960, p. 15; Halperin 1988, pp. 194-249).

ἐν μέσῳ . . . ζῷα. It is not always easy to convey the theological geography of the throne (cf. 5:6, 22:1-2; and notes). The text probably means that the four beings support, and together constitute, the throne. As in Ezek 1, LXX, John uses the term ζῷα, "animals," to convey the Jewish concept of *hayyot*, which can be translated as "lives," as "living beings," or as "animals." The four monstrous beings of Ezekiel, which might be cherubim, represent the peak of the angelic hierarchy and appear frequently in Jewish mystical literature. John's account differs in certain ways from Ezekiel's model. Each of the beings has a single face that is different from that of the other beings, while in Ezekiel each has four faces: those of a man, a lion, a bull, and an eagle (Ezek 1:10). They have, moreover, the six wings of the seraphim in Isa 6:2, while in Ezek 1:6 they each have four (just as they do in *Apoc. Abr.* 18:5-7, a text in which the living beings seem to be identified with the cherubim; 10:9). In John the creatures are "full" of eyes, while in Ezek 1:18 the eyes cover instead the wheels of the chariot-throne, which are called *ophannim* and are themselves considered to be angelic beings of the highest level. Ezek 1:20, on the other hand, asserts that "the spirit of the living creature was in the wheels," thus suggesting that the living beings and the wheels might be the same. Thus this passage reveals John's characteristic habit of blending together elements from various parts of the same vision or from various visions, even drawn from different prophets; whether or not it is the account of an ecstatic experience, the vision of the throne in the Apocalypse appears to be a conflation of the accounts in Isaiah and Ezekiel (see notes to 1:4; 4:9-10; 22:3).

4:9-10 δώσουσιν . . . βαλοῦσιν. Many exegetes believe that the future indicatives of the two verses have an iterative function, and that therefore they should be translated, "Every time they will give . . . , they will also fall . . . and they will worship . . . and they will cast. . . ." In the rest of the book, however, ὅταν never has an iterative sense (cf. 12:4), and when it is used with the future in the postclassical period it does not necessarily indicate iteration (cf. variants on Luke 13:28). I would propose that vv. 9-11 look ahead to the exaltation of the Lamb described in ch. 5 (cf. Corsini 1980, pp. 191-92). This exaltation follows the victory of the Lamb, who can finally open the seven seals; it is not an event that has been or that can be repeated (cf. Rom 6:10, etc.). Falling as an act of adoration could be a realistic detail: perhaps one designed to emphasize the natural disproportion between the one who adores and the one who is adored (cf. 1:17; in this case the "elders" could be humans), or else a characteristic of angelic adoration, as in 4QShirShabb: "The [cheru]bs fall down before him and b[les]s" (4Q405 frr. 20-22, 2:7). In this case we must ask if this falling in adoration assumes that angels cannot do other than "fall" in adoration, as they have no joints (see Introduction, p. 24, n. 70; cf., e.g., *Gen. Rab.* 65:21 and Halperin 1988, pp. 137 and 149-53). In any case, the idea is traditional: Ruth 2:10; 2 Sam 1:2; Job 1:20; *1 Enoch (BS)* 48:5.

5:1 ἐπὶ τὴν δεξιὰν τοῦ καθημένου. As in 1:20, "upon the right" means "in the right hand." The ancient world, both pagan and Jewish, attributed greater importance to the right; the NT, for instance, has the judgment scene of Matt 25:32-46 in which the sheep are put on the right and the goats on the left. In the Apocalypse left and right are explicitly contrasted only in reference to the feet of the angel who appears at the beginning of ch. 10, but nonetheless the greater importance and the superiority of the right are still in evidence (cf. Fabbro 1995). That the seven stars in chs. 1–2 are said to be in the right hand of the Risen One probably indicates his total control over the seven beings, and the position of the scroll in the right hand of the person "seated on the throne" (a detail that is repeated in 5:7) likewise suggests a particularly close relationship between the scroll and the one who holds it in his hand.

βιβλίον . . . ὄπισθεν. This is an opisthograph: a scroll with writing both on the inside — the front face when it is open — and the outside — the back face. As the scroll is sealed, and must therefore be rolled, it is not quite clear how John can see that it has writing on the inside as well. It is not necessary, however, for the inside of the scroll to be visible; on the one hand, one would expect that a scroll with writing on the outside would have it also on the inside, and, on the other, the most important model for this scroll, both prophetically and theologically, appears in Ezek 2:9 (in spite of the possible analogy with 1 Enoch [BS] 39:2), and as that scroll is an opisthograph, it is logical to assume that this one is too.

κατεσφραγισμένον . . . ἑπτά. The seven seals represent the first group of seven objects that John sees together. They provide the structure of the subsequent visions, in which they appear in a numbered sequence, deliberately dividing the text into seven stages that are marked by the use of the ordinal numbers from "first" to "seventh" and that constitute a so-called "septet" (needless to say, the literary and theological model for all successive "septets" is the heptameron of Gen 1:1–2:4a; but see comments on 9:5). The literary technique creates the structure whereby John develops and deepens his material by stages. He sees a complex vision with seven distinct elements, and from each element he develops further visions. The seventh and last of these is in itself a new and complex vision and may include seven elements that are then developed into seven visions and so on, like a Russian doll. For the idea of a scroll with seven seals see 4QProtoEsther^a (4Q550), one of the possible models of the book of Esther, in which the king finds a scroll "sealed with the seven seals of the ring of Darius, his father."

5:2 ἄγγελον . . . μεγάλῃ. The term "strong" occurs seven times in the Apocalypse as an adjective and two times as a noun. When it is a noun, it is always in the plural and indicates a category of human beings destined to meet a nasty end (6:15; 19:18). As an adjective it is used three times to describe an angel (here; 10:1; 18:21) and once each to describe a voice (18:2), the city of Babylon (18:10), the thunder (19:6), and the Lord God (18:8). Thus in the majority of cases the word is used to refer to angelic or angelomorphic figures rather than to humans. We might ask whether "strong," like "great," refers not so much to the unusual muscularity of the angel (only 18:21 seems to suggest that) as to its spiritual force, or at least to its superhuman greatness.

5:3 ἐν τῷ οὐρανῷ . . . τῆς γῆς. The tripartite division of the cosmos corresponds to that in Phil 2:10 ("So that at the name of Jesus every knee should bow, of those who are in heaven, on earth, and under the earth"). Like Paul, John is referring here to the inhabitants of the three parts of the cosmos, most likely as an allusion to the entirety of spiritual beings, human, angelic, and demonic, the worship of whom is forbidden in Exod 20:4 and Deut 4:17-18.

5:5 ὁ λέων . . . Ἰούδα. The connection between Judah and the lion is traditional, stemming back at least to Jacob's blessing (Gen 49:9). Equally traditional, in Christian circles, is the emphasis on Jesus' descent from the tribe of Judah (Matt 1:2-3; Luke 3:33; Heb 7:14).

ἡ ῥίζα Δαυίδ. The "root of Jesse" appears in Isa 11:10, where it is prophesied that it will "stand as a signal" in the last days. The term "root" can therefore refer to descendants, to those who proceed from Jesse, to his seed. In 22:16, however ("I am the root and the offspring of David"), "root" indicates not the descendants but the ancestors of David, not the root that is produced by David but the root from which David is produced, while the idea of *descent* is expressed by γένος, "offspring" or "lineage." This person, who in the end will be identified with the Risen One, is both the ancestor of David (the preexisting Christ) and his descendant (the human Jesus).

5:6 ἐν μέσῳ τοῦ θρόνου . . . πρεσβυτέρων. This is the usual theological geography of the throne (see comments on 4:6). John seemingly intends to say that even as the Lamb is sacrificed from eternity, so is he enthroned from eternity; even before the end of the world and of time, he is already on the Father's throne. He is clearly distinguished in v. 7 from the person seated on the throne; the relationship between them is not clearly defined, but whatever it is, the Lamb is found on his throne. The element of "now and not yet" that originates with the church's experience is projected onto the vision of the Godhead and his power.

ἀρνίον . . . ἐσφαγμένον. With these words we are at the heart of the mystery of Christian revelation. Jesus Christ, who was introduced in v. 5 as a "lion," appears here as a "lamb" and indeed as a slaughtered lamb: one that has been sacrificed (see Introduction, p. 32 and n. 102). The text emphasizes the fact that the Lamb is standing. This verb appears more than twenty times in the Apocalypse, and although it can be used to indicate the position of Christ or the lamb (3:20; 5:6; 14:1), it most often refers to angels (7:1, 11; 8:2 and 3; 10:5 and 8; 11:4[?]; 19:17), to the holy ones and the resurrected (7:9; 11:11; 15:2;

20:12), or to the devil (12:4 and 18). John uses the word in a way consistent with Jewish thought, according to which angels always stand upright in their activity of praise and prayer to God (for Qumranic texts see ShirShabb [4Q405] fr. 23, 1:5), while sitting is a sign of God's dignity (cf. 3 Enoch 16:3-5; Introduction, p. 24, n. 70; and comment on 4:9-10). After the annunciation of a victorious lion, the appearance of a "slaughtered lamb" is surprising. The victory of an eschatological lion over an eagle, which probably represents Roman power, is one of the features of 4 Ezra 11:37–12:3, and thus by substituting the Lamb John here initiates his polemic with contemporary Jewish ideas and with the unfulfilled hope that the lion of Judah will triumph over the pagan eagle. In a typical instance of the theology of reversal John identifies the lion with the Lamb, and his victory with sacrificial death. The term ἀρνίον occurs twenty-nine times in the Apocalypse. The number has no recondite significance: that there is no particular arithmetical importance to the number of times that such an important term occurs suggests to me that critics at least sometimes accord significance to the number of occurrences of a term (see comment on 1:6) when the number is actually a matter of sheer chance.

The "[seven] spirits" who appeared in the form of burning torches in 4:5 return here and are "sent out to all the earth." Their sending out underlines the connection between sevenness and this world as well, possibly its temporal duration (see comment on 4:5). John does not seem to think of the Spirit as being merely sevenfold, but (especially if the numeral in "seven spirits" is not original to the text) as being represented by two series of seven beings, the "horns" and the "eyes." If the Lamb contains within itself all the fullness of the Spirit that is sent out over the earth, and if this Spirit is represented by two series of seven beings, it may follow that the Lamb recapitulates in himself both old and new economies. The seven horns and the seven eyes would thus represent the old and new covenants, the two phases of spiritual intervention in salvation history.

5:7   καί . . . εἴληφεν. The coming of the Lamb, whom we have just seen already sitting "in the midst of the throne," probably has a theological significance, which is connected with the title/epithet ὁ ἐρχόμενος (see comment on 1:4).

5:8   ἔχοντες . . . χρυσᾶς. The details of the scene (which are not in themselves very realistic, as one does not play a harp while holding full bowls) indicates both the priestly and liturgical dimensions of the figures and their role as mediators between the "holy ones" (see following comments) and God. We might wonder whether the fact that the creatures and the elders are the same in their function implies that they are also the same in their nature. What John describes seems to be an angelic liturgy, in which angels intercede for men.

θυμιαμάτων . . . τῶν ἁγίων. 8:3-4 also states that "incense" is connected to "the prayers of all the holy ones." The context suggests a spiritual significance to the worship: not only to the bloody sacrifice but also to the offering of incense (θυμίαμα must be the mixture prescribed in Exod 30:34-36; for the prayer as incense, see Ps 141:2). The identity of the holy ones poses a problem similar to that encountered in certain Qumranic texts, where it is never quite clear whether the holy ones are the followers of the sect or the holy angels (see 14:10). The clarity of those other passages, however, in which John refers, for instance, to the "endurance" of the holy ones or even to their "blood" (13:10; 16:6; 17:6, etc.), suggests that the term refers to believers in this passage too. It is a usage typical of marginalized religious groups, who distinguish themselves from other groups by reference to their own sanctity.

5:9 ᾠδὴν καινήν. In the Apocalypse the "song" of the holy ones is always a "new song." This is repeated in 14:3 and finally explained in 15:3 by a reference to Moses' song of victory, the song that the ancient servant of God raised to God at the moment of God's triumph over the forces of evil by plunging Pharaoh into the sea (Exod 15:1-21). The newness is the Christian interpretation: Moses' song corresponds to the canticle to the Lamb, and the real victory is the sacrifice on the cross. This passage is important for an understanding of the significance of the scroll and the opening of the seals, which is possible only after Christ's sacrifice. This sacrifice is the foundation of the church of the saved, both from Israel ("every tribe") and from the Gentiles ("and language and people and nation"). If the scroll, which contains a written text, represents revelation, and the opening of the seals indicates the fullness of revelation, then this fullness is made possible by the royal triumph of Christ. This explains the allusion to a kingdom "upon the earth" that belongs to "priests" (see 1:6): the millennial priestly reign (20:4-6). The text's insistence on the priestly nature of this kingdom suggests that it contains a place of worship, which may be thoroughly spiritual but which is still located on an earth that is not yet the "new" earth of 21:1 (see comments on 3:12 and 21).

5:11 Καὶ εἶδον. The final vision of the passage, which is also auditory, begins from the throne and expands the visionary's view to include the entire cosmos, in a return to the perspective of v. 3. The space "under the earth" is still there, and this time the sea is included (see v. 13), which shows that the vision is not yet that of the "new heaven and the new earth" but fits the cosmic reign of Christ over this world: the millennium. The generic reference to "every creature" (πᾶν κτίσμα) indicates both the physical and spiritual beings of a world that still exists and in which evil seems to have been neutralized.

φωνήν . . . πολλῶν. The ranks of the angels are now distinguished from the throne, the living creatures, and the elders. Heaven's inhabitants are arrayed in concentric circles, in descending order of importance, around its logical and ontological center, the throne, on which are the "seated one" and the Lamb.

5:12 τὴν δύναμιν . . . καὶ εὐλογίαν. Critics have long commented on the oddity of this expression, where a single article serves for seven nouns, as if they constituted a formula or a single word (Charles I 1920, p. 149; Bousset 1906, pp. 261-62). The theory that the expression is liturgical (see the other doxologies: that with three members in 4:9, that with four in 5:13, and that with seven in 7:12) has now been confirmed by the example of the sevenfold doxologies in *ShirShabb* (Newsom 1985, p. 177).

6:1 μίαν . . . σφραγίδων. Here the cardinal number ("one") is used to indicate the ordinal number ("first"), according to the Hebrew practice, which also appears in 9:12. It is typical of the septets that they be ordered around a list of elements that are numbered explicitly. There are numbered lists also in *ShirShabb* (*MasadaShirShabb* 2 and 4Q403 1 and 2; see Newsom 1985, pp. 175-78), which adds weight to the theory that sevenfold structures might derive from a mystical interpretation of Sabbath liturgies.

Ἔρχου. The command — or invitation — to "Come!" repeated four times by the four living creatures, is followed by the appearance of four horses of different colors, ridden by figures who at first glance are different, and who are usually interpreted as angelic figures of various types; this scene is an elaboration of Zech 1:8, where the prophet sees horses of different colors ridden by figures who are angels of God. At the end of the Apocalypse, in 22:17-20, the same command is given three more times, bringing the total number of repetitions to seven — perhaps not a mere coincidence. The seventh and last time, the name of the one who is invited to come is also given: the "Lord Jesus." This strengthens the argument that the conqueror on the white horse, whose appearance follows the first occurrence of the invitation, is a christological figure.

6:2 τόξον. This is the only appearance of the word "bow" in the entire NT. If we are to consider it a weapon of attack, we must presume that there are also arrows, although they are not mentioned in the text, and the absence of arrows might in fact suggest an alternative interpretation. The term "bow" might be an echo of Gen 9:13 (also τόξον in the LXX), where it means the rainbow, which marks the end of the flood and is the sign of peace between man and God. In this case it would indicate, like the ἶρις of 4:3 and 10:1, that the figure comes from the very heart of God. His actions in this case would not be precisely warlike but would have as their goal the establishment of a pact — possibly a new one — with humanity, on the model of that made in the time of Noah. All of this would lead us to suppose that the rider of the white horse is Christ incarnate in Jesus (see comment on 10:1).

ἐξῆλθεν . . . νικήσῃ. The expression "to go out as a victor — in order that someone might have victory" occurs innumerable times in the Bible, and does not necessarily signify the violence of war; it can mean "to assert oneself" or "to take the upper hand." LXX, in fact, translates it as εἰς τέλος, with a couple of exceptions, in which it has εἰς νῖκος-νεῖκος. (1 Cor 15:54, on the other hand, citing Isa 25:8, rejects the translation of LXX and renders the concept as νῖκος "victory.") John includes a repetition in the expression, maybe to make the phrase mean "with a complete and absolute victory" (see 3:17). On the other hand, the repetition — the insertion of the term "victor" in the conventional phrase "went out in order that he might have victory" — might be part of John's program of creating internal references within the text, and in particular with the seven letters of the first chapter and their promises "to the victor" (for the crown of the victor see comments on 3:11). In this way the rider and the white horse would represent the necessary spread of Christianity over the whole earth, a spread that Christ began, which the church continues, and which cannot be completed before the beginning of the end and its pains (see, e.g., Matt 24:14/Mark 13:10).

6:4   καὶ ἵνα . . . σφάξουσιν. This is the method devised by God and carried out by Gabriel for destroying the giants in *1 Enoch* 10:9: the holy angels of God do not themselves kill, but rather order matters in such a way that the sinners destroy each other. This mutual destruction among the wicked also characterizes some of the major negative figures of the Apocalypse, such as the beast and the prostitute of ch. 17. Note that the generic plural "they" refers *(ad sensum)* to the enemies of God who are on earth (see comments on 12:6).

6:6   Χοῖνιξ. The choenix is a unit of volume for measuring solids such as grain. It is slightly more than a liter, and was the daily ration of wheat for a man. The structure of the sentence spoken by the voice is an echo of 2 Kings 7:1; there, however, much larger measurements of wheat and barley are sold at extremely low prices to mark the end of the famine and the return of God's favor; grain, barley, wine, and oil are referred to together in the context of famine in Joel 1:10-11 (the passage used in ch. 9).

6:8   ἵππος χλωρός. The association of death with the color green — a color generally associated with life and growth — seems strange to many, and for this reason it is sometimes translated "greenish" (see Corsini 1980, pp. 203, 208ff.) or even "pale," or subjected to rather farfetched explanations, for instance, that sickly green or yellow is the color of bodies left unburied during times of plague. The text, however, does say "green." Perhaps it does so precisely because of the conventional significance of the color, thus link-ing life with the kind of death that Death himself brings (see Vanni 1980, pp. 485-86). There are other colors whose symbolic significance is equally obvi-ous. The connection between white, victory, and virginity is made clear in the text (see also 14:4); its opposite, black, represents darkness, in the sense of divine punishment (see 16:10); red, in v. 4, is the color of the blood of vio-lent death and represents the mutual human slaughter of war. The figure on the white horse, with his bow and crown, is not actually shown killing, al-though he is destined for victory. The figure on the red horse removes peace from the earth, but it is humans who actually slaughter each other. Even the figure on the black horse is not actually told to kill anyone. The scale in his hand is not a weapon; it weighs scarce and expensive food in a time of war or other disaster. The actual task of killing "over the fourth part of the earth" is reserved for Death and Hades, who make use of a "sword," "famine," "death," and "wild beasts."

John uses ῥομφαία for sword, deliberately distinguishing it from the μάχαιρα of the second rider; the term appears six times in the Apocalypse, and on the other five occasions (1:16; 2:12, 16; 19:15, 21) the sword always comes from the mouth of a divine and/or angelic figure. Thus it does not seem to be a human weapon but rather one handled by the superhuman and angelic fig-ures called Death and Hades (see 1:18). The only other time the term appears in the NT is in the prophecy of Simeon, who tells Mary that a sword will "pierce" her soul (Luke 2:35). This sword, which we understand metaphori-cally, is brandished by an angel of God, or may actually be an angelic being it-self, "Sword." μάχαιρα can also have a spiritual meaning (see Eph 6:17; Heb 4:12), but it is ordinarily used of the weapon that humans use to kill each other. In view of the possible parallel with 1 Chr 21 (LXX), in which the ῥομφαία (of God or of the angel) is the plague that punishes Israel and threat-ens Jerusalem, I imagine that here also ῥομφαία indicates plague, or at least death from disease. If this theory is correct, there is no redundancy within the passage, as the function of this rider is distinguished from that of the second rider, who brings about the violent death of many by the hands of others. Death and Hades would thus be responsible for all human deaths — death caused by plague or disease, famine, old age, wild beasts — except for those caused by other humans, for which the second rider would be responsible. This interpretation would explain the "green" as being the color of that death which is due to the inherently mortal nature of life rather than to the actions of other humans. In both the Greek of LXX and the Hebrew of MT, however, the term for "death" includes death by plague or pestilence, and thus "sword, hunger, and death" could mean war, hunger, and plague (see 4QpPsª [4Q171]

1-2). In this reading — which is perfectly valid — the role of the rider on the red horse is duplicated.

6:9 θυσιαστηρίου. This is the altar of sacrifice, even though in 8:3-4 it clearly seems to be the same as the altar of incense. In the spiritual Christian temple the prayer of the holy ones is indeed one with the sacrifice of the martyrs, and there must therefore be a single altar whereon is offered the perfect sacrifice, on the model of the sacrifice of the Lamb-Christ. The substitution of prayer for temple sacrifice — "the offering of the lips in compliance with the decree of law will be like the pleasant aroma of justice " — had already been contemplated at Qumran, where worship was offered "without the flesh of burnt offerings and without the fats of sacrifice" (1QS 9:3-6; cf. CD 6:12). It may seem strange that the souls of the dead — those slaughtered like the sacrificial victims in the temple and like the Lamb — are *under* the altar. The term "soul" (ψυχή) probably means "life" (see 8:9; 16:3), which is a principle residing in the blood; the context explicitly recalls that their blood has been shed. In the Jerusalem temple (see Introduction, p. 32), it is precisely under the altar of sacrifice that the blood of the sacrificial victims flowed (Lev 17:27; *m. Pes.* 5; *m. Yoma* 5:6; *m. Mid.* 3:2), and it was thus possible to imagine that the victims' life ran under the altar and entered into the earth. This detail of blood under the altar must have been well known in first-century Palestinian Judaism, even as a result of criticism by the Essenes who argued from Scripture (see *TS* 52:12 and 53:5-6, which echoes Lev 17:13 and Deut 12:24) that the blood from the sacrifices should not be channeled into the valley of Kedron but rather should disappear down a shaft (*TS* 32:12-15 and see *m. Hul.* 2:9). It must have been a lively debate, in view also of the symbolic value of that river of water and blood (the water of purification was mixed with the blood) which in some way flowed out of the temple and calls to mind the Christian reworking of the theme in John 19:34 and 1 John 5:6-7.

6:10-11 Ἕως πότε . . . πληρωθῶσιν. This idea — that the end would come only when a certain number either of the living (2 *Bar.* 23:4-5) or of converts (Rom 11:25-26) had been reached — was a fairly common one (see *1 Enoch* 47:4 [*BS*]). There is a similar protest on the part of the souls of the just in *4 Ezra* 4:33-37. Besides the scriptural origin of some elements (the "Until when?" for instance, is probably derived from Ps 79:5 or Zech 1:12), this is one of the cases in which the parallel between *4 Ezra* and the Apocalypse is too close to be mere coincidence. Just as John announces the coming of a victorious lion, as occurs in *4 Ezra,* and then introduces the slaughtered Lamb instead, so here, I believe, does he deliberately set himself against *4 Ezra* (or against his ideas) when he specifies that those who must be fulfilled are those who have been killed. By exalting a victory that is obtained through a form of death which is a way of witnessing, he is clearly making a statement against worldly triumphalism. John uses the term "fulfilled," and at no point says that the fulfillment of the martyrs consists in their reaching a certain number. The verb "fulfill," moreover, is the same one as is generally used to mean the fulfillment of Scripture. John might therefore be thinking that the fullness of testimony would be brought about by the slaughter of the faithful, regardless of their numbers. This might in turn be linked to a reflection on martyrdom (inasmuch as it is analogous to the sacrifice of the Lamb) as the fulfillment of Scripture, or even as a new covenant that completes the old one. For the "white robe" see the comments on 2:10 and 3:4.

ἐπὶ τῆς γῆς. The meaning of the passage changes dramatically depending on whether γῆ means the inhabited world or Israel, the Land.

6:12 τὴν σφραγῖδα τὴν ἕκτην. This passage is woven out of echoes from the prophets, primarily ones concerned with the visitation of the LORD. It is a tapestry of apocalyptic tropes that are so common that it is difficult to identify their origins precisely. The sources most likely to have been John's inspiration are Joel 3:1 (= 3:4) (the great day, the darkening of the sun and the moon of blood quoted in Acts 2:20); Amos 8:9 (the black sun; the "sackcloth" appears in the following verse; this passage lies behind Mark 13:24-25 and parallels); Isa 13:9-10 (the day, wrath, sun, moon, stars; this passage also lies behind Mark 13:24-25 and parallels); Isa 34:4 (the heavens being rolled up like a scroll, the stars falling like leaves of a fig tree, and the reference to mountains in this immediate context; also an inspiration for Mark 13:24-25 and parallels). The "great quake" probably comes from Ezek 38:19, where it is aimed against "the land of Israel" and where mountains are also mentioned (see also Jer 10:22, LXX). The image of the sky being rolled up like a scroll becomes intelligible if one believes that God "spread out" the vault of heaven like a scroll. When God draws it back, it rolls up on itself as a scroll would do, and the stars, which hang from the vault of heaven, fall to earth. The falling of the stars is the disintegration of the "hosts of heaven" (Isa 34:4) — the destruction of the rebel angels' power. It is accompanied by the fall of the mountains, which appear here for the first time together with the islands (see 16:20). The islands usually represent eastern kingdoms like Greece and, later, Rome, and they are spiritual entities capable of trembling and experiencing fear, as we see most clearly in Ezek 26:15-18, where the "princes of the sea" also figure. Contemporary uncertainty about the relation of islands to solid land (see Introduction, p. 29) allowed the possibility that they might move (like the Symplegades, for instance). If the mountains are seen as the demonic powers behind the strength of pagan kingdoms (see comments on 17:9-10), then their relationship to the islands and to the kings is clear; everyone who accepts the power structures of this world, from kings to slaves, will ask the mountains, in the words of Hos 10:8, to hide them from the face of God and to protect them from the wrath of the Lamb. As γῆ is contrasted to the sky, it probably does not refer to the Holy Land but to the whole earth.

The scene in which the kings seek refuge under the mountains and among the rocks has several sources; the rocks come from Isa 2:10, 21, while in Hos 10:8 the idolatrous Israelites plead with the mountains and the hills. The context is different from that in Hosea. There the wicked desire the end of the physical world, while here the enemies of God seem to be making a desperate plea for protection. Something similar happens in Luke 23:30, in a passage found only in that Gospel; on the way to Golgotha Jesus cites accurately the words of Hosea, prophesying that the inhabitants of Jerusalem will utter them when their city is destroyed. This destruction (whether in 70 CE or at the end of the world) is understood to be a direct consequence of the killing of Jesus (the "green wood" of the new, Christianity, as opposed to the "old wood" of Judaism: Luke 23:31). In any case, in the Apocalypse the mountains have no choice but to fall, any more than do the fallen angels and, at least according to a Qumranic text, their equally sinful offspring the giants ("And their sons, whose height was like that of the cedars and whose bodies were like mountains, indeed fell"; CD 2:18-19). The Face is an object of fear for some (20:11), while others have received a promise that they will look upon it, and so they do (22:3-4 and comments); its relation to the Lamb, to whose wrath it is here juxtaposed, is not clear.

σεισμὸς μέγας ἐγένετο. This "great quake" is a cosmic upheaval, and does not necessarily involve a disturbance of the physical earth (see Matt 8:23-27, where the same phrase is used to indicate a storm "on the sea"). In the NT the adjective "great" often qualifies this noun, at times in an apocalyptic context (Luke 21:11) but not always (see Acts 16:26, where there is an identical phrase). In any case, it is always a sign of divine intervention: it points to salvific intervention in the passage from Acts, while in Matt 28:2 it indicates the presence of "an angel of the Lord, descending from heaven." For us the pertinent question is what meaning might be attributed to a movement of the earth or of another element, a movement that was sometimes believed to be very intense, but localized. All religious people would agree that it had a spiritual element, and in Jewish or Christian circles its nature would be understood to be angelic. In the passage in Matthew where Jesus calms the storm he rebukes the winds and the sea, and, the evangelist concludes, "The men were amazed" (Matt 8:27), thus contrasting the reaction of mere humans, who are amazed, and the angelic or spiritual beings, who are not amazed because they know Jesus (see Matt 8:29); this interpretation assumes that there is an angelomorphic nature behind the waves, the sea, the winds, and perhaps the storm itself.

7:1 εἶδον τέσσαρας ἀγγέλους. The image of the four punishing angels restrained by another angel, perhaps their leader, appears in *2 Bar.* 6:4-5, where four angels wait "at the four corners of the city" to set fire to it and the fifth restrains them long enough for the sacred temple furnishings to be salvaged. It is possible that *2 Baruch* took inspiration from the Apocalypse, although there are many differences in the details; here, for instance, the fifth angel arises from the East, while in *2 Baruch* he comes down from heaven. See an analogous scene also in *1 Enoch (BS)* 66:1 and comments on 9:14-15. If by γῆ John means the Holy Land (as the biblical source of this passage, which is Ezek 7:2 [see also 9:1-8], induces us to believe), the similarity between the texts is even stronger. The presence of the sea would suggest that John has the whole earth in mind, but nonetheless the context of 7:1-8 does suggest that the scene takes place within the borders of Israel.

κρατοῦντας . . . ἀνέμους. A comparison with 1:18, 2:1, and 9:14 probably suggests strongly that these winds, too, which are certainly connected with the four corners of the earth (see Dan 7:2; Zech 2:10; 4 Ezra 13:5), are to be considered as angelic beings. 4 Ezra 3:19 also mentions "four doors," which might be those by which the angel-winds enter and leave the earth (see also comments on 16:4).

7:2 ἀναβαίνοντα . . . ἡλίου. This reference to Isa 41:25 takes on christological significance when it appears in a Christian text (see Luke 1:78). The immediate context suggests that the passage refers at least primarily to the salvation of Israel; that destruction is postponed until the saved are marked with a seal is probably derived from Ezek 9:4, which in turn is a reworking of Exod 12. This interpretation is suggested both by the list of those saved from the twelve tribes and by the literary precedent of Ezek 9:1-8 in which we meet six men (actually angels) who massacre those inhabitants of Jerusalem who do not receive a mark from a seventh man, who guides the other six.

7:2-3 σφραγῖδα . . . σφραγίσωμεν. "Seal" and "to mark with a seal" occur eight and thirteen times respectively in the text with two basic meanings. A seal can represent closing: the seven seals on the scroll, the sealing of the abyss (20:3), the sealing of the utterance of the seven thunders (10:4), or the words of the prophecy (22:10). A seal can also be a distinguishing mark, as in those marked with a seal here and in 9:4. In either case, whether it is attached to words, to saved human beings, or to things, the seal is always a sign of the presence or power of God (see 4QShir^b [4Q511] fr. 30, 3). The χάραγμα, the

"brand" of the beast, is a demonic imitation of the "seal" of God, to which it is
contrasted (see comments on 13:16).

7:4 ἑκατὸν τεσσεράκοντα τέσσαρες. This number, the square of twelve,
is the first three-figured number to appear in the book. The Greeks and the
Jews, who had neither arabic numbers nor the number "zero," used the letters
of the alphabet to indicate the value of numbers. The twenty-four letters of
the Greek alphabet, with the addition of three extra letters (ancient graphic
symbols that had fallen out of use), usually followed by an apostrophe, represented the units from 1 to 9, the tens from 10 to 90, and the hundreds from 100
to 900. Thus α' = 1, ω' = 800, and ⱶ' *(sampi)* = 900. The thousands, from 1000
to 900,000, were represented by the same letters, preceded by another symbol,
so that ͵α = 1000 and ͵ω = 800,000. This their way of representing and of
thinking about numbers was different from ours: numbers like 1 or 40 or 300
or 1000 corresponded to a single letter-symbol, while 360, for instance, was
represented by two letter symbols: that for 300 and that for 60. Moreover, the
position of the symbols does not matter: α' is always 1, and ι' is always ten,
whatever their order. They were most commonly written in descending order,
as in this text, or in ascending order: Plutarch, discussing a legend about 7777
Argives, writes "seven and seventy and seven hundred and seven thousand"
(*Mor.* 245d). Our system of symbols enables us to "see" immediately a connection between, for instance, 4 and 40; the sum of the two, 44, appears as the
same symbol written twice, which gives it a certain solidity that is absent in
Greek, where 44 is usually written as μδ' (ΜΔ'), and there is no visible similarity between the two symbols (see 13:18). Thousands (or "chiliads") are per
se a tribal or military division characteristic in ancient Israel (e.g., Exod 18:21,
25; see Num 1:16, where the "thousands of Israel" appear) — one that was revived at Qumran. It is not clear to what extent this revival was symbolic since
thousands, together with hundreds and tens, appear both in texts about the
organization of the sect's ritual life and in texts about the eschatological battle
(1QS 2:20-22; CD 13:2 [the so-called "Rule of the Dwelling in the Encamp-
ments"]; 1QM [and 1Q33] 2 and 3, 5:3-4 [where the first thousand is divided
into seven formations], and 12:4; 4Q491 fr. 13.2). Those Qumranic texts that
describe the eschatological army (1QM) usually assume that it will be organized around the number "seven" (seven formations, seven lines, seven jave-
lin throws); the cavalry, however, seems to consist of 6000 troops, 500 from
each tribe (1QM 6:8-11: a difficult text to understand). This tells us simply that
it would have been natural for a first-century Jew who knew the Bible to
imagine a community of the elect or an eschatological army organized in
groups of a thousand.

The list of the twelve sons of Jacob-Israel corresponds neither in order nor in members to those found in Genesis (e.g., 35:23-26). Judah, the fourth son of Jacob, born from Leah, is named first, ahead of the firstborn Reuben; the change makes sense in light of the fact that the kings of Israel, and Jesus himself, come from the tribe of Judah (see 5:5). The disappearance of Dan is usually accounted for by the idea that the Antichrist would be a Danite, as well as by the unfavorable traditions about Dan (see Judg 18). In any case, the issue is complicated by the fact that Joseph's two sons Ephraim and Manasseh, whom Jacob adopted in his old age (see Gen 48), had replaced their father in the list of the patriarchs as progenitors of two "half-tribes" (thus maintaining the number of tribes at twelve, despite the presence of thirteen names in the list). John's list is odd in that it contains Joseph's name as well as Manasseh's but not Ephraim's. Perhaps John simply wanted to have a list of twelve names that exalted Judah and excluded Dan, and was not interested in other details.

7:9 εἶδον . . . ὄχλος. The utterance of the number 144,000 leads into a vision, not only of people whose number the visionary had heard pronounced, but of a "great throng" (ὄχλος πολύς). This literary device occurs several times in the book: a certain reality is announced, and is followed by a vision of something larger, of which only a part had been announced. The beginning of ch. 6, where the victorious lion is announced and then the Lamb appears, follows this pattern inasmuch as Judaism (the lion of Judah) is only a part of the (theologically speaking) larger reality of Christianity. The latter does not negate the former — the sacrifice of the Lamb, which is at the heart of the Jewish religion, is the true victory of the lion of Judah — but includes the former within itself. The throng itself is varied and, if I am correct, includes the saved from within Israel (the "tribes"), along with the saved of the rest of the earth ("peoples" and "nations" and "languages"). The whole church has many parts, and only one, that composed of the Jews, bears a number. The number of 144,000, who are the army of the Lamb (see comments on 14:1 and 4), seems to be half of something else: 288,000 is indeed the number of soldiers in the army of David (1 Chr 27:1-15). Perhaps John wants to emphasize that the church is made up of two halves: those who come from the circumcision, and those who come from paganism. The two halves are not balanced in numbers since only that half composed of the Jews is numbered and the sum of the two halves is so great that "no one could count it"; the implication is that the Gentiles are more numerous. Nonetheless, from a theological point of view they are halves, and the Jewish half has a particularly honorable calling, although its number is still a multiple of 6 (see comments on 13:18). That the crowd cannot be counted means that God's promise to Abraham — that he will give him innumerable descendants, like the stars in heaven and the sand of the sea (Gen 15:5; 22:17; 32:13, etc.) — has finally been fulfilled (see also note to 12:18). Lastly this mystical innumerability, which is reached by the Christian church thanks to the presence of the pagans, may signify that the church cannot be conquered by Satan, whose power is always countable (see notes to 3:11 and 19:12).

φοίνικες . . . αὐτῶν. Palms were symbols of victory in the entire Greek and Hellenistic world (e.g., Plutarch, *Mor.* 723b); in an example of theological reversal the palm becomes a symbol of martyrdom within Christianity, because the Lamb's victory is precisely in his sacrifice. Can this passage mean that all the saved ones must have been physically killed? Perhaps their death could be a form of spiritual death: one that is indeed modeled on the sacrifice of the Lamb, but that could be understood in terms of a Pauline theology of conversion and baptism (see Rom 6:3-7, etc.). Nonetheless, a reading of the Apocalypse does give one the impression of a militant Christianity that did not seek the spilling of its members' blood, but that certainly did not fear it.

7:11 πάντες οἱ ἄγγελοι. The scene of 5:11, of the angelic court in its entirety, is revisited here, but with the order of the elements altered. In 5:11 we have, arranged outward from the center, the throne, the living creatures, the elders, and the angels. Here, instead, we have the throne, the elders, the living creatures, and the angels. That the four living creatures and the twenty-four elders appear interchangeable lends weight to the notion that the elders too are angelic figures.

7:12 εὐλογία. In spite of the parallels between them, there are differences between the praises offered by the angels here and those offered by humans in v. 10. The humans attribute "salvation" to God, but this does not appear in the sevenfold list of elements with which the angels praise God; that it is a list of seven is deliberate (see comments on 5:12). The humans' praise, moreover, is directed to "our God, to him who sits on the throne, and to the Lamb," whereas that of the angels is directed simply "to our God." It seems that humans cannot address God except through the mediation of the Lamb (see comments on 22:3).

7:13-17 It would seem that in the last part of this chapter the promises made in 3:4-5 are fulfilled. This section of ch. 7 comes at the end of the sequence of events that follow the opening of the sixth seal (6:12) and seems to show some development relative to those events that follow the opening of the fifth. There (6:9-11) we encountered the "souls of those slaughtered"; they are "underneath the sacrificial altar" and are given "a white robe," which temporarily satisfies their impatience for justice until such time as "the ones who are to be killed" are "fulfilled" (see comments on 6:11). Here we see human figures (see 7:9) who are already wearing "white robes" because they have passed through a bloody persecution during which they "washed" and "bleached" their robes "in the blood of the Lamb." No altar is mentioned here; these figures are "before the throne of God" in "his temple," where they "render [priestly?] service to him day and night." There are so many of them that "no one could count" them (7:9), which suggests that they represent the whole body of the saved, of whom those under the altar were the first fruits. That John, in v. 15b, shifts to the future tense, looking forward to the content of ch. 21, further suggests that this passage is a development of the preceding one. What is John describing here? We have suggested that this innumerable "throng" includes in its ranks the "one hundred forty-four thousands"; now we must suppose that it also includes "the souls of those slaughtered" who were "underneath the sacrificial altar," but who are no longer waiting passively but rather are serving in the temple, now that their "fellow servants and their brothers" have been fulfilled. Perhaps those who were slain correspond with the 144,000 and represent all those among the saved who are of the circumcision, or perhaps those who were slain were their first fruits and the 144,000 are their totality.

The condition of all of the saved is not clear. The presence of the temple, despite the use of the future tense, seems to make clear that this is not the final blessedness of the New Jerusalem. I would suggest two possible alternative interpretations. According to the first of these, the blessedness described here is a celestial anticipation of that described in ch. 20 as the earthly millennium. "He that sits on the throne," who "will abide upon them," seems to be God, possibly present in the person of the Lamb "in the midst of the throne": Jesus Christ, the king of the millennium (20:4, 6). The "temple" is that which will presumably exist in the "city, the beloved one" (20:9), and the "white robe" is the (spiritual) body of the first resurrection. That these figures are endowed with priestly roles further confirms their royal status (5:10), which will be realized in the millennium. According to the other possible interpretation, the blessedness described here represents an intermediate state of proximity to God (he that "sits on the throne"), in his heavenly temple, which will be named explicitly for the first time in 11:19. The image of the white robe suggests this blessedness, or might very hypothetically signify the "vehicle" for the disincarnate soul (see comments on 3:4).

7:14 τῆς θλίψεως τῆς μεγάλης. That the tribulation is defined as "great" does not mean that John has in mind a universal persecution of Christianity. Rather, it is great because it is the superhuman and spiritual clash between believers and the forces of Satan (see comments on 1:10). Christians can triumph only by washing their robes in the blood of the Lamb. It is difficult to say whether this phrase refers symbolically to baptism or literally to martyrdom because the connection between baptism by water and bloody martyrdom is extremely close.

7:16 οὐδὲ μὴ πέσῃ . . . καῦμα. John makes free use of Isa 49:10, a song of rejoicing at the return of the exiles who in Isa 48:20 are invited to "go out of Babylon." The text from deutero-Isaiah has eschatological overtones ("on the day of salvation," 49:8) and, after stating that the returning exiles will not hunger or thirst, goes on to declare that "neither the scorching nor the sun shall strike them" (49:10; LXX reads οὐδὲ πατάξει αὐτοὺς ὁ καύσων οὐδὲ ὁ ἥλιος) "Scorching" or "burning" is the etymological meaning of "seraph" and is the word used to describe the "fiery" poisonous serpents of Num 21:6 as well as the mysterious flying dragons of Isa 14:29 and 30:6. They must have been a kind of angelomorphic being that God could send to punish Israel and that could be considered demonic in nature. John does not say any more that the sun or the "scorching" will be kept from striking the holy people, but from "falling on them" (for "fall" see comments on 2:5). We have already seen the fall of the stars (6:13) and of the mountains (6:16), and we will shortly see the fall of a large, burning star (8:10). I believe that with the fall of the sun and the πᾶν καῦμα John refers to the attack of the rebel angels whose power over humans began with their fall from heaven. The term καῦμα probably means "something blazing, scorching" (in classical Greek the term could also refer to a burning coal). Thus what we have here is stars, that is, devils (it will be common in Christian folklore to define the devil as a lump of burning coal).

8:1 σιγή. The liturgy of the angels falls silent when the prayers of men rise up to God (see 8:3) so that God can hear them (thus Bauckham 1993, pp. 70-83 and cross references). But there is no rabbinic teaching on this theme before the end of the 3rd century, and earlier sources connect the silence of the angels with moments of revelation: angels are silent when God is speaking (thus Halperin 1988, pp. 137-41). Further, there are moments of silence connected neither to human prayer nor to divine self-revelation in the angelic liturgies discovered at Qumran and Masada (see Newsom 1985, p. 56), in which we also find the expression "voice of silence" (4Q405 frr. 20-22, 2:7, 12). And *T. Adam,* which contains traditions that can be related to worship before 70 CE, records a moment of silence among the angels in the "twelfth hour" of the night (i.e., at daybreak, since the day begins at sunset) at the same time as the offering of incense (Bauckham 1993, pp. 70-83). The silence could also be interpreted as a return to the silence of creation (see *4 Ezra* 6:39; 7:30, which has a silence of "seven days"; Pseudo-Philo, *Lib. Ant. Bib.* 60.2; see also the critical position of *2 Bar.* 3:7-8).

The question of the amount of time remains; why on earth does John say that the silence lasts "half an hour"? The answers commonly given are that he wanted to indicate a short time, or that he was making a reference to an actual half-hour pause within the temple liturgy. The latter hypothesis, although it has been reinforced by some of the texts newly discovered, is still difficult to prove since our knowledge of contemporary liturgies and of the time spans involved in them is very incomplete. As to the former hypothesis, John does not say at all that the silence in heaven lasts for half an hour, but rather that there is silence "for something like" half an hour. He thereby makes clear that the time is *not* half an hour but that it does have a connection to that amount of time whose characteristic feature lies in being half of something.

Rather than entering into a discussion of how short a period of time half an hour is, therefore, we do better to reflect on the presence in the book of "halved" times, of which this is the first. I will begin with the basic hypothesis that the significance of periods of time as well as of measures lies not so much in the unit of measurement (days, weeks, months, years, cubits, stades, etc.) as in the numerical value attached to them, which is where the deeper meaning of the passage, the meaning that we would call symbolic, is located. To establish fully the interpretive validity of this point, we would have to compare all such cases within the text, but for now let us restrict ourselves to the observation that the most important "halved" period in the text is that of the "half week" of days or years (three and a half days or years). This halved period is derived from Daniel, where it indicates the length of the persecution; in the Apocalypse it seems to refer to a period during which the holy ones are overwhelmed on the earth by the forces of evil (see comments on 11:3). Whatever the real duration within human history of this half-hour period of silence (in *Apoc. Abr.* 28:5 there is a correspondence between an hour and a hundred years), if its being halved is intended as a reference to such a period of suffering, then it follows that John thinks that martyrdom is true prayer, or at least thinks that the Christian God reveals himself in martyrdom. When she is being persecuted then the church is truly praying and witnessing, and her prayer and witness are so welcome in heaven that they temporarily silence the angelic liturgy. Just as the martyrdom of the faithful is true prayer, so the sacrifice of the Lamb is the true revelation, and before this mystery the heavens — that is, the angels — can do nothing but fall silent. It may, finally, be possible that the silence in heaven is also the silence of God (see Ign. *Eph.* 19, where he speaks of "deafening mysteries, formed in the silence of God," and comments on 11:3, 13).

8:2 εἶδον . . . ἀγγέλους. This group of angels is introduced by the article, as if the reader were already aware of their existence. At the beginning of the book John talked about "seven spirits that are in front of his throne" (1:4), who later appear as "seven torches of fire" still "before the throne" (4:5). The seven angels who appear here might be the same angelic/spiritual beings (see 5:6 and comments). In a very fragmentary, and possibly apocalyptic, text from Qumran (4QNarrative [4Q458]) the isolated expression "first angel" appears, which suggests the presence of a group or list of angels (it is impossible to say whether this first angel has a special role or honor, as in Apoc 21:9).

ἐδόθησαν . . . σάλπιγγες. During the period of silence in heaven (and therefore, if I am correct, of persecution on earth) divine providence does not remain inactive. When the souls under the altar complained, they were told to "rest a short time more," but a white robe was also given to each of them (ἐδόθη αὐτοῖς). In like manner here, during the half-hour of silence among the angels "seven trumpets [i.e., one each] were given to them (ἐδόθησαν αὐτοῖς)." I believe that the parallel, which is strengthened by the use of *passivum divinum*, is deliberate: while the prayers and sacrifices of the persecuted rise up to reach God, those who have already been sacrificed wait for the fulfillment of promises — a fulfillment that has already begun — and the angels prepare themselves for action.

8:3 τὸ θυσιαστήριον τὸ χρυσοῦν. This verse shows that there is a single altar in the heavenly temple "before the throne." It is a "sacrificial altar," but it is also described as being "golden," and it is the place where the "incense" is offered (see comments on 6:9). In the earthly temple there were two altars; that "of the sacrifices" — that is, of the blood offerings — was covered with copper (or bronze: Exod 27:2; 38:2; 1 Kings 8:64; 9:25, etc.) and that of the incense was covered with gold (Exod 30:1-10; 37:25-28; 1 Kings 6:22, etc.) and was even called "the golden altar" (Num 4:11). John is making the point that heavenly worship, the angelic liturgy that is the pattern for that on earth, involves only one altar, upon which occurs the perfect sacrifice, pleasing to God: the offering of incense, which means prayers. This is a projection into the heavenly realm of the Christian awareness that bloody sacrifices in an earthly temple are useless since the already accomplished sacrifice of Christ rendered animal sacrifice obsolete (see also Heb 13:10). Thus only one altar is needed for the purely spiritual worship in heaven (see comments on 9:14 for its angelic aspects). The implication is that earthly (Jewish) worship, which has two altars to represent the duality of its physical and spiritual aspects, is a corruption and that the Christian approach in which (personal) sacrifice and prayer become synonymous is the only proper one. That prayer should be seen as having replaced animal sacrifice may well be a characteristic attitude of a minority group that has been excluded from the temple. CD 11:20ff. recalls Prov 15:8 in stating that "the sacrifice of the wicked one is an abomination, but the prayer of the just one is like an agreeable offering." Jewish opinion never turned against animal sacrifice per se but against sacrifice performed by "the wicked." For the sectarians at Qumran all other Jews, and especially the authorities in charge of worship in Jerusalem, were wicked, followers of the "wicked Priest," and thus no sacrifice performed in the earthly temple was actually pleasing to God. Unlike the Apocalypse, however, *ShirShabb* seems to refer to a kind of sacrificial worship among the ranks of the angels (see comments on 3:12 and 6:9). This proves that both Christian groups and radical Jewish groups could dissociate themselves from the worship at Jerusalem, but that apparently only Christian groups rejected in theory the possibility that sacrificial practice might be renewed even in the eschatological future (baptist groups besides Essenes and Christians must have developed an alternative form of worship, but the sources about such groups are so confused that it is impossible to arrive at any definite positions; see Thomas 1935 and Klijn-Reinink 1973).

8:5 σεισμός. The word appears at the end of a list that includes beings of angelic nature (thunders, voices, lightnings), and it does not seem to be essentially different from these others (see comments on 6:12). This quake is probably an earthquake: as the "fire" from the heavenly throne is thrown to the earth, so here are several instances of phenomena that begin in heaven (the thunders, voices, and lightnings) and end on earth (the quake). We can also note that the angel does not throw incense onto the earth but rather "fire," which might be another angelic or spiritual being (it is possible but less likely that the angel casts to the earth an entire censer full of heavenly fire). The fall of this fire seems to be the cause of the "quake." Perhaps this is also a veiled reference to the fall of Satan and his acolytes, who were cast from heaven to earth. Thunders, voices, and a quake occur together also in *Apoc. Abr.* 30:8, where they are the tenth plague to strike the pagans.

8:7 καὶ πῦρ . . . κατεκάη. At the sound of the first three trumpets fire, or something burning, is thrown or falls on the earth and into the sea, rivers, and springs. This is a development of the image in the previous verse, in which the angel threw fire to the earth. The presence of the seas and of fresh water imply that this γῆ refers to the whole earth and not just to Israel. At the sound of the first four trumpets the "third part" of some cosmic entity comes to harm (and the "third part" of mankind will be killed after the sounding of the third trumpet: 9:15, 18). In certain contexts John makes a theological point of dividing the matter under discussion into three parts, of which one is destroyed. The original source of the image is Ezek 5, which is echoed in Zech 13:8-9 in reference to the punishment of God on Israel and Jerusalem; we find it again in 16:19, where, during another "great quake," the "city, the great one" is divided "into three parts." It may also reappear in 11:1-2 (see comments).

8:8 ὡς ὄρος μέγα. The presence of "something like" and of the adjective "great" almost certainly means that the being who is "thrown" (by God, with *passivum divinum?*) is a spiritual being, an angel (see comments on 6:12; 17:9-10).

8:9 τὸ τρίτον τῶν πλοίων. This reference to "ships" is unexpected and is not very obvious. The "ships" are in fact the only man-made items that are damaged or destroyed in the wake of the trumpets' sounding. I believe that John is trying to establish a connection between this passage and 18:19, which records the wealth of those who "have ships in the sea" (these two passages are the only places where the word "ship" appears). This connection does not necessarily mean that John is referring to the same historic event, but that there is a parallel between the fall of mountains, stars, and fire from heaven, and the fall of the city: the same figures are harmed in both cases, because the earthly city seems to be some kind of historical expression of the demonic power that was cast out of heaven. This power is on the side of "the rich," while the true faithful are "the poor" (see Introduction, p. 17 and comments on 17:5).

8:10 ἔπεσεν . . . ἀστὴρ μέγας. Both the phrase and the concept pertain to the Enochic tradition (see, e.g., *1 Enoch* 86:1 [*BD*]: "and I looked, and behold, a star fell down from heaven"): in the Enochic tradition falling stars are symbols of the fall of the rebel angels' chief (see Luke 10:18 and comments on 9:1 and 12:4, 9). That the star is compared to "a torch" might mean that it is like one of the spirits of God; the term λαμπάς appears only here and in 4:5. If this line of argument is valid, then the angelic figure is of the highest level, at least in its origins.

8:11 ἐκ τῶν ὑδάτων ὅτι ἐπικράνθησαν. The "bitter waters" must be a reference to the waters of Marah (Exod 15:23). After the events at Marah God promised the Israelites that if they would obey all his statutes he would not afflict them with the diseases with which he afflicted the Egyptians (Exod 15:26). This verse of the Apocalypse is seemingly intended to make the reader or hearer reflect on the example of Israel (for the "plagues of Egypt" as a threat to the Jews, see comments on 15:1). The same is true of "wormwood." In Jeremiah God always threatens to feed wormwood with "poisonous water" to Israel (Jer 9:14; in LXX [9:15] the wormwood is absent, but there is "water of gall," i.e., very bitter; see also Jer 8:14, LXX) or to the prophets of Israel (Jer 23:15; here, too, LXX does not mention wormwood as food, but has "bitter water" as a drink). Wormwood and bitter water are thus closely connected to the story of Israel both past (the waters of Marah) and future (Jeremiah's threats).

8:12 ἐπλήγη . . . τῶν ἀστέρων. Sun and Moon are two of the seven rebel angels who abandoned the plan of God from the beginning. The darkening of a third of the sources of light (which is spiritual or angelic) parallels the Sa-

tanic dominion over a part of the angelic hosts — a dominion that is elsewhere portrayed as a direct action by the "dragon," who "threw . . . to the
earth" a third of the stars (see 12:4 and comments). We are not told here who
it is that strikes the stars, but John might be using the passive voice to imply
that God's will is responsible, thus emphasizing God's power over the forces
of evil. The darkening of each day and night by a third (of their duration?)
looks forward to the time when they will disappear altogether. It could also be
connected to the shortening of "those days" of Matt 24:22.

8:13 Καὶ . . . ἤκουσα. From a purely literary point of view, John likes to
divide his seven part lists into two subgroups of four and three elements,
which he distinguishes from each other in various ways. Here he uses the appearance of the eagle to mark the division between the first four trumpets,
whose effects are described briefly, and the last three: these last three are associated with the three repetitions of "woe," and the description of them lasts
until the appearance of the seven bowls (chs. 15–16). It is consistent with
John's usual practice that he should expand in this manner on the last three
items in a septet. For the use of "woe," which may be connected with Ezek
13:18, see 4QShir^b (4Q511) fr. 63, 3:5.

ἑνός . . . πετομένου. This is the first time that we find εἷς–μία–ἕν used as an
adjective. In some cases it is clear that John is using the term to indicate the
uniqueness of the thing he is describing (e.g., 21:21: "Each of the gates . . . was
made of a single pearl"; see 17:12, 13, 17; 18:8, 10, 16, 19), while in others he
might simply be using it as an indefinite article (possibly here and in 9:13;
18:21; 19:17). The eagle is one of the animals that has a positive significance for
John. The fourth of the living creatures near the throne of God is ὅμοιον ἀετῷ
πετομένῳ (4:7), and God gives "the two wings of the eagle, the great one" to
the woman so that she can take refuge in the desert (see comments on 12:14).
As the eagle appears only in these contexts, it seems plain that we are not dealing with just any eagle but rather with an instrument of God's word; if this is
so, then "the great voice" is not the eagle's own loud cry but a manifestation
of "the great voice" (see comments on 1:10-11). What is more, as the eagle is
flying in "high heaven" where we will later meet "another angel" on a mission
of proclamation (14:6), it is possible that this proclaiming eagle is itself a spiritual angelomorphic being. Eagles and stars are both embroidered on the veil
of the temple, which represents the vault of heaven (see Introduction, p. 32)
and thus are conceptually similar (and the word μεσουράνημα, "high heaven,"
can mean the zenith, but it can also be used for the culmination of a star or
constellation).

τοὺς κατοικοῦντας . . . γῆς. This is a favorite expression of John's (but see
also 1 Enoch [BS] 37:5 and passim), and it occurs here for the third time. We

will come across it a total of eleven times, usually with ἐπί and the genitive (3:10; 6:10; 8:13; 11:10 [twice]; 13:8, 14 [twice]; 17:8), once with ἐν and the dative (13:12), and once more with the accusative and no preposition (17:2). The verb "to dwell" indicates either the habitation of the earth by humans susceptible of sin and ruin, or else the dwelling on the earth of the devil (2:13; see 18:2, ἐγένετο κατοικητήριον δαιμονίων), or of an angel in peril (2:13). Otherwise John uses σκηνόω to indicate the dwelling in heaven, or the dwelling of God among men in the New Jerusalem (12:12; 13:6 and 7:15; 21:3). It is almost always impossible to determine with absolute certainty whether γῆ here refers to the populated world (which I believe it does in this passage at least) or to the Holy Land and its inhabitants, the Jews. If the latter is the case, then the three "woes" are directed to Israel.

ἐκ τῶν . . . φωνῶν. The three "woes" are not just three sounds articulated by the flying eagle but — very concretely — their contents, which is everything that happens when the last three seals are opened. Therefore, the "woes" can originate "from (ἐκ) the remaining voices of the trumpet of the three angels."

9:1 καὶ εἶδον . . . εἰς τὴν γῆν. The sentence is Enochic in tone (see 8:10) and refers to the fall of the angels, although the conceptual context is different from that of the Enochic tradition, which does not stress as clearly as does John that the angelic beings who destroy and torture the earth and its inhabitants are firmly under God's control and can accomplish nothing that he has not determined. This is a constant theme in the Apocalypse (see, e.g., 7:1-3). The forces of evil begin their activity at the sound of an angelic trumpet; this immediately makes plain that their activity is directed in some way by God, and the entire chapter seems to be dedicated to underlining further this concept. The punishing angels are no less evil for being under God's control, but on the other hand their evil does not lessen the fact that they are acting in obedience to God; this same concept appears in the case of the "wicked angel of the LORD" of the preexilic tradition (Levison 1995, pp. 464-65). The handing over of the key shows that God maintains his dominion even over the forces of darkness. V. 4 makes explicit that these evil spirits must not harm the flora of the earth, or γῆ, which has already been burned by the fire of the first trumpet. Notwithstanding this, it is possible that γῆ refers to the same land (or earth) from which come those men "who do not have the seal of God" — that is, the unsanctified portion of those inhabitants mentioned at the end of ch. 8. Thus, while the first four trumpets heralded attacks made on non-human entities, with humans being harmed only incidentally (the ships in 8:9 are destroyed, and their occupants presumably drowned, as a consequence of the attack on the seas, and the humans who die in v. 11 do so as a result of the attack on the waters of rivers and springs), the three "woes" involve humanity directly. The "key of the pit of the abyss" appears here with the definite article, perhaps to make plain that John has already talked about it. It could in fact coincide with the "keys of Death and of Hades" (1:18) that are held firmly in the hands of the Risen One. Even if this is not so, it is still clear that John wants to emphasize God's control over everything that happens in his narrative. Even the "pit of the abyss" — the place that, theologically speaking, should be the farthest from divine providence (see 4QTNaph [4Q215] fr. 2, 2; 1QS 9:16; and especially 4QBerᵃ [4Q286] fr. 7, 2:4-5) — is so entirely under his power that not even "the star fallen from heaven" could open it if the key had not been given to him (ἐδόθη, *passivum divinum;* see comments on 9:11). Even the locusts of vv. 3-11 exercise a very limited freedom, the extent of which is circumscribed by a series of passive verbs. They are given (ἐδόθη) only a certain kind of power; it is said to them (ἐρρέθη) what they may not touch and whom they must harm; it is granted to them (ἐδόθη) not to kill but only to torment "for five months." Limits are thus set for the quality, extent, and duration of their power. I do not believe that we can infer from the text the existence of that shadowy feminine world that some exegesis claims to identify in the mind of John (Pippin 1992 and 1994): a subterranean world in rebellion against the will of God, a world that is both threatening and dangerously free, and that is simultaneously dreaded and unconsciously desired by the visionary. John's pre-Galilean cosmos does not contain any areas that lie outside of God's control. God is a totalitarian figure, whose absolute, androcentric, and patriarchal power may indeed seem primitive and even crude to today's hesitant theologies, but I don't think the text allows for any other reading.

9:5   καὶ ἐδόθη αὐτοῖς. "And it was granted *them.*" These are the "locusts," who are the subject of the following ἵνα μὴ ἀποκτείνουσιν αὐτούς, "that they not kill *them.*" These are the "men," subject of βασανισθήσονται, "they be tormented." The accumulation of pronouns renders the sentence quite obscure, especially in English.

μῆνας πέντε. This period of time presents problems for commentators. The most common explanation, here as above, is that John wants to indicate a short period of time (see comments on 8:1 and Vanni 1980, p. 491). The only other place in the book where the number "five" appears is in ch. 17, where John says that five of the seven heads of the beast, which are also "mountains" and "kings," have already "fallen." With respect to that passage (see comments ad loc.) I will argue that the entities in question are the demonic sovereigns who dominated the first five periods of human history. In the light of this theory it becomes interesting that the present chapter (particularly from v. 20

onward) has a strong anti-idolatrous theme. I think that John might be making a connection between, on the one hand, these "five months" that are dominated by a "king" who is "the angel of the abyss" and who has both Greek and Hebrew names (v. 11), suggesting that he can dominate and corrupt both pagan and Jewish worlds, and on the other hand the five eras prior to the birth of Jesus Christ during which human history was dominated by Satan. There is nothing in the text to suggest that this period should be considered short, unless, perhaps, one takes the eternity of God as one's unit of measurement. In any case, it is not clear why an intervention of God should be described as being brief: it is not a period of persecution of the holy ones, but rather of torment of others. The main interpretive problem lies in determining whether John really means to refer to the first five periods of human history that are in the past (Corsini 1980, p. 266), or rather to a moment in the future, which recalls and reverses past history in the course of its eschatological drama. If it is the former, then it is possible that the first five elements in this septet might also refer not to the end of time but rather to the first five eras of human history. Could there be a unified pattern behind the text, such that the first five elements in any septet always refer to the past?

There have been a variety of critical answers to this. In the other septets, as in this one, it is difficult to locate a precise sequence that clearly corresponds to speculations on the cosmic week (see Introduction, p. 20). If we take the current example of the seven trumpets and compare the order of the events described to that of the seven days of creation (Gen 1:1–2:4a), the comparison suggests that there is no such deliberate correspondence. At the sounding of the first trumpet fire, hail (for which see Exod 9:13-35), and blood burn up a third of the land, a third of the trees, and all of the grass; land, trees, and grass are precisely the elements created on the third day. At the second trumpet's sound a mountain of fire turns a third of the sea to blood and destroys a third of its living creatures and of the ships; the sea was created on the third day, the creatures who "creep" in it on the fifth day, the ships do not feature at all in the account of creation, and the transformation of water into blood calls to mind the first of the plagues of Egypt (Exod 7:20). At the sound of the third trumpet a burning star strikes a third of the rivers and springs and causes the death of many men; rivers are not mentioned at all in the six days of creation (the first river appears in Gen 2:20, and Gen 2:5-6 suggest that there were no rivers until that moment) and men were created on the sixth day. At the fourth trumpet a third part of the heavenly lights are darkened; these lights were indeed created on the fourth day, but their darkening calls to mind the ninth plague of Egypt (Exod 10:21-23). With the fifth trumpet, finally, it is the turn of men to be tortured; man was created on the sixth day. With the exception of the correspondence between the fourth trumpet and the fourth day of creation, no pattern of parallels emerges, and there does not even seem to be a clear order; men were killed in the ships (second trumpet) and by the waters of wormwood (third trumpet) long before the torments aimed directly at them after the sound of the fifth trumpet. There is no way to link the events associated with the six trumpets to six past periods of salvation history in such a way as to support the hypothesis of a parallel with the cosmic week, and while various trumpets do refer to the events of the exodus, they do not do so in chronological order.

As for the chronological location of the events John describes, we can note that it is common in prophetic texts for verbs in the past tense to refer to future events. The visionary sees events take place that he later refers to as being in his own past because it was in the past that he saw them, although the events that he foresaw are themselves in the future with regard to the time, whether real or fictitious, at which the vision occurs. As a literary phenomenon this was called "tense interchange" (ἐναλλαγή) by the ancient grammarians. Therefore, that the verbs are in the past tense does not prevent us from interpreting the entire scene as referring to the future. The alternative interpretation requires that we treat the future tense verbs in v. 6 as if they refer to the past; the verbs in question are introduced by the expression "in those days," which in itself gives no indication of where in time the action is located. This is very problematic, though, because the verse is almost an afterthought, an additional, unexpected explanation that John inserts into the description of the vision and in fact the next verb, in v. 8, is in the past tense again. Thus it is likely that John used the future tense deliberately, precisely for the purpose of indicating that the events he is describing are in the future.

9:7 ὡς στέφανοι. For the false crowns of the monsters, see the comments on 3:11.

9:8 ὡς τρίχας γυναικῶν. The plural term "women" occurs only twice in the book, here and in 14:4, where John speaks of virgin men who "have not defiled themselves with women." Women are thus a negative presence and are, or should be, feared by men. The effect of John's statements is rendered all the stronger by virtue of appearing in phrases that are not strictly necessary to the argument and that simply take for granted the negative nature of the feminine. Virgin men have not defiled themselves with women, and demonic monsters composed of elements from different animals have "faces of men" but "hair of women"; in certain contexts it must have seemed normal that the worst devils had women's hair (see *Apoc. Zeph.* 4:4; 6:8). In 4:7 the third of the living creatures has a man's face but definitely not a woman's hair. The detail of women's hair is probably intended to suggest a dangerous seductive ability. There must have been speculation about the fact that even the angels were susceptible to the sight of women's hair, which might have been precisely the instrument of their seduction (see 1 Cor 11:10 and comments on 3:18).

9:9 ὡς φωνὴ ἁρμάτων. This detail is drawn from Joel (2:5), the book that provides the literary antecedent for the entire passage (see the "lion's teeth" in Joel 1:6). The prophet describes the coming of the LORD (ἡμέρα κυρίου: Joel 2:1, LXX) as being like an infestation of locusts who destroy the land and terrorize its inhabitants (1:2; 2:1); it is clear from the context that the land is Israel and its inhabitants are "the people" (1:9, 16; 2:1, 12-18).

9:10 ἀδικῆσαι τοὺς ἀνθρώπους. Within the septet of the seals, as in that of the trumpets, the angels' roles are always linked to human destiny. The seven seals, in particular the fifth and the sixth, describe human realities, but the agents that the visionary sees are in all cases angels, from the figure on the white horse in 6:2 to the angelic court in 7:11. Conversely, while the events surrounding the sounding of the trumpets are on the face of it primarily concerned with the fall of the angels, the account always emphasizes the consequences of the events for human beings, beginning with the "ships" of the second trumpet (8:9). It is difficult to imagine the very existence of angels without making some reference to humans.

9:11 Ἀπολλύων, or "The Destroyer," is probably an allusion to Apollo. That the king of the demons has two names, one Greek and one Hebrew (like the kings of the Hasmonean dynasty), shows his power over both nations, and, contrary to what some of the biblical references cited above would seem to suggest, appears to show that John is not talking only about Israel. Just as the church of the faithful is composed of Jews and pagans (see 7:9 and comments), so, for John, the entire world is composed of Jews and "Greeks" or Gentiles. This distinction is part of a theological rather than an ethnic view of humanity.

The Hebrew name "Abaddon" was originally the name of a place, like Hades or Sheol, but it seems to have been personified in at least one poetic text discovered at Qumran: "saved . . . from the pit and from the Sheol of Abaddon" (*Hodayot* [1QH–4QH] 11:19), while in other such texts it appears as a place (1QH–4QH, line 32 and 4QDibHam[a] [4Q405] 7:8). The "angel of the abyss," the king of the demonic monsters who come out of the pit, must be the same "star" to whom the "key of the pit" was given (see comments on 17:9). A similar expression was used at Qumran as part of a description of a couple of demonic beings: "and [cursed be . . . the ange]l of the pit and the sp[irit of des]truction in al[l] the designs of [your] g[uilty] inclination" (4QBer[a] [4Q286] fr. 7, 2:7; for Death and Hades see 1:18; 6:8; 20:13, 14). The scene in 20:1-3 would suggest that this king-star is none other than Satan.

9:14 λέγοντα. The parallel with 16:7 shows quite indisputably that this altar can talk. We must therefore ask what sort of thing this altar is that can speak, or that has a "voice" of its own, or that has "another angel" that comes from it who has power over fire and whose particular (and perhaps only) role is that of shouting "with a great voice" (see 14:18).

The first parallel is a visual one with the throne. The four "corners" of the altar correspond to the four *hayyot* of the throne; fire is also present at the throne, and voices and angelic or angelomorphic beings are continually coming from it. There is also a structural or functional parallel that runs deeper. As every lamb that is slaughtered "ascends" to the altar to be offered to God in the fire, so the slain Lamb ascends triumphantly onto the Father's throne because his victory is intimately connected with his sacrificial death. If, then, the sacrifice of Christ is from eternity (see comments on 13:7), just so is it celebrated from eternity on the altar of the heavenly temple as the perfect model of the imperfect sacrifices offered in the earthly temple and of the sacrifices of the martyrs (see comments on 6:9). Thus the altar and the throne are both heavenly entities with voices and angels of their own; they seem to be angelic beings themselves, in the sense that we have been discovering in the course of our reading of the Apocalypse. Nevertheless, they do not seem to overlap completely since they perform complementary functions. The throne appears as the revelation of God to the human world (or as the angel of such a revelation), whereas the altar is often an instrument that humans use to direct themselves toward God. This function of the altar as an intermediary appears in the fact that human prayers and incense are offered on top of it, while under it the souls of the martyrs wait to be enthroned as victors with Christ. Thus the altar embodies the spiritual continuum between martyrdom and prayer (see comments on 8:1 and 3). There are, finally, interesting analogies in the *Apocalypse of Abraham,* where the "altar of the mountain" of sacrifice is made of "men" who are immediately identified as "angels" (12:9 and 13:1); these angelic altars themselves then ascend to God, carrying with them the victims offered by Abraham (15:1).

ἐπὶ τῷ ποταμῷ . . . Εὐφράτῃ. The Euphrates, the "great river," is named twice in the book, here and in 16:12. In both cases it is associated with the presence of dreaded beings, whose destructive power is waiting to break forth. Here the four (punishing?) angels are ready to "kill the third part of mankind." The most obvious interpretation is that "mankind" refers to all of humanity. The account has some odd features. In the first place the four angels, whom we would expect to be associated with the four corners of the earth or with the four winds that have been restrained since the opening of the sixth seal (7:1), are now bound at the Euphrates (an association of "angels of punishment" with the "powers of the waters" can be found in *1 Enoch* [*BS*] 66:1; the destruction they bring [the Flood] will reach "all who live and dwell upon the earth"). Also, the Euphrates becomes the conceptual boundary of the inhabited world, beyond which no humans live. In the Qumranic *Genesis Apocryphon,* however, we find that the Euphrates is indeed the eastern boundary of the land, but of the Holy Land that God promised to Israel and that Abraham visited in an elaboration on Gen 13:17 (1QapGen 21). Therefore, on the basis of the promises of universal dominion that are made to Abraham in the Bible (Gen 13:14-15; 15:8; 27:28-29), the land of Israel was held to extend from the Nile to the Euphrates, which implies that the land and the people that become the object of God's wrath at the sound of the sixth trumpet could be primarily the land of Israel and its inhabitants. This interpretation stands in obvious parallel to the events surrounding the pouring out of the sixth bowl: the Euphrates dries up and prepares the way for the kings from the East (16:12). Clearly the scene (especially 16:12; see comments) might be historically linked to fear of the Parthians. Nonetheless, the text never actually says that the four angels cross the Euphrates when they are set free, nor is the reader yet told what will happen when the sixth cup is poured out. If anything, that the angels are four in number might suggest that they will spread out (perhaps at the head of the angelic cavalry; see v. 18) from where they are bound toward the four corners of the earth. If so, then the significance of the Euphrates lies not in its being the eastern boundary of Israel but rather in its flowing from Eden (Gen 2:14), and thus in its vicinity to the place from which humanity first began to populate the earth. I think, therefore, that the "third part of mankind" who are destined to perish with the sixth trumpet is more likely a third of the human race and not just a third of Israel.

9:17 Καὶ οὕτως . . . ὁράσει. When the sixth seal was opened, John first heard the number of those marked with the seal and then saw a crowd that could not be counted (7:4, 9); likewise here when the sixth trumpet is sounded, he first hears the number of the horses in the cavalry (two myriads of myriads) and then sees them. It is clear here that what he sees and what he hears are the same thing rather than two separate things, and the parallel with ch. 7 thus suggests that there is one and not two entities in that passage also. The group of those marked with the seal is not contrasted to the crowd that could not be counted, but both refer to the church of the saved in its component parts.

θώρακας . . . θειώδεις. The adjectives do not seem to describe the substance from which the breastplates are made but rather their external appearance and color. The colors correspond to the three plagues (fire, smoke, and sulfur) that issue from the mouths of the lionlike horses; by "hyacinth" is meant not the flower, but the intense blue of suffocating smoke. It is also possible that "hyacinth" might be the precious stone of the same name and color that we see in the foundations of the New Jerusalem (see 21:20); if so, then fire, sulfur, and hyacinth might be the materials from which the breastplates of these angelic creatures are made, and the hyacinth might accordingly be an indication that the creatures are part of the angelic hosts that are faithful to God (see comments on 15:6 for the possibility of angels dressed in precious stones, and comments on 17:4 for the role of hyacinth; the fire coming from their mouths is also characteristic of the divine forces; see 11:5 and comments on 11:3). Fire and sulfur, finally, insofar as they are instruments of divine punishment, are utterly outside of Satanic control (see 20:10) and thus are fitting attributes of God's punishing angels.

9:19 ὅμοιαι ὄφεσιν. There are similarities between these horses and the locusts of the fifth trumpet. Both sorts of monsters have attributes of horses and of lions, and both have power to inflict harm with their tails. Unlike the locusts, however, these horses kill.

9:20 οἱ λοιποὶ τῶν ἀνθρώπων. The "remainder" are not always a holy remnant but can also, as in this case, have negative connotations. The final verses of this vision — verses that focus primarily on idolatry — are traditional in their vocabulary and phraseology, drawing on Isa 2:8 (against the house of Jacob, which is guilty of idolatry) and Ps 115:4-7. The final list of sins (murders, poisonings, prostitution, thefts) is knit together from the traditional accusations that can be directed both against pagans (see Rom 1:29) and against Jews. In the latter case "prostitution" is the same as idolatry (see comments on 17:1 and Introduction, p. 26). The term πορνεία, like the verb πορνεύω, means any illicit sexual activity, and should perhaps be translated "fornication," if we were sure that "the remainder of mankind" here means all of sinful humanity and not just the remnant of the Jews (see comments on 14:8).

οὐδὲ μετενόησαν. This failure to repent after the three plagues links these figures to Pharaoh with his hardened heart, and to the Egyptians of Exod 7–10 who changed their minds only after the tenth plague. In the Apocalypse it is only in 11:13 that "the rest" appear to repent (see comments). Their failure to repent of their prostitution links these "men" closely to the followers of Jezebel (see 2:20 and comments).

10:1 ἄλλον . . . ἰσχυρόν. It is not clear whom this angel is "other" than. There was another "strong angel" in 5:2, and perhaps John means that this strong angel is different from that one. Or perhaps he wants to distinguish this angel from the four who were liberated in 9:15 (the last angels to have been defined as such), or perhaps from the sixth angel, who was responsible for liberating them. Whatever the case, this angel is distinct from the seven with the trumpets, and stands outside their group. That he is of the highest level and is connected with the very presence of God is shown by the fact that "his feet [were] like pillars of fire," which is a reference to the pillar of smoke and fire that preceded the Israelites in Exod 13:21-22.

This figure shares many characteristics of the risen Christ: the "cloud" (see 1:7), the "rainbow" (which recalls the rainbow around the throne in 4:3), the "face . . . like the sun" (see 1:16), the "feet" like "fire" (see 1:15; 2:18), the "scroll" in his "hand" (see 5:8 and 5:1) that is now "open" and which must be that which the Lamb opened between 6:1 and 8:1, his dominion over land and sea (see 5:13), his "great voice" (see 1:10, where the vision of Christ is introduced), his likeness to a lion (see 5:5; for the "roar" as a messianic characteristic, see *4 Ezra* 11:37). For these reasons many scholars used to hold that this "strong angel" is Christ; some still do (Gundry 1994). All of the references listed above are to parts of the book that the reader or hearer has already encountered, which suggests that John does indeed want to lead his audience to make a connection between this figure and Christ (for the importance of constant reference to what John has said earlier in the text, see Mealy 1992, especially p. 94). There are differences, however, as well as these many similarities. In 1:7 Christ is said to come "with the clouds," whereas the angel here is "wrapped in a cloud," the "scroll" is "open," which assumes that the seven seals have been opened, but it is also possibly "small"; the dominion over "land" and "sea" does not extend as far as the universal dominion ascribed to Christ in 5:13, where it is said to include the "heaven" and the realm "under the earth." The omission of the realms above the heavenly vault and below the earth from his dominion seems to me to be one of the most interesting aspects of this figure, along with the emphasis on the lionlike aspect of his nature at the expense of the lamblike. The figure has an unmistakably christological dimension, but it is somehow partial and limited.

The nature of this angel is also revealed in his actions. In the first place he swears "by him who lives forever and ever" (v. 6), exactly echoing the words of Christ in 1:18: "and, lo, I am the one who lives forever and ever." If John really wanted to make it clear that this angel is Christ, he surely would not have used this exact phrase to identify the authority by whom the angel swears — an authority who must therefore be superior to himself. This argument holds regardless of what identity is ascribed to "the one who lives" (see note to 10:6). In the second place he gives the "small scroll, opened" to John directly without intermediaries so that he may "swallow" it and thus acquire the ability to "prophesy." Why on earth would this angel make John swallow a "little" scroll, especially since this same scroll is described in v. 8 as being "open," therefore inviting us to think that it is the same as the only other scroll mentioned in the book, the one whose seals were opened by the Lamb? (When John uses a diminutive Greek term to describe the scroll that he ate, this does not necessarily mean that it is smaller than the one opened by the Lamb. Herm. 1.2 [*Vis.* 1.2], 1.4 uses the same terms as does John, in a way that suggests they are interchangeable.) The whole scene, finally, is directed by a "voice from heaven" (vv. 4, 8) that both John and the angel obey; this would be odd if the angel were really Christ.

These difficulties will be less severe if the angel is "the angel of Jesus Christ." In fact, if the "scroll" is the same as that which appears in 5:1, then the figure "seated on the throne" may very well be God the Father, who gives the sealed scroll to the Lamb (5:8), who in turn opens all seven seals (6:1–8:1). Now "another angel" — other, that is, than the seven angels who have been sounding the trumpets — gives a small, opened scroll to John. If the scroll represents revelation, then this chain of events recapitulates the structure of 1:1 in which revelation originates with God, is passed on by Jesus Christ who acts by means of his angel, and finally reaches John. In the last passage the scroll might become "small" because it has to be swallowed by John, who is a physically finite human being, or perhaps because it does not contain the fullness of revelation, which would be consistent with the fact that the voices of the thunders are never written down, as well as with the fact that the scroll appears before the seventh trumpet sounds. For the connection between the "rainbow" and the "head" of an angel, see *Apoc. Abr.* 11:3 (which is about Iaoel; see comments on 1:1); for the issue of huge size, see the angel or "power" Jesus (and the feminine angel–Holy Spirit) in the *Revelation* of Elchasai in Epiphanius, *Pan.* 19.4.1-2 (GCS 25, p. 221), and the Risen One accompanied by two angels in the *Gospel of Peter* (fr. 1.10 [40]). See also "the Elect One and the other forces [the human army?] on earth [and] over the sea" (*1 Enoch* [BS] 61:10).

10:3 αἱ ἑπτὰ βρονταί. It is strange that John uses the article since he has not mentioned these "seven thunders" before; that they are numbered suggests that they are different from the other "thunders" mentioned in the book. If the thunders are angelic figures (see comments on 4:5), we can imagine that John would see them as being characterized by appearing in sevens like the angels in the septets, the spirits, the angels of the churches, the mountains, the kings, the heads, and so on. John does not see the thunders but hears "their voices," so it must be from their voices that he perceives that there are seven of them. They must therefore sound one after the other, in such a way that they can be identified separately and counted, as is suggested by the use of the number "seven," which is often linked to a temporal succession. It would be risky to attempt to identify them precisely. They are certainly possessed of some knowledge, which John believes he can access sufficiently well to be able to write it down (v. 4); they reveal this knowledge, but it must then be sealed up and therefore does not become part of the scroll that by now is open and no longer sealed. The thunders are probably among God's means of self-revelation; in primitive Christianity there was a close relationship between thunder and revelation, which explains the epithet "Sons of Thunder" that Jesus himself gives to James and John, as well as the existence of a Nag Hammadi text that consists of a single discourse on revelation and is entitled "Thunder" (NHC 6.2). The closest connection we can make is with the "seven spirits" that John has named four times (1:4; 3:1; 4:5; 5:6) and that he does not mention again in the rest of the book (see comments on 14:13). This connection is reinforced by the fact that the seven spirits, although they are "of God," are also the "seven eyes" (and perhaps the "seven horns") of the Lamb (see comments on 5:6) and are "had" by Christ (3:1). The seven thunders in our passage make their utterance when the christological angel shouts, which further strengthens their connection with a christological figure; it is possible to ask ourselves whether the "voices" of the thunders sound in unison with the "shout" (lit. "roar") of the angel.

10:4 φωνὴν ἐκ τοῦ οὐρανοῦ. This is the first appearance of this expression, which is the usual way of translating the Hebrew *bath qol* (lit. "daughter [of a] voice"). In Jewish tradition, it is not only hypostatized and at times considered equivalent to the Spirit (Charlesworth 1985, pp. 25-26), but John 12:28-29 shows how it could be taken for thunder or for an angel. There is no doubt that it comes from God, but it is difficult to say whether it is the same as Jesus Christ or the Spirit or is another angelic-spiritual being.

10:6 ἐν τῷ ζῶντι . . . αἰώνων. The title might be that of God (4:9, 10; 15:7) or of the risen and glorified Jesus Christ (1:18). The reference to the creation of heaven, earth, and sea (see 4:11) suggests that the "one who lives" is God. We must also bear in mind, however, that in 3:14 Christ is called "the beginning of the creation of God," that in every branch of Judaism and Christianity there were people who believed that the act of creation itself was carried out by a manifestation of God (the creative Word, the Son), and that it is therefore possible that the "one who lives" is the heavenly Christ. It is not as strange as it may seem to us that the epithets of what we consider the first and second persons of the Trinity are used interchangeably. Within the terms of a worldview that interprets every reality that we would call "spiritual" in angelological or angelomorphic terms, there is a place for a continuum of substance between God and man or even between God and the depths of the abyss. The various levels of angels are the intermediate stages: the various points at which this continuum is realized at the level of phenomena. Therefore, epithets and images can "slip" between one level and the next.

χρόνος . . . ἔσται. In vv. 5-7 John recalls and modifies Dan 12:7: "And I heard the man clothed in linen, who was on the waters of the river, and he raised his right hand and his left hand toward heaven, and he swore by the one who lives forever that it would be for a time, times, and half a time, and that when the shattering of the power [lit. "of the hand"] of the holy people comes to an end, all these things would be accomplished." The shift from "man" to "angel" is not an alteration, but a clarification of what is already in Daniel (see 21:17); on the other hand, the oath taken only with the right may come from Deut 32:40ff., in the last part of the Song of Moses, where God himself (or possibly his angel) vows to take bloody revenge on his enemies; this may well indicate John's desire to be very specific about the way in which God's mystery is realized (but see also Isa 62:8). The most interesting change, however, is in the chronological notation. The Hebrew text of Dan 12:7 differs in this detail from Dan 7:25 ("a time, times, and half a time"; see also 12:7, LXX); in 12:7 LXX makes the meaning consistent with 7:25, but MT, Theod., and the Vg. read "a time of times and half of a time." This renders the prophecy more mysterious and the period of time longer, up to "a year of years," which would be 360, 364, or 365 years depending on the calendar being used (assuming it was a solar one). Faced with two interpretive options that were probably current in his own day, John takes another route and denies that there will still be such a thing as time at the sound of the trumpet (see 1:3).

10:7 καὶ ἐτελέσθη. The καί might mean "thus" or "and so," or it might be a Hebrew literary construction, although there is no equivalent term in the text of Daniel translated above. The past tense of the verb ("was completed") might be John's way of suggesting a past in the future, and thus should be translated with the future perfect "will have been completed." Alternatively, it might be a prophetic tense interchange (see comments to 9:6). In this instance John is seeing what has yet to come as if it had already happened or at least had already been determined. The meaning, then, would be: "will certainly be completed."

εὐηγγέλισεν. "proclaimed with good report." The difficulty lies in understanding who the prophets are. Are they the followers of Jesus, the new prophets of the gospel, or does John mean that the prophets of the "old economy" are included in the very same divine plan of evangelization? Comparison with 14:6 inclines toward the second option.

10:8 Καὶ ἡ φωνή. The translation maintains the Greek anacoluthon.

10:9 Λάβε . . . αὐτό. The scene recalls Ezek 2–3, where the prophet receives and obeys an order to swallow a scroll. John repeats several times that the scroll, whether it is large or small, is nonetheless "open" after the revelatory action of the Lamb. Also in Ezek 2:10 the writing is unrolled (ἀνείλησεν αὐτὴν ἐνώπιόν μου, LXX) and read by the prophet. (For a Freudian interpretation of the passage see Halperin 1993, in particular pp. 133-34 and pp. 1-38, for hypotheses from other scholars; for criticism see Lupieri 1999; for another prophet who "devours" the words of God see Jer 15:16.) It was fairly common in Hellenistic medicine as well as in magic for patients to eat strips of papyrus or another material on which various formulae were written. The practice is extremely ancient and is mentioned in Akkadian texts and present in many cultures. Second Temple Judaism must have been familiar with the rituals involved in preparing "bitter waters," the concoction that women suspected of adultery were made to drink by the priests (Num 5:11-31; the detail of "bitterness" is absent from LXX; for bitter water in the Apocalypse see 8:11). In this ritual the priest wrote the words of the curse on a sheet of papyrus, which he then washed; the water in which he washed it, which somehow contained the words of the curse, was drunk by the woman under suspicion. In this case, then, we have a text that is drunk rather than eaten, and whose effects were considered a proof of adultery (e.g., *m. Sot.* 3:4). Nonetheless, I think it safe to assume that a first-century Jew would not see the practice of swallowing a written text as particularly abstruse.

10:10   ἐπικράνθη . . . μου. John continues with his adaptation of Ezek 2–3. The prophet of the exile said that the scroll tasted "as sweet as honey" but did not mention its effect on his stomach, although he mentions his stomach in the same verse (3:3). John might mean that the scroll he ate was the same as that which Ezekiel ate, containing the same revelation that had been given to the prophet of old, but that now it is not merely a "sweet" message of salvation and liberation after suffering but also involves condemnation and thus bitter. In those passages where John is most obviously concerned with adapting an earlier prophecy or relating it to his present, he tends to portray the moment of crisis as nearer, more inevitable, and more terrible than does his source (see comments on 10:6 and 14:20).

10:11   Δεῖ σε . . . πολλοῖς. We are not told who utters this sentence; it might be the angels, or the plural might merely be a method of rendering a passive without a subject. In any case, its function is to connect different parts of the book. Its primary significance is that the visionary is ordered to repeat his prophetic activity with respect to the figures listed. We should note that this expression "prophesy about" does not necessarily mean "prophesy against" and thus tells us nothing about whether the new prophecy is negative or positive in content. Moreover, if John has already prophesied "about numerous peoples and nations and languages and kings," then "tribes" is now missing from the list. I believe that this is not simply a stylistic decision to vary a repeated list but that it indicates that from this point on he will be paying particular attention to the destiny of the nations and that it should be considered different from, and at times opposed to, that of the people of Israel. The next time they are mentioned, two verses on (11:2), the nations "will trample on the holy city"; it is obvious that the histories of Israel and of the nations will follow different paths, and the results might explain the bitterness John feels (see also Prov 5:3-4). Whether or not terms that refer literally to historical and ethnic matters in fact require a spiritual interpretation is another issue (see comments on 21:25-26).

11:1 Verses 1 and 2 give us a sense of the mystical geography of the "holy city," which can only be Jerusalem, in view also of its dependence on Ezek 40, which provides the inspiration for the new scene and for the idea of measuring the temple. In the first place, the "court, the one outside the temple," is theologically "thrown out" and abandoned to the mercy of the nations, representing the pagan occupation of Jerusalem, which lasts forty-two months — the three and a half years of the persecution of Dan 7:25. The outer court is thus that part of Israel which has been lost, contaminated by contact with the Gentiles. The entire Jewish (and Christian) religious world, which is spiritually represented by the figure of Jerusalem, is divided into three parts: the temple, the altar (with those who worship in it), and the court (see comments on 16:19). The "temple" represents the presence of God, the altar and those who worship there the community of the true faithful, the followers of Jesus Christ, and the court represents the remnant of Israel, which has already been condemned, the historic Judea and Jerusalem. The "holy city" therefore represents the mystical or theological dimension of earthly reality — that Israel of which the Christian community forms the really saved and holy part. It is consistent with the role of the altar that the earthly church can be identified in it (see comments on 7:13-17); the prayers and sacrifices made through it reach God. I do not know whether or to what extent it is possible to identify a precise Eucharistic theology within the Apocalypse, but Christian liturgy repeats the sacrifice of the Lamb Christ and thus transforms the church into the altar in the fullest sense.

Many critics prefer a more historical reading to this indisputably spiritual one. In prophetic contexts and in this passage itself, measuring represents the salvation of that which is measured, inasmuch as it is the object of special attention and protection from God (see Ezek 40 and *1 Enoch* 61). It has been inferred from this that John is not, or at least not only, prophesying the spiritual salvation of the followers of Jesus but also the physical salvation of the temple in Jerusalem, despite the fact that the city will be occupied by the pagans of the Roman army. This leads some critics to date the redaction of the Apocalypse before the destruction of the temple in 70 CE, at the very beginning of the war (thus after 66), or at least when it was already obvious that Jerusalem was going to fall into the hands of Titus, who was not expected to burn the temple. However, John does not seem to pay so much attention to the earthly temple elsewhere in the Apocalypse, and, moreover, he carefully emphasizes the absence of the temple in the New Jerusalem also because of the need to find a theological justification for the destruction of the earthly temple, which had been contaminated by humans and no longer had a purpose to serve (see Acts 7:48). John is more interested in insisting that the presence of God (the temple) and the true church (the altar) will outlive the destruction of Jerusalem than in fretting over the survival of Jewish physical worship (which does not appear in the book: what is the use of lambs and other animals for sacrifice if Christians have the Lamb?).

Taken together, these verses prepare the reader of the text to do without the physical Jerusalem, and not to persevere with deluded notions about the survival of a building that has outlived its usefulness. Qumran also gives us at least one text in which the true temple is the (eschatological) community of the elect ("And among the holy ones, God makes (some) hol[y] for himself like an everlasting sanctuary"; 4QShir^b [4Q511] fr. 35, 2-3), and another in which the community is the building that is measured (*Hodayot* [1QH–4QH] 14:26). Moreover, and still at Qumran, Jerusalem is the "holy city" by antonomasia even when the claim is made that the true faithful must abandon her (e.g., "the house of Peleg, who left the holy city and leaned on God in the age of Israel's unfaithfulness"; CD 20:22-23). In our passage also John defines the city as "holy" precisely as he is proclaiming that she will be trampled on, which in a Jewish framework implies that she will be contaminated. Is this simply a case of a traditional mode of expression that survives into the moment of defilement, or does John perhaps think that God's presence in faithful Christians makes such continuity possible, even after the loss of the earthly and Jewish Jerusalem? The tripartite division of the temple was traditional; there was speculation about its relation to the tripartite division of the cosmos into heaven, earth, and sea (see Josephus, *A.J.* 3[4.4].123; and comments on 16:19; 21:12).

κάλαμος . . . ῥάβδῳ. Ezekiel, and the visionaries who take their inspiration from him, speak only of a "reed" (sometimes a golden one; see 21:15), but John here finds it necessary to say that this reed is "similar to a staff." The term "staff" appears three more times in the text, always in citations of Ps 2:8-

9: it is the "staff of iron" with which the Messiah will shepherd the nations. This should perhaps alert the reader that the scene of measuring that follows will not be simply a protection for the holy part of Israel but will include an element of condemnation involving the nations as well.

λέγων. John does not say who the speaker is. The previous verb is passive, and thus the logical subject of the whole sentence should be God or his angel. Given the Christian nature of the text, and given God's method of revelation as outlined in the opening of the book, the subject must be the risen Christ or his angel, which would be consistent with v. 3, which also begins with the first person.

11:3 τοῖς δυσὶν μάρτυσίν μου. "My two witnesses" appear *ex abrupto* with the definite article, as if they were familiar to the reader of the text (see 10:3; on the legal necessity and sufficiency of two witnesses see Num 35:30; Deut 17:6; 19:15; Matt 18:16; John 8:17; Heb 10:28). "The two olive trees and the two lampstands" are also new (the other occasion where lampstands appear is at the beginning of the book, where there are seven rather than two), but the article is there because John is recalling Zech 4:3, 11-14 and therefore speaking of "those two" olive trees that Zechariah prophesied. In citing the biblical text, however, he makes a significant alteration; Zechariah sees one "lampstand all of gold," which is "the Lord of the whole earth," and two olive trees, which are the "two anointed ones who stand beside" him. John's two prophets do not seem to be anointed, and the lampstand, a figure already used to represent churches in peril, cannot now take on a theological or christological significance; thus John replaces Zechariah's single lampstand and applies the figure to humans — extraordinary ones, to be sure — who are clearly distinct from the "Lord of the earth." The Lord of the earth in turn seems to be distinct from the speaker, unless v. 4 is the beginning of an address by John, in which case the direct discourse by the figure who commissions his witnesses ends with the end of v. 3. If this is the case, the "Lord of the earth" must be the risen Christ, in front of whom the two olive trees/lampstands/witnesses stand, in a sort of little heavenly court in which human beings are elevated to the dignity of angels. If, on the other hand, this is still part of the discourse of the original speaker that goes on to include the description of the witnesses, perhaps up to v. 6, and if this figure is Christ, then the "Lord" must be God the Father. If it is Christ's angel speaking in his name, then the "Lord" could still be Christ. It will be made clear later in the narration, when the two witnesses are killed, that they are human; for now they are shown as capable of performing the miracles of Elijah (preventing rain) and of Moses (turning water into blood and smiting the earth with plagues). John's contemporaries might have seen the duration of the witnesses' activity — three and a half years — as a reference to Elijah since it was by this time an established idea that the drought controlled by Elijah (see 1 Kings 17:1–18:46) lasted three and a half years (see Luke 4:25 and James 5:17). The witnesses seem to be more powerful than Moses and Elijah, in that they can act "as many times as they desire."

At this point we have already seen water turn to blood and plagues afflict mankind (8:8 and 9:18, 20) at the hands of punishing angels who always acted under the strict control of God; their activity was restricted in time and manner (a third of the water, three plagues, for five months), and they did not have the same degree of freedom as do the two witnesses. The fire that "comes out of their mouth" is a superhuman trait that we encountered in the angelic "horses" of 9:17. It can also be attributed to more or less demonic monsters like Leviathan in Job (41:10-12) or to God himself (2 Sam 22:9 = Ps 18:9), but on at least one occasion it is attributed to a prophet, Jeremiah, to whom God says, "I am now making my words in your mouth a fire, and this people wood, and the fire shall devour them" (Jer 5:14). Therefore, the fire coming out of the mouth of God's prophet can devour the "house of Israel" (Jer 5:15). The ability to "devour enemies," however, seems to characterize only the fire of God, which is described as an angelomorphic being that "goes before" him (Ps 97:3), or, more commonly, as a fire that descends from heaven, as in the story of Elijah (2 Kings 1:10, and see comments on 20:9). The connection to the mouth probably derives from the "breath of the mouth" of God. This was originally a creative and life-giving spirit (see Ps 33:6 [32:6, LXX]; Gen 2:7), but it is also interpreted as a deadly breath of punishment that becomes a messianic characteristic (Isa 11:4; 2 Thess 2:8) and that is sometimes expounded on extensively (4 Ezra 13:10: *Emisit de ore suo sicut flatum ignis et de labiis eius spiritus flammae et de lingua eius emittebat scintillas et tempestates;* "He sent forth from his mouth as it were a breath of fire, and from his lips flaming puffs, and from his tongue he shot forth storms and sparks"; see 4 *Ezra* 13:4, where this fire is said to be the burning voice of the messiah who destroys the wicked; see comments on 19:21). For a figure who may not be messianic but is certainly extraordinary, see "and who will endure the flow of my lips?" (4Q491c fr. 1, l. 17; this is still the so-called *Song of Michael;* see comments on 3:21). In any case, all the details agree in suggesting that we are dealing with some form of preaching, as is demonstrated also by a strange parallel in the *Hymns* from Qumran, where the Teacher of Righteousness proclaims, "But you, my God, you have placed in my mouth as it were an early rain for all [the thirsty] and a spring of living water; and they [i.e., my words] will not fail to open the skies, they will not stop but will become a torrent overflowing" (*Hodayot* [1QH–4QH] 16:16-17). The opening or closing of the heavens corresponds to the mercy or rejection of God, conveyed by the preaching of his man.

The identity of the two figures has not been satisfactorily explained. The usual approach is to concentrate on the analogies with Elijah and Moses, but even in antiquity there were doubts about this interpretation since both witnesses seem to belong completely within the NT economy, and thus to be Christian figures such as, for instance, the new Elijah and the new Moses, that is, John the Baptist and Jesus (both killed by wicked kings, emanations from the "beast"), who will return at the end of time. Some have seen them as Christian realizations of Jewish reflections on the end-times return of two biblical figures who were believed never to have died (Enoch and Elijah, in a manner similar to the reinterpretation of the *Apocalypse of Elijah*), while others see in them Peter and Paul, who were killed in Rome (the "city") by Nero (the "beast" and therefore the Antichrist).

In any case, we are dealing with two figures who are connected with eschatology and whom John presents as belonging to the future, although it is not clear with respect to what they are in the future. That they are not named and are capable of being interpreted in a variety of ways probably means that John does not want to give enough information to enable the reader to arrive at a definitive interpretation. As they are "witnesses," their activity ought to coincide with that of the church, which would explain the fact that they are "lampstands" (see 1:20). Thus they probably are "corporate personalities" — figures who appear to be individuals but actually represent more complex human groups, such as kingdoms or peoples, in which case they would represent the two parts of militant Christianity (see comments on 13:5).

ἡμέρας . . . ἑξήκοντα. The duration of the two witnesses' activity, "one thousand two hundred and sixty days," is the same as 42 months of 30 days each, and is a literary device used to link the new figures directly with the measuring of the temple in the preceding verses. This length of time recalls the "three times and a half" (where "time" is taken to mean "year"; a half week of years, to be precise) that is attributed to the abomination of desolation in Dan 9:27 (see 7:25; 8:14; 12:7, 11, 12). John uses the traditional Hebrew solar calendar, which is made of twelve months of thirty days each, with an extra day inserted once every three-month season, to create a year of 364 days. If one does not count the extra days, this is the only calendar according to which 42 months is the equivalent of 1,260 days. The use of this calendar in the temple was abandoned amid some debate, probably in the Seleucid period, in favor of a lunisolar calendar corresponding to that which Seleucus I had imposed from 312 BCE. With minor local differences, this year marks the beginning of the Greek era in the entire Greek East; the "Greek calendar" became so important that it was not even replaced by the Julian calendar, and even survived into the Islamic era. The adoption in the temple of the lunisolar calendar was perhaps a political necessity, and was certainly a sign of "modernization": to the best of our knowledge the older, solar calendar did not include provisions for adapting to the astronomic solar year, which is longer than 365 days. The innovation was never really accepted by the most observant Jews such as the Essenes, who continued to calculate the holy days on the basis of the old priestly calendar since it was inconceivable to them that they should calculate on the basis of the Greek calendar used by the pagans; from their perspective even sacred time, the time observed in the temple at Jerusalem, had fallen under the control of Satan and his ranks. John seems to consider the old solar calendar to be the only one suitable for calculating the sacred time of what he sees and hears. Whatever might be the actual duration in human history of the events in his vision, the mission of the two witnesses and the trampling of Jerusalem are calculated according to this old calendar. That John does not include the extra days (besides the numerological advantages of not doing so; see comments on 12:6) might mean that he does not think that the events he describes will really last three and a half years of human history; in this case they would actually last 1,274 days (with years of 364 days) rather than 1,260. The important thing is still that however the period is expressed, in terms of months or of days, it is a "halved" period — a half week of years or of "times" (see 12:14).

11:6 πατάξαι τὴν γῆν. Here again the question arises of what this γῆ refers to. The two witnesses act on "heaven," on "the waters" and then on γῆ: which suggests that it is the whole earth. The epithet "the Lord of the earth," which might mean God or Christ, also points in this direction: it certainly does not merely indicate lordship over Israel. Notwithstanding this, that they are introduced immediately after the temple is measured and that they are said to act for the same length of time as that during which the holy city will be trampled suggest that although their power is of significance to the entire cosmos, it will be directed with particular attention to the Holy Land. Moreover, the fact that they strike this land with "plagues" suggests to the reader and hearer that it somehow corresponds to ancient Egypt.

11:7 τὸ θηρίον . . . ἐκ τῆς ἀβύσσου. Like the witnesses, the "beast" appears unexpectedly and is preceded by the definite article, although it has not been mentioned before. Earlier we saw smoke rising from the abyss and monstrous locusts come from that smoke (9:2-3); they have as their king "the angel of the abyss," whose name John told us both in Greek and in Hebrew (9:11). Thus, regardless of the comparisons that the reader will later be able to make with "the beast" that will rise out of "the sea" (13:1) and with "the beast" that will come up from "the abyss" (17:8), at this stage we already have reason to associate this beast with demonic forces. Simply by being a beast, however, it is directly linked to the assorted beasts and wild animals that populate apocalyptic texts at least as early as Daniel and 1 *Enoch (BD)* and that usually represent men (princes or peoples) or human political entities (kingdoms). The enemy of the two witnesses, therefore, must be the human dimension or expression of a demonic power.

11:8 τῆς πόλεως τῆς μεγάλης. This is the first time the expression "the city, the great one" appears in the Apocalypse (it will recur eight times in all; in 11:8; 16:19; 17:18; 18:10, 16, 18, 19, 21), and John explains what city is involved. Up to this moment he has spoken twice of "cities." In 3:12 he announced "the name of the city of my God, the new Jerusalem," and he looked forward to its descent "out of heaven" in the same context as he predicted a "temple of my God," which will evidently be new and spiritual since "the victor" will be one of its "pillars." Then, at the beginning of ch. 11, he turned his attention to the "holy city," which, he says, will be trampled "for forty-two months" by the "nations" (11:2). Up to this point, therefore, he has spoken exclusively about the "city" of Jerusalem — the future one that is promised by God, and the transient one that is destined to be occupied by a pagan army. Now we learn why the "holy city" is destined to be profaned by the Gentiles: it is there that the beast who comes up from the abyss, a manifestation of Satan, is victorious (see comments on 11:7). Its citizens, together with the rest of wicked humanity, rejoice at the murder of the two witnesses. Their attitude against the church is a continuation — almost a historical one — of the attitude of those who crucified Jesus.

The title "great city" is biblical. By and large "great (and usually fortified) cities" are the cities of pre-conquest Canaan (Num 13:29; Deut 1:28; 6:10; 9:1; Josh 14:12; and its literary echo in 1 Macc 5:26), with the exception of 1 Kings 4:13, where the expression refers to the feudal territories of one of Solomon's officials. In the singular, "great" is applied to Sidon (Josh 19:28 and 2 Sam 24:6 in variants) and once to Babylon (Dan 4:27). "Great city" sometimes describes Gibeon (Josh 10:2) and Ephron (1 Macc 5:46), but it is used more often of Nineveh. This usage appears first in a rather unclear and hard-to-date passage in Gen 10:11-12, but after that mainly in texts from the Hellenistic era, in which the memory of the ancient city is shading into legend: Jdt 1:1 and above all Jonah 1:2; 3:2, 3; 4:11. We can observe that the definition of greatness often comes before a sudden and at times dramatic change of situation: the city is conquered by the Hebrews, or is at least converted. Jerusalem can also aspire to a greatness of its own, inasmuch as it is the seat of a "great king," who is God (Ps 48:2; cf. 47:3), or it is rebuilt "wide and large" (Neh 7:4); however, the verse most relevant for us appears in a prophecy of Jeremiah: "and many nations will pass by this city, and all of them will say to one another, 'Why has the LORD dealt in this way with this great city?'" (Jer 22:8). Here too the title gives dramatic emphasis to the change of fortunes awaiting the city: the "great city" is already destined to be destroyed. This is why John uses the expression while explaining Jerusalem's sin, after he has announced that the city will be trampled by pagan feet.

Up to this point in the narrative, Jerusalem is the only city that John has mentioned, and the reader or hearer of the text does not know that this "city, the great one" will later be identified as Babylon. This passage does, however, bring to light several aspects of the city. The first is both historical and theological: the city is the place of the crucifixion. The reference is to a particular historical event, which is recounted for its deeper significance: it is the final sin, which (as the killing of the witnesses shows) is not repented of, and it will therefore lead to destruction. The second aspect is theological: the city, which is no longer "holy" but rather "great" like pagan cities, is now seen by God in the same category as Sodom, which was destroyed by fire, and Egypt, which was afflicted with plagues. The sin took place in Jerusalem: Satan triumphed there, and there the punishment of God will strike. We should note, finally, that even in the reworking of this passage in the *Apocalypse of Elijah* (a reworking that obviously does not mention the crucifixion) the "great city" is still Jerusalem (*Apoc. El.* 4:13; see the "holy place" in *Apoc. El.* 4:7, and comments on Apoc 11:9).

πνευματικῶς. The adverb appears in the NT only here and in 1 Cor 2:14 (and in variants of 1 Cor 2:13). In both contexts it refers to a wisdom that comes from the Spirit and is not accessible to certain categories of people: Paul speaks explicitly of interpreting (ἀνακρίνεται). John's assertion is of particular importance for our understanding of the Apocalypse because it shows his awareness that the text he is composing requires a level of spiritual interpretation that goes beyond the letter. The "great city" is not the Sodom or the Egypt of human experience, but corresponds to them according to the wisdom of the Spirit (see comments on 17:5). After the Genesis account Sodom becomes a common biblical model for Jerusalem or Israel insofar as they are human sites of sin and betrayal (Deut 29:22; 32:32; Isa 1:9-10; 3:9; Jer 23:14; Lam 4:6; see Loader 1990). There is a particularly forceful example in Ezek 16:46-56, where the sins of Jerusalem are said to be greater than those of Sodom, her "sister." This anti-Jerusalem sentiment appears also in the NT (see the reworking of Isa 1:9 in Rom 9:29; see also Matt 11:21-23. Some sort of connection between Sodom and Jerusalem appears also in a couple of tiny fragments from Qumran, recently discussed by Tigchelaar 2004. Here, too, the attention is focused more on idolatry than sexuality). The fate of Sodom is also, however, on several occasions used as a threat against the enemies of

Israel: Edom in Jer 49:18, Moab in Zeph 2:9, and Babylon in Isa 13:19 and Jer 50:40. In the NT cities that do not welcome the gospel are threatened with the same fate (Matt 10:15; Luke 10:12), as is perhaps the entire unbelieving world (Luke 17:28-32) at the parousia. Josephus's comment is striking: "If the Romans had delayed [in punishing] these malefactors . . . the city [Jerusalem] . . . would have had its part in the fires of the region of Sodom" (*J.W.* 5[13.6].566).

The sin of Sodom has very little to do with sodomy. Jude 7 explains that "Sodom and Gomorrah and the surrounding cities, fornicated in the same manner as [the angels]" by the pursuit of "a different flesh," namely, the "flesh" of the angels (see Loader 1990, pp. 122-24). The sin of the inhabitants of Sodom is thus the human complement to the sin of the angels; they go against their nature by having sexual relations with non-human entities, for whom there is no expectation of reproduction. That the angels have a "flesh" of their own is taken for granted in *1 Enoch* 6–7 *(BW)*, appears in *1 Enoch* 86:4 *(BD)*, and is stated explicitly in *1 Enoch* 69:5 *(BS; see Apoc 14:4)*; if the fallen angels are the pagan gods, then unnatural relations with them means that "fornication" or "prostitution" which prophetic texts use to describe Israel's idolatry. Idolatrous prostitution is the (sinful) human answer to the angels' sin (this probably explains the reasoning behind the gnostic exaltation of the inhabitants of Sodom). In this light the juxtaposition of Sodom and Egypt appears even more natural, since the latter is the very exemplar of idolatry. Egypt's condemnation is transferred to Jerusalem, and Jerusalem is "spiritually" considered to be Egypt as early as Ezek 9, where the angels of God pass through the city, slaughtering the guilty Jews and saving only those few who bear a sign, in a clear reference to the events of Exod 12. Finally, there is a pseudo-Mosaic text from Qumran that shows how a minority Jewish group could associate Israel and Egypt as being destined for the same punishment and condemnation, and attribute the decision to God himself: "Egypt and Israel I will destroy and deliver up to the sword" (4QpsMoses[c] [4Q388[a]] fr. 1, 5; see comments on 15:1).

11:9 καὶ βλέπουσιν . . . τὸ πτῶμα. The "tribes" reappear in the list, confirming that the Jewish world is involved too, although the use of partitives shows that not all of them are looking on and rejoicing. The two witnesses, moreover, are active after the crucifixion, and thus during a period when the church has already come into being ("those who bow down" in v. 1). As this takes place in Jerusalem, we might ask what the γῆ is whose inhabitants appear in this scene. It is possible that John was thinking primarily of the land of Israel, in which, however, there must have been "those who dwell" in the whole earth since Jerusalem is the spiritual center of the world (see Acts 2:9-11).

ἡμέρας . . . ἥμισυ. The half week appears here, quite unexpectedly, in the form of a half week of days. This is a characteristic of the witnesses: they are active for a half week of years, and their death lasts a half week of days. As Jesus in the Fourth Gospel is active for three years, so the witnesses are active for three and a half years; as Jesus lay in the tomb for three days, so the two witnesses lie in the tomb for three and a half days. The Apocalypse emphasizes details such as this for the purpose of creating internal consistency: John has decided that the period of time associated with the two witnesses, in death as in life, is the half week. In this passage the period of three and a half days can be seen to be consistent with the speculation on the half week that is associated with the two witnesses. This makes an important contribution to the secure dating of *Apoc. El.* 4:14 in the Christian era (see O. S. Wintermute, in Charlesworth I 1983, p. 725). This detail is reproduced there, but without any context that might explain it; thus we can see it as an ancient reworking of our passage (see comments on 11:7 and Introduction, p. 22). The translation reproduces John's use of "corpses" and "corpse" (collective singular, twice).

11:11 πνεῦμα ζωῆς. John constructs the resurrection scene on Ezekiel's model; the "spirit of life" comes from Ezek 37:5 (LXX), while the rest of the verse parallels 37:10 (εἰσῆθεν εἰς αὐτούς . . . καὶ ἔστησαν ἐπὶ τῶν ποδῶν αὐτῶν, LXX). It is not quite clear what "a spirit of life from God" is. It would be easy to identify it as the Spirit of God, who is life-giving, but John takes "a spirit of life" directly from Ezekiel, without the definite article, and thus would seem to have in mind an entity that the reader is not yet acquainted with. It must therefore be a spiritual being sent by God for this particular task. A look at the context of Ezekiel's vision may help us to understand John's. Ezekiel sees a valley full of dry bones that God brings back to life, forming "a vast army" (συναγωγή, LXX); God then explains that the bones are the "house of Israel," who were victims of their own lack of faith, and whom he is now bringing "up from [their] graves" (Ezek 37:11-12). Ezekiel's account is highly allegorical; the prophet does not have in mind the resurrection of individuals but rather the reconstitution of a scattered people. It seems at first glance that John is saying something different, as he is concerned with the story of only two individuals. However, if the two witnesses do in fact represent the entire church, their corporate dimension could explain why John decided to refer to a vision about the entire chosen people in discussing the case of two individual human beings.

11:13 τὸ δέκατον . . . ἑπτά. Efforts have been made to give this detail a historical interpretation, whether by attempting to identify an earthquake that actually occurred somewhere (probably in Asia Minor, which is more susceptible to seismic activity than other Mediterranean regions) or by trying to calculate the size of the city in question. If the fall of a tenth of the city led to 7000 deaths, then the entire city had a population of 70,000. This might be roughly the size of Jerusalem, and considerably less than that of Rome. However, John does not talk about "inhabitants" but rather about "names of men," which would mean only adult males: should we therefore conclude that the city had about 350,000 inhabitants? Or should we not take the text at its word when it talks of "names of men" but only when it talks of a "tenth" and of 7,000? The book does not indicate that John has a particular taste for population statistics or archeology that would lead him to give the real number of the city's inhabitants. He is saying that God, having allowed the city to be trampled on for a half week (of years), and having sent his two witnesses for this entire period, has allowed them to be killed and to lie dead for another half week (of days); now, at the moment in which he calls them back to life and takes them up into heaven, he demands from the guilty city a sort of "tithe of blood." Moreover, if this 7,000 really is a tenth part of something, it is worth remembering that 70,000 males (ἑβδομήκοντα χιλιάδες ἀνδρῶν, LXX) is precisely the number that God (or his angel, named "Death") killed in Israel as a punishment for David's attempt to take a census (2 Sam 24:15-16; 1 Chr 21:14-15). On that occasion God repented of the harm he was doing and, after sending "Death" against Israel for three days, stayed the hand of the angel who had begun to destroy Jerusalem. In both cases, therefore, only a part of the population dies and the survivors, and certainly David, seem to repent. The clearest reference is, however, to 1 Kings 19:18 (quoted in Rom 11:4) in which God tells Elijah that he has kept for himself "seven thousand men" (ἑπτὰ χιλιάδες ἀνδρῶν, LXX), together with Isa 6:13, which tells us that the remnant is precisely a "tenth part" of the people (see Giblin, cited in Bauckham 1993, p. 282). This is another case of the theology of reversal: what used to be the holy remnant of Israel is now perishing (in fact, Isa 6:13 says that the "tenth" is destined to be destroyed anew), while the remnant, meaning all the others, show signs of repentance. The destruction of its "rest" identifies the fate of the city with that of, for instance, the Philistines (Isa 14:30, "and your remnant I will kill"; see comments on 9:20) or with the enemies of Israel (see 1QM 14:5; 18:2-3).

ἔδωκαν . . . τοῦ οὐρανοῦ. This time "the rest," even if they are motivated only by fear, appear to repent to the point of giving "glory to the God of heaven." Up to this point nothing that the angels have done has produced any sign of conversion, but now there is finally a positive result. Critics have generally seen this as an expression of the idea that it is Christianity, as testified by the two witnesses, that has produced conversion. However, the passage does not treat the giving of thanks as if it is connected to the testimony of the witnesses; on the contrary, the witnesses are clearly said to have tormented the inhabitants of the earth, and those inhabitants rejoice over their death and show no sign of penitence. The resurrection creates fear, and fear in its turn, after quake, fall, and death, leads to thanksgiving. If John wants to describe the success of the first Christian martyrs, it is strange that he twice emphasizes that conversion is a result of fear. None of this settles the question of whether the rest are simply the inhabitants of the city who survived the earthquake, or whether they are all the surviving humans, both in the city and elsewhere. The immediate context suggests that they are from the city, but the next verses, in which the cosmic reign of Christ is announced by the seventh trumpet, give the scene a universal dimension. If we attend to this dimension and read the passage alongside v. 18, we should perhaps interpret the fear as that awe of God which John expresses four times with the verb φοβέομαι (11:18; 14:7; 15:4; 19:5); however, the noun φόβος seems to be used only for the experience of negative figures (18:10, 15, in both of which the fear is of torment [βασανισμός], for which see 11:10). The sending of the witnesses appears to the reader to be a positive move devised by God to limit the effects of the trampling: the city that was holy and is now reduced to being the outer court of the temple is trampled by the Gentiles just as is this one. I think this demands a spiritual interpretation, to the effect that historical Israel has become so corrupt as to be reduced to the status of an outer court of the temple at the mercy of the pagans. But if Israel is guilty of having abandoned her role in the history of salvation by crucifying "the Lord," the church has now taken on the role of bearing witness to the message before both Jews and pagans. The obstinacy of the unbelievers demands that the witnesses deliver a forceful message, probably one of judgment. Thus the beast's attack on them should probably be seen as both a symbolic representation of the historical life of the church and a prefiguration of eschatological events. The half week of days between their death and God's intervention is the equivalent of the half hour of silence in heaven and of the half week of years during which Jerusalem is trampled. This draws us into the heart of John's theodicy: what appears to be God's absence, his silence, his failure to intervene, his acceptance of the triumph of evil, is in fact a silence that he owes to his servants, so that in their suffering and trial they can really pray, and he can manifest himself. So the heavens are silent, and God does not act. The believer can find comfort in the certainty not only that the silence itself is part of God's mercy, but also that the persecution, however long it lasts in the human experience of events, still lasts for only half a time. The apparent triumph of the beast and the defeat of the believers in reality are the moment in which God receives real human prayers.

It is not clear whether the text's entire account of the witnesses is included within the discourse of the Voice, or whether the Voice says only what is in v. 3 and the rest is from John. Although it is not, strictly speaking, a vision (John never mentions "seeing" what he describes), it is difficult to distinguish the account from the visions as it is written in the same register. Together with the vision of the angel carrying the little open scroll, this account constitutes an expansion of the description of the events that follow on the sounding of the sixth trumpet (the intervention of the angelic cavalry provoked by the freeing of the four angels). We saw a similar structural phenomenon in regard to the sixth seal when John, after describing the events immediately following its opening (6:12-17), saw for the first time the four angels and the angel restraining them, heard the number of the "one hundred forty-four thousand," and finally saw the throng that no one could count. We can note that in these expansions John himself becomes an actor in the visions (the conversation with one of the elders in 7:13-14, the swallowing of the scroll, and the prophetic commissioning in 10:8-11). John is not involved in the events surrounding those seals or trumpets on which he does not elaborate — the first five from each septet. Another instance of his involvement in the vision is his being given the reed and ordered to go and measure the three elements of the temple (11:1-2). At first glance it is odd that John never reports that he obeyed this order: we can either admit that this is odd or we can see the order as referring to a spiritual measuring that John does in fact carry out in the rest of the book.

11:15 Ἐγένετο ἡ βασιλεία. The "Lord of the earth" already appeared after the sounding of the sixth trumpet (v. 4), as did the "God of heaven" (v. 13); perhaps the recognition by the "rest" was necessary for the historical realization of the kingdom. The world is in the hands of "our Lord and of his Anointed." The figure of Christ, here as elsewhere, is very closely united with that of God, to the extent that there is only a single reign, as the singular of the verb "will reign" underlines. It is certain, however, that two divine figures are involved, unless we understand "our Lord" to be "his [God's] Anointed." In any case, the proclamation of the cosmic reign, with the consequences that are described in the following verses, must be the completion of the "mystery" that the "christological" angel announced in 10:7. The whole passage describing the first events after the sound of the trumpet (up to and including 11:9) is brimming with internal references to the rest of the text. John echoes ch. 4 in particular, where a scene of *proskynesis* like this is prophesied. The adoration of God by the twenty-four is a recurrent theme in the text; John seems to use it as a way of drawing attention to particularly solemn moments, especially those in which the lordship of God and/or Christ is proclaimed (see 4:10; 5:8, 14; 7:11 [?]; 11:16; 19:4). The title "Almighty," which is reserved for

God and is often used in invocations (see 1:8; 4:8; 15:3; 16:7, 14; 19:6, 15; 21:22), also adds solemnity to the elders' hymn of thanksgiving (Εὐχαριστοῦμεν). We may note that while the "great voices" exalt the lordship of God and Christ (v. 15), the hymn of the elders is addressed exclusively to God, and does not contain explicitly Christian elements. The power and reign of God are followed by the anger of the nations, then, in answer, comes the anger of God (see comments on 14:10), and finally the judgment of the dead with the reward and punishment, apparently of living and dead together. The hymn thus seems to be a means of summarizing events that have already taken place in salvation history (the anger of the nations and of God), while at the same time it looks forward to events that John has yet to recount.

There are three categories of good humans, those who receive the reward of God: the "servants" of God, who are called "prophets"; the "holy ones"; and "those who fear [God's] name," who are also defined as "the small and the great." This tripartite definition accords well with an ideal notion of the perfect Israel, guided by the prophets, made up of a holy people, and supported by a good number of *timentes deum,* uncircumcised Gentiles who fit the definition "small and great." This phrase occurs five times in the book; twice (here and in 19:5) it refers to those who fear God, twice (13:16; 19:18) to evildoers who are victims of the beast or are killed by the sword of the Word, and once (20:12, where the order is reversed — "great and small") to all the dead who have yet to be judged: a group made of humans of all sorts. The two titles imply that "those who fear God's name" are a large and varied congregation of the faithful, whose origins seem to lie beyond the world of Judaism. If we undertake the risky enterprise of reconstructing the social and theological realities of primitive Christianity on the basis of the clues we find in phrases such as these, we will find a church with no hierarchy besides the charismatic leaders, the "prophets," who guide it; it is composed of a group of Jewish Christians, the "holy ones," and another group, already somewhat bigger, of pagan Christians, the "small and great . . . who fear" God. Or this is at least what John seems to be wishing.

11:17 ὁ ὢν καὶ ὁ ἦν. The divine attribute first mentioned in 1:4 (see comments) reappears here, without the third element. John does not define God as "he who is coming" either here or in 16:5, where the expression appears for the last time. In these contexts (in both cases God is being praised, by the elders or by a particular angel) the lordship of God has already been fully realized, probably by means of the triumph of Christ. There is no more reason for God to "come" to his creation, as he is now fully present in it. In a text like John's, which is always poised between the "already" and the "not yet," this passage leans toward the "already."

11:18 τοὺς μικροὺς καὶ τοὺς μεγάλους. Trying to explain these accusatives is an almost hopeless task (and many manuscripts and editors have corrected the text). I think John meant: "Those who fear your name — it does not matter whether they are small or great (in the church)." The phrase could be considered an irregular absolute accusative (as it is not syntactically "absolute").

διαφθεῖραι . . . γῆν. This sentence looks forward to the fate that awaits the prostitute (see 19:2) and is linked to the apostrophe against Babylon in Jer 51:25, where the prophet calls the city a "destroying mountain . . . that destroys the whole earth" (but Jer 28:25 LXX has τὸ ὄρος τὸ διεφθαρμένον, τὸ διαφθεῖρον πᾶσαν τὴν γῆν). God applies the principle of "an eye for an eye" to the enemies of the γῆ. It is not that John has any ecological concerns: he does not bat an eyelid as the angels wreak untold havoc on the world under God's orders or at least under his control. The central problem here is once again that of determining what γῆ refers to here and who it is who is destroying it (the terms φθείρω and διαφθείρω refer to "destruction," but also corruption or moral contamination). The passage before the seventh trumpet opens with the measuring of the Jerusalem temple and concludes with the partial collapse of the "city" that is historically identified as Jerusalem. In the immediate context of the elders' hymn, the only identifiable enemies are the "nations," whose anger provokes God's anger; thus there is here a destructive action to which God responds with similar destruction. If John is continuing with the same subject, then the γῆ that is the object of destruction on the part of the nations is most probably Israel, whose destroyers and/or corrupters are thus the nations and their allies, the false Jews whom John opposes. There is a similar phrase in the *WS* that seems to strengthen this interpretation: "The covenant of your peace you engraved for them [. . .] to muster the arm[ies] of your [ch]osen ones according to its thousands and its myriads together with your holy ones [and with] your angels, to have the upper hand in the battle [and destroy] the rebels (the enemies?) of earth in the lawsuit of your judgments" (1QM 12:3-5). Finally, in 1 Cor 3:17 we read, "If anyone destroys God's temple, God will destroy him" (εἴ τις τὸν ναὸν τοῦ θεοῦ φθείρει, φθερεῖ τοῦτον ὁ θεός). In Paul's letter, however, the sentence — which seems to be proverbial — has taken on a spiritual meaning; "God's holy temple" is no longer that in Jerusalem, but rather is made up of the Corinthian Christians.

11:19 ὁ ναός . . . ἐν τῷ οὐρανῷ. The focus shifts to the heavenly temple, which was in some way announced in 7:15. John frequently speaks of a spiritual temple (see, e.g., 3:12), but up to this point he has made no mention of a temple "in heaven." There is ample witness to the existence of such a temple in apocalyptic literature, at least since *1 Enoch* 9:1 (the Greek version has now been confirmed by an Aramaic fragment), and a large number of the Jews of John's time believed in it. A model both of the cosmos and of the earthly temple, it had been with God from the beginning and was shown to Adam (who thereby acquired his gift of prophetic knowledge), to Moses and then to David and/or Solomon, who reproduced it in Jerusalem. Inasmuch as it was the ideal model of the earthly temple, radical Jewish groups saw it as being in tension with this earthly temple (the second temple and the Herodian reconstruction were seen as imperfect copies of Solomon's), and thus open to the charge of being "made with human hands" like an idol (see Stephen's speech in Acts 7:48). According to John's account, once this temple was opened the "ark of [the] covenant" — the true spiritual and heavenly heart of Judaism — became visible, unlike the earthly ark, which by now was lost without a trace (the second temple, notoriously, was empty). In the context of John's theology, as in much of primitive Christianity, the Christian event is the fulfillment of the mystery of Jewish revelation. The tearing of the "veil of the temple" at the moment of Jesus' death, according to Matt 27:51, probably means that the mystery of redemption is being fulfilled and revealed. Here the visible apparition of the ark points ahead to the "signs" that will also appear (to everybody, which is why they are "signs") in the following verses. It is meaningful for the literary structure of the book that the temple's opening is reaffirmed in 15:5, which describes the same event, thus framing everything that happens after the sounding of the seventh trumpet. As in the previous septets, after a description of the immediate consequences of the angel's action we see an expansion of the scene, which in this case includes a series of signs and visions. At the end of this comes the announcement of the next septet, that of the plagues in the bowls, which has its origins in the last element of the preceding sequence. Thus the repetition of the temple's opening, three chapters from the first account of the event, emphasizes that what comes in between is a single section within the structure of the account, at the end of the seven trumpets and at the beginning of the seven bowls.

ἀστραπαί . . . μεγάλη. The revelation causes a series of cosmic disturbances between heaven and earth. In Matt 27:51, 54 as well, the tearing of the veil of the temple brings about a "quake." The list here includes elements that we have already seen, and this may help us to understand its meaning. We have, first, "lightnings and voices and thunders": the order is the same as when they come forth from the throne of God in 4:5, in which context we interpreted them as angelic beings who mediate between the divine and human spheres. Their presence here suggests a parallel between the throne and the celestial temple; the temple and the ark inside it are, like the throne, locations of God's presence, of which the "lightnings and voices and thunders" are signs. The revelation is also a revelation of judgment against sinful humanity, however, and thus it has a threatening aspect that could be glimpsed in the lightning and thunder, and which is now shown fully in the "quake and great hail" (see *Apoc. Abr.* 30:8). The first time it is mentioned (in 6:12), the "quake" accompanies cosmic disturbances connected with the opening of the sixth seal in the "great day of [God's] rage"; the last time (in 11:13), in the context of the resurrection and ascension of the two witnesses, it accompanies the fall of "the tenth part of the city" and the death of "seven thousand" men. The next occasion, in 8:5, comes at the end of a series of events in which there are also angels and which are very similar to these: "thunders and voices and lightnings and a quake." In this case the manifestation accompanies the fire of the heavenly altar being thrown on the earth. This confirms the connection with the celestial temple through the altar within it, and also strengthens our argument that the whole series of signs shows the revelation of the divine mystery descending from heaven to earth. This revelation has a dual aspect, as the hymn of the elders has just shown: the salvation of the faithful and the destruction of the destroyers of the earth. This latter aspect is underlined by the last element of the series, the "great hail" that we saw earlier in 8:7 (see comments). There it was thrown to the earth, together with fire and blood, at the sound of the first trumpet; thus it was still a fire that descended on the earth (in this case, to burn a third of it). For the meaning of the adjective "great" see the comments on 1:10; for the last appearance of the "quake" and of the "hail" see the comments on 16:17, 21.

12:1 γυνή . . . δώδεκα. The first "great sign . . . in heaven" appears here: a sign over whose interpretation exegetes have been divided from the beginning. There have been a number of extreme interpretations, from those that see the passage as a messianic Jewish apocalypse without Christian content that John has simply taken on, to those who claim that this is a vision of the Madonna (the traditional iconography of the Immaculate Conception is based on this passage). This is the second woman to appear in the text, and, like the first (Jezebel in 2:20), she is a mother. But while Jezebel has "children" (τέκνα) whom Christ threatens to "kill with death" (2:23), this woman is described as giving birth to "a son, a male" whom Satan wants to "swallow," and she also has a "seed" against whose "remnant" Satan goes to "make war" (12:17). The two female figures thus have parallel but antithetical characteristics: the first is the enemy of Christ (and the friend of Satan: 2:24), and the second is the enemy of Satan. The woman in heaven is "wrapped in the sun, and the moon was under her feet, and a crown of twelve stars on her head."

This image is derived from Joseph's dream in Gen 37:9 in which the patriarch, while still a young man, dreamt that "the sun, the moon, and eleven stars bowed down" to him; the dream earned the envy of his brothers and a reproach from his father, who, however, interpreted the dream correctly, "Shall we indeed come, I and your mother and your brothers, and bow to the ground before you?" (ἐπὶ τὴν γῆν in 37:10 LXX might lead the reader to think that the scene is being moved from a celestial arena, where there are stars, to an earthly one). The symbology must therefore represent the whole of Israel in the loins of Jacob, Rachel, and the twelve patriarchs. If the "crown" (see comments on 3:11) is the sign of victory, then it must also signify dominion or superiority to the "stars."

It seems logical to conclude that the woman is a heavenly representation of Israel (which is a feminine word in Hebrew, and is always represented as a woman in the prophetic tradition of the OT) — of that faithful Israel which is also true Christianity, as is made apparent at the end of the chapter in which "the remnant of her seed . . . keep the commandments of God and have the testimony of Jesus" (v. 17). The woman is "in heaven," that intermediate site outside the categories of space and time where visions can exist (see comments on 4:2, 4; 17:10). That heaven is not subject to temporal or spatial laws accounts for one of the most disconcerting features in apocalyptic texts: ch. 12 moves back and forth continually between past, present, and future, with only one clear linear movement — the movement of the scene from heaven to earth. In v. 1 the woman is in heaven, as is the dragon in v. 3. However, by v. 4a the dragon has thrown to the earth "the third part of the stars in heaven" (i.e., the angels), and in v. 4b he is still in heaven, where the battle with Michael takes place only in v. 7. It is not until v. 9 that he is finally "thrown down to earth" together with "his angels" (i.e., the stars). As for the woman, in v. 6 she is said to have already fled "into the desert," but in v. 13 she seems to be within reach of the dragon (perhaps on the earth), so that in v. 14 she is given "the two wings of an eagle, the great one, . . . in order that she might fly to the desert" and thus escape the dragon. Thus time is flattened out, and the events of salvation history are unfurled repeatedly before the eyes of the visionary, without any necessary correspondence between the order of events in the vision and the order in which they are realized on earth in the human events that parallel, and are consequent upon, those in heaven.

12:2 ὠδίνουσα. Critics were amazed when in the *Hymns* of Qumran they came across a passage — by now famous — attributed to the Teacher of Righteousness, which described two pregnant women in the pains of labor. In the light of our text the Qumranic passage was often interpreted as being messianic, despite the danger of projecting ideas more than two hundred years backward in time (see Dupont-Sommer 1955, pp. 174-88). It became clear, however, that the image of a laboring woman has strong roots in Judaism, and that there was no need to look for the sources of our text in the literature of pagan mythology (Apollo, Leto, Pytho), as NT criticism typically did before Qumran (Delcor 1957, especially pp. 339-40). This is a literal translation of 1QH–4QH 11:7-18 (see in particular García Martínez 1994, pp. 331-32 and Moraldi 1986², pp. 372ff.).

> I was in distress like one who gives birth the first time when her pains come on her and a pang (racks) her ripples (the mouth of her womb?) to bring about birth in the crucible of the pregnant woman, for children reached the edge of death. And she who is expecting a man is racked by her pains, for a male is born from the edge of death, and there comes out from the pains of Sheol, from the crucible of the pregnant woman, a wonderful counselor with his strength, and a man comes out (free, unharmed) from the ripples. In the woman pregnant with him rush all the pains; and all the sharp agonies of their birth and the terror (comes) to those who are pregnant with them, and at his birth all the labor-pains come suddenly in the crucible of the pregnant woman. And she who is pregnant with a serpent (is) with a terrible pain, and the edges of the pit (reach) all works of terror. The foundations of the wall shake, like a ship on the surface of the sea, and the clouds answer at the top of their voice. Those who sit on the dry land ("dust") as well as those who move about on the waters are terrified by the voice of the water. And their wise men are for them like sailors on the high seas (the depths?), for all their wisdom has been (will be?) swallowed up by the voice of the waters, by the boiling of the depths over (against?) the springs of water: they [are thrown] on high (to form) huge waves and the billows (the gates?) of water, with clamorous voice. And when they rush out, [Sheol and Abaddon] open; [all] the arrows of the pit are in pursuit of them; their voice makes itself heard all the way down in the pit. And the gates of [Sheol] open [for all] the works of the serpent. And the doors of the pit close upon the one who is pregnant with evil, and everlasting bolts behind all the spirits of the serpent.

This is a fascinating text, the real and deep meaning of which is difficult to ascertain. Some phrases bear a striking similarity to John's, with which they share biblical origins, and like which they are used in an apocalyptic context such that they could be said to breathe the same atmosphere. The devil is identified with the serpent, who is considered a spiritual being, to the point that his followers (a collection of demonic beings?) are called "the spirits of the serpent." There is Abaddon, which is probably personified, just as "the arrows of the pit" are probably hypostatized ("angelomorphically"). Both "clouds" and "waters" have a voice, and the expression is not just a literary way to depict a storm at sea; the terror of those who live on the land and sail on the sea also finds close literary parallels in the Apocalypse.

Nonetheless the Teacher of Righteousness and John are talking about different things. The Teacher of Righteousness begins this passage by comparing himself to a pregnant woman, and then develops the antithetical contrast between the two pregnant women: the one with positive connotations, who is "expectant with a man" and "gives birth to a male" who will be a "wonderful counselor" and "a man," and the one with negative connotations, who is pregnant with "a serpent" (or "the serpent") and who gives birth to something that is not described in the passage. If the Teacher of Righteousness is the laboring woman, then what he gives birth to should be the teaching of righteousness, which is opposed to the wicked doctrine of the sect's enemies (maybe this is an allusion to the Wicked Priest). Or perhaps he gives birth to the community of believers that constitutes the body for his spiritual teaching. This instruction and/or community has an indisputable salvific value, and thus could be called "male" or "man," and the title "wonderful counselor" (which is messianic, at least in Christian texts, and comes from Isa 28:29) be applied to it. There is, therefore, quite a strong similarity with those Pauline passages in which the apostle compares himself to a mother who suffers the pains of childbirth, whether for a particular community (Gal 4:19) or seemingly for all believers (Rom 8:19-23). A new people is being born, a people of "adopted sons" and "redeemed," and this birth informs the image of labor. The Teacher of Righteousness and Paul share the idea that something new in human terms is about to be born, thanks to the believing community that they are bringing to birth. Both are far from the enthusiasm in Isa 66:7-8, which also announces the birth of a male (the new people), but a birth that is sudden and painless. Rather, they seem to apply to themselves those biblical images according to which men can also suffer labor pains (see Jer 30:6; again for the Teacher of Righteousness, and in the *Hodayot*, see 1QH–4QH 13:30-31). The analogy with John is weaker here, as we cannot imagine that John thinks he is seeing himself in the heavenly woman. There is a fundamental parallel, however, in that John is also dealing with the birth of a male in and from Israel. This male might be the fullness of the promise and thus the Christian messiah as an individual, or he might be the holy and chosen people, Christianity as the true Israel (as a corporate personality; see comments on 12:5).

12:3 δράκων . . . διαδήματα. At Satan's first appearance, still in heaven, he is shown as a being with royal qualities ("diadems on its heads"), who is similar in all aspects to the beast whom John will describe coming up from the sea in the next chapter (see 13:1). That they have the same external charac-teristics shows the deep and substantial unity of the forces of evil: Satan and the two beasts are a sort of evil "trinity." For John's use of διάδημα see the comments on 3:11. For possible meanings of the heads and horns see the com-ments on 17:9 and 12.

12:4 ἡ οὐρά . . . τῶν ἀστέρων. Satan shows that his power is in his tail, as is that of the horse-locusts, the power of whose scorpion tails John stresses in 9:3, 10 (fifth trumpet). The phrase "the third part of the stars" does not so much tell us exactly what proportion of the angels followed Satan, as it recalls events mentioned earlier in the account of the septet of the trumpets when, at the sound of the fourth trumpet, "the third part of the sun . . . and the third part of the moon and the third part of the stars" were hit (8:12). There are ma-jor differences between this passage and the events of the fourth trumpet, however. Sun and moon do not seem to be affected by the Satanic activity here, whereas there the "third part" of every heavenly body was "hit." More-over, there the agent was not specified and the passive voice of the verb seemed to suggest that the subject was God. Finally, the stars were darkened, rather than falling, when they were struck. Thus while there is an indisputable echo of formal elements from the fourth and fifth trumpets, the situations in question are different.

Critics have identified Dan 8:10 as one of the antecedents of this passage: the so-called "vision of the ram and the goat." Daniel witnesses the victory of Alexander the Great (the goat), then the four reigns of the Diadochi (the four horns), from one of which grows the "little horn" that grows into a great power. This is Antiochus Epiphanes, who rises up so high that he fights against "the host of heaven" and throws some of them down to the earth, along with some of the stars, and tramples on them. In the next verse Antiochus is said to take the daily sacrifice away from the prince of the host: that is, from God. The passage, with the heavenly hosts and the stars, is about the holy people of Israel and their spiritual guides (see Dan 12:3), the victims of Antiochus's aggression. The Greek versions modify the text, and, while LXX pursues its own course, Theod. translates, "and (a part) of the power of the heavens and the stars fell to earth, and he trampled on them."

Thus we see here the fall of part of the stars, which is in some way caused by an anatomical appendage (in this case a horn) of an animal, traditionally the location of the animal's power. This shows how an image derived from the myth of the fall of the angels flows into the tradition of Daniel, although the myth does not actually appear in Daniel (a text that is in reaction against apocalypses of the Enochic tradition; see Introduction, p. 16, and Boccaccini 1987, pp. 267-99). John, by contrast, knows and uses the Enochic texts, and is well aware of the most developed version of the myth of the fallen angels, according to which they have a supreme leader. The extent and importance of his reflection on the "third part" suggest that he might well have developed the image without having gone through Dan 8:10. He says that Satan himself cast to the earth a third of the stars in heaven, in accordance with the traditional narrative of the fall of the angels, whereby the rebel angels go to earth of their own free will and their chief leads the way. Only a few lines further on, however, John offers the account that is for him the deepest and truest, and that will be the account that predominates in later Christian tradition: that the evil angels did not choose to leave heaven, but were cast out after a bitter battle by the heavenly host who were still faithful to God (see comments on 12:7). Thus Satan's responsibility with regard to the other angels is a moral one, and here too the real effective agent is God working through his angels.

12:5 καὶ ἔτεκεν υἱὸν ἄρσεν. The quotation from the Psalm (see following comments) points to this being a messianic birth on the part of a heavenly figure with the characteristics of Israel. The heavenly birth of a "male" who is immediately "snatched" from his mother and kept by God while waiting for unspecified future events has been the source of considerable difficulties in traditional exegesis, which struggles to see the story of Jesus Christ in this account, and has been subject to radical interpretations, according to which the passage reflects expectations that are only Jewish or even pagan in origin, and not actually Christian (see, e.g., *4 Ezra* 13:26, *Ipse est quem conservat Altissimus multis temporibus* ["He is the one, whom the Highest keeps for many ages"] or *1 Enoch* 48:6; 62:7 [*BS*]; see also Charles I 1920, pp. 299-300 and references, and Massyngberde Ford 1975, p. 191; for feminist interpretation that emphasizes the androcentric and patriarchal aspects of the passage see Pippin 1992, pp. 82-86, 105-7).

The scene fits rather uncomfortably into a Christian pattern of salvation history; Satan appears here still possessed of all his powers, and seems indeed to be cast out of heaven precisely for his attempt to interfere with God's plans and to devour the woman's "male son." What was his real sin, and when was it committed? The authors of apocalyptic texts were forced to reconcile a variety of traditions (see Introduction, pp. 14-19), which is precisely what John is doing when he defines Satan as "the ancient serpent" (ὁ ὄφις ὁ ἀρχαῖος [12:9]), in reference to the sin of Eden. What is the relationship between this scene and the Genesis account? The whole issue has probably been cast in the wrong terms. John's visions draw us into a dimension in which the Lamb has been slain and the names of the saved and the damned have been written in heavenly books since before the establishment of the world (13:8; 17:8).

Christ's sacrifice does not come before creation according to our chronology, but in the timeless reality of God it has happened from eternity and for eternity. In this timeless reality everything had already happened before time existed, including the sin of Satan and his angels and the birth of a messianic figure who can therefore be kept close to God and his throne — these events are independent of what will take place in history, when there is such a thing as history. John does not see the vision of the woman and the dragon as a description of the order of events, but rather as an understandable explanation that God prepared for him of heavenly events before or outside of the created world. As he knew from eternity of the treachery of Satan, God had ordered from eternity the salvation of humanity by means of the sacrifice of the Lamb and the birth of a messianic figure.

Satan's sin, when he is still with God, is precisely his opposition to the plan of salvation that was made necessary by his sin. Theologically speaking, this leaves all the initiative with God; Satan (like Judas in John 13:26-30) simply falls into the trap that God laid for him. All the events of salvation history, from Eve's sin to the Incarnation to the end of the world, are both logically and soteriologically the consequences of what *is* in God's realm. In God's eternal present these events simply "are," with no temporal connotation, and thus John can see them regardless of whether, in salvation history as it is experienced by humans, they take place in the past, present, or future relative to John's own place in that history. Thus he sees the Messiah being born in heaven, of Israel, and he sees him being saved by God despite the threat from Satan. His vision certainly corresponds to traditional Jewish images, and it is also possible that it somehow reflects the birth of Jesus and his persecution by Herod, according to the account in the First Gospel. This, however, is all somewhat peripheral to John's point. The historical event of Jesus was certainly fundamental to primitive Christianity and to what we can imagine of the personal faith of the visionary of Patmos, but the human story of Jesus could have been quite different — could have happened, for instance, in another time or place. What matters is that everything has "already" happened in God, and only because of this can it happen in history, be seen or foreseen by John, or come to pass again at the end of time. Our passage is a "Jewish" text in the sense that its author is a Jew who is using earlier Jewish traditions and perhaps Jewish texts, but to claim that it is not a Christian text is to propose a falsely historicist reading that does not bear in mind apocalyptic modes of thought, and applies modern conceptual categories to a text almost two thousand years old.

12:6 ἡμέρας . . . ἑξήκοντα. The same period appears for the third time, and will do so again at the start of ch. 13. Besides three and a half years John has two different methods of describing the same period: "forty-two months" and "one thousand two hundred and sixty days." He uses the former to indicate the duration of persecution or evil acts on the part of hostile powers (the trampling of the temple by the nations in 11:2 and the "authority . . . to act" of the beast in 13:5), and the second to indicate God's protection (the sending of the two witnesses in 11:3 and, here, the nourishing of the woman). John may refer to the number of days when he is describing God's acts as a way of showing that, however long Satan's power might last, divine providence is there every day (see Vanni 1980, pp. 490-91).

This still leaves the question of what John intended by borrowing from Daniel the period of a half week of years. There are several hypotheses; some claim that the period indicates a precise span of time, whether past, present, or future with respect to John and to the moment of his vision, others that the number indicates a period that cannot be easily determined. Some of those who believe it to be a precise reference to a definite period close to John's own time also observe that this period lasts roughly as long as the war with Rome, from 66 CE to the destruction of the temple in 70 CE. But this passage seems to have rather a broader reference than that, and to suggest events that transcend those of the war, as meaningful and as tragic as those events were to John. The topic here is Satanic activity and divine providence.

We noted above the significance of the two periods of 42 months and of 1260 days (see comments on 11:3). Now we should inquire whether, besides their function of indicating time, these numbers might not also have a numerological significance. We must allow that numerological thought is very foreign to our own way of thinking, and that although we, like the ancients, can observe numerical patterns, we usually do not know the mystical significance that they attached to them. That said, we can observe some of the peculiar features of these numbers. First of all, 42 is the product of 6 and 7, and can also be seen to some extent as a "multiple" of 12, as it is the product of 12 and 3½, 3½ being to some degree the "key" to the numbers in this passage. 1260 is a multiple of 42 ($\times$ 30), 12 ($\times$ 105), 7 ($\times$ 180) and 3½ ($\times$ 360). This last means not only that 1260 is the number of days in 3½ "solar" years of 360 days (as noted in 11:3) but also that if we posit a year of 1260 days, then one "day" of that year would be precisely 3½ days, which brings us to the mysterious 3½ days that the two witnesses lie unburied (11:9-11). Their death lasts precisely 1/360 of their activity: one day out of a year.

The two numbers that seem to have the greatest significance in the book, 7 and 12, were seen by the ancients as being mysteriously or mystically linked by being, respectively, the sum and the product of 3 and 4. All of these numbers — which we can call "base" numbers — are thus included in 42 and 1260.

Moreover, like 12, both 42 and 1260 are "rectangular" numbers. While modern methods of counting have "square" numbers, the ancients speculated about "triangular" and "rectangular" numbers (see Bauckham 1993, pp. 390-94: I draw on this here and in my comments on 13:18). When counting with pebbles (see comments on 2:17), square and rectangular numbers are those that correspond to a square and to a rectangle, which have on each side as many pebbles as the numbers of which they are the product. For instance, 4 is the square of 2 because it corresponds to a square with a side of 2, and 6 is the rectangle of 2 and 3 because it corresponds to a rectangle with sides of 2 and 3. Because all the sides of a square are the same, a square number is the product of a number multiplied by itself: a rectangular number, on the other hand, is the product of two consecutive numbers, such that it corresponds to a rectangle whose longer side is one unit longer than its shorter side. The following diagram, in which one should imagine a pebble for every number, will make this clearer.

26	17	10	5	2	1		31	21	13	7	3	1	2
27	18	11	6	3	4		32	22	14	8	4	5	6
28	19	12	7	8	9		33	23	15	9	10	11	12
29	30	21	22	23	24		34	24	16	17	18	19	20
30	21	22	23	24	25		35	25	26	27	28	29	30
31	32	33	34	35	36		36	37	38	39	40	41	42

The first figure is a square; the square numbers appear in the righthand column and are the squares of the cardinal numbers from 1 to 6 in order. The second figure is a rectangle with one side a unit shorter than the other side; the rectangular numbers appear in the right-hand column and correspond to the products of consecutive numbers from $1 \times 2 (= 2)$ to $6 \times 7 (= 42)$. 1260 is the rectangular (i.e., the product) of 35 and 36; but 35 is a product of 7 ($\times$ 5), and 36 is the square of 6 as well as being 12×3 (and the "triangular" of 8, for which see comments on 13:18). We could look at this in many ways, but two of them seem to be inescapable: 42 indicates 6 weeks (of months), and 1260 one year (360) of half weeks (of days). This would suggest that John situates his prophecies in the context of speculations about weeks and half weeks that were common in Jewish apocalypticism both of the Enochic tradition and of the tradition that stems from Daniel. These derive in their turn from meditations on the cosmic week and on the 70 years of the exile — the period of Israel's earthly suffering. This period — a week of decades — was seen as the equivalent of 10 weeks of years (Grabbe 1987, pp. 67-72) and gave rise to prophecies about the end times and about the duration of the persecution that would accompany them. These calculations were always reckoned in weeks (of years or of an unspecified period; see Lupieri 1992). This was further associated with the measurement of time in jubilees, that is, in periods of 7 weeks (49) of years (e.g., *Jub.* 50:4; for *4 Ezra*, see Lupieri 1992, pp. 121-24). Thus John's "forty-two (months)" might mean that Satan is given only six of the seven weeks (42 out of 49 "periods") that constitute either the entirety of cosmic history (in which case the cosmic week becomes a week of weeks, or a jubilee), or else the time of the final persecution (for a possible apocalyptic interpretation of the 42 generations in the genealogy of Matt 1:2-17, see Lupieri 2005). The two hypotheses do not necessarily contradict each other because the end time can reflect and summarize the whole of human history (see comments on 17:9, 10). On the other hand, the year of half weeks confirms that God has complete and global sovereignty (an entire sacred year) as opposed to the severely limited jubilee that is granted to Satan. Thus the numerical values would underline the antithetical aspect of what, in absolute terms, is the same period of time according to the contrast that we noted with many hesitations at the beginning of this comment.

Finally, concerning the act of nourishing, the generic "they" is a relatively usual way to construct an impersonal third plural instead of a passive form (in this case: "She would be nourished" [by God? by his angels?]; see 13:16 and 18:14).

12:7 ὁ Μιχαήλ. "Michael" takes the article ("the Michael"), as in Jude 9. It seems that Michael's name, like that of his adversary "the Satan," may also denote his role, perhaps on the basis of the name's meaning ("Who is like God?" see 13:4, "Who is like the beast?"). If this is the case, then several angelomorphic beings could fill the role of "Michael" as and when it was necessary (see comment on 20:1).

12:9 ἐβλήθη. John always uses the term "thrown" to indicate the evil angels' fall to earth: a fall that is not of their own choosing (see v. 4). This creates various parallels within salvation history since the throwing down of Satan anticipates the casting out of Adam and Eve before the beginning of human history. "Nor was their place found anymore" in v. 8 is a common expression, which was also used at Qumran ("And the sons of iniquity will not be found any more"; 4QSapWorkAᵃ [4Q418] fr. 69, 8).

12:10 ὁ κατηγορῶν. The use of the present is odd at first glance, because logically one would expect the past. Some scholars think that the term is intended to be understood as a past tense (see 22:8), others that it is another translation (like the "accuser" earlier in the verse) of the meaning of the Hebrew term "Satan," along the lines of "the one who leads . . . astray" in v. 9 (notice the paronomastic of ὁ κατήγωρ; the construction is similar to "victor . . . that he might be victorious" in 6:2). In this verse we see again the close connection between the doings of angels and of men, as well as between their natures: the "great voice" calls those accused by Satan, who must be humans, "our brothers." We can also observe that Satan appears to be constantly engaged in accusing men: that he is an accuser by antonomasia. If these observations are correct, then what we have here is a moment outside of salvation history, and this eternal dimension accounts for the use of the present tense that creates problems in a superficial reading.

12:11 καὶ αὐτοί . . . αὐτόν. This further stresses the parallels between angelic and human activity. Satan is defeated by the angels who have remained faithful to God, and at the same time is defeated by men. Men can in fact be said to have defeated him even before human history (note the use of the aorist) by means of the blood of the Lamb who was sacrificed from all eternity. There is thus a total interpenetration of the extrahistorical and transcendent dimension proper to God on the one hand and the human dimension of salvation history on the other: an interpenetration that cannot but be disturbing to a modern reader. Satan was already defeated, not only by angels but also by men (the holy ones, obviously), even before he persecuted them and made "war" (v. 17) against them on earth.

12:12 εὐφραίνεσθε . . . οὐρανοί. This is the only place in the Apocalypse where the term "heavens" appears in the plural, since it is a reference to Isa 49:13 (LXX). For σκηνόω and κατοικέω, see the comments to 8:13. Satan loses his place in heaven, and his activity is confined to the earth and the sea, whence the "beasts" will emerge in the following chapters. John contrasts the shortness of the time or the "littleness" of the occasion allowed to Satan with the "greatness" of his wrath; from the devil's perspective the remainder of human history, until the fulfillment of the promise (the coming of the Messiah and/or the end of time?), is a short time compared to the lost eternity and, at all events, to the times that belong to God. This same theme emerges from a fragmentary passage of 4Q491, a text quite close to WS that recounts a hortatory speech to be delivered by the chief of the seven priests to encourage his soldiers after a military defeat. The speech includes ". . . a short time for Belial, and a covenant of God (is) peace [for I]srael in all the appointed times [of eternity]" (fr. 11, 2:18). Satan's activity is thus characterized by the shortness of the time available to him.

12:14 αἱ δύο . . . τοῦ ἀετοῦ. The "wings" are a token of God's special mercy, as we see in 4Q504 (= 4QDibHam^a), the *Words of the Luminaries,* a text that has prayers for every day of the week; the title may indicate that these prayers were taught by the "Luminaries" — namely, the angel-stars. Fr. 6.6-8 of this text has a sort of mystical paraphrase of Deut 32:11 and Exod 19:4 combined: "You have lifted us wonderfully [upon the wings of] eagles, and you have brought us to you. And like the eagle which weans its brood, circles [over its chicks], stretches its wings, takes him, and carries it upon [its pinions]" (the pronoun is in the masculine singular because Deut 32 speaks about Jacob). Thus there is a strong tradition not only about "wings of God" as a sign of his protection (e.g., Ps 17:8 [16:8, LXX] and 2 *Bar.* 41:4) but also about the wings of God being like the wings of an eagle. This is the third and last time that the term "eagle" appears in the book to describe entities that we would call angelic or angelomorphic. The adjective "great" denotes the superhuman and supernatural nature of the wings (see comments on 1:10 and also Ezek 17:3). The existence of precise biblical literary antecedents for this image (the two winged women in Zech 5:9) demonstrates that there is no need to look to outlandish mythical sources to understand John's text.

12:15 ἔβαλεν . . . ὕδωρ. Satan, like the Risen One, acts by means of "his mouth." Satan and his angels, like God and his chief angels, can send forth "spirits," possibly angelomorphic ones (see 16:13); even evil angels retain some traces of the ability to produce, if not to create. If what comes from the mouth is only "words," here we should understand it to be a reference to Satan's role as deceiver (he might be uttering pagan religions, or non-Christian or non-prophetic interpretations of the Law). If, however, it is a matter of physical persecution, we will have to recognize a similar, and not only verbal, function to the "sword" that comes from the mouth of the warrior of God.

ἵνα αὐτήν . . . ποιήσῃ. This is another paronomastic play on words that depends on the repetition of the root of the term "river" (ποταμός). Satan is trying to imitate God by producing a flood of his own, and for this reason he uses the same instrument (the "river") that will become the sign of salvation in the new creation, and which the Judaism of the time used as an image of God's intervention in the last period of history (see 22:1). Differently from Genesis, where the "earth" was powerless against God's deeds (Gen 7:10-12), here the earth is hypostatized and is shown as remaining faithful to God, still resisting Satan's seduction, and opposing him by defending the woman. This is the last time that the "earth" — the old one, that is — is on God's side; when it reappears, it is already "marveling after" the beast (see 13:3 and 1:5). Thus the fate of the earth is decided. The image of the earth as having a "mouth" that can "swallow" is a fairly common one; the earth usually swallows enemies or adversaries for the purpose of protecting the holy ones (Num 16:30-34; see 4QNarrative A [4Q458] fr. 2, 2:4: "and she swallowed all the uncircumcised ones"), but sometimes it swallows objects for the purpose of protecting them (2 *Bar.* 6:8-10).

12:18 καὶ ἐστάθη . . . θαλάσσης. This expression, which comes about halfway through the text, functions as a kind of keystone to the book by marking a change of perspective from heaven to earth, from the divine to the human sphere, and from the extrahistorical to the historical. Satan, who has lost his power in heaven, now unleashes his wrath on the earth and the sea. Since the woman is protected for half of a week of times (therefore, not forever), he turns his aggression on "the remnant of her seed," who are identified as both Jews and Christians together. Here as elsewhere John seems to see Judaism and Christianity as a single conceptual reality; in the expression "those who keep the commandments of God and have the testimony of Jesus" the καί might be used in an explanatory sense, meaning "and thus," "and therefore." The real object of Satan's wrath is holy Israel, which always has been and always will be Christian.

This verse describes the high point of Satan's campaign, the moment when he succeeds in setting himself up on "the sand of the sea." I believe the expression ἄμμος τῆς θαλάσσης means not "beach," "shore," or "bank of the sea," but rather "sand of the sea." This is such a different thing that Gen 22:17, which is echoed in Dan 3:36 and then in Heb 11:12, finds it necessary to make clear that it is talking about "the sand by the shore of the sea" (τὴν ἄμμον τὴν παρὰ τὸ χεῖλος τῆς θαλάσσης, LXX). Thus if John had wanted to say that Satan had established himself on the seashore, he would have been able to make use of the biblical texts. He says "sand" instead, because "sand of the sea" is a traditional metaphor for the people of Israel, a metaphor that has its roots in God's oft-repeated promise, made for the first time in Gen 22:17. The promise to Abraham speaks of the "stars of the sky" and the "sand of the sea" (Gen 22:17 and see Gen 15:5; 32:13, etc.).

This might indicate that there are two aspects to the people of Israel, a heavenly one (see Dan 8:10; 12:3) and an earthly one. The heavenly Israel is safe, now and forever, and thus the heavens can "rejoice" (v. 12; where the connection between angelic and heavenly natures is also in play). Satan managed to "drag" with his tail only a third part of the stars of the sky (v. 4) and now that he can act only on the earth and the sea, he takes possession of "the sand of the sea." Thus, despite his defeat in heaven, he seems to have won a partial victory here in taking control of the people of Israel under their earthly, if not their heavenly, aspect. Taking the "sand of the sea" (Israel according to the flesh) as his base, he can establish himself in his power and can manifest in the highest degree his ephemeral and transitory glory by setting up a trinity of his own with the two beasts; it is not by chance that the beasts emerge from the "sea" and the "earth" — the two parts of the cosmos that he now has under his power. We can note, however, that even this image contains within itself evidence of Satan's inferiority and inadequacy. We have to look only at the image of the christological angel in ch. 10, whom John sees "standing on the sea and on the land" with his right hand "raised . . . toward heaven" (10:5), to see how far Satan, standing on the unstable "sand of the sea," is from the representatives of God.

13:1 ἔχον . . . ἑπτά. The "beast . . . with ten horns and seven heads" is what it is because it includes within itself all the beasts that appear in Dan 7:3-7. The Daniel passage has four monsters, of which the third has four heads and the fourth has ten horns. The first three, moreover, are compared to a lion, a leopard, and a bear respectively: to the same animals, that is, that appear here in v. 2. John's beast is thus the sum of Daniel's beasts, which also "came up out of the sea" (Dan 7:3). Daniel's beasts are part of his reflection on the four phases of recent human history, phases that are identified with four universal empires (Babylonian, Median, Persian, and Alexander's with the Diadochi — the ten horns are the Seleucid kings). The four beasts are "four kingdoms [according to the Greek and the Vg.; the Aramaic has "four kings"] that will arise out of the earth" (Dan 7:17). By recalling the "ten diadems" John shows that his own interpretation of the visions is the same as Daniel's in that his beasts also refer to sovereigns, and represent the political and military power of the ancient world (for διάδημα see comments on 3:11). By combining the four into a single beast, however, he seemingly intends to say that there is no real difference among the empires that succeed each other in human history: they share a single nature that is as evil as the Satanic power that sustains them.

The mystical identification of the beasts with Satan (see 12:1) does not lie only in the number of heads and horns; Satan himself is said to give to them "his power and his throne and great authority" (see comments on 17:3, and for the meaning of "great" see 1:10). All of human history is under the power of Satan, and the various kingdoms of this world come directly and exclusively from him (see Luke 4:5-6, "He showed him in an instant all the kingdoms of the world. And the devil said to him, 'To you I will give all this authority and their glory, for it has been given over [*passivum divinum*] to me, and I give it to anyone I please'"). Although for John the Roman Empire was the most blatant example of this sort of universal power, nonetheless in describing the beast he is at pains to avoid identifying it with any single histori-cal phenomenon; the beast gathers up in itself all the power of this world.

But while this vision is not informed by any particular political agenda, at least as we would understand it today, John's views are certainly very far from any kind of Constantinian order. As many and varied as are the scholarly in-terpretations of the beast, they almost always agree that its vision expresses the Satanic nature of earthly power and the radical difference between this power and Christianity. This must have been one of the reasons why the Apocalypse created such problems for bishops at the Byzantine court, as well as, earlier, for Eusebius. On the other hand, the text's distaste for historical manifestations of power is one of the factors that contributes to its popularity among politically active contemporary theologians and, more broadly, among minority Christian groups (see Introduction, p. 11).

ὄνομα[τα] βλασφημίας. The terms "blasphemy/blaspheme" are used four times in the first six verses of this chapter to describe one of the characteris-tics of the beast who comes up from the sea. Before this point "blasphemy" appeared only in 2:9, where the Risen One says that he knows "the blasphemy coming from those who say they are Jews and are not, but are a synagogue of Satan." The others accused of blasphemy in the book are the men who do not repent after the plagues of the fourth, fifth, and sixth bowls (16:9, 11, 21) and the scarlet beast on whom the prostitute sits (17:3). The NT bears witness that Christians and non-Christian Jews frequently accused each other of blas-phemy. On the one hand are the Jewish accusations that Jesus is guilty of blas-phemy (Mark 2:7; 14:64; Matt 9:3; 26:65; Luke 5:21; John 10:33, 36), while on the other are Christian claims that Jewish reactions to Jesus and his followers constitute blasphemy (Mark 15:29; Matt 27:39; Acts 13:45; 18:6; Luke 22:65 and 23:39 are in a different category because here Luke has only wicked Jews blas-pheme Jesus). The prophetic traditions recognize as belonging to a particular category of blasphemy that of the pagans who "blaspheme the Name (of God)" because of the behavior of the Jews. "Because of you my name is blas-phemed among the nations" (δι᾽ ὑμᾶς διαπαντὸς τὸ ὄνομά μου βλασφημεῖται ἐν τοῖς ἔθνεσι: Isa 52:5, LXX; see Ezek 36:20). This verse is so useful for polemi-cal purposes that Paul quotes it (Rom 2:24; for the same idea applied to the case of the Christian faithful see 1 Tim 6:1; Tit 2:5, and perhaps 2 Pet 2:2). Thus ch. 2 of the Apocalypse expresses the notion that non-Christian Jews blas-pheme when they reject Christianity, while in other passages pagan figures blaspheme, although it is always possible that they do so in response to the Jews.

13:3 ὡς ἐσφαγμένην . . . ἐθεραπεύθη. The healing of the mortal wound is a feature that distinguishes this beast from other evil figures (see 13:12-14).

The expression "as though slaughtered" is a reference to the wound of the Lamb (see in particular 5:6, 9, 12), to which it is counterposed, almost explicitly, in 13:8 (see comments on 13:7). The wound represents a Satanic attempt to imitate the death and resurrection of Jesus Christ, for the purpose of tricking "the entire earth" and claiming the worship that properly belongs to Christ.

Contemporary scholars often see this passage as a reference to Nero's suicide and to a popular legend that the emperor had never died but had been saved in some dramatic fashion in the East, and would return at the head of an army of Parthians to take his revenge on Rome and on the empire he had led. This so-called legend of *Nero redivivus* seems to have been quite widely dispersed; the suicidal emperor, in all his grandiose madness, had such a hold over the popular imagination that his return could seem almost desirable. Some pretenders took advantage of this credulity to set themselves up as "false Neros" while, both at the popular level and among the more cultivated, Domitian was seen as a "second Nero" on the basis both of his behavior and of his physical resemblance to the dead emperor (some similarities were purposefully underlined through the official coinage of the Flavian emperor).

In fact, the wounded beast's identity with the resurrected emperor is not as straightforward as it might seem. The pagan legend that was the basis of the pretender's claims did not actually anticipate that Nero would die and rise again (see *Sib. Or.* 4:119-24 and 137-39; 5:33-34, 136-54, 215-24, 363-70; 8:70ff., 139-59). Only *Sib. Or.* 5:367 ("he will immediately seize the one [feminine — possibly Rome?] because of whom he perished") seems to expect that Nero will die before he comes back (but Yarbro Collins 1976, pp. 180-81, claims that the verse is an allusion to Nero's political ruin and not to his physical death). In some Jewish and Christian circles Beliar, to whose self-manifestation are attributed the features of the Antichrist, also assumes some features that can be seen as characteristic of Nero (*Sib. Or.* 3:63-74 [Beliar will come "from the Sebastenoi," which could mean "Samaritans" or else "Augusti"; there is nothing else in the context to suggest the Roman emperors]; *Asc. Isa.* 4:2-12 ["killer of his mother," persecutor, "king," killer of "one of the twelve"]) but without any mention of death or resurrection, nor yet of a "return." We must therefore conclude that John was drawing on more than one of the various versions in which the legend existed (Bauckham 1993, p. 423) and that, although most of those versions did not talk about death and resurrection, he altered it significantly to serve his own theological agenda. If the redaction of the Apocalypse dates from the time of Domitian, and if Domitian is represented by the beast or its wounded head, then we must assume that John took a legend about the evil of a past emperor reappearing in a new and equally evil emperor and transformed this legend into one about the death and resurrection of a single figure. The two legends tend in opposite directions and probably arise in different cultural contexts. The first bears witness to the hope felt in some popular strata of society that a beloved emperor who had never actually died would come back from the East, while the second is extremely critical of the current emperor, whose real or presumed evil it explains somewhat symbolically by portraying him as a specter of the past. Thus from the perspective of the history of ideas we can construct two different hypotheses to explain the text, hypotheses that cannot both be adopted. While John may indeed have been aware of various conflicting legends about some sort of return of Nero, it seems to me that his interest lies elsewhere, and that echoes of these legends that appear in this text are of secondary importance.

ἐθαυμάσθη . . . γῆ. The expression "the entire earth" shows that the γῆ here means the whole world, hypostatized as marveling and as inclined to accept the apparent victory of Satan (v. 4). We can explain the plural forms in v. 4 ("they bowed down") by referring them to the inhabitants of the earth who were named earlier in the sentence (see 8:9 for a possibly similar phenomenon).

13:5 μῆνας . . . δύο. This is the fourth and last appearance of this period of time, which is so important to the conceptual consistency of chs. 11–15. That the heavenly temple is said twice to have been opened lends unity to this passage, which seems in its entirety to be an expansion of the events following the sounding of the seventh trumpet (see 11:19 and 15:5 with comments; for the concept of "expansion" see comments on 8:13). This unity is further emphasized by other details, such as John's statement that the appearance of the "seven angels with seven plagues, the last ones" (the septet of the angels with the bowls), is "another sign in the sky, great and wondrous" (15:1), words that are a clear echo of 12:1. The entire block of chs. 11–15 is thus enclosed by parallel scenes and phrases. The four indicators of periods of time (see comments on 12:6) link the events of the seventh trumpet with those of the sixth; the first two come within the last scenes of the sixth trumpet (11:2 and 3), and the last two within the first scenes of the seventh trumpet (12:6 and 13:5). They appear in chiastic order: 42 months in 11:2, 1260 days in 11:3, 1260 days in 12:6, and finally 42 months again in 13:5. Is this significant? The four scenes marked out by these four periods of time appear in ascending order. The first — the measuring of the temple and the prophecy of the trampling of Jerusalem — is quite short (11:1-2), the second — the prophecy of two witnesses and their struggle with the beast (11:3-13) — is longer, and the third and fourth are both longer still and are roughly equal in length: the third — the heavenly woman, the messianic birth, and the struggle with Satan — fills all of ch. 12 (vv. 1-18), and the fourth — the account of Satan on earth and of the beasts — all of ch.

13 (vv. 1-18). The length of the successive scenes would indicate that the narrative is rising to a literary climax.

The internal connection between the scenes is also rather peculiar. If the first 42 months correspond to the first 1260 days (11:2 and 11:3), then it follows that the two witnesses are active while Jerusalem is being trampled. Moreover, John says not far from here that "when they have completed their testimony, the beast that comes up out of the abyss will make war with them and will defeat them" (11:7). This is consistent with what he says about "the beast that comes up from the sea" (13:1), to whom it "was granted to make war on the holy ones and to defeat them" (13:7) and who also has "authority . . . to act," which lasts "forty-two months" (13:5). So on reading ch. 13 the reader should know for certain that the two witnesses are active at the same time as is the beast, even if the activity of the beast is described only after the affair of the woman. We can thus adopt a hypothesis that the 1260 days during which the witnesses are active are a divine response to the 42 months of the beast's activity, while the 1260 days during which heavenly Israel is nourished in the desert are a divine response to the 42 months during which earthly Jerusalem is trampled. According to this hypothesis, the four scenes are arranged in two pairs that alternate with each other. This means that the four scenes are arranged chiastically with regard to the way in which the periods of time are described, that as regards the length of the scene itself they are arranged in such a way as to build to a climax, and that from the point of view of the correspondences in content they alternate (A/B//A/B).

Is there any meaning to this, and, if so, what is it? From a logical, if not from a chronological, point of view (see comments on 12:5) the heavenly events — the Messiah's birth, the dragon's attempt on the woman, and the subsequent clash between Satan and Michael — precede all the earthly events — the trampling of Jerusalem, the activity of the witnesses, the flight and refuge in the desert, and the activity of the two beasts. John says that each of these lasts a half week of years, bringing the total to two half weeks of Satanic activity and two more half weeks of divine intervention. The most obvious response to this would be to combine the two half weeks to make a whole week, which would thus represent all of human history under its two aspects — the activity of Satan and that of God — which both contrast and parallel each other. It is difficult to assign a chronological order to the various episodes, however. Do the 42 months in which the beast is active — a period that reaches its peak in Jerusalem with the killing of the two witnesses — precede, follow, or coincide with the 42 months during which Jerusalem is being trampled? And do the 1260 days of the witnesses' activity — a period that comes to an end in the earthly Jerusalem — precede, follow, or coincide with the 1260 days during which heavenly Israel is nourished in the desert?

I would suggest that John deliberately planned the structural oddities I noted above — with scenes rearranging themselves according to what aspect of them is under consideration — to prevent the reader from interpreting the scenes as descriptions of events that succeed each other in history. Instead he is probably describing different aspects of the entire history of salvation that would fulfill the prophecy of the half week, and he describes these aspects without saying anything about the actual duration of the historical events. Thus the different ways of expressing periods of time (42 months and 1260 days) are used to indicate the different theological value of the contrasting forms of activity: Satan's power lasts for six out of seven possible "weeks," while the providential action of God covers every day of the whole sacred (and cosmic) "year" (see comments on 12:6). The half week of years would in that case represent the whole of salvation history: the ongoing conflict between Satan and God that begins and ends in heaven, independently from human history on earth. The various pairings of periods and figures in the book (such as the two witnesses) would then show that the providence of God is broad enough to embrace both the old and the new economies. John points out both the distinction and the continuity between these two economies. If Christianity is the true Israel, then the true Jews are and always have been Christians too, and can be represented by one of the pair of witnesses, who are disciples of Christ; Christians, on the other hand, have always been a part of salvation history, even that of the past, and thus have always had their part in the miraculous works of divine providence recounted in the Bible, such as the miracles of Elijah and Moses. John takes the story of the exodus, when Israel was protected and nourished by God in the desert, as a model for all of history. After giving birth in heaven to the Messiah Israel is constantly threatened by the dragon, who knows that God's promise will be fulfilled in her and that she will bring about his own destruction. Satan must resist to the utmost the birth of the Messiah into history, because that birth is the means by which God's plan will be fulfilled and his own defeat sealed. The mission of the two witnesses and the protection of the woman in the desert are God's strategies for confounding Satan on earth. Satan, however, although he knows he has only a "little time" left (12:12), still has it within his power to bring about the main contradiction in the history of salvation: the death of the Messiah at the hands of his own people and therefore the double economy that becomes necessary when the historical heirs of the first economy fail in their fidelity to the fruit that had always been promised to them.

13:7 ἐδόθη αὐτῷ ἐξουσία . . . ἔθνος. The passive voice of the verb "to grant" (lit. "to give") suggests that however terrifying Satan's power appears to men, it is really only the appearance of power that God permits him to exercise briefly (12:12) or for a specified period of time (42 months). Notwithstanding this, Satan does have the power to operate in the spiritual realm; the beast, in close imitation of Daniel (see in particular chs. 7 and 8), can act against God and his holy ones by "blaspheming." He has absolute power over the face of the earth; the tribes, indeed "every tribe," appear again in the list of those who are subject to him, showing that even historical Israel has bowed to the power of the beast. This universal dimension is apparent in v. 8, where we read that "all those who dwell upon the earth will bow down to it." At first glance this seems strange because we have only just heard (in vv. 3-4) that the whole earth marveled and bowed down to the dragon. Is there a reason for this repetition, and for the fact that the passage is in the future tense? Most likely it is not actually a repetition at all, and the switch to the future tense is indeed significant. No subject for "bow down" is explicitly given in v. 4, but we presume the subject to be the inhabitants of "the entire earth" that was just mentioned in v. 3. John probably means that all over the face of the earth people bow down before the beast, but he does not actually say that all the inhabitants worship it. The sentence, with its verb in the aorist, probably describes the subjection that has always been typical of the political and religious life of pagans, to rulers who are both idolatrous and divinized. In v. 7, after the beast's victory over the holy ones, its power reaches even to Israel ("every tribe and tongue and people and nation"). Only after this is it possible to say: "All those who dwell upon the earth will bow down to it." Here γῆ could refer either to the whole world or to the Holy Land of Israel that has by now become part of the pagan world in its subjection to the beast.

Thus the passage includes two phases that are soteriologically and perhaps also chronologically consecutive: first the whole earth bends to the power of the beast, and then the holy nation follows suit. Even here, however, Satan's victory is not absolute: in a syntactically abrupt passage in v. 8 John tells us that those who are subject to the beast are those who do not have their names written in the "scroll of life": the scroll that was mentioned earlier in 3:5 (see comments) and whose function we will see toward the end of the book. Here it is called the "scroll of life of the Lamb" to show that salvation, which is guaranteed to those and only to those whose name is written in it, comes through Christ. John makes immediately clear that salvation is not restricted to those who are Christian in historical terms — to those who have followed the message preached by Jesus of Nazareth. Salvation is universal and is somehow "retroactive" with respect to the historical event of the Incarnation since in God's reality, which John is witnessing, the Lamb has been slain "from the establishment of the world." This phrase is parallel to that in 17:8, which leads us to believe that the names of the saved were written on the scroll of life "from the establishment of the world"; even here the syntax allows that the time in question could be that at which the names were written rather than the time at which the Lamb was sacrificed. At this stage, however, the ordinary reader is not yet aware of 17:8, and thus John most likely means to say that both the sacrifice of the Lamb and the salvation that his sacrifice brings have existed from the foundation of the world. Faced with the discontinuous presence of Satan, John affirms the unchangeable stability of the "scroll of life" that is the Lamb's book and that existed before the world itself.

In this context it is particularly significant that John places the sacrifice of the Lamb outside of time and history because it is here that he mentions for the first time that "one of its [the beast's] heads" was "as though slaughtered to death, and the wound of its death was healed." All that the Satanic imitation of God can accomplish is for the second person of the demonic trinity, the beast who comes up from the sea, to have one head mortally wounded and then healed. The healing is expressed in the passive voice ("was healed" in 13:3, 12), which suggests that this too happens only because God permits it. Moreover, if the beast's seven heads are somehow linked to the unfolding of human history in seven periods (see comments on 17:9-11), then John's phrasing means that the Satanic imitation of the Lamb's sacrifice occurs in one, and one only, of these historical phases, and thus cannot possibly have the same universal value or efficacy as Christ's sacrifice, which is from eternity and forever.

13:10 εἴ τις εἰς αἰχμαλωσίαν . . . ἀποκτανθῆναι. The rejection of the law of "an eye for an eye" and the acceptance of the suffering brought about by Satan and evil men is part of the novelty of Christianity. The famous saying, "he who lives by the sword will die by the sword" (see Matt 26:52), is consistent with the principle of "an eye for an eye," and there would have been no need to announce it here with the sort of expressions that are used to mark a new, special, or difficult revelation ("he who has ears, let him hear") or that make an appeal to "perseverance." It is so heralded here because victory is attained only through death, and in the time before the end that remains to the faithful there is room only for an ethic of nonviolence and nonintervention. If and when there is war, it will be waged by God, and the follower of the slain Lamb can only wait.

This faithful waiting does not seem to be the same as seeking martyrdom, nor even as letting oneself be killed or die rather than tolerating contamination, as praised in a text nearly contemporary with the Apocalypse (the affair of Taxo in T. Mos. 9:1-7; see J. Priest in Charlesworth I 1983, pp. 922-23 and 931). There does not seem to be any intention to try to speed along the progress toward the end, nor to force God's hand and make him act immediately to avenge the blood of the just. That John chooses to say right here that martyrdom must be accepted must mean that he sees martyrdom as a realistic possibility for those whose names are written in the book of life and who do not bow down to the beast. The sentence is probably intended to be universal in its application, also because there are no verbs that can tie it to any precise time, but its appearance at the end of the first description of the beast from the sea does show that the authority represented by the beast must have been somehow persecuting Christians (see 2:13). Contemporaries of John who read or heard about the beast would have asked questions — and not rhetorical questions — about the response that was required of them. This is further evidence not only that it is legitimate to explain the beast as a representation including the political power of the day but that John actually expects such an explanation.

13:11 ἄλλο θηρίον. The second beast completes the Satanic trinity. Satan is imitating God; the beast from the sea who undergoes a false resurrection is an imitation of Christ (note καὶ ἔζησεν in v. 14, which repeats the precise expression in 2:8), and the beast who here comes up out of the earth is an imitation of the prophetic and religious function of the Spirit. Although it is defined as a "false prophet" only in 16:13, the aspect of false spirituality is already apparent here, and in fact it is characterized by its deceptiveness (it is a "dragon" disguised as a "lamb"), by its power of speech, and by its priestly function. It even performs Elijah's miracle (which had cultic significance: Elijah made fire come down from heaven to consume the sacrificial animal in 1 Kings 18:20-40) and other "great signs" that are not described. Most of all, it is responsible for establishing the new worship of the beast from the sea; its greatest sin is that of persuading "those that dwell . . . on the earth" to "make an image to the beast." This is the ancient sin of Aaron, the first priest of Israel, who led the people to idolatry in the desert by making a golden calf and establishing it as an object of worship (Exod 32). This second beast is thus a religious power in the service of the political and military power represented by the first beast. It is primarily an allusion to the imperial cult that was celebrated throughout a large part of the Roman Empire, and was particularly important in the East (the "sea," inasmuch as it is the site of the "islands," that is, of pagan kingdoms, is a mythologized projection of the Mediterranean, the Great Sea in the West from which came Rome and its power). John's words, here as elsewhere, take on a more generalized meaning, just as the divinization of sovereigns was not a local phenomenon but a widely diffused practice even outside the empire.

A remarkable number of references to Jewish religious practices are used in the description of the false prophet-beast, which suggests that it may not represent only, or primarily, pagan religions, but also the corrupt form of Judaism that has compromised with the pagan world. The γῆ which is mentioned four times in four verses, may actually be Israel, and in any case the beast might be a savage parody of the universalistic pretensions of non-Christian Judaism. If so, John would echo the traditional prophetic accusation that Israel has become corrupt and has devoted herself to idolatry. Those priests and people who fought to stop the Romans from erecting a statue of Caligula in the temple in 40 CE, having now rejected the Messiah who was sent to them, appear to bear not only the spiritual guilt of paganism but also the guilt of having rejected their proper place in salvation history and serving instead the religious interests of the pagan world — of Satan and of the beast from the sea. The idea of two beasts, one from the sea and one from the earth, appears elsewhere in the Judaism of this era; 4 Ezra 6:49-52 says, in a passage about God's deeds on the fifth day of creation, "then you kept in existence two living beings (animas) that you created; the name of the one you called Behemoth, and the name of the other Leviathan. And you separated one from the other, for the seventh part where the water had gathered together could not hold them (both). And you gave Behemoth one of the parts that had been dried up on the third day, to live in it, where there are a thousand mountains; but to Leviathan you gave the seventh part, the watery part; and you have kept them to be eaten by whom you wish and when you wish" (for the notion of the banquet see comments on 19:17). John seems to have taken up the idea and applied it to the text of Daniel (in which the visionary sees the beasts rise out of the sea as a pattern for future beasts — the kingdoms that will arise from the earth); but he divides the nature of the beasts into two parts, of which the first is primarily political and the second primarily religious. In 4 Ezra 13:3, where the Messiah rises out of "the heart of the sea," the author is not devising a different cosmology but simply stressing that God's power is universal and reaches so deep into the abyss that it can keep God's Anointed One hidden there.

13:12   τὸ θηρίον . . . αὐτοῦ. The mortal wound sustained by one of the first beast's heads was enough to kill the whole beast and not merely that head. John uses this detail to develop a general critical reflection on political power in itself rather than on any particular emperor whose death would not necessarily bring about the end of the empire. Those scholars who believe that John is drawing on the myth of Nero redivivus see this as an allusion to Nero's death and to the Italian civil war that followed, during which the Roman Empire was in serious danger of utter collapse. This theory assumes, however, that it was Vespasian who restored the empire, as the propaganda of the Flavian dynasty claims. But in this case there is no more need for the legend of Nero redivivus since at no point in Vespasian's imperial propaganda is there any hint of a relationship between the Flavii and Nero, from whom the first two Flavii try to separate themselves as much as possible, even eliminating the "false Neros." Thus if the beast who was healed represents the restoration of the empire by Vespasian, it follows that John is talking about the affairs of the Roman Empire in general terms. In this case the wounding of the head would be a reference not to the real or presumed suicide of Nero, but to the troubles of the empire in 69 CE, the year of the three emperors. The identification of Vespasian with Nero would then be the result of further historical manipulation on John's part, and could be difficult for his contemporaries to understand.

13:14 τὴν πληγὴν τῆς μαχαίρης. Here we are told that the beast's mortal wound was inflicted by a sword. By placing the definite article before the noun John even seems to be suggesting that he is referring to a particular sword that the reader is familiar with, and thus might be referring to one of the two earlier occurrences of the term μάχαιρα. The closer one is only four verses away in 13:10, but there the sword, named without the use of the article, appears to be that which is used to persecute Christians, and thus is very unlikely to be the one referred to here. The reference might therefore be to the "large," and therefore superhuman, μάχαιρα that is given to an angelic figure in 6:4. The subject who gives the sword to the angel does not appear, but the verse seems to be an instance of the *passivum divinum*.

13:16 καὶ ποιεῖ πάντας. The cluster of repetitions of the verb ποιεῖν, which occurs 10 times in this chapter out of a total of 30 in the book as a whole, might be intended to suggest the desperate frenzy with which evil works on the earth during the short time that is allowed to Satan (12:12).

χάραγμα. The "brand" of the beast is the Satanic equivalent of the "seal" of God (see 7:2-4, 9:4). Just as the servants of God had his seal on their foreheads (and only there), so now do the beast's followers receive its mark on their foreheads and right hands. There are several ways to account for the precise reference to the right hand, which from now on is simply referred to as "the hand" (14:9; 20:4; this verse is the last time that the term "right" occurs in the Apocalypse; see comments on 5:1). We can discount the hypothesis that it refers to the practice of branding runaway slaves; they were sometimes branded on their foreheads but not on their hands, and in any case the analogy does not work well as the figures in question here are not attempting to run away (see comments on 17:5).

Two other theories are worth considering. The reference might be to commercial or mercantile activity mentioned in the context (see comments on 18:11-14); John shows little sympathy for such activity (see comments on 8:9) for religious reasons that will become apparent later on. In this case the pertinent feature would be a connection between commerce and "handedness" so strong as to suggest that Satan has control over the hand most involved in commercial transactions. Most scholars, however, are not convinced by attempts to identify behind John's text particular situations within the commercial life of late antiquity. This leaves open the other valid hypothesis: that the placing of the "name of the beast" on "their right hand or on their forehead" is a polemical and almost sarcastic allusion to the Jewish practice of using *tefillim* or phylacteries (Charles I 1920, pp. 362-63) These are little strips of parchment or papyrus, inscribed with important biblical passages, that are rolled up, enclosed in boxes, and bound around the head and the left hand in obedience to the biblical dictate of Deut 6:8 ("bind [these precepts] as a sign on your hand, and they will be as a pendant between your eyes" [LXX: καὶ ἀφάψεις αὐτὰ εἰς σημεῖον ἐπὶ τῆς χειρός σου, καὶ ἔσται ἀσάλευτον πρὸ ὀφθαλμῶν σου] and see Isa 44:5, "another will write on his hand 'the LORD's' and will be called by the name of Israel" [LXX: ἐπιγράψει χειρὶ αὐτοῦ, τοῦ θεοῦ εἰμι, καὶ ἐπὶ τῷ ὀνόματι Ἰσραὴλ βοήσεται]). In this case, then, this passage continues the preceding verses' polemic against non-Christian observant Judaism, a polemic centered on the erection and worship of the statue. The followers of this kind of Judaism have the name or the number of the beast on their hands and foreheads rather than the name and word of God; they are marked, in other words, by the idolatrous historical manifestation of Satan (see comments on 17:5).

From a numerological perspective we can observe that the term "brand," which is used only to refer to the mark of the beast, appears seven times in the text, despite the claims of those exegetes who insist that John never repeats seven times any words connected with Satan or with the forces of evil (Bauckham 1993, p. 36). The term "forehead," which appears eight times, seems to be used only for human beings (faithful and/or followers of the beast) and for the prostitute of 17:5, while the beast has "the names" written on its "heads" (13:1). *Hodayot* [1QH–4QH] 3:3-4 (". . . from your hand every seal [. . .] the sons of man according to his [or: their?] intelligence [. . .") is too fragmentary to be of any use.

13:18 ψηφισάτω τὸν ἀριθμόν. The verb ψηφίζω, from ψῆφος (see comments on 2:17), means "to calculate"; in this case it probably refers to a particular form of calculation known as "gematria." Since every letter is a number (see comments on 7:4), every word has a numerical value equivalent to the sum of its letters. This could give rise to puzzles, particularly in the case of proper names, such as the graffiti in Pompeii that reads "I love her whose number is 545." Sadly we are not able now to reconstruct the girl's name since we do not even know how many letters there were in it; but we can be sure that the message made sense at least to a group of friends who were accustomed to play around with the equivalences of letters and numbers. In Christian circles it was noted, for instance, that the name Ἰησοῦς has the numerical value of 888 (see *Sib. Or.* 1:328-29). As "the Lord's day," the day of resurrection, was considered to be the eighth day of the week (because it came after the Sabbath, the seventh day of the week), the number "eight" took on very positive connotations for Christians. Thus it must have appeared extremely meaningful and prophetical that the numerical value of Jesus' name was eight, ten eights, and a hundred eights: everything pointed toward the mystery of the resurrection.

Another form of calculation based on gematria is isopsephism. A meaningful connection, at the least, was held to exist between two words, names, or sentences that had the same numerical value. There are cases of isopsephism recorded in Greek and Hebrew: critics most often note the case of Nero, which is recorded by Suetonius (*Nero* 39); the emperor's name, if transliterated into Greek, has a value of 1005, the same value as the Greek phrase "killed his mother." In this case a person's name corresponds to a sentence that says something about that person. Within the rabbinical tradition there are attempts to use this method to interpret biblical terms: the "shoot" of Isa 11:1 has a value of 138, the same as "Messiah Menachem"; the phrase "mighty waters" in Ezek 43:2 has a value of 342, the same as "Angel Gabriel" (see Bauckham 1993, pp. 386-87). John has just said that the "name" of the beast has a "number" (13:17; see 15:2), and thus when he tells the reader to calculate "the number of the beast" he is possibly referring to the number of its name. Since he then gives the numerical value himself, the invitation to "calculate the number" is usually understood as an invitation to use the techniques of gematria to work out the beast's name.

ἀριθμὸς γὰρ ἀνθρώπου ἐστίν. This sentence is usually understood to mean that behind the image of the beast is a human being whose name has this number. We should note, however, the parallel with the "the measure of a man" in 21:17 (μέτρον ἀνθρώπου; Mussies 1971, p. 82); John explains here that "of a man" means "of an angel" (ἀνθρώπου ὅ ἐστιν ἀγγέλου), which places us in a typically apocalyptic conceptual framework, in which several different animals can represent various kinds of humans, monsters and composite animals often represent demonic beings, and "men" represent angelic figures (see comments on 21:17). Throughout the rest of the book, however, the term "men" (in the plural) does certainly mean human beings, and on the few other occasions when it is used in the singular, it probably, with the exception of these two instances, refers to a human as well. This is evident in the expression "similar to a son of man" (in 1:13; see comments on this and on 14:14), which describes a heavenly figure, but emphasizes precisely his human aspects. The word is also used in 9:5, where John speaks of the "torment of a scorpion when it stings a man," and thus cannot be referring to an angel. This leaves the two occurrences of the noun in the singular that we have noted. I would suggest that the parallel with 21:17 is very important, and that at the very least we should infer from it that the expression "number of a man" does not necessarily mean that there is a human being hiding behind the symbol of the beast; we should be open to the possibility that the being in question is primarily or exclusively angelic or angelomorphic, and thus Satanic. This possibility finds support in *1 Enoch* 49:13 *(BS)*, where "the number of Kasbeel," whatever its numerological meaning, must be referred to the head of the rebellious angels, Semeyaza (see Caquot–Geoltrain 1963).

ἐξακόσιοι ἑξήκοντα ἕξ. 666 is probably the most famous number in the Apocalypse. It also remains the most mysterious, although there have been innumerable attempts to explain it. Even the variant 616 (ἐξακόσιοι δέκα ἕξ), which is so old as to be known to Irenaeus (who rightly rejects it; see *Adv. haer.* 5.30.1), has given rise to various interpretations, and some scholars believe that the variant emerged precisely out of the desire to identify the beast with some specific person: this is Irenaeus's own view. In any case, the oldest records of attempts to interpret the number 666 come to us from Irenaeus (*Adv. haer.* 5.30.3). He lists three interpretations, the first of which he himself prefers: Τειταν, Ευανθας, Λατεινος. He dismisses as baseless other interpretations current at the time, and unfortunately for us does not record them. It would be very interesting to know what they are, because they surely are opposed to his own interpretation of the text and probably are connected with the expectation of an imminent end, an expectation that he rejects.

Ευανθας *(Euanthas)* is a very difficult name for us to understand. Some scholars think there is a play on the name of Gessius Florus, the Roman general who tried to conquer Jerusalem but was defeated in 66 CE. As *Florus* is etymologically related to *flos,* the Latin word for "flower," and as the Greek for flower is ἄνθος, the name Euanthas could suggest that the beast is identified with Gessius Florus. This reconstruction is highly speculative and does not explain the prefix EY- ("good"; see εὐανθής: blooming rich in flowers" or gay-colored): why should Gessius Florus be called a "good flower?" Rather it is worth noting that in the gnostic *Apocryphon of John* (NHC 2.1; 3.1; 4.1; BG 8502.2) *Euanthen* is the name of one of the 365 angels/demons who cooperate in creating man (he was in charge of the "left underarm": 16, 8; NHL, p. 107). This proves that at least in some Christian circles the name was considered the name of an angel or a demon. Also εὐάν *(euhan),* a cry in the Bacchanals (I thank A. Nicolotti, of Turin, who drew my attention to it), is considered a synonym for Σατάν in Theophilus of Antioch, *Ad Autol.* 2.28.6 (via the connection to Eve, who introduced deception in human history thanks to her sin with the Snake-Satan, and whose name appears in the LXX always in its accusative form Εὔαν [Gen 4:1, 25 and Tob 8:6; Gen 3:20 has the nominative Ζωή). See also Clement of Alexandria, *Protr.* 12.2 and Epiphanius, *De fide* 10.7. According to the *Lexicon* of Hesychius (s.v.), Εὔας was also a name for Bacchus (and εὐάν an Indian name for ivy, the plant that was sacred to him) — therefore, a pagan deity. Λατεινος is the Greek transliteration of *Latinus,* and this points to a Roman figure, possibly, some emperor. Τειταν, on the other hand, is a way of writing Τιταν (and is pronounced the same way) that makes the numbers come out right and has, as Irenaeus observes, six letters. The "Titan" in question must have been a pagan deity, probably Apollo, who is called Titan in some inscriptions; the sun god had been known by that name as early as Empedocles (fr. 38 in Diels 1901; see Irenaeus, *Ad haer.* 5.30.3) and also appears by this name in the poetic works of Ezekiel, a Hellenistic Jewish poet active in Egypt in the 2nd century BCE (*Exagoge* 217; see Charlesworth II 1985, p. 817). This product of the calculation of 666 might also be connected with Ἀπολλύων in 9:11, which is probably an allusion to Apollo and reflects the demonic nature of the sun and the stars. Irenaeus has nothing to say about this, however, and steers us away from further hypotheses, but I think the parallel between the titanic opposition to the gods of the sky and the Genesis account of the Tower of Babel–Babylon (Corsini 1980, p. 343) is very interesting. There is also a possible parallel between the Titans and the rebel angels, not to mention the traditional apocalyptic interpretation of the Babel episode, according to which it was built by the "giants" — the offspring of angels and women.

So out of the three names recorded, one suggests a political, and the other two a theological or, better, demonological interpretation of 666. For nearly two millennia the main attempts to interpret this passage have pursued one of these two routes. We should also note that one of the terms is a transliteration from Latin into Greek; ancient exegesis was always aware that the calculation had to be carried out with letters/numbers in Greek and in no other language. Finally, all three terms are proper names, which lends weight to the idea that the number of the beast points to a name, if not necessarily to the name of a human being. Notwithstanding this, the number has at times been understood to be the number of years in a given period; as the year 1288 approached, many Christians believed and hoped that 666 was the number of years that the "mahometan heresy" would endure after the Hejira in 622. 1288 passed without major incidents, as did 1332 (twice 666) and 1998 (three times 666). Scientific criticism today does not look for chronographic interpretations of the number.

In the past nonconformist and anti-Catholic Christian groups tended to

215

identify the various beasts with the papacy of the time; Ubertino da Casale observed that the name of Benedict XI (1303-4) transliterated into Greek is Βενεδικτος, which has the value of 666. Osiander took a broader approach, observing that εκκλησια ιταλικα (*Ecclesia Italica,* transliterated into Greek) produces the same number. The Jesuit Luis de Alcazar responded to this early in the 17th century by observing that 666 also corresponds to a phrase derived from 1 John 2:16: ἡ ἀλαζονεία βίου ("the false wisdom that comes from life," *sapientia carnis*). Luther also offered an anti-Roman explanation, suggesting that the number comes from the Hebrew *rwmyywt,* something like "roman-nes." Luther was probably responsible for the official abandonment of the idea that the number must necessarily correspond to a proper name, and he was certainly responsible for the enduring popularity of the notion that the calculation did not have to be made on the basis of a Greek term. This gave rise to numerous attempts to calculate the numerical value of various words from the book, mainly in Hebrew but also in Aramaic (the expression "King of kings and Lord of lords" in 17:14 and 19:16, if translated into Aramaic, produces a phrase whose value is 777).

In the 19th century no fewer than four scholars arrived independently at the solution most widely accepted today: "Nero Caesar" should be written in Hebrew as *nrwn qsr,* which has the numerical value of 666. It is remarkable also that *nrw qsr,* a precise transcription from the Latin, produces 616 (see the discussion, authoritative in its own way, in Charles I 1920, pp. 364-68). The only difficulty with this is that the term Caesar (Καῖσαρ) was usually rendered in the Hebrew as *qysr;* more recently, however, a text discovered in a cave near Wadi Murabba'at dated from the second year of Nero's reign, uses *qsr* to indicate the Roman emperor. This discovery has been taken as definitive proof of the theory that the number of the beast points to Nero, and has overshadowed all other hypotheses. Some scholars claim that this is not a case of simple gematria but a real isopsephism since θηρίον transliterated into Hebrew gives *trywn,* whose value is 666, while the genitive θηρίου becomes *tryw,* which gives 616; according to Bauckham (1993, pp. 388-90), this is a "genuine alternative tradition." What we have then is an isopsephism (beast = Nero Caesar) that is carried out entirely in Hebrew, with terms transliterated from Greek or Latin, and is then put back into Greek. This would have been comprehensible to the text's first readers, as they were all Jewish Christians who knew the numerical value of "Nero Caesar" in Hebrew.

The modern anti-Roman interpretation of the number (and of the whole text) has its origins in northern European Protestant criticism, and the idea that the term in question was in Hebrew comes from the personal influence of Luther. With the passage of time "scientific" criticism has become increasingly secular and has come to interpret the text strictly according to the dictates of the historical-critical method and to deny that it has any prophetic application to the present. Thus the text's anti-Romanism is understood not in religious but in historical and political terms and is thus rendered acceptable to Protestant and Catholic, secular and religious, and European and third-world scholars. Those who believe that the text is a book of prophecies that are still valid today, as well as theologians with political commitments, also accept the Neronian theory as a first stage of an interpretation that sees the beast as foreshadowing the tyrannies that regularly appear on the stage of human history, whether that of Hitler (see Barclay 1958-59) or of Saddam Hussein (see Pippin 1992, p. 46).

It thus seems acceptable to all parties today that the number of the beast points to Nero, but there are still a couple of points that require clarification. First of all, there is nothing in the text to indicate that the name must be in any particular language. Everybody made use of gematria, but, as far as I know, we do not have ancient examples of interlinguistic gematria — of a text in one language that calculates the numerical value of a name in another. Foreign names are always transliterated in the language of the text where we find the number. Here, however, we have Latin terms that are turned into Greek and then transliterated into Hebrew, and that in Hebrew are subjected to calculations that produce a numerical value that is then referred to a Greek text. No one in the ancient world ever contemplated such a strange route to the solution of the puzzle. Secondly, the text does not tell us how many letters there are in the name (and "Nero Caesar" is actually two names). This is a crucial point; if we do not know the number of letters in the name, there will always be an unlimited number of possibilities, each as likely as the next. As for the number 666 itself, it is a "triangular" number (see Bauckham 1993, pp. 390-94, and my comments on 12:6). Triangular numbers are the sums of the series of consecutive numbers beginning with 1. The first triangular number after 1 is 3, the sum of 1 and 2; the next is 6, the sum of 1, 2, and 3; the third is 10, the sum of 1, 2, 3 and 4, and so on, as we see below:

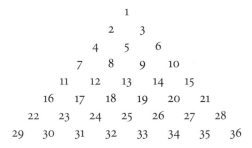

The numbers are arranged in an equilateral triangle, with the same number of units on each side; the righthand side consists of the triangular numbers (in this case up to 36, which is the triangular of 8 — the sum of the first 8 numbers). 666 is special because it is the triangular of 36, which is itself a triangular. This is a rare phenomenon because, as the triangle above gets larger, triangular numbers occur proportionally less frequently, and so also do triangulars of triangulars.

666, therefore, has the following characteristics. First of all, it is a number with three terms, all of which contain 6 (ἑξακόσιοι ἑξήκοντα ἕξ); six, ten sixes, and a hundred sixes. This is the same phenomenon that we saw earlier with the number 8 in the case of Ἰησοῦς. Secondly it is the triangular of 36, which is the square of 6 and the triangular of 8, an even rarer phenomenon; the next number to be both square and triangular is 1225. The number of the beast thus seems to be related to the length of its activity, which we have identified as 6 weeks (see comments on 12:6). It used to be the case that 6, being a unit short of 7, was seen as the number of imperfection, but since there is no support for this theory in sources contemporary with John it has been abandoned (Yarbro Collins 1984, p. 1272). The connection between 6 and Satan is very strong, however: the golden statue of Nebuchadnezzar, which is connected to Babylon, is said to be 60 cubits high and 6 cubits wide (see Dan 3:1, a passage that John uses here; see comments on 13:15). Thus our inquiry also reveals a connection with the number 8: at first glance this is startling because 8, insofar as it indicates the eighth day, the Lord's day, ought to have positive connotations in a Christian text. My interpretation of ch. 17 (see comments on 17:11) should make it clear why John sees the demonic world as being connected both to 6 and to 8 (a single connection would not be meaningful: Kraft 1974, pp. 183-84, argues that John overlooked the possible connection between 666 and 8 in Apoc 17:11). Whatever is the case, and regardless of the greater or lesser plausibility of the frequently farfetched interlinguistic and arithmological games, to identify the number 666 with the name of a particular Roman emperor is to oversimplify and to run against the grain of a text that strives to be cosmic in its application. There may be some meaning in numbers' correspondence with a particular name, but this contingent aspect of the prophecy should remain secondary to its broader application. The beast is the incarnation of Satan, who is the sum and source of the evil in all earthly power.

14:1 τὸ ἀρνίον. The Lamb, like the forces of evil, is no longer in heaven, on or near the throne, but is rather on earth, and at its most sacred point, Mount Zion. This seems to be the logical choice (the Messiah of 4 Ezra

also establishes himself on Zion in *4 Ezra* 13:36) since it is the site that God chose for his dwelling, but we must note that there is no mention here of the city, the temple, or the altar, but only of the mountain. It is quite common for God to show himself on mountains (Horeb, Sinai, Zion, the Mount of Olives . . .) as these mountains are the earthly equivalent of the "mountain of God that is his throne," which Enoch saw at the extreme ends of the world surrounded by six other sacred mountains that were also angelic beings (*1 Enoch* 25:3). The earth and its inhabitants and the sea have all gone over to the beast who set himself on the sands of the sea, and the holy mountain is the only place left for the Lamb to establish himself. Thus the absence of the city and the temple are significant: inasmuch as they are physical entities, they are lost.

τὸ ὄνομα. As the "brand" was the beast's name or number, so the "seal" of God that is put on the foreheads of his servants (see 7:2-4; 9:4), is "the name [of the Lamb] and the name of his Father." This name is thus the first (2:3) and the last (22:4) to appear in the book, and John has shown since 2:17 that he considers it a central element of the Christian mystery. His Christian reading of Judaism leads John to combine two things in a way that would not be acceptable to a non-Christian Jew: next to the unutterable name of a God who is now known as "Father" we find the equally powerful name of the "Son" (2:18). The newness of Christianity lies precisely in the union of these two names (2:17), along with the exaltation of the name of Christ that is characteristic of all primitive Christianity (see Phil 2:9-10) and that finds in the baptismal formula the sign of the actualization of its power. It is the Name that saves.

14:2 ἤκουσα φωνήν. The passage is full of references to the preceding chapters. The "voice from heaven" could be the same voice that was heard in 10:4 and 8 and perhaps in 11:12 ("a great voice from heaven"); it appears again later in this chapter (v. 13), and it is not clear whether it is the same as the "other voice from heaven" that John hears in 18:4. In all the other cases besides this one the "voice from heaven" gives orders, which often involve the visionary or require action from human beings (this includes the "voice . . . like that of a trumpet" that calls John from heaven in 4:1). John also hears "great voices" in 11:15 and "a great voice" in heaven (rather than "from heaven") in 12:10 and 19:1; but like most of the voices he hears, these are voices of praise or of revelation. As for the "voice of many waters," John always (in 1:15, here, and in 19:6) hears a voice that is "like" a voice of many waters. The same is the case with the "voice of thunder" (6:1, here, and 19:6), although in 10:3 it is the thunders' own voices that John hears. The explanation for this use of "many waters" lies in John's fidelity to his model (Ezek 1:24). The case of the "voice of thunder" is rather more difficult (see comments on 19:6). In *Hodayot*, differently from John's text, the voice "like that of waters" is the voice of the enemies (1QH–4QH 10:27). The voice is also "like that of lyrists playing on their lyres" (κιθαρῳδῶν κιθαριζόντων ἐν ταῖς κιθάραις αὐτῶν; the assonance of the Greek is lost in the translation). Lyres appear in the text several times: in 5:8 they are in the hands of the "four living creatures and the twenty-four elders"; in 15:2 in the hands of "the conquerors of the beast."

In all these cases the scene takes place in heaven, probably near the throne of God. We are told immediately what the voice says; here, as on the other two occasions where there are lyres, it is a "new song" (5:9; 15:3; see comments on 5:9). By and large it is a heavenly song that only the "one hundred forty-four thousand" can learn. We may observe that thus far nothing has been said to suggest that this group of humans is an army. If anything, they seem to be comparable to the Levites whose songs and music accompanied the temple services, and their priestly status is precisely a human parallel to angelic worship.

It is not quite clear how John sees the scene unfolding. At the beginning we must be on the earth, although "Mount Zion" brings us near to heaven, from which the voice seems to be coming. But since the subject of "they sing" is not given, we must ask whether the "hundred forty-four thousand" are already singing "before the throne and before the four living creatures and the elders," or whether the song comes from the angelic ranks, who are not explicitly named in the text. Those who make up the "one hundred forty-four thousand" seem to be distinct from the earth, from which they were "purchased" (see comments on 14:4). John probably means that the holy mountain is the place where heaven and earth meet, and that they have come together as a result of the holiness of those "purchased," which is described next. It is thanks to them that the "throne" — meaning the presence of God — is on Zion, although it is very difficult to be sure whether this is physical Zion or its spiritual parallel.

Finally, when does John think this scene comes to pass? Is it something that has been prepared from all eternity by God, or does John see the moment at which it takes place or will take place? And are the "one hundred forty-four thousand" living humans or the souls of the dead, or are they perhaps resurrected humans? We can speculate on the fact that their priestly status suggests the kingdom and the priesthood that we have associated with the millennium (see comments on 20:6, 9); this would explain why Mount Zion still exists at least partially as an earthly reality.

14:4 μετὰ γυναικῶν οὐκ ἐμολύνθησαν. Three explanations of this phrase are more plausible than the others. According to the first, the 144,000 constitute an army that is kept in readiness for the eschatological battle and thus observes the ban on sexual relations customary for soldiers in a time of war (Deut 23:10-12). However (apart from the number involved; see comments on 7:4), the primary emphasis of the passage is on the priestly aspect of the group. Thus, according to the second explanation, the 144,000 abstain from sexual relations as do priests officiating in the temple. Both of these hypotheses see John as being conceptually in line with the spirituality of Qumran and of the celibate Essenes. John's purpose is more general than this, however: the exhortation to virginity (see following comments) is not to an occasional practice under particular circumstances, nor to chastity after conversion. When he says that the men "have not defiled" themselves, he is making reference to the behavior of the fallen angels, who decided to "lie together with them — with those women — and defiled themselves" (*1 Enoch* 9:8). According to the Aramaic text of *1 Enoch* 10:11, they "joined themselves with women to be defiled by them in their impurity" (for the verb, see Lev 18:20; for the concept outside the Enochic literature see *2 Bar.* 56:11-14). These "virgins" are thus those humans who, unlike the inhabitants of Sodom (see comments on 11:8), knew what kind of behavior was the proper response to the sin of the angels and acted accordingly (see Yarbro Collins 1987, p. 89).

Perhaps John thinks that the "one hundred forty-four thousand" are destined to fill the spaces left in heaven by those angels who let themselves be "dragged" by the tail of the dragon (12:4). In *Apoc. Abr.* 13:14 Abraham is actually promised "the garment that in heaven" used to belong to Azazel, the leader of the rebel angels (for the exchange of their "places" see *Apoc. Abr.* 13:7-8). The substitution of a man for an angel is in keeping with the interchangeability of roles that permeates our text; it suggests the possibility that the holy dead might become angels (see Matt 22:30), or even that holy — meaning continent — humans might be said to become angels while alive, inasmuch as their holiness gives them a foretaste of the joys of heaven. *4 Ezra* 7:125 says that "the faces of those who practiced sexual self-control shall shine more than the stars" (implying that they are superior to the angels); this is a reinterpretation of Dan 12:3, according to which the "teachers of righteousness" are destined to "shine like the stars." In *4 Ezra* 6:32 we also see that perpetual chastity is required of those who receive true revelations; this is another conjunction of virginity, prophecy, and angelic life. The consciousness of being a holy and/or angelic army, and the associated exaltation of virginity, will later be characteristic of the monastic movement, and it will become traditional for Christian exegesis to see the "one hundred forty-four thousand" as a prophecy of the monastic "army."

παρθένοι. The only time John mentions virginity he does so in relation to men. Female figures are never referred to as virgins: Jezebel has "children"

(2:23); the woman in the sky is seen giving birth (12:2); the prostitute is certainly not a virgin (17:2), and as for the "bride" of the final chapters she is nowhere explicitly said to be a virgin (contrary to most criticism, including such nontraditional approaches as that of Pippin 1992, p. 80). John does not say that the "bride of the Lamb" is a virgin; he probably believed that she was but considered the fact to be of secondary importance. When describing female figures he emphasizes their maternal nature (see comments on 17:5) and treats virginity as a male prerogative.

ἠγοράσθησαν ἀπὸ τῶν ἀνθρώπων. John uses the term "purchase" six times. With the exception of the first occurrence in 3:18, the other occasions refer either to an act of the Lamb or else to its opposite, a reprehensible action on the part of the forces of evil. The Lamb's purchase is described three times. The first occasion is in 5:9-10, where the living creatures and elders singing the "new song" proclaim the Lamb's worthiness; by allowing himself to be "slaughtered" he "purchased for God, by [his] blood, men of every tribe and language and people and nation and . . . made them a kingdom and priests." The other two occurrences of the term are in this chapter and are very similar to 5:9-10. Here, however, the object of the purchase is explicitly said to be the "one hundred forty-four thousand" who were "taken away from the earth" and "from among men, a first offering for God and for the Lamb." "Earth" and "men" indicate their origin, from which they are separated (ἀπό). If they are a "first offering," then they are not all of the saved, but have nonetheless been "purchased" like all of the saved ("from every tribe and language and people and nation" [5:9], which, in view of the inclusion of "tribe," must include Judaism). "Earth" and "men" here, like "world" in the Fourth Gospel, refer to something negative: something from which the faithful must separate themselves. If the "one hundred forty-four thousand" really do represent Jewish Christianity, then γῆ might actually be the Holy Land. At all events we can suppose that there is a connection between the earthly dimension and Judaism, and one that will be of considerable import in Christianity, particularly from the 2nd century onward and in gnostic circles. The Lamb's "purchase" is contrasted to the "buying and selling" controlled by Satan in 13:17, a passage that contains the only occurrence in the text of the term "to sell," in a context that stresses the commercial and monetary aspect (see comments on 18:3). The Lamb, by way of contrast, does not sell but only buys, and does so only "by his blood."

14:6 ἄλλον ἄγγελον. Whom is this "other" angel other than? Perhaps he is other than the "Lamb" (v. 1) or than the "voice" (v. 2). John did not "see" the voice, however, as it does not seem to be hypostatized, and perhaps represents a plurality of voices, as "they sing" in v. 3 would suggest. He might be "other" than the "seventh" angel with the trumpet in 11:15. In any case, this is the first of three "other angels" who perform a revelatory role in the central part of this chapter, a role that is perhaps the root of their "otherness." We are in a period of transition: the Lamb has appeared with the royal and priestly "first offering" of the faithful (which is not presented as an army), but nothing seems to be happening, although this chosen and numbered group is said to "follow the Lamb wherever he goes." The long-expected conflict will not come to pass until chs. 19–20. Now the proclamation of the three angels confirms to the reader or hearer who has contemplated the forces of evil and the ranks of the Lamb that the judgment has come, that Babylon has fallen, and that the followers of the beast will be punished.

εὐαγγέλιον . . . εὐαγγελίσαι. This is the only appearance of the term "gospel" in the book, and the only appearance of the phrase "eternal gospel" in the whole of the NT. It is also the only appearance of the adjective "eternal" in the book, in contrast to the usage of John, where "eternal" is used 17 times, always with "life" (while the expression "eternal life" never appears in the Apocalypse). John sees the message of salvation as being one and from all eternity: there is no separation between "old" and "new," and therefore the gospel is "eternal." The paronomastic play on words εὐαγγέλιον and εὐαγγελίσαι is lost in the translation.

ἐπὶ τοὺς καθημένους . . . λαόν. There are two possible interpretations of this expression. "Those who reside on the earth" might be all human beings: in this case, the first καί is explicative and "every nation and tribe and language and people" explains who are the inhabitants of the earth, among whom are the people of Israel, the "tribe." Alternatively, γῆ might refer to Israel, in which case the καί is a conjunction: all the others are the remainder of the earth's inhabitants, and "tribe" is a reference to the Jews of the diaspora. I think the first option is more plausible. In any case, John is probably returning to the list in Dan 3:4 and 7 (the context of which he has already used in ch. 13), and adding "tribe." Daniel is speaking of the whole world's surrender to Antiochus — that is, to the forces of evil; John stresses the broader and deeper triumph of the gospel, which is not only eternal but also universal.

14:8 ἔπεσεν Βαβυλὼν ἡ μεγάλη. V. 7 proclaimed that "judgment" was imminent and inevitable; now a new character, Babylon, appears *ex abrupto*. We must ask what the intended reader of the text would have made of this. Up to this point Jerusalem has been the only city named by John, who treats it almost as two different entities. There is the "new" city, which is probably eschatological, as it will be revealed only in ch. 21 and explicitly called "Jerusalem" (see 3:12). Then there is a transient entity that is corrupted and is destined to be trampled by the Gentiles. This latter is not given a name, but is said to be the site of the crucifixion, and to be "spiritually . . . called Sodom and Egypt" (11:8). The implication is that the earthly Jerusalem seems no longer to be worthy of her own name, and that her true nature is best described by the use of pagan geographical terms that symbolize idolatry — Egypt — and sinful relations with angels — Sodom (which is also idolatrous; see comments on 11:8). Like Babylon in this verse, the earthly Jerusalem has been called the "city, the great one" (11:8), and a tenth of her has been said to "fall" (11:13). Up to this point the word "fall" (which here is taken from Isa 21:9; see Jer 51:8) has been used to indicate an act of prostration on the part of a positive figure, or else the fall of stars or mountains; the only other city that is said to fall is the unnamed one in 11:13 that we have identified with Jerusalem. The adjective "great," which is borrowed from Dan 4:27, is appropriate if by "fall" we understand a change in condition.

As soon as Babylon is introduced, she is characterized by "her prostitution." This is more than simply the common prophetic term for the idolatry of Jerusalem and the Jews (see comments on 17:1). From a theological perspective only someone who already has a relationship with God — particularly a spousal relationship, as in the case of Israel — can be said to "prostitute" herself in betraying him. The pagans have never known the true God, and thus their idolatry, although no less sinful, is not considered to be prostitution. This is why historical Babylon in the OT is described in all sorts of ways, even "virgin" (Isa 47:1), but is never called "prostitute." In the early part of the book John himself links prostitution, or fornication, with the consumption of food offered to idols and calls it a scandal before the eyes of the children of Israel (2:14) and the sin of the followers of Jezebel (2:20). Moreover, the only other previous occurrence of the phrase "her prostitution" is in reference to Jezebel (2:21). What the name of Jezebel recalls is precisely Israel's idolatrous corruption. The last important feature here is that Babylon is said to have given her "wine" of prostitution to "all the nations" to drink. This suggests that she is somehow apart from "all" the nations; theologically speaking, it is not clear why a pagan entity should be said to prostitute herself with other pagans. Rather, this accusation is the one reserved by all the prophets for Israel.

Despite this reasoning, most contemporary exegesis thinks that the Babylon is an alias for Rome rather than for Israel. Babylon would have been a suitable alias both for reasons of political prudence and for theological reasons, since Babylon was the supreme pagan power that had destroyed Jerusalem in the past, just as Rome had destroyed her or was on the point of destroying her, threatening Christianity in the process. When Babylon and the destruction of Jerusalem in 586 BCE are mentioned in Jewish apocalyptic writing of John's time, it really refers to Rome and to the destruction of Jerusalem in 70 CE (see Introduction, pp. 21-22). Jewish Christians would also have been in the habit of referring to the imperial capital as "Babylon," as we see from 1 Pet 5:13, which declares itself to have been written ἐν Βαβυλῶνι but which must have been written in Rome (some mss. actually say Ῥώμη). While it is true that "prostitute" is usually a reference to Israel or Jerusalem rather than to Babylon, it is also true that Tyre is defined that way at least once (Isa 23:16-17), showing that it is indeed possible for a pagan city to "prostitute" herself (but see comments on 17:5). Ch. 11, where the "the city, the great one" is identified with Jerusalem, the site of the crucifixion, presents an obstacle to this theory, but the difficulty can be resolved either by supposing that there were two great cities and that the one in ch. 11 (Jerusalem) is not the same as the one in 17:8 (Babylon/Rome), or else — more sharply — by suggesting that Rome is so far corrupted as to be the site of all the world's evil, including, from a spiritual point of view, the crucifixion itself. If so, then Rome contains within herself corrupt Jerusalem (thus, if I have understood correctly, Vanni 1980², p. 69; but in Vanni 1980, p. 481 Jerusalem is said to be "the equivalent . . . of Rome herself"). From a purely logical perspective, John's reasoning would be the exact opposite of what we have assumed: the issue is not that Jerusalem has lost her identity by becoming corrupt and has taken on the identity of pagan Babylon, but that pagan Rome, which is naturally identified with Babylon, takes on the responsibility even for the corruption of Jerusalem. As regards numbers, the name "Babylon" appears six times, which, in view of its connection with the beast, may not be accidental. The term "prostitution" appears seven times (see comments on 13:17): six times in the expression "her prostitution" and once as "their [said of men] prostitution" (but see comments on 9:20).

14:10 ἐκ τοῦ οἴνου . . . τῆς ὀργῆς. The third "other angel" declares eternal punishment "also" for the followers of the beast. The "also" in v. 10 must mean that John is adding something to what he has already said; in fact, in v. 8 he said that "all the nations" would "drink the wine of the wrath." At this stage it is not clear whether the worshipers of the beast come from among the nations, in which case the third angel is elaborating on a part of the second angel's message, or whether they are other than the nations, in which case the third angel is talking about the idolatrous corruption of Israel.

The punishment begins with "drinking the wine of the wrath." The term "wine" appears eight times in the Apocalypse. On two occasions it is accompanied by "oil" and indicates the physical drink (6:6; 18:13). On the other six occasions it is used metaphorically, and on five of these it is the "wine of wrath" (on the sixth it is the "wine of prostitution," which we will encounter shortly). The term "wrath" (θυμός) appears ten times: the first time it refers to the "great wrath" of Satan (12:12), while on the other occasions it is the wrath "of God," who is named seven out of the nine times. The "wrath of God" would thus seem to be a response to the "wrath" of Satan. John treats the "wine of wrath" as a single concept that he can insert freely into already heavily laden sentences as if it were a single word (see 19:15: "of the wine of the wrath of the rage of God"). In v. 8, describing the deeds of Babylon, he says that she gives all the people to drink of the "wine of the wrath of her prostitution." This is an odd expression: what does wrath have to do with prostitution? The answer is found here, in v. 10, with the "wine of the wrath of God." John means that the nations who drink the "wine of her prostitution" (see 17:2), under the illusion that they are fornicating with the prostitute, are actually drinking "the wine of the wrath of God," and thus are drinking their own condemnation (see 1 Cor 11:29; Pesce 1990, pp. 495-513).

The third angel, then, explains two things. First of all, the "wrath" of v. 8 is not the wrath of the prostitute, or of Satan or anyone else, but the "wrath of God"; "all the nations" are thus already condemned. Secondly, those who worship the beast (and whose willing prostration "to the beast and to its image," along with their taking of the "brand," are stressed twice in vv. 9 and 11) will face the same fate, since they drink that same "wine of wrath." John seems to be making a distinction between the Gentiles with whom Babylon prostitutes herself and these others who prefer the mark of the beast to the seal of the Lamb. It seems that the second group's guilt is actually heavier than the first's, to the extent that for them the wine of wrath is actually poured "unmixed into the cup of the rage [of God]" (v. 10). The term "rage" (ὀργή) appears six times in the book, always with reference to God's activity, from the somewhat oxymoronic "rage of the Lamb" in 6:16 to the "rage of God, the almighty" in 19:15. That which is represented by the term "cup" is also always under God's control (see comments on 17:4). Moreover, on the other three of the four appearances of the term the "cup" is connected with Babylon, who receives it (16:19), holds it (17:4), and drinks from it (18:6). Thus, if our interpretation is valid, the "cup of God's rage" always points to God's action in relation to a Jewish reality, by whose "prostitution" he has been betrayed. "Cup," "wine," "wrath," and "rage" are terms from the biblical and prophetic tradition. We can note that here it is not Babylon herself who is said to drink, but rather that she gives to others to drink — to "all the nations" and then to those who "bow down to the beast." Babylon appears almost to be an instrument of the wrath of God, although she is not any less guilty for it. There is a parallel with Jer 51:7 (28:7, LXX), where Babylon is defined as a "golden cup in the hand of the LORD, who makes all the earth drunken; the nations drank of her wine." There is similar language, although without reference to Babylon, in, for instance, Ps 75:9, where the "wine" is also said to be "unmixed" (ἀκράτου; 74:9, LXX). In this case the topic is more general, since those drinking are "the wicked of the earth" (ἁμαρτολοὶ τῆς γῆς, LXX). These examples should be sufficient proof that it was a successful polemical *topos,* capable of being deployed also against the Jewish people to whom God can give the wine of defeat and disaster (Ps 60:5 [LXX 59:5]: ἐπότισας ἡμᾶς οἶνον; also see comments on 17:4 and 18:6).

14:11 ὁ καπνός . . . ἀναβαίνει. The punishment of the beast's worshipers connects them closely with Babylon, whose smoke "rises forever and ever" also in 19:3. This further confirms the theory that there is a single theological reality underlying Babylon and the worshipers of the beast, who represent Jerusalem and non-Christian Jews respectively. The expression "they have no rest, day or night, those who bow down to the beast and to its image" is a deliberate distortion of the actions of the "four living creatures," who also "have no rest day or night" from their prayer (4:8). The phrase also shows the worshipers of the beast and his image being engaged in "priestly" activity at the very moment of their punishment, which might be another reference to Jewish worship. The image of smoke rising up forever comes from Isa 34:10, where the prophet describes the fate of Edom, which will also burn "night and day." The primary model, however, must be the fate of Sodom and Gomorrah (Gen 19:28; the detail of "fire and brimstone" occurs in v. 24). All the biblical descriptions of wicked cities who were punished are applied to whatever historical reality is hidden under the name of Babylon (and the reference to Sodom recalls 11:8; see comments).

14:12 ἡ ὑπομονὴ τῶν ἁγίων. The "endurance of the holy ones" is an echo of 13:10; there the phrase follows a warning of the persecution awaiting those who do not receive the brand of the beast, while here it follows the description of the punishment that awaits those who did accept it. The holy ones are described in two ways here as well, in a clearer reference to the two economies: that of the Law and that of Jesus Christ (see 6:9 and 12:17); the "faith of Jesus" recalls 2:13. All three of these passages refer to persecution: 12:17 to the war unleashed by Satan, 6:9 to the "slaughtered" under the altar, and 2:13 to the martyrdom of Antipas. Thus the acceptance or rejection of the brand is closely connected with the persecution of the faithful and is behind the references to their "endurance."

14:13 φωνῆς ἐκ τοῦ οὐρανοῦ. This is another appearance of the "voice from heaven" that was heard in v. 2. This time it orders the visionary to "write," which is John's method of indicating that what follows is important and should be attended to. What follows is in fact a beatitude, whose subject is "the dead"; it is logical that the "endurance of the holy ones" during persecution should be followed by a discourse on the martyrdom that can result from persecution. The text does not explicitly mention killing, but in the context the reference to "those who die in the Lord from this time onward" can mean only one thing.

λέγει τὸ πνεῦμα. The Spirit appears suddenly, and his words are recorded in direct speech. After the seven pronouncements attributed to the Spirit in the seven messages of chs. 2 and 3, this happens only here and at the end of the book (22:17), and his words are therefore very important. He promises to the faithful that "rest" which in v. 11 was denied to the worshipers of the beast and which was granted to those other dead whose "souls" John saw "underneath the sacrificial altar" (6:9-11). "Those who die . . . from this time onward" are probably the "fulfillment" of the dead that is predicted there: the martyrs whom we define as "Christian" and are the fullness of those who die for God. The Spirit's appearance is unexpected, and is usually explained as an authoritative confirmation of the "voice from heaven," but we may wonder whether it does not rather indicate the real, spiritual nature of the Voice. If so, then this is not the abrupt appearance of a new figure but rather John's explanation of so crucial a point as the promise of a reward to those faithful who die "in the Lord." The authority of the "voice from heaven" lies in its being the voice of the Spirit, or in its being the Spirit in person.

14:14 Καὶ εἶδον . . . ἰδού. The series of auditions is followed by a complex vision in which four heavenly figures — one "similar to a son of man" and three "other angels" — are engaged in the dual activity of "reaping" and gathering grapes, both on the earth. There is a prophetic precedent in Joel 4:13, where reaping (of grain) and grape pressing represent the judgment of punishing the nations (LXX has ὅτι πεπλήθυνται τὰ κακὰ αὐτῶν) in the valley of Jehoshaphat. Critics are divided on the meaning of this dual action in the Apocalypse. There is general agreement that this is a judgment scene, but some think that the double judgment is one of salvation: a gathering of the elect, or of forgiven and saved sinners (thus Corsini 1980, pp. 383-84; for a text in which reaping and grape picking are put in a positive light see Isa 62:8-9), while others think that it is one of condemnation, and still others that it is mixed, with the saved being gathered with the grain (as in such passages as Mark 4:29 or John 4:35) and the condemned with the grapes (nobody suggests that the grapes are saved and the grain condemned).

καθήμενον . . . χρυσοῦν. It is not easy to identify the figure "sitting on the cloud," even though he is described in some detail. The most obvious possibility is that he is the risen Christ, whose coming "with the clouds" was announced in 1:7 (this is the seventh and last occurrence of the term "cloud").

Luke 21:27 says that the "Son of Man" will come "in a cloud": a phrase that interprets Dan 7:13 as involving a single cloud rather than several. The whiteness of the cloud recalls the "bright cloud" of the transfiguration (Matt 17:5), which would seem to confirm that the figure is Christ (for the use of "white" see comments on 3:4). Likewise, when a figure is said three times in three verses to be "sitting," in parallel with the one seated on the throne in the vision in ch. 4 and with the figure of the Risen One, who says of himself that he is "seated with the Father . . . on his throne," the implication is that this figure is superior to the angels. Finally, the "crown of gold" seems to be a reference to the victory of the risen Christ (see comments on 3:11).

Notwithstanding this, it seems strange that Christ should take orders from "another angel" (other than whom?) even if that angel comes from the temple and if the scene might therefore indicate the submission of Christ to the will of the Father, who alone knows the day of the harvest, unknown to the Son and the angels (see Matt 24:36). This might therefore be another appearance of the christological angel of ch. 10, who was introduced as "another angel" "wrapped in a cloud" (10:1; see comments). In any case, John must have thought that these events were extremely important since they are accompanied by angels of the highest level — or possibly even by the risen Christ himself — and by a series of commands always uttered "with a great voice" from the heavenly temple (v. 15) and from the "sacrificial altar" (v. 18). For another "son of man" sitting on the throne of his glory and acting as an eschatological judge, see *1 Enoch (BS)* 46:1-4; 47:3–48:6; 61:8; and 62:5. This Son of Man or "Elect One" is probably identified with Enoch at 71:14, 17, while in *T. Abr.* 12:1–13:3 (rec. A) we find yet another "son of man"/"son of Adam" acting as a judge. He is a just man who was killed, and whose blood is well known in the NT (Luke 11:51 and parallel): Abel (see Chialà 1997, pp. 303-40). The subsequent fortune of Abel varies in different religious traditions; under the name of Hibil Ziua he has even become a divine intermediary among the Mandaeans.

14:15 ἦλθεν ἡ ὥρα. It seems certain that this expression refers to the coming of judgment, as it follows closely on and echoes v. 7 and does not appear anywhere else in the book (although in 18:10 the same words are used in a different order to indicate the judgment and condemnation of Babylon).

ἐξηράνθη ὁ θερισμός. The expression probably means that the harvest is fully ripe, although John uses exactly the same verb in 16:12 with reference to the drying up of the waters of the Euphrates. It is most commonly used to mean the death of a plant, from the parable of the sower (Mark 4:6 and parallels) to the withered fig tree (Mark 11:20 and parallel). The term is also used with reference to the sickness of human body parts, like that of the hand miraculously healed in Mark 3:1, or to the drying of "the source of the blood" of the woman in Mark 5:29, and the rigidity of the demoniac's body in Mark 9:18. It is used metaphorically in the discourse on the vine and the branches: "Whoever does not abide in me is thrown outside like a branch and *withers;* and they gather him, throw him into the fire, and he burns" (John 15:6). Finally, there is Isa 40:7: "the grass withered" (ἐξηράνθη ὁ χόρτος), which is taken up in 1 Pet 1:24. All of this suggests that John's choice of the verb might cast some light on the meaning of the "harvest of the earth."

14:16 ἔβαλεν . . . ἐπὶ τὴν γῆν. This is rather an odd gesture, as one can hardly be said to "reap" anything by "throwing" a sickle. In the rest of the book the only things "thrown to earth" (usually, like here and in v. 19, εἰς τὴν γῆν) are Satan and his angels or stars (see 6:13; 12:4, 9, 13), the "fire" from the heavenly altar (8:5), and the "hail and fire mixed with blood" (8:7): all negative entities that pose a threat to humans. It is possible that these "sharp sickles" might be devils themselves, inasmuch as they are angels of punishment, and, if so, then their absolute dependence on God is emphasized yet again when they are cast down from heaven to earth by "other angels." God probably uses their rebellion as an instrument in his own providential harvesting of the earth's grain and grapes — his gathering and judging of all its evil. We could thus identify the christological angel "sitting on the cloud" with Michael in 12:7 (this would have a precise parallel in Herm. 3.69[*Sim.* 8.3].3, for which see Brox 1991, pp. 362-65).

14:17 δρέπανον. Lucius Annaeus Cornutus associates this term with vine growing (see Lang 1881, p. 51) to explain the iconography of Pan, who holds a sickle in his right hand. Cornutus's primary hypothesis is that he uses it to "clean" the vines. To "clean" the vines, however, means to prune them and cut back superfluous branches, not to gather the grapes, and either task would demand a smaller tool than that used to reap.

14:18 ἔχων . . . πυρός. It stands to reason that an angel who comes from the altar would have power over fire. This, however, seems to be a precise reference to the angel in 8:5 who cast to earth the fire taken from the altar (see comments on 14:16). The highlighting of this detail seems to set the stage for the judgment of condemnation. Since an "angel of the waters" appears in 16:5, it has been suggested that these two angels are the members of a group originally made up of four angels, who are given charge over the four elements, in a Jewish development of a pagan concept (Betz 1966; see comments on 16:4).

τοὺς βότρυας . . . αἱ σταφυλαί. For the prophets the vineyard is usually Israel (Isa 5:7; 27:2-3; Jer 2:21; 5:10; 6:9; 12:10; Ezek 15:1-8; 17:6-10; 19:10-14; Hos 10:1; see Ps 80:9-17), and the association is continued in the parable of the tenants in the vineyard (Mark 12:1-12 and parallels) and the parable of the two sons (Matt 21:28-32). This passage is probably therefore principally concerned with the destiny of non-Christian Jews. This seems to be confirmed by several differences between this scene of the grape gathering and that of the harvest. In this scene, not only do both angels come from the temple but the second, the one bearing the orders to gather the grapes, comes "from the sacrificial altar," from the very heart of temple worship. John uses the harvest to declare that everything happens exactly according to the will of God (the second angel comes out of the temple) and the grape picking to emphasize that everything that happens is closely connected to the heart of worship.

ἤκμασαν. John seemingly wants to highlight the contrast between the withering of the grain (v. 15) and the peak of the grapes' ripeness.

14:19 τὸν μέγαν. "Which is great." This accusative is difficult to explain (see 11:18). The only other accusative in the sentence is "the winepress," which is feminine (τὴν ληνόν), while the other two nouns are masculine but genitive. We can suppose that it is an apposition of "wrath" to show the real greatness of God's wrath, as opposed to the "great wrath" of Satan (12:12).

14:20 ἐπατήθη ἡ ληνός. The expression "trample the winepress" is common in LXX, and may have no special symbolic significance but simply be a literal reference to the pressing of the grapes (as in Neh 13:15). However, πατέω, the word we translate "trample," is the word traditionally used to indicate the persecuting and contaminating presence of the enemies of God in the Holy City; John uses it in this sense in 11:2 (the antecedent must be Isa 63:18 or Zech 12:3, for which LXX uses the verb καταπατέω; in the NT see Luke 21:24). God responds by "trampling the winepress" of the "peoples" (see Isa 63:2-3, 6, which John echoes in 19:15). In Lam 1:15, however, the motif is applied to Jerusalem, which is "trodden," or "trampled," by God (ληνὸν ἐπάτησε κύριος παρθένῳ θυγατρὶ Ἰούδα, LXX). It is thus possible that this passage refers to Israel.

ἔξωθεν τῆς πόλεως. John makes a connection between being "cast out" and being "trampled" (11:2). In Matt 5:13, when the "salt of the earth" has lost its taste it is "thrown out to be trampled by people" (this passage can be read as a polemic against that Judaism which loses its strength by failing to recognize Jesus, and thus loses its place as the "salt of the earth"). Zech 14:10 and Joel 4:12 both situate the harvest and grape picking in the "valley of Jehoshaphat" and thus outside the city, but the precise location of particular "presses" mentioned in prophetic texts is secondary; what we have is a theological rather than a geographical location, as is recognized throughout the NT (Mark 4:11; 12:8; Luke 13:25, 28; John 6:37; 12:31; 1 Cor 5:12-13, etc.). Jesus' crucifixion outside the city (John 19:17, 20) is given salvific significance in Heb 13:12-13. I think, however, that the decisive phrase is "winepress of the wrath of God"; the wine that comes from such a winepress must of necessity be a "wine of wrath" (see comments on 14:10).

αἷμα . . . τῶν ἵππων. Now we find that we are dealing with "blood" rather than with wine. There is literary precedent for this image in *1 Enoch* 100:3: "the horse shall walk through the blood of sinners up to his chest; and the chariot shall sink down up to its top"; this is the only appearance of the image prior to the Apocalypse, although it enjoyed some popularity subsequently (Bauckham 1993, pp. 41-44). It seems that the Christian prophet intends to correct Enoch by saying that at the moment of judgment there will be even more blood than he had foreseen. The parallel with *1 Enoch* presents an obstacle to the optimistic interpretation of the scene whereby the blood is the saving blood of Christ, who was crucified outside of the city, and the horses are the demonic forces who drown in it, like Pharaoh's cavalry (see Corsini 1980, pp. 385-86).

σταδίων χιλίων ἑξακοσίων. This number also seems to point to Israel. In Isa 63:6 God declares that he "trampled" the peoples and "poured out their blood on the earth"; it seems that here John wants to give the measurements of that earth or land, to clarify who and what he is discussing. Critics have noted that "one thousand six hundred stades" was held to be the length of Israel (Bauckham 1993, p. 48 with further literature). *TS* confirms that there were Jewish speculations on the dimensions of Israel or Jerusalem that were based on the number 1600 (which, being a hundred times the square of 4, lent itself to measures of length or breadth, in view of the four corners of the earth or the four walls of the temple and/or Jerusalem). In this scroll the outer wall of the eschatological city is in fact given as "one thousand six hundred cubits" (11Q19 40:9-15; see comments on 21:16-17). The number, therefore, suggests that the city is Jerusalem and that those "trodden" by the "wrath" are the Jews.

In conclusion, then, it is likely that the harvest and the grape gathering both represent a judgment of condemnation that is applied first to the Gentiles and then to Israel. Thus we see once again the theological division of humanity into two parts of which John is so fond, whether he is talking about the faithful or, as in this case, about the world "outside."

15:1 ἄλλο . . . οὐρανῷ. The series of visions and auditions that began in 11:15 with the sound of the seventh trumpet ends here with "another sign in the sky," this time "great and wondrous." As it consists of "seven angels with seven plagues, the last ones," it also initiates the last septet, that of the bowls (see comments on 8:13 and Introduction, p. 4). John's choice of terms ("last," "had been completed") shows both that he is attending to the structure of his book and that this structure is approaching its climax. This septet is usually called "the Septet of the Bowls" because these are the instruments used to pour out the "plagues" (actually the main object of the septet), which John describes with deliberate references to Exodus.

To whom are the seven plagues directed? In *Apoc. Abr.* 30 the ten eschatological plagues are destined for the Gentiles. In Exodus the ten plagues afflict the Egyptians, an idolatrous nation that John has already used as a spiritual representation of the city of the crucifixion (11:8). Our phrase, however, seems to be a precise reference to Lev 26 and Deut 28; in these passages the covenant has been sealed and, as in all ancient contracts, there is a list of the blessings and curses awaiting the parties (in this case the people of Israel) dependent on whether they keep or break the conditions of the covenant. In Deut 28:59-60 we read, "The LORD will transmit you your plagues, plagues great and wondrous (πληγὰν μεγάλας καὶ θαυμαστάς). He will bring back upon you all the diseases of Egypt, the evil one (πᾶσαν τὴν ὀδύνην Αἰγύπτου τὴν πονηράν)." Thus it is clear in Deut 28 that Jews who do not obey the covenant are destined to receive Egypt's fate and all its plagues (see comments on 16:2). The number of the plagues probably comes from Lev 26, where God says four times that if Israel does not obey him he will punish them "sevenfold for your sins" (Lev 26:18, 21, 24, 27). LXX on one occasion has, "I will lay on you seven plagues, according to your sins" (προσθήσω ὑμῖν πληγὰς ἑπτὰ κατὰ τὰς ἁμαρτίας ὑμῶν; Lev 26:21). John's reasons for using septets are complex (see comments on 1:4; 2:10; 4:5), but this connection with Lev 26 is significant: the recurrence of the number seven seems to imply that God is here carrying out what he had promised, and thus it suggests strongly that it is Israel that is being punished. This interpretation allows us to account for the septet of the plagues without demanding that we commit ourselves to any specific notion of the relationship between the septets and the cosmic week.

15:2 ὡς θάλασσαν . . . πυρί. The vision of a sea made of crystal is traditional (see comments on 4:6), as is its connection with the vault of heaven. What is new and interesting here is that this sea is "mixed with fire." In *1 Enoch* 14:8-25 there is fire in some form in every heaven or level of the vision: it serves as a means both of explaining the existence of lightning in the sky, and of assigning it a purpose (in *1 Enoch* 14:17 lightning and stars occupy the same heaven). John, however, seems to show no interest in explaining the "scientific" mysteries of the cosmos, and thus there must be some other reason for this alteration in the vault of heaven. The best explanation is probably that suggested in 8:7, where the reference to "hail and fire mixed with blood" (these are the only two occurrences of the word "mixed") being "thrown to the earth" (see comments ad loc.) implies that there is a kind of fire that can

233

be mixed with heavenly entities, some of which are then cast to the earth with disastrous consequences, while others stay in heaven. If this fire is connected with the judgment of condemnation against sinful humanity, then this alteration in heaven indicates that God's will is being realized throughout the cosmos: the wrath of God "has been completed" (15:1). If it is the fire of persecution, as numerous commentators suggest, then its presence in the vault of heaven, and therefore under their feet, serves to highlight the triumph of the "conquerors" as well, perhaps, as to indicate that even persecution is part of God's plan, since fire is always and everywhere subject to God.

τοὺς νικῶντας. On the vault of heaven, mingled with the fire of the judgment awaiting the wicked (but see comments above), the "conquerors" can stand upright, possibly as a sign of victory, or of their absorption into the angelic dimension. The many promises made to the "victor" in the epistles of the early chapters should leave no doubt that these are human. The victory of the faithful, won through "the blood of the Lamb," appears to be outside of time (see comments on 12:11). The heavenly ranks are already complete (John says "the" conquerors, which implies that they are all there), although there is no question that, at the time John wrote the book, the conflict with the beast could not be said to be over, at least on this earth. John twice says that the beast is given power to "defeat" the holy ones (11:7; 13:7), and also says twice that the holy ones have "conquered" or "defeated" the beast (12:11 and 15:2). On the first occasion he describes the means of the victory, which is won through the blood of the Lamb — that is, through apparent defeat — and on the second he emphasizes the completeness of the victory over evil in all its forms — the beast, its image, and the number of its name. This is a full-fledged theology of reversal: the moment of Satan's victory within history is the moment of his real defeat. In keeping with the model of the crucifixion, which is the real beginning of the end for the devil's power on earth, every apparent victory on his part is, in the spiritual world, a repetition of God's triumph.

15:3 τὴν ᾠδὴν Μωϋσέως . . . τοῦ ἀρνίου. This is the explanation of the "new song" (see comments on 5:9). The hymnlike passage is a collage of biblical references, some from books that are not in the canon today (e.g. *1 Enoch* 9:4). "All the nations" reappear at the close of the song, but this time they are not enemies but converts who come to "bow down before" the true God, presumably in Jerusalem, as it is the only place where one can "bow down before" God. The sentence is a fairly accurate echo of Ps 86:9 (see Isa 2:2-3; 45:14; Jer 16:19, etc.) and puts "the nations" in a thoroughly positive light for the first time in the text. The surrender of the nations has been on the cards since 2:26, where the "victor" was promised "authority over the nations" (see comments ad loc.), and it is logical that it should take place here, immediately after God has been proclaimed "king of the nations" (following Jer 10:7; see also 2:28). This is something more than a surrender, however; the psalm foresees a conversion at some point in the future. Between describing Satan's success in all the earth and recounting a series of plagues that do not seem to achieve their intended effect, John reaffirms the definitive and universal triumph ("all the nations") of the Christian message. On the other hand, just as there is an Israel that will be saved and one that is condemned, so are there some nations who will be saved and others who are condemned. John has said several times — with regard to the crowd that could not be counted, for instance — that the group of the saved is from "all nations and tribes and peoples and languages" (7:9); the accent here is on the completeness of the Gentiles' salvation. At those points in the narrative where it appears that "the nations" are completely and utterly destroyed (20:8-9), the reader will have the assurance that this destruction does not nullify the salvation that exists for "all the nations." Finally, the verse prepares the way for the nations to enter into the New Jerusalem (see comments on 21:24).

15:4 τὰ δικαιώματά σου. A comparison with 19:8 and with the usage of the term throughout the NT (Paul in particular) shows that it seems to refer to a decision or act of God whereby a sinner is justified or can justify himself by submitting to the will of God. "Justification" can thus be said to be of God, as it is here, as well as of "the holy ones," as it is in 19:8 (see comments ad loc.).

15:5 ἠνοίγη . . . ἐν τῷ οὐρανῷ. All the events of this transitional phase, which opens the septet of the bowls, take place under the close control of the heavenly temple, meaning under the direct control of God. The second opening of the temple performs a structural role in the text (see comments on 11:9), but it also has a more profound meaning, probably associated with the strange and weighty description of the temple as the "temple of the tent of the testimony" (but see comments on 21:3. Instead of the usual μαρτυρία John here uses μαρτύριον, the term used by LXX in the expression "tent of the testimony"). By "testimony" is intended the Ten Commandments, or rather the tablets that ratify the covenant and that are preserved in the ark, which in its turn is placed in the tabernacle or dwelling (the "tent"): the mobile temple that accompanied the Israelites during the exodus (see Exod 25, in particular vv. 16, 22, 26). To say that the tent of the testimony is in heaven is consistent with the position of those Jews who held that since the temple in Jerusalem was empty, it no longer had any normative authority. The "opening" probably means that there is a process of revelation taking place: the "last" mysteries are realized, the mysteries of the "wrath of God," those brought out of the temple by the seven angels. Possibly God is laying out terms for a new covenant with men, a new "testimony" that will be the only valid one because it comes directly from that dwelling that was Moses' model (Exod 25:9). The mention of the "nations" in v. 4 should tend to give the scene a universal meaning, but John's emphasis on the "testimony" perhaps suggests that his primary focus is shifting back to Israel and its destiny.

15:6 οἱ ἑπτὰ ἄγγελοι. Besides their provenance from within the temple, the clothing of these angels, which is similar to that of the Risen One in 1:13, shows that they are of the highest level. They receive the golden bowls directly from one — perhaps the first — of the four living creatures of God's throne. The focus on "linen" (the only time the word appears in the text) and on its "purity" and "brightness" implies that they have a priestly function, since Jewish priestly vestments were made of absolutely pure white linen and had to be kept in a state of absolute purity. These seven angels, therefore, are the ones who officiate in the heavenly temple in priestly roles: this phenomenon has recently received absolute confirmation from such Qumranic texts as *ShirShabb* (see comments on 1:6). Not only is the heavenly temple, after having fulfilled its role as a model, the true temple, but the true priesthood is that of the angels. Finally, other Qumranic texts such as *WS* make clear that the priests in eschatological times would operate in groups of seven (see Introduction, p. 19, and comments on 12:12; see also comments on 17:1).

15:8 ἐγεμίσθη . . . τῆς δόξης. The word "smoke" appears a total of twelve times in the book. On the other eleven occasions it is linked to an angelic-demonic or evil entity, and only here is it said to come from the very heart of God: from his "glory" and "power," which are two ways of denoting the presence of God (for the glory of God see Luke 2:9, and for his power Mark 14:62 and parallels; for power and glory together see Mark 13:26 and parallels). The scene is influenced by Isa 6: the "smoke" that fills the temple comes from Isa 6:4, and the "glory" perhaps from Isa 6:1 (which is the way LXX translates the "robe of God"). John's statement that nobody could enter the temple because of the smoke recalls occasions on which the "cloud" of God's presence fills the tabernacle during the exodus (Exod 40:34) and especially Solomon's temple (1 Kings 8:10-11 and 2 Chr 5:13-14). These OT passages stress the fact that the priests could not minister in the temple because of the presence of the cloud, and something similar seems to happen here, as the seven angelic priests come out of the temple just as the Solomonic priests are said to have done. This is a paradoxical situation: the temple is open, but "no one" can go in until "the seven plagues were completed." If the heavenly temple is the place to which the prayers of Israel are brought by the angels, then perhaps John means that during the time of the plagues the heavenly temple no longer receives these prayers.

16:2 εἰς τὴν γῆν . . . πονηρόν. There are similarities between the first four bowls and the first four trumpets. The trumpets afflicted "earth," "sea," "rivers and springs," and "sun . . . moon . . . and stars" in that order (8:7-12), and the plagues poured from the bowls reach "earth," "sea," "rivers and springs," and "sun." The main difference is that when the "plagues" reach these parts of the world they afflict living beings and in particular "men," either explicitly, in the case of the first and fourth, or implicitly, in the case of the third, while the second plague afflicts "every living soul . . . in the sea." Moreover, here all of the beings reached by the plague are afflicted, while only "the third part" died at the sound of the trumpets (with the exception of "all green grass" in 8:7). This difference in the objects and in the intensity of the suffering indicates that the situation is worsening. The first plague corresponds to the sixth plague of Egypt, which caused "festering boils" (Exod 9:9-10). John's decision to begin with the sixth plague is probably connected with Deut 28 (see comments on 15:1), where "sores" or "ulcers" are the only punishment with which God twice threatens Israel: "The LORD will strike you with the sore of Egypt" (Deut 28:27; LXX: πατάξαι σε κύριος ἕλκει Αἰγυπτίῳ) and "The LORD will strike you . . . with a foul sore" (Deut 28:35, LXX: πατάξαι σε κύριος ἐν ἕλκει πονηρῷ). If John is thinking about Israel's betrayal, then this "sore, wicked and evil," is the most fitting of the plagues of Egypt. And if Judaism is indeed his subject, then it is also fitting that the only ones afflicted are "men, those who had the brand of the beast and those who bowed down to its image" (see comments on 13:16).

16:3 αἷμα ὡς νεκροῦ. This calls to mind the first plague of Egypt (Exod 7:17-21) and the disasters caused by the sound of the second trumpet (8:8-9). In the latter case and here, however, the sea and its creatures are struck, whereas in Exodus it is the river of Egypt and all the other bodies of water (as with the third bowl). Despite the analogy, there are also differences between the cases of the second trumpet and the second bowl. In ch. 8 the water of the sea turned to "blood," while here it becomes "blood like that of a dead man." Here, moreover, death reaches "every living soul," while there only "the third part of the creatures" perished. In Exod 7:18, 21 the fish in the Nile are said to die as a result of the waters being turned into blood, and thus a connection does exist, although here there is an even more deliberate emphasis on death, expressed in the contrast between "blood like that of a dead man" and "living souls." The fact that the blood is like that "of a dead man" is probably intended to make absolutely clear that it is the contaminating blood of a human corpse. No observant Jew would dream of allowing himself to come into contact with this substance (see Luke 10:30-32). Nothing is said here of the "ships" mentioned in 8:9, but by this point it is clear that the sea has become utterly contaminated and lifeless, full of defiling carcasses.

16:4 εἰς τοὺς ποταμούς . . . αἷμα. The plague of the third bowl reaches the same bodies of water as does the third trumpet (8:10-11), and turns them all into blood, as in the first plague of Egypt (see comments above). Here, however, it is the "angel of the waters" who tells us the consequences of this transformation. This new kind of angel appears quite unexpectedly, but there are angels of the waters in *1 Enoch* 66:1-2 (*BS;* the text is still linked to the figure of Noah. See comments on 14:18 for a possible connection with the angel "with power over fire"). These are punishing angels, who are ready to unleash the flood but are restrained by the orders of God (for the notion of angels being held back see 7:1-3 and 9:14-15 above). A fragmentary text from Qumran has also preserved ". . . of the ear]th, the angels of the fire and the spirits of the clouds [. . .". (4QBer^b [4Q287] fr. 2, 4) in which it seems possible to identify angelic-spiritual beings in charge of earth (?), fire, and clouds — the waters are probably mentioned in one of the gaps of the text. Thus the waters have angels of their own. This is not surprising: without any notion of gravity how would one explain the movement of the water in a river, for instance? It must be moved by an angel (see John 5:4). Every body of water has its own angel, and our passage shows that there is a sort of superintendent, "the angel of the waters," at the head of the angels of the individual bodies of water. This angel sees God destroy the waters that God himself had entrusted to him, but rather than protesting he acknowledges the justice of God and his deeds: this justice is confirmed authoritatively by the "sacrificial altar" (v. 7) that, by speaking, reveals its own angelomorphic nature.

The angel of the waters calls God "holy" as well as "just": the term is ὅσιος, which in the Apocalypse is used only to indicate God's holiness and his special purity, as distinct from human holiness (in fact, "the holy men" on the next line are ἅγιοι; see v. 6). The expression "just and holy" appears in the song of Moses (Deut 32:4), which was already referenced in 15:4, the only other occurrence in the text of ὅσιος. The holiness or perfect purity of God is proclaimed by the angel of the waters at the very moment that God transforms the water — the typical instrument of purification — into the blood of a corpse — an instrument of the worst contamination. God's act thus deprives the observant Jew of the very possibility of purifying himself and thus of observing the Law. This severe decision can be seen as God's response to the spilling of the "blood of prophets and of holy men" (see comments on 18:24): human acts that have already made observance impossible *de facto.* In prophetic language, and in much of primitive Christianity, Jerusalem and official Judaism were accused of having spilled the blood of the prophets and even of being responsible for the blood of all the righteous beginning with Abel (Matt 23:33-37). This spilled blood defiles the city, the temple, and thus worship itself. Just as God responds to the wrath of Satan and to the rage of the peoples with his own wrath and rage (see comments on 14:10), so here he responds to those who contaminate the purity of worship by the spilling of blood with the transformation of water into blood, which makes it impure. The justice of God does not break the covenant because he responds to blood with blood (see Exod 21:24).

This all makes sense if the source of the offense is Judaism, to whom God entrusted worship and the norms of purity. From a Christian point of view real purity and cult become possible after the sacrifice of Christ, whose blood replaces the water of purification as the means of salvation (see 1 John 5:6). Even if all the waters of the earth were turned into the blood of a corpse, purification would become impossible only for Jews, while Christianity would still have the means of its own salvation in the blood of the living Christ.

Finally, we can observe that not only is the drinking of blood the height of wickedness, and explicitly forbidden by the Law (Lev 17:10-11, etc.), but it is also the worst of the giants' sins and is what provoked the earth's protest and God's response (1 *Enoch* 7:5). To sum up, in the Apocalypse we are still, or once again, in a worldview according to which the punishment is inherent within the crime: the drinking of blood is both the worst sin and the worst punishment imaginable. Thus God's reaction here is no longer a flood of water, whose transience and ineffectiveness even the Bible acknowledges (Gen 8:21), but rather the definitive transformation into blood of all the earth's existing waters.

16:8 ἐπὶ τὸν ἥλιον. When the fourth trumpet sounded, the third part of the sun, moon, and stars were struck, and one third of their light was darkened (8:12). Now the whole sun is afflicted, but, rather than becoming dark, its flame is intensified to the point that it can "scorch men with fire." But although the sun behaves differently in this case, with disastrous consequences for men ("scorched . . . with a great heat" is a so-called internal accusative; see 17:6), the result is similar to that which followed on the sounding of the seventh trumpet: humans do not repent (see 9:20-21). The damaging and dangerous presence of the sun and the "great scorching" (καῦμα μέγα) recall 7:16; these men are undergoing precisely what it was promised that the holy ones would not undergo.

Who are these "men"? The plagues of the first three bowls seemed to be aimed at Israel, but here (and in vv. 11 and 21) there is a recurrence of the "blaspheming of the name of God": the sin of the beast who came up from the sea. The "blaspheming of the name" is often a pagan sin, committed in reaction to the sight of Israel's infidelity (see comments on 13:6). Perhaps John reserved the first three plagues primarily for Israel and extends the other four to include the pagans, whose involvement in the last three is quite clear.

16:9 δοῦναι δόξαν. This expression places these impenitents in a parallel relationship with those of 9:20 — the sixth trumpet — and in an antithetical relationship with the penitents of 11:13. The same thing happens in v. 11 — the sixth bowl — as a function of other details ("God of heaven," which recalls 11:13, and "their works," which recalls 9:20). The textual echoes that link the fourth and fifth bowls to elements of the sixth and seventh trumpets weaken an interpretation that rests only on parallels between those components that occupy the same place within their respective septets; I do not think John is committed to quite that great an extent to maintaining mechanical correspondences between the various parts of his work. For a possible connection with the plagues of Egypt see the comments on 16:21.

16:10 τὸν θρόνον τοῦ θηρίου. The darkness of the fifth plague recalls the ninth plague of Egypt, and with the dark the beast returns — presumably the beast that "came up from the sea." This beast has certain royal characteristics, in imitation of the kingship of Christ. The three appearances of a "throne" connected with the forces of evil (see comments on 2:13) must all be references to the same being; just as the Lamb sits on the throne of the Father, so in the Satanic trinity the beast who comes up from the sea sits on the throne of Satan. The letter to the church at Pergamum (2:13) probably involves a reference to a local imperial cult, but the geographical reference in this verse need not be so precise; the "kingdom" of the beast must be the whole earth, while for those who see the beast as the Antichrist the site of his temporary triumph must be Jerusalem.

ἐγένετο . . . ἐσκοτωμένη. We have already seen two moments of darkening after the fourth and fifth trumpets (see 8:12 and 9:2); now darkness falls on the kingdom of the beast, which is probably the earthly manifestation of Satan's power. It must be an earthly power because the ones who feel its effects are very probably humans: humans, more than angels, can be said to "gnaw their tongues because of the pain." The closest parallel to the general idea is the "outer darkness," where "there will be weeping and gnashing of teeth." Matthew is very fond of this phrase, and always uses it in polemics against non-Christian Jews; the "heirs of the kingdom" will be flung into this outer darkness (while many converts "from east and west" will be welcomed into the kingdom; 8:11-12) along with the guest without the "wedding robe" (22:13) and the "worthless slave" (the one who hid his "talent" in the ground; 25:30; for "weeping and gnashing of teeth" without darkness, see Matt 13:42, 50 and 24:51). It is hard to determine whether this fact, along with the mention of "sores" in v. 11 — the "sore" of the first plague (see comments on 16:2), is intended to make the entire passage a polemic against non-Christian Jews, or simply to indicate that some of them are also among those affected.

16:12 τὸν ποταμόν . . . Εὐφράτην. The Euphrates appears again, but this time there is no mention of angels, and the river is certainly considered as belonging to, or at least being on the borders of, the East. Perhaps it is the eastern boundary of the ideal Israel (see 9:14 and comments). Most critics think that it represented an ideal boundary to the Roman Empire, beyond which lay the threatening presence of the Parthian Empire. Thus the "kings" who must cross it on dry land are usually interpreted as negative presences, perhaps bringing political or demonic persecution (see also *1 Enoch* [BS] 56:5ff. and 4Q491 fr. 11, 1:12, cited in comments on 3:21). The expression "where the sun rises," however, has strongly christological overtones (see Luke 1:78), just as "prepare the way" is evangelical in tone (see Isa 40:3 in Mark 1:3; there is a Qumranic parallel in 1QS 9:19-20). "Be prepared," moreover, is probably a *passivum divinum.*

The text has nothing negative to say about these kings, nor does it tell us how many of them there are or what they do. They could be angels or humans with a punitive function who are hostile to the forces of evil. These last, indeed, react immediately by producing "three impure spirits" who will gather "the kings of the entire inhabited world" for the purpose of "war." Thus the "kings . . . from where the sun rises" are placed in contrast to the "kings of the entire inhabited world," which are allies of the forces of evil from which they are gathered (the Teacher of Righteousness also saw enemy nations "join together"; *Hodayot* [1QH–4QH] 14:7). This brings a cosmic dimension to the conflict, which is now between "the entire inhabited world" and "the rising of the sun." I think that the "kings . . . who come from where the sun rises" may be the King himself — Christ — together with his faithful, who are defined precisely as "kings" and his "kingdom" (1:6; 5:10, etc.). This is certainly consistent with the fact that the hostile forces come together at Armageddon, where the conflict in ch. 19 will presumably take place (but see comments on 19:14).

Passing with dry feet through water that has been miraculously dried up is characteristic in the Bible of the forces of good, such as Moses crossing the Red Sea (Exod 14:21-31, where the miracle is effected by means of "a strong east wind" that ἐποίησε τὴν θάλασσαν ξηράν; v. 21, LXX) or Joshua crossing the Jordan διὰ ξηρᾶς (Josh 3:15–4:18). This double portent serves as a model for other bodies of water such as the Nile (see MT of 2 Kings 19:24 = Isa 37:25) and most particularly the Euphrates in the section of Isaiah that underlies this passage. In Isa 11:15-16 the prophet foresees that God "with his scorching blow . . . will split [the Euphrates] into seven rivulets and make a way to cross on foot," in analogy to what he did with the "sea of Egypt." The purpose of the miracle was to allow the return from the East of the "remnant" of the tribes who had been deported to Assyria. In *4 Ezra* 13:40-47 the miracle is doubled: the waters withdraw both when the exiles leave and when they return triumphant from their centuries-long sojourn in a distant land. The idea that the exiles can remain in strange lands without contamination and that the lost tribes will return in triumph as the end of the world approaches was, and indeed still is, very popular. Recently in Israel, for instance, there has been a upsurge of apocalyptic ideas connected with the "return" to the Holy Land of Ethiopian Jews whom some rabbis deemed to be the lost tribes themselves. This expectation of a return from the East must have contributed to the Jewish adoption of the anti-Roman legend of *Nero redivivus* (see comments on 13:3), one outcome of which is the strange connection between Jews, Nero, and the Antichrist found well into the 3rd century in Commodianus (*Carmen de duobus populus, sive Apologeticum* 825-935).

16:13 ἐκ τοῦ στόματος τοῦ ψευδοπροφήτου. The "false prophet" appears rather abruptly, and John offers no explanation of who he is; it is only in 19:20 that he is identified with "the beast that comes up from the land." A Jewish convert to Christianity would have taken for granted that the "false prophecy" was non-Christian Judaism; the epithet "false prophet" seems to have been specially reserved for Jewish figures (Acts 13:6), or, at any rate, for religious adversaries whom the author saw as a threat, whether contemporary or eschatological (Mark 13:22; Matt 7:15; 24:11, 24; 2 Pet 2:1). The term is the equivalent of the Hebrew "prophet of lies"; for its use in Qumranic texts, and thus in religious polemics within Judaism, see *Hodayot* [1QH–4QH] 12(ex 14):16, and the polemic of 4QMyst[b] ([4Q300] fr. 1, 2:2-3).

The intractable exegetical question is that of whether the false prophet is identified only with the beast who comes up from the land or whether John sees him as an incarnation of some particular human figure. John says nothing about his physical appearance: is it human or animal? As the false prophet does in fact take the place of the beast, who disappears from the scene, it is of secondary importance for our purposes whether or not the two figures are coextensive: what is important is that they are expressions of the same reality. The demonic, and therefore angelic, dimension of the dragon, beast, and false prophet is shown by their ability to produce spiritual beings from their mouths. This is an imitation of God's creative power and of the ability of the spiritual forces of heaven to emit other angelomorphic beings (see comments on 12:15). From the perspective of a Jewish Christian, Israel's falling off means that Judaism is no longer spiritually represented by Michael or an angel of

God, but rather by a beast like the one who represents pagan political power, or else by a false prophet.

πνεύματα . . . ὡς βάτραχοι. It is unclear whether John means that these are "impure spirits" who are "like frogs" or whether they are "impure like frogs" (see Lev 11:10). In any case, their presence here could be accounted for by the fact that frogs are the second plague of Egypt (Exod 7:26–8:11). The parallel is appropriate, although the appearance of the frogs is not directly connected to the pouring out of the sixth cup; in Exod 8:7 we read that the "magicians" of Egypt also managed to produce frogs. This is therefore a plague that the forces of evil can manage. Acts 13:6 shows that "magician" can be connected to "false prophet" and to "Jew." This is yet another link between Egypt and Judaism, along with idolatrous paganism and Satan himself.

16:14 ἐκπορεύεται ἐπί. The expression probably means that these spirits are poured like a liquid over the kings, in a Satanic imitation of the anointing of a king. Satan intends to anoint his own kings with an evil spiritual unction and set himself and them in opposition to God and his Anointed, and to his faithful kings.

τῆς ἡμέρας . . . τοῦ θεοῦ. The "great day" is that of "wrath" (see 6:17).

16:15 ἔρχομαι ὡς κλέπτης. This phrase, which apparently interrupts the logical development both of ideas and of events (the content of v. 16 follows on that of v. 14), used to be taken either as a sign of John's literary failings or as the result of a transcription error or even a gloss. Actually, though, the section following the sixth bowl is organized around alternating motifs: first the way is prepared for the kings from the East, then the Satanic response is prepared, then the coming of Christ is promised, together with the third blessing of the book, and finally the forces of evil are gathered at Harmagedon. The coming of Christ thus relates to the coming of the kings, and the gathering assembly at Harmagedon to the "gathering for war." "Coming like a thief" was a trope commonly used in Christianity to indicate that the "day of the Lord," just mentioned in v. 14, would come suddenly and unexpectedly (1 Thess 5:2; 1 Pet 4:15; see Matt 24:43). The promise to "come" is thus threatening for the wicked, as we can see from the parallel with 3:3, where the threat is directed to whoever is not "awake." Keeping awake, like "keeping" in 3:3, receives a blessing here, but the element of threat persists in the negative formulation "that he may not walk naked, and that man not see his indecency." The "indecency" (like the "shame" of 3:18) is a euphemism for the genitals, whose exposure was considered to be dangerous. (See comments on 3:18 for the connection between the prohibition of nudity and the presence of God or his angels.) The verb "keep" appears eleven times in the text, and only here does it have "garments" as its object; usually it is the Law or the word of God that is kept.

Nonetheless, "garments" have already been mentioned three times in the vicinity of 3:3, and always with an allegorical sense. It not clear what John means by the exhortation to keep garments so as not to go around naked. The garments are probably the "white garments" that can be worn by living beings and whose meaning seems to depend on the context; here they might indicate bodily purity, the observance of the Law, faith (in God through Christ), or possibly all of these and more.

16:16 συνήγαγεν . . . Ἀρμαγεδών. *Magedon* is Megiddo, the site of Josiah's death and of the disaster of the nation of Israel in 609 BCE. Josiah was the first of a succession of Israelite kings to choose, or to find themselves on, the wrong side in the struggle between Babylon and Egypt; a pattern that eventually led to the destruction of the kingdom at the hands of Nebuchadnezzar. An observant Jew of the 1st century would have seen Josiah as a holy king who, like David (see 2 Kings 22:2; 2 Chr 34:2), had put an end to paganism in the temple and throughout the kingdom and reestablished obedience to the Law, in an attempt to avoid the disasters with which God had threatened the people, and which were recorded in a scroll "of the Law" that had been conveniently rediscovered during the restoration of the temple (2 Kings 22:3–23:3; 2 Chr 34:14-33). Josiah was a pro-Babylonian, anti-Assyrian sovereign who attempted the impossible task of stopping the Egyptian army on their march north, where the newly ascended Pharaoh Necho, who understood the extent of the Babylonian threat, was attempting to go to the aid of the floundering Assyrian Empire. Assyria fell in 606, and the Egyptian army was finally defeated at Carchemish in 605; but the army of Judah was destroyed and the king killed at Megiddo (2 Chr 35:20-25; see 2 Kings 23:29-30).

Megiddo is thus the site of Egypt's military victory over Israel and her holy king. What better place could there be for the forces of evil, which are spiritually linked to Egypt, to meet the forces of good in the hope of vanquishing them? But John does not say Megiddo; he says *Har Magedon,* something like "the mountain of Megiddo" (in Hebrew). The city of Megiddo was situated on a small mountain, or *tell,* but the conflict had definitely taken place on a plain, where war chariots could be used (2 Chr 35:22, 24). John might have made it a mountain to indicate Megiddo's spiritual dimension; it is the site of the victory of evil, and is thus the evil counterpart of Mount Zion, which was mentioned in 14:1 (there are scholars who think that Megiddo, like Egypt, represents the corruption of Jerusalem; see the discussion in Beagley 1987, pp. 87ff.).

16:17 ἐπὶ τὸν ἀέρα. The contents of the seventh bowl are poured out "on the air." The air had already been darkened by the smoke that "rose" from the abyss at the sound of the fifth trumpet (9:2; see comments on 9:1-11); here, however, the invasion of the space between heaven and earth comes from above and is directed by heaven. A "great voice" speaks; it does not have the definite article and thus is not *the* Voice, which is great by antonomasia, but it nonetheless comes "out of the temple" and "from the throne," confirming that, according to the spiritual geography of heaven, the throne of God is found within the heavenly temple (see comments on 11:19). The Voice utters a single, solemn word, which could be rendered with "It is accomplished," "It was," or "It has happened." A similar phrase appears in the plural in 21:6, at the beginning of a self-declaration of the one "who sits on the throne," and, according to the Fourth Gospel (John 19:30), Jesus' last word from the cross is similar: "It is finished." The implication is that whatever happens in history, however terrible it may appear, happens also in the spiritual dimension of God and in fulfillment of his will. After thus reassuring his readers, John goes on to the account of what does happen: "and there were lightnings and voices and thunders, and there was a great quake." The phenomena increase in power, and other elements that elsewhere appear alone are added to the group of "lightnings . . . voices . . . thunders" (see 4:5; 8:5; 11:19 and comments). Among these elements is the "great quake" of 6:12 and 11:13: a quake that, while not specifically described as "great," is already linked to "lightnings . . . voices . . . thunders" in 8:5 and 11:19. By twice calling it "great" and stating that there has never been its equal "since man has been on the earth," John is emphasizing that this quake is unique, as if it were independent of the other three. This is the last time that the quake and the group "lightnings . . . voices . . . thunders" appear in the book. The "great hail" of 11:19 is missing here, but it makes its final appearance in v. 21, after two verses apparently describing the effects of the "great quake" (see following comments), and it is also described as being extraordinary. This seems to be the climactic occurrence of this type of divine intervention in the world, and in fact the seventh plague marks the end of the last septet.

16:19 ἐγένετο . . . μέρη. This is the first of the seemingly devastating effects of the "great quake." Its presence connects this passage to the opening of the sixth seal (6:12-17), where the function of the "great quake" is unclear (it might be the fall of the stars; see comments on 6:12). In any case, the great day of wrath appears here too (6:17), and the enemies of God, with the "kings of the earth" at their head, address the "mountains" (6:15-16).

There is also a close parallel with 11:13, where the "great quake" is connected with the resurrection and ascension into heaven of the two witnesses, and where "a tenth part" of "the city" falls. Here, however, the city is called "the great one" and is not said to fall but to "come to be in three parts"; it is "the cities of the nations" that fall, and the "city, the great one" is thus distinguished from "the cities of the nations," among whom it is not included. Its division into three parts is reminiscent of speculations on the importance of the "third part" and the spiritual division of the temple into three (see comments on 11:1-2). The tripartite division of the city originates in Ezek 5, where the prophet, acting on orders from God, takes a sharp sword, shaves his head and beard, weighs the hair, and divides it into three parts, which he then burns, cuts up with a sword, and scatters to the wind. At the end he declares "this is Jerusalem" (5:5), and explains his actions by relating them to the coming siege and deportation. Jerusalem has been "more rebellious than the nations" (5:7), and has "defiled [the] sanctuary" (5:11); therefore, God will "do what I have never yet done, and the like of which I will never do again" (5:9). This similarity of our passage to this one from Ezekiel leads me to believe that the "city, the great one," which is distinct from "the cities of the nations" and "comes to be in three parts," is Jerusalem (see 11:8).

Βαβυλὼν . . . τοῦ θεοῦ. "Babylon the great" closely parallels "the city, the great one." The name of the city appears for the second time (see 14:8), as does the term "cup" (see 14:10). This verse is characteristic of John's method; first he introduces the several elements of his composition, and then he takes them up one by one, gradually leading the reader toward a fuller understanding. In 14:8 he introduced an angel who proclaimed the fall of Babylon "the great," which appeared as the one who gives to the nations to drink "the wine of the wrath of her prostitution" (not as the one who drinks it herself). No cup is mentioned at this point, nor is the identity of Babylon revealed; the text says only that she is "great" (see comments on 1:10), like the "city, the great one" of 11:8. Shortly after this the "wine of the wrath of God" is given in "the cup of his rage" to those who have received the brand of the beast (see comments on 14:10). In our verse these separate elements are brought into a closer relation. Here Babylon is the one given the "cup of the wine of the wrath of [God's] rage"; she does not have to drink it yet (see comments on 18:6) and perhaps is given it so that she can give it to the nations to drink, as in ch. 14, as the means whereby God makes manifest his wrath (see comments on 14:8).

The expression "was remembered" is also ambiguous, as God can remember humans either in mercy or in wrath; the context suggests the latter, but the text does not make it explicit. As well as receiving the cup, Babylon is brought into closer proximity with the "city, the great one," although she is not verbatim identified with it. Depending on how καί is understood, "Babylon, the great" can be identified either with the "city, the great one" or with one of the "cities of the nations" (after all, in 14:8 John said that Babylon was "fallen"), or it can be seen as distinct from them all. But although nothing is stated explicitly, the alert reader will be aware that Babylon is brought into proximity with "the city, the great one" and will consider the implications.

16:20 πᾶσα . . . εὑρέθησαν. The movement of the islands and mountains, like the "great quake," echoes the opening of the sixth seal (see 6:14). As we noted there, the "islands" must be the pagan kingdoms of the West, and the "mountains" the angelic-demonic representatives of pagan kings and kingdoms. In this context the islands are personalized to the point that they can be said to "flee" (like the earth in 20:11), and the expression "no mountains were found" links them closely with Satan and his angels (12:8) as well as with the "earth" and "heaven" (20:11). Finally, we should note that the disappearance of the mountains is proclaimed shortly after Harmagedon, the "mountain of Megiddo," is mentioned; the (bilingual) believer would be left in no doubt as to the eventual outcome of the conflict whose first stages he was witnessing.

16:21 χάλαζα . . . τοῦ οὐρανοῦ. This is the last appearance of the "great hail" that we saw in 11:19, and its appearance serves to strengthen the parallel between this passage and that (see comments on 16:17). It also serves to connect this "plague of hail" — the seventh and last plague of the Apocalypse — with the seventh plague of Egypt (Exod 9:13-35). Other details accentuate this connection. The assertion that there had never been a quake as great as this one on the earth "since man has been on the earth" (v. 18) is a fairly accurate echo of the repeated affirmation that the seventh plague was "the heaviest hail . . . that had ever fallen in Egypt from the day it was founded until now" (Exod 9:18, 24). The Egyptian hail was also accompanied by lightning and thunder (Exod 9:23-24, 29, 33-34), as well as by a mysterious fire (Exod 9:23) that calls to mind the fire that has appeared on several occasions: with hail (8:7), with "lightning . . . voices . . . thunders" (4:5 and particularly 8:5), alone (at the beginning of the section with the seven plagues, in 15:2, and as a central element in the fourth plague, which would otherwise be the only apocalyptic plague not to have a connection with the plagues of Exodus).

It is possible that John got the idea of the hailstones' weight — "of a talent" — from the devastating experience of Roman catapults, as recorded by Josephus (*J.W.* 5[6.3].270). It may be significant, however, that John describes the hail as "coming down from heaven." The verb "come down" is used ten times, and always refers to a descent "from heaven" (nine times explicitly, and once implicitly, in 12:12). In these nine cases the subject of the verb is Jerusalem ("new" or "heavenly"; three times), an angel (three times), a fire (twice), and the devil (once). Thus they are primarily angelic or angelomorphic entities, and the hail should also be considered as belonging to this category (see comments on 4:1 and 8:7). This would account for the use of the epithet "great" (see comments on 1:10).

The blasphemy of the impenitents recalls vv. 9 and 11 (as well as the parallels noted in the comments on 13:16). The failure of the plagues to achieve their goal — a failure that is particularly emphasized in the cases of the fourth, fifth, and seventh plagues — once again recalls Egypt and the hardening of Pharaoh's heart, which occurs after every plague in the Exodus account.

The final sentence, "because the plague of it is great, very much so," is possibly a comment on John's part (see 17:14). That the hail comes "from heaven" probably means that it is sent by God, but the text does not say explicitly who the "men" are to whom it is sent. They are clearly the successors of the Egyptians, but the OT description of Joshua's victory over Gibeon shows that hail was also effective against other pagans: "The LORD threw down huge stones [LXX: λίθους χαλάζης] from heaven on them . . . and there were more who died because of the hailstones [LXX: τοὺς λίθους τῆς χαλάζης] than the Israelites killed with the sword" (Josh 10:11). Hailstones also strike the Assyrians on God's commands (Isa 30:30) but another passage from Isaiah — the passage about the cornerstone of which much was made in primitive Christianity — is more pertinent to our concerns. In this oracle against "those who rule [LXX: ἄρχοντες] this people in Jerusalem" (Isa 28:14), God threatens that "hail will sweep away the [your] refuge of lies" (Isa 28:17, Hebrew; LXX has a different text). The immediate context tells us the origin of this hail that will be unleashed on the rulers of Jerusalem and on their refuge (which is probably the spiritual edifice of their "covenant [LXX: διαθήκη] with Death . . . and Sheol"; v. 18): by means of the hail God "will rage as in the valley of Gibeon to do his deed" (v. 21). God's miraculous intervention against Gibeon is turned against Jerusalem and its unworthy rulers. This shows first of all that hail can be used as a punishment for Israel when she strays, and secondly that God's anger against the nations can be turned against Israel. Not only Egypt with its plagues but any nation stricken by God within biblical history can become the model for Israel's own destiny (see comments on 17:6).

17:1 τὸ κρίμα . . . μεγάλης. This is the first appearance of one of the book's most famous figures: "the prostitute, the great one." It is also the first occurrence of πόρνη, although we have already encountered πορνεία and πορνεύω. Up to this point John has used the verb only to indicate the "prostitution" that accompanies "eating food offered to idols" (2:14, 20), whereas he has used the noun three times to indicate the sins of Jezebel (2:21), of the impenitent idolaters (9:21 and comments), and of Babylon (14:8). Of these three passages the last is the closest to the present one, as the "wine of her prostitution" (17:2) echoes "the wine of the wrath of her prostitution"

(14:8), and this wine is to be drunk by "all the nations" (14:8) and by "those who inhabit the earth" (17:2). This internal echo is strengthened by the appearance of "the kings of the earth" who "fornicated" with her. The "kings of the earth" are first mentioned in 1:5, and appear a total of nine times in the course of the book, on one occasion being referred to as "the kings of the whole world" (16:14). They perform a variety of functions; in some contexts they are Christ's subjects and show no signs of being unfaithful to him (1:5), but more often they represent Christ's enemies (beginning with 6:15). After this passage the verb πορνεύω occurs only twice, and on both occasions "the kings of the earth" are the subject. Nonetheless they remain very ambiguous, especially in 21:24 (see comments ad loc.).

All this leads us to expect that the "prostitute, the great one," will be identified with "Babylon the great," as indeed she is in v. 5. If Babylon is the prostitute, however, we must ask what it means that she prostitutes herself with "the kings of the earth" or that she gives to drink "to the nations." The biblical passages that might account for one or the other of these seem to lead in two different directions. The pages of the prophets are full of the whoredom of Jerusalem (see comments on 14:8); we have only to turn to Isa 1:21, "How the faithful city has become a prostitute!" (LXX: πῶς ἐγένετο πόρνη πόλις πιστὴ Σιὼν πλήρης κρίσεως) and Jer 2:20, "On every high hill and under every green tree you sprawled and prostituted yourself" (LXX: πορεύσομαι ἐπὶ πάντα βουνὸν ὑψηλόν . . . ἐκεῖ διαχυθήσομαι ἐν τῇ πορνείᾳ μου). The bitterest texts are in Ezekiel, particularly chs. 16 and 23, which seem to be the source of many of the images adopted by John. Not only does Ezekiel address Jerusalem directly as a "prostitute" (16:35), call her the sister of Sodom (16:46; see comments on 11:8) and of Samaria (16:46 and all of ch. 23), and identify her prostitution with idolatrous worship (16:15-25, 31, 47; 23:37), but he also says that she prostitutes herself with Egyptians (16:26; 23:19, 21, 27), with Assyrians (16:28; 23:12, 23), and with Babylonians ("sons of Babylon and all the Chaldeans" 16:29; 23:14-17, 23). Ezekiel says that Jerusalem's prostitution is greater even than Samaria's (23:11, LXX: καὶ τὴν πορνείαν αὐτῆς ὑπὲρ τὴν πορνείαν τῆς ἀδελφῆς αὐτῆς) and that it is mainly with foreign military officials (23:12, 23, "governors and commanders"; LXX: ἡγουμένους/ἡγεμόνας καὶ στρατηγούς).

The motif of prostitution, then, suggests that the female figure is an image of Jerusalem. This suggestion is strengthened if the "kings of the earth" are the pagan rulers of the nations, particularly in the light of the imperial cult and of the forms of idolatrous worship reserved for kings (see also the interpretation of the "kings of the earth" as angelic figures in *1 Enoch* [BS]: Chialà 1997, pp. 157ff.). In the eyes of a Jew, whether Christian or not, there is a very close connection between the king of a nation and that nation's angel: its pagan god or evil spirit (see Dan 10:13: ὁ ἄρχων βασιλείας Περσῶν, LXX); prostitution and idolatry are the same.

As regards evidence from outside the biblical tradition, there is what seems to me a decisive confirmation in the *Halakhic Letter* from Qumran, which contains ideas previously believed to have emerged in Israel in the 1st century CE but actually dating from the second half of the 2nd century BCE; the pagans, for instance, are considered to be a source and a vehicle of defilement, and their offerings to the temple (the text makes explicit mention of grain offerings and sacrifices) must be rejected. On the subject of the "sacrifice of the Gentiles" the text, which is fragmentary and difficult to interpret, asserts that "this is like she who whored with him," that is, to accept them (4QMMT "B" 8-9; see Qimron–Strugnell 1994, pp. 46-47, 149-50). "Prostitution," therefore, is not necessarily adherence to pagan worship or the Gentile way of life, but can also be the mere acceptance of sacrifices from the Gentiles: the Qumranic text and John's connection between "prostitution" and "eating food offered to idols" are mutually illuminating. The authors of the *HL* see the sacrifices of pagans as nothing other than food offered to idols.

Isa 23:17, however, seems to suggest quite another direction. In this passage Tyre, after being compared to a "forgotten prostitute" (23:16, LXX: πόλις πόρνη ἐπιλελησμένη), returns to her "trade . . . with all the kingdoms of the world on the face of the earth!" The word for "to trade with" may also mean a form of prostitution, but the LXX sees only the commercial aspect: (ἔσται ἐμπόριον πάσαις ταῖς βασιλείαις τῆς οἰκουμένης ἐπὶ πρόσωπον τῆς γῆς). Moreover, the fact that inhabitants of the earth are drunk with the "wine" that the prostitute pours out points toward historical Babylon being "the prostitute, the great one." Jeremiah sees Babylon as the instrument chosen by God to make all the earth drunk (Jer 51:7, cited in comments on 14:10). Babylon is, however, not the only human instrument chosen by God to bear the cup of the wine of his wrath, and in fact the instrument need not even be a political entity outside of Israel: Jeremiah himself is charged by God with the task of making "all the nations" drunk (Jer 25:15-16 [32:15-16 LXX]: λάβε τὸ ποτήριον τοῦ οἴνου τοῦ ἀκράτου τούτου ἐκ χειρός μου καὶ ποτιεῖς πάντα τὰ ἔθνη). We find here the "unmixed" wine that we saw in 14:10; there it seemed to be a particularly harsh response on God's part to his people's betrayal, but here it appears to be reserved for the "nations." In the following verses, however, Jeremiah lists the "nations" to whom he gives the cup, and at the head of the list we find "Jerusalem and the towns of Judah, its kings and its princes" (Jer 25:18 [32:18, LXX]: τὴν Ἰερουσαλὴμ καὶ τὰς πόλεις Ἰούδα καὶ βασιλεῖς Ἰούδα καὶ ἄρχοντας αὐτοῦ). The next in line, and thus the closest to Jerusalem, is "Pharaoh king of Egypt." This juxtaposition of Israel and Egypt is well established in Jeremiah; it appears also in 9:5, where Egypt and Judah, in that order, are numbered among those who will be punished for being "circumcised only in the foreskin" (i.e., not in the heart; see Jer 4:4). For a Qumranic formulation of this idea see the comments on 11:8.

By this point we can advance the thesis that, at least from Jeremiah onward, when Jerusalem sins she is compared to the Gentiles, and her punishment to theirs. Moreover, in her course of depravity and prostitution she realizes the connection between Egypt and her destiny that was threatened in Deut 28 and that John takes up explicitly in 11:8 (also see comments on 16:2). In Num 11:33, "the Lᴏʀᴅ struck the people with a very great plague" (LXX: ἐπάταξε κύριος τὸν λαὸν πληγὴν μεγάλην σφόδρα), thus confirming his intention to treat Israel like Egypt. (Among the best contemporary works on Babylon in the Apocalypse are Beagley 1987 and Corsini 2002.)

τῆς καθημένης . . . πολλῶν. Neither a human prostitute nor a city can be "seated on many waters." The reference to many waters is usually taken to be a reference to the historical Babylon, which was located on one of the most famous rivers of the ancient world, at the center of an equally famous system of canals. Jer 51:12-13 is directed against "the inhabitants of Babylon," and the city herself is addressed directly as "you who live on mighty waters" (28:12-13, LXX: ἐπὶ τοὺς κατοικοῦντας βαβυλῶνα κατασκηνοῦντας ἐφ᾽ ὕδασι πολλοῖς). The literal sense of the verse is as well adapted to Babylon as it is ill adapted to Rome or, still more, to Jerusalem. Whatever the contemporary reality to which John refers with the name of Babylon (see comments on 17:15), the reference to it in this sentence must be symbolic: only God "builds his dwellings on the waters" (Ps 104[103]:3) and "sits enthroned over the flood" (a possible translation of Ps 29[28]:10).

17:3 Καὶ ἀπήνεγκέν με . . . εἶδον. Up to this point John has not actually seen Babylon or the prostitute, both of whom have been vividly announced to him by angels (14:8 and 17:1-2). Only now is John taken "into a desert" to see what has been announced. It is not at all clear why Babylon appears "in a desert," as neither historical Babylon nor Rome has any connection with the desert. Israel, on the other hand, has a number of links with the desert, which is the site of flight and refuge (from Egypt and the Pharaoh) as well as of the sin of idolatry (Exod 32) that makes her like Egypt (primitive Christianity makes full polemical use of the Exodus narrative; see Stephen's speech in Acts 7:39-43). John would have stressed in this manner that the scene shifts and that he is taken by an angel "in spirit into a desert" (see Mark 1:12 and parallels) only if he wanted his readers or hearers to think about the desert; but the desert is mentioned in the text only in ch. 12, in connection to the woman who takes refuge there (12:6, 14) despite Satan's attempts to prevent her. I think that John intends to indicate the temporary victory of Satan, who has succeeded in leading Israel into idolatry, as during the exodus.

γυναῖκα . . . θηρίον. The woman is usually taken to be a representation of Rome, who sits like a queen over her universal empire. In any case, she is the "prostitute" with whom "the kings of the earth fornicated." The beast is generally agreed to represent power and thus the kings of the earth, who might be the Roman emperors; if this is the case, then the woman is sitting on the beast as a sign of her intimacy with those who fornicate with her. Moreover, the angel's announcement is about a "prostitute . . . who sits on many waters" (v. 1), but John sees instead a "woman sitting on a scarlet beast." If the woman is the prostitute, then the scarlet beast must be the same as the many waters, and we can begin to see what John has in mind. It is not very persuasive to suggest that Rome is fornicating with her own empire; it is much more likely that John is using traditional forms to lament Israel and Jerusalem's fornication with pagan power. If the "woman/prostitute" is Rome, it is unlikely that the "beast" could be the Roman Empire, and vice versa. Finally, if to sit on the beast indicates a dominant position with respect to the nations, then, however strange it may seem to us, a 1st-century reader of the Bible would understand the one who sits like a queen (without actually being a queen any more) to be Jerusalem: "How like a widow she sits, she [that was] the great one among the nations, a princess among the provinces!" (Lam 1:1). There is further proof in 4QapLamA (4Q179) that takes up and expands on Lamentations along traditional lines: "[How] solitary [sits] the [g]rea[t] city [Jerusa]lem (once) f[ull of pe]ople; the princess of all the nation[s] has become desolate like an abandoned (woman)" (fr. 2, 4-5); there is a basic continuity of concepts between Jeremiah, the Qumranic text, and John, for all of whom a lament on Jerusalem's destruction involves the affirmation of her greatness and universal royalty (see comments on 9:14 and 17:18).

Notwithstanding this evidence, there is a powerful prejudice in favor of the notion that when any text connected in any way with the Christian scriptures speaks of a woman of ill repute it must be a reference to Rome — a prejudice so powerful that even a Qumranic text known as *Wiles of the Wicked Woman* has been interpreted as a reference to Rome. The female figure in this text leads astray "the righteous chosen ones" — the member of the group whose ideas the text defends — and she is portrayed as follows: "In the city squares she veils herself, and in the gates of the village she stations herself" (4Q184, 12 and 14). There is no possibility that this is a reference to Rome rather than to a hostile Jewish group such as the Pharisees.

The interpretation of this passage that I accept is as follows: the woman is the same one whom God saved in the desert and who now returns from the desert as a "prostitute"; if it is not the same woman, then John must have "forgotten" the woman of ch. 12, who in that case does not appear again anywhere in the book. The devil has thus succeeded in reaching her through the offices of the beast who represents him, and the woman has prostituted herself with the beast, which is to say that she has accepted pagan power and idolatry; at the same time she has refused to acknowledge the historical Jesus as the expected Christ, the Son whom she, insofar as she is Israel, has been destined by God from all eternity to bear. Satan's triumph would seem complete, were it not that the angel brought John into the desert not to show him the prostitute but rather "the condemnation of the prostitute" (17:1); once again John stresses that everything that happens is under God's control, and reminds the reader that every victory of the forces of evil is merely illusory. He may also be reflecting again on that fact that the "condemnation" is made manifest, or is definitely decided, at the very moment of evil's apparent victory.

κόκκινον . . . δέκα. This beast shares some features with the beast from the sea (13:1) and with Satan himself (12:3). The color "scarlet" connects this beast with the "dragon, fiery red" (12:3; see comments on 17:4), as well as linking it closely to the woman who wears "purple and scarlet" (17:4); John, as usual, is emphasizing the unity of the forces of evil. The presence of the "names of blasphemy" (see 13:1) also connects this beast with the one from the sea (but see comments on 17:8). The first and most obvious explanation is that the beast, by representing what we call "political power," points to the Roman Empire — the supreme political power at the time of the book's composition. That the "seven heads" are "seven kings" suggests, by virtue of the analogy with the ten horns of Dan 7:24, that John is thinking of a succession of seven emperors; one could apply to this succession the prophecy in v. 10 and thus date the text accurately within the reign of the sixth emperor. The numbers do not come out right, however (see comments on 17:9-10). Also in Dan 2:36-45, if we count the explanations of the five parts of the statue, the fifth part of which is explained in three separate ways, we reach a total of seven kingdoms, which represent not the reigns of seven individual sovereigns within a single empire, but rather seven universal empires. In like manner the beast of the Apocalypse may very well represent the totality of earthly political power, which comes from Satan. It is certainly possible that it also refers to the Roman Empire, but I am convinced that John's primary meaning is that any and all human power as it is manifest in history is always an expression of Satanic power; the Roman Empire is merely one such manifestation.

17:4 περιβεβλημένη . . . μαργαρίταις. The sentence parallels 18:16, where the city appears περιβεβλημένη βύσσινον καὶ πορφυροῦν καὶ κόκκινον καὶ κεχρυσωμένη χρυσίῳ καὶ λίθῳ τιμίῳ καὶ μαργαρίτῃ. It is not surprising that the two sentences are so similar since in 17:18 the "woman" is identified with the "city, the great one." What may surprise the reader — and is usually ignored by critics — are the extraordinary parallels with the decoration of the tabernacle that Moses built in the wilderness, and with the most sacred elements of the vestments of Aaron and thus of the high priest. The tabernacle itself was made of curtains of "fine . . . linen, and hyacinth, purple and scarlet" (Exod 26:1; 36:8), and the wooden columns (or "planks") are "adorned with gold" (Exod 26:29; 36:34). The veil of the Holy of Holies is also made of "hyacinth, purple and scarlet, and of fine . . . linen" and hung on four pillars of acacia "adorned with gold" (Exod 36:31-32; 36:35-36; for the continuation of this tradition closer to John's own era see *TS* 3 and 10). For the gilding, LXX primarily uses terms related to καταχρυσόω, but for the veil Exod 26:31-32 says, καταπέτασμα ἐξ ὑακίνθου καὶ πορφύρας καὶ κοκκίνου . . . καὶ βίσσου . . . καί . . . στύλων . . . κεχρυσωμένων χρυσίῳ ("veil of hyacinth and of purple and of scarlet . . . and of fine linen . . . and . . . of columns . . . adorned with gold"). Whether or not John is using LXX, it is clear that he is referring to these biblical passages, although he is altering them to his purposes.

The similarities between the tabernacle as described in Exodus and the woman/prostitute make sense if the woman represents a Jewish entity, but are very difficult to account for if she represents something pagan. If we turn to the Exodus descriptions of the most sacred parts of Aaron's priestly vestments — the ephod and the "breastplate of judgment" that hangs over the chest from the shoulder-pieces of the ephod (see comments on 2:17 and *m. Yoma* 3:4) — we find further, and incontrovertible, evidence that John wants his reader — a Jewish Christian like himself who was familiar with the components of his Jewish religious world — to be thinking about the heart of Jewish religiosity. The vestments of the high priest were also the sign of his priestly power, and during part of the occupation (from 6 to 36 CE) they were confiscated by the Romans, who had assumed the power of the last Hasmonean kings, and were given back to the high priest only for the chief festivals (Josephus, *A.J.* 15[11.4].403-8; 18[4.3].90-95, 20[1.1-2].6-14; Josephus shows how difficult this was for observant Jews, who were afraid that contact with pagans would contaminate the most sacred objects in Judaism). The ephod, the shoulder pieces, and the breastplate were all made of "gold, hyacinth, purple, scarlet, and fine linen" — a list that is repeated at least eight times in Exodus (28:5-6 = 39:1-2 [twice]; 28:8 = 28:15 = 39:5 = 39:8. The robe of the ephod is made from the same materials, except for the linen; 28:33 = 39:24). The ephod and the breastplate also have precious stones: two on the shoulder pieces of the ephod and twelve on the breastplate, set in four rows of three (see comments on 2:17 and 12:6). The names of the twelve tribes were engraved on these in the manner of "seals"; in two groups of six on the ephod and one on each stone of the breastplate (Exod 28:9-11 [see 39:6] and 28:17-21 [see 39:10-14]). The tradition that when Aaron was "before the LORD" he wore on his heart and shoulders stones engraved with names, like seals, is most likely the source of the important Johannine motif of the "seals" and the "marks" that are inscribed with opposing names and are worn by the holy ones and by the wicked (see comments on 13:16 and 17:5; for the engraving of the Name on the "white pebble" see comments on 2:17).

The traditional character of the colors and the materials is confirmed by a passage in *WS* that describes the group of seven priests who will accompany the army of true Jews to their eschatological conflict with the sons of darkness: there "shall go out seven priests of the sons of Aaron, robed with garments of fine white linen . . . and they shall gird on a belt of intertwined fine linen, hyacinth and purple and scarlet" (1QM 7:9-11). Even these "garments of war, which they shall not bring into the sanctuary," reproduce the distinctive elements of the sacred priestly vestments.

Exodus always talks about precious "stones," while John uses only the singular. The expression "precious stone" appears four times: here, in the parallel passage in 18:16, in 18:12 in the list of the objects that are traded in the "city, the great one," and in the foundations of the heavenly Jerusalem in 21:19; the expression "very precious stone" is also used in relation to the New Jerusalem (21:11, which also includes "stone of jasper," previously used in 4:3 to describe the appearance of the one "seated on the throne"). Babylon, on the other hand, is compared to "a stone, like a great millstone" (18:21). The eight occurrences of the word "stone" show that it can be used both positively, to represent the splendor of God or of Jerusalem, and negatively, to denote the corruption of this splendor in Babylon. If Babylon is a representation of the degeneration of Jerusalem and Judaism, then the "great millstone" is actually the very same "precious stone," and it has followed Judaism's course from the heights of glory to the depths of shame.

We should ask whether there is any significance in the shift from the plural in Exodus to the singular, or in other differences with respect to the biblical model, such as the appearance of "pearls" and the omission of "hyacinth." The term "pearl" appears five times in the same context as "precious stone"; here, in 18:16 (in the singular), in 18:12, and in 21:21 (once in the singular and once in the plural). Thus John always uses "precious stone" in the singular, but only sometimes does so with "pearl." This usage might be connected to the theological reflection in ch. 21. The precious stones in Exodus are engraved with the names of the patriarchs, so as to represent Judaism before God, whereas in John's Christian vision the twelve precious stones that make up the "foundations" of the New Jerusalem are engraved with the names of the twelve apostles and represent the Christian church. The names of the patriarchs are preserved in the New Jerusalem, but on the twelve "pearls" that form the "gates" of the city. There are no pearls in the priestly vestments, nor in any part of the temple: the OT does not mention them, and thus the biblical traditions give no reason to consider them holy. There is, however, the well-known passage from Matt 7:6, "Do not give what is holy to dogs; and do not throw your pearls before swine." "Dogs" and "swine," both impure animals, are grouped together and contrasted with "your pearls" and "what is holy" — the part of the offering that is presented in the temple and is destined to be food for the priests. There must have been some honor ascribed to pearls if they were to be used symbolically in connection with the holy food of priests. There is also a very fragmentary Qumranic text in which Wisdom appears as an elegant woman in "purple," "scarlet," "gold," and "pearls" (as well, probably, as other materials mentioned in the lacunae; 4QBeat [4Q525] fr. 2, 3:5-7). This shows both that within Jewish tradition pearls could appear in lists of precious materials alongside those that characterized priestly vestments, and that they could be used in the description of a hypostatized female figure as important as Wisdom.

John's use of pearls in the New Jerusalem does not deny the salvific role of Judaism, but rather gives evidence of a symbolic shift rooted in Christian reflections on Christ and the apostles as the "stone" and the "foundation" of the church (see comments on 21:12, 14). If, and only if, Babylon represents the corruption of Jerusalem, does it make sense that there must still be pearls in it, together with the "fine linen" (18:12, 16) that characterizes the holy ones in ch. 19 (for those commentators who believe that Babylon is Rome, the "fine linen" must have different meanings in different contexts; Bauckham 1993, p. 369). In John's eyes Jerusalem and Israel sinned very grievously when they dragged the sacred attributes of the tabernacle and of the Aaronic vestments into prostitution with the beast. There is clear prophetic precedent here also: Ezekiel accused Jerusalem of willingly profaning the sanctuary and even of spreading a banquet of prostitution for her pagan lovers with God's "oil" and "incense" (Ezek 23:39, 41).

However, it seems that the woman has not dragged quite everything into her prostitution with the beast: the various biblical lists all include "hyacinth," which does not appear here. The term indicates a fabric dyed with the so-called "violet purple," which was probably dark blue. The term appears in the Apocalypse only to describe a blue precious stone in the foundation of the New Jerusalem (21:20), and in reference to the breastplates of the angelic cavalry (9:17). Thus hyacinth remains under God's immediate control, connected

both to salvation, as part of the apostolic foundation of the eschatological Jerusalem, and to the instruments of divine justice. The direct connection between hyacinth and God also appears in *1 Enoch* 71:2 *(BS)*, where, in a heavenly vision, we find "light of . . . fire . . . shining like hyacinth." This
interpretation might be compatible with what Josephus has to say about the
symbolic value of "hyacinth and fine linen, scarlet and purple": the purple
represents the sea and fine linen the earth because of their origins (purple dye
comes from mollusks and linen is a plant fiber), while on the basis of their
colors scarlet and hyacinth represent fire and air respectively (*J.W.* 5[5.4].212-
13). Does John mean that of the four the "heavenly" element (the heavens being blue in color) remains faithful to God?

ποτήριον χρυσοῦν. This is the "cup" of 14:10 and 16:19, now firmly in the
hand of the prostitute/Babylon, who received it at the end of the last chapter.
The text does not say that she has to drink from it, and thus it seems that she
still uses it to give drink to others. That it is "golden," a detail possibly derived
from Jer 51:7 (see comments on 14:10-11 and 17:1), shows that it is an instrument of divine action. Coming at the moment when Babylon appears at the
height of her powers, this detail emphasizes once again that everything is under God's control.

γέμον . . . αὐτῆς. John describes the contents of the cup, which seem to
represent the destiny of those with whom the woman prostitutes herself, by
using a term that points clearly to the corruption of Judaism. "Abomination"
(βδέλυγμα) is the ultimate impurity; Dan 9:27 (11:31; 12:11) identifies it with
the idolatrous worship in the temple in Jerusalem (see Mark 13:14; Matt 24:15).
For its exclusion from the New Jerusalem, see 21:27. "Abomination," like
"prostitution," is a technical term used in prophetic language to denote Israel's idolatry.

17:5 ἐπὶ τὸ μέτωπον . . . γεγραμμένον. Most contemporary exegesis cites
this passage as definitive historical proof that the prostitute is none other
than Rome. Some passages in Seneca and Juvenal have been taken as evidence
that Roman prostitutes in the brothels of the imperial era used to make themselves known to potential clients by wearing around their heads a strip of fabric with their names written on it. John would thus have been alluding to this
particular habit as a way of helping his more careful reader correctly to identify the woman. It has become apparent recently that Latin sources do not in
fact permit this interpretation (Beagley 1987, p. 102), which arose from the su-
perimposition on the text of the sexual practices of a less distant world used
to *belle époque* and pre-war brothels. Despite this, the old interpretation of
the verse has survived simply because it is convenient (see, e.g., Bauckham
1993, who goes so far as to think that prostitutes went around *the streets* of

Rome with their names written on their foreheads). Even if Seneca or Juvenal had actually said what a couple of generations of scholars believed them to have said, it would surely have been rather odd for a Jew like John to have been familiar with the habits of the Roman stews, or to expect the Christian Jews of Asia Minor who were the first readers of his book to be sufficiently *au fait* with the lascivious secrets of the Suburra to understand the allusion (and, if not for ethical reasons, at least for reasons of purity).

Having dealt with this issue we next need to look for the real significance of the fact that the Apocalypse is brimming with figures who bear on their foreheads either a "seal" or a "mark" (the latter being also on their hands) with a name or number indicating their allegiance to the ranks of God or of Satan (for the term "forehead," which appears also in 7:3; 9:4; 13:16; 14:1, 9; 20:4; and 22:4, see comments on 13:6). There is no reason to suspect that John turned, in the sole case of the woman/city/prostitute, to models other than those he used in the rest of the book, nor that a (fictional) practice of Roman prostitutes could have seemed so important to John that he would have based on it a recurrent image that he applies not only to the forces of evil but also to the ranks of the holy ones.

We have found the source for the woman's clothing and jewelry in Exodus, which also furnishes evidence that the detail of the name on her forehead is derived from Jewish religious practice. It is the πέταλον, the golden rosette of the high priest, which is described more than once (Exod 28:36-38; 39:30-31) and which was probably a priestly substitute for the royal crown (see Lev 8:9 and Ezek 21:31; a crown is mentioned also in the rescript of Claudius recorded by Josephus, *A.J.* 20[1.2].12). The high priest wore this rosette of "pure gold" (χρυσοῦν καθαρόν) on his forehead over his turban so that it would be visible when he approached God. On it, "like the engraving of a seal," was written "Holy *(qodeš)* to the LORD" (LXX: ἁγίασμα κυρίου; see Zech 14:20; Greek sources from the Second Temple period mention only the Name; see Josephus, *J.W.* 5[5.7].235: "Around it [a 'tiara' of fine linen and hyacinth] there was another crown of gold, inscribed with the sacred letters: these are four vowels"). The term *qodeš*, meaning "sacred" or "holy," indicates the state of exceptional purity in which Aaron (and, through him, the people) has to be when he appears before God. This state would be unattainable if God did not purify the people himself, which is why LXX interprets the term as relating to an action; "sanctification" is the act of rendering pure that which is not pure.

The function of the πέταλον was to remind God of his ability and duty to sanctify Israel by blotting out her sins. By means of it, Aaron will "take up and carry away the sins of the holy things" (Exod 28:38, LXX: ἐξαρεῖ Ἀαρὼν τὰ ἁμαρτήματα τῶν ἁγίων). Once decontextualized, the sentence had been taken to mean "to take away the sins of the holy ones," where the "holy ones" are the Jews (see its "Christian reading" in John 1:29, discussed below). In making the "holy offering that the Israelites consecrate as their sacred donations" they could "sanctify" or make pure their sins, and it is the πέταλον itself that makes this possible by being the guarantee of God's merciful aid, of his acceptance of the offering and, in short, of Jewish ritual life. Because of this, "it will be on Aaron's forehead forever, acceptable for them (the Jews) before the Lord"; LXX: καὶ ἔσται ἐπὶ τοῦ μετώπου Ἀαρὼν διαπαντὸς δεκτὸν αὐτοῖς ἔναντι κυρίου).

The primary function of the πέταλον occurs on the great Day of Atonement *(Yom hak-Kippurim)*, the symbolism of which probably leaves its impression both on the mind of the Jewish John and on the conceptual structure of the Apocalypse. This was the day that the sin of Israel was carried off by a goat into the desert, into the place of Satan (Azazel), the lowest point of a unified cosmos whose highest point was God's temple in Jerusalem, where the blood of the sacrifice was shed (see Destro–Pesce 1992 and Destro–Pesce 1995).

The basic idea of the connections between blood, Jerusalem, and the temple and between sin and the desert permeates the entire book, although it is transformed by the Christian perspective and by John's radical criticism of non-Christian Jewish institutions, which he regards as obsolete. The golden rosette had such an important place in Jewish worship that the expression "to wear the πέταλον" meant "to officiate as a priest" (Policrates, the bishop of Ephesus at the end of the 2nd century, uses the expression for the apostle John in Eusebius, *Hist. eccl.* 3.31.3 and 5.24.3). The priestly role of purifying sins was an extremely important theme in primitive Christianity, which saw Jesus as the true High Priest (see, e.g., the Christology of Hebrews) who offered himself as the victim in a sacrifice really acceptable to God (see John 17:19: ὑπὲρ αὐτῶν ἐγὼ ἁγιάζω ἐμαυτόν, which echoes the ἁγίασμα of the πέταλον) so as to render acceptable the life of the faithful (Phil 4:18). Exod 28:38 (quoted above) is also a source of John 1:29 ("Here is the Lamb of God, who takes away [ὁ αἴρων] the sin of the world") and is in fact behind the author's alteration of Isaiah's text about the sacrificed lamb: in the gospel the Lamb does not merely "take the sins on himself" (Isa 53:12, LXX: ἁμαρτίας . . . ἀνήνεγκε) but actually takes them away as Aaron does.

The conceptual context I have described here, rather than some shady and foreign practice, is behind John's insistence on the name written on the forehead, both of the good and of the evil. In particular, both the Exodus description of the ephod and the breastplate and the description of the πέταλον say specifically that the letters are engraved "like (the engraving of) a seal." The terms used in LXX suggest a work in relief (Exod 28:36: καὶ ἐκτυπόσεις ἐν αὐτῷ ἐκτύπωμα σφραγίδος; Exod 39:31, in LXX at the end of ch. 36: καὶ ἔγραψεν ἐπ᾽ αὐτοῦ γράμματα ἐκτετυπωμένα σφραγίδος), but in any case the biblical expressions stress the role of the letters as models or archetypes. Just as a seal functions as a model by creating repeated images of itself, so these holy letters are the first source of Israel's salvation, which is constantly renewed by their repeatedly appearing before God. The Christian and Johannine re-interpretations of Judaism replace the Hebrew letters with "the Name" that alone can give salvation: that of Christ united with that of the Father (see comments on 14:1), which name now functions as a seal and appears on the foreheads of the elect: the nation of priests and martyrs of whom Jesus Christ is the model. This reinterpretation is probably behind the motifs of the 144,000 signed with the seal and of the holy ones who bear on their foreheads the seal with the Name. Opposing the elect and the holy ones are Babylon and the reprobates, and *their* foreheads bear a mark with the name of the beast whose role as the enemy of the Christ is evident throughout the book. Just as faithful Jews wear phylacteries, so the worshipers of the beast wear its mark on their foreheads and hands (see comments on 17:4 and 13:16), and the city/ prostitute, which is full of priestly symbols, bears on her forehead the name of her own corruption, just as the high priest wore the πέταλον. In Ezek 28:13 the precious stones and the engravings from the Aaronic breastplate are apparently applied to the description of the prince of Tyre, and thus it is not impossible that Babylon and those bearing the mark are in fact pagans. However, the best explanation of this passage is to be found in the polemic against non-Christian Judaism that permeates John's entire work. Judaism, represented by the city of the temple, has dragged the most sacred things into her idolatrous prostitution, and reached the depth of degradation when she failed to acknowledge Jesus as the Messiah and killed him in collaboration with the Roman and pro-Roman authorities who held the power to institute and remove the high priests, as well as the insignia of the high priest's authority.

μυστήριον . . . μεγάλη. It is unclear whether the term "mystery" is part of the inscription or whether it is a remark on the part of John or of the angel, intended to highlight the importance of this revelation and of the mystery that is gradually unfolding. In any case, the word shows that John attaches very particular importance to what is said here. The term μυστήριον appears four times in the text. The first and last times it refers to a mystery that is revealed to John: the mystery "of the seven stars" and "of the woman and of the beast" (see comments on 1:20 and 17:7). The other two times the mystery is not explained, although John does give clues as to its interpretation. The "mystery of God" that is "completed" with the "seven plagues, the last ones," appears in 10:7, while the mystery here is connected to the spiritual name of the woman-prostitute. It would appear that the text wants to contrast two mysteries, one of God and the other of Satan. The mystery of God consists in his justice, which will be completed above all with Israel but also with the pagan world that is entangled with Israel in a relationship of mutual corruption. The mystery of Satan is an exact complement to this; it consists in the ultimate degradation of Israel and Jerusalem, which take on the name and the spiritual role of Egypt, Sodom, and Babylon. Israel has taken the riches that were given to her as a guarantee of her "sanctification" and has thrown them before dogs and swine (see Matt 7:6 and comments on 22:15), so that rather than bringing about the salvation of the whole world they have become the ruin both of idolatrous Israel and of the nations that remained pagan. This is the mystery of Satan: the irreparable corruption of Israel and the subsequent overturning of salvation history, which should have brought salvation to the Gentiles through Jesus' earthly ministry. With the death of Christ and the condemnation of Israel that followed, Satan seems to have assumed final and complete possession over human history and his "war against the remnant of [the woman's] seed" (12:17) seems to have achieved its goal. Only a few faithful followers of Jesus remain to continue the struggle against the beast.

Modern exegetes will find in this line of argument a potentially fatal logical (or methodological) difficulty: why on earth would John have chosen to represent Jerusalem, or the non-Christian Judaism of his time, with something as notoriously pagan and anti-Jewish as the biblical Babylon that destroyed her? Actually John is placing himself in a tradition of spiritual reflection whereby every biblical pagan city or nation that God threatens or punishes becomes a model of idolatrous Jerusalem. The OT threatens the unfaithful people (of Israel) and their rulers with the fate of Egypt (see comments on 15:1 and 16:2), of Sodom and Gomorrah (see comments on 11:8 and 14:11), and of Gibeon (see comments on 16:21).

The case of Tyre is complex because Ezek 26–28 describes the city and its ruler in terms that are derived from Jewish religion and worship (such as, perhaps, the reference to Aaron's breastplate in Ezek 28:13). Behind this story may be the historical fact that since the time when Solomon and Hiram collaborated on the construction of the temple (1 Kings 5:1-2 [15-16, LXX]) Tyre had been a long-term ally of Jerusalem, and its fall thus looked like a fall from a condition similar to Jerusalem's. This would explain why Ezekiel could say that the "prince of Tyre" — the angelic or angelomorphic representative of the city — was like a "cherub" whom God installed on his "holy mountain" (Ezek 28:14; LXX: ἐν ὄρει ἁγίῳ θεοῦ), from which God now "cast [him] to the ground" (Ezek 28:17: this is the source of the traditional interpretation, which goes from Origen to Jewish and Muslim legends of the Middle Ages, according to which Hiram himself is Satan; Halperin 1988, pp. 241-47). Moreover, the coins of Tyre (tetradrachma or silver shekels) were until the end of the Second Temple still the official currency used in temple transactions, which rendered them somehow "sacred" and reinforced the connection between Tyre, the temple, and Jerusalem. The destinies of the two cities thus become interchangeable.

A fragmentary commentary on the prophet Nahum found in the fourth cave at Qumran (4QpNah) gives further evidence that prophecies of misfortune originally directed at Israel's enemies were habitually applied to Israel herself and to her rulers. Nah 2–3 contain oracles against the city and the princes of Nineveh, which at the end of the 7th century BCE was called "city of bloodshed" and "prostitute," full of "sorcery"; she is threatened with terrible suffering. The Qumran sectarians, hostile as they were to the religious and civil authorities of Jerusalem, saw all theses oracles as being fulfilled with regard to their enemies. As far as it is possible to make out, the "prostitute" is the community of the Pharisees, which deceives the other Jews, rulers and people, as well as proselytes and sympathizers from other nations (Nah 3:4: "who led astray nations through her prostitution"). Egypt (mentioned in v. 9) represents the allies of those in power, perhaps a group of apostate Essenes, or the mysterious "house of Peleg." Nahum threatened Nineveh with destruction; God would strip her, laying bare her genitals before nations and kingdoms (3:5), would cast at her the abomination (3:6), and finally she would become drunk (3:11). Despite the condition of the text, it is possible to determine that after referring to Nineveh's drunkenness the text goes on to talk about "their cup" that followed Manasseh, the royal house of the Hasmoneans or Herodians. This suggests that the drunkenness was understood to be a punishment for Jerusalem's rulers (see comments on 17:1). Moreover, Nah 3:13 talks about a population of women opening the "gates of your land" to the enemies, and the Essene exegete interprets the land as being "the whole region of Israel to the sea" (4QpNah, fr. 5).

The same process of identifying past figures in present events is carried out by the Qumranic commentary on Habakkuk (1QpHab), in which the Chaldeans of Hab 1:7-9 become the Kittim — possibly the Romans — who, in a paraphrase of Habakkuk, "trample the Land with [their] horses and their animals and come from far off, from the islands of the sea, to devour all the nations like an eagle, insatiable" (1QpHab 3:10-12). The most interesting parts of the commentary for our purposes are in columns 9 and 12. In the former the exegete comments on Hab 2:8a, "since you pillaged many peoples, all the rest of the nations will pillage you," and applies the text to "the last priests of

Jerusalem, who will accumulate riches and loot from plundering the nations. However, in the end of days their riches and loot will be given into the hands of the army of the Kittim." He next comments on Hab 2:8b ("For the human blood [spilt] and the violence [done] to the country, the city, and all who dwell in it"), saying, "Its interpretation concerns the [Wi]cked Priest, whom, for his wickedness against the Teacher of Righteousness and the members of his council, God delivered into the hands of his enemies to disgrace him with a punishment, to destroy him with bitterness of soul for having acted wickedly against His Elect."

These verses are evidence of an internal conflict within Judaism so severe as to merit, in Essene eyes, the intervention of pagan armies to punish the Jerusalem authorities who shed the blood of the founder of the sect, considered the Elect of the LORD. The punishment (described in col. 10) will involve "sulphurous fire" being poured on their enemies (the priests of Jerusalem?), while the community of the Spreader of the Lie — a leader of the Pharisees who was hostile to the Teacher of Righteousness — will become "a city built with blood" (a phrase not present in Habakkuk but suggested by 2:8b). Immediately after this, commenting on Hab 2:15, the exegete informs us that the Wicked Priest unsuccessfully attempted to eliminate the exiled Teacher of Righteousness, and that this act of violence is the spilling of blood that Habakkuk prophesied. Finally in column 12, in a comment on Hab 2:17 (which is a repetition of 2:8b), the exegete says: "Its interpretation: the city is Jerusalem in which the Wicked Priest ("Wicked" is added in superscript) has performed repulsive acts and defiled the sanctuary of God. And violence (done to) the country is the cities of Judah, which he plundered of the possessions of the poor." The poor who are robbed must be the true faithful, the followers of the Teacher of Righteousness. From a strictly historical point of view it would appear that the persecution was primarily economic in nature (the text speaks of "theft") and that there was little bloodshed; the Essenes' sense that they were persecuted for being the true Israel accounts for the forcefulness of the rhetoric. The Teacher of Righteousness was not killed, but the founder of primitive Christianity was, and was followed in death by leaders of the community like Stephen and James; all of them were killed in Jerusalem, and their deaths were ascribed to the religious and political leaders of the Jews. Whatever was originally meant by "city of blood" in the biblical context, for at least some among the early followers of Jesus it could be none other than Jerusalem, and thus it was to Jerusalem that they applied the prophecies of punishment against pagan cities, just as the prophets of old and the Qumranic commentators had done and continued to do.

ἡ μήτηρ τῶν πορνῶν. This is the only appearance in the text of the term "mother," and the motherhood it refers to is corrupt. Jezebel has "children," as does the heavenly (and later earthly) "woman" of ch. 12. We can also suppose that the New Jerusalem, described as a "bride," is somehow destined to be a mother. However, the prostitute is the only one actually called "mother," indeed "the mother of the prostitutes." The first two women must have had male children (and the woman of ch. 12 possibly only male children), but here we have a woman-prostitute who is the mother of women-prostitutes (in a text with no accents it is possible to read it as πόρνων, meaning male prostitutes or fornicators, but — as far as I know — no ancient commentator considered this for a moment, and Humphrey 1995, p. 108 makes little sense in saying that πορνῶν could be either male or female). An analogy can be made with the gnostic notion that Israel's femininity was a sign of her imperfection and negativity; without going too far down this road we can note that the development of the time was such that in some Christian circles the split with Judaism was seen in cosmic and symbolically sexual terms. In any case, the prostitute is a mother in different ways, as she is the mother τῶν πορνῶν καὶ τῶν βδελυγμάτων τῆς γῆς. We saw in v. 4 that John seems to have used the term βδελύγματα to indicate the abomination of Israel's corruption; if this is also the case here, then the term γῆ might refer to the Holy Land, as the repeated juxtaposition of abomination and prostitution would suggest.

17:6 μεθύουσαν ἐκ τοῦ αἵματος. Finally we reach one of the central elements that characterize Babylon and that John has been gradually building toward: her deep connection with blood, which she drinks (see comments on 16:4). The phrase assumes that Babylon has drunk from the "cup" that she holds "in her hand" (see comments on 18:6). The text specifies at the outset that this is "the blood of the holy ones and . . . the blood of the witnesses of Jesus"; it is not, therefore, the blood of enemies nor of Babylon herself (which makes it impossible to see this passage as a parallel to the often-quoted verses from Isa 49:26, where Israel's enemies are destined to "be drunk . . . with their own blood as wine," or to Isa 34:7, where "the land [of the Idumeans] will be drunk on [their] blood"). Implicit in the fact of being drunk on blood is the punishment of the city that has been awaited since v. 1, but that does not yet appear; the woman seems to be relishing her drunkenness, much to the amazement of John, who had perhaps been expecting to witness her punishment and suffering.

It appears from the context that the city is responsible for the bloodshed. (These details highlight both the similarities and the differences between "Babylon" and those against whom the third plague is directed, who "poured out the blood of just men and prophets" and have therefore been given blood to drink [16:6; see comments on 16:4]. The blood was shed by those who are now given blood to drink, but it does not seem to be the same blood, nor to be their own: the blood they are given to drink is that into which the water of the rivers and springs was transformed. The drinking of blood [without drunkenness] is a punishment, and for the creatures of the sea it is fatal [16:3]. Thus while there is a basic similarity between the two passages, there are also differences.) The following two chapters will expound on the relationship between "Babylon" and "blood," but for now we encounter the fact itself: Babylon wallows in blood and becomes drunk on it. If we look for a biblical source for a "city of blood," we will find none other than Jerusalem, as Ezekiel proclaims. It is likely that Ezek 22:2, with its reference to the judgment of the city ("And you, son of man, won't you judge the city of blood?; LXX: καὶ σὺ υἱὲ ἀνθρώπου εἰ κρινεῖς τὴν πόλιν τῶν αἱμάτων;) is one of the passages from which John drew his inspiration. The spilling of innocent blood in Jerusalem (ὦ πόλις ἐκχέουσα αἵματα ἐν μέσῳ αὐτῆς; 22:3, LXX) by the city's "princes" or its authorities is a recurring theme in Ezekiel (in ch. 22 alone see also vv. 6, 9, 12, and 27).

Ezekiel might also provide one of the reasons why Israel must be a woman: the sinful behavior of the Israelites is "like the uncleanness of a woman in her menstrual period" (Ezek 37:17, LXX: κατὰ τὴν ἀκαθαρσίαν τῆς ἀποκαθημένης), and, therefore, God declares, "I poured out my wrath upon them for the blood they had shed upon the land" (v. 18). There are two elements to Ezekiel's meditation. From the perspective of observance, the guilty city has become as impure as it is possible to be because the blood she shed is that of a menstruating woman; if we add to this the fact that she is already impure because she is a prostitute and thus has been defiled by men who do not respect the purity laws, we can see that she has reached a level of impurity that would be difficult for a man to attain. Moreover, if shedding the blood of her own innocent citizens is equivalent to the impurity of a menstruating woman, then the blood she sheds is her own impure blood, and this bloodshed will therefore be punished by the pouring out of the wrath of God, in accordance with the normal pattern whereby the punishment corresponds to the sin being punished (see comments on 16:4).

These are variations on a central theme: Jerusalem has shed innocent blood and therefore has been or will be punished by God. In the nonbiblical texts found at Qumran there are not only clear restatements of the biblical prohibitions (e.g., *TS* 52:11) or radical developments of normal positions (e.g., *TS* 32:12-15 [about the blood of the offerings]; 4Q493, 5-6 [laws pertaining to priests in battles]), but also some traces of speculations that further emphasize the relationship between Jerusalem, or the Jewish world, and blood as a source of contamination. In the summary of salvation history found in CD the descendants of the patriarchs, who have gone down to Egypt, "walked in the stubbornness of their hearts . . . and they ate blood and their males were cut off in the wilderness. . . . The very first to enter the covenant made themselves guilty and were delivered up to the sword" (CD 3:5-11). The basic elements of this position are similar to John's. Israel is in Egypt and becomes contaminated by ingesting blood, for which she is cut off; the emphasis is on the fact that those who had entered the covenant, and in fact had been the first to do so, were delivered up to the sword (perhaps a punishing angel of that name). Two columns later the text declares that the temple is also contaminated because the Israelites, in particular the priestly authorities, have had sexual relations with menstruating women (5:6-7).

The most interesting text for us, along with the 1QpHab commentary mentioned in regard to v. 5, is 4QTest (4Q175), which, after commentaries on a variety of scriptural texts, comments on *Pseudo-Joshua* (also known as the *Psalms of Joshua*), a parabiblical elaboration that was previously unknown, but fragments of which were discovered in the same cave (4Q379). *Pseudo-Joshua* expands the curses of Josh 6:26 against the rebuilders of Jericho, saying that their rebuilding is a curse for the whole of Israel, to the extent that they "will shed blo]od like water upon the ramparts of the daughter of Zion and in the precincts of Jerusalem" (4Q175, 21-30; 4Q379, 2:7-14; see Newsom 1988, pp. 56-73, in particular 68-73). The blood on the walls of Jerusalem (that may refer to an event during some war) is one of the consequences of the "profanation of the Land" (meaning the Holy Land) that was brought about by those who rebuilt Jericho. 4QTest puts it even more strongly, stating that the prophecy of *Pseudo-Joshua*, which originally referred to Jericho ("They will rebuild [this city and er]ect for it a rampart and towers to make it into a fortress [or refuge] of wickedness"), is actually a prophetic reference to Jerusalem herself, in accordance with the exegetical practice of applying to Jerusalem biblical curses originally directed to her enemies (see comments on 16:21).

Finally, I would suggest that Nahum's application to Nineveh of the epithet "city of blood" might have been precisely what led to the prophecies against Nineveh being transferred to Jerusalem (see comments on 17:5). Any persecuted Jewish minority had no doubts as to who was responsible for the shedding of innocent blood. It is also worth noting that even Jewish groups who were not hostile to Jerusalem saw the city as being the site of the shedding of innocent blood (e.g., 2 *Bar.* 64:2).

ἐθαύμασα . . . μέγα. John is probably echoing Hab 1:5 (MT): "Look among the peoples, amazed with amazement" (this is the only appearance in the Bible of an internal accusative with the verb "to be amazed"; for amazement as a sign of repressed sexual desire [Pippin 1992, p. 57] see Lupieri 1999). Although the historical context of Habakkuk is difficult to reconstruct, it seems that the amazement is caused by the approach of the powerful "Chaldean" military machine, which will return to the throne of Jerusalem the rightful ruler whose place was usurped by an illegitimate sovereign supported by Egypt and/or Assyria. This took place around 605 BCE; Habakkuk was possibly of the anti-Egyptian party, and saw the Babylonians as the instrument of the divine punishment that was about to strike Jerusalem for its sin in forming an alliance with Egypt and thus frustrating Josiah's political and religious project (see comments on 16:16). Like Jeremiah, Habakkuk sees the alliance with Egypt and the abandonment of Josiah's policies as bringing about Jerusalem's imminent ruin (Haak 1992). Whatever the prophet's original context and meaning, at Qumran (1QpHab) this passage received a thoroughly anti-Jerusalemite reading whereby the oppressors were the ruling Hasmonean party of the day, and their allies the priests and Pharisees. The Qumranic commentator actually seems to read "look, traitors" (Hab 1:5, LXX) for "look among the peoples." If the prostitute is Jerusalem (who is Egypt) then John is writing in a context consistent with the prophetic atmosphere of Habakkuk, just as Jerusalem's destruction by a pagan power is consistent with the whole of the prophetic biblical tradition. John does not identify two pagan powers that would correspond with the ancient Egyptians and Babylonians; this may be because the Parthian threat was distant at the time he was writing, or it may be primarily because the strong polarizing tendencies of his thought admit a single evil world, whose monsters, beasts, heads, and horns are all set in motion by Satan. It matters little which historical human force destroys Jerusalem; whoever it is, it is the beast.

17:7 τὸ μυστήριον . . . θηρίου. The woman and the beast are united in a single evil mystery; indeed, their union itself is the tragic and terrible mystery of Satan's apparent triumph in history (see comments on 17:5). In this verse John says that the beast "bears" the woman, and the concept is promptly repeated three times from the perspective of the woman; she "sits upon" it in v. 9, "is seated" in v. 15, and finally "has rule over" it in v. 18. These are probably all references to the same phenomenon, and John's insistence on the images of bearing / sitting on / ruling is fully understandable if they express figuratively the real relationship between the woman and the beast, which is the "mystery" of Satan's victory. It is also worth noting that although the angel says he will reveal "the mystery of the woman and of the beast," he actually reveals the mystery of the beast first and only later unveils that of the woman. That the woman comes last suggests that it is she who really interests John and is the object of his amazement (not the beast). In light of the basic theological premises of salvation history (God's love for his people) it is not the natural wickedness of the beast but the transformation of the woman into a prostitute that strikes horror into the heart of the Jewish-Christian visionary.

17:8 ἦν . . . ὑπάγει. The first definition given to the beast parallels the tripartite definition of God that we saw at the start of the book (1:4, 8; 4:8; see comments ad loc.) and as such is designed to show the beast's inferiority. The beast, like God, is seen in relation to time, but in contrast to God's eternal being it is characterized by having been only in the past, as not being in the present, and as having only a fleeting and ephemeral existence in the future. The definition is repeated at the end of the verse (ἦν καὶ οὐκ ἔστιν καὶ παρέσται) and taken up again in v. 11, with a different third term being used on each occasion to suggest different details; on each occasion, however, the third term points to the fact that the beast itself is destined for destruction (see comments on 17:11).

The beast who is destined to "come up from the abyss" combines within itself the characteristics of the dragon who is Satan and those of the beast who "comes up from the sea" and seems to be distinct from Satan. In ch. 12 the dragon/serpent/Satan has seven heads, ten horns, and seven diadems (12:3), and thus its royalty is associated with its heads. In ch. 13 the beast from the sea has ten horns, seven heads, and ten diadems (13:1), and its royalty is thus connected to its horns. This beast has seven heads, ten horns, and no diadems. In v. 9, however, the seven heads are said to be "kings," which indicates that they are the seat of its royalty, as in the case of the dragon; in v. 12, the horns are also called "kings," and are thus the seat of royalty, as in the case of the beast from the sea. The beast from the sea, moreover, had "on his heads a name of blasphemy" (13:1), whereas this one is "full of names of blasphemy" (17:3) just as the four living creatures were "full of eyes" (4:6, 8), which is to say that they were completely covered with them. This seems to indicate a still greater degree of idolatrous corruption (see comments on 13:1).

The "beast from the land" who appeared in 13:11 and was later replaced by the "false prophet" of 16:13 has vanished, and its religious and priestly role, as indicated by its clothing and attributes, has been assumed by the city/prostitute (see Corsini 1980, p. 455); the "false prophet" reappears only in 19:20, after the destruction and disappearance of Babylon (the name appears for the last time in 18:21; for parallels between the text's treatment of Babylon and of Satan, see comments ad loc.). From that point in ch. 19 a distinction will be made between the destinies of the "beast" and of the "dragon": the "beast" is cast into the "marsh of fire" (19:20), while the final vicissitudes of the dragon, who is again explicitly identified with the "serpent" and with "Satan," are described in ch. 20. The beast and the dragon are distinguished for the last time in 20:10. Thus from ch. 13 onward Satan acts through two emissaries who are members of a trinity of whom he is the third, in an evil imitation of the divine Trinity. The beast from the earth, since it is at the head of a corrupt religion and worship, corresponds to the Spirit; it is a deceiving spirit, described as a "false prophet." The false prophet, in his turn, acts through the city/prostitute. When the city/prostitute is destroyed, the false prophet reappears, but only for the purpose of receiving his punishment. The beast from the sea and the dragon/Satan are distinguished at the beginning, but in the relationship of prostitution and fornication with the woman they are superimposed so that they seem to be a single figure. Just as the divinity of the Son is expressed in such a way that he seems to merge with the Father, so in the Satanic trinity Satan and the beast from the sea merge into a single beast that "bears" the city/prostitute. In the act of bearing the woman, which appears to represent Satan's triumph, he must perform to the fullest extent of his power: it is as if all of the Satanic energy is concentrated on the moment in which the forces of evil enter into a relationship with the woman. Satan's defiance of God lies in his seduction of the woman whom he had failed to kill in ch. 12: when he has seduced her, then he can destroy her. But even when he does so, he is carrying out the will of God (17:17), although this does not lessen his guilt. In fact, when he tries to do battle with the Lamb by means of his emissaries, they are defeated and punished. Like the monsters of the OT (e.g., Ezek 29:3-5; Job 40:15–41:26) and like Beliar of the Qumran texts, Satan, despite his apparent victories, is revealed in his true nature as the tragic dupe of God. John's vision is thoroughly unified and perfectly biblical. That the beast of ch. 17 takes on some of the characteristics of the dragon/Satan and of the beast from the sea helps us to explain the first two elements of its three-part definition. It is probably a reference to Satan: Satan's origin in God accounts for the fact that it "was," and the statement that it "is not" in spite of its attempts to exist (παρέσται) refers to Satan's fall. The third element of the definition, then, according to which the beast is destined in the future to "come up from the abyss and go to perdition," is most likely a precise reference to the fate of Satan during the "millennium" as described in 20:2-10 (see comments ad loc.), while another description of events of the millennium appears also in 17:11 (see comments ad loc.).

It is unclear whether the vision refers to historical or to pre- or metahistorical events. On the one hand, the fact that the beast "is not" any more whereas it once "was" indicates that Satan has already been cast out of heaven; but on the other hand, he still has to "come up from the abyss," which places the action before the battle of "Gog and Magog" (see 20:7-9; the "abyss" is in 20:3). Thus it seems that we are within salvation history. There are still at least three possible interpretations. According to the first and most probable, the vision describes Satan at a time before he has been cast into the abyss from which he will rise, and thus shows him as being at liberty to act on earth and in history. Thus both his first defeat at Harmagedon, after which he will be chained "for a thousand years," and his liberation and final defeat at Gog and Magog are eschatological events. According to the second and less plausible interpretation, Satan at this point is already in the abyss, from which he will rise only once. There is no chronological distinction between his being cast out of heaven and being thrown into the abyss, and the whole history coincides with the millennium. The third interpretation, like the first, sees Satan's fall as taking place in stages, but defines those stages differently: Satan is thrown down to earth at the beginning of history and cast into the abyss when he kills Jesus. Satan's apparent victory is really his defeat; thus the millennium is the time of the church on earth (for other interpretations see comments on 20:1-9). This last interpretation cannot easily be reconciled with the theory that the woman/city/prostitute represents Jerusalem or Rome or any other historical city: if Satan is chained in the abyss at the moment of Jesus' crucifixion, and the beast and the false prophet are cast into the marsh of fire (19:20), then he would not be at liberty to destroy Jerusalem or Rome (17:16). I understand the text as saying that the city is destroyed before the time of the first battle (in 19:19-21). If this is not the case, then we must abandon any hope of connecting the Apocalypse with known or datable historical events and accept that it refers entirely to symbolic and atemporal realities.

βλεπόντων τὸ θηρίον. It is quite obvious that "seeing the beast" is the reason for the wonder of "those who dwell upon the earth." What is difficult to explain is the genitive of the participle. We can suppose it is an irregular absolute genitive, which is not syntactically "absolute."

17:9 Ὧδε . . . σοφίαν. The term νοῦς appears only here and in 13:18, where there is a parallel phrase, the similarity of whose terms to these cannot be mere coincidence. In 13:18 John tells us the number of the beast; here he offers a more thorough explanation of it. The repetition is probably intended to indicate that the same reality is being revealed in both cases and that in both cases the revelation is of particular importance. As regards the meaning of the terms in question, νοῦς probably indicates the human capacity to penetrate the mystery, while σοφία (of which this is the last appearance) is used on its other two appearances of an attribute of the Lamb (5:12) or of God (7:12). Taken as a whole, the phrase and the parallel in 13:18 indicate that the revelation comes from God and can thus be understood only by those who are predisposed to understand it.

αἱ ἑπτά . . . εἰσίν. The "seven heads" are said to be "seven mountains." The most common explanation, which is almost universally accepted, is that this is a reference to Rome, a city on seven hills. John, however, never says anything about hills. The term ὄρος, which appears eight times in the text, means only "mountain." In the term's other appearances, with the possible exception of 21:10, John might be using it to describe an angelic being. This is consistent with those apocalyptic traditions that involve "seven mountains": "And I saw there the seven stars, (which) were like great, burning mountains . . . the spirits of the angels who have united themselves with women" (see all of *1 Enoch* 18:13–19:1 [*BW*], the parallel passage in *1 Enoch* 21:3-6 [*BW*], and *1 Enoch* 108:4; for the seven mountains/thrones who are faithful to God see the Introduction, pp. 29-30, and comments on 14:1). In both good and evil a "mountain" is an earthly manifestation of an angelic reality (and "star" is its heavenly equivalent). In *1 Enoch* 52:2ff. *(BS)*, for instance, we see six mountains of different metals that, following Dan 2, represent the six earthly reigns that will precede the coming of the Messiah, and that were created "by the authority of the Messiah, so that he may give orders and be praised upon the earth." The six mountains are destined to melt "like a honeycomb" before him "and become helpless before (or under) his feet" (*1 Enoch* 52:6 [*BS*]; see Ps 97:5). This passage is probably echoing speculations concerning the cosmic week (see comments on 9:5 and 12:6), but what concerns us is that the kingdoms or periods are represented by mountains and are destined to be defeated together in the final conflict with the Messiah (see comments on 17:10). I believe that John is using images common in the apocalyptic traditions of his age to stress that the beast with its seven heads represents power throughout human history: the direct expression of Satan's fallen angelic nature (the relationship between mountains and devils or gods is widely accepted even in texts that are not part of the Enochic tradition, such as *2 Bar.* 36:5: "And the head of the mountains was humiliated"; see 4Q380 fr. 2, 2-3: ". . . mountains and hills [. . .] those who rely on them shall shudder [. . .").

In the Greek literature before John's time the hills of Rome are usually denoted by the word λόφοι, which appears in the composite ἑπτάλοφος, typically used in imperial propaganda to refer to Rome as being on seven hills. In Latin texts we commonly find *colles* and *montes,* and in poetic works also *arces,* to signify the Roman *colles,* but there are few parallels in Greek texts that are not themselves based on an anti-Roman reading of the Apocalypse (see Lupieri 1990, pp. 391-92 n. 38, for the interpretation of a sestertius of Vespasian that figures Rome and is dated 71 CE). It is possible that John is expecting Rome to receive, at the end, an exemplary punishment, or even an overturning of its destiny such as that which Jerusalem had undergone, but I do not believe that is what he has in mind here.

ὅπου . . . ἐπ' αὐτῶν. John has already said that the female figure is seated on "many waters" and "on the beast"; now he underlines that she is sitting on the seven mountains. It would appear that "many waters," "beast," and "seven mountains" are different ways of describing the same thing. John might insist on the fact that the woman is sitting on the mountains to indicate that he is referring to a city (see the Introduction, pp. 30-31, and comments on 21:16). If the sin of Jerusalem is his topic, the implication is that Jerusalem has abandoned the holy mountain of Zion to prostitute herself on the pagan high places, which are identified with the seven angels/devils who sinned from the beginning, or to sin with those manifestations of them that are represented by the pagan emperors and the enemies of Israel. The atmosphere is similar to that of traditional prophetic texts.

καὶ βασιλεῖς . . . εἰσιν. As well as being mountains, the seven heads of the beast are also "kings." These seven sovereigns are generally held to be the Roman emperors, who should be identified on the basis of v. 10. The *Damascus Document* offers a contemporary explanation of the terms in Deut 32:33: "The 'serpents' are the kings of the peoples, and the 'wine' is their paths, and the 'asps' head' (this word is usually translated 'poison,' but the Hebrew has *rwš*, which means 'head,' and the Qumranic interpretation is based on this meaning) is the head of the kings of Greece" (CD 8:10-11). Another text from Qumran explains a prophecy of Nahum against some "mountains" as being directed against the pagan enemies: Bashan refers to the Kittim, Lebanon to its leaders, and Carmel to its king (4QpNah [4Q169] on Nah 1:4). Biblical "heads" and "mountains" can thus be understood as kings. It is still not quite clear, however, why John should identify the seven hills of Rome, the city/prostitute, with the emperors, or why Rome should be said to sit on the emperors (if anything, it should be the emperors who sit on Rome and at the head of the empire).

If we allow, on the other hand, that the mountains and the stars are angelic being hostile to God, it is not surprising that John (like the Qumranic commentators on Nahum) should consider them in mystical terms to be the spiritual structure of various earthly kingdoms, the real rulers of this world, the demonic sovereigns who appear to dominate human history. There is also Isa 14, according to which the king of Babylon is the star ("son of the morning") who was cast out of heaven, and who exclaims in his pride, "I will raise up my throne over the stars of the heavens; I will sit on a high mountain over the high mountains that are toward the north" (Isa 14:14, LXX; note the parallel between the stars of the heavens and the mountains of the north). There is, again, Ezek 28, which presents the figure of the angel/king of Tyre, but the principal reference is to Dan 10, with the angels/princes who are the spiritual heads of the kingdoms of the nations (and see the four angels, one of whom is called "Babel" and rules over "Persia" in the pseudo-Daniel text of 4Q552 and 553). Hippolytus also asserts that "all nations are entrusted to the angels, as John says in the Apocalypse" (*In Dan.* 3.9.10). In texts of the Enochic tradition the *Book of Dream Visions* mentions seventy angels/shepherds to whom the flock of Israel is successively entrusted; they exceed the limits set out for them, and thus at the end of the story (and of history) they are cast into the "abyss, full of fire and flames" in which the "stars" burn (*1 Enoch* 89:59–90:25). A similar idea appears in 4QpsMoses^e (4Q390), a Qumranic text (which is probably apocalyptic) whose author sees part of the history of the Second Temple during which Israel, in his opinion, suffered a period of degradation as a punishment for the Jews, who were abandoned by God "to the hands of the angels of destruction, and they will rule over them" (fr. 2, 1). Apart from his use of symbolic numbers John does not seem to be thinking of any particular sovereign but rather of earthly reigns in general, inasmuch as they are expressions of the power of evil angels. *WS* (1QM, 1Q33) contains speculations on Deut 7:1 and Josh 24:11 that show that the earthly kingdoms were precisely seven in number and were under the control of Satan, and that "the poor" are destined to "fell the hordes of Belial, the seven peoples of futility" (11:8-9; see comments on 2:6).

17:10 οἱ πέντε . . . μεῖναι. When the "kings" are identified with the Roman emperors, the verse is commonly used to attempt to determine the date of the work, or at least the date of John's visions. If five emperors have already "fallen," one "is," and the other "has not yet come," then John must have lived, or at least wanted to indicate that his visions took place, during the reign of the sixth. But who was the sixth Roman emperor? If we begin counting with Augustus (who never actually accepted the title of emperor or king), then the sixth is Galba, who reigned for a few months after Nero's death. Since his reign was of little importance, it is often said that John began counting with Julius Caesar, the founder of the Julian-Claudian dynasty; this is what Suetonius will do, although there is even better reason here to bear in mind that Caesar was never king or emperor. According to this approach, the sixth emperor is Nero, and Galba is the one who reigns for "a short while." Some scholars believe that John wrote during the reign of Galba's successor, Otho, but intended his readers to believe that he was writing in the time of Nero. He already knows that Galba's reign will be very short, and wants to present this after-the-fact knowledge as a prophecy of the future. If this is the case, then the text was written and published in 69, during the few months of Otho's contested reign, which John, however, did not realize was precarious.

Many other scholars find this hypothesis improbable, thinking it unlikely that, in view of the civil war of 69, John could have imagined Otho's reign to stand much chance of survival. Many, consequently, believe that the three emperors of 69 were too ephemeral to figure in the reckoning; if they are passed over, Nero is the sixth and Vespasian is the seventh. This school of thought sees John as writing at the beginning of Vespasian's reign with the expectation that the new emperor would follow the example of his three predecessors and meet a swift end. Even more in this case than in the last, John displays little in the way of political far-sightedess, but is inclined to tinker carefully with the text to give the impression that he was writing during the reign of the sixth emperor while he was actually living during the reign of the seventh.

Those scholars, on the other hand, who assign to the work a date during the reign of Domitian believe that John was well acquainted with the succession of the emperors and also well aware that neither Caesar nor Augustus was ever strictly speaking an emperor. The first real emperor, according to this reckoning, is Tiberius; if the three short-lived emperors after Nero are passed over, then the sixth is Titus and the seventh Domitian. In this scenario, as in the previous one, John deliberately implies that the composition of the text (or at least of the visions) is earlier than its actual date, and shows little prophetic skill with regard to the length of Domitian's reign, which he hoped would reach its end speedily. Solutions dating the text within the reign of Trajan have also been proposed, with different lists of emperors, but this hypothesis has been abandoned.

While it is not beyond the bounds of possibility that John did indeed toy with one of these lines of reasoning, it is surely much more likely that he is reflecting on the view of salvation history that sees it as being divided into seven phases or reigns. There is no necessity to follow Hippolytus (*In Dan.* 4.23.6) in thinking that these are millennia. For one thing, not only are the reflections on the cosmic week in *2 Baruch* not concerned with millennia, but they deal with periods of unequal length (Lupieri 1992, p. 128; see Introduction, p. 21). The Johannine reading of history as divided into seven periods has both similarities to and differences from that of *2 Baruch*. If we allow that the mountains/kings are the angelic princes of this world and are expressed concretely in the succession of pagan empires that rule over it, then the verse means that five periods have passed and that John is living during the sixth. Unlike *2 Baruch*, this view sees all of history in the hands of these Satanic powers, against whom there are no periods of light. The seventh mountain/king has not yet appeared, but "when he comes, he must remain a short while."

We are thus in the sixth period, the one that "is." Although the text does not allow us to make a precise calculation based on millennia as Hippolytus suggests, he is probably right about the basic idea. The short reign of the seventh mountain/king thus corresponds with the Satanic attack on the Logos at the battle of Harmagedon, an attack that fails and is followed by the millennial earthly reign of Christ, through whom God takes full possession of human time. Thus the whole of the seventh period is under the control of God, the beast and the false prophet spend it alive in the marsh of fire, and Satan is imprisoned in the abyss (see following comments).

It is not surprising, finally, that John can see all of the beast's seven heads at the same time, even though they represent historical periods of the past, present, and future. All apocalyptic visions take for granted that all of time is continually present in the eternity of God (see comments on 12:1). *2 Bar.* 48:2, 13 and particularly 54:3 even show us how this simultaneous presence of periods is possible: the "heads of the times," who correspond to John's "mountains/kings," are angels whom God can call together at any moment so as to take in at a single glance all of the periods represented by their ruling angels (see *Apoc. Abr.* 9:5 and 21:1).

17:11 ὃ ἦν . . . ἔστιν. This should perhaps be translated, in analogy to the divine title (see comments on 1:4), as "the Was and is not" (reading ὁ ἦν).

αὐτός . . . ὑπάγει. This is possibly a reference to the final battle of Gog and Magog (see also Num 24:23-24, LXX, where a similar sentence seemingly refers to the eschatological fate of Og and the other enemies of Israel; see also comments on 20:8). The figure indicated with the masculine pronoun is possibly Satan in the fullness of his nature, who contains within himself all of the power of the beast ("consists of the seven," i.e., of the mountain/kings discussed above). He returns at the end of the millennium, the seventh period of history, and wants to be the eighth period himself. However, as God has already claimed the seventh period, the cosmic Sabbath, by means of the messianic reign, it is inconceivable that Satan should take control of the eighth period, the Lord's day of the cosmic week. This belongs to God and to Christ, whose power has no limits and extends outside of time (as we will see, the old heaven will be no more, and there will be perpetual day [see 20:11 and 21:23-25], which means that time will cease to exist) in an eternity that cannot be measured. John avoids measuring or defining the time of God precisely because it is actually outside of time and thus of the very possibility of measurement: measurable time is that which is under Satan's control.

There are a number of stages to God's intervention: first he reestablishes control over the seventh period, which thus becomes a millennium, or rather "the millennium" (the only period of time associated with a number indicating totality), then he renders all other calculation impossible by destroying time itself and restoring an atemporal eternity over which he reigns supreme. As long as there is time that can be measured, Satan can hope or attempt to make a comeback.

Most scholars avoid such a "spiritual" reading of the text and claim that the male figure is a Roman emperor: *Nero redivivus,* who comes back as the eighth emperor after his real or apparent death, thus accounting for the phrase, translated "he is the eighth, and is (one) of the seven (past emperors)." This interpretation is possible only if καὶ ἐκ τῶν ἑπτά ἐστιν means "and is *one* of the seven," which is not syntactically impossible (see Acts 21:8), but see Lupieri 1990, pp. 394-95 n. 47; Mussies 1971, p. 96 remarks that ἐκ τῶν ἑπτά is not a partitive form here.

17:12   τὰ δέκα . . . εἰσιν. These ten horns, like the seven heads, come from Dan 7:7 (see 7:20, 24). The horns are monarchs in Daniel as well, and appear on the last of the four beasts. It is not clear where John sees them (here and in the earlier passages 12:3 and 13:1), but he says that these rulers will all come to power together. Therefore, like the ten horns in Daniel, these too belong to the same beast and constitute a single unit. This, as well as the fact that they will have power "for one hour only" and will all fight the Lamb and be defeated, suggests that they do not follow each other in succession. In any case, these horns/kings are different from the seven heads/mountains/kings, who do succeed each other in time, and, if my interpretation is correct, over long periods of time. Moreover, while five of the heads are in the past, one in the present, and only one in the future, the horns are all active in the future (note the presence in both verses of the adverb οὔπω, which can only mean "not yet" in both cases, as opposed to the argument in Corsini 1980, p. 434). Despite this it has been argued that the seven heads represent the seven first important emperors, without the three short-lived ones of 69, and the ten horns represent all of them, including those of 69. This runs counter both to logic (since the same emperors are considered both as short lived and as not) and to the text (see Lupieri 1990, p. 393 n. 42).

It is difficult to be sure what John is alluding to. We can note in the first place that he is taking up again the description of the beast from the sea in 13:1, whose royalty is located in its horns, and then that, following Dan 7, the horns, unlike the heads, most likely represent human sovereigns. Since ten and its multiples represent completeness, these might represent all the earthly kings who "will do battle with the Lamb." This "battle," which was mentioned in 13:4 and 7, is now presented for the first time as a war fought by the Lamb, in anticipation of chs. 19 and 20. While in ch. 13, however, the beast was said to "make war on the holy ones and to defeat them" (v. 7), now these kings "will do battle with the Lamb, and the Lamb will defeat them." The allusions to chs. 19 and 20 leave room for at least three possible interpretations. The ten kings might take part in the first eschatological conflict, traditionally said to be that of Harmagedon (ch. 19), or in the second, that of "Gog and Magog" (ch. 20), or maybe John is referring to both of these events. According to this last hypothesis the two conflicts would coincide, and the "millennium" would no longer be a real period in time but would merely be symbolic.

The bulk of the internal allusions support the first interpretation. The alliance between the beast and the kings is made explicit only in 19:19, whereas neither of them appears in the conflict of ch. 20, during which the beast is already in the marsh of fire. In addition, the definition of the Lamb as "Lord of lords and King of kings" corresponds to that of the Word in 19:16 (see comments on 19:11): "King of kings and Lord of lords." These are the only two appearances of the phrase, a dual occurrence of the "Hebrew superlative" (like "Holy of Holies" or "Song of Songs"). It also seems that only in ch. 19 does Christ fight a "war": although the Lamb is not named in 20:9, we can certainly imagine that he is besieged at "the camp of the holy ones," but the situation there is resolved by a "fire . . . from heaven" that "devours" the enemies, and thus never actually develops into a battle as it does in 19:19-21. The only possible allusion in our verse to demonic activity after the millennium lies in the detail that the power of horn/kings is said to last "for one hour only," just as only "a short time" is allowed to Satan in 20:3. However, the "one hour only" (which appears only in chs. 17 and 18) might be in reference to something else, while the "short time," which is a characteristic of Satanic activity, is probably a reference to 6:11. If this line of reasoning is valid, then the ten horns, like the ten horns of Daniel, are connected with the last of the heads, the seventh one that has yet to come and that will last a short time (v. 10). In this case it would not be connected to John's present but rather to the time of the conflict that comes shortly before the coming of the millennium. A typical reader, however, does not yet know that there will be a millennium, although he understands for the first time in the text that there will be a direct military conflict between the forces of evil and those of the Lamb, and that this conflict will bring about the final victory of the good.

17:13 τὴν δύναμιν . . . διδόασιν. See 13:2, 4, where Satan gives his power and authority to the beast. The concept appears again in v. 17, where John explains that this "power" is their royal power. What we have here is probably a reference to the fact that pagan kings dedicated themselves to their gods as the ideological foundation of their power. The alliance between the kings and Satan consists in an exchange of "power" in two directions: Satan helps his supporters, giving his power to the beast, and the kings of the nations put their authority in his hands.

17:14 ὅτι κύριος . . . πιστοί. This ending might be an addition by John rather than by the angel; see 20:3. The royal epithets that are usually applied to God belong naturally in the formulas of prayer (see *Hodayot* [1QH–4QH]

18:8: "See, you are prince of gods and king of the glorious ones and lord of every spirit and ruler of every creature").

17:15   Τὰ ὕδατα. The waters that were announced at the beginning of the chapter and then seemingly forgotten reappear here. As it seems unlikely that a prostitute could sit on a beast and on the waters at the same time, we must assume that there is a symbolic equivalence between the two. The waters represent pagan humanity ("peoples and throngs and nations and languages"), not including the "tribes." Thus the beast is pagan political power, a manifestation of the power of Satan.

17:16   οὗτοι. This is masculine, although it is applied to the beast and the horns, which are both neuter terms in Greek. Whether they are men or angels, John thinks of them as male.

μισήσουσιν τὴν πόρνην . . . ἐν πυρί. The destruction of Babylon/the prostitute has been anticipated at least since 14:8. The turn of events, however, can be explained only by recourse to biblical antecedents: "Babylon" is destroyed by her own allies, who thus carry out the will of God. The preceding verses would lead us to expect that the kings and the beast would make war against the Lamb rather than against Babylon, with whom they seem united in corruption. Such a reversal, however, is often predicted by the prophets with reference to Jerusalem, who is destined to be destroyed by her own foreign and idolatrous allies and "lovers." Once more the primary model is Ezekiel, which describes at length, particularly in chs. 16, 19, and 23, the destiny of Israel and of Jerusalem, the "prostitute" and the "bloody one" who will be "desolate," left "naked and bare," and "burned" by her own lovers (it is interesting that neither Ezekiel nor John says explicitly that the city will be "killed"). The eating of the flesh probably derives from Mic 3:3-4, which in LXX reads: ὃν τρόπον κατέφαγον τὰς σάρκας τοῦ λαοῦ μου . . . οὕτως κεκράξονται . . . καὶ οὐκ εἰσακούσεται αὐτῶν ("Just as they devoured the flesh of my people, . . . so will they cry out . . . but no hearing will be given to them"). Micah's invective is directed against the authorities of Jerusalem. Every expression in our passage has many biblical echoes besides those of Ezekiel; there is, for instance, Isa 1:7: "Your country lies desolate, your cities are burned with fire; in your very presence aliens devour your land; it will be desolate, destroyed like Sodom." Certainly burning was the usual fate of a destroyed city, but it might nevertheless be significant that this detail of fire is taken up in a lament over Jerusalem found at Qumran (4QapLamA [4Q179] fr. 1, 1:5).

We may also note that the entire scene of ch. 17, from the description of the city's sin of prostitution to the vision of its destruction, is all set in the "desert" of v. 3. Apart from its reference to the symbology of Kippur (see comments on 17:5), this detail serves to recall the events of the exodus as they appear, for instance, in Ezek 20:13 and 21. While Israel was in the desert God did not destroy her completely for her sins, but now, after her definitive sin, God's action against her also becomes definitive. The final verses of this chapter are the most important for the argument that the city/prostitute represents Jerusalem or at least a Jewish entity (among other things, the condemnation to be "burned with fire" in Lev 21:9 is reserved for the daughters of priests who defile themselves through prostitution; LXX: ἐπὶ πυρὸς κατακαυθήσεται). The passage aims to bring all of human history, which had seemingly been abandoned into Satan's hands, back under the power of God. John always stresses that Satan's deeds are under God's control, and here he repeats with some force that the destruction of Jerusalem is carried out by the same forces of evil with whom she became corrupt, in accordance with God's will. The end of the city and of the temple need not alarm the Jew who has become Christian because everything that happens happens according to the will of God.

The more difficult question is that of when all this will take place. We have seen that the most logical moment for the activity of the ten "horns" is at the beginning of the millennium: their battle against the Lamb, in alliance with the beast, would then be the conflict described in ch. 19. If this is the case, then the destruction of the city, by the horns and the beast acting together, should signal the beginning of the action, and thus of the royal "power," of these evil forces. The close parallel between vv. 17 and 13, which focus on the union of purpose among the Satanic powers, shows that the war against the Lamb and the destruction of the city/prostitute are closely connected. The underlying concept is, I believe, that Satan has finally succeeded in seducing Israel/Jerusalem and thus can do what he has always desired, that is, destroy God's beloved city, but that this destruction, which seems to show Satan's victory, is really a fulfillment of the will of God, who means to punish Jewish betrayal. Satan has already determined his own destiny, and now all he can do is to make the final fatal mistake of attacking the Lamb directly. This conflict will be the end of the forces of evil, and will open the way for Christ's millennial reign.

It is hard to say how far apart Satan's two attacks, on "Babylon" and on the Lamb, are chronologically. The frequent occurrence of the future tense makes plain that they are both thought of as coming in the future (relative to the time of the vision), but I do not think there is sufficient material to warrant a hypothesis about the time that John thought of as separating the two events. If Jerusalem had already fallen by the time that John was writing, then this is a prophecy *ex eventu,* at least as regards the time of the redaction, but the expression "for one hour only" (v. 12) does not tell us that the attack on the Lamb follows closely. It is nonetheless interesting to note the logical, if not the chronological, connection between the ruin of Jerusalem and the time of the end; Satan is destined to destroy the city and only afterward to attack the Lamb.

17:18 ἡ γυνή . . . μεγάλη. The vision in the desert that opened at the beginning of the chapter comes to an end with the angelic explanation of the true nature of the woman. The term ἔρημος, which appeared twice in ch. 12, does not occur again after this point, but its derivative ἐρημόω, "to make desolate" or to "lay waste," which appeared for the first time in 17:16, will occur twice more, in 18:17 and 19. The extraordinary impact of Dan 9:27 (the "abomination of desolation") tended to fix the use of the abstract ἐρήμωσις as indicating idolatrous prostitution (the presence of an idol) in the temple (see 1 Macc 1:54; Mark 13:14; Matt 24:15); in Luke 21:20, however, the term is used to indicate the "desolation" of Jerusalem probably caused by the "armies" surrounding it, while in itself the verb "to desolate" is not necessarily connected with Jerusalem (see Matt 12:25; Luke 11:17). Following his usual *crescendo* pattern, John brings the series of references to a close by explaining that the "woman," whom we now see in the desert, is "the city, the great one." The expression is used a total of eight times, seven as ἡ πόλις ἡ μεγάλη and the final time (18:21) as ἡ μεγάλη πόλις (it is difficult to know whether there is any significance to these numbers). Up to this point the "great city" cannot be other than Jerusalem (see comments on 11:8; 14:8; 16:19); if John says here that the "woman" is "the city, the great one," then it cannot but be a reference to the two times in the previous passage where he explains what "the city, the great one" is. This justifies the presence of the definite article. Those exegetes (and they are in the majority) who think that there are two or more "great cities" in the text account for the article by saying that it is not a reference to the earlier passages in which "the city, the great one" was named, but is rather an expression of John's desire to make quite clear that this is not just any "great city" but is that which "has rule over the kings of the earth," namely, Rome, the capital of the universal empire.

This negative dimension of Jerusalem should come as no surprise: in the Apocalypse we see Israel split into its two dimensions of holiness and of sin just as happens in the preparation of the expiatory goat (see comments on 17:5). The only "woman" who is the seat of the promise now becomes a "prostitute" and at the end of the book will reappear as a "bride." Hosea's wife/prostitute (Hos 1:2), the symbol that contains the contradictory aspects of Israel's chosenness and betrayal, has been split into her component parts so that the negative part can be destroyed (see comments on 19:7 and 21:2).

ἡ ἔχουσα . . . γῆς. This royalty can be a characteristic of Jerusalem (see comments on 17:3), whose ideal reign was seen as extending as far as the Euphrates (see comments on 9:14) or, in a universalistic and/or messianic context, over the whole world. In a text a little more recent than the Apocalypse the reign of David and Solomon is recalled in remarkably exalted terms: "the city of Zion then dominated all the lands and the regions" (*2 Bar.* 61:7). Even the "reign" of Zerubbabel, whose role as the last Davidic sovereign lent him an increasingly messianic quality, was seen as being universal (see Sacchi 1976). Among those biblical passages that explicitly attribute royal status to Jerusalem Ezek 16 stands out: v. 13 (in Hebrew; LXX omits the detail) records how Jerusalem, when she enjoyed God's favor, was "fit to be a queen," but later God laments, in the words of the prophet, "You . . . took your beautiful vases of my gold and my silver among those I had given you, and made for yourself male images, and with them played the whore" (v. 17).

Thus royalty and idolatrous prostitution are linked in Jerusalem. That the Bible sometimes refers to Babylon as a queen should not oblige us to interpret this passage as a reference to Rome, nor should the fact that some passages in John might be references to prophetic texts that call Babylon queen; by this point Jerusalem has absorbed into herself the attributes and epithets of Israel's enemies (see comments on 17:5). As for the "kings of the earth," we remarked in 17:1 that these are ambiguous figures. In some messianic texts such as the famous second Psalm, dominion over the kings of the earth, who are seen as on the verge of rebellion, is said to come from Zion (Ps 2:6), and their rebellion is merely another episode in the rule of "the LORD and his Anointed" (v. 2). In her depravity and prostitution with the pagans Jerusalem acquires a sort of power (to "have rule over the kings of the earth" is the same as "to sit on the beast") that is a painful imitation of that power planned for her by God. It is an illusory power, like that of Satan, but it is the only one that he is able to provide her with, and that only temporarily. In view of the hostility between this Jerusalem and the Christian Messiah the "rule over the kings of the earth" renders the city an enemy of the "King of kings and Lord of lords" (17:14; 19:16).

18:1 Μετὰ ταῦτα . . . οὐρανοῦ. This phrase is transitional, marking a change of scene. With the vision of the prostitute and the beast in the desert over, we now see two interventions "from heaven" on the part of angelic figures who use revelatory words and gestures to further show the destiny of the city/prostitute. The first figure is "another angel," who, although more briefly described than the "other angels" of 5:2 and 8:3, shares with them enough attributes to characterize him as a christological angel (see also 10:1 and comments on 18:4). The fact that "the earth was illuminated by his glory" is taken directly from Ezek 43:2 (LXX has a slightly embroidered text: καὶ ἡ γῆ ἐξέλαμπεν ὡς φέγγος ἀπὸ τῆς δόξης κυκλόθεν: "And the earth shone like a flame from the glory all around"). In a number of places John uses this scene from Ezekiel, which is about the triumphal return of God, with his Glory, to the rebuilt temple in Jerusalem as it appeared in the prophet's vision. In the same verse (still in the Hebrew) Ezekiel records that the "voice" of the Glory is "like the sound of many waters"; John gives the same definition to the voices of the Risen One (in 1:15) and of some angels (19:6). The same passage tells us that the Glory comes "from where the sun rises" (43:1-2, 4), as do the "other angel" of 7:2 and the "kings" of 16:12 (see comments ad loc.). Ezekiel also asserts that the vision he is seeing is identical to the one he had seen "when [God] came to destroy the city," the city being Jerusalem (Ezek 43:3; the mss. have "when I had gone," which must be a theological emendation; LXX alters it still more, perhaps due to a misunderstanding of the Hebrew: τοῦ χρῖσαι τὴν πόλιν, "to anoint the city"). John is thus saying again what he has said so many times before: that what happened in Ezekiel's time is happening or is about to happen again in his own time. The city, which is once again a prostitute, this time for good, must be destroyed so that the Glory of God can return. The city presents an obstacle to the Glory of God, and its destruction signals the return of that Glory. Because we are dealing with late Second Temple Judaism, the Glory is itself an angelomorphic figure, and because this is a Christian text, it is also a christological figure.

18:2 Ἔπεσεν ἔπεσεν. This verse and the following one recall 14:8, which was also spoken by "another angel." John returns both to the fall of Babylon (with the same quotation from Isa 21:9) and to the "wine of the wrath of her prostitution" and expands them by describing the results of the fall and additional details about other categories of evildoers as well as the "nations."

18:3 οἱ ἔμποροι . . . ἐπλούτησαν. The "merchants," who will be mentioned four times in this chapter, always with negative connotations, make their first appearance here. John shows little sympathy for the "ships" (see v. 19 and comments on 8:9) and passes a negative judgment against those who buy and sell (see comments on 14:4). On eight other occasions where the terms "rich," "riches," and "become rich" appear, it is also with negative connotations: the exceptions are 2:9, 3:18, and 5:12. Who are these "merchants," and what do they represent? The most obvious biblical antecedents are the prophetic laments on the fall of Tyre (Isa 23; Ezek 27), with all its merchants and mariners and riches. Some of John's expressions also appear to be direct quotations (e.g., 18:23c, which comes from Isa 23:8) and thus leave no doubt that John has in mind those passages from the prophets. However, "Judah and the land of Israel" (v. 17) figure in the list of merchants who did trade with Tyre (Ezek 27:12-25), and in Neh 13:16 there are merchants from Tyre who sell their wares in Jerusalem on the Sabbath and are thrown out of the city by the Jewish reformer. The banker Tobiah, who has set up shop in the temple, is "thrown outside" with his wares (vv. 5-8). At the end "the merchants and sellers of all kinds of merchandise" on the Sabbath are removed not only from the temple but also from the city, and even from the surrounding area (Neh 13:20-21; for Tyre and Jerusalem see comments on 17:5). The removal from the temple of bankers and merchants is the model for a well-known NT episode that was so important in primitive Christianity as to appear in all four Gospels: the so-called "cleansing of the temple" by Jesus (Mark 11:15 and parallels). Only Mark and Matthew include the expulsion of the buyers as well, and only Matthew has a single category for "sellers and buyers" or real merchants who both buy and sell, although the evangelist does not tell us what their ware is. Here again it is Matthew's Gospel that is closest to the Apocalypse. These sources are not very helpful in determining the precise nature of John's merchants, as some of them are Jewish and some pagan. Nor can we learn a great deal from the connection with γῆ: regardless of whether γῆ here means the whole world or just the land of Israel, John might be referring to the merchants who live on the land, to the merchants who belong to it, or, finally, to those who make the land their ware (see comments on 18:23).

18:4 Ἐξέλθατε . . . ἐξ αὐτῆς. As elsewhere (e.g., 10:1-4), the appearance of an angel with christological characteristics is followed by a "voice from heaven" that confirms or details the angel's words and actions. The similarity with the opening of ch. 10 is strengthened by the fact that this "other angel" now "cries with a strong voice," just as the earlier one "cried with a great voice" before the intervention of the "voice." In the manner of angelic figures of the OT the "voice" addresses that "people," whom it defines as its own, indicating that it is speaking in the name of God, but then immediately (v. 5) refers to God in the third person, to show that it is distinct from him. In any case, the "people" must mean the followers of Jesus.

The voice's first words come directly from Jer 51:45 (in Hebrew), which is an exhortation to leave Babylon, with several parallels (see Isa 48:20; 52:11; Jer 50:8; 51:6) that are taken up in the NT (2 Cor 6:17). The Gospels adapt the ancient prophetic notion to the new reality; in his so-called "apocalyptic discourse" Jesus exhorts believers to leave Judea before its destruction (Matt 24:15-20; Mark 13:14-18), or even to abandon Jerusalem, which is "surrounded by armies" (Luke 21:20-22). The passage from Luke is most interesting because it also contains the desolation as a characteristic of Jerusalem's future (see comments on 17:18). Finally, the exhortation in Heb 13:13 to "go to him outside the camp," meaning out of Judaism, demands a thoroughly spiritual interpretation (see comments on 20:9 and 21:1).

These passages prove that from the beginning of Christian thought biblical phrases about the enemies of the chosen people could be applied to Jerusalem and Judaism. This attitude, which is typical of a religious minority, expresses itself in terms of separation and abandonment (of the temple, of Jerusalem, of the Land) both by individual preachers or observant followers and by entire groups (for John the Baptist and Bannas see Lupieri 1997, pp. 8off.; for Yehudah ben Dortai and the problems associated with observance see Sussmann 1994 in Qimron–Strugnell 1994, p. 192). The most famous of the Qumranic texts are quite explicit on this point. The segregation in the desert (Isa 40:3) and the conviction that "this is the time for making ready the path to the desert" appear in the *Rule of the Community* (1QS 8: 13-14 and 9:19-20). CD is a fertile source. Its comments on Ezek 44:15 are clear; the "priests" are "the converts of Israel who left the land of Judah"; the "Levites" are "those who joined them," and the "sons of Zadok" are "the chosen of Israel, those called by their own names, who rise at the end of days" (CD 3:21–4:4). "The path that was discovered by those who entered the new covenant in the land of Damascus" is such that they no longer "enter the temple to kindle his altar in vain" (CD 6:11-19; for the separation of the "house of Peleg" see the text of CD 20:22-23, quoted in the comments on 11:1-2). The fragmentary 4Q522, in its conviction that Jerusalem was at that time occupied and defiled by pagans, also insists on the separation: "Now let us establish the t[ent of mee]ting far from [. . .]Eleazer [to transport] the t[ent of mee]ting away from the house [of . . ." (fr. 9, 2:12-13). Separation from a contaminated Jerusalem is thus a common theme among significant groups of Jews before 70 CE.

18:5 ἐκολλήθησαν . . . ἁμαρτίαι. The sins of the city are piled one on top of the other in a great heap that reaches to heaven. That a mass of human sins can reach to heaven is a fairly common *topos* (see, e.g., 1 Enoch 9:2); the antecedent to this passage must be the description of Sodom's sins in Gen 18:20. In *4 Ezra* 11:43 the lion (the Messiah) says something similar *(Et ascendit contumelia tua usque ad Altissimum)* to the eagle (the Roman Empire).

18:6 ἀπόδοτε . . . διπλᾶ. It is not at all clear whom the "voice" is addressing at this point; the earlier exhortation in the second person plural ("go out") is addressed to (Christian) "people," who would not be in a position to punish the city. The plural here seems to be generic. The "voice" is calling together the enemies, or perhaps some punitive angelic figures who are not otherwise addressed in the immediate context. The law of "an eye for an eye" is traditionally applied to Israel's enemies. Ps 137:8, speaking of the city personified as "daughter of Babylon," says, "Happy shall they be who pay you back what you have done to us!" (Ps 136:8, LXX: μακάριος ὃς ἀνταποδώσει σοι τὸ ἀνταπόδομά σου ὃ ἀνταπέδωκας ἡμῖν; see Jer 50:15, 29).

John emphasizes that the city will not only be repaid for what she has done, but that she will be repaid twofold. The phrase "double it in double fashion" contains an internal accusative and appears in almost identical form in Job 42:10 ("[the LORD] doubled it twice"). The idea of a "double" punishment is, however, typically applied to Jerusalem and Israel (see Beagley 1987, p. 98). In Isa 40:2 Israel is said to "have received from the LORD's hand double for all her sins" (LXX: ἐδέξατο ἐκ χειρὸς κυρίου διπλᾶ τὰ ἁμαρτήματα αὐτῆς), and in Jer 16:18 God promises to "doubly repay their iniquity and their sins, because they have polluted my land with the carcasses of their abominations" (LXX: καὶ ἀνταποδώσω διπλᾶς τὰς κακίας αὐτῶν καὶ τὰς ἁμαρτίας αὐτῶν ἐφ᾽ αἷς ἐβεβήλωσαν τὴν γῆν μου ἐν τοῖς θνησιμαίοις τῶν βδελυγμάτων αὐτῶν). These abominations here refer to idolatrous ritual sacrifices performed by the Israelites, the carcasses of which defile God's holy land. Thus while it was expected that God would punish Israel's enemies according to the law of "an eye for an eye," the tradition held that he would punish Israel and Jerusalem twofold (there is a comment on Isa 40:1-5 in the fragmentary 4QTanh [4Q176] frr. 1-2, end of col. 1). This is probably due to the Israelites' awareness that their sins were never "simple" but always inherently involved betrayal and infidelity and were thus more serious than the sins of other nations and deserving of more severe punishment.

God's love for Israel, and his choice of her as his firstborn, are the first reason for punishment: "For that reason you have poured on us your rage [and] your [jealou]sy with all the intensity of your anger" (4QDibHamᵃ [4Q504] 3, particularly 10-11). This must have been a very live question in John's day, since much of *4 Ezra* consists of a theodicy that sets out to explain why God always punishes Israel in a way that seems, at least to human eyes, to be disproportionate to her sins, particularly when the disaster of Zion is compared to the well-being of sinful Babylon (see, e.g., *4 Ezra* 3:2, 28, 31). John takes a stance on this problem in our passage: while *4 Ezra* seeks comfort in the inscrutability of God's judgments (4:11), John, as a Christian, claims to know full well why Israel and Jerusalem are being punished. Jerusalem/Babylon is as unforgivable as Sodom, receives the "plagues" (vv. 4 and 8) like Egypt, and finally is forced to drink of the cup from which she gave others to drink. John here brings to its conclusion what he said earlier (see in particular 17:6 and comments): the prostitute Babylon drinks blood from a cup that comes from God (see comments on 14:8; 16:19; 17:1, 4). Numerous prophetic passages, such as Isa 51:17 and Jer 13:12-14, say that this "cup" is destined for Israel; Ezek 23:32-34 in particular says that Jerusalem drinks the cup of her "sister Samaria" and "gnaws its shards." The cup in Hab 2:16, finally, according to the Qumranic commentary 1QpHab (see comments on 17:5-6), was said to be held in reserve by God for the Jewish authorities.

We have proceeded here in the only way possible when dealing with a text so rich in allusions and in deliberately cryptic passages. What we have is a cluster of ideas or images — punishment according to the law of "an eye for an eye," the doubling of punishment in response to sin, punishment described as the drinking of the cup of God — some of which can refer to different entities — Israel's enemies, sinful Israel herself — while at least one refers to a particular entity: the doubling of the penalty refers only to Jerusalem/Israel. In such a case, as in iconology, the element that is not ambiguous should be taken as the determining symbol of the entire scene, and the meaning of the others brought into harmony to it.

18:7 Κάθημαι . . . εἰμί. This verse echoes in several details the address to Babylon in Isa 47, where the city is defined as "mistress of the kingdoms" (47:5) and believes that she will be "mistress forever" (47:7) and will not "sit as a widow or know the loss of children" (47:8); but in "one day" she will be afflicted both by the loss of children and by widowhood (47:9). There is, therefore, a clear reference to Babylon. However, the prophecy should be applied to Jerusalem and Israel, since in Lam 1:1 the prophet says of Jerusalem, "How like a widow she has become, she that was great among the nations! She that was a princess among the provinces has become subject to tribute." Lam 1:2 contains another example of that reversal of fortunes in her relationship with her lovers that we have seen in regard to the prostitute: "among all her lovers she has no one to comfort her; all her friends . . . have become her enemies." Finally, 2 *Bar.* 67:2 has a very interesting parallel to this: the nations, boasting before their idols about the destruction of Jerusalem, exclaim that "she who has trodden others down for such a long time has been trodden down; and she who has subjugated has been subjugated." By this point it should be quite certain that John intends to refer to Jerusalem and Israel rather than to Rome.

18:9 Καὶ κλαύσουσιν. Verses 9 and 10 are the first and the most synthetic of three parallel laments that introduce into the proceedings the "kings of the earth" (vv. 9-10), the "merchants" (vv. 11-17a), the "helmsmen" and "seamen," and "all those who practice trade by sea" (vv. 17b-20). The three passages are very similar in structure. In all three the figures are said to "weep" and mourn, and in all three they are said to "stand afar" to look on the ruins of the city and their words are reported in direct discourse. Their words also conform to a common pattern, beginning in all cases with "Woe, woe, O great city" and ending by observing that she met her "judgment" or was "laid waste" in "a single hour."

We can note at the outset that by means of the "kings," "merchants," "helmsmen," and "those who practice trade" both land and sea are involved in the lament for the "great city"; in contrast, "heaven" appears at the end of the tripartite lament and is exhorted to "rejoice" (v. 20). The contrast is strong and deliberate, and indeed characterizes the cosmos of the Apocalypse from at least as early as 12:12, where Satan falls and the "heavens" can "rejoice" while "woe" is destined to reach "land and sea." Our passage is an obvious echo of 12:12. The kings, merchants, and those who go on the sea are the holders of human power over land and sea: by contrasting them to heaven and to the "holy ones and the apostles and the prophets" of v. 20, John shows that they represent that part of humanity in subjection to Satan — those "kings" with whom the prostitute fornicated (17:2 and 18:3). However, John adds something here to what he said there: since the city/prostitute was devoured by the beast and the kings who are its ten horns, then these kings, who weep from afar at the sight of the destroyed city, afraid "of her torment," cannot be the same kings as those who destroyed her. The lament appears rather abruptly, as did the destruction of the city by the beast and the horns who are destined to fight against the Lamb (17:14). There seems to be a rupture within the forces of evil, with Satan and the various beasts on one side, and on the other the city/prostitute and the three categories of people who are lamenting over her; if this is the case, then the "ten horns" do not represent all of the "kings of the earth" but only a group of them. That the lamenting kings are fearful, moreover, suggests that they are afraid of being involved themselves, and of ending up in the same condition as the city. They are and remain accomplices of the city/prostitute to an even greater extent than those "kings of the earth" who, according to Lam 4:12, were incredulous at the fall of Jerusalem.

The laments also include three pairs of "woes," whose relation to the "woes" of chs. 8–11 is unclear. Could John perhaps mean that the "great city" is now receiving double the "woes" that "those who dwell on the earth" (8:13) or the "land and sea" (12:12) are destined to receive? This would be consistent with what we noted in the comments on v. 6.

βλέπωσιν . . . πυρώσεως. See Gen 19:28 and comments on 14:11.

18:10 μιᾷ ὥρᾳ. John repeats three times (vv. 10, 17, and 19, as well as "in a single day" in v. 8) that the city is destroyed quickly, which is an element typical of divine punishment; the repetition suggests that he views it as important. It may be another reference to the destruction of Sodom, like the one in Lam 4:6. There are other possible parallels, such as Isa 47:9 (already referenced in vv. 7-8) or Num 16:20, which shows how swiftly God acts to punish rebellion among the Israelites. The destruction lasts exactly as long as the power of the ten horns (17:12); however long the event takes in terms of human history, from a theological point of view it is a single act on God's part.

18:11-13   The list of objects that make up the "cargo" of the merchants alternates, in a way that initially looks very odd, between accusatives and genitives. Much has been written about the syntactical confusion of this sentence, but actually the list operates on two distinct logical levels. The first accusative, "a cargo," supports an initial series of genitives, each of them indicating a precious substance of which only a little amount is worth a great deal (from "gold" to "scarlet"). These are not yet manufactured goods, but merely very precious raw materials. John distinguishes from these "every thyine wood," which is also a precious substance but which is required in larger quantities. This, like "cargo," is in the accusative, as is the following term, which I have rendered as "article" because σκεῦος, "vessel," was used on the basis of the Hebrew to indicate any object or instrument, from the "vessels" in the temple to the "vase of election" of Rom 9:23. As does "cargo," "every article" supports a series of genitives indicating the materials from which the objects/vases are made; ivory, precious wood (before which "every article" is repeated for the second time; we can note that here the "precious wood" has been made into an object/vase, while the thyine wood was uncarved), bronze, iron, and marble.

Having finished the series of articles and their materials, John takes up the list again, and returns, appropriately, to the accusative, recording spices, incenses, and foods whose value seems to be in inverse proportion to the amount required. He begins with rare and valuable substances that are needed only in small quantities (from "cinnamon" to "incense") and proceeds through increasingly common foods such as wine, oil, flour, and wheat. These last terms indicate large amounts of agrarian produce, which were transported in great quantities. Still in the accusative, John goes on, as in a rhetorical climax, to describe huge masses of materials being transported; for the first of these he uses collective terms ("herds" and "flocks"). He does not make explicit the species in question (such as "of cattle" or "of sheep") since these are already implied by the collective terms. After these, however, he does not use any more collective terms, but rather names the various categories of which the groups are comprised, putting them, correctly, in the genitive: "and [herds] of horses and [ranks] of chariots and [throngs] of [human] bodies." Thus the genitives can be explained as dependent on the collective nouns whose presence in the list is implicit after "herds and flocks." Finally, John concludes the list with a normal accusative plural ("souls"), which belongs on the same logical level as "cargo" and is followed by its genitive ("of men"), to make clear that these are not just any "lives," such as those of the marine animals in 16:13.

The "bodies" must be servants, as, for instance, in Gen 36:6, where Esau is said to take with him "his wives, his sons, his daughters, and all the bodies of his household." The expression "souls of men" appears as an object of commerce in Ezek 27:13, and thus might also be a reference to slaves. As we can see, John distinguishes the "bodies," which are genitive and depend on an implied collective noun, from the "souls," in the accusative, which supports a specifying genitive. Thus "bodies" and "souls" occupy different logical and syntactic levels, and should not be merged together. If John had simply meant to say "men" or "slaves," he would have said it, as he does elsewhere. His intent is to distinguish the commercial traffic of human bodies from that of human souls.

We may note in passing that there are twenty-nine items in the list of cargo; there is no foundation for the argument (see Bauckham 1993, particularly p. 31) that the number is 28, or 7 × 4, which would suggest the completeness (7) of the goods that come from the four corners of the earth and are destined for Rome. In any case, the whole list seems to have been composed with considerable care and a moderate degree of syntactical liberty. Many of its elements appear in Ezek 27:12-24, where the prophet lists the mercantile objects that poured into Tyre before its anticipated fall. The purpose of both lists, then, is to show the enormous wealth of a corrupt city that is about to be conquered and destroyed. We may also note, however, that the first part of the list includes the principal materials used in the furnishing of the temple and in the priestly vestments, including that "fine linen" whose presence here and in v. 16 some critics find perplexing since everywhere else its whiteness is associated with positive figures (see 17:4; 18:16 and comments). All the other materials mentioned can be found in connection both with good and with evil, but John uses "fine linen" exclusively in association with holiness, prayer, and purity. What function could it have in Rome? If the city in question is not Rome but a corrupt Jerusalem, then it makes perfect sense to find in the list sacred and priestly linen reduced to a mere mercantile commodity. Here, too, the unambiguous image or symbol should be taken as a guide to the interpretation of the more ambivalent or neutral objects of the list.

18:12 σιρικοῦ. The only passage in the OT to feature silk is the story of Jerusalem in Ezek 16. The prophet says that when Jerusalem reached the age of puberty she was beloved of God, who washed away her blood, fed her with fine flour, oil, and honey, and covered her with jewels and precious clothes, gold, silver, linen, and silk until she was "fit to be a queen" and her "fame spread among the nations" (vv. 8-14). Immediately afterward, however, Jerusalem prostituted herself and used the things that God had given her to make idols for herself and to prostitute herself on their altars (vv. 15-19). There are many parallels between this passage and ours, and the fact that the OT does not mention silk anywhere else seems to me a clear indication that John is referring to Jerusalem.

πᾶν ξύλον θύϊνον. The term indicates a valuable wood, known in antiquity for its resistance to damage, resinous and fragrant when burned (Homer, *Od.* 5.60). It came from the Arar tree, which has been known to botanists since the early 1900s as *Tetraclinis articulata* but used to be known as *Callitris quadrivalvis* or *Thuja articulata*. Today it grows only on the Atlantic coast of Morocco, in Malta, and in a very small area of Spain. It is probably one of the two trees that the Latins called "citrus," whose wood, which was variegated if taken from the roots, was extremely expensive and was used primarily in the construction of luxury tables, which were very much in fashion in the late republic and the imperial era. The tree gradually vanished from Egypt and the rest of North Africa (see Pliny, *Nat. hist.* 13.29.91–30.102; Olck 1899). The wood was also prized for construction (it was still used in the 9th century in the mosque at Cordoba — now the cathedral), but during the Middle Ages it was used only for its resin (sandarac). It is not certain whether John had so much botanical knowledge that he would make a point of choosing this precise tree rather than another. He probably meant to refer to a wood with which we are not familiar but that was freely used by Solomon in 1 Kings 10 and 2 Chr 2 and 9. In Hebrew it is called *almuggim* or *algummim*, which LXX renders as ξύλα πεύκινα (2 Chr 2:8 [7 in the Hebrew]; 9:10-11) or ξύλα πελεκητά (1 Kings 10:11-12 [twice]) and the Vg. as *ligna thyina* (1 Kings 10:11-12 [twice]; 2 Chr 9:10-11; but as *ligna pinea* in 2 Chr 2:8). This wood, which was probably resinous, came from Lebanon and was brought to Jerusalem by Hiram, king of Tyre and friend of Solomon.

The context in 1 Kings and 2 Chronicles is the splendor of Solomon's reign as expressed in the building of the temple and the palace in Jerusalem. We find here several elements that also appear in our "cargo," such as chariots and horses, as well as gold and silver, ivory (for the throne), incense (of the palace), and materials for the construction of the temple; most importantly, we find "the kings of the earth" — in fact, "all the kings of the earth" whom Solomon is said to excel in wealth and in wisdom, and over whom he "rules" (2 Chr 9:22-26 and parallels). Moreover, in 2 Chr 9:14 (= 1 Kings 10:15) we find all together "the traders and merchants . . . and all the kings of Arabia and the governors of the land" (LXX has τῶν ἐμπόρων καὶ πάντων τῶν βασιλέων τοῦ πέραν καὶ τῶν σατραπῶν τῆς γῆς: "the merchants and all the kings from far away and [all] the governors of the earth," which gives a universal significance to the text). Finally, we can observe that these very passages, which describe Hiram's collaboration with Solomon, are the foundation of the theological connection between Tyre and Jerusalem.

σκεῦος . . . χαλκοῦ . . . καὶ μαρμάρου. If all the elements of the list are references to the worship at Jerusalem and to the wealth of Solomon, then also the vessels/articles "of bronze" are a reference to the numerous bronze instruments in the temple and especially to the receptacles for the purification of offerings and the enormous basin known as "the sea" that contained water for the purification of the priests (1 Kings 7:23-39; 2 Kings 25:13-17; 2 Chr 4:1-6, etc.). The vessels/articles "of marble" might be the stone basins of various sizes, hollowed out with a lathe that the most observant Jews used to hold water for purification, as we have learned from recent discoveries at ʿAin Feshkha and Jerusalem (see John 2:6; see Avigad 1990, pp. 82ff. and 86-89; see also *m. Yoma Tob* 2:3).

18:14 ἡ ὀπώρα . . . ψυχῆς. The cluster of genitives renders this expression rather unwieldy (for the order of words, see 13:3 and 11). The object in question, "seasonal fruit," might be either the object of the city's desire (its imported goods) or else, as is perhaps more likely, the result of the city's "soul's desire" and thus that which the city produces and is prepared to sell to the pagans in exchange for their goods. I think the sentence is yet another version of the usual accusation that Israel has abandoned her vocation as the salt of the earth, the seat of the salvific promise that includes the pagans, for the sake of trading with them, which means entering into idolatrous covenants with them. Rather than preserving the holy things that were entrusted to her (probably so that she could give them freely to the nations at the coming of Christ), Israel has treated them as her own property and even as objects of commerce, and has handed Jesus over to the Romans so that she may be allowed to keep them; for this reason they will be taken from her, and what had been destined for her by God will instead be given to the Christians.

καὶ πάντα . . . τὰ λαμπρά. If the interpretation I have been proposing is the correct one, then the "sumptuous things and the splendid things" represent Jewish worship, with its sacrificial victims (the sumptuous things; lit. "fat, greasy") and its splendors. This all came to an end in 70 CE, at least as a public phenomenon, and this sentence seems to reflect the Christian awareness that Jewish sacrificial worship had lost its meaning and that God had decided to put a permanent end to it.

18:17 πᾶς κυβερνήτης . . . ἐργάζονται. The text distinguishes four categories of people who travel by sea. The first are helmsmen or captains who are able to sail on the open sea; then come those "who sail locally" (see *m. Ned.* 3:6, where the text distinguishes between "those who go from Accra to Jaffa" and "those who sail at large"). Next come "seamen," who are not given a fuller description but may be the helmsmen's crews, and in last place come those who practice trade by sea, probably marine merchants as distinct from the land merchants in the previous verses. These seem to be the same as "those who have ships in the sea" (v. 19) and are thus both merchants and ship-owners, two categories that often coincided in antiquity.

18:20 Εὐφραίνου. Like "the heavens" in 12:12, "heaven" is here invited to rejoice. The only other people of whom John says that "they rejoice" are "those who dwell on the land," who rejoice at the murder of the two witnesses. It may be rather alienating to contemporary sensibilities that not only do the wicked rejoice at the suffering of the righteous but the heavens, with the "holy ones and the apostles and the prophets" (who dwell in heaven, or at least are destined to do so), rejoice at the punishment of the wicked. This phenomenon is one of the results of a theology of reversal. The overthrowing of the wicked, who are victorious within history, coincides with the eschatological salvation of the righteous. Since the "cry of Abel," who asks God to exterminate the seed of Cain (1 Enoch 22:7), apocalyptic texts, including Christian ones, give considerable evidence of a thirst for justice that at times looks very much like a thirst for revenge, especially when the extermination and punishment of the wicked take place before the eyes of the righteous (see, e.g., 1 Enoch 56:8 or 62:6 [BS]). This attitude is born, in the first place, of the frustration of those who see themselves as the suffering righteous while witnessing the earthly happiness of the wicked; the anticipation of the future pain of the wicked, often in a very physical and human otherworld, provides some comfort amid present anguish. In the second place, the threat of the pains of hell can provide a disincentive for those members of the religious community who might be susceptible to external and worldly (and thus ultimately diabolic) temptations.

Both of these motivations may be at work for John, although his visions have little to say about the fate of the damned after death (in fact, John's lack of interest in the subject is one of the literary reasons for the wealth of apocryphal texts that fill this "gap"). He seems to be focusing on the "historic" destiny of the foes, whose destruction is described in ways that leave little room for a mystical reading such as an interpretation that sees the various massacres as symbolic language created to describe the destruction of evil and thus really about the salvation of sinners. In any case, the future suffering of others might have been intended as a corrective to the present sufferings of those followers of Jesus who shared John's views, as well, judging from the threats in the opening letters (2:5, 16, 22-23; 3:3), as a disincentive for Christians of other persuasions whose behavior John believed to be sinful or ambiguous.

ἔκρινεν . . . αὐτῆς. There are two possible explanations for the phrase. According to the first, God appears to avenge the wrongs suffered by his people; he takes on himself the task of *carrying out* the judgment that Israel would pass against her enemies if she were able. According to the second and more probable interpretation, God turns away the judgment of condemnation that would strike even spiritual Israel, since all humans are sinners, and redirects it against Israel's enemies; people are saved because of God's merciful will and not because of their own righteousness or holiness (for the meaning of ἐκ see 6:10 and 15:2).

18:21 βληθήσεται . . . ἔτι. "Babylon" is destined to undergo the same treatment as Satan and his angels, who were "thrown down" so that their place was "not found anymore" in heaven (see 12:8-9). In 11:2 (with ἐκβάλλω) the outer court of the temple is also "thrown outside." There seems to be a pattern underlying various scenes of the book. A part of the angels, first created and loved by God (the "third part"; 12:4), is "thrown," a part of the temple (the third element; see comments on 11:1-2) is "thrown," and now "Babylon" "will be thrown." This seems to be consistent with my argument that Babylon is Jerusalem (a great city "in three parts" in 16:19), which was first loved and is now "thrown" by God, as we read in Jer 23:39, where "the city" and its inhabitants are referred to as a "burden" and cast far away from the face of God. The biblical precedents for the scene are Jer 51:63-64 (28:63, LXX), in which God tells the prophet to tie "a stone" to the scroll containing his prophecy and to throw it "into the middle of the Euphrates," prophesying that "thus shall Babylon sink"; and Ezek 26:12, where Tyre is told that her "stones" will be "cast into the middle of the sea" by her victorious enemies. In John gestures of this sort are performed not by humans but by an angel. This one "lifts up" (from the earth? to heaven? see Jer 23:39) the "stone" and casts it "into the sea." Babylon's end is the same as that of Pharaoh of Egypt (Exod 15:1), who ended up in the sea without human intervention, as is recorded among the curses against Egypt in 4Q158 (4QReworked Pentateuchª, fr. 14, 1:7-8: ". . . Thrown] into the middle of the sea, into the depths of the abyss [. . ."), a sentence based on a pun on the correspondence between "sea" and "abyss" (of Sheol).

John's image takes up several passages from earlier chapters where we saw "a large star, burning like a torch," fall from heaven "upon the springs of water" (8:10) and "something like a great mountain, burning with fire, . . . thrown into the sea" (8:8), not to mention "a star fallen from heaven to the earth" (9:1). The thing thrown in this case is rather less noble, being neither a spiritual star nor a mountain, but merely "a stone," possibly carved out of a mountain. It must have a certain dignity of its own to be described as "great" (see 1:10), even if it has degenerated enough to be compared to a millstone, the same stone that in Mark 9:42 and parallels drags into the sea those who "scandalize . . . these little ones" (Mark uses the term βέβληται). Satan's fall from heaven thus becomes the model for all later falls. In the synoptic Gospels as well, when something, whether a pig or a mountain, is thrown into the sea, it is usually something that can be interpreted as demonic, or at any rate as connected to the forces of evil (see Mark 5:13 and parallels and 11:23 and parallel). The gesture of the "strong" angel, which the visionary witnesses and the angel immediately explains, is intensely prophetic; it is the divine guarantee of the fall of Babylon. This means that at the time at which John situates his composition in literary terms, the city has yet to fall (which explains the future tense of the verbs), but it does not mean that the book was written before the destruction of Jerusalem (see Introduction, p. 44).

18:22-23 φωνὴ κιθαρῳδῶν . . . ἀκουσθῇ ἐν σοὶ ἔτι. The address to the city that is destined for destruction includes several elements from biblical prophecies. The bulk of the passage comes from various places in Jeremiah that lament over or threaten Jerusalem; in Jer 25:10 we find the bridegroom, the bride, the millstone (either domestic or from the mill), and the lamp. This must have been a recurring theme in Jeremiah's preaching, as we find it repeated in part in 7:34 and 16:9 (the bride and bridegroom) as well as in Bar 2:23 (the bride and the bridegroom). The voice of the bride and bridegroom, representing the promise of a future restoration for Jerusalem and for the "cities of Judah," appears also in Jer 33:10-11. John is quoting exactly from a famous *topos* which refers exclusively to Jerusalem's destiny. The "craftsmen" must be "the artisans and the smiths" who were deported from Jerusalem in Jer 24:1. Their presence should be profoundly significant because "the work of the artisan" is an idolatrous activity that "the house of Israel" is forbidden to engage in, according to Jer 10:9. The echo of Jeremiah, therefore, anchors John's work still more firmly to Jerusalem and her destruction (there is a similar lament, also for Jerusalem, in 2 *Bar.* 10:6-19). "Lyres," together with "kettledrums" and "wine," appear in Isa 24:8 in a threat uttered against a land and an enemy city that are unnamed, but whose inhabitants are said to have "transgressed the laws" and "broken the everlasting covenant" (Isa 24:5); the silencing of "lyres" and "songs" and the prospect that a city "will never be found again" appear in Ezek 26:13 and 21 in a threat directed to Tyre (see comments on 17:5).

Among the many "voices" there is also that "of a millstone," which should properly be a "sound." The same occurs with the voices "of flute players and of trumpeters" (one does not hear their voices while they play, but the sound of their instruments), although the translation is less harsh. It is quite common in Hebrew, especially in poetic texts, that the sound of a musical instrument is called a "voice." The millstone can be considered as such, or its voice may refer to the singing of the maids who turned it. John is faithful to Jer 25:10, which has "voice of millstones" (or: "voice of the milling maids") in Hebrew, while LXX interprets otherwise.

18:23 ὅτι οἱ ἔμποροί σου . . . ἔθνη. The end of the address consists of two parts of sentences in close parallel, underlined by the anaphoric repetition of ὅτι. Within this parallel structure, which places the verbs in the central position in each part, there is a syntactic chiasmus, since "merchants" and "all the nations," the respective subjects of the verbs, are at opposite ends. I do not know whether this is intended to place "merchants" and "nations" in symbolic opposition. As regards the content, the first part of the parallel is almost a direct quotation from the last part of Isa 23:8 ("whose merchants were princes, whose traders were the honored ones of the earth"; LXX: οἱ ἔμποροι αὐτῆς ἔνδοξοι ἄρχοντες τῆς γῆς, "her merchants were glorious princes of the earth"), which originally referred to Tyre, while the magic potion for poisoning seems to be connected with Isa 47:9, where Babylon is an enchantress, or with Nah 3:4, where the city/witch is Nineveh (but see comments on 17:5).

The phrase "your merchants" reopens the ambiguity we saw earlier; are these merchants who belong to the city or live in her, or do they do business with her and take her as their merchandise (see οἱ ἔμποροι τούτων in v. 15; vv. 11, 14; and comments on 18:3)? As for the "chief men of the earth," the question is once again what γῆ really means here. The "chief men" must be the same as those in 6:15 who, together with the "kings of the earth," seek refuge among rocks and mountains. We can also note that these two passages contain the only occurrences in the NT of the term μεγιστᾶνες, along with Mark 6:21, where it is used to indicate the dignitaries of Herod's court. The context of its use in Mark, for what it is worth, recalls Jewish "kings" and "chief men," albeit evil ones.

Finally, the fact that "all the nations" are afflicted by the city's poison might suggest that the city is not part of "all the nations."

18:24 αἷμα . . . γῆς. These may be the words of the angel or of John, but, in any case, they bring to a close the scene of the strong angel with the millstone with a return to the theme of spilled blood, which is typical of polemics against Jerusalem (see comments on 16:4). The presence of the "blood of prophets" in particular (see 16:6), together with the blood of "all those slaughtered upon the earth" (see 6:9), is a clear parallel to Matt 23:34-35, 37, quoted earlier, in which Jesus threatens to bring against the Jews "all the righteous blood shed on earth" (see Matt 27:25, "His blood [Jesus', deemed as "righteous" in 27:19] be on us and on our children").

19**:1** ὡς φωνήν . . . πολλοῦ. The use of "like" and of the adjective "great" (both of which, however, are absent in parts of the tradition) suggests that what John hears is not a real voice, analogous to a human voice (see following comments). The expression "like the . . . voice of a large throng" (which occurs again in v. 6) is drawn once again from Dan 10:6 (and see *Ps. Sol.* 8:2), which was used earlier in Apoc 1:13-15. There, however, the figure who appeared (the Risen One) had a voice "like the voice of many waters" (which also recurs in v. 6). Besides its appearance in this verse, the "large throng" appears only in 7:9, where it is used of the throng of the saved in white robes who, in 7:10, "shout with a great voice." Is the "great voice" of 19:1 the same as that of 7:10?

λεγόντων. This genitive plural is usually explained as a *constructio ad sensum* on the genitive plural of a name that is implied: "voice/crowd of (men and/or angels) who said" (see 7:9); strictly speaking, the one who speaks ought to be that which is "like a voice." Could this voice possibly be several beings or voices? See also λεγόντων in v. 6, which can be explained in various ways (as agreeing with "crowd," "waters," and "thunders" or as agreeing only with "thunders"; as referring to the three "voices" but attracted to the genitive because it is preceded by two genitives).

19:2 ἔφθειρεν . . . αὐτῆς. In 11:18 John foresaw the destruction of those "who destroy the land"; here we learn that "the prostitute, the great one," "destroyed the earth/land." The quotation from Jer 51:25 is certainly a reference to Babylon (see comments on 11:18). We can note that Jeremiah speaks of "the whole earth," whereas in both passages (here and 11:18) John simply says γῆ, "earth" or "land," which leaves open the possibility that he means Israel, the Land, by antonomasia. If so, then it would make perfect sense that the destruction comes about "through her prostitution"; it would be another repetition of the prophetic *topos* about unworthy guides leading Israel to her ruin (see comments on 3:17 and 17:9).

19:3 δεύτερον. The term "Hallelujah" appears four times in the first six verses of this chapter, and nowhere else in the book, nor indeed in the NT. Three times it is the first word uttered by "something like a voice." It is unclear why John stresses the fact that this is a second utterance, unless he wants to make clear that this is the same plural subject that uttered the preceding doxology (see comments on 19:4 and 6). He apparently wants to accentuate this plurality, although he mentions hearing only "something like a great voice."

19:4 ἔπεσαν. This is the last of the repeated gestures of adoration on the part of the twenty-four elders. This scene of worship was introduced in 4:10 and appears in 5:8, 14, 7:11, 11:16, and here. There are slight variations as regards who "fall" to the ground and what they proclaim. In this passage the elders and living creatures fall and bow down, and all say "Amen" and "Hallelujah" (the "Amen" is uttered only by the living creatures in 5:14, and by everybody in 7:12). What is new here is the "Hallelujah." The destruction of the city/prostitute is the cause of repeated rejoicing (the double "Hallelujah" may correspond antithetically to the double "Woe") from the "large throng in heaven," and the scene of adoration makes clear not only that its destruction is in accord with the will of God ("Amen") but also that the associated joy ("Hallelujah") reaches "God . . . who sits on the throne." We may observe, however, that by the time it reaches the throne the shout of exultation has lost its descriptive content ("prostitute . . . blood . . . smoke") and arrives reduced to its bare essentials ("Amen, Hallelujah").

19:5 φωνὴ ἀπὸ τοῦ θρόνου. The response from the throne is not long in coming. The "Voice" confirms that here indeed is reason for universal rejoicing, expressed as "Praise our God"; here also, however, any hint of the original motive for the rejoicing (the destruction of the prostitute) vanishes and is replaced by the invitation to praise.

19:6 ἤκουσα . . . ἰσχυρῶν. The three instances of "something like a voice" correspond to the "something like a voice of a large throng" in v. 1, to "like a voice of many waters" in 1:15 and 14:2, and probably to "like a voice of great thunder" in 14:2, which recalls "like a voice of thunder" in 6:1. It is apparently deliberate on John's part that the three things "like voices" make their final appearance together. Their appearances in the text are ordered in a *crescendo*, and the third "something like a voice" is expressed in a slightly different way from the previous ones: the first time it appeared it was "like a voice of thunder," then "like a voice of great thunder," and finally "like a voice of strong thunders," in a return to the plurality of the voices of thunders in ch. 10. Although this is clearly deliberate, its significance is not entirely clear. Is there a theological purpose to the variations in the description of the third member, a purpose that might be relevant to the definition of God (see comments on 11:17), or is it a matter of style or of some other factor? It is hard to imagine that there could be any substantive significance to the case of "like a voice of thunder/great thunder/strong thunders," except, possibly, that these variations reflect John's sense of the simultaneous multiplicity and individuality of the voice/voices, a multiplicity and individuality that can be expressed by using plural verbs with singular subjects ("voice"; see v. 1 and possibly also v. 6). Could this be a special way of communicating the unison of angels and holy ones? Similar linguistic liberty is taken in *ShirShabb*, whose editor wrote about the intentional violations of syntax and of the ordinary meaning of terms in a text that tries to communicate something of the elusive transcendence of a heavenly reality (Newsom 1985, p. 49).

John seems to know and reproduce the language of ancient Jewish mysticism — a language that would have been lost to us were it not for the fortuitous discoveries in the Judean desert. Should we suppose that there were real ecstatic experiences behind texts similar to this one? At all events, it is clear that John has scant regard for the laws of elegant prose. On the other hand, part of the fascination that the Apocalypse exerts comes precisely from its apparently intentional carelessness, which gives to the book a linguistic color that has few known parallels (see 22:3-4).

Ἀλληλουϊά. The "Hallelujah" that bursts from the "large throng" in heaven reaches the throne by means of the elders and living creatures, is confirmed by the "voice . . . from the throne," and now spreads throughout the cosmos by the mediation of the three "like voices" that come from the "large throng . . . many waters and . . . strong thunders" and that seem to belong to all the inhabitants of heaven in unison. It is a choral response to the invitation in the preceding verse and, like the invitation, does not make any reference to the prostitute. In fact, the "prostitute" and her "prostitution" are not mentioned again after 19:2. Just as the "woman" of ch. 12 seems to vanish "into the desert" (Pippin 1992, p. 72), so the prostitute vanishes, or at least appears to, in a superficial reading of the text. We must in fact imagine that she has been burned up and her flesh devoured by the "horns" and the "beast," as was foreseen in 17:16, or that she has been "thrown," as was prophesied in 18:21, and has disappeared completely ("shall never again be found"; ibid.); in the latter case she would have avoided eternal pain. But as all the wicked, living and dead, end up in the marsh of fire (20:14-15), would not the prostitute do so also?

19:7 ὁ γάμος τοῦ ἀρνίου. The negative elements that filled the chapter's first and second hymns of exaltation are now left behind; this chorus announces the positive motives for rejoicing. The "reign" of v. 6 is recalled (for which see comments on 20:4), and the "marriage of the Lamb" appears for the first time, together with "his woman" and, in v. 8, the "fine linen, bright, pure." These three are all connected, as the fine linen is the garment with which the woman "has prepared herself" for a marriage that could not take place without her. In keeping with his usual pattern of gradual revelation, John does not tell us until 21:9 the identity of this last woman in the book. I will follow his example for the moment and simply point out that, after the "prostitute" and her "prostitution" have been mentioned for the last time (in v. 2), the "woman" can appear, and John can mention the marriage for the first time.

There is clearly an antithetical connection between the "woman/prostitute" of ch. 17 and this new woman who appears when the other disappears: until the first is destroyed there can be no marriage. Why is this? If the last woman in the Apocalypse is, as we shall see, the church, and if the prostitute were Rome, then John would be binding the (eschatological) marriage of the

Lamb to victory over the Roman Empire, the manifestation of idolatrous Satanic power. It is not, however, the Lamb who destroys the prostitute but rather the Satanic forces (see comments on 17:16) who are still so alive and active after the destruction of the city that they challenge the Lamb on two separate occasions; the marriage will take place only after the final victory. The city/prostitute, all in all, is a secondary figure, a transitory instrument of the forces of evil, who use her and then destroy her.

So why, then, do John's female figures follow one after the other? First of all, the heavenly woman disappears "into the desert" and is not mentioned again. Then John sees the prostitute, also "in a desert." Let us assume that both figures are really the same woman — Israel, who has been seduced by Satan in the desert (see comments on 17:3). Now, if the bride of the Lamb is the church, *verus Israel*, it is theologically as well as logically necessary that the prostitute/Israel who has been corrupted by Satanic idolatry must disappear to make way for the text's final and definitive woman to appear. If this is correct, then the three great feminine figures of the Apocalypse all describe a unified reality: first the heavenly and the earthly Israel, the holder of the promise, then the historical Israel, corrupted by Satanic power, and finally the eschatological Israel, the church of Jesus Christ. This does not necessarily mean that each woman appearing in the text is actually the same, but rather that what we see as the "woman symbol" (and what for John was not unlike the male angelomorphic figures he describes; see comments on 21:9 and 1:20) has a single meaning throughout the text. By presenting the church of Jesus Christ as a woman who is destined for marriage to the Lamb, John emphasizes both the continuity and the newness of the new religious movement with respect to Judaism: what is entirely new is actually presented as something that has been restored after having been irretrievably lost. It is no coincidence that in 21:2 the new and holy Jerusalem descends again from that same "heaven" that the heavenly woman abandoned to flee into the "desert" in 12:6: a heaven that the prostitute has never known.

19:8 βύσσινον . . . καθαρόν. "Fine linen" appeared earlier as something negative — as an object of commerce in 18:12 and then as the robe of the prostitute Jerusalem in 18:16 — but here and in v. 14 (where it is "white, pure") fine linen finally appears in its true splendor as a spiritual "Christian" linen. Its radiance and its spiritual significance are immediately explained as representing "the justifications of the holy ones." The expression probably means that the "holy ones" are not such by their own merit or nature, but that they have been "justified" or "made just" by God (see comments on 15:4). Salvation can be given freely only by God, and cannot be achieved by humans by means of observance or virtue (Christianity is a product of a form of Judaism that is opposed to the position of *Ezra;* see Introduction, pp. 13-14). Much less, John insists, is salvation an *object of commerce,* something that can be bought and sold, which is what non-Christian Judaism had reduced it too; the only legitimate theological transaction is the purchase that Jesus Christ made with his own blood. It seems to me that by contrasting "fine linen" to "fine linen, bright, pure" John again intends to distance himself and his followers from official Judaism and Jewish worship with its purity laws and priestly vestments; even Jewish purity, in his opinion, had become an object of commerce and no longer brings salvation (for the baptismal symbolism connected with white robes and for the relationship between water and the salvific blood of the cross see comments on 19:13 and 14).

19:9 Καὶ λέγει μοι. Up to this point the "voices" have expressed themselves only in the plural: the abrupt change of subject is somewhat disconcerting. This new figure is male and has authority; he orders John to write (see 1:19), utters one of the seven blessings (see 1:3 and comments), announces for a second time the marriage of the Lamb, to whose "supper" all those "called" are now invited, and finally he declares the words of God to be true. The invitation to the marriage supper comes immediately after the reference to the "justifications of the holy ones," which strongly suggests that it is the direct consequence of that justification. Once again we can compare a text of the Apocalypse to a passage from Matthew, in this case with the parable of the wedding banquet (Matt 22:2-14). The first Gospel (unlike Luke 14:16-24) not only makes the presence of the guests dependent on a "wedding robe" (the "fine linen" of the Apocalypse) but also ties the entire scene to the vicissitudes of Judaism and the destruction by fire of the "city" (Jerusalem).

19:10 καὶ ἔπεσα . . . αὐτῷ. The refusal to accept John's worship has parallels in contemporary apocalypses, in which a visionary is prompted by a vision of angelic glory to worship the angel, who rejects the worship (see Tob 12:16-22; *Asc. Isa.* 7:18-23; 8:1–10:15; *2 Enoch* 1:4-8; Stuckenbruck 1995). For all the gigantic and splendid angels that John has seen, only here and in the parallel scene in 22:8-9 does he make a gesture of worship, and find his gesture rejected. Neither here nor in ch. 22 is the speaker described. John is moved to worship not by his external appearance but by what he says. His words do not seem to be particularly extraordinary in themselves, but coming at the culmination of all the words that precede them they bring John to the point at which he throws himself to the ground to worship the one who reveals them. Indeed, since the beginning of the chapter he has been listening to heavenly "voices" who, although manifold, speak in unison and who apparently sum up in themselves all the "voices" heard by him and other prophets and announce to him a disorienting and thrilling series of events. The city/prostitute has been judged and condemned to the fire; the news reaches the throne of God; all the heavens rejoice; marvelous announcements follow one after the other — the reign of God, the marriage of the Lamb and his woman, the giving of white linen robes for the salvation of men. Finally, the "called" are invited to the supper, thus fulfilling the promises of God. For John, this is the high point of the revelation; those "called to the marriage supper of the Lamb" are "blessed," and in this invitation the word of God is shown to be true. In other words, salvation is brought about by means of the Christian victory. This is indeed the heart of the revelation. John believes that this proclamation — the new Christian reality that replaces non-Christian Judaism — can come only from a divine figure, and thus he attempts to worship him, but he is mistaken in doing so, and his gesture is rejected.

The text does not tell us who the speaker is, nor even that it is an angel (which may constitute a departure from the traditional terms of the apocalyptic *topos;* but see comments on 22:8-9). The figure who addresses John describes himself as a "fellow servant" of his and of his "brothers" to whom also has been given "the testimony of Jesus," which is "the spirit of prophecy." This last detail, which is added in explanation either by the speaker or by John himself and which comes at the moment of the speaker's disappearance from the text, is significant. Whoever the figure is, whether angel or saint or an ancient prophet now in heaven, what is important is that he means to present himself simply as a prophet and not as a divine being (for the "prophets" as "brothers" see 22:9 and comments). John's words represent a further element in his polemic against those Jews who do not acknowledge Jesus; if the prophetic spirit bears witness to Jesus, then Jesus should have been recognized by whoever reads the Scriptures. The figure's reproach to John, who sees the declaration that the words of God are true as evidence of a divine revelation, really represents the condemnation of non-Christian Judaism, which does not recognize the fulfillment of the prophecies in Jesus or the church.

19:11 εἶδον . . . ἠνεῳγμένον. The rebuff of his attempted worship has put John back on the right path, so to speak, and made him able to receive the next revelations. After a series of auditions (the last time the phrase "I saw" appeared was in 18:1; since then there have been a series of recurrences of the verb "to hear," from the "I heard" of 18:4 to that of 19:6) John now returns to seeing complex scenes ("I saw" will appear nine times up to 21:2, and in 21:3 the return of "I heard" will mark a new transition). For the second and last time heaven opens. Differently from 6:14, where the sky was opened by the wrath of God, John here describes primarily or exclusively the salvific aspects of God's opening of heaven, an opening that thus has more in common with that of the "door" in 4:1. The beginning of ch. 4 also marked the end of a long series of auditions (the dictation of the seven messages) and the beginning of the largest section of the visions; now that it is heaven itself that opens and not merely a door in it, it seems reasonable to assume that the visions that follow will be the most important ones.

καὶ ἰδοὺ ἵππος λευκός. On some occasions the vision is revealed gradually, and John at first sees only the details that surround or underlie what will eventually prove to be the main object of the vision (see 1:12-13 ["lampstands"], 4:2 ["throne"], 14:14 ["clouds"], here ["horse"], and 20:11 ["throne"]). The vision in 6:1-8 of the four horses (white, red, black, and green) and the four figures sitting on them is analogous to this, as is the vision in 9:17 of the monstrous cavalry; in this case John describes the "horses" in detail but describes the riders only by their armors. Something along the same lines also happens in 4:4, where he sees first of all "twenty-four thrones . . . around the throne" and then "seated on the thrones twenty-four elders"; other cases are ambiguous, as, for instance, 4:6, where he sees "in the middle of the throne and around the throne . . . four living creatures," and 5:6, where he sees "in the midst of the throne and the four living creatures, and in the midst of the elders, a Lamb standing." None of these characters are ever defined as angels, and the normal angels do not receive the same attention. This pattern does not hold for female figures, whether negative or positive (in 17:3 we immediately see "a woman sitting on a scarlet beast" rather than first the beast and then the woman, and in 12:1 we see "a woman wrapped in the sun, and the moon was under her feet . . ."). When a single masculine figure, usually a seated one, is revealed in this gradual way, not only does John not say that it is an angel, but he does not even explain what he is, and on only one occasion before this one does he give the figure's name.

ὁ καθήμενος. The description of the figure "sitting" on the white horse is so detailed that it lasts until v. 16 (v. 14 describes the figure's followers). Many of his distinguishing features not only come from ancient prophetic visions but recall word-for-word, or nearly so, visions that John had earlier in the book. This raises the hermeneutical problem of whether the one sitting on the horse is a new figure with respect to those earlier figures who were also mostly "sitting," or whether he represents the full revelation of a single figure, whose name and attributes we finally learn.

The name, which seems to be the central element of the revelation, is complex. First of all, John says that "he has a name written that no one knows save himself" (v. 12), but then he goes on to reveal it as "the Word of God." The obvious reference is to John's Gospel, and in particular to John 1:1, but the Logos as God's manifestation, "Word," creative power, intermediary, "Firstborn Son," "first among the angels," and revelation of the transcendent

Father can also be found in Hellenistic Judaism, particularly in Philo of Alexandria (e.g., *De conf. ling.* 146). This idea comes from the Stoic and Platonic tradition, entered learned Alexandrian Jewish circles probably through Philo, and was appropriated by an important segment of primitive Christianity, which took it as the basis of its Christology. This is the only time that the term "Logos" is used in the Apocalypse to refer to a character, but the expression is deeply rooted both in the book's immediate and distant context. At the beginning of the description the "Word of God" is called "true" (ἀληθινός . . . ὁ λόγος τοῦ θεοῦ; vv. 11-13), which is a deliberate echo of the "true words of God" (οἱ λόγοι ἀληθινοὶ τοῦ θεοῦ) in v. 9, the mere mention of which caused John to fall down in adoration. Moreover, the Word is also defined as "faithful" (πιστός; "faithful and true" in v. 11). On the one hand, this is an anticipation of 21:5 and 22:6, where the expression "faithful and true words" will reappear; on the other, it is a double quotation of 1:5, where Jesus Christ is called "the faithful witness" (ὁ μάρτυς ὁ πιστός) or possibly "the Witness, the Faithful" (this is the first recurrence both of "witness" and of "faithful") and of 3:14, where "the Amen" is defined as "the faithful and true witness." This implies that John wants to identify Jesus Christ with the Amen and with the Logos, and that he is using the passage with the Logos to bring together into one the various definitions that are scattered throughout the book. If we go on to analyze the occurrences of the expression "true" (when it appears without "the faithful"), we find that the "true" one is defined in 3:7 as "the holy one . . . who has the key of David" and the absolute power to open and close and that in 6:10 the term is used of "the Master, the holy and true" who is called on to "judge" by the souls of "those slaughtered for the word of God." It seems likely that John intended all these passages to point toward this one. He uses the same strategy when he gives the Logos his last title in this passage: "King of kings and Lord of lords" (βασιλεὺς βασιλέων καὶ κύριος κυρίων; v. 16), which recalls not only that in 17:14 the Lamb is κύριος κυρίων ἐστὶν καὶ βασιλεὺς βασιλέων but also that in 1:5 Jesus Christ is said to be "the Ruler of the kings of the earth" (ὁ ἄρχων τῶν βασιλέων τῆς γῆς). By his frequent use of parallel phrases with slight differences John implies that Jesus Christ, the Lamb, and the Word are the same. In view of this passage's central place within the book's internal structure we might ask whether "Word of God" is that "new name" which is characteristic of the Christian message and whose revelation has been anticipated since 2:17. The newness of the name being revealed is further emphasized by the declaration that "no man knows [it] save he himself" (v. 12); if it was not previously known to men, then for them it is indeed a "new name."

This figure's appearance on the scene parallels that of the four horsemen of ch. 6, and is analogous in particular to 6:2 (the "victor" seated on the "white horse") and antithetical to 6:8, which describes the appearance of the only one of the horsemen whose name John reveals: "And, lo, a green horse, and he who was sitting upon it; his name was [the] Death" (for the "green" see comments on 6:8). The Word takes fully on himself the characteristics of the only other figure seated on a white horse (see comments on 6:2 and 10:1) and is opposed to the figure on the green horse as life is opposed to death.

ἐν δικαιοσύνῃ . . . πολεμεῖ. This expression introduces one of the important new elements in this passage. On the one hand, one might expect that "the true" would be said to judge "by means of righteousness" as this would recall a rich series of passages from "true and just are his judgments" (19:2; a direct quotation of the words of the altar in 16:7, words that in turn echo the song of Moses or of the Lamb in 15:3, explaining that the "ways" of the song must be understood to mean "judgments") to the words of the angel of the waters who proclaims, "You are just . . . because you have decreed [in Greek the same verb that means "to judge"] these things" (16:5), and to the invitation to the "true" to judge (6:10). Thus this passage reinforces the connection between "true," "judgment," and "righteousness" by explaining that the Word of God is the author of the judgment.

The same sentence also says that the one sitting on the horse does not confine himself to judging with righteousness but also judges and "makes war." There is a strong connection in Jewish traditions between judgment and the (eschatological) battle. "Then the sword of God will pounce in the era of judgment and all the sons of the t[ru]th will awaken, to destroy [the sons of] wickedness, and all the sons of guilt will no longer exist" (Hodayot [1QH–4QH] 14:29-30). John highlights the detail that "a sharp sword" comes from the "mouth" of the Logos (v. 15). The sword is thus no longer a punishing angel from God but rather is dependent on the Logos, and the battle is merely a superficial manifestation of the judgment uttered by his "mouth," although it is not any the less terrible for that. This is the last time that the verb "make war" appears in the text, and John explains its meaning: if God is to fight, through the mediation of the Logos, then the fight must consist in a righteous judgment of condemnation against whoever dares oppose him. This probably means, moreover, that all the scenes of battle, whether they are announced, have taken place (as, e.g., 12:7-9), or are expected to take place in the future, must be interpreted as scenes of judgment.

The element of condemnation that accompanies the righteous judgment is worth noting not only because, in the perspective of the Apocalypse, it involves seeing justice done in response to blood (6:10; 19:2), but because throughout primitive Christianity salvation did not consist in being judged by God and absolved (since sinful human nature would render that impossible) but rather in escaping judgment, in not being judged, because the saved are "justified" through Jesus Christ. Judgment thus represents salvation for the justified (i.e., for those who believe and thereby accept salvation) and condemnation for unbelievers (see especially Rom 3:21-26).

19:12 γεγραμμένον. John does not say where the name is written. As he has just mentioned the "head" and the "diadems," we may imagine that this name, unlike that written on the "garment" and on the "thigh," is written on the head, as is usual in the case of written names (see 19:16 and comments). The diadems are "many," but they have no number; see the comments to 3:11 and 7:9.

19:13 περιβεβλημένος . . . αἵματι. The subject is still "he who was sitting." Critics largely agree that the expression refers to Christ's salvific death and thus that the "blood" in which the Word has dipped his garment is his own. The ancient pattern for this idea is Jacob's blessing of Judah, in which the patriarch "plunges his garments into wine" (πλυνεῖ ἐν οἴνῳ τὴν στολὴν αὐτοῦ; Gen 49:11, LXX); the switch from wine to blood enabled the first Christians to see the passage as a prophecy of Jesus' saving death, which gave rise to phrases such as that of Apoc 7:14 (see comments), which is probably being echoed here. This passage also represents the last appearance of the term "blood," and thus draws together and concludes the series of expressions that begins with "he who has . . . freed us from our sins by means of his blood" (1:5). The salvific dimension of Christ's blood is mentioned no fewer than five times in the book (1:5; 5:9; 7:14; 12:11; 19:13). The "garment" must thus be Jesus' body: 7:14 (στολή) and 3:4 (ἱμάτιον) seem to show that an article of clothing can represent a body.

19:14 στρατεύματα. These are cavalry, like the troops in 9:16 to whom they are contrasted with respect to their horses and clothing, their clothing being the only detail used to describe their persons in both passages. John does not tell us the nature of the riders even here, but he does use masculine adjectives to describe them, whereas the term "troops" is neutral (see comments on 19:19). Further, while the Satanic army has a number, heard by John at 9:16, here there is no number (see comments on 19:12 and 19). The army is "in heaven" (see *Hodayot* [1QH–4QH] 11:35) and follows the Word as the members of the "one hundred forty-four thousand" (who were also male) followed the Lamb in 14:4. John nowhere tells us the color of the clothing of the "one hundred forty-four thousand," but the "great throng" mentioned immediately after them in 7:9 are characterized by their "white robes," just as the heavenly army is now characterized by its whiteness: their clothes are not simply white, but of "fine linen, white, pure." The immediate echo is thus of 19:8 (see comments ad loc.). If, however, white fine linen is "the justifications of the holy ones," then these followers of the Word, like the followers of the Lamb, must also be humans justified by God and thus "in heaven."

19:15   ἐκ τοῦ στόματος αὐτοῦ. The "sharp sword" that comes "from his mouth" recalls the opening vision of 1:16 and the echoes of it in the letters (2:12 and 16) and looks ahead to the vision of the conflict in v. 21. What is relatively new in this passage is the task of "smiting the nations," which is also given to this sword (probably on the model of Isa 11:4: "He shall strike the earth with the rod of his mouth"; LXX: πατάξει γῆν τῷ λόγῳ τοῦ στόματος αὐτοῦ: "he will strike the earth with the word of his mouth") and not only to the "scepter/rod of iron" (see Ps 2:9) that is mentioned immediately after it, and that was already promised to the "male child" of the woman in 12:5 (see also the "son" in Ps 2:7) and to the "victor" by Christ himself in 2:27. Judaism clearly contains the notion that God or the Messiah might judge and punish by means of the "mouth": "May you be [. . .] with the power of your [mouth.] With your sceptre may you lay waste the earth, and with the breath of your lips may you kill the wicked" (1QSb [*Rule of the Blessings* = 1Q28b] 5:23-25; see comments on 19:21); it is the development of the narrative that is novel here. We can note in passing that here as well the "victorious" human being receives the same marks of victory as Christ himself.

αὐτὸς πατεῖ τὴν ληνόν. This is the last appearance in the text of the terms "trample," "winepress," "wine," "wrath," and "rage"; like the rest of the description of the Word, these sum up and bring to a conclusion the series of similar phrases that are spread, in this case, throughout the second part of the book (in particular, 14:8, 10, 19-20; 16:19; and 18:3). John is saying that what had earlier been announced is about to take place; the narrative is approaching the military conflict whose function is judgment. The expression "wrath of the rage" (like "anger of wrath") is very common in LXX (beginning with Exod 32:12), is generally used to describe an emotion "of God," and is also frequently used to describe the nature of a "day": the last day of human history, which is precisely the day of judgment. It appears at least once at Qumran (4QShir^b [4Q511] fr. 35, 2), where we also find clusters of genitives like the ones in our passage, which usually appear without articles ("the colors of the light of the spirit of the holy of holies": 4Q405 fr. 23, 8; see ibid., ll. 11-12).

19:16   καὶ ἔχει . . . γεγραμμένον. If the "garment" is the body, or, in any case, some sort of reality connected with the Incarnation, then it would make sense that the royalty of the Logos is associated with his doings in the flesh. In fact, it is on the cross that he comes into his kingdom. Thus it is possible that the "thigh" might also be a reference to the bodily nature assumed by the Logos. The term, which can mean "thigh," "femur," "hip," "knee," or "leg," appears only here in the NT, and its occurrences in LXX are not very helpful. In the Apocalypse, moreover, when a "name" is "written" on part of the body, whether of a good figure or an evil one, it is usually on the head (the "forehead") or at most on the hand (the right hand; see comments on 13:16). The writing of a name on a robe or a thigh evokes Hellenistic statuary, in particular that of the Egyptian tradition, where names, attributes, and dedications of and to the gods were sometimes engraved on robes and legs. It would be very strange, however, if John had decided to pattern his Logos after statues of the gods: things that he considered Satanic. Some scholars think that the expression indicates a military belt or some kind of bandolier, which would be "over his clothes and on the hip." One may wonder whether John might possibly be thinking of something similar to those mysterious letters (usually called *gammadia*) that appear in paleo-Christian portraiture, for instance, on the white robes of the saints, as in the mosaic of Sant' Apollinare in Ravenna, or even of Christ, as in the apsidal mosaic in San Vitale, also in Ravenna, where Christ is shown seated on the throne holding the scroll with its seven seals. In these cases those Greek letters are both on the clothing and on the legs of the figures. For "King of kings" see the comments on 19:11 and 17:14.

19:17 εἶδον ἕνα ἄγγελον. The second vision in this part of the account again figures an angel (for the use of εἷς see comments on 8:13), who, like several of the "other angels," has "a great voice" (see comments on 10:1 and 18:4). This new angel stands "in the sun," which seems to imply that as the definitive battle approaches, God, through his angels, has taken back direct control of all of creation including the sun, which, inasmuch as it is a planet, had rebelled. At the same time it seemingly implies that the earth has been abandoned to the battle between the opposing forces.

λέγων . . . ὀρνέοις. The invitation to the birds comes from Ezek 39, where the prophet, addressed as a "son of man," is ordered by God to invite the birds of prey and the wild animals to tear apart and devour the remnant of the army of Gog, the king of Magog, which God has destroyed (Ezek 39:4, 17-20; see comments on 20:8). Some of the details of John's work are very similar to the words of Ezekiel (e.g., the reference to "horses" and "cavalry"), but in other places he departs from his model. The invitation is addressed only to birds and not to wild beasts, John speaks of various kinds of human victims as well as the horses, and he makes the vision universal by saying that they will eat "the flesh of all, of freemen and of slaves, and of small and of great" (note the chiasmus), whereas Ezekiel speaks only of warriors who become "rams . . . lambs . . . goats . . . bulls, all of them fatlings," for the sacrifice prepared by God. The idea that the end is a great sacrificial banquet prepared by God had some footing in apocalyptic traditions before or during John's time (for *4 Ezra* 6:49-52, quoted in comments on 13:11, see following comments).

The derivation from Ezekiel seemingly explains the appearance of the "birds," which is otherwise rather hard to account for. The only other birds mentioned as such (in the Apocalypse and in the NT) are the "impure" ones in 18:2 who take refuge in the ruins of Babylon. John specifies that the invitation is directed to all the birds who fly ἐν μεσουρανήματι; this is an internal reference to 8:13 and 14:6, where an "eagle" and "another angel" are said to fly ἐν μεσουρανήματι. This is of little help, however, unless John intends to present the birds at the supper as angelic figures. The birds also recall one of the signs of the end mentioned by Jesus, "wherever the corpse is, there the eagles will gather" (Matt 24:28; Luke 17:37), a phrase that in its turn recalls Job 39:30. All that the appearance of the phrase in the Gospels does is to give evidence of the popularity of the apocalyptic *topos,* to which we probably owe the existence of this scene.

εἰς τὸ δεῖπνον . . . θεοῦ. The only other "supper" that is mentioned in the book and to which all are invited is that of "the marriage supper of the Lamb," which was mentioned in 19:9. As this will not be mentioned again, nor described among the events to follow, we may ask whether the current passage should not perhaps be understood allegorically, such that the supper of the birds "flying in high heaven" is in fact the supper of the holy ones who are invited to the marriage of the Lamb. We should note, however, that the term "flesh" (which appears a total of seven times in the text) is only ever used in a different context as the "flesh" of the city/prostitute, which is also "eaten" in 17:16. There the flesh is eaten by the ten horns and the beast — that is, the kings of the earth and Satan, or those very enemies of the Word (v. 19) who are about to be defeated here. Those who punish Jerusalem thus receive the same punishment, and this event is one of the signs of the beginning of the end.

As regards the list of enemies, we can note that they are largely the same as those who asked the mountains to protect them from the rage of the Lamb in 6:15. A similar list in a judgment scene appears in *1 Enoch* 63:12 *(BS).* For an eschatological feast on the flesh of enemies, see *4 Ezra* 6:49-52 (see comments on 13:11), echoed by *2 Bar.* 29:4. In these non-Christian apocalypses the beasts of sea and land, Leviathan and Behemoth, are the ones who are devoured at the end by the human survivors, as a banquet spread for them by God; here, however, the two beasts are thrown "alive" into the "marsh of fire" while it is primarily human flesh that is devoured by animals. Thus while there is a tradition of common images, John clearly takes his own path, possibly for polemical reasons. We can also note that in the non-Christian texts the expression those "who are left" are always the Jewish survivors whereas in John, here as often elsewhere, "the rest" are destroyed (see comments on 19:21).

19:20 τὸ θηρίον . . . τῇ εἰκόνι αὐτοῦ. The verse explains that the "false prophet" who appeared suddenly in 16:13 alongside the dragon and the beast is none other than the "beast coming up out of the land" in 13:11. Its deceptions, which are briefly described here, are indeed the same as those of ch. 13 (the "signs" in 13:13; "before the beast" in 13:14; the "brand" in 13:16; the worship of its image in 13:15). This is a form of idolatrous worship whose role as a source of false prophecy we have explained by interpreting it as a corruption of Judaism (see comments on 16:13). That the explanation of the false prophet's true identity comes three chapters after his initial appearance is one of the signs that John had thought through the reception of the book at many levels, and expected it to receive a careful and reflective reading. The arrangement of vv. 19-20 suggests that "the beast and the kings of the earth" probably represent the pagan world, whereas the false prophet and those whom he deceived represent a Judaism that has, in John's view, become corrupted. After the destruction of Jerusalem/Babylon this universal conflict brings to an end the warlike interlude that began at Harmagedon (16:16): in the same passage, that is, where the beast and the false prophet appeared together for the first time under those names. The whole of the pagan world and what is left of non-Christian Judaism are destroyed, beginning with their spiritual leaders who are captured "alive" and thrown into the fire (John here adapts Dan 7:11, where "the beast was put to death, and its body destroyed and given over to be burnt with fire" [LXX does not have the word "destroyed"]; see comments on 20:3).

εἰς τὴν λίμνην . . . ἐν θείῳ. The "marsh" of fire appears only in these last chapters. "Fire" and "sulphur" together are a traditional form of punishment for God's enemies from Sodom and Gomorrah (Gen 19:24) to Gog (Ezek 38:22). We will discuss the idea of temporary or eternal punishment in fire in relation to 20:3; for the present we can note that in describing a marsh or lake of fire (Luke uses the term λίμνη for the lake/sea of Gennesaret, e.g., 5:1). John is combining two images of punishment: that in water (the flood) and that in fire (from heaven, as for Sodom, or in a furnace, as in, e.g., Dan 3:11; *1 Enoch* 54:6). This idea is seemingly recent and is also developed in a passage of *1 Enoch (BS)* connected with the figure of Noah, where water of fire and sulphur are used as a punishment for the angels "who perverted those who dwell upon the earth" (67:5-7). There is also in play the ancient explanation of hot springs, or springs whose water varied in temperature. When they put out hot water, it meant that the angels were being punished in the bowels of the earth; when the water was cold, then the angels had gotten out (*1 Enoch* 67:11-13). Another text is specific about the position of "the fiery abyss" that is "to the right of that house," the house being the Jerusalem temple (*1 Enoch* 90:26).

"Flames of sulphur," finally, are probably the foundation of Sheol (4QBeat [4Q525] fr. 15, 6).

The syntactical structure of the sentence is similar to that of 1:15. As in that passage, the translation repeats the noun with which the participle possibly agrees (on a logical more than a syntactical or grammatical basis).

19:21 οἱ λοιποὶ . . . ῥομφαίᾳ. Who are "the rest"? Here they do not seem to be the corrupt remnant of Israel but, perhaps more simply, all the others, apart from the beast and the false prophet. If my interpretation is correct, "the rest" are all human beings who are not Christians. The white-robed army on the white horses do not appear to perform any function; when the beast and the false prophet are "seized" and then "thrown" (for the use of "thrown" see comments on 12:9 and 18:21), the verbs used are passive without any agent specified: could it be the *passivum divinum?* Does the Word act alone, or should we assume that there is angelic involvement that is not mentioned? In any case, the cavalry described in v. 14 do not seem to be involved. All the others — the human members of the Satanic army — are judged by the sword that comes from the mouth of the Logos: we can deduce that the army of the holy ones function as witnesses rather than as combatants (see comments on 18:20; for the notion that the "rest" might be destroyed, see comments on 11:13). The killing is done by the sword that came out of the mouth of the Word. The messianic figure thus fights and kills (which is to say that he judges and condemns) with his word (see comments on 19:15). There is a very important parallel to this in the vision of *4 Ezra* 12:1-3, where the words of the Messiah/lion upset the transformations of the eagle/empire so badly that it bursts into flames and is burned to ash. *4 Ezra* 13:9 further emphasizes that the Messiah acts by means of his words in his conflict with hostile powers: "He neither lifted his hand nor held a spear or any weapon of war." The only weapon he uses is the multiform "fire" that comes from his mouth in 13:10 (see comments on 9:17 and 11:3): *Et ubicumque exibat vox de ore eius, ardescebant omnes qui audiebant voces eius* ("And wherever [his] voice came forth from his mouth, all who heard his utterances burned"; *4 Ezra* 13:4). There is, finally, a text from Qumran in which, like "fire" (see comments on 11:3), the "sword" characterizes the actions of the prophet or the man of God: "You have made (or will make) my mouth like a sharpened sword and have opened my mouth to the words of holiness" (4QBarki Napshi^c [4Q436] fr. 1, 7).

20:1 εἶδον . . . οὐρανοῦ. John reworks the description of two "other angels" with christological characteristics (see 10:1 and 18:1); here it is even more difficult than earlier to determine whether all these angels are really christological figures. The new angelic figure is distinct from the Word. The Word is not mentioned again by that name, that is thus seemingly a title reflecting the roles of warrior and judge that he has performed. It seems logical that the judgment would be entrusted to the "Word" of God (but see comments on 20:12). This angel, like the other angels who come down from heaven, has such great power (he has the job of binding Satan, the most powerful of the rebel angels, and thus of performing the role of Michael; see comments on 12:7) that he holds "the key of the abyss" that was temporarily given in 9:1 (the verb is in the *passivum divinum*) to the "star (angel), fallen from heaven." That the key has changed hands shows that God is always in complete control of the entire cosmos, including the abyss where Satan is to be "thrown" to be punished. Far from being his own kingdom, a place far from the world and from God's rule, the abyss is Satan's prison (see comments on 20:3). Rather, Satan's temporary and partial power over the forces of evil and over human history (see comments on 9:1 and 13:7) is at an end.

20:2 ἐκράτησεν. The verb is the same one used to indicate the power over the seven star/angels that was possessed by the heavenly figure who appears to John at the beginning of the book (2:1; see also the recurrence of the expression "in/on his right": 20:1 = 1:20; see 1:16 and 2:1). Whether or not this figure is a christological angel, the analogies to the Risen One are plain.

ἔδησεν . . . ἔτη. The first reference in the text to the "millennium" refers to the duration of Satan's first punishment. That there is a temporary torment before the final torment is a common theme of apocalypses in the Enochic tradition (see *1 Enoch* 10:6-7). In *1 Enoch* 10:12 *(BW)* the intermediate punishment lasts "seventy generations"; in *1 Enoch* 18:16 it lasts "for a myriad [ten thousand] centuries" or a thousand millennia (in the Greek; the Ethiopic is corrupt); in *1 Enoch* 21:6 it lasts "ten thousand years" (also in the Greek and one Ethiopic manuscript; the other Ethiopic mss. have "ten thousand ages").

At Qumran there are also hints of a transitory punishment at the same time as the "blessing" of the righteous and after the "visit" of God: "and all the ages of their generation (they shall spend) in bitter weeping and hard evils in the abysses of darkness until their destruction without there being a remnant or a survivor for them" (1QS 4:13-14). 11QMelkizedek, which describes the events of the tenth and last jubilee in human history, in the reconstruction of the fragments proposed years ago (Puech 1987), contains a text that could be understood as a description of the temporary torment of Beliar in the fire, which is followed by a rebellion that is followed in its turn by something (possibly an attack) having to do with the wall of Jerusalem. The editor's translation runs: ". . .] et lui-mê[me] annoncera [. . .] consume[ront] Bélial par le feu [. . . as]semblée (?) [. . .] Bélial et se rebelleront les (?) [. . .]

par les desseins de leur coeur [. . . a lacuna of almost a full line] avec le[s] mur[s] de Judah [. . .] le rempart de Jér[usalem (?) . . .] un mur et pour po[s]er une [co]lonne et [. . ." (3:6-19, p. 491; = 11Q13 3 fr. 5 + 7, 6-10; García Martínez–Tigchelaar 1997, p. 1209).

The concept makes another appearance in 2 *Bar.* 36:11, which belongs to the last phase of ancient Jewish apocalypticism. Thus it is not surprising to find the same conceptual pattern in John. If the duration of a temporary period of torment is given as a fairly large round number of years, it does not necessarily follow that every apocalyptic writer believed the period would last precisely that long. In the Apocalypse a period of "a thousand years," and indeed the number "one thousand" by itself, does not appear anywhere else but in this chapter, and thus we have no internal parallels within the book that might indicate any other particular meaning. On the other hand, it might be significant that in two of the Enochic passages cited above the period of provisional punishments is indicated by a multiple of a thousand. In any case, the number, being a multiple of ten, is intended to suggest the completeness of the period of time (see Yarbro Collins 1984, pp. 1242ff.). This seems to me to be the significant point; whether or not the millennium is actually a thousand years, it is a complete rather than a partial period. John, what is more, introduces this period to indicate the duration not of the messianic reign but of the transitory punishment of Satan; the messianic reign will last as long as the punishment and not vice versa. The "millennium" is thus primarily associated with the history of Satan.

The passage can be read as following and elaborating on 17:9-11 (see comments ad loc.). With the battle of Harmagedon Satan, the beast, and the false prophet attempt to establish for the seventh time a Satanic dominion over the created world, but their defeat marks their disappearance from the scene for the period of which they aimed to take control; the time and space that they left open can thus be occupied by the reign of the victorious Christ.

20:3 ἔβαλεν . . . καὶ ἐσφράγισεν. Not only the concept of temporary torment but also the type of punishment are fully consonant with the Enochic tradition. In 1 *Enoch* 10:4-7 *(BW)* we read: "And the Lord said to Raphael, 'Bind Azaza'el hand and foot (and) throw him into the darkness!' And he made a hole in the desert that was in Duda'el and cast him there, and he threw on top of him rugged and sharp rocks . . . in order that he may be sent into the fire on the great day of judgment." All the rebel angels are eventually destined for the fire (see 1 *Enoch* 10:13-14), but in the meantime their leader is cast down below the earth. For the use of σφραγίζω, see the comments on 7:2-3.

ἵνα μή . . . ἔθνη. The expression apparently means that, despite the massacre that has just ended, there are still "nations" that Satan can lead astray. This is the first of a series of more or less real logical problems within the text, problems associated with the "nations," which always appear to have been completely destroyed but then reappear unexpectedly. John might, however, be referring to the "nations" who were judged, killed, and devoured by the "birds" at the end of the battle of Harmagedon. This would imply not that these nations are still susceptible to deception at the time of the account, but simply that Satan will return to deceive the nations at the end of the thousand years during which he is unable to harm them. Immediately afterward, in fact, John announces that God will temporarily liberate Satan for the very purpose of deceiving the nations for the last time (see comments on 20:8-9).

μικρὸν χρόνον. Satan's activity is, as always, characterized by being of short duration (see 12:12 and comments). But here, however long the period of his liberty between the millennium and his eternal torment (and God's triumph) will be in terms of human history, in reality it seems to be a "short time." It parallels the "short while" of the war at the beginning of the seventh king's reign (see 17:10) and corresponds to the rapidity with which he "goes to perdition" as announced in 17:11. John stresses this for hortatory reasons: Satan's dominion is always brief and will pass quickly.

20:4 εἶδον . . . ἐκάθισαν. This is another gradual vision (as is always the case when John sees somebody sitting on a throne: 4:2, 4; 20:4, 11; see comments in 19:11). It places those seated on the thrones in parallel with those seated on white horses in 19:14, who were also introduced in a gradual vision and were not described. A "judgment" is entrusted to "they that sat upon" the thrones: it is probably not yet the final judgment, which will be carried out by the one "sitting upon . . . the great white throne" in vv. 12-15. Just as there is a twofold battle and a twofold punishment, so must there be a twofold judgment. In fact, if the battle is really the same as the judgment (see 19:11 and comments), then these first judges must also be warriors. They might also be the cavalry of the Word, who did not seem to have any role and who, unless this is they here, disappeared from the scene without a trace. In any case, that this judgment is "given to them" (probably a *passivum divinum*) emphasizes their dependence on God's will. Just as these judges are not described, so it is left unclear what or whom they are called to judge.

The sentence continues with an anacoluthon that leaves the reader quite at sea, and there is nothing to clarify the relationship in which "they that sat" on the thrones stands to the "souls" (who must be the same as those in 6:9-11) or to those who "would not worship the beast" or receive the brand (see 13:15-17). In 6:9 we have "the souls of those slaughtered for the word of God and for the testimony that they held."

The "word of God" appears here also; the "testimony" is made more explicit by the presence of Jesus' name, and the "slaughtered souls" here become the "decapitated" ones (the verb, *hapax* in the NT, indicates execution by an axe, precisely a two-edged one). This last change is less perplexing if we consider that "slaughter" describes the mode of the Lamb's death, and of the death of animals sacrificed by the Jews (at least since the reforms of John Hyrcanus; see Introduction, p. 32 and n. 102), whereas a blow from a two-edged axe might be the means by which animals were killed in pagan sacrifices (e.g., Homer, *Il.* 17.520; *Od.* 3.442). If this is what John has in mind, then the double definition is open to several interpretations, from a historical/political one according to which the Christians are the victims both of pagans and of non-Christian Jews, to a more strictly religious interpretation whereby the sacrifices of the Jews are now no different from those of the pagans. In any case, the important point is that the true faithful are killed. We can also note that in 6:10 the souls of the slaughtered cry out for judgment "with a great voice," and thus it makes sense that in 20:4 they would be "given judgment." Moreover, in 6:11 they receive the "white robe" that has been promised to the faithful since 3:4 and was worn by the "great throng" in 7:9. This detail also recalls the army of the Word's horsemen and their fine linen robes, whose meaning John finally explained (see comments on 19:14).

Finally, in 6:11 we also read that the "brothers" of the "souls" were expected to be "killed"; this is precisely what happens to those who resisted the beast in ch. 13, which strengthens the case that it is they who appear in this verse. The souls of those who were beheaded and those who resisted the beast are not, thus, those who are judged, but are rather themselves the judges. And since fighting is equivalent to judging, it follows that they are also the horsemen of the Word who, like the judges, are not described. The battle is the judgment. The idea that the faithful members of the true community are called to judge all the rest of the humanity is a common one: one has only to think of the well-known passage in 1 Cor 6:2-3 where Paul asserts that Christians will be called on to judge the "world" and even "the angels" (by which are meant the fallen angels), or to Matt 19:28, where Jesus promises the Twelve: "When the Son of Man is seated upon the throne of his glory, you . . . will also sit on twelve thrones, judging the twelve tribes of Israel" (see also Luke 22:30).

τὸν λόγον τοῦ θεοῦ. This is the last occurrence of this expression in the book, and follows shortly after the appearance of the person whose name is the Word of God (19:13). The terms are absolutely identical, and John probably expects the careful reader to reflect on this. In the context, and in view of the parallel with "the testimony of Jesus," I would suggest that the underlying concept is Christianity's full reclamation of its Jewish heritage. If Christ is the

314

Word of God, then every word uttered by God, from the words of the creation through the words of the prophets to the whole of Scripture — in short, all the divine content of the Jewish message — is Christian. Thus all those who have been "killed" for the faith in every age have the testimony of Jesus. Christ's death on the cross is the pattern not only for the present sufferings of his followers but also for the sufferings of all the past victims of Satanic power.

καὶ ἔζησαν . . . ἔτη. This phrase introduces the new element in this passage. If the interpretation I have been proposing is correct, then John has already several times seen the "souls" and those who died for the faith, and now he sees them "live" again. When the Word passes the judgment of condemnation, it brings about the death of non-believers and the much-emphasized eating of their "flesh" by the birds. But this battle and judgment are also the battle and judgment of those seated on the horses and on the thrones, who come back to "live" a real life, that is, with a body. They are no longer either "souls" (the term does not occur again) or "dead," but rather they live in such a way that John can speak of "resurrection" (see comments on 20:5). This first resurrection becomes a reign as well. John has already foreseen or prophesied future kingdoms several times. It seems that there are two distinct kingdoms: the "kingdom of the world of our Lord and of his Anointed" that will endure "forever and ever" (see 11:15) and the reign "upon the earth" that is also a "priesthood," which the Lamb gives to men through his blood and which is proclaimed in 5:10. In this verse and in the two preceding John announces the coming of this second kingdom, whose priestly nature appears in v. 6. As it is an earthly reign, we may expect it not to be eternal, and John indeed stresses its duration: "a thousand years" (vv. 4-7, four times). This idea of the reign "with Christ" (see also v. 6) is roughly equivalent to the common Jewish idea of a messianic reign on earth; Scripture and tradition were examined for clues in the discussion about its duration (from forty years to seven thousand, according to the rabbinic traditions collected by Billerbeck in Strack IV/2, pp. 948-1115).

The Enochic tradition connects the eschatological period with some kind of thousand: the blessed ones of the earth "will sire thousands" (*1 Enoch* 10:17 [*BW*], confirmed by 4QEn); this probably means that they will live to see the thousandth generation of their descendants (thus CD 7:6; 19:1; 20:22; 4QpPs[a] [4Q171] 3:1; 4:2-3; *Jub.* 23:37, on the other hand, has them living for almost a thousand years, which is probably evidence of speculations on the life of Adam [Gen 5:5]). We have seen (Introduction, pp. 21-22) that in *4 Ezra* the eschatological era lasts 400 years during the last part of the sixth millennium, and that in *2 Baruch* it lasts an indeterminate period of time during the second part of the seventh cosmic day.

If my calculations are correct, John has the reign of the resurrected with Christ occupying the seventh period of human history. Christian exegetes, who are usually attentive to discontinuities between the Apocalypse and non-Christian Judaism, stress the way in which John's hasty treatment of the millennial reign removes from it all those elements of well-being, wealth and abundance that are typical of much of the Jewish tradition (see, e.g., 1 Enoch 62:13-16 [BS], 11QBer = 11Q14, and 4Q285) and that are a constant presence in Christian millenialistic literature written after John. If earthly well-being is an essential constituent of the millennium as it is anticipated by millennialists, then John's millennium is not "millennialist." Moreover, John does not seem to base his ideas about the duration of the millennium on his speculations about the kingdom, but rather on the duration of Satan's temporary imprisonment after the Logos's battle/judgment. In other words, Christ's reign on earth is the positive aspect of Satan's imprisonment in the abyss.

20:5 οἱ λοιποὶ τῶν νεκρῶν. For the "rest" as the rest of the condemned, see comments on 11:13. It is not fully clear to whom John is referring here, which is problematic since it is quite an important question for the general interpretation of this part of the book. If we knew for certain who is *not* resurrected, we would understand more fully who *is* resurrected. We can first exclude from consideration the possibility that this "rest" is the same as that in 19:21. That "rest" seem to have been those killed all at once in the conflict with the Logos, whereas these are all the dead except for those who were resurrected for the millennial reign. According to the literal sense of the text, the only ones who rise again now are two groups of the slain: those in ch. 6 and those in ch. 13. Only martyrs, therefore, are resurrected. Whether or not John understood this martyrdom in a sense that we would call symbolic is another question altogether (see comments on 20:13).

αὕτη . . . πρώτη. Here and in the next verse John talks about a "resurrection, the first one." In what follows he does not mention any other resurrection, which has led some scholars to believe that there is only one resurrection. When he talks about death, however, it is either simply of "death" unqualified by adjectives, or of the "second death." Although he never explicitly names the first death, a second death presupposes a first, just as a first resurrection demands that there be at least a second. The two eschatological realities are linked, as v. 6 shows. The first resurrection must follow the first death of those who rise now and is definitive, which is to say that those who rise in the first resurrection will not die again. There is, however, a second death, which was first mentioned in 2:11 and will be explained only in 20:14 and 21:8, awaiting at least some of those who do not rise now. In v. 12 John sees "the dead . . . standing" to be judged. Those who did not rise at the first resurrection will find themselves facing judgment. This is not, therefore, really a "second" resurrection because each dead individual rises only once; rather, it is a resurrection that takes place on a second occasion, about a "millennium" after the first. Apart from the chronological separation between the two resurrections, the present tense of the narrative gives this passage the flavor of John 5:28-29: "The hour is coming when all who are in their graves will hear his voice [the Son of Man's] and will come out — those who have done good to a resurrection of life, and those who have done evil to a resurrection of judgment."

20:6 ἔσονται ἱερεῖς. The "reign" brings with it the priesthood of the risen. Whether or not this priesthood of the faithful is understood in a spiritual sense, it demands a place of worship, spiritual or otherwise, in which it can be conducted (see comments on 20:9).

20:8 πλανῆσαι . . . τῆς γῆς. In an obvious echo of v. 3, which set the scene, John reintroduces "the nations," despite the fact that they were destroyed in 19:15 and 21. For us, this creates a logical difficulty that critics have resolved in a variety of ways. The prevailing opinion used to be that this incongruity was the result of clumsy redaction. Either John working on an earlier Jewish source, or a later redactor working on John's text had taken from their context phrases originally close to each other, with the effect of creating two apocalyptic conflicts from a source that contained only one (the parallel passage in *4 Ezra* 13:5 being used to prove the existence of a Jewish source: *Et ecce congregabatur multitudo hominum, quorum non erat numerus de quattuor ventis caeli, ut debellarent hominem:* "And, lo, an innumerable multitude of men were gathered together from the four winds of heaven, to make war against the man [the Messiah]"; see 13:34). Thus the reference to the leading astray of the nations would have come before their killing, which would have taken place only once.

Today most scholars have a higher opinion of the literary abilities of the NT authors and tend to explain incongruities within the text in terms of content. According to this view, the author was well aware that what he was writing was at first glance complex and even contained internal contradictions, but he had reasons for writing as he did, and it is our job to understand them. There are several ways — not all of them satisfactory — of dealing with the problem posed by the nations' reappearance after their destruction.

The first and most radical approach is to see incongruities within the text as being placed there deliberately by John to persuade the careful reader to abandon the literal meaning of the text. Several scholars have pursued this rather intriguing path (see Corsini 1983 and 2002). According to this approach, when the nations are killed by the sword that comes from the mouth of the Logos, what is really happening is that they are being converted by Christian preaching; the devouring of their "flesh" really indicates their spiritual salvation and the only blood spilled is that of Jesus Christ. The theological realities of Satan's defeat and of universal salvation had taken place once and for all at the moment of Jesus' death; in dying he gave life to the world that killed him, and in his apparent defeat he defeated the Evil One. This is a radical reading of that theology of reversal of which clear indications are present in the text. This interpretation develops the Christian and apocalyptic theme of the "now and not yet"; salvation has already come to pass in God by the eternal sacrifice of the Son and now is coming to pass within history by means of the cross, but while it is already complete and perfect it still has to be realized in the conversion of the whole world. The crucifixion is the only salvific event, and the millennium does not occupy chronological time; the text refers on different occasions to the same moment, "the" moment, the crucial moment of Jesus' redemptive death. The Apocalypse, the first christological treatise in Christian literary history, is not about the end of the world but, as is consistent with the most radical elements of the Fourth Gospel, has a fully realized eschatology.

It is plain that at this point the discussion is not concerned with the interpretation of individual passages, but rather with the meaning of the whole book. It is best to pass over the details (see comments on 14:20) and tackle the question beginning with its basic elements. If the reading I have described above is correct, then we must accept that John's intention was to write a book in code that reviews the common themes of the Jewish and Christian apocalyptic literature of his day with a view to bringing the careful reader of the text to see the contradictions within it. This careful reader had to understand that the contradictions do not belong to the text itself but rather arise from an apocalyptic vision of the world that expects that the end will be preceded by a millennial reign on the earth: a vision that the author rejects. Thus John's book would actually be antimillennialist, and we would be forced to admit that for nearly 2,000 years hardly anybody has understood John's literary strategy, as there should have been no doubts as to his antimillennialist orthodoxy. This is an intriguing interpretation from a hermeneutical point of view, but it is rather difficult to support from a historical perspective.

Recent years have seen the formulation of a new hypothesis that seeks to eliminate the contradictions by bringing together into one the scenes of judgment and battle. The conceptual presupposition of this school is that time is inherently relative in apocalyptic literature, where God's achronic time and human historical time are superimposed. Its claim is, briefly, that John describes the single event of the judgment from different points of view. For all the saved the entire event of the judgment corresponds to a "millennium" of joy on earth, while the damned experience it as destruction, devouring, and condemnation (Mealy 1992). The basis for this hypothesis was elaborated several decades ago and has undergone occasional revivals since then (Metzger and Schüssler Fiorenza, discussed in Mealy 1992, pp. 47-58 and 36-46 respectively). It begins with the intuition that the nations who rise "upon the plain of the earth" (v. 9) from its "four corners" might be the pagan dead, whom Satan and his acolytes deceived after they were cast out of heaven and earth and established their dominion only under the earth. There is an inherent contradiction lurking here since the pagan dead would thus seem to rise twice, once to "come up" on the surface of the earth where they are killed by fire that comes down from heaven, and once again to be judged together with all of the dead (in vv. 12-15). This problem is resolved if there is only one judgment, which is seen first as battle and then as judgment. In sum, this hypothesis claims that the judgment takes place only once, but is recounted on four separate occasions; from the perspective of the holy ones it is seen as the victory at Harmagedon (19:11–20:3) and as the judgment and reign (20:4-6), while from the perspective of the damned it appears as the defeat of Gog and Magog (20:7-10) and as the judgment of condemnation (20:11-15).

This theory draws support from Ezek 39, in which the birds are invited to devour the corpses of the wicked; this passage appears in the chapter where Ezekiel describes the battle of Gog, king of Magog. John quotes the chapter in reference to the battle of Harmagedon, which might indeed be a hint on his part that the two conflicts are actually one. There are some difficulties, however. If we accept the hypothesis, then we must hold that all the chronographic details in the text are meaningless and that the fire that comes down from heaven in v. 9 is the same as the "marsh of fire" (Mealy 1992, pp. 178-79), even though the two fires seem to come from opposite geographic directions. Rather, the fire from heaven "devours" the nations just as the "birds, those flying in high heaven . . . eat the flesh" of the dead (19:17-18); the structural analogy is with the birds rather than with the marsh that does not devour those thrown into it but rather torments them "day and night forever and ever" (v. 10). It does seem that the two fires are different in nature; that which comes from heaven is protective (the text is practically a quotation of 2 Kings 1:10 and 12 [1:10, LXX: καὶ κατέβη πῦρ ἐκ τοῦ οὐρανοῦ καὶ κατέφαγεν αὐτόν, "And fire came down from heaven and swallowed him"]), while that of the marsh is punitive (for its origins, see comments on 19:20).

Moreover, in v. 11 we see the earth and the heaven flee in John's vision of the dead, a vision that is apparently made possible by the flight of the earth, which lays bare the lower regions (Mealy 1992, pp. 167-68). If this is a single event, then why in v. 9 are the same dead said to "come up on the surface of the earth?" If the earth flees and disappears immediately, then the conflict/judgment cannot take place on an earth that is no longer there.

An analysis of the details of the two battles/judgments — that of Harmagedon and that of Gog and Magog — shows that they should not actually be seen as overlapping. In the first case there is a heavenly cavalry made up of holy ones who have been killed but have been brought to life by the presence and the blood of Christ, who is the Word and the Lamb. When they appear as an army, before the battle the holy ones have not yet risen, but we can assume that when they are restored to life they will resume their bodies. The enemy army is composed of wicked figures who are apparently alive but who are spiritually dead inasmuch as Satan and his emissaries are their leaders. The holy ones are not described, but these figures are put into various categories (kings, commanders, etc., right down to slaves and the "small"); they are all killed, and after their death their flesh is eaten and they thus lose their bodies. In the second case there is an army of risen holy ones, presumably under the leadership of Christ with whom they reign, and an enemy army that is led by Satan, this time on his own, and is made up of "nations" who are not described more fully, and who rise "upon the plain of the earth."

Let us accept the hypothesis that in the second conflict the evil army is an army of the dead that includes those killed in the preceding chapter. In this case the two conflicts mirror each other logically: slain holy ones against living nations at Harmagedon and evil slain dead against living holy ones at Gog and Magog. In the first conflict the dead are spiritually alive and defeat and judge the living who are spiritually dead; in the second the dead both in body and spirit are defeated by those who live both in body and in spirit. In addition to this structural harmony other textual details support this interpretation. The text stresses that the wicked at Harmagedon are first killed and then eaten by birds who fly in the sky; there are several insistent references to the flesh of these dead. The wicked of Gog and Magog, on the other hand, are immediately "devoured" by the fire that comes down from heaven; they are not killed first and there is no mention of flesh or bodies. This might imply that their nature is spiritual, like that of the "souls" and of the slain holy ones in ch. 19. It may also be significant that whereas before the first conflict Satan makes use of the two beasts to deceive the earth's living and corporeal inhabitants, in the second conflict he acts alone as a degenerate spiritual entity who corrupts the bodiless dead. John might be giving these some sort of last chance by allowing them the option of refusing Satan's seduction; in choosing to follow Satan they show their own stubbornness and thus the justice of their punishment. This would place us in a cultural climate similar to that which produced the various narratives of the *descensus ad inferos,* in which it appears that the dead still have a choice between salvation and damnation, although in the context of the common belief that the dead will repeat the choices that shaped their lives. This reading is not compatible with a resurrection of the wicked before Gog and Magog, as such a resurrection would create a new set of incongruities; they would have a new, brief life, then a second death (by the fire from heaven), then another resurrection and a final punishment (which would amount to a third death). Both the holy ones (who are all "martyrs" and have thus already fought for the faith) and the damned each fight one battle when they are alive (in which they die physically) and one when they are dead. After their second battle they rise, the holy ones to the millennial reign, the first fruits of their eternal reward, and the wicked to eternal damnation.

The general outline of salvation history involves a certain initial pessimism about human prospects; after the expulsion of Satan from heaven all of human history, with few exceptions, is in his hands. Thanks to Jesus, however, the followers of the good muster their strength and manage to turn the situation around. Thus there are two conflict/judgments followed by resurrections, one at the beginning and one at the end of Satan's temporary torment, and the text's numerous chronological references do have meaning, although the numbers are probably symbolic. Satan's temporary imprisonment (a reversed *descensus ad inferos*) really does occupy time, as does Christ's reign on the earth; during this time the beast and the false prophet experience the torment of the marsh of fire, which will become eternal only when Satan joins them ("forever and ever"; 14:11 and 20:10). The holy ones also have a foretaste of their beatitude during the "thousand years" on the earth; the "cosmic reign" that follows it will be eternal ("forever and ever"; 11:15 and 22:5).

τὸν Γὼγ καὶ Μαγώγ. John is recalling the story of "Gog, of the land of Magog," from Ezek 38–39 (see also 1QM 11:16: "you shall carry out sentence on Gog and on all his gathering"). It is worth noticing that Gog was more important in eschatological and messianic contexts than is usually appreciated. As an example, Num 24:7-8 (an oracle of Balaam) in LXX reads, differently from MT, "A man will come from his [Jacob's] seed, and be the lord of many nations. And his kingdom will be exalted over Gog, and his kingdom will grow. [But] God guided him [the man?] out of Egypt, like the glory of the unicorn with him. He will eat the nations of his enemies." The best text for Apoc 20:8 says "*the* Gog and Magog." It is therefore not certain that John thinks there is a second prince called Magog; he means to say only that he has seen the fulfillment of the prophecy about Gog and Magog, whatever these terms mean in Ezekiel. The transformation of a place name into a person's name does, however, occur quite frequently also in non-Christian Jewish traditions (see *3 Enoch* 45:5 and P. Alexander's cross references in Charlesworth I 1983, p. 298, note *u*). This transformation (facilitated by the fact that Ezek 38–39 contains two oracles on Gog and Magog; see Mealy 1992, pp. 131-32) produces an eschatological pairing that has negative connotations thanks either to the collective imagination or to precise historical and literary references that we cannot reconstruct with certainty (like the equivalent figures in Jewish and Christian apocalypses, the "two witnesses" in ch. 11 are another eschatological pairing, but have positive connotations).

In any case, the appearance of "Gog and Magog" here must be the earliest occurrence of the expression; it is found in later Jewish texts as well as Christian ones, which suggests that there might have been a Jewish interpretive tradition from which both John and the later Jewish texts derive (unfortunately gaps in the text of the Qumranic commentary 4QpIsᵃ leave it unclear whether the term "Magog," added to Isa 11 [frr. 8-10, 3:18-25, García Martínez 1994, p. 186], indicates the name of a place, a nation, or an individual). The alternative is to imagine that the concept or interpretive possibility that John initiated was so popular that it found its way into the world of non-Christian Jewish apocalyptic traditions.

20:9 τὴν παρεμβολήν . . . ἠγαπημένην. The "city, the beloved one," can only be Jerusalem, although there is no exact biblical parallel; the woman "beloved" of God is all of Israel, and often when God's love is described the context is Israel's betrayal or God's punishment (see Jer 11:15, LXX: "What abomination (βδέλυγμα) has [my] beloved done in my house?"). The appearance of the city right in the middle of the millennium is rather startling, especially if one believes that the Apocalypse is preoccupied with the destruction of 70 CE. Does John perhaps imagine that Jerusalem will be rebuilt on this earth during Christ's millennial reign? If so, does he imagine this millennial Jerusalem as having a temple? If so, what kind of worship could take place in it? Some commentators respond to this difficulty by suggesting that John is making use here of traditional Jewish sources that expect the temple to be reconstructed during the messianic millennium, and that he found it inadvisable or impossible to remove the references of Jerusalem that occur within his sources, although they do not fit well into the scheme of his work.

Our first task is to determine whether or not "camp" and "city" are two distinct entities. Both terms are direct objects of a single verb ("encircled in siege") in a context that is full of military terms. We can infer from this that the καί that joins the two objects is epexegetic and thus that the meaning is "the camp of the holy ones, that is, the city." This brings us into a realm of military symbology that may certainly be derived from numerous biblical expressions (e.g., 2 Kings 6:14) but that is very close to the one we find in the Qumran scrolls. For the Essenes, "camp" is any place occupied by one of their communities (e.g., CD 7:6; 12:22-23 and passim; the term obviously has its roots in the exodus: see the "twelve camps" of 4QShir^b [4Q511] fr. 2, 1:7), and Jerusalem is "the first of the camps" (see the *HL* [4QMMT "B" 29ff., 58-62], where the "tent of meeting" is the sanctuary and the "camp" is Jerusalem, also called the "holy camp" and "head, first of the camps of Israel"; see Qimron–Strugnell 1994, pp. 48-53). This close connection between priestly and military dimensions appears also in a fragment of *ShirShabb* (see comments on 1:6) that reads, "the most holy ones . . . are honored in all the camps of the gods and revered by the councils of men" (4Q400 fr. 2, 1-2).

It is not always clear whether the phrases "holy ones" and "most holy ones" refer to angels (as is likely), to the holy dead, or to the members of the sect; in the Apocalypse the holy ones are usually the elect, meaning the faithful (see comments on 5:8). "Camp of the holy ones" is the community of believers, which also constitutes the city that is "beloved" by God and is thus different from any other human place. We do not have to infer from this that John anticipated the reconstruction of physical Jerusalem, or that he was incapable of exercising discernment in his use of traditional sources. More simply, the "church of the holy ones," however and wherever it is "built," even if this building is spiritual rather than physical, always becomes Jerusalem, the object of God's love. Jerusalem is also both physically and spiritually the only place where those faithful to the Lamb can be priests and kings. What we see here is another stage in the ideal movement from physical Jerusalem, which by now is irretrievably lost because of her sins, to the spiritual and eschatological "city" that comes from God and is thus the only true substitute possible for the old Jerusalem.

After encountering the Christian church as a temple and spiritual altar that is preserved from the destruction taking place in John's historical present (see comments on 11:1-2), we now see the community of those who rose in the millennium; this community is the spiritual substitute for the Jerusalem of the old economy, and is the last thing to be created by humans before the descent of the "new" Jerusalem that comes "from God" (see comments on 21:10). God's merciful love for the Christian spiritual Jerusalem is manifested throughout the stages of its coming into being: by the "measuring" in 11:1, by the fire coming down in 20:9, and again in the "measuring" in 21:15-17; the culmination of this love is, of course, the marriage of the Lamb (see Heb 13:13 in comments on 21:2 and see comments on 18:4).

20:11 ἔφυγεν . . . οὐρανός. In 13:3 the "marveling" earth follows the beast and is ready to accept Satan's apparent victory; it should therefore come as no surprise that it flees and vanishes as the islands flee and the mountains vanish in 16:20 (for the fear of "his countenance" see 6:16 and 4 Ezra 13:3). This verse contains a reappearance of the clause "and no place was found for them," which John uses only in regard to Satan and his angels in 12:8. The demoniza-tion of the earth is thus complete. Why heaven follows the earth is less clear. Perhaps it is implicated by the collaboration with the beast coming from the earth in 13:13 (see comments on 20:13). Perhaps it has become no more than a barrier that must be torn or opened from time to time to permit contact with God, and the time has come for it to be removed altogether (see comments on 4:1 and 20:13). Perhaps the old heaven has become useless as a result of the end of chronological and astronomical time, which itself is the result of the condemnation of the planets and the unfaithful stars (see comments on 17:11 and 21:23-26). If there are no stars, there is no need for a heaven. Whatever the case, it was commonly held in primitive Christianity that heaven and earth were destined to perish simultaneously on the day of judgment: "The present heavens and earth have been reserved for fire, being kept until the day of judgment and destruction of the godless" (2 Pet 3:7).

20:12 εἶδον τοὺς νεκρούς. There must have been varying opinions among primitive Christian groups about the nature of the judgment of the living and of the dead, and there was no clear consensus as to the order of events. Besides the passage from Rom 2:8-9 quoted above about the prece-dence of the Jews (a precedence that may also be understood in a non-chronological sense), 1 Thess 4:16-17 foresees that "the dead in Christ will rise first" and will then be "caught up by means of the clouds" together with those still living; the destiny of the wicked is not indicated. John's treatment sounds quite unique: when all the wicked have been killed, then the holy dead rise. The risen neither die again nor face judgment, but reign for "a thousand years" while Satan is imprisoned. At the end of the millennium the wicked dead are defeated, and then all the dead, who at this stage are all those who have not risen, are judged. There is no sign in the text of the faithful who are still alive when the Word appears. Might they be part of the heavenly cavalry? They are certainly not in the Satanic armies. Does John perhaps think that at the end of history all of the faithful will have died as martyrs, or will in any case already be dead? This is not impossible, although it is a minority opinion among Christians: "And yet, when the Son of Man comes, will he find faith on earth?" (Luke 18:8, in the context of a parable about the judgment of God; for the absence of living faithful at the time of the battle see Mealy 1992, pp. 90-91).

καὶ βιβλία . . . ἠνοίχθη. Heavenly scrolls or tablets are a *topos* of apocalyp-tic literature (Mal 3:16; *Jub.* 30:22; *1 Enoch* 90:20 [BD]; 4 Ezra 6:20; 2 Bar. 24:1;

Asc. Isa. 9:22; see also 4QTLevi arᵈ [4Q541 fr. 7], where in a different context we find the "Great Sea" being reduced to silence and scrolls "of wisdom" being opened). Here the scene is taken from Dan 7:10, which in turn reflects the judicial practices of the Hellenistic courts. Qumran was also aware that God kept a written record of the names "of all their armies . . . and the num[ber of the ju]st" (see 1QM 12:2). The relatively new element here lies in John's having added to the scroll that records the deeds of the dead "another scroll . . . which is the one of life" (but see the text of *Jub.* 30:22, which has something of the same sort). The relationship of this scroll to the "scroll of life" in 3:5, 13:8, and 17:8 is plain. The names of the saved must be in this scroll, which is a sign of the mercy of God, who saves whom he will. The scroll can be seen as an alternative to the scrolls recording the good and evil deeds of the dead; whoever's name is included in the scroll of life is pardoned of the evil deeds he may have committed and is saved. As the "scroll of life" is also the "scroll of the Lamb" (13:8; 17:8; 21:27), so is the blood of the Lamb the true means of salvation. We are told twice (13:8 and 17:8) that the names are written or the blood of the Lamb is shed "from the establishment of the world"; the consequence of this would be a clear predeterminism (as is typical of apocalyptic literature), which is permeated by ideas from the Pauline tradition about free salvation and justification by faith. Precisely in this context, however, John says twice that the dead are judged "according to their works." His insistence on works suggests that John probably sees danger in overly Pauline ideas that are too disengaged from a way of thinking that connects salvation to retribution (see, e.g., Col 3:9).

20:13 ἔδωκεν . . . νεκρούς. The sea is often linked to the earth, both in the memory of the account of creation (e.g., 10:6 and 14:7) and in the account of the catastrophes (e.g., 7:2-3 and 12:12). Its disappearance, along with that of earth and heaven, might be the result of the cosmic guilt that is glimpsed in chs. 12 and 13. Satan falls "from heaven," the first beast comes "from the sea," and the second "from the earth [land]." Thus all of creation somehow participates in sin, and must disappear to make room for the new creation (for the fact that the sea is not replaced by a new sea, see comments on 22:1). The only reason why the old sea does not vanish immediately with earth and heaven is that it is needed to perform its final function of giving up the dead. These last figures might be all those who have been drowned in the course of history and thus ended up "in the sea" rather than being buried in the earth; more particularly they might be those who were on the "third part of the ships" that were destroyed in 8:9. In any case, the depth of the sea might reach down as far as the subterranean abyss and the place of the dead; indeed, in this same context the other dead are given up by Death and Hades (in *1 Enoch* 51:1 [BS]

Sheol and hell or earth and Sheol deliver up the dead, depending on the mss. [see Isaac, in Charlesworth I 1983, p. 36, note *a* on 51]; in *4Ezra* 4:42 and 7:32 it is Hades, the earth and "the chambers" [or storerooms], whereas in *2 Bar.* 42:8 it appears to be the earth alone, although the phrase is ambiguous).

Here Death and Hades seem to be hypostatized, or rather to show their angelomorphic nature. Like other punishing angels in other apocalypses, they are punished in their turn; the expression "and they were judged, each according to their works" in v. 13 might include them. We have to imagine, although John does not say so, that they belong to Satan's entourage or that, like the shepherd angels of the Enochic tradition, they have exceeded the limits that God placed on their actions (see *1 Enoch* 90:22-25 and *4 Ezra* 8:53: *In infernum fugit corruptio in oblivione*, "Corruption has fled into Hades to be forgotten"). Within the structure of vv. 11-15 the dead appear in two waves, and John twice speaks of "judgment." The first time, in v. 12, he sees "the dead . . . standing before the throne," which is something that only angelic or angelomorphic figures have done up to this point; he does not say where these dead come from. Then the scrolls are opened and the dead are judged on the basis of what is written there as well as "according to their works." At this point John says that the sea and then Death and Hades give up their dead, who are judged "each according to their works": the scrolls are not mentioned again. The punishment of Death and Hades (but not of the sea) follows, and then the punishment of "whoever was not found written in the scroll of life."

This last expression unites the two appearances of the dead, since the scroll is the point of reference for "each," namely, for all of the dead. But despite this it seems that John means to distinguish between two categories of the dead. If this is so, the first category consists of the righteous who were not martyred. These did not rise for the millennium, but remained faithful to God in Hades (or perhaps were at rest with God?) and thus already appear now "standing before the throne" awaiting the judgment that will be their salvation. The other category would consist of all the dead sinners whom God abandoned to the sea, Death, and Hades. This is clearly a hypothetical interpretation, as it is perfectly possible that this is a single vision being unfolded gradually (such that John sees all the dead at once and mentions their judgment, then says where they come from and repeats the modality of the judgment). Nonetheless the hypothesis permits us to solve the hermeneutical problem created by the impression that the Apocalypse restricts salvation to martyrs who were slain for the faith, or else demands martyrdom for all the faithful (see comments on 20:12).

The text does not tell us whether these dead are Jews or Gentiles, but it seems reasonable to suppose that all the dead, including pagans, are taken into consideration here. John does not even say what became of the members of the armies of the "nations" who were devoured by the "fire" in v. 9. Whether or not I am correct in the hypothesis that these were the pagan dead, we can still presume that they are among the dead who are judged here, although we cannot say what group they belong to. It is not even clear what sort of anthropology John espouses; sometimes he talks of the "souls" of the slain, but generally he refers to the dead. Nor is it clear how he envisages the resurrection and whether or not he thinks that souls will be reunited with the bodies from which they were separated. The giving up of the dead by the sea, Death, and Hades seems to refer to the whole of the body and the vital principle, or just to the body; at least in the case of the sea, the bodies alone and not the souls of the drowned ended up there (the "living souls" in 16:3 must be something else; see 8:9 and comments ad loc.). John does not even say whether or not those still to be judged and those already judged are resurrected, and we have to infer it from the reference to the "second death" and from a negative sentence in v. 5 (see following note).

20:14 οὖτος . . . δεύτερός ἐστιν. The phrase is exactly parallel to αὕτη ἡ ἀνάστασις ἡ πρώτη in v. 5, and this parallel represents another invitation to interpret the second death as being connected, if only antithetically, with the first resurrection. If and when there is a first resurrection, there will be no second death, and vice versa. We must rather imagine a second wave of resurrections until the second death can take place; just as only the living can die, so only those who have come back to life (see vv. 4-5) can die again. V. 5 ("The rest of the dead did not live until the thousand years were completed") should be understood to mean that at the conclusion of the thousand years the rest of the dead will also come back to life. See also 21:8.

20:15 εἴ τις οὐχ εὑρέθη. This verse seems to presuppose the presence both of those whose names are written in the book of life and of those whose names are not written in it (see Dan 12:1). This implies that while the first resurrection concerns only the first fruits of the saved, this time both those condemned and those not condemned are present. The marsh of fire receives the dead in stages; first the beast and the false prophet, then the devil, Death, and Hades, and finally all the dead whose names are not written in the book. John does not say where the marsh is.

21

:1 εἶδον . . . ἔτι. In a few brief words (some of them drawn from Isa 65:17) John announces that he has seen an entirely new universe, newly created by God. The new heaven and the new earth serve as the necessary backdrop to the manifestation of the New Jerusalem (on which, see following comments), which fully occupies the visionary's and the reader's attention. For the disappearance of the sea, see comments on 22:1.

21:2 τὴν πόλιν . . . καταβαίνουσαν. The last section of the book, up to 22:5, is fully occupied with the vision of the New Jerusalem and of some of its characteristics and future inhabitants. This vision, in other words, is the culmination of the entire book, and John uses some formal means to highlight its special status. First of all, this is the last time that he declares that he has "seen" something (in v. 22, the last appearance of εἶδον in the text, John says that he did *not* see [any temple]). Everything from now on is "shown" to him by a heavenly agent (see comments on 21:9). Moreover, whereas previously John usually introduced new visions with the expression καὶ εἶδον preceding the object of the vision, in this case he first announces the object and then says that he "saw" it. The only other exception to the rule, which is thus a significant parallel to this passage, is his use of ὤφθη in 12:1, in the verse where the "woman . . . in heaven" appears for the first time (as opposed to 11:19 and 12:2). The first and last times that a "woman" (or "*the* woman") appears in heaven or from heaven John underlines the importance of the event by using a solemn phrase (as opposed, e.g., to 17:3). The coming of "the city of my God" — the "name" of which will be written on the "victor" who is mystically transformed into "a pillar in the temple of God" — was first announced in 3:12; now John finally sees the "New Jerusalem coming down out of heaven from God" (an almost identical phrase to that in 3:12). It is worth noting that the name of Jerusalem appears in the book only and always to indicate the "new" reality; the "city . . . where also their Lord was crucified" (11:8) is called, not Jerusalem but Egypt, Sodom, and, if I am correct in my interpretation, Babylon. Even when it is given positive connotations although still under its earthly aspect, it is not named but appears as the "holy city" (see comments on 11:1-2) or "the city, the beloved one" (20:9). It seems that John wants to emphasize the movement from holiness to love. The arrival of the only entity worthy of bearing the name "Jerusalem" demands a new cosmos, that new and final creation which John briefly describes in v. 1. The New Jerusalem comes down from a new heaven onto a new earth, indeed, onto its highest point, the eschatological Zion (see comments on 21:16).

John accounts for this descent by referring to the then-well-established concept of a heavenly Jerusalem. The idea that there was a model of the holy city in God's keeping went along with the idea of a heavenly temple (see comments on 11:19) and may have been facilitated by the identification of Jerusalem with the temple. When Ezekiel saw the future temple in a vision, he was brought to a city that could only be a Jerusalem that did not yet exist (Ezek 40:2). The city, like the temple, is the preexistent model on which the earthly

city is built (see comments on 21:21). According to some non-Christian apocalyptic texts very close in time to John's, the heavenly Jerusalem is as old as
paradise (and thus older than the earth; *4 Ezra* 3:6), was occasionally revealed
to exceptional figures after Adam (to Abraham during the sacrifice in *4 Ezra*
3:14 and *2 Bar.* 4:4; to Moses, together with its measurements, in *2 Bar.* 4:5;
59:4, and Pseudo-Philo, *Lib. Ant. Bib.* 19:10), and is now kept by God until it is
revealed during the last times (*2 Bar.* 4:2-6). In *4 Ezra* 9:38–10:57 an old
woman is transfigured into the heavenly Jerusalem (for the appearance of the
eschatological city see *4 Ezra* 7:6-9, 26 and 13:36). John does not, strictly
speaking, ever talk about a "heavenly" Jerusalem (the adjective does not appear in the book), but the New Jerusalem comes "down out of heaven" and
thus must have been there before being seen by the visionary. It is no coincidence that the expression "heavenly Jerusalem" appears in Heb 12:22, where
the author uses it to describe Christian spiritual reality to his readers.

It may seem rather strange that a Christian author should conclude the
history of salvation with a Jewish entity like Jerusalem. But the career of the
city/woman throughout the book shows the extent to which the idea of Israel
came to assume a dual aspect in the eyes of Jesus' followers. Although Christians felt that their anger at the Jews was officially justified by the death of Jesus, it could not eliminate some level of awareness of their own origins. Even
when Christianity becomes strong enough to try to destroy historical Judaism, it will never deny its spiritual dependence on an idealized Judaism, perhaps an ancient and "pure" Judaism distinct from that in the time of Jesus or
of the church. This can operate differently in other religious contexts, even
those that are also culturally dependent on Judaism; in the Mandaean legend,
for instance, Jerusalem is destroyed by the revealer of Mandaeanism himself,
whereas here the destruction is the work of hostile and demonic forces and
not of the Lamb. John provides a particularly intense and painful example of
the relationship of a complex and multifaceted Christianity to its origins:
torn between attraction and repulsion, between rejection (theological rather
than historical) of its own past and nostalgia for its roots. The cross in Jerusalem unites and divides what we today consider two separate religions (see
Heb 13:13-14: "Let us then go to him outside the camp and bear the abuse he
endured [i.e., the cross]. For here we have no lasting city, but we are looking
for the city that is to come"). As for the translation ("And the holy city, a New
Jerusalem, I saw coming down"), it could equally well be translated as "And
the city, the holy Jerusalem, I saw come down new" (see comments on 21:10).

ἠτοιμασμένην . . . κεκοσμημένην. We saw the Lamb's "woman" being prepared in 19:7 and wrapping herself in "fine linen, bright, pure" in 19:8, where
its meaning was also explained; now she appears "prepared like a bride." The

change of her clothing may be a traditional expression of the change in Jerusalem's destiny, and her assumption of glorious clothes of her return to the grace of God (see Isa 52:1, where the expression "holy city" also appears), in contrast to the desolation and nakedness that indicates her abandonment by God (see comments on 17:16 and the scene in Zech 3:1-6 where Joshua is undressed and reclothed). Something of this sort appears in a very fragmentary Qumranic text: ". . .] and the hardness of her face will change into brilliance and her menstruation and her clothes [. . ." (4QNarrative [4Q462] fr. 1, 16). This fragment is of interest to us also because in line 19 the scribe crossed out "Israel" and wrote "Jerusalem," which means that the two names could ideally be interchangeable, so that the city's destiny and the people's destiny would be the same.

John does not yet say (and will not until v. 9) that this is the bride of the Lamb, but by this point the reader should understand that this is so. We learn here also that the "woman" who was announced in 19:7 by the celestial chorus is a "city," the New Jerusalem. John probably uses the term "city" to indicate a spiritual place inhabited by humans, a community of the faithful. In this sense all three of the women who appear to John are alike in that they represent a group of human beings. It is common in prophetic language to say that the bride of God, besides being Israel, is Jerusalem in the real sense. To those passages already discussed in connection with the "prostitute" in ch. 17 we should add Isa 54 and 62, which John knew well and used frequently. In particular we should note Isa 62:5, where the Hebrew reads: "For as a young man marries a young woman, so shall your sons marry you, and as the bridegroom rejoices over the bride, so shall your God rejoice over you." LXX, possibly to avoid the suggestion of incest, adapts this to read: "As a young man lives together with a virgin, so will your sons live; and it will come about that in the manner that a bridegroom rejoices over a bride, so shall the Lord rejoice over you." The incest vanishes and the inhabitation (intended to be of Jerusalem) by her sons is compared to the joy that a young bridegroom feels in lying with his virgin bride (we may wonder whether the translators had a mystical interpretation of the passage in mind, since the inhabitation of Jerusalem is enduring, whereas a virgin can only be "inhabited" once; the Hebrew says "young woman" [*btwlh*] and not necessarily "virgin," although LXX does sometimes interpret the term to mean virgin; see Isa 7:14). From our point of view the important aspect of this text is that the joy of the bridegroom is shared by the sons (i.e., of the bride; see also 4QGrace after Meals [4Q434ᵃ] fr. 1, 6, where in one line of text Jerusalem is compared first to a mother and then to a bride). In John the bridegroom is the Lamb, who takes the place of the OT God; a conceptual pattern like that in the Hebrew of Isa 62:5 would imply that the faithful share in the spousal joy of Christ inasmuch as they are also bridegrooms of the New Jerusalem. This point is made by many contemporary commentators, especially those who make use of psychoanalytical techniques; according to this type of exegesis, the participation of the "sons" in the bridal joy of the Lamb (a participation possibly also present in Mark 2:19 and parallels), which implies their identification with the Son/groom, offers a resolution of the Oedipal complex of the text's (male) readers (Raguse 1993, in particular pp. 198ff.).

Certainly the faithful can hope to enter the New Jerusalem, whose "gates will surely not be closed" (21:25; 22:14), but the marriage is that of the Lamb alone. The holy ones enter in and inhabit the city, which is both a spiritual place prepared by God for the faithful and, at the same time, the community of its inhabitants. Insofar as it is the church, the community of the faithful, it is the bride of Christ, and thus the faithful are not the bridegrooms of the city but rather in her and with her they become the human consort of God. It is consistent with those elements within primitive Christianity that were to be taken up by Gnosticism and developed radically, that all the faithful, including men, should take on a feminine role in relation to Christ the bridegroom. In their relationship with the Father the faithful are identified with Christ, but in the relationship between Christ and the church they are identified with the church rather than Christ.

As for God's preparing of a place, the Fourth Gospel also declares that Christ will "prepare a place" in heaven for his followers (John 14:2), but here the "city . . . prepared" suggests rather that God prepared a city as the reward. The closest text is thus Heb 11:16: "Therefore God is not ashamed to be called their God; indeed, he has prepared a city for them." The author of Hebrews is talking about the patriarchs and the holy ones of the Bible who died in faith and trust in God that God will not betray. The city is the "heavenly . . . motherland" (Heb 11:14, 16), the heavenly Christian Jerusalem that, as in the Apocalypse, welcomes the holy ones of the Old Covenant together with the faithful of the New. There is very similar language in *4 Ezra* 8:52, where this idea is brought into the present: "For you . . . ; a city has been built."

21:3 ἡ σκηνή . . . ἀνθρώπων. This verse and the following are spoken by a "great voice," the last Voice to appear in the text, which comes from the "throne" as it does elsewhere (4:5; 16:17; 19:5). This is another way in which John stresses the importance of the revelation, which comes from the heart of the God who reveals himself. The first definition of the New Jerusalem, which is somehow expressed by God himself, describes it as "the abode," literally "the tent," the place of dwelling, the tabernacle from Exodus. Insofar as it is "the abode of God among men," the whole city assumes from the first the traditional function of the temple (see comments on 21.22), with a terminology that goes back to the first Christian generation (see Heb 13:10, whatever the phrase may mean there). If, however, the new city is the "abode" or "tent," then we can reread and reinterpret the other two passages in which John uses the term: 13:6 and 15:5. In the first the beast utters blasphemies against God's name "and his abode, that is, those who abide in heaven," and in the latter we see "the temple of the tent of the testimony . . . in heaven." In both cases, then, John seems to mean the New Jerusalem, which is not yet called by its own name but which is "in heaven." Having held back the name Jerusalem until the end of the book and of the revelation, he uses the term "abode" to describe the heavenly reality before its eschatological revelation.

An investigation of the three occurrences of the word σκηνή shows that the city is both God's dwelling among men (21:3 and see 7:15) and the heavenly dwelling of the holy ones (13:6). Coming down to the new earth, the new city is ready to become the true and final meeting place of God and man. Finally, if the abode/tent is the city, then the phrase "the temple of the tent" ceases to be redundant and makes more sense. All the words of the Voice from the throne recall biblical expressions, particularly from Ezekiel and Isaiah. The most interesting is the phrase "and they will be his peoples," which is a deliberate Johannine adaptation of a phrase that appears repeatedly in the Bible beginning with Lev 26:12, in which God, addressing the Israelites, announces that he will be "your God" and calls them "my people" (see comments on 21:7). The phrase "my peoples" does not appear in the OT, where God has only one people, but John uses the plural deliberately to emphasize the newness brought by the Christian church.

21:5-6 ὁ καθήμενος . . . δωρεάν. This is the last appearance in the text of the figure "who sits on the throne," who first appeared in 4:2, at the start of the visions. When the "great voice from the throne" is silent, he begins to speak in words of particular solemnity. These words echo Isa 43:19 (LXX: ἰδοὺ ἐγώ ποιῶ καινά, "Lo, I do new things") or 65:17 (Hebrew: "For I create new heavens and a new earth"; in LXX the text is impersonal), and clearly recalls v. 1. It indeed seems that for a new creation to come into being the old one must disappear or be destroyed (see 4QGrace after Meals [4Q434[a]] fr. 1, 2-3: ". . . to [de]stroy peoples and he will eliminate nations and the wicked [. . .] renew the works of the heavens and of the earth, and they will rejoice and (with) his glory will be filled [all the earth"; 4QTNaph [4Q215] fr. 4: ". . .] to destroy the earth [with] his anger and to renew [. . .]"; 4QBer[b] [4Q287] fr. 3, 2-4).

The whole discourse is brimming with biblical references and with phrases that have appeared earlier in the book, especially in the early chapters, and that anticipate the last pages. The passage thus functions as an internal nexus within the book and also contains the last command to "write" and the penultimate reference to the "faithful and true words" (see 19:9 and 22:6).

The purpose of v. 6 is apparently to help the reader understand who the unnamed figure on the throne really is. At first glance, however, these references are somewhat surprising. The first word, γέγοναν, recalls the γέγονεν of 16:17, but there the speaker precisely was the "great voice from the throne" who has now fallen silent. The two self-definitions that follow — "the Alpha and the Omega" and "the beginning and the end" — appear several times in the text from 1:8 to 22:13, at times in reference to "Lord God . . . Almighty" (1:8) and at times to Christ (22:13). It is this detail, then, that renders the passage particularly important as it indicates the full divinity of Christ who is now seated on the throne of his Father (3:21), to the point that the words uttered by the Father and by the Son are interchangeable. It would be tempting to identify the activity of the Spirit, which is one and sevenfold, in the "great voice" that comes from the throne, like the Voices and Thunders and Torches of fire. That the word of the Spirit is confirmed, although not reproduced precisely, probably indicates here the specific function of the Spirit who is summoned or sent to act in particular situations, while the one seated on the throne most likely expresses the complex whole of God's activity by using the verb in the plural (γέγοναν). The gift of water anticipates 22:17 and the description of the water of life in the definitive Jerusalem; that the one seated on the throne proclaims his ability to give this water (see Isa 55:1 and John 7:37) expresses once more the full divinity of Christ.

21:7 ὁ νικῶν . . . ταῦτα. This is the eighth and last appearance of the "victor" who was mentioned seven times in the seven opening letters (this appearance is the sixth in the nominative; it is unclear whether there is any arithmological significance to this, but one might think that the anacoluthons in 2:26 and 3:12, 21 are the result of John's desire to keep ὁ νικῶν in the nominative). The victor's reward is presented as an "inheritance," an important term in ancient Christianity but one that appears only here in the book. The "things" that he inherits must be those "new" things that have just been (re)made by the one seated on the throne (in v. 5). To the promise of inheritance is added that of sonship with respect to God, which echoes and blends two famous biblical expressions (which are quoted together also in Heb 1:5-6). The first, in the form "your/their God" and "my people," is found in Lev 26:12 and reappears in Ezek 11:20 and 37:27 and Zech 8:8; the second, in the form "his father" and "my son," appears in 2 Sam 7:14 and in 1 Chr 17:13, 22:10, and 28:6, all in reference to God's particular predilection for Solomon. While in v. 3 the "great voice from the throne" had altered the first expression by speaking of "peoples," now the one sitting on the throne extends the promise to all faithful individuals in a new form that arises from the combination of the two expressions. This new alteration on John's part is not as clear as the earlier one. Hypothetically, however, if the speaker is Christ/God, then it makes sense that he would emphasize his own divinity, thus preserving the rights of the faithful to sonship while explicitly reserving the paternity for God (see Matt 23:9, which has no synoptic parallel).

Unlike all the earlier visions, the vision of the New Jerusalem contains few references to the fate of the wicked. This, like a tragic subtheme, surfaces here where the "marsh, the one burning with fire and sulphur," is mentioned for the last time, together with the "second death," and in v. 27, where damnation is mentioned in negative terms as exclusion from the destination of the blessed. After the end of the vision the theme appears for the final time in the form of a diptych of contrasting destinies in the same manner as here; the blessing and curse of saints and sinners in 22:14-15 makes use of the symbology of inclusion and exclusion. The lists of sinners in these three places share significant elements, a fact that emphasizes the book's underlying unity of composition, by means of the use of the same phrases both in the text of the visions and in the literary framework (see comments on 22:15).

21:9 εἷς . . . ἀγγέλων. This is the angelic figure that appeared to John in 17:1, "one of" or "the first of the seven" (see comments ad loc.). The modern reader may find it confusing that the participle γεμόντων, "full," "overflowing," refers to the angels rather than to the bowls. Perhaps the angels themselves are "full" of the plagues that they have to pour out, just as the living creatures appeared to John "full of eyes" (4:6). The nature of an angelic being is the same as its role, in antithetical parallelism to the beast, who was also "full of names of blasphemy" (17:3). In any case, whether it is the angels or the bowls that are "full," their fullness is expressed with a present participle, although this is the end of the account and John has already seen and, in ch. 16, described the pouring out and emptying of the seven bowls and the consequences that followed. There are two possible explanations for this, one dealing with form and the other with content. According to the first, "full" is an epithet that does not describe their actual condition, but rather a characteristic quality. According to the second, John is trying to convey to the reader that although he had already witnessed the pouring out of the bowls, the scene actually anticipated events still to come; we are still in that atemporal time typical of the world of visions (see comments on 12:1), and in the last moments of the final vision the angels (or the bowls) are still "full."

Δεῦρο, δείξω . . . ἀρνίου. This is another deliberate and explicit recall of 17:1; not only does the same angel appear to John to show him a "woman" but begins with the same words: "Come here, I will show you." John uses the verb "to show" (δεικνύω/δείκνυμι) only in particularly solemn contexts: at the beginning and end of the book (1:1 and 22:6) and at the start of the visions (4:1) as well as in 17:1 and four times in this last vision of the New Jerusalem (21:9, 10; 22:1, 8; I do not know whether there is any arithmological significance in the fact that the term occurs eight times). There is an antithetical parallelism with the beginning of ch. 17, where the subject was the "prostitute" of "the beast," while here it is "the bride . . . of the Lamb," which makes perfect sense if the two women represent two opposing phases in the mystical history of Israel/Jerusalem.

21:10 ἀπήνεγκέν με . . . ὑψηλόν. John continues the antithetical parallelism with the beginning of ch. 17 and the vision of the prostitute. In ch. 17 also he was "carried . . . in spirit" by the same angel, but to a "desert." The expression "in spirit" recalls other important passages (as noted above) such as the beginning of the book (1:10) and the beginning of the visions (4:2). The first implication of this has less to do with the importance of the New Jerusalem in the book's general structure than it does with the importance of the prostitute. This fact supports the argument we have been developing, since it is unlikely that John would give such a central position in the universal story of salvation to a theologically marginal entity like Rome. John was taken into the "desert" to see the prostitute, who appeared to him on "seven mountains"; here the vision takes place on a "mountain, great and high." It is natural that a revelation, or a moment of particular significance, should take place on a mountain (see comments on 14:1; within the NT see the choosing of the Twelve [Mark 3:12 and parallel], the Sermon on the Mount [Matt 5:1], the transfiguration [Mark 9:2 and parallels], and the meeting with the risen Christ in Galilee [Matt 28:16]). The situation here is different, however. It derives once again from Ezek 40:2, where the prophet is led to "a very high mountain" (LXX: ἐπ᾽ ὄρος ὑψηλὸν σφόδρα) and there sees "something like the construction of a city" (LXX: ὡσεὶ οἰκοδομὴ πόλεως), and the vision on or from an elevated place is indeed a common *topos* (Matt 4:8; even the devil brings Jesus εἰς ὄρος ὑψηλὸν λίαν).

But despite this context, John appears to have in mind the eschatological Zion (see Heb 12:22: "you have come to Mount Zion and to the city of the living God, the heavenly Jerusalem"; προσεληλύθατε Σιὼν ὄρει καὶ πόλει θεοῦ ζῶντος Ἰερουσαλὴμ ἐπουρανίῳ). There must have been speculation about the great height of the mount of the eschatological Jerusalem (the "great and high" in our verse might be a superlative). According to some rabbinic meditations, Sinai, Carmel, and Tabor will come together with Zion to raise up and sustain the eschatological temple and/or city (Strack IV, p. 885 and n. aη, pp. 930-31. This note contains several rabbinic texts with mountains that

move, talk, and complain, and the city that sits "on the mountains" is Jerusalem and certainly not Rome; see comments on 17:9). According to 4 Ezra
13:35-36, the mountain on which the eschatological city will appear *parata et
aedificata* ("already prepared and built up") is a Zion not made by human
hands, a "great mountain" formed by the Messiah himself (4 Ezra 13:6).

As for the rest, if the final Jerusalem is at last the seat of God's self-
revelation, then he must have a throne worthy of his Glory (v. 11) and thus a
mountain-throne whose peak is the point of contact between heaven and
earth (see comments on 21:16). John does not explicitly say, however, that the
city is on this or any other mountain, but rather that he was placed on the
mountain to see the city. In our comments on v. 16 we will infer that the New
Jerusalem is in fact, as one would expect, on a mountain.

21:11 ὁ φωστήρ. John probably draws the idea of Jerusalem as light from
the beginning of Isa 60, where God himself is the radiance of Jerusalem and
the city is compared to a star: "And the nations shall proceed to your light,
and kings to the brightness of your dawn" (v. 3). If John is really referring to
this passage from Isaiah, then maybe he is doing so to alert the careful reader
of the text to the presence of the nations and the kings even here, at the time
of Jerusalem's final manifestation. The connection with the star, moreover,
leads the reader to reflect on John's chosen term, φωστήρ, which usually
means a star inasmuch as it is a "luminary" (see the use of the term in Phil
2:15, where the members of the community are compared to φωστῆρες; it is
uncertain what is the intended meaning of the title of 4QDibHam, *Words of
the Luminaries*, which contains prayers for every day of the week). David is
also defined as "light like the light of the sun" in a text exalting him that belongs to a collection of apocryphal Psalms found at Qumran (11QPSᵃ [11Q5]
27:2).

Some exegetes maintain that the "splendor" of Jerusalem here means its
"star," that is, Christ himself, who will be presented as a "star" in 22:16 (see
comments ad loc.). This is a very interesting possibility because it implies that
what is "similar to a very precious stone" is actually Christ, and the internal
reference is to 4:3, where the one seated on the throne is described, as here, as
being "like a stone of crystalline jasper."

21:12 ἔχουσα . . . πυλῶνας δώδεκα. Like the mountain, the wall is said to
be "great and high," which may mean that it is as high as the mountain, and
that John was placed on the mountain so that he could see over the wall into
the city (see comments 21:16). John does not dwell on the dimensions of the
wall, but begins to talk about its gates. It was a common idea that the eschatological Jerusalem should have twelve gates named after the twelve patriarchs;
the list, like their orientation and number (three for every direction), first ap-

pears in Ezek 48:31-34 and is taken up in several later texts. It appears in an Aramaic text called *New Jerusalem (NJ)*, of which at least five examples were found at Qumran (4Q554 fr. 1, 1-2; the order is different than in Ezekiel) and in the *TS* (39:12-13; see comments below). This insistence on the twelve gates also makes sense in the context of speculations on the temple (and thus on Jerusalem) as a model of heaven and of the entire cosmos: heaven itself had twelve gates (*1 Enoch* 33:36 [*BW*], now confirmed by 4QEn^c ar [4Q204], which completes the Ethiopic text; see *1 Enoch* 76 [*BA*], confirmed by 4QEnastr ar^{b-c}). In other words, the heavenly temple and the heavenly Jerusalem are the model of the spiritual world (in fact, the elements of the cosmos such as the firmament are part of the heavenly temple; e.g., *1 Enoch* 14 and *ShirShabb* [see Newsom 1984, pp. 39-47]), and the earthly temple and the earthly Jerusalem, physical copies of the heavenly model, are in their turn models of the physical cosmos. See comments on 4:1 and 11:1-2.

21:14 τὸ τεῖχος . . . θεμελίους δώδεκα. It is unclear what it means for the wall to have twelve foundations — whether the foundation is made up of twelve strata that run under the entire wall, or whether there are twelve distinct foundations each under a different section of the wall (perhaps corresponding to the twelve gates or, at any rate, three on a side). The huge blocks of stone used in the Herodian reconstruction of the temple might have had a part in the formation of the concept, in which case the twelve foundations would be twelve levels running under the wall's entire perimeter (like the levels of the stones in the Herodian structure; see Introduction, p. 31. The fresco in the synagogue at Dura Europus is not very helpful because of problems of perspective; there appear to be seven differently colored surrounding walls with the temple in the middle or possibly behind them, held up by a double base consisting of two rows of white stones placed on two rows of pink stones [Goodenough 1964, pp. 42-46 and tab. XI]). See *4 Ezra* 10:27 for the presence of "foundations" in a vision of the heavenly Jerusalem almost contemporary with John's.

John's description of the wall is the beginning of his description of the city's architecture, the first impression of which is one of splendor (v. 11). The description runs from v. 12 to v. 21 and proceeds in a rather strange way, returning occasionally to the same subjects and adding details each time. We see the gates and the foundations — the two series of twelve entities that are numbered but not measured (see comments on 17:3 for the "names written"). The "twelve angels" who appear only here (v. 12) must be the angels of the tribes (the Greek can also be read as "and on the gates twelve angels and names written, which [both the angels and the names] are of the twelve tribes"). Just as every church has its own angel with God, so it makes sense that every tribe is represented in this way. There is no further mention of a single angel for Israel; indeed, at this point it seems that Michael is destined to fill a more universal role than his traditional one of protecting the holy people (see comments on 20:1). In any case, the presence of the "angels" seems sufficient to guarantee the tribes' entrance through their twelve gates; in fact, as no other gates are named, whoever enters Jerusalem must pass through the gates of the twelve tribes, which is rather remarkable in a Christian text. This question had occurred to the Essenes. In the passage from the *TS* quoted above (39:12-13) the names of the patriarchs are indeed given to twelve gates, but to the gates of the inner wall, within the eschatological temple, that divides the "court of the Jews" from that of the women; thus only circumcised adult Jewish men without physical defects and in a state of purity could pass through them. John, by contrast, places the names on the outer wall of the city so that everybody will have to pass through them, which implies that the necessary purity is spiritual. Only thus can the whole city be called the "holy Jerusalem" (see comments on 21:10).

In view of the connection between angels and stars, some scholars equate the group of twelve angels surrounding the New Jerusalem with the twelve stars that form the crown of the "woman" in ch. 12. This is an intriguing possibility, given the correspondence between those twelve stars and the twelve patriarchs (on the basis of Gen 37:10; see comments on 12:1). In her time in heaven before her descent to the earth the woman is already surrounded by the angels/patriarchs of the tribes whom, coming full circle, we rediscover around the New Jerusalem, the last "woman" of the text.

Let us look at the twelve foundations in detail. The idea that the church is spiritually built on the foundation of the apostles was quite common in Christianity; there is the celebrated passage in Matthew (16:18) about Peter, the foundation of the church, and Eph 2:20 talks explicitly about the "apostles and prophets" as the foundations of the community. 1 Cor 3:12 provides us with a list of symbolic materials (from gold to straw) on which a community could be more or less firmly built, and Heb 11:10 presents the *civitas Christiana* awaited by the Hebrews as "the city that has foundations." John is almost certainly inspired by Isa 54:11-12, where the eschatological Jerusalem appears founded on, and built out of, precious stones (see Isa 60:17 and Tob 13:17).

Luckily a commentary on Isaiah's text was found at Qumran, a fragment of which (4QpIs^d = 4Q164) includes the explanations given to the "foundations of sapphire," "battlements" or "pinnacles of rubies," and "gates of jewels [probably: carbuncle]" in Isa 54:11-12. It is an allegorical interpretation according to which the various parts of the city/temple are the members of the

community. It says of the foundation of sapphire: "They will found the counsel of the community, [the] priests and the peo[ple . . .] the assembly of their
elect, like a sapphire stone in the midst of stones." The "battlements/pinnacles
of ruby" are the "twelve [chiefs of the priests, who] illuminate with the judgment of the Urim and the Thummim[. . . ." The "gates of jewels" are "the
chiefs of the tribes of Israel for the e[nd of the days. . . ." The "gates," therefore,
are still connected to the twelve tribes (thanks to the influence of Ezekiel since
Isaiah does not even mention the number of the gates), but not to their past
patriarchs; instead, they are connected with the heads (members of the elect
community) who will represent the tribes at the end of days.

John's insertion of the "angels" beside the names shows the same inclination to make use of exemplary figures who are not exactly the same as the human patriarchs of history. John makes use of their heavenly representatives,
but his approach is not too far from that of the Qumranic text, since the sectarians believed that they had angels in their midst (see comments on 3:18)
and that they themselves were somehow like angels (see comments on 5:8 and
20:9). The other two elements, however, are even more interesting; first of all,
the foundations are people and, secondly, there are twelve "pinnacles" or
"battlements" (probably the "merlons of the battlements"; Isaiah does not
give even this number) because the sectarians identify twelve figures, the
leaders of the priests of their community. John's decision to identify twelve
foundations moves his text in exactly the same conceptual direction. For
other speculations on the stones of the breastplate see Pseudo-Philo, *Lib. Ant.
Bib.* 26:4-13 (where there are twenty-four stones) and *2 Bar.* 6:7 (where there
are forty-eight of them). See the comments on 3:12 for the idea that parts of
the temple (and, by extension, the city) are spiritually alive.

21:15 μέτρον . . . μετρήσῃ. This scene of measuring is in obvious contrast
to that of 11:1, although both derive from the beginning of Ezek 40. There it
was John who was charged with the task of measuring part of the "holy city,"
and he did not record its dimensions; here the task falls to the angel who had
reappeared in v. 9. There John used "a reed similar to a staff" to measure (see
comments on 11:1); here the reed, like a good part of the city being measured,
is "golden."

21:16 ἡ πόλις . . . ἐστίν. Ezekiel (48:16, 30-35) described the eschatological city as being square, and the idea must have been fairly widespread in
John's day. Josephus records the existence of a prophecy according to which
the end of the world would come when the the temple square became actually
square (*J.W.* 6[5.4].311), and there is reason to believe that Herod's architects
deliberately designed the square so that it would not have four right angles in
an attempt to avoid the danger threatened by the prophecy (see Introduction,

p. 31). According to Ezekiel's description, the wall was 4500 cubits (about 2.3 kilometers) long on each side, giving a total perimeter of 18,000 (Ezek 48:35). The dimensions of the outer wall of eschatological Jerusalem appear in col. 40:9-15 of the *TS:* the wall is "about one thousand six [hundred] cubits" long on each side. The rather strange "about" is explained by the fact that we have no round number for the walls, but the length of the inside of the wall is 1590 cubits and of its outside is 1604 cubits. (The two figures are the result of our calculation, since the text as we have it provides ciphers for the segments rather than for the total; Johannes Maier argues that there must have been towers at the corners of the perimeter wall — the text is not clear on this point — and that each side would thus be a little longer; see Maier 1989, pp. 23-62; see also the measurements given in a text similar to the *Temple Scroll:* 4Q364-365 or 4QReworked Pentateuch[b, c] fr. 28, 2).

What is interesting about this is that the author wanted to get the number 1600, even if it was not produced by his calculations. There must have been some arithmological significance to the number; it is, indeed, the number we encountered in 14:20 ("one thousand six hundred stades"; see comments ad loc.). This is further confirmed in our passage, where the city measures "twelve thousand stades." The first and most obvious feature of this number is its connection with "twelve." It makes sense that a wall with twelve gates and twelve foundations would also be twelve thousand measures long. What is less obvious is that 12,000 is seven and a half times 1600. That there is a connection between the two numbers can also be deduced from the fact that they are the only two numbers in the book given in stades. This might mean that the measure of God's providential mercy is more than seven times that of his wrath (see Matt 18:21-22). Besides the symbolic value of the numbers, another detail that is often overlooked is that John gives 12,000 stades as the measure of the city; he then adds that the length, breadth and height of the city are the same, but nowhere does he say that 12,000 stades is the length of one side of the city. Thus the perimeter would be over 2200 kilometers (if a stade is about 185 meters), and the measurement John gives would be a deliberate adaptation or explanation of Ezek 48:35. If this is the case, then one side is 3000 stades, which is still a disproportionate length relative to actual human cities (about 550 kilometers) but would at least involve an indirect biblical reference. Unfortunately the passage in which Ezekiel gives the dimensions of the wall around the temple area (which in Ezekiel is separate from the city) is rather unclear both in Greek and in Hebrew, and it is not possible to be certain whether he is talking about "cubits" or "reeds" (Ezek 42:15-20 and 45:2). He says that the wall is square and measures 500 reeds (or cubits) on each side; if John had read "500 reeds," which must have been Ezekiel's original idea, then since the reed is "six long cubits" in length (Ezek 40:5), the temple wall would be 3000 cubits long.

This brings us to the crucial point in the description of the form of the New Jerusalem. John says that the length, breadth, and height of the city are equal. In recent years this has been very widely understood as implying that the city is cubic in shape. The cube, with its perfectly balanced dimensions, is thought to have served as a sign of perfection and, hard as it is to imagine, a cubic Jerusalem would not be out of place in the end times. The literature that is usually used as a resource for a better understanding of biblical texts, however, shows no sign of any other cubic city (M. Piantelli, of the University of Turin, tells me that there are Indian texts that tell the story of three cubic cities with metal walls [of *ayar,* silver, and gold] that appear on the clouds and are the location of the resurrection of the dead Asuras; but it is hard to construct a persuasive historical connection with the Apocalypse). Neither have I been able to find any ancient text that suggests that the cube was seen as a perfect shape. The Greek term κύβος basically means "die" (for games), and the adjective derived from it, κυβικός, means first of all "like a die." Dice are not a symbol of perfection, least of all of moral perfection. When Methodius of Olympus mocks Origen's idea that the resurrected body might be spherical (the sphere being indeed a sign of perfection), he objects that it might also be cubic or pyramidal, but this only implies that the cube was not considered a sign of perfection (Methodius, *De resurrectione, Synopsis* 11, in Photius, *Bibliotheca,* cod. 234). As for the Jerusalem temple, Ezra 6:3 says that the new building, by the orders of Cyrus, was to be 60 cubits high and wide. The text appears to be incomplete, as the length is missing, but we can imagine that it was also 60 cubits. Even this does not necessarily mean that the temple is a cube, because the Second Temple (or at least Herod's temple) was equal in its dimensions but was shaped like a "T" (see Introduction, p. 31 and n. 98).

Having said this much about the idea of a "cube," we can turn to the text. John does not call the city cubical, but "foursquare." He also uses the expression κεῖται — "is laid out," "stretches," or "extends" — which is more appropriate to a flat shape that is laid out on a surface such as a square than it is to a volume like a cube, which can hardly be said to be "laid out." The verb is used in Greek to indicate the appearance of normal human cities, which are not cubes. A phrase from Matthew is particularly helpful here; "You are the light of the world. A city that lies on a mountain cannot be hidden" (κειμένη ἐπάνω ὄρους; Matt 5:14). Jerusalem is built on a "mountain" — Mount Zion — and the New Jerusalem, the Christian community, will be exactly like the "city" in Matthew, a source of light on a high mountain. I do not think it is necessary for the reader to force himself to imagine something deliberately foreign to

human experience; instead of such a bizarre object as a cubic city we can simply imagine a city built on the top of a very high mountain (it matters little
whether the mountain is 3000 or 12,000 stades high), which it covers, reaching down into the valley until it is surrounded by a very long wall in the shape
of a square. The center of the city, probably the square of v. 21, is on the summit of the mountain, and is also the site of God's throne, just as in the case of
the earthly temple Herod's leveling created the "square" on which the temple
was built. Thus the mountain (Zion) and the city (Jerusalem) that covers it
share an identity, as was in fact traditional (see an apocryphal Psalm, a
"Hymn to Zion" found at Qumran in which Zion has both "marvellous
squares" and "glorious breasts"; 11QPs^a [11Q5] 22:5). John's New Jerusalem is
indeed enormous, but it is not absurd.

21:17 ἑκατόν . . . πηχῶν. Although John does not say explicitly that the
"hundred forty-four cubits" represents the height of the wall, this seems to be
the most obvious interpretation. Ezekiel has little to say about its height; in
40:5 he says that the wall outside the temple was destined to be one reed high
(which is six long cubits or seven ordinary cubits), and in 40:14 he speaks
about "pilasters" sixty cubits high. Both *TS*, however, and *NJ* (for which a
"reed" is seven cubits long and thus most measurements are in multiples of
seven) are rich in details and agree on some of them. The wall around the city
is usually 49 cubits (or seven reeds) high, and is often 7 (*TS* 40) or 14 cubits
thick (*NJ* [4Q554] fr., 2) at the foundations. Both texts foresee towers. *TS* has a
total of 12, each 70 cubits high (col. 40) within which the gates are set, whereas
NJ describes two towers at each gate, one on either side, and other towers, for
a total of 1432, each one 10 reeds (thus also 70 cubits) high (col. 2:15-18). This
gives a construction over 30 meters high all told, or the equivalent of a modern building over ten stories high. John more than doubles this measure. A
wall about 65 meters high is not quite the Empire State Building, but, if one
bears in mind that it is at least 550 kilometers long, it certainly merits the description "great and high" (v. 12), particularly in relation to the technology of
the day.

Those who argue that the New Jerusalem is a cube think that its wall is
12,000 stades high, and many exegetes thus believe that the measurement of
144 cubits refers to the thickness of the wall. This causes new problems, however; it gives us a wall about 65 meters thick, either 550 or 2200 kilometers
high, with a perimeter of either 2200 or 8800 kilometers, within which the
city "is laid out." The question has been raised how John could see the city on
the other side of such a wall, and it has been suggested in reply that the wall
was transparent (but see comments on 21:18). Obviously everybody is aware
that these measurements have great symbolic value. The "one hundred forty-

four" is not only the square of twelve (and thus in perfect harmony with a city in which everything is counted or measured on the base of twelve) but is also the number, in thousands, of the "virgins" who "follow the Lamb" (see comments on 7:4 and 14:1 and 4). It is both possible and reasonable to suppose that these "blameless" ones (14:5), who, if they accompany the Lamb everywhere, must have been at his side also during the battle (17:14), are somehow connected with the spiritual defensive wall of the New City. For the spiritual "walls" of Qumran and of 2 *Baruch* see comments on 3:12 and on the next two verses.

μέτρον . . . ἀγγέλου. John here takes up and modifies Deut 3:11, where the expression "cubit of a man" (LXX: ἐν πήχει ἀνδρός) indicates the unit of measure used to give the dimensions of Og, king of Bashan, the last descendant of the giants. This is a very interesting reference indeed; we learn from the context that the enemy cities destroyed by the Israelites were "fortress towns" with "high walls" (Deut 3:5) "up to heaven" (Deut 1:28). But if Og is the last of the giants, the sinful sons of the sinful angels, then it is no accident that our text refers back to it while discussing a "wall" that, thanks to the "hundred forty-four" (cubits) and to the "twelve thousand" (stades), could also represent the final victory of the "hundred forty-four thousand" who, as we have seen, are the men who in some manner replace the sinful angels (see comments on 14:4).

In the second place, John was well aware of the prophetic, biblical (e.g., Dan 10:5), and Enochic (e.g., 1 *Enoch* 87:2) traditions whereby some of the "men" seen in visions are angelic figures (while the animals in the visions represent humans, e.g., Dan 8:3 and 1 *Enoch* 85–90), and is indicating that he is using the same symbology. John uses the term "man" in the singular only in one other expression, which is an absolute parallel to this and in which he speaks not of measure but of the "number of a man." I think he is doing here what we have often seen him do: explaining the meaning of an expression he used in earlier chapters (see comments on 13:18).

21:18 ἡ ἐνδώμησις . . . καθαρῷ. Both the "splendor" of Jerusalem and the one seated on the throne (4:3) are "like" jasper and, in particular, "crystalline jasper" (v. 11). We do not always know exactly what the names of precious stones in ancient texts refer to. When a Greek spoke of "crystal," he meant an especially bright gem, possibly one that was transparent, which we usually render as "carbuncle." The adjective that derives from it, however ("crystalline"), can be used to describe various things, from glass to natural crystal to diamond. That they are "like" crystalline jasper probably means that the phrases describe a human/divine nature — thus ultimately Christ — who transcends the physicality of the "jasper" that is really found in nature.

Here, however, the "wall" and the "first foundation" (in v. 19) are actually of jasper, and not just "like" it. The term "jasper" does not appear anywhere else, and it is therefore acceptable for us to look for a possible conceptual link between the one "seated on the throne," the "splendor," the "wall," and its "first foundation." In a vision of a "man with a measuring line in his hand," who intends to measure the "width" and "length" of Jerusalem, Zechariah hears God say that Jerusalem will no longer have walls, but that "I will be a wall of fire all around it . . . and I will be the glory within it" (Zech 2:1-5). We can therefore expect that there is some kind of connection between the wall and God. I think that the gems themselves represent their human dimension, whereas being "like" the gems represents the ineffability of the mystery of the Incarnation, of the presence of God in humanity. Thus the wall and the first foundation would be Christ's human imitators. If this is so, then it is a confirmation of the hypothesis that there is a connection between the wall and the "hundred forty-four thousand" imitators of Christ. If we go on to consider that the imitation of Christ consists in witness, which is martyrdom, then the "jasper" might point to the bond between Christ and those who imitate him. In the eyes of the faithful it is a precious bond, a bond of blood, that reaches the first foundation, the apostles. This does not necessarily mean that John has in mind the martyrdom of Peter, considered to be the first of the Twelve, but that bearing witness to the point of shedding one's blood is the first foundation of apostolicity. I would not like to go any further than this and try to identify the symbolic value (symbolic, at least, to us) of each precious stone recorded in the following verses, but only want to point out that they correspond to a fair degree (certainly ten out of the twelve) to the gems in the breastplate of the high priest (see Exod 28:17-20 and 39:10-13). This brings the New Jerusalem and the prostitute still closer to each other (see comments on 17:4). It is sufficient to note here that the surviving fragments of the Qumranic *NJ* contain architectonic elements in "sapphire" ("gates" and buildings) and of "rubies" (other buildings; 2Q24 fr. 3, 2; 4Q554 fr. 2, 2:14-15), but it is very difficult to construct interpretations of the individual gems that will bear close examination.

We must, however, say something about the "gold." It is common to describe a beloved and desired object as golden. In the case of Jerusalem there may also be a historical memory of the profusion of gold in Herod's temple, whose opulence has left indelible traces in rabbinic tradition (e.g., *m. Sheq.* 4:4) as well as in Josephus (e.g., *J. W.* 5[5.1-7].184-237). To see the place of gold in Jewish images of the eschatological Jerusalem one has only to turn to some fragments of *NJ*, which is full of golden objects and buildings: ". . .] this wall is pure gold[. . ." (this must refer to the city wall or part of it), and: ". . .] all their stones [. . .] . . . overlaid with gold" (11Q18 fr. 10 and 11; former frr. 23 and 24; see García Martínez 1992, pp. 190ff.). John uses two synonymous terms to indicate "gold": χρυσός and χρυσίον. The former appears four times, always in connection with evil entities (the monsters of the abyss in 9:7 and the city/prostitute in 17:4 and 18:12 and 16); the latter three times (for a total of seven appearances), always in connection with the side of the good. The first appearance is in 3:18, where gold is "fired" and offered by John to the lukewarm Laodiceans, and the last two are here, in vv. 18 and 21, where it is used to describe the city and its square. In these last cases, and only here, is the gold said to be "pure." John thereby deliberately distinguishes χρυσίον from χρυσός according to whether the object in question is positive or negative (the adjective "golden" is almost always used for objects connected with God and worship, the only exception being 9:20; see comments on 17:4). In vv. 18 and 21 the "pure gold" is compared to "pure glass" and "transparent glass." Despite some variants (and despite the fact that a different reading of v. 21 is syntactically possible) these expressions do not mean that the gold is transparent (a rather unlikely phenomenon, even in the New Jerusalem) but that it is as pure as glass when it is transparent. John imagines the city (of gold), its squares (also of gold), and its wall (of jasper) as shining, but not as transparent (see comments on 21:17).

21:21 δώδεκα . . . μαργαρῖται. The image of "gates" as "pearls" seems very odd, especially as we always use the term "gate" to translate two different Greek words, θύρα, the real "door" (see 3:8), and πυλῶν, which really means "entrance," or an opening built into a structure (see Matt 26:71 and especially Acts 12:13, which reads τὴν θύραν τοῦ πυλῶνος). John is probably thinking of the twelve entrance towers in the wall of the eschatological city (each at least 144 cubits high), each of which consists of a single pearl about whose natural dimensions there can be no doubt. Amid the dazzle of light, gold, and precious stones that fills the New Jerusalem there is a place for pearls, and it is no more daring to imagine a foundation made of emerald than an entrance made of a pearl. Indeed, when John insists that each entrance is made of a single pearl, perhaps his intention is to highlight the extraordinary and incomparable value of God's new creation, which will have pearls of this size — not in the millennium but in the definitive reign of God. Finally, it is just possible that John's images might have been to some degree influenced by the existence of a feminine ornament called the "city of gold." This is mentioned no fewer than three times in the Mishna (*m. Shab.* 6:1; *m. 'Eduy.* 2:7; *m. Kel.* 11:8), and in the commentaries on these passages in the Talmud, it appears to be a reference to something that was used in the past. In response to the question of what it was, *t.b. Shab.* 59b replies: "A Jerusalem of gold, like the one that

Aqibah made for his wife." *T.b. Sot.* 49b says that it is a "bridal crown of gold" of the sort forbidden after the repression of Lusius Quietus (117-18 CE). It appears from the discussion that this must have been a coronet or a tiara made all of gold or with parts made of fabric that represented the city, although some modern writers think that it was a medallion that could also be worn on the head. I am not aware of any sources that mention precious stones or pearls on such an ornament, but I would be curious to see how it represented the walls and gates of the city.

21:22 ναὸν οὐκ εἶδον. With this "saw no temple" John begins the last section of this great vision of the New Jerusalem, which will continue until 22:5. This last part is the summit of the book's concluding vision and is particularly densely and richly furnished with internal echoes. Let us observe the most visible phenomena, such as the relationship between the opening and closing verses that enclose the whole passage; the lordship of God (21:22 and 22:5), the lack of any need for the sun (21:23 and 22:5), the fact that God is the light of the city (21:23 and 22:5), the royalty of human figures (21:24 and 22:5), the absence of night (21:25 and 22:5), and the presence of God and the Lamb together (21:22, 23 and 22:1, 3). After describing the external appearance of the whole and of the walls and gates (21:10-21), John begins to portray the inside of the city, with reference to the square (in v. 21). John remarks that there is no temple on this square, however, where it would seem natural and obvious that the temple should be. Regardless of whether or not the earthly Jerusalem had already been destroyed by Titus at the time that he wrote, John makes it clear here that there is no longer any need for a physical temple.

For the majority of Jews, including Christian ones, the destruction of the temple in 70 CE raised the problem of how they could continue to observe the Law without a temple in which to offer sacrifices; it is possible that worship was begun again in some reduced form, but, if so, it certainly did not happen immediately nor in a form at all comparable to that of the past. The theoretical premises for adaptation to the new situation were already well known within Judaism and the Bible itself, and not only in those groups like the Essenes who thought that the temple of their day was contaminated. In Jer 3:14-18 — a section written after 587 BCE — the writer foresees a time when there will be no ark, and nobody will even talk about it or lament its loss or think about rebuilding it, because its place will have been filled by Jerusalem: "At that time Jerusalem shall be called the throne of the LORD" (3:17).

Within Christianity Jesus' words about the destruction of the temple (Mark 13:2 and parallels) and Stephen's discourse on the temple being "made by human hands" (Acts 7:48) bear witness that the temple is not necessary. John the Baptist preached that remission of sins was possible in the Jordan, far from the temple, without sacrifices or offerings but on the basis of repentance alone, and the success of his message showed that the time was ripe for new forms of Judaism.

The texts of Qumran, however, while they believed that the physical temple of their own time was contaminated or destined for ruin, foresaw that it would be rebuilt so that worship could be reestablished (thus *TS* and *NJ*). In later Judaism it fell to the rabbis to develop alternatives to the temple and its worship by heightening the Pharisaic spirituality that was already well established before 70 CE, and which involved a life centered around the synagogue, the exaltation of the family table as a religious site like the altar, and an individual moral life, rich in prayer and good deeds, that could be conducted without need of the temple. The Pharisees were lay teachers and built a lay religiosity that survived 70 and extended its influence over all of Judaism; Jewish religious life came increasingly under the control of the rabbis, who gradually took control from the descendants of priestly families who were too bound to the physical temple. This is one of the reasons for which John wrote the Apocalypse: the temple has probably already been, or is perhaps about to be destroyed, and John is saying that there is no more need for the temple nor for the human city that houses it, since God has decreed that there will be a new world with a New Jerusalem that has no temple. The presence of God himself ("The Lord, God Almighty") means that there is no need for any such building, and thus what the Romans have just done or are about to do will not prevent the salvation of the faithful.

καὶ τὸ ἀρνίον. Here and in the next verse (καὶ ὁ λύχνος αὐτῆς τὸ ἀρνίον) the appearance of the Lamb at the end of a phrase like this used to be taken as a sure sign that John was acting as a redactor and adding the Lamb to a Jewish text that spoke only of God and used singular verbs. As there are no exact sources, it is difficult to determine whether this is the case, but I would point out that it does not seem necessary to assume that in v. 23 John was acting as a redactor and sewing up or altering an original document, since the text says that "the Glory of God gave her light, and the Lamb is her lamp." It makes sense that the Lamb, the incarnate and sacrificed Christ, should be the means whereby the divine light makes itself visible. It is also worth noting that John says that the Glory of God "gave light" to the city; this is the only aorist in a text otherwise full of present or future verbs. Perhaps this means that God has given light from all eternity to this New Jerusalem, which he has preserved from all eternity, and that therefore the Lamb can now be its lamp (see comments on 22:5).

21:23 ἡ πόλις . . . σελήνης. This is not merely the logical consequence of God's illuminating the city, nor is it simply the realization of Isa 60:19-20;

apart from anything else, Isaiah expected that there would be a spiritual sun (God) *and a moon:* "Your sun shall no more go down, or your moon disappear" — during the eternal day, there will always be a full moon, an eternal Passover festival without lunar phases. In Gen 8:22 God promised that "All the days of the earth . . . day and night shall not cease"; the disappearance of the night is a sign that the old world is finished. John is emphasizing here that as the old heaven no longer exists, neither do the old celestial luminaries nor the old stars. The luminary of the city is Christ, who has just been called "lamp" (in v. 11; whereas 2 *Bar.* 17:4, 18:1-2, and 59:2 stress repeatedly that "the Law" alone is a lamp and a light to the faithful). At the beginning of the book John spoke of seven "lampstands," but did not mention any lamps on them. We remarked in that context that there was a correspondence between lamps and stars; see the comments on 1:20. Now Christ is about to reveal himself as "the star" that is the source of light (22:16). We can also note that John says a lot about "stars" in the first part of the book (from the first "seven" in 1:16 to the last "twelve" in 12:1), but that after he records that Satan had dragged a third of them down from heaven (12:4) he does not mention stars again until the last definitive and truly luminous star, Christ in 22:16. We can assume that Christ is the only star in the new heaven that appears in 21:1, which will certainly not contain planets such as the sun and the moon.

This means that there will be no more pagan gods, no more Fate, and no more chronological time (see *1 Enoch* 56:4, and in particular 58:3, 6 [*BS*]; see also Chialà 1997, p. 244). This last detail represents the final defeat of Satan, whose power is bound to time, indeed to a "little time" (see comments on 12:12); this "little time" refers to the duration of the first creation, a time that is certainly "little" in comparison to God's eternity. The absence of night, which is repeatedly stressed, means that this eternity of light is conceived as a day that has no end (see also *1 Enoch* 50:1 [*BS*]). Taken together, these last verses are in full agreement with our theory about Satan's connection with the seven periods of history and about his inability to be the eighth period (see comments on 17:11). This day without end is the eternal and definitive day, and should not be considered as the "eighth" since it is part of a new creation, outside of the old time and thus of Satan's power; this book has a remarkable level of conceptual and formal consistency. As for light, it is fitting that its presence is taken for granted at the end of time, at least for the blessed; in *4 Ezra* 7:39-44 the day of judgment itself will be a light that lasts seven years.

21:24 καὶ περιπατήσουσιν . . . γῆς. The "nations" and even "the kings of the earth" who were massacred not only at the end of ch. 19 but also at the end of ch. 20 make a reappearance. In the late 19th and early 20th centuries critics saw this inconsistency as evidence of redactional work, and even today the re-appearance of the kings of the earth poses problems, even for the most confident exegetes (see Raguse 1993, pp. 200-201). If we are to have any success with a text so intransigent to so many methods, and are to make sense of this apparently contradictory passage, we must first ask what role it plays in its context. There are numerous biblical and nonbiblical passages to support the idea that the nations of the earth and their kings will come to the earthly Jerusalem in the last days bringing gifts, perhaps on the pattern of what was thought to have actually happened during the time of Solomon and his temple. The strength of this tradition is shown in a Qumranic text that, after praising "David" (or his eschatological successor), who "will sit before you [God] on the throne of Israel forever," contains this phrase: "And all the nations will see your glory, because you have made yourself holy in the middle of your people Israel. And to your great Name they will carry their offerings: silver, gold, precious stones, with all the treasures of their country to honor your people and Zion your holy city and your wonderful house" (4QDibHam[a] [4Q504] fr. 1-2, 4:6-12; see 1QM 12:13-14: "Open your gate[s] continuously so that the wealth of nations can be brought to you! Their kings shall wait on you," and the realization of Ps 68:30-31 in 1QpPs [1Q16] fr. 9). Our passage is an almost verbal quotation from Isa 60:3 (quoted in comments on 21:11), with one fundamental alteration; Isaiah speaks of "nations" and then, in 60:12, says, "the nation and the kingdom that will not serve you shall perish; those nations shall be utterly laid waste" (for the continuation of the idea, see 2 *Bar.* 72:4). John, on the other hand, does not talk here about "peoples" (as he does in 21:3) but instead brings to walk in the light of Jerusalem those very "nations" who had been or were to be exterminated (there are many more possible parallels; see, e.g., Ps 22:28; Isa 2:3; Mic 4:1-2; Tob 13:13; Hag 2:7; Zech 2:15; 8:22-23). What is more, while 11:2 prophesied that the nations "will trample" (πατήσουσιν) the holy city, this verse now prophesies that these same nations "will walk" (περιπατήσουσιν) in the light of the holy Jerusalem. The nations have thus been considerably transformed in the course of the Apocalypse, even though the Greek records it with only a small lexical shift.

This is the last appearance of the phrase "kings of the earth," as well as of the terms "king" and "earth," just as the first appearance of the phrase in 1:5, where Jesus Christ is called "the prince of the kings of the earth," was the first appearance of both terms. We noted earlier that while some kings of the earth fight against the Lamb, others seem to be quite willing to be his subjects (see comments on 17:1 and 18). I think the texts support the notion that there are at least two groups of "kings" or "kings of the earth," one of enemies and one of subjects of the Lamb (but see comments on 18:9).

It is worth reviewing briefly the occasions on which the terms "king," "kingdom," and "reign" have definitely positive connotations and are used in regard to human beings, or at least to beings other than God and Christ. We have already mentioned the case of 1:5; immediately after this, in 1:6, John says, "and made of us a kingdom"; next, in 1:9, he talks about the "kingdom and endurance of Jesus" as a quality of the faithful. After this he does not mention "kings" or "kingdoms" again until ch. 5, where, talking about those redeemed by the Lamb in 5:10, he says, "and made of them for our God a kingdom . . . and they will reign upon the earth." Up to this point in the work "king," "kingdom," and "reign" have referred exclusively to the reign of the faithful, which is twice said to be "of" or "on" the earth. From here on the text deals with kings and kingdoms that have negative connotations or that, in a couple of cases, are ambiguous. In 17:14, however, the Lamb is defined as the "King of kings," and in 19:16 the Word is also said to be "King of kings." Then, in ch. 20, it is said of those who rose in the first resurrection that "they will live and reign with Christ for a thousand years" (20:4), a concept that is repeated in 20:6: "and will reign with him for a thousand years." Finally, at the end of the vision of the New Jerusalem, the faithful of the city "reign forever and ever" (22:5, the seventh and last appearance of the verb "to reign," which is always used in a positive sense). At this point it seems not only reasonable but also necessary to conclude that the "kings of the earth" in this passage are none other than the blessed faithful, and particularly those companions of Christ's millennial kingdom who have reigned on earth, rather than any of the sovereigns under Satan's protection (see following comments.)

21:25-26 οἱ πυλῶνες . . . τῶν ἐθνῶν. Scholars have seen these two verses as another sign of John's carelessness in composition. Obviously, they say, it must be the kings of the earth who bring the glory and the honor of the nations into the New Jerusalem; therefore, John, without obvious breaks in the text, speaks first of the nations and the kings of the earth who bring their glory to Jerusalem, then says that the gates are open and that there is no night, and then repeats that the kings of the earth bring the glory and honor of the nations into the city. I think that there is in fact no repetition within the text, and that it means exactly what it says. In reality, three different groups are mentioned. There are the "nations" in v. 24, of whom it is not yet said that they enter Jerusalem but merely that they "walk by the help of her light" (see Matt 5:14, quoted in comments on 21:16); there are the "kings of the earth" who "bring" to the city "their glory" (which is distinct from that of the nations); and there are the "gates," which will always be opened and, since they are the subject of the verb, will in their turn bring into the city "the glory and the honor of the nations." Since the "gates" bear the names and the angels of the twelve tribes, the symbolism is quite clear; at the end, in the final Jerusalem, Judaism will fulfill the mission for which God destined it, that of bringing the nations to salvation and faith.

"Historical" Judaism prostituted itself with the pagans and in doing so not only failed to save them but even damned itself. Eschatological Judaism, however, will take up its proper role again. It will act as a filter ("no profane thing will enter it"; v. 27), and will allow only "the glory and the honor of the nations" to enter. I translate as "honor" the word τιμή, which can be understood to mean "value": that which is precious or has worth among the nations, that which the Lamb bought with the price of his own blood. The context makes clear that the Judaism of the last days is spiritualized; the insertion of "lies" next to "abomination" makes clear that observance is no longer what divides good from evil (see comments on 22:15). The Jewish gates will let in only "those who are written in the Lamb's scroll of life," namely, the followers of Christ ("from the establishment of the world"; 17:8). At the heart of John's message is the conviction that the Judaism of the last days, rather than building barriers or "fences" around the Law, will consist of twelve gates eternally thrown open to welcome those who have converted from paganism. The deeply passionate Judaism of the Christian John is clear here, and it is probably here that John reaches the best equilibrium available to a Jewish Christian of his day. Primitive Christianity was well aware that salvation comes through Judaism; this is evident even in Paul (see Rom 11:11-32). John expresses the idea by the image of the nations passing through the twelve gates; in a spiritual sense the nations enter into Judaism and thus into the economy of salvation, but the Judaism into which they enter is its Christian perfection, which is built on the foundation of the apostles.

There are still a number of exegetical problems, one of which I think cannot be easily resolved. Even if we allow that the "kings of the earth" are those who rose with Christ in the millennial kingdom, their socioreligious composition (to use contemporary terminology) remains unclear, as does that of the "nations." In the first place, it seems that nobody but the "kings of the earth" and the better part of the nations are saved. If, as is possible (see 20:4), only martyrs are included in the first resurrection, then the "nations" include all the other righteous. If this is the case, however, then the term "nations" must be understood as being completely spiritualized and as bearing no relation to the genetic ethnicity of this group of the saved. The alternative is to imagine that the first resurrection involved only holy Christian Jews, and that converted pagans arrive now, after their resurrection, through the gates of spiritual Judaism. It is still undetermined whether martyrdom/testimony necessarily involves the physical shedding of blood or whether this also should be understood in a spiritual sense, but notwithstanding this uncertainty, I think that the term "nations" here indicates a spiritual paganism; everybody, whether Jewish or pagan by origin, has to pass through spiritual Judaism to enter into the new and holy Jerusalem.

21:27 πᾶν κοινόν. For other details see the comments on 22:15. There was a tendency to view the sacred nature of the temple, which is defined also by internal architectural boundaries that cannot be crossed by, for instance, the uncircumcised or women, as extending to include the whole city. At the end of the 1st century the degrees of purity necessary to cross the various boundaries were understood differently by different groups of Jews. The Mishna (*m. Kel.* 1:6-9) describes ten concentric levels associated with different degrees of purity that are conceptually centered on the "Holy of Holies," which only the high priest could enter when in a condition of absolute purity. According to *TS* and CD, Jerusalem's sanctity was such that all sexual activity was, or should be, forbidden, no menstruating woman should enter, and nobody should die there (CD 11:21–12:2; *TS* 45:11-17; see Milgrom 1978). This would obviously have made normal family life quite impossible within the city. The main problem is precisely the presence of a sacred place such as the temple within a profane place, the site of daily life such as a city. Ezekiel, in his utopian vision of the reconstruction of the temple and Jerusalem, understood this perfectly. Probably inspired by traditions such as that in Exod 33:7, from which it appears that the "tent" (see comments on 21:3) was located outside the camp (see comments on 20:9), he suggested that the temple should be built in the middle of the sacred land, which would be reserved only for priests and which would not be taken away or removed from them, and that the city would be built some distance away, on "profane" land (see Ezek 48:9-21 and especially v. 15). Although it is quite impossible to achieve in practical terms, this plan was conceived precisely to avoid those difficulties that did in fact arise and that today, within a religiously diverse society, continue to make cohabitation difficult in Jerusalem.

22:1 ἔδειξέν μοι . . . ἀρνίου. The same angelic figure now shows John the heart of the city. At the end of the book, and of salvation history, God and the Lamb sit on the throne, finally and eternally together. The lightnings, voices, and thunders (4:5) that were necessary earlier no longer "come forth" from the throne, and instead the "river" of God's merciful and life-giving providence flows from it. The presence of the water of life in this shining vision, with its obvious reference to baptism, also recalls that "spirit of life" which comes "from God" (11:11). It was a fairly common notion both in Judaism and in primitive Christianity that at the end of time there will be a spiritual river, or that the Spirit will appear in the form of a river (1QH–4QH 16:4-37; like rivers of fire, 1QH–4QH 11:26-36). The image may have been lent force by the movement from sprinkling to baptism as the sacramental instrument of salvation (see "he will baptize you with the Holy Spirit"; Mark 1:8 and parallels), which is the Christian successor to the sprinkling in Ezek 36:25. John inserts the eschatological Jordan, which gives life to the Dead Sea in Ezek 47, into a passage that draws heavily from Zechariah (ch. 14, but also the Jerusalem spring in 13:1); he probably considers it as the definitive and constant emission of the life-giving Spirit (for the idea of a "holy source" or spring in and from the temple, see *ShirShabb* [4Q400] fr. 1, 1:7 and comments by Newsom 1985, p. 44). Whatever might be the reality made manifest in the "throne," the image of the "river" coming forth "from the throne of God and of the Lamb" anticipates what will, in terms appropriate both to the Greek mind-set and their theology, be called "the procession of the Spirit from the Father and the Son." For "coming forth from the throne" as a characteristic of angelic beings, see comments on 4:5. John is not alone in using the concept of "living water" (John 4:10-11; 7:38); see 1QS[b] 1:3-6 and CD 19(ex 7-8):30-35.

λαμπρὸν ὡς κρύσταλλον. The old heaven has ceased to exist, and in the order of the new creation God's throne is placed in the privileged position at the height of Jerusalem, where divine and human come together, no longer separated by the vault of heaven. The heritage of that heaven, which used to support the throne of God, has passed to the river of the water of life, which flows from under the throne and whose light, "bright like crystal," recalls the "crystalline" heaven of the old order (see 21:11). That heaven was "like a sea . . . similar to crystal" (4:6), but now there is a river that is "like crystal," while the presence of the sea in ch. 4, though traditional, now shows the imperfect and provisional nature of the old creation. The sea no longer exists; it seems crude, when faced with this final, luminous vision, to imagine, as some scholars have done, that this river must flow into some new, future sea of the water of life. Besides the fact that John explicitly denies it (21:1), this idea would have seemed downright comical to a 1st-century Jew, even a Christian one, who must have known that sea water belongs to the category of "smitten water" and thus has at most the second degree of purity, which is inadequate for the water of sprinkling (*m. Miqw.* 1:8). Perhaps this is why there are no eschatological seas, but only rivers and springs. Above all, however, John is concerned with the constant and eternal flowing of the Spirit of God, who gives life to the new world: there is no need for seas.

22:2 ἐν μέσῳ . . . ἐκεῖθεν. The order of the objects is disturbing to a modern reader. John takes up Ezek 47:12, which says that every kind of fruit tree grows on the two banks of the eschatological river, and decides to reduce the tree/wood to one (the uniqueness of Christ's sacrifice means that there cannot be a multiplicity of trees) but to keep the detail. I am not comfortable with the theory that John is unaware of the inconsistency, and prefer instead to see this as another example of that mystical geography of the sacred which we have seen in the previous visions of the throne of God (see comments on 4:6). I think that John was trying to communicate something mystical and made a deliberate choice about how to do so. If the "tree/wood of life" is said to be "on one side of the river" and then, immediately after, to be "on the other" side of the same river, and the whole to be "in the middle of her square" ("her" referring to the city), the meaning must be that the tree/wood grows in the center and that the river flows from below it (perhaps from within the roots; see the spring that flows from below the "vine" in 2 *Bar.* 36:2-4). But the middle of the square must naturally have been occupied by the throne, the place of God's presence, from below which the river flows (in v. 1). I think that this is precisely the point; John wants to tell the attentive reader that the "tree of life" is the wood of the cross and is the real throne of Christ/God, and that the river flows from it (see comments on 22:3). For the connection with the "tree of life" in Genesis see comments on 2:7.

ξύλον . . . δώδεκα. This "tree/wood of life" is what is referred to in the promise in 2:7 (see comments ad loc.), and the details of the fruits that ripen "each month" are taken from Ezek 47:12. That there are twelve fruits, as many as the months of the year, is John's addition. This is the only place in the text where the number "twelve" is mentioned in connection with the temporal dimension, but the main reference is to the twelve tribes (see following comments). According to the original text of *Jub.* 21:12 and of *T. Levi* 9:13 (and 4QTLevi ar^b [4Q214] fr. 1), wood for sacrifice could be taken from only twelve kinds of trees, which were therefore the most sacred among the trees; thus there was a connection between the tree's sacred nature and the number "twelve."

καὶ τὰ φύλλα . . . τῶν ἐθνῶν. John is still drawing on Ezek 47:12, which says that "their fruits [of the trees that grow on the banks of the eschatological river] will be like food, and their leaves will be like medicine" (see also 4 *Ezra* 7:53). He interprets the distinction between food and medicine as a prefiguration of the two categories of the saved who are destined to enter the New Jerusalem. One group will be ready to receive nourishment from the fruits of the cross, while the others will (first?) need to be cured and healed by its leaves. There must be a connection between the first group and the twelve fruits and between the other group and the leaves, which cannot be counted, or whose number at any rate is not recorded in the text. This subdivision within the world of the saved calls to mind other subdivisions that we have come across in the course of the book, from the "hundred forty-four thousand" (a multiple of twelve) and the "throng" without number in ch. 7, to the "kings of the earth" and the "nations" at the end of ch. 21 (see the "peoples" of God in 21:3). The "nations" are the same as in 21:24 and 26; by clinging spiritually to the cross (nourishing themselves with the leaves of the tree) they are able to be "healed."

22:3 πᾶν κατάθεμα . . . ἔτι. The immediate antecedent is Zech 14:11, part of a brief apocalypse (ch. 14). John uses several elements of this: the eschatological river of living water that flows from Jerusalem, the eternal day without day or night, the reign of the Lord over the whole earth, the lifting up of Jerusalem while the rest of the world becomes a plain, the annual pilgrimage to Jerusalem by the survivors among the nations, and, finally, this phrase: "Never again shall there be vow of extermination (LXX: καὶ ἀνάθεμα οὐκ ἔσται ἔτι), and Jerusalem shall abide in security." The Hebrew term *ḥrm* indicates the kind of vow with which an Israelite sovereign or military leader consecrated an enemy entity — such as a Canaanite city and its inhabitants — to God, and thus to total destruction. What does it have to do with our context? One might think in terms of God's repentance in Gen 8:21, and his decision to "never again curse the earth"; this would then be a new covenant between God and men, like the one after the flood, within which the blood of Christ will be the seal of a new and eternal peace. This is certainly one possible solution, but it is odd that John should refer to it in passing. I think it is more likely that John's κατάθεμα corresponds to the ἀνάθεμα of LXX: there will no longer be a vow of extermination nor holy war between Israel and the pagans. John is repeating the same concept that is expressed in the preceding lines: eschatological Judaism will be the means of salvation for the nations rather than the means of their ruin. Israel will still consecrate the nations to God, but will do so by healing all of them and leading them into the New Jerusalem rather than by slaughtering them.

ὁ θρόνος . . . ἀρνίου. The first thing to appear to John in heaven was "a throne" with one seated on it, who remains unnamed throughout the book (see 4:2). The last thing he sees is also a throne, actually "the throne," and now the name of those seated on it is written above: "God and the Lamb" (22:1 and 3). This not only confirms the terms of the seventh promise, in the seventh letter, but is probably also intended to resolve the ambiguity we have noted about the nature of the one "sitting on the throne," who at times seems to be most like God the Father and at times more like Christ (at least according to our way of thinking). John is saying that the two beings (I do not think it historically justifiable to use the term "persons") interpenetrate each other in such a way that the attributes of full divinity are predicated of the Son and that the result is unity (see John 10:30).

The literary consequences of this and the following verse may strike us as odd or awkward, as will inevitably be the case in a book that expresses its theology in images adopted by a Christian Jew at the end of the 1st century. After saying that the throne is "of God and of the Lamb," John carries on using singular personal pronouns — "his servants," "his face," "his name" — where we would expect the plural ("their face," or even "their names"). One could of course attribute this, as many have, to the work of a redactor or to John's carelessness, but I believe that the phenomenon can be explained in two different ways or, rather, in one way that operates on two different levels. The first level involves a reflection on the union (which today we would call "substantial") between the Lamb and God, which makes it possible to use singular expressions that refer both to God and to the Lamb. John himself suggests this interpretation of his texts: in 14:1 he says that the "hundred forty-four thousand" bear "his [the Lamb's] name and the name of his Father written [singular] on their foreheads." In the same manner our passage says that "his servants" have "his name . . . on their foreheads." This can only mean that the Name (probably the name of God, self-revealing in Christ) is a single name for a divine entity that is both singular and plural at the same time (see comments on 19:6).

The second interpretive level involves the "throne" to which, from a grammatical point of view, all the pronouns in the phrase can be understood to refer. But who or what is this "throne" that talks, and from which come forth voices, thunders, lights, perhaps spiritual burning torches, and now also the river of the water of life? I have already suggested that the throne is identified with the "tree/wood" or the cross on which the Lamb offers himself up "from the establishment of the world" (13:8; see also comments on 22:2), and that it is probably an angelomorphic being (in the *Gospel of Peter* the cross moves and speaks; fr. 1, 10 [40]), as were the angelic "thrones" that were certainly part of later mystical traditions and now, having been found in Qumranic texts, can also be identified in Col 1:16 (see comments on 1:4). The Jewish mystical traditions, as evidenced by texts considerably later than the 1st century, give evidence that the throne of God, which is his chariot (again on the model of Ezekiel's vision), is exalted and is, above all, regarded as being his manifestation, visible to those who ascend to the *merkabah*. In texts of this sort the chariot/throne has one or more faces (that, or those, of the "living creatures") and one or more names that are considered secret and/or incommunicable (see Halperin 1988). In view of the chronological distance between the two sets of texts, it would be unwise to push this comparison any further, but nonetheless in John we may indeed have a throne that is somehow the visible manifestation, albeit a very spiritualized one, of the invisible God and that therefore, although in the New Jerusalem rather than in the physical temple, can be the object of priestly activity, can show its face, and can allow its name to be written on the forehead of its servants. In a theology like John's, which operates by overlapping images and which one might well define as oneiric because it follows the laws of visions rather than those of the waking consciousness, it should come as no surprise if this name, inasmuch as it is the name of the self-revealing God or of his first self-revelation, should in the last analysis be a/the name/s of Christ/God.

22:5 φωτὸς λύχνου. The idea that the new Jerusalem has no need of the light of a physical lamp has two functions in the text. On the one hand it reaffirms that the true and spiritual lamp is the Lamb, and on the other it recalls the description of the fate of Babylon where John says, "Light of lamp shall never again shine in you" (18:23). This is a close verbal echo, but what in ch. 18 was a curse here becomes a blessing, a sign that the physicality that needs a physical lamp has been left behind. The destinies of the two cities run along parallel tracks, thus giving us further reason to see in the New Jerusalem the eschatological salvation of the old Jerusalem, who in historical terms had debased herself to become Babylon. We may note that the connection of the "sun," the first planetary star, with the "lamp" reinforces the connection between the angel, star, and lamp that we proposed earlier (see comments on 21:23).

βασιλεύσουσιν . . . αἰώνων. For this "reign" see the comments on 21:24. This formula takes up that of 11:15 ("and he will reign forever and ever"), where the subject was "our Lord and his Anointed" (a singular verb with plural subjects; see comments on 22:3). This means that it is the eternal and definitive reign, as distinct from the millennial reign, and that the prophecies about it have been fulfilled. This brings to a close the vision of the New Jerusalem and the most specifically visionary part of the book.

22:6 Καὶ εἶπέν μοι. From here on the rest of the book is composed of a series of interjections by speakers whose identities are not easy to determine. For the most part they are expressions taken up from elsewhere in the book, often from the first part. These concluding phrases are probably intended to guard against errors of interpretation by explaining to the reader the true nature of some of the figures who have appeared in the book. In the next verses it will become apparent that the figure who speaks here is an angel, probably the same as the one who appeared in 21:9. For the first thing he says, about the "faithful and true words," see 4 *Ezra* 15:2, where the revealing figure orders the visionary to write the *sermones prophetiae* ("words of the prophecy") because they are *fideles et veri* ("faithful and true"). The rest of what he says recalls 1:1, with one addition; it is "the Lord, the God of the spirits of the prophets," who sends the angel. In the concluding moments of the book John reaffirms the divinity of Christ by pointing to him as the author of the prophecies. For the figure of the "Lord of the Spirits" see 1 Enoch 37:2 (BS), and for its sources and parallels, including Qumran, see Chialà 1997, pp. 142ff.

22:8 Κἀγὼ Ἰωάννης. As in the beginning, John states his own name (1:9) but immediately declares that he fell again into error. Both the scene and the terms used are very close to those in 19:9-10. Here also his error seems understandable; besides everything he has told and shown John, this angel utters a phrase concerning the "faithful and true words," which is the same as that uttered by the one seated on the throne in 21:5. After the scene in 19:9 this ought not to take John by surprise, but the angel also applies to himself the phrase "to come soon" (see 2:5, 16, [25]; 3:11). At this point John tries to worship him, probably mistaking him for Christ/God. That John should show that he is incapable of understanding what he sees by making the same mistake twice within three chapters indicates that this is close to his heart. Notwithstanding the reflections of contemporary criticism about the angelic or angelomorphic Christology of the Apocalypse, John's point is that it is easy to mistake a particularly authoritative angel for Christ himself, but that it is wrong to do so. This particular angel, since he is not Christ, must be "his angel," the one sent to his "servants" to reveal and to prophesy. He is also the first of the seven angels of the bowls, or at least nothing in the text suggests that he might be any other angel. Inasmuch as he is the angel of Christ, he may also constitute the various christological angels whom we have analyzed in the course of the book (see comments on 22:16). It is certainly possible, although difficult to prove for sure, that behind John's repeated error lies his desire to prevent or criticize worship directed to the angels (Eph 1:21; Col 2:15) or to limit excessive forms of veneration of certain of the prophets, which run the risk of confusing the sent with the sender.

22:9 τῶν ἀδελφῶν . . . προφητῶν. For the brotherhood between prophets and apocalyptic writers see 4 Ezra 12:12: "your brother Daniel," and comments on 1:12. If we keep this in mind we will not interpret this passage as if it referred exclusively to Christian prophets and we will not necessarily imagine behind them a confraternity of prophets active in the early communities. Their role as prophets makes visionaries "brothers," regardless of the age they lived in. John saw all "prophets," past and present, as "evangelized" and thus somehow part of the same economy of salvation; but that is a different issue (see 14:6).

22:10 Καὶ λέγει μοι. The figure speaking here must be the same angel as before; he certainly speaks with authority, telling John to "not seal" the content of the vision, because "the moment is near." Besides the internal references (see 10:4), this is a revision of Dan 8:26 and 12:4, 9-13, where the prophet was told by the interpreting angel to keep sealed up the message that he had received up until the time of the end. This ancient literary fiction is useless now in that John believes that that moment has come. This is the only way to make sense of the "correction" of Daniel's text, a text that undermines interpretations of the Apocalypse that try to deny its eschatological tension or that see the book merely as an example of realized eschatology.

22:11 ὁ ἀδικῶν ἀδικησάτω ἔτι. It is unclear who utters this phrase; it is probably the same angel, but it might also be John. In any case, it follows logically from the assertion that the moment is near and sketches the basic form of an interim ethic. Whatever the scriptural antecedents might be (Dan 12:10 and perhaps Ezek 3:27), here the faithful are instructed not to intervene in history. Actions, battles, judgments — in a word, everything — is the work of God and his angels or of the slain holy ones (see comments on 20:4), the only exception being the desperate struggles by Satan and his supporters (see comments on 13:16). The concepts of "justice" and "purity" that John appeals to here should probably be understood in an ethical sense rather than in reference to the observance that we have seen John criticize; in any case, he does not call his readers to set themselves against the injustice and impurity of others, but rather to practice justice and purity themselves. This verse stands in the way of a political or interventionist interpretation of the text. We must either remove the verse — without any paleographic justification — or we must admit that it confirms our earlier impressions that the imminence of the end does not justify Christians in actively rebelling against Rome or against Satan or against any injustice; they should wait for God to step into human history. As little as it appeals to contemporary tastes, the text holds that the only possible form of witness is martyrdom — the imitation of and identification with the slain Lamb. John shows the difficult road of the victorious Christian, who must pass by way of his own defeat and death.

22:12 Ἰδοὺ ἔρχομαι ταχύ. These words are probably the beginning of the direct interjection on the part of Christ, as we see not from the assertion that he is coming "soon" but from the subsequent role he is to play as judge and, most of all, from the fact that he introduces himself as the Alpha and the Omega, something that an angel could not do. Immediately after the command not to intervene issued in the preceding verse — a crucial moment as regards the response required of the faithful — it becomes clear that the Risen One has appeared on the scene. Not to act, and not actively to seek martyrdom (see comments on 13:10), must have seemed a difficult thing in tense times (see 2:13), and one of John's motives for writing the book must have been precisely that of encouraging the faithful to have trust. God has always intervened in history, and does and will continue to do so; it is not the task of humans to change the course of events, especially now that "the moment is near." As for the "payment" that Christ brings, it makes sense that at the end everyone will receive the correct "pay" (see *4 Ezra* 7:35).

22:14 Μακάριοι. The last blessing of the book must be uttered by Christ. It follows from the preceding sentences in terms both of logic and of content. The washing of the robes still indicates the imitation of Christ's sacrifice (7:14) that brings with it the "authority . . . over the wood of life" or the ability to avail oneself of the cross, which in turn makes possible the entrance into the New Jerusalem through the twelve "gates," the Christian version of Judaism. This is a verbal as well as a conceptual reference to the end of the vision of the New Jerusalem (21:22–22:5).

22:15 ἔξω οἱ κύνες. There was a lively polemic between observant groups about the presence of dogs in Jerusalem, as we can see in *HL*, found at Qumran (4QMMT and parallels; lines 58-59 of the reconstructed text; see Qimron–Strugnell 1994, p. 163 and the comments of Sussmann 1994, pp.189-90; for the equation of dogs and pigs see comments on 17:4 and 5 and Lupieri 1997, p. 77; on the whole subject see Philonenko 1997). John is thus making use of an expression that would have been very familiar in the internal polemics of 1st-century Judaism. The context, however, clearly shows that he is actually referring to people: the "dogs" are ethically impure men (see Phil 3:2). Coming at the beginning of a list of sinners, the term operates as an epitome. The whole list is thus set apart from the lists that are plentiful in Judaism, including at Qumran, and that are used to indicate those categories of persons in a state of impurity who could not enter into Jerusalem or into the community (e.g. CD 15:15-17; 1QM 7:3-7; *TS* 46:16-18; 48:14-17; in Qumranic texts those listed are often excluded because of the presence of angels among the "holy ones"). Taken as it is, the phrase is a violent one, and has historically been used in an anti-Semitic sense: Nazi youth organizations cried, "Out with the dogs!" as they expelled Jews from German universities in the late 1930s.

The speaker here is presumably still Christ.

22:16 Ἐγὼ Ἰησοῦς. John waits until this moment to announce the identity of the figure who has been speaking probably since v. 12. It is common in mss. of Christian texts for "Christ" to be added whenever the name "Jesus" appears, and vice versa, but in this case the manuscript tradition is solidly in favor of using "Jesus" alone. In this sentence, and in this concluding section of the book, John stresses the identity between Jesus and Christ/God, perhaps in response to interpretations that tend to see them as distinct figures, and that will be rampant within Christianity in the next century (see Simonetti 1986, especially pp. 445-46). To distinguish God from the angels and integrate Jesus Christ fully into the divinity, John stresses that it was Jesus who sent the angel to testify. This places Jesus above the angels, and makes it impossible to consider him as an entity distinct from Christ. John says, to sum up, that the man Jesus is God inasmuch as he is Christ, and reaffirms this in the next words. Jesus says not only that he is descended from David in the flesh (in response to the expectation of a Davidic Messiah; see, e.g., 4QpGen^a [4Q252] 5:3-4), but also that he is "the root" of David (see 5:5) or the source from which David came. If this is so, then Jesus, inasmuch as he is Christ, is preexistent and came before David (see comments on 5:5). Christ's preexistence is not merely human, but pertains also to the angels and to the stars. He is "the star": not only one (*the* one?) that gives true light (see 21:11) but the "bright" one "of the early morning," the one shining from the beginning. This "original" nature of Jesus Christ as a star is probably a reference to origins, to the creation (see 3:14). The phrase represents not only the unveiling of the content of the promise made in 2:28, but also another statement of John's position on the preexistence of Jesus Christ and on the eternal value of his sacrifice (see comments on 12:5 and 13:7). Finally, it is worth noting that when Jesus speaks he addresses his listeners directly with the "you" form. This is the first time that this happens here, and it has not happened since John addressed his readers and listeners at the beginning of the book (see 1:4, 9); we are leaving behind the narrative dimension of the work, and the characters are entering into conversation with those to whom the text is directed.

22:17 τὸ πνεῦμα . . . Ἔρχου. Jesus has finished his own self-revelation, and now the Spirit and the Bride — that is, the New Jerusalem — appear on the scene. It is not true that all the women in the book are silent or are reduced to silence (see comments on 2:20); the Bride says only one word, to be sure, but she does say that one word, and as it is uttered in unison with the Spirit it is a prophetic word. The expression raises the exegetical problem of understanding who it is that is invited to "Come." The most logical option is that they are addressing Jesus himself, who has just finished speaking; this is supported by the rest of the verse, which runs, "And let him who hears say, 'Come!'" At this point the issue becomes complicated because, if we accept that it is Jesus who is invited to come, then it is not clear who utters the whole phrase and who it is that listens. "Him who hears" is probably the believer of John's own day who hears the text being read (see 1:3 and 22:18). John also, however, has presented himself as "him who hears" (in v. 8) with the same present participle as is used here; that was rather unclear in its context, which suggests that John used the form deliberately to create an internal reference. It seems more likely, however, that John utters the entire sentence and that the imperative addresses his readers/listeners. He steps out of the narrative level to interject after the Spirit and the Bride have spoken; their word, uttered in a loud voice, resounds among those who are listening to the text, and John interjects to urge them to respond, with a sort of liturgical formula.

καὶ ὁ διψῶν . . . δωρεάν. At this point it becomes an almost hopeless task to figure out who utters the invitation to the thirsty, and who it is that is thirsty. The least complicated solution is that the "thirsty" is again the Christian believer and that the invitation is again issued by John. But what does the phrase really mean, and what does it mean that "whoever desires" is invited to "take the water of life free of charge?" Does John have the authority to issue such an invitation, or should we assume that it is at least an angel — the one who must, as we will see, utter the following verses? Among the several possible interpretations, I support the following one. "Him who hears" is the ordinary believer, who cannot read but only listen, but "him who is thirsty" is the more privileged reader, who has the time and the means to read and meditate on the text. This latter, if he "desires," will find within the text "the water of life"; the prophetic spirit who makes himself known and will save him "free of charge" so that he can share in the promised salvation. According to this interpretation, the phrases about the hearer and the thirsty are both uttered by John, who is playing with different senses of the verb "come." In the case of the thirsty this means not an eschatological coming but an approach to the text, which will become a source of revelation for him.

22:18 Μαρτυρῶ ἐγώ. I believe that the speaker here is once again the angel who was sent by Jesus to "testify" in v. 16. It might possibly be John (see 1:2) or Jesus himself, the ultimate "witness" (e.g., 1:5), but is most likely the angel whose witness has just been mentioned. Jesus says that the angel was sent by him to "testify . . . to you," and now the speaker says that he testifies "to everyone who listens." It is those listening to the reading of the Apocalypse who are addressed in the second person plural in the direct discourses. The immediate consequence of the fact that the book is "testified" by an angel and is thus part of God's authentic message to men is the curse on whoever "adds to" or "takes away from" the text. This is a formula encountered in biblical passages of a normative character (Deut 4:2; 13:1; 29:19). In this context it might be rather an index of the precariousness of John's situation; as we saw in the opening letters, John could not always count on strong support or a majority standing within the churches he writes to (see Introduction, p. 42). There is nothing else of this sort in the rest of the NT.

22:20 Δέγει ὁ μαρτυρῶν . . . Ἰησοῦ. The book's last sentence before the closing formula explains that the witness who is speaking is the same as he who is "coming soon" and thus is either the angel or Jesus. The interpretive decision depends on who has been identified as delivering the final exhortation to Jesus to "come." I think that it is uttered by the same angel/witness, who thus distinguishes himself from Jesus yet again. Alternatively the invitation to Jesus could be a sort of choral formula (see 1 Cor 16:22), perhaps a fragment of an ancient liturgy, which is uttered in response to the witness's statement that he is coming "soon." It seems to me, however, that John is repeating that the angel must come and is deliberately linking the coming of the angel to the expectation of Christ's coming. This makes sense if the angel is still the first of the seven angels with the seven bowls. His coming would then coincide with the pouring out of his bowl and thus with the beginning of that end in which the Savior will come to reign with his saints.

22:21 Ἡ χάρις . . . πάντων. The formula of closing greetings is often brief, both in Greek and in specifically Christian epistles. This one contains the most common elements: the reference to "grace," to its divine origin and to those to whom it is directed. All of Paul's letters contain the same structure, with various elaborations. The variant "with the saints" or "with all the saints" is ideological in orientation (see 1:1 in variants).

Index of Modern Authors

Index of Names

Juvenal, 257, 258

Kasbeel, 214
Koresh, David. *See* Howell, Vernon
   Wayne

Latinus, 215
Lazarus, 108
Leah, 150
Leto, 190
Leviathan, 175, 210, 308
Lucifer, 124
Luke, 42
Lusius Quietus, 346
Luther, Martin, 6, 7, 216

Macarius of Magnesia, 28
Madonna, the, 188
Magog, 321
Manasseh, 39, 150, 262
Marcion, 2
Mary, 33, 37, 144
Matthew, 9, 38
Melchizedek, 23, 24
Menachem, 213
Metatron, 24, 33, 115
Methodius, 3
Michael, 28, 98, 99, 111, 115, 189, 197, 205,
   230, 242, 311, 338
Mohammed, 30
Montanus, 2
Moon, Sun Myung, 10
Moses, 44, 113, 141, 170, 174, 175, 176, 187,
   206, 236, 238, 241, 254, 304, 329

Nadab, 134
Nahum, 262, 272
Nebuchadnezzar, 20, 21, 22, 133, 218
Necho, 244
Nero, 6, 7, 8, 176, 203, 204, 210, 211, 213,
   217, 242, 244, 273, 274, 276
Nicholas, 116
Noah, 98, 143, 238, 309

Og, 275, 343
Origen, 3, 262, 341
Osiander, 216

Otho, 273

Pan, 230
Papias, 1, 3, 9
Paul, vii, 2, 9, 36, 37, 39, 43, 108, 112, 116,
   121, 123, 139, 176, 186, 191, 202, 235, 363
Peleg, 173, 262, 284
Peter, 9, 36, 98, 126, 176, 344
Petrus Joannis Olivi, 6
Pharaoh, 141, 166, 232, 248, 250, 251, 293
Philip, 36, 37, 38, 39
Philo, 24, 31, 303
Policrates, 259
Pompey, 35
Pytho, 190

Ra'ami'el, 135
Rachel, 189
Raphael, 115, 312
Reuben, 150

Saddam Hussein, 217
Saladin, 5
Satan, 10, 28, 43, 99, 103, 116, 119, 120, 123,
   124, 129, 132, 136, 151, 152, 156, 161, 163,
   166, 177, 178, 179, 188, 191, 192, 193, 194,
   195, 197, 198, 199, 200, 201, 202, 204,
   205, 206, 207, 208, 209, 211, 212, 214, 215,
   218, 222, 226, 227, 230, 231, 234, 235, 239,
   240, 243, 247, 251, 252, 253, 258, 259, 261,
   262, 267, 268, 269, 270, 271, 273, 274,
   275, 277, 278, 279, 280, 281, 287, 293,
   299, 308, 311, 312, 313, 316, 318, 319, 320,
   321, 323, 324, 325, 326, 348, 350, 359
Saul (Paul), 42
Seleucus I, 176
Seneca, 257, 258
Simeon, 36, 37, 144
Solomon, 31, 127, 178, 187, 236, 261, 281,
   290, 291, 349
Spener, 6
Stephen, 187, 251, 263, 346
Suetonius, 273
Sybil, 25

Tabitha, 22
Taxo, 208

Index of Places

Index of Subjects

Index of References